BANK MANAGEMENT

Concepts and Issues

BANK MANAGEMENT

Concepts and Issues

EDITED BY

John R. Brick

Michigan State University

ROBERT F. DAME, INC.
1905 Huguenot Road
Richmond, Virginia 23235

ISBN 0-936328-00-2
Library of Congress Catalog No. 80-68804

PRINTED IN THE UNITED STATES OF AMERICA

Designed and typeset by Publications Development
Co. of Texas, Crockett Texas.
Production Editor: Nancy Marcus Land

PREFACE

Throughout the 1970s a rapidly escalating inflation rate coupled with erratic monetary policies resulted in an extremely volatile financial environment. Depository-type financial institutions which traditionally loaned on a longer-term basis than their sources of funds repeatedly found themselves in a profit squeeze. When interest rates increased, the costs of liabilities tended to increase more rapidly than the returns generated by assets. Furthermore, during periods of rising interest rates many savers bypassed banks and thrift institutions in order to obtain higher yields than those allowed under the provisions of Regulation Q. To cope with this *disintermediation* and in response to the demands of inflation-ravaged savers, regulators allowed institutions to tie the interest rate on certain types of deposits to the prevailing market rate. Thus armed with the new money market certificates in mid-1978, institutions began competing aggressively for funds and in the process, further escalated their cost. Not surprisingly, many bankers had difficulty coping with the problems created by a volatile interest rate environment. Contributing to the bank manager's dilemma was a rapidly changing regulatory and competitive environment.

By the late 1970s and early 1980s, it became increasingly apparent that many traditional bank management practices were inadequate to cope with these conditions. New types of assets and liabilities as well as more effective risk-management strategies became necessary. Similarly, increased emphasis on pricing loans and services, profitability analysis, cost control, and analysis of the competitive and regulatory implications of decisions would be required to ensure profitability and sustained growth. The purpose of this book is to address these issues through the use of selected readings and thus provide an overview of the contemporary bank management process.

The selection of articles in this book was based on several criteria, two of which bear special mention. First, it was necessary that each article focus on a topic with important managerial or decision-making implications. In this way each article contributes to the mainstream of the book—bank management. In order to reflect the environment within which banks are now operating and the dramatic changes mentioned above, it was also essential that most of the articles be current. Thirty of the forty-two articles were published since 1977. The other articles date back to 1972 but the underlying concepts and issues are as relevant now as when the articles were written. Some of the earlier articles reflect a bias toward men in bank management positions that is rapidly changing. Although no attempt was made to edit the use of the pronoun "he," it should be understood that banks are managed by qualified individuals of both sexes.

This book is designed for use in courses on *bank management* and the *management of financial institutions*. The material in this book has been used in such courses at the graduate and undergraduate levels at Michigan State University. The book is also appropriate for banking practitioners wishing to update and expand their knowledge. Many of the concepts and issues covered in the broad spectrum of readings also apply to the activities of savings and loan associations, credit unions, and mutual savings banks. Accordingly, the book is an appropriate educational vehicle for the managers of these institutions.

The organizational structure of the book is as follows:

Part   I   Asset Management
Part   II   Liability and Capital Management
Part III   International Banking
Part IV   Asset-Liability Management
Part   V   Costs and Profitability Concepts
Part VI   Regulatory Issues

Parts I and II are further divided into several sections. Part I deals with cash management and reserves, commercial lending, consumer and mortgage lending, and investments. Part II is made up of a section on deposits and another section on borrowed funds and capital. This structure enables the articles to be used sequentially in order to "package" a course or an in-house training program. An alternative is to use the articles independently.

As is the case with most books, several acknowledgments are in order. First, to the extent that this book contributes to the management process of banks and other depository-type institutions, we are deeply indebted to the authors of the various articles. They are to be commended for their valuable contributions to the literature. In addition, we are grateful to the copyright holders for granting permission to reprint these articles and thus propagate important management concepts and issues. Finally, the editor would like to acknowledge the assistance of Isabel Simpson and Nancy Land, as well as the encouragement of Robert F. Dame whose idea has become a reality.

John R. Brick

East Lansing, Michigan

August, 1980

CONTENTS

Part I
ASSET MANAGEMENT

A. CASH MANAGEMENT AND RESERVES

Part I of this book deals with topics related to asset management and is divided into four sections: cash management and reserves, commercial lending, consumer and mortgage lending, and investments. In the first section of Part I the article by Charles M. Lucas, Marcos T. Jones, and Thom B. Thurston provides a detailed explanation of federal funds and repurchase agreements. Since the cash position of commercial banks can swing dramatically from one day to the next and these market instruments repre-sent both outlets and sources of funds for as little as one day, they are extremely important elements in the cash and reserve management process within commercial banks. The second article in this section is by Robert E. Knight and provides a summary of operating guidelines for efficient reserve management. An understanding of these guidelines is essential since penalties are imposed for reserve deficiencies and excess reserves result in foregone income.

FEDERAL FUNDS AND REPURCHASE AGREEMENTS*

Charles M. Lucas, Marcos T. Jones and Thom B. Thurston

The markets for Federal funds and repurchase agreements (RPs) are among the most important financial markets in the United States. Using these instruments, many banks, large corporations, and nonbank financial firms trade large amounts of liquid funds with one another for periods as short as one day. Such institutions provide and use much of the credit made available in the United States and typically manage their financial positions carefully and aggressively. The interest rate on overnight (one day) Federal funds measures the return on the most liquid of all financial assets, and for this reason is critical to investment decisions. That is, financial managers compare this rate to yields on all other investments before choosing the combinations of maturities of the financial assets in which they will invest or the term over which they will borrow.

The Federal funds market is also important because it is related to the conduct of Federal Reserve monetary policy. The interest rate on Federal funds is highly sensitive to Federal Reserve actions that supply reserves to member commercial banks, and the rate influences commercial bank decisions concerning loans to business, individual, and other borrowers. Moreover, interest rates paid on other short-term financial assets—commercial paper and Treasury bills, for example— usually move up or down roughly in

*Reprinted from the *Quarterly Review*, Summer 1977, pp. 33-48, with permission from the Federal Reserve Bank of New York and the authors.

parallel with the Federal funds rate. Thus the rate also influences the cost of credit obtained from sources other than commercial banks.

Frequently, the Federal funds market is described as one in which commercial banks borrow and lend excess reserve balances held at the Federal Reserve, hence the name Federal funds. While banks often use the Federal funds market for this purpose, growth and change in the market have made this description highly oversimplified. Many active market participants do not hold balances at the Federal Reserve. These include commercial banks that are not members of the Federal Reserve System, thrift institutions, certain agencies of the United States Government, and branches and agencies of foreign banks operating on United States soil. Moreover, this broad set of market participants borrows and lends amounts far beyond the modest total of excess reserve balances. Currently, borrowings of Federal funds outstanding average $45 billion to $50 billion daily.

A closely related market for short-term funds is the market for RPs involving United States Government and Federal agency securities.[1] This market includes many of the same participants that trade Federal funds, but it also includes large nonfinancial corporations, state and local governments, and dealers in United States Government and Federal agency securities. The RP market has expanded rapidly of late, and its workings are perhaps less widely known than those of the Federal funds market.

Although the Federal funds and RP markets are distinct, they share many common features. Both, for example, primarily involve transactions for one business day, although transactions with maturities of up to several weeks are not uncommon. In both markets, commercial banks that are members of the Federal Reserve System can acquire funds not subject to reserve requirements. A lesser known but nevertheless very important common element is the fact that transactions in both markets are settled in what are known as "immediately available funds". Indeed, some observers see the two markets as so closely related that they might appropriately be grouped together under a broader designation—"the markets for short-term immediately available funds". For an elaboration of the nature and uses of immediately available funds, see pages 8 and 9.

The main purpose of this article is to review major recent developments in the markets for Federal funds and RPs. The most significant changes are the dramatic growth of the volume of transactions and of the number and type of institutions active in these markets. At the same time, the language of the market has been changing, mostly because of the evolution in market practices. It is, therefore, necessary to begin with definitions of some terms most frequently used by market participants.

---

[1] The term "Federal agency" is used here in its popular meaning, which refers both to Federal agencies, such as the Commodity Credit Corporation, and to Federally sponsored quasi-public corporations, such as the Federal National Mortgage Association.

FEDERAL FUNDS

Federal funds transactions are frequently described as the borrowing and lending of "excess reserve" balances among commercial banks.[2] This description of Federal funds was accurate years ago but is now seriously deficient, even though it still appears in the financial press. While such commercial bank use of the market persists in substantial volume, Federal funds transactions are no longer confined to the borrowing and lending of excess reserve balances. Moreover—and this is a key point—a Federal funds transaction does not necessarily involve transfer of a reserve balance, even though such a transfer usually does occur. For example, a commercial bank can borrow the "correspondent balances" held with it by other banks. The execution of such a transaction involves only accounting entries on the books of both the borrower and lender.

The most useful description of Federal funds has several elements, some based on regulations, others simply on market convention. In practice, Federal funds are overnight loans that are settled in immediately available funds. Only a limited group of institutions are in a position to borrow in this fashion, mostly commercial banks and some other financial institutions such as agencies of foreign banks. If a member bank borrows Federal funds, Federal Reserve regulations do not require it to hold reserves against the borrowing, as it must for funds acquired in the form of demand or time deposits. But, under Federal Reserve regulations, member banks are permitted to borrow reserve-free funds only from a certain group of institutions. This group includes other commercial banks, Federal agencies, savings and loan associations, mutual savings banks, domestic agencies and branches of foreign banks, and, to a limited degree, Government securities dealers. Market convention has adjusted to these regulatory restrictions, and a Federal funds borrowing has come to mean an overnight loan not just between two commercial banks but between any two of the group of institutions from which member banks may borrow free of reserve requirements. A savings and loan association, for example, can lend Federal funds to an agency of a foreign bank.

This description makes it easy to see that the Federal funds market is by no means limited to the lending of excess reserves. Many of the institutions that participate in the market are not members of the Federal Reserve System and, therefore, do not have reserve accounts. Moreover, the excess reserves

---

[2] A fundamental difficulty with this notion of Federal funds borrowing is that the use of the term "excess reserves" is very imprecise. No distinction is made between the actual excess reserves held in a bank's reserve account and what might be called "potential" excess reserves. Clearly, an individual bank can control the amount of excess reserves it has available to sell in the Federal funds market most easily by selling assets and converting the proceeds into balances at a Federal Reserve Bank. In this sense, the potential excess reserves of an individual bank are nearly as large as its total earning asset portfolio.

of individual member banks are normally very small in relation to their total reserves. The excess reserves characterization of Federal funds borrowing suggests that total activity in the market is likewise rather modest. While this was once true, it no longer is. In recent years, daily outstanding borrowings by member banks in the Federal funds market have approached $50 billion, or about 40 percent more than the *total* reserves they hold. Some individual banks continually borrow as much as four times their required reserves in the Federal funds market.

Fairly recently, banks have begun to borrow immediately available funds for periods longer than a single business day. This form of borrowing was developed by agencies of Canadian banks located in the United States. The transactions are arranged among the same institutions which participate in the overnight market and are similar in all respects except maturity. For these reasons, the transactions have come to be called "term Federal funds" transactions.

The Federal funds and term Federal funds transactions described above are normally "unsecured". This means that the lending institutions have no guarantee of repayment other than the promise of the borrower. For this reason, unsecured Federal funds transactions are done only by institutions that enjoy a very high degree of mutual confidence. At times, however, a lender of Federal funds will ask that the transaction be "secured". This means that the borrower must pledge an asset, usually a Government or Federal agency security, as "collateral" against the loan. The borrower may either set aside the collateral in a custody account or actually deliver it to the lender. However, secured Federal funds transactions are not very common.[3]

REPURCHASE AGREEMENTS

A repurchase agreement (RP) is an acquisition of immediately available funds through the sale of securities, together with a simultaneous agreement to repurchase them at a later date. RPs are most commonly made for one business day, though longer maturities are also frequent. The funds that a member bank acquires in this manner are free of reserve requirements so long as the securities involved are those of the United States Government or Federal agencies. When an RP is arranged, the acquirer of funds agrees to sell to the provider of funds United States Government or Federal agency securities in exchange for immediately available funds. At the maturity of the agreement, the transaction is reversed, again using immediately available funds. Market insiders use different terms to describe the RP, including "repo" and "buy back".

---

[3] Banks chartered in certain states face regulations that require collateral to be provided for the portion of an individual Federal funds transaction in excess of some proportion of the lender's combined capital and surplus.

Those who supply or acquire funds view RPs as involving little risk. Transactions are usually arranged only among institutions enjoying a high degree of confidence in one another. In addition, contracts are usually of very short maturity. Protection against any residual risk can be incorporated in an RP contract by establishing a differential—called a margin—between the quantity of funds supplied and the market value of the securities involved. The margin can protect either party to the transaction, but not both. It protects the supplier of funds if the value of the securities exceeds the quantity of funds supplied. It protects the taker of funds if the securities are of less value than the amount of funds supplied. The supplier of funds generally considers the consequences of default by the other party to be minor, because the securities acquired are obligations either issued or guaranteed by the Federal Government. Another element of risk arises from the possibility that the price of the securities may fall between the time the RP is arranged and the time of any default. For this reason, the margin is most often set to protect the supplier of funds.

This article is concerned with RPs involving only United States Government and Federal agency securities, but it should be noted in passing that an RP can involve any sort of asset which the supplier of funds is willing to accept. RPs involving other assets are executed to a limited degree, for example using certificates of deposit of large banks.

Transactions are executed in several ways, but two appraoches are most common. One approach is for the securities to be both sold and repurchased at the same price, with charges representing the agreed-upon rate of return added to the principal at the maturity of the contract. The second approach involves setting a higher price for repayment than for selling.

The term "reverse repurchase agreement" is sometimes thought to be quite different from an RP. In fact, it refers to exactly the same transaction viewed from the perspective of the supplier of funds rather than the recipient. Compare the two views of the transaction: The recipient of funds sells a security to obtain funds, and "repurchases" it at maturity by redelivery of funds. In a reverse RP, the supplier of funds buys a security by delivering funds when the agreement is made and "resells" the security for immediately available funds on maturity of the contract. From the perspective of the party acquiring funds, the term "repurchase agreement" seems apt, and from that of the supplier of funds, the transaction is exactly the "reverse". However, whether funds are acquired or supplied, the transaction is usually referred to in the marketplace simply as an RP.

THE MARKETS FOR FEDERAL FUNDS AND RPs

There is no central physical marketplace for Federal funds; the market consists of a loosely structured telephone network connecting the major participants. These participants, as already mentioned, include commercial

IMMEDIATELY AVAILABLE FUNDS

The Means of Settlement for Transactions in Federal Funds and RPs

An essential feature of both Federal funds and RPs is that transactions are settled in "immediately available funds". Therefore it is necessary to specify precisely what such funds are. Immediately available funds are two related but distinct types of financial claims: (1) deposit liabilities of Federal Reserve Banks and (2) certain "collected" liabilities of commercial banks that may be transferred or withdrawn during a business day on the order of account holders.

Federal Reserve Banks, of course, are "banks for banks", and deposits are held there mainly by commercial banks that are members of the Federal Reserve System in order to satisfy the reserve requirements imposed on members. These deposits have special features, however. Along with currency and coin, they are the only form of money created directly by a Federal authority. This reflects the fact that these deposits are the direct liabilities of the Federal Reserve Banks. In addition, the Federal Reserve operates a nationwide electronic communications network over which these deposits can be transferred anywhere in the country within a business day. Deposits at Federal Reserve Banks are therefore termed immediately available funds, since they can be converted to cash or transferred anywhere in the United States within a single day on demand.

Immediately available funds also consist of certain collected liabilities of commercial banks. This group of liabilities include a portion of a bank's demand and time deposits, as well as certain other liabilities which are used very much like deposits but which are classed separately for accounting or regulatory reasons. These liabilities are termed immediately available funds because commercial banks permit them to be withdrawn in cash or used for payment without question within a single day. The immediate and unquestioned use of these bank liabilities for payment depends on the fact that they are collected, a feature which can be illustrated by describing how an individual's checking deposit with a bank becomes collected.

Typically, an individual increases his bank balance by depositing checks payable to him drawn on the same or some other bank. When the check is drawn on some other bank, the individual is normally unable to withdraw or otherwise use the funds on the same day that the deposit is made. Fre-

banks and those other financial institutions from which, under Federal Reserve regulations, member banks can buy reserve-free Federal funds. The market also includes a small group of firms that act as brokers for Federal funds. These firms neither lend nor borrow but arrange transactions between borrowers and lenders in exchange for a very small percentage commission.

quently, several days elapse, during which time the credit to the depositor's account is only provisional and the check is in the process of being collected. That is, it is cleared and then payment is received by the depositor's bank from the bank on which the check is drawn. Payment may be received in any one of several forms: a deposit at a Federal Reserve Bank, a collected deposit at another commercial bank, or conceivably in currency or coin. Whatever the case, once collected, the individual's balance can be transferred on his order.

Alternatively, a depositor may receive payment to his account in immediately available funds. In this case, the funds can be withdrawn in cash or otherwise used on the day of receipt with no intervening period for collection. For credit to be received immediately, the deposit must be made in some form other than the common check. The most obvious alternative is cash, used frequently for small deposits but only rarely for sizable transactions because of the risk of loss.

More commonly, when the depositor wishes to receive immediately available funds, the transfer is accomplished through the Federal Reserve electronic communications network. This network is used either within or between Federal Reserve Districts. Any member bank may send or receive immediately available funds—in the form of reserve deposits—to or from any other member bank, and the entire transfer takes place within one business day. The use of the Federal Reserve network can be accomplished indirectly by individuals or institutions other than member banks. This requires the transfer of a depositor's collected balance from one member bank to another, in effect using a reserve balance at the Federal Reserve as a means of payment between banks. If the transaction results in a transfer of funds from one account to another within a single bank, only balance-sheet entries are affected since there need be no actual movement of funds over the Federal Reserve network.

Immediately available funds can be used by a customer of a commercial bank to make payment in any sort of transaction. Among the principal users are sizable financial, business, and government institutions. In practice, such funds are used only for large transactions including, for example, payment for purchase of a financial asset, for raw materials, or for a construction contract. In all these cases, immediately available funds are used as a means of payment because the parties to the transactions wish to use them. Thus, not all transactions involving the use of immediately available funds are related to either the Federal funds or the repurchase agreement markets.

All major participants employ traders. These individuals make the actual telephone contact on behalf of lending or borrowing institutions, making offers to borrow or lend at specific interest rates. They also negotiate any differences between the rate bid by a borrower and that offered by a lender. Transactions are usually executed in lots of $1 million or more. Frequently, but not always, settlement of the transaction requires transfer of funds over the Federal Reserve wire transfer network, first when the agreement is reached and again the next day when repayment is made.

Many banks, particularly medium-sized and large ones, frequently borrow and lend Federal funds on the same day, thereby performing an intermediary function in the Federal funds market. Such banks channel funds from banks with lesser need for funds to banks with greater need for them, frequently borrowing from smaller banks and lending to larger ones. Over the past decade, more medium-sized regional banks have begun to act as intermediaries. In addition, many more banks during this period have come to borrow significantly more than they lend; that is, they have become continual net borrowers.

In recent years a growing portion of the market has consisted of large banks' borrowing of correspondent balances from small banks. Historically, these correspondent balances earned no interest. But both large and small banks have come to regard correspondent relationships as convenient bases for arranging Federal funds transactions. Small banks now intentionally accumulate large balances, selling off daily the excess not needed for the clearing of checks or for other purposes. In such cases, it is not necessary to transfer funds over the Federal Reserve wire transfer network, and reserve balances need not change ownership. Rather, bookkeeping entries are posted by both the borrower and lender to reflect the fact that a noninterest-bearing correspondent demand balance has been converted into a Federal funds borrowing.

No central physical marketplace for repurchase agreements exists either. Transactions are arranged by telephone, largely on a direct basis between the parties supplying and acquiring funds but increasingly through a small group of market specialists. These specialists, mostly Government securities dealers, arrange a repurchase agreement with one party to acquire funds and a reverse repurchase agreement with another party to supply funds. They earn a profit by acquiring funds more cheaply than they supply them.

Large banks and Government securities dealers are the primary seekers of funds in the RP market. Banks use the market as one among many sources of funds, but have a distinct advantage over other institutions as acquirers of funds because they hold large portfolios of United States Government and Federal agency securities. Moreover, because the supplier of funds receives securities, and because member banks acquiring funds need not hold reserves against RPs regardless of the source of funds, the RP market attracts a wider array of participants than does the Federal funds market. Government securities dealers use the market as a source of funds to finance their holdings of Government and agency securities. Many types of institutions supply immediately available funds in this market, but large nonfinancial corporations and state and local governments dominate.

Typically, participants on both sides of the RP market have lists of customers with whom they routinely do business. Each of the largest participants uses an "RP trader", an individual whose job it is to contact other traders and to negotiate the best arrangements possible. A trader begins the day with information on the amount of funds he must supply or acquire. His objective is to arrange transactions at the maximum return obtainable if he is to provide funds and at the minimum cost possible if he is to acquire funds.

With these definitions and descriptions in mind, it is possible to discuss in some detail the roles of the major institutional participants in the markets for immediately available funds. It is appropriate to begin with an examination of the role played by commercial banks, who are currently the most important of those who obtain funds in these markets. Moreover, the reserve position adjustments that banks make in the markets for immediately available funds are important links in transmitting the effects of monetary policy throughout the financial system.

COMMERCIAL BANKS AND
IMMEDIATELY AVAILABLE FUNDS

Commercial banks are the largest and most active participants in the markets for immediately available funds. Banks use these markets for several purposes, among which is the day-to-day adjustment of reserve positions. Large banks have made such adjustments in the Federal funds market for over fifty years and continue to do so in substantial volume. But commercial bank use of both the Federal funds and the RP markets is best understood in the much broader context of how banks obtain and use funds. In addition, bank operations in the Federal funds and RP markets have been heavily influenced by changes in the regulations that govern bank activities.

The traditional view of banks has been that they accept deposit liabilities from customers and use the funds to lend or invest. In the process, they make a profit by earning more in interest on loans and investments than their cost of operations, including interest they pay on deposits. This approach has undergone significant modification over the past decade at least, particularly at large banks. In place of a passive stance, banks have become active solicitors of funds in the open markets. Moreover, they have developed liabilities in addition to standard demand and savings accounts. Fifteen years ago, for example, banks developed and began to exploit the negotiable certificate of deposit (CD). More recently, Euro-dollars, commercial paper issued by bank holding companies, and other instruments have been developed and used as sources of funds. Large banks set a target for the total amount of liabilities they will attempt to secure, basing that target on the total of loans and investments thought to be profitable. The overall approach, summarized here in its barest outlines, is generally known as "liability management".

The spread of the practice of liability management has had two related effects on commercial bank activity in the Federal funds market. First, instead of just engaging in relatively small trades for the purpose of making daily reserve adjustments, today banks may rely on this market to meet a desired proportion of liabilities. Thus, they at times borrow amounts that are large relative to their total assets or liabilities. Second, instead of individual banks lending as often as they borrow, some banks are continual net borrowers, while others are continual lenders. The borrowers use the market both to offset the impact on their reserve holdings of day-to-day inflows and outflows of deposits and as an ongoing source of funds to finance loans and investments. The lenders, usually smaller banks, treat Federal funds as a highly liquid interest-earning short-term asset.

ORIGINS OF THE FEDERAL FUNDS MARKET

Commercial banks were entirely responsible for the origination and early development of the Federal funds market. The market began among a small number of New York City banks in the early 1920's. Some banks frequently found themselves in reserve deficit positions and, therefore, were forced to borrow from the Federal Reserve discount window. Others frequently had unanticipated excess reserve holdings, and these balances did not earn any interest. Under these circumstances, an obvious opportunity for mutual benefit existed, and bank managers devised a mechanism to realize these benefits. They exchanged drafts drawn on Federal Reserve balances and so created the Federal funds market. A lending bank made payment by delivering a draft on a reserve account on the day a borrowing was arranged. Such drafts, in contrast to a common check, could be collected on the day they were presented to the Federal Reserve. To accomplish the repayment, the borrowing bank gave a clearinghouse check made out to the lender to be collected the following day. The repayment check was for a slightly larger sum to reflect the interest due.

This practice spread to other cities in subsequent years, but the amounts traded remained small, and the markets remained largely confined to local areas. Only large banks participated in the market, and transactions were undertaken only to adjust for relatively small deficits or excesses in reserves. Many individual banks found that they were able to lend in the market one day, but had to borrow the next.

Toward the end of the 1920's, the market began to expand to include interregional as well as intracity transactions. Trading of funds between regions was made possible by the Federal Reserve wire transfer facilities, which permitted the movements of funds from one city to another without the use of drafts. By this time, daily borrowing reached about $250 million. With the 1929 stock market crash and the ensuing depression, however, interest rates fell substantially and banks developed a strong preference for holding cash, reflected in large holdings of excess reserves. These developments cut short the growth of the Federal funds market, but the brief appearance of wire trading of Federal funds in the late 1920's set the stage for rapid development of the market after World War II.

FEDERAL FUNDS IN THE POSTWAR ERA

In the three decades since the end of World War II, the Federal funds market has changed in at least two fundamental respects. First, both the number of banks participating in the market and aggregate trading volume in Federal funds have grown enormously. Second, most large banks, which formerly alternated between borrowing and lending, have become continual net borrowers, which small banks not previously active in the market have entered the market, primarily as continual lenders.

The changing role of the large banks is evidence that liability management has been added to daily reserve position adjustment as a motive for participation in the Federal funds market. A continuous and steady supply of funds is available to large banks once they have established market contacts with sellers. As a result, Federal funds have become an important source of liabilities because of their availability and the low cost of executing transactions over the Federal Reserve wire network, and because these funds are not subject to reserve requirements or interest rate ceilings.

Smaller banks have been introduced to the market primarily through correspondent relationships with large banks. Immediately after World War II, small banks held relatively large amounts of their assets in cash. The practice was understandable at that time, because interest rates were very low and because a high value was placed on liquidity due to the vivid memories of the prewar depression. Interest rates began to rise in the 1950's, however, increasing the interest earnings foregone by holding large amounts of cash. With large banks willing to borrow and interest rates rising, a few small banks began to lend their cash balances to large banks in the form of Federal funds. Such overnight lending provided virtually the same liquidity as cash.

By the early 1960's, banks of all sizes and types had become familiar with the advantages of participation in the Federal funds market. Two major rulings by bank regulators in these years also served to encourage trading of Federal funds.

In 1963, the Comptroller of the Currency issued rulings that eliminated restrictions on the amounts that a nationally chartered bank could lend to any one bank. Formerly, unsecured lending to a single borrower in Federal funds had been restricted to 10 percent of the lending bank's combined capital and surplus. Though this limit applied to all nationally chartered banks, it effectively restricted the activities only of the small banks in this group. The 1963 ruling declared Federal funds transactions to be purchases and sales, not borrowings and lendings. In so ruling, the Comptroller effectively removed the restrictions that had kept small banks from placing relatively large amounts of funds in the Federal funds market.

In 1964, a ruling by the Federal Reserve Board made it clear that member banks could legally purchase correspondent balances of nonmember banks as Federal funds. Prior to this ruling, the practice of purchasing correspondent balances had not been as widespread.

Together these rulings served to encourage the sale of Federal funds by small banks, and to reinforce the spread of liability management techniques among large correspondent banks. Small banks were now in a position to ask their correspondents to engage in Federal funds transactions under the threat that their funds would otherwise be moved to a competitor. Faced with a potential loss of balances, large correspondent banks began to buy Federal funds regularly in large amounts from small banks.

The net purchases of Federal funds by large commercial banks have increased enormously since the regulatory changes. But as the lower two segments of Chart 1 show, the growth has occurred sporadically. Spurts of rapid growth in this market have generally taken place during periods when short-term interest rates were either rising rapidly or at high levels. The Federal funds rate, as Chart 2 shows, has reached several postwar peaks in the last fifteen years. At such times, large banks sought funds most aggressively. They put considerable effort into developing new correspondent relationships and into attracting larger amounts of funds from existing ones. Smaller banks were induced to increase their lending by the high interest rates offered. The volume of funds traded in the market declined somewhat during periods of lower short-term interest rates, but once developed, the correspondent relationships have tended to remain active.

The rapid postwar development of the Federal funds market led to a reversal in 1965 of the long-standing relationship between the Federal funds rate and the Federal Reserve discount rate. Prior to that time, the discount rate had served as an effective ceiling on the Federal funds rate. This was because many banks borrowed Federal funds only occasionally and in relatively small amounts, and were therefore able to accomplish such short-term adjustments at the discount window as an alternative to Federal funds borrowing. This use of the discount window occurred whenever the Federal funds rate approached the discount rate. As banks turned to the discount

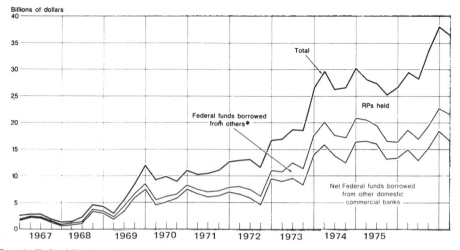

Chart 1 Federal Funds and RPs Held by 46 Large Domestic Commercial Banks (*Includes borrowings from those institutions other than domestic commercial banks from which member banks may borrow free of reserve requirements.)

Percent

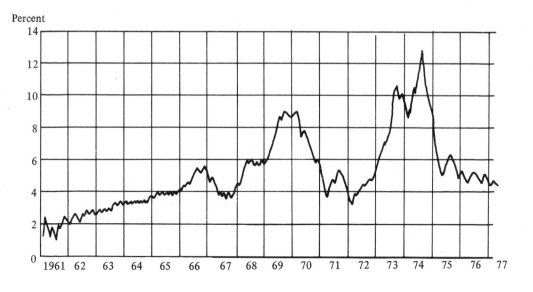

Chart 2 Interest Rate on Federal Funds

window, demand for Federal funds diminished, and upward rate pressures slackened.

With the rise in liability management practices in the early 1960's, banks borrowed Federal funds more frequently and in larger amounts. Such borrowing could not be done at the discount window, which has always been available only for short-term adjustments by individual banks. As a result, banks using the Federal funds market for liability management purposes continued bidding for Federal funds as the rate rose to and exceeded the discount rate. This happened for the first time in 1965, when tightening monetary policy pushed the Federal funds rate upward. The Federal funds rate has been above the discount rate for much of the period since.

Another significant change in the market came in 1970. Federal Reserve Regulation D, which specifies those deposits of member banks that are subject to reserve requirements, had previously exempted Federal funds borrowing from reserve requirements so long as the lender was a commercial bank. An amendment to the regulation, along with a formal interpretation, extended the exemption to several other types of nonbank institutions, including agencies of the United States Government, savings and loan associations, mutual savings banks, as well as agencies and branches of foreign banks operating in this country. By 1970, some banks had already begun to borrow Federal funds from these nonbank institutions, and the regulatory change removed any doubt that the practice was acceptable. This change was particularly important, for it provided explicit regulatory approval for banks to borrow Federal funds from selected lenders outside the banking community, just as banks do by issuing CDs, demand deposits, or any other type of liability.

Commercial banks are able to obtain immediately available funds through repurchase agreements as well as through Federal funds transactions. The growth of RP activity by commercial banks, like that of Federal funds, has been influenced by regulatory changes. In 1969, Federal Reserve Regulation D was amended to restrict the exemption from reserve requirements only to those funds raised through RPs involving United States Government or Federal agency securities. This action practically eliminated bank trading in those RPs which involve other sorts of financial claims. At the same time, however, it removed any questions about the status of RPs involving Government securities.

RECENT DEVELOPMENTS IN THE BANKING SECTOR

Some rather dramatic events occurred in the markets for immediately available funds beginning in 1973. Monetary policy was tightened that year in response to rapid inflation and a booming economy. The tightening placed severe pressure on the banking system—which had a limited supply of funds and faced strong demand for loans, particularly from businesses. Under these circumstances, banks with a strong liability management orientation turned to any and all potential sources of funds. In early 1973, large banks began to borrow heavily in the CD market. This borrowing was facilitated by the suspension in May 1973 of interest rate ceilings on all maturities of large denomination CDs. From early 1973 through mid-1974, CD borrowing jumped by about $38 billion. Large banks sought short-term open market funds to meet loan demands much more heavily than before, taking in about $18 billion of additional Federal funds and RPs during the same period.

The United States economy went through a sharp recession between late 1973 and early 1975. Demand for credit from commercial banks as well as other lenders remained strong for a time, but progressively weakened through the later stages of the downslide and into the recovery which began in mid-1975. With loans contracting, large banks gradually reduced their lending rates and also sought liabilities with lessened intensity. Their CDs dropped sharply, falling by $28 billion between early 1975 and late 1976. Commercial bank acquisition of Federal funds and RPs, however, did not follow the pattern set in the CD market. Holdings of these funds declined by only about $4 billion in late 1974 and 1975, then grew by about $17 billion in 1976. This reflected a continuing basic growth of the markets for Federal funds and RPs.

The basic growth also was manifest in the continuing entry of banks into the markets for immediately available funds. Call reports of member banks of the Federal Reserve System show that in 1969 about 55 percent of all member banks either bought or sold Federal funds. By 1976, the proportion of member banks that was in the market had climbed to 88 percent. Most of the new entrants to the market were small banks.

Thus, even in the early 1970's many commercial banks were newcomers to the markets for immediately available funds. These markets broadened and deepened in stages which typically occurred in periods of high interest rates. The concentration of entry in such periods is due at least partially to sizable start-up expenditures for trading in immediately available funds. Start-up costs are incurred mostly by borrowers, and mainly involve expenses of finding and establishing a trading relationship with potential suppliers of funds. The expenditures are more easily justified when interest rates (and potential earnings) are high. Once established, trading relationships tend to remain active even after interest rates fall.

Other developments also contributed to the greater acquisition of Federal funds and RPs by banks during 1975 and 1976. In 1974, the Treasury changed the way it handled its deposits at commercial banks (Tax and Loan Accounts). Such accounts had been held at banks for decades. Beginning in August 1974, however, most of these balances were transferred to the twelve Federal Reserve Banks. This reduced the volume of Government and agency securities that commercial banks were required to hold as pledged collateral against Treasury deposits. Once free from this purpose, these securities were available for use in the market for repurchase agreements.

With loan demand light in 1975, commercial banks began to accumulate large amounts of additional Government and agency securities. The process was significantly aided by the large amounts of new Government securities the Treasury sold in order to finance the sizable deficits the Federal Government was running. These securities were heavily used by large banks to acquire funds in repurchase agreements since they could be financed in this way at a cost below their interest yield. At about the same time, the effects of the recession led corporations to reduce inventories and expenditures for fixed plant and equipment. This enabled corporations to begin to rebuild their liquidity, partly through the purchase of Government securities and also by supplying funds to the RP market. The use of RPs grew rapidly as corporations increasingly came to view repurchase agreements as income-generating substitutes for demand deposits at commercial banks.

Quite separately, small banks and nonbank financial institutions were also increasing their offerings of immediately available funds. Both types of institutions experienced a decline in loan demand from corporate and other borrowers with the onset of the recession. But individuals stepped up their savings in the form of deposits with small banks and with nonbank thrift institutions. With increasing deposit inflows and declining demand for loans, these institutions looked for alternative investments and became active suppliers of immediately available funds.

THE ROLE OF GOVERNMENT SECURITIES DEALERS

Government securities dealers are the second major group of participants active in the markets for immediately available funds. Dealers are in the markets primarily to acquire funds, but they also supply funds under some circumstances. In some ways dealers act as financial intermediaries, but their operations also have speculative features. Dealers earn income in two ways: "carry income" and "trading profits". Carry income (or loss) refers to the difference between the interest yield of a dealer's portfolio and the cost of the funds which support that portfolio. Trading profits refer to the gain (or loss) a dealer earns by selling securities for more (or less) than he paid for them.

Government securities dealers often hold sizable positions in United States Government and Federal agency securities. These positions are highly leveraged in that the dealers borrow a very high percentage of the cost of purchasing securities. The search for low cost money to finance his position is a central part of the operations of any successful Government securities dealer. This search led the dealer community to promote the use of the repurchase agreement shortly after World War II. RPs were offered mainly to large corporations, which found them attractive because the short maturities of the RP contracts made them much like demand deposits, with the added advantage of earning income. The use of RPs by dealers has expanded ever since, in part because more corporations and others have come to accept the repurchase agreement as a reliable short-term money market instrument. Dealers have also come to vary the size of their positions much more than before, in response to the greater variability of interest rates and securities prices in recent years. These larger swings in position, which are evident in Chart 3, have been accompanied by higher average positions, which in turn have contributed to the increased use of RPs by dealers.

Because of greater interest rate variability, and in an effort to broaden their activities, Government securities dealers have developed new trading techniques and expanded the use of others. One of the greatly expanded techniques enables dealers to act essentially as brokers in the RP markets. They obtain funds in exchange for securities in one transaction and simultaneously release funds in exchange for securities in a separate transaction. When the maturities of the two transactions—one a repurchase agreement and the other a reverse repurchase agreement—are identical, the two are said to be "matched". The dealer profits by obtaining funds at a cost slightly lower than the return he receives for the funds he supplies. After arranging such a pair of transactions, a dealer is exposed to credit risk (the possibility of default), but not to market risk (changes in the value of the portfolio due to changes in market prices).

A commonly used variant of the "matched" agreement gives the dealer greater opportunity to try to take advantage of movements in interest rates. A dealer may deliberately not "match" the maturity of an RP with the maturity of a reverse RP. Usually the RP is for a period shorter than the reverse RP, establishing what is called a "tail". The "tail" refers to the difference in the maturities of the two transactions. If during this period the dealer is able to refinance the reverse RP with an RP at a lower cost, he makes a profit; if not, he loses money.

Billions of dollars

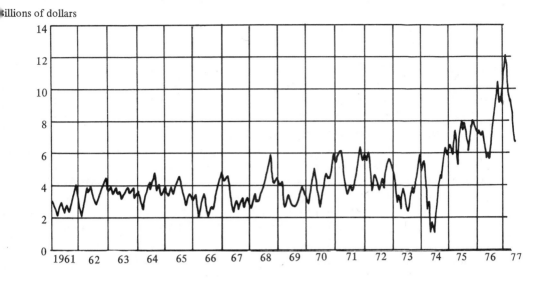

Chart 3 Dealer Positions in United States Government and Federal Agency Securities

Another use of the reverse RP has been developed more recently. Reverse RPs are now used frequently to facilitate "short sales" of Government and Federal agency securities.[4] In the past, dealers wishing to establish such positions had to borrow securities from commercial banks, usually at an interest fee of 50 basis points (½ percent). Now dealers often acquire securities elsewhere under reverse RPs and frequently through this device reduce the cost of obtaining securities for the purpose of short sales.

Use of the reverse RP to facilitate the short sale has led to the appearance of a new subsector of the repurchase agreement market, known as the "specific issue market". The subsector has developed because, for purposes of a short sale, a dealer tries to obtain the exact issue whose price he expects to fall. In a usual reverse RP, the specific securities to be exchanged are rarely discussed (though their maturity should exceed that of the reverse RP), since the parties to the agreement are primarily concerned with the cost of the money involved. The placement of securities in the specific issue market is advantageous for both principals to the transaction. Since it is apparent that the dealer is interested in a particular issue, the holder of the securities is able to negotiate with the dealer and can often get funds at a slightly lower cost than if he were to place the securities in the overall RP market.

---

[4]The dealer does not own the securities that he promises to deliver in a short sale. He "covers" the short by buying in the open market the particular security he has promised to deliver. Trading profits can be earned during periods of falling securities prices if the securities that were sold short became available at below-contract prices prior to the agreed-upon delivery date.

CORPORATIONS AND THE RP MARKET

Up to this point, the analysis has concentrated on the major demanders of Federal funds and RPs. The discussion of major nonbank suppliers begins with nonfinancial corporations. They have been supplying funds through RPs against Government and agency securities for about thirty years.

The principal reason corporations hold cash and other short-term liquid assets is to bridge timing gaps between receipts and expenditures. Large quantities of funds are accumulated in anticipation of payments for dividends, corporate taxes, payrolls, and other regular expenses. In addition, corporations also accumulate short-term liquid assets in anticipation of expenditures for plant and equipment. In general, corporate liquidity is related to economic conditions and expectations about the future course of the economy and interest rates. Liquidity is often low—i.e., corporations have small amounts of liquid assets and large amounts of short-term borrowing—in periods of rapid economic expansion. Liquidity is rebuilt by reducing short-term borrowings and acquiring liquid assets during an economic slowdown or the early stages of an expansion.

Corporations have traditionally held significant amounts of their liquid assets in the form of demand deposits at commercial banks. Such balances have not earned interest since 1933, but this was not of great significance during the low interest rate periods of the depression and just after World War II. Interest rates began to climb in the late 1950's, and the higher rates have had a significant impact on how corporations handle their liquidity positions. They constituted an inducement to develop "cash management" techniques in some ways parallel to the "liability management" techniques adopted by banks during the same period. Cash management consists of a variety of procedures designed to achieve four goals: to speed up the receipt of payments due; to slow down the disbursement of payments owed; to keep a corporation's demand deposits to a minimum because they earn no interest; and to earn the maximum return on liquid asset holdings.

Repurchase agreements are particularly useful as tools of cash management. They generate income for the supplier of funds and are generally regarded as secure. Their key advantage is flexibility, primarily because they can be arranged for periods as short as one day. Few if any other income-generating assets have this feature. Regulations prevent banks from issuing CDs with maturities of less than thirty days; commercial paper and bankers' acceptances can be obtained for shorter periods, but as a practical matter not for one day. None of these instruments are viewed as being quite as secure as repurchase agreements, where there is a margin between the amount of funds supplied and the value of the securities. Corporations can buy Government securities or other financial assets and hold them for short periods, but the transaction costs can be relatively high and the possibility of capital loss reduces the attractiveness of such alternatives. The overnight feature of RPs means that corporations treat them as if they are income-earning demand deposits.

Corporations make heavy use of a particular form of RP known as the "continuing contract". Under such a contract, a corporation will agree to provide a specific volume of funds to a bank or a dealer for a certain period of time. However, during the life of the contract the repurchase agreement is treated almost as if it were reestablished each day. That is, earnings are calculated daily, often related to the prevailing overnight RP rate. Either party has the right to withdraw at any time, although this right is seldom used. The principal advantage of the continuing contract over the daily renewals of an RP is that securities and funds are exchanged only at the beginning and at the end of the contract. The continuing contract therefore significantly reduces transactions costs, compared with daily RPs. An additional feature of the continuing contract RP is the seller's right of substitution, under which securities of equal value may be used to replace those originally involved in the RP. This option does not appear in all continuing contracts but, where it does appear, it is frequently exercised.

Another RP arrangement rather similar to the continuing contract specifies neither a definite period nor a fixed amount. Arrangements are made by banks chiefly for their corporate customers. The corporation concentrates all its demand balances in a single account at that bank daily. Before the bank closes its books each day, the corporation's balance in this account is determined, and any excess over a specified minimum is automatically converted into an RP. The following morning the funds are moved from the RP back to the corporation's demand balance for use during the day. Such automatic arrangements for the conversion of demand deposits to RPs are often included in packages of services offered by banks to their corporate customers. Among the services in such packages are lines of credit, payroll administration, and the use of safekeeping facilities. Payment for such service packages is usually not made on the basis of a stated fee. Instead, average or minimum demand deposit balances—called compensating balances—are usually required.

RPs also can be used to provide liquidity for somewhat longer periods, for example, to allow the accumulation of funds for a tax or dividend payment. This option is particularly attractive to corporations if the income that can be earned on a longer RP exceeds that available on an overnight RP. One or several RPs can be written, as liquidity is accumulated over the period prior to a payment date, with the contracts maturing on the day disbursements, must be made. The RP has less commanding advantages over other money market assets for longer periods, however. Commercial paper can frequently be tailored to mature on a specific day, and Treasury bills that mature very close to the desired date can often be purchased. RPs are nevertheless used very frequently for such purposes, primarily because they can be arranged easily and quickly once a corporation has established a routine trading relationship with market participants.

The volume of corporate RPs has grown dramatically in the 1970's. This growth has not been smooth, but has occurred in bursts. Monetary policy was quite restrictive through 1969 and into 1970, and again in 1973 and early 1974. During these periods, interest rates, particularly on short-term instruments, reached very high levels. The interest income foregone by holding demand deposits was obviously very high, and corporate treasurers responded by accelerating the development of cash management techniques in general and increasing the use of RPs. In effect, the periods of high interest rates helped corporations meet the cost of developing these new techniques, and the high rates then attainable explain the apparent paradox that corporations provided a growing volume of funds to the RP market when they were most strapped for cash.

Interest rates fell rather quickly once the economy entered the 1974-75 recession. For a time, as they had in the earlier periods of declining interest rates, corporations reduced their supply of funds to the RP market. By early 1975, however, corporations began to expand their RP activity rapidly. The apparently atypical increase in RP activity was brought on by the combination of several forces. Most important, the RP became widely accepted as an instrument of cash management for corporations. During preceding periods, many corporations did not participate in the RP market due either to restrictions in their by-laws or to lack of familiarity with the instrument among corporate treasurers. But by the mid-1970's, by-laws of many corporations had been changed, and the instrument had become widely accepted. Coincidentally, by 1974 many corporations felt that their liquidity had reached dangerously low levels, and rebuilding liquidity thus became a high priority. Reductions in capital expenditures and inventories were possible as the economy turned downward, thereby reducing corporate borrowing needs and contributing to improved cash flow. Corporations were able to begin to accumulate liquid assets as soon as cash flow began to improve after the worst of the recession was over, a process that has continued since. Significant portions of the new-found corporate liquidity were placed either in outright purchases of Government securities or in repurchase agreements against such securities.

State and local government units have entered the RP market only in recent years but have quickly become major suppliers of funds. The RP is particularly well suited to their needs. These governments usually are required by law to hold their assets in the most secure form, generally in bank deposits or Government and Federal agency securities. The RP provides a way of meeting these requirements while earning income on short-term investments.

Tax receipts of state and local governments never match exactly the timing pattern of their expenditures, thereby creating the need for them either to borrow or to invest for short periods at various times of the year. Until recently their major investment alternative to deposits has been Treasury bills. As the advantages of the RP have become more widely recognized, these governments have switched more of their liquid investments into RPs.

In 1972, the Congress passed revenue-sharing legislation which increased the total volume of Federal money flowing to states and localities. The revenue-sharing payments are concentrated at the beginning of each calendar quarter, and state and local governments have invested large portions of these funds in RPs until needed.

THE ROLE OF NONBANK FINANCIAL INSTITUTIONS

Several types of nonbank financial institutions are active in the markets for immediately available funds. These include mutual savings banks, savings and loan associations, branches and agencies of foreign banks that operate on United States soil, and Edge Act corporations. (The latter are affiliates of United States commercial banks empowered to engage in international or foreign banking in the United States or abroad.) All of these institutions are active primarily in the market for Federal funds, and generally do not enter into repurchase agreements in volume. They generally lend Federal funds to commercial banks, although under certain circumstances agencies and branches of foreign banks will borrow from banks or other nonbank lenders.

The appearance of all these institutions in the Federal funds market has occurred relatively recently. Their entry has dramatically changed the function of the Federal funds market, allowing the banking system to draw funds from a wide array of institutions, instead of just reallocating reserves. The expanded borrowing ability of banks serves to integrate more closely the United States financial structure, and to help break down the barriers which have traditionally existed among various types of financial institutions.

The agencies and branches of foreign banks have also become active participants in the Federal funds market. These institutions deal with or represent foreign commercial banks, which trade in both the money markets of their home countries and in the Euro-currency markets. Through the Federal funds market, the agencies and branches of foreign banks provide a link between the various markets abroad and the United States commercial banking system.

The participation of these institutions in United States financial markets mirrors the activities of United States commercial banks overseas. In the last three decades, overseas branch networks of United States banks have grown significantly in both the scale and range of their operations, and these networks have provided United States banks with easy access to foreign and international financial markets. Entry into the Federal funds market by agencies and branches of foreign banks, therefore, has contributed to the continuing integration of credit markets and banking in the United States and abroad.

THE ROLE OF THE FEDERAL RESERVE

The Federal Reserve is important to the markets for Federal funds and RPs for two quite different reasons. One is that Federal Reserve regulations play a very important role in the markets by limiting the type and terms of transactions member banks may undertake. A second is that actions taken by the Federal Reserve in the normal conduct of monetary policy have a major influence on the levels of interest rates in general and on the Federal funds rate in particular. Federal Reserve monetary policy is oriented toward achieving steady and sustained growth of the economy, along with reasonably stable prices. Such a sound economy depends on a multiplicity of factors, one of which is the capacity of the commercial banking system to extend loans and create deposits. These capacities, in turn, are strongly influenced by the interest rate on Federal funds and the supply of reserves to member banks.

The Federal Reserve controls the supply of reserves through open market operations, mainly via outright purchases and sales of Government and Federal agency securities. An outright purchase of securities provides reserves permanently, while a sale permanently reduces the total supply of reserves. But the Federal Reserve also needs to provide and absorb reserves for short periods, mainly to accommodate the seasonal needs of banks for reserves and to offset the effects on reserves of day-to-day changes in currency in circulation, in the Treasury's balance at Federal Reserve Banks, and in Federal Reserve float. Reserves can be supplied temporarily by use of repurchase agreements, and absorbed temporarily through "matched sale-purchase transactions", which most market participants call reverse RPs.

A full historical treatment of Federal Reserve use of the RP and matched sale-purchase transaction would require another article, but a few highlights are important because they have influenced the development of the RP market. Federal Reserve use of the RP dates back to 1917, but extensive use of the instrument began only in the postwar period. Matched sale-purchase transactions were first used to absorb reserves in 1966. The technique was introduced at the time of a sudden, temporary increase in float arising from a widespread interruption of airline service. The amount of reserves needed to be absorbed at that time was too large to be handled by *outright* sales of securities by the Federal Reserve without disturbing the financial markets.

Until 1972, Federal Reserve RPs were executed at a rate fixed by the Federal Reserve, usually the discount rate. In that year the Federal Reserve instituted a competitive bidding procedure whereby the rate on RPs was set as a result of Government securities dealer offerings of securities in relation to Federal Reserve needs to provide reserves. Shortly thereafter, dealers were permitted to offer to the Federal Reserve any securities they obtained in separate transactions with other market participants. Until 1975, RPs were done by the Federal Reserve only with nonbank Government securities dealers. At that time, the practice was changed to include commercial bank Government securities dealer departments. All these changes contributed to the acceptability, flexibility, and utility of the RP.

Federal Reserve use of RPs and matched sale-purchase transactions for temporary reserve adjustment has grown sharply in the past few years, but for generally different reasons than those which explain the increase in the use of RPs by banks and others. The increase has arisen in large part from a change in Treasury procedures for handling its cash balances. Prior to August 1974, the Treasury received payments into accounts at commercial banks, and generally moved funds into its balance at the Federal Reserve only as funds were needed to make payments on behalf of the Federal Government.

Under this scheme, Treasury balances in commercial banks fluctuated widely, but the Treasury balance at the Federal Reserve was reasonably stable. In August 1974, the Treasury began to move its balances more quickly into its accounts at the Federal Reserve Banks, which climbed by several billion dollars over a period of several months. This policy has led to much wider fluctuation in these accounts. This in turn has created greater variability in the supply of reserves available to the banking system which the Federal Reserve usually offsets by temporary adjustments to reserves through RPs or matched sale-purchase transactions.

SOME MAJOR IMPLICATIONS

The Federal funds and RP markets have grown dramatically since World War II, but particularly in the past few years. This growth is due in part to changes in the regulations which govern the operations of commercial banks, but is more basically due to the changing practices and behavior of all participants in these markets. The circumstances influencing each group of market participants have differed in detail, but for all, the quite high interest rates since the mid-1960's have provided the major motivation.

In addition, technological development has made participation less costly. Growth—both in trading volume and in the number of institutions participating in the markets—has not been even. Periods of most rapid growth in these markets have occurred when interest rates were rising toward or stood at postwar peaks. For the most part the markets for immediately available funds have contracted as interest rates fell from successive peaks, but never by as much as in the earlier periods of expansion.

The growth in the Federal funds and RP markets has several implications. Most importantly, the markets have expanded to include a broader range of domestic and international financial institutions and corporations. They use the markets as a link in a worldwide network that transfers interest-sensitive dollar balances to wherever they are in greatest demand. To be sure, mechanisms to move funds to high-demand uses have existed for some time, but the Federal funds and RP markets help make the task easier and more efficient by bringing interest-sensitive funds into a central marketplace from a broader arena. For example, most individuals who hold deposits at thrift institutions do not move their funds quickly from one investment to another in response to small interest rate changes. But thrift institutions can lend in the Federal funds market, in effect allowing the small deposits of individuals to be combined and placed directly in the national markets for short-term credit. Similar considerations apply with respect to international credit flows.

These developments have some implications for the conduct of Federal Reserve monetary policy. Policy actions significantly influence the Federal funds and RP markets, which commercial banks now use as sources of funds more extensively than ever before. Hence any change in the availability of funds in these markets probably has a more direct impact than before on the cost to banks of making loans and on the rates they charge. Moreover, many more small banks and nonbank financial institutions have become quite active in the markets. Through this mechanism, Federal Reserve monetary policy is felt more quickly and directly by a broader range of the financial institutions, including those that provide a major portion of the total credit available in the United States economy.

United States and international financial markets have also become more closely integrated in recent years. There are multiple linkages among the various markets, but they center on the activities in this country and abroad of multinational corporations and of United States and foreign commercial banks. These institutions borrow and lend sizable amounts in both the United States and international markets, and are sensitive to the margins between borrowing and lending rates in different countries. For example, if short-term interest rates in the United States were higher than abroad, the differential would quickly draw funds from other uses abroad and channel liquidity into the United States financial markets. These flows would tend to reduce the differential between interest rates abroad and in this country.

But the flows of credit induced by such interest rate differentials may not be in keeping with Federal Reserve policy objectives at the time. For example, a restrictive monetary policy works to reduce spending by individuals and businesses, partly because it makes borrowing more expensive and difficult to obtain. The effects of such policies on the domestic economy could be dampened if large corporations and financial institutions can readily obtain credit elsewhere.

While high interest rates and inflation have encouraged growth of the Federal funds and RP markets, the evolution of technology, particularly the use of computer facilities, has also played an important part. The new and changing technology speeds the transfer of funds, reduces the cost of record keeping, and increases the availability of information concerning investment opportunities. It seems certain that technological change will continue at a rapid rate, thereby reducing further the costs of arranging and executing financial transactions and reinforcing the already strong trend toward aggressive financial management.

The rapid growth of the markets for Federal funds and RPs in recent years can be viewed as part of a pervasive trend in all United States financial markets toward more aggressive portfolio management by holders of financial assets. This trend will clearly continue to be a strong influence on the markets. Participants will no doubt devise new trading techniques, refine existing ones, and attract others into the marketplace. But the Federal funds and RP markets are only two of many markets for short-term financial claims, and their growth relative to others will be heavily influenced by the regulatory and legal framework in which they operate. These markets could be significantly affected by several proposals for financial reform that have been put forth in recent years, some in the form of legislative proposals introduced in the Congress.

Of particular note in this respect are the increasing number of arguments heard in favor of relaxing or eliminating prohibitions against the payment of interest on demand deposits and the payment of interest on member bank reserve accounts. Such proposals, if enacted, would probably have minor effects on the Federal funds market insofar as it is used by banks for reserve adjustment purposes, but would more heavily affect the use of both the Federal funds and RP markets as sources of funds on a continuing basis by banks. The effect any legislation will have on the markets will, of course, depend on the exact provisions. But one fact seems clear; legislative and regulatory changes can channel the pressure emanating from aggressive financial management into or away from the Federal funds and RP markets, but it is unlikely that financial management itself can be forced to return to the tamer posture of a decade and more ago.

GUIDELINES FOR EFFICIENT RESERVE MANAGEMENT[†]

Robert E. Knight[*]

2

Efficient reserve management is important to every member of the Federal Reserve System. Under present regulations, member banks are required to maintain reserves against deposits and other selected liabilities. These reserves must be held either as vault cash or in a deposit account at a Federal Reserve Bank. Since such assets earn no explicit interest, bank profits can potentially be increased by minimizing holdings of excess reserves. However, if a bank experiences a reserve deficiency, a penalty may be charged.[1] In view of the

[†] Reprinted from the *Monthly Review*, November 1977, pp. 11-23, with permission from the Federal Reserve Bank of Kansas City and the author.

[*] The author is President of the Alliance National Bank, Alliance, Nebraska.

[1] The penalty is based on the amount of the reserve deficiency. Regulation D states that the "penalty will be assessed at a rate of 2 per cent per annum above the lowest rate applicable to borrowings by each member bank from its Federal Reserve Bank on the first day of the calendar month in which the deficiencies occurred."

Although the penalty provides banks with an economic incentive for meeting reserve requirements, the potential threat of regulatory action is usually of greater significance. If a state member bank persists with a reserve deficiency, the Federal Reserve is authorized to suspend its membership privileges. In the case of a national bank, the Federal Reserve may direct the Comptroller of the Currency to initiate legal action to remove a bank's charter. In either case, a less drastic option would be for the Federal Reserve to exercise close surveillance over the bank's activities in order to ensure that reserve requirements were satisfied.

The potential costs of reserve deficiencies, therefore, can considerably exceed those associated with the penalty rate of interest. As a result, the concerns of banks in managing reserves must extend beyond the immediate trade-off between the likely penalty on a deficiency and the rate of interest which could be earned on loanable funds. In economic terms, banks should seek to maximize profits subject to the constraint that adequate provision is made for required reserves.

desirability to banks of avoiding either unused excess reserves or penalties on deficiencies, this article presents guidelines for efficient reserve management. Before turning to this general objective, though, the System's regulations concerning reserve requirements are summarized.

REGULATORY PROVISIONS

System reserve requirements against deposits are based on net demand deposits and on gross time and savings deposits. Net demand deposits are defined as gross demand deposits minus the sum of cash items in process of collection and demand balances due from domestic commercial banks. As can be seen in Table 1, the reserve schedule for demand balances is graduated, rising with the amount of demand deposits held. The requirements for time deposits are a function of both the amount and initial maturity of such deposits, with shorter maturities being subject to higher requirements. By comparison, the reserve requirement for savings deposits does not vary with deposit size. In addition to these requirements, reserves must also be

Table 1
Member Bank Reserve
Requirements
September 15, 1977

Type of Deposit	Percentage Reserve Requirement
Net Demand Deposits	
First $2 million	7.0
Next $8 million	9.5
Next $90 million	11.75
Next $300 million	12.75
Amount over $400 million	16.25
Savings Deposits	3.0
Time Deposits Maturing in	
30 to 179 days	
First $5 million	3.0
Over $5 million	6.0
180 days to 4 years	2.5*
4 years or more	1.0*

*The average reserve requirement on all time and savings deposits must be at least 3 per cent, the minimum specified in the Federal Reserve Act.

> Throughout this article, "reserve assessment" period refers to the week during which deposits and other reservable liabilities determine the magnitude of reserves a bank must hold. The "reserve maintenance" or "settlement" period is 2 weeks later and refers to the week during which the reserves are required to be maintained.

held against a variety of nondeposit sources of funds.[2] The specific balance sheet items subject to reserve requirements and the levels of those requirements are set by the Board of Governors and are changed when economic and financial conditions warrant. Details concerning the requirements at any time may be found in Regulations D and M of the Federal Reserve System.

Present procedures for meeting reserve requirements are designed to give banks some degree of flexibility and to minimize the uncertainty about the amount of reserves which must be held. One factor contributing to this flexibility is the ability of banks to average reserves. In calculating required reserves, banks average the daily totals of deposits and other items subject to requirements over a one-week period.[3] Similarly, reserves are averaged over a 1-week period. The ability to average reserves means that banks do not have to meet minimum targets for reserves on each individual day. A reserve shortfall early in the settlement week can be offset with an excess later in the week, while a reserve excess early in the period can be balanced by a subsequent deficiency. However, if a sizable surplus develops toward the end of a settlement week, a bank is not allowed to "overdraw" its account at the Federal Reserve in an effort to reduce its average balance to the required level.[4]

---

[2] Nondeposit transactions subject to reserve requirements include, under certain conditions, funds obtained by a bank through the issuance of obligations by affiliates, funds obtained through a bank's sale of ineligible acceptances or "finance bills," net balances due from domestic banks to foreign branches, assets acquired by foreign branches from domestic offices, loans made by foreign branches to U.S. residents, and borrowings from foreign banks by domestic banks.

[3] An exception exists in the case of balance sheet items involving foreign banks and branches. In these cases, the base period for calculating required reserves is the 4 weeks ending 2 weeks before the beginning of the 4-week reserve maintenance period. Although the reserve maintenance period is 4 weeks, banks are expected to meet requirements during each of the 4 weeks. Since the main difference in the case of foreign transactions is one of timing, the general guidelines for optimal reserve management, described later, are not altered.

[4] In practice, standard reporting forms in use at most Reserve Banks do not require member banks to average either the items subject to reserve requirements or the reserves maintained. On those forms, for example, daily figures for net demand deposits are summed to obtain the total of net demand deposits on seven consecutive days. Reserve requirements for net demand deposits are adjusted to make allowance for the fact that these totals are seven times the average net demand deposit size of the bank. Similarly, reserves held are computed as the sum of reserves maintained on each of seven days. This procedure permits a bank experiencing a reserve excess or deficiency to adjust its reserves by the calculated dollar amount of the excess or deficiency. Specifically, a bank does not need to compute the change in reserves necessary to lower or raise the average by a stipulated amount. The result, in effect, allows banks to average deposits and reserves over 1-week periods.

EXAMPLE

Suppose a bank's cumulative required reserves for 1 week are $7 million. This requirement could be satisfied by holding $1 million in reserves on each of 7 days or by holding any combination which would total $7 million over the week. For instance, the bank could hold $7 million for 1 day and nothing on the other 6 days of the week. Alternatively, if the bank held $1.5 million on each of the first 4 days of a settlement week, the bank's cumulative reserve position at the end of 4 days would be $6 million. The bank would then be $1 million short of its $7 million target, and would be required to hold $1 million cumulatively over the remaining 3 days. One possibility would be to keep $333,333 in reserves on each of the 3 days.

However, suppose the bank were to hold $1.5 million in reserves on each of the first 6 days of the settlement week. At the end of the sixth day its cumulative reserve position would be $9 million. With only $7 million required for the week, the bank might wish to invest the $2 million excess in the Federal funds market for 1 day. Such action, however, would not be permissible. Since the bank's actual balance at the Reserve Bank is $1.5 million, this amount is the maximum the bank could sell without overdrawing its reserve account.

To reduce bank uncertainty about the amount of reserves that must be held, the Federal Reserve introduced lagged reserve requirements in 1968. Previously, the reserve and deposit periods had been coincident, with the result that banks were unable to determine their required reserves before the end of the settlement period and often held large amounts of excess reserves to protect against unanticipated losses of funds. Since 1968, required reserves for any settlement week have been based on deposits (and other liabilities subject to reserve requirements) held 2 weeks earlier. Consequently, required reserves can be known with certainty at the beginning of any settlement period. Reserves which must be kept at the Federal Reserve are determined by deducting a bank's holdings of vault cash during the reserve assessment period from total required reserves.[5] (See Example, p. 33.)

A carry-over procedure provides banks with additional latitude in managing reserves and also allows them to make full use of all reserves maintained. Under this provision, a bank is permitted to carry a reserve excess or deficiency forward into the next reserve period. Reserves can be carried over only 1 week, however, and the maximum amount of the carry-over is limited to 2 per cent of *total cumulative reserves required* for the current settlement week. Total cumulative reserves required represent the aggregate reserves a bank must hold against deposits and other reservable liabilities; they are the

---

[5] In determining the deduction, banks are to include with vault cash all currency and coin in transit to or from a Reserve Bank during the reserve assessment week.

EXAMPLE

Suppose that at the end of a reserve assessment week a bank determines that its required reserves to be maintained 2 weeks later are $5 million. This figure would be derived by multiplying the relevant reserve requirement percentages by the amounts of deposits and other reservable liabilities held during the week. Suppose also that during the week the bank had $1.2 million in vault cash. Then, the balance the bank would be expected to maintain at the Federal Reserve during the settlement week beginning 1 week hence could be $3.8 million. Note, however, that this total may subsequently be adjusted when allowance is made for the reserve carry-over.

---

required reserves before any adjustments are made for the carry-over from the previous week or for vault cash maintained 2 weeks earlier. In practice, a bank which has a reserve excess one week is automatically permitted to incur a reserve deficiency in the following period up to the amount of its actual carry-over. Similarly, 'if a bank carries a reserve deficiency forward into the following period, it must hold excess reserves at least equal to the amount of the deficiency to avoid being subject to a penalty.[6] If the bank held more reserves in the second period than were necessary to offset the deficiency, the additional excess would be eligible for carry-over to the succeeding period, subject to the 2 per cent limitation.

To obtain maximum benefit from the carry-over allowance a bank should seek to alternate weeks of reserve excesses and deficiencies, while holding those excesses and deficiencies to amounts allowable for carry-over. As indicated in the example (p. 34), a bank with an excess carry-over should seek to establish a deficiency in the following week. Two consecutive weeks of excess reserves would mean that a bank had not utilized the carry-over available from the first week and had foregone potential interest earnings on that excess. Similarly, 2 consecutive weeks of reserve deficiencies would subject a bank to a penalty on the deficiency incurred during the first week and on any portion of the deficiency of the second week not offset in the following period.

The principles of efficient reserve management require banks to establish a target range for reserves held at the Federal Reserve. The derivation and meaning of this range will be analyzed in a subsequent section of this article. However, one boundary of this range will always be the amount of reserves a bank should maintain at the Reserve Bank if the bank wishes to establish a zero reserve carry-over to the next period. As the foregoing analysis shows, this amount is equal to the reserve requirements based on deposits and other

---

[6] If a bank has a reserve deficiency in excess of the 2 per cent limitation, a penalty may be assessed on the deficiency over the 2 per cent limit, regardless of the amount of reserves held in the following period.

EXAMPLE

Suppose a bank's required reserves for the current settlement week are $6.5 million. The maximum carry-over the bank would be allowed would be 2 percent of $6.5 million or $130,000. Assume further the bank has a zero carry-over from the previous week and that it experiences an actual excess of $110,000 in the current week. The bank would then have a carry-over excess of $110,000 to the following settlement period.

During the next settlement week, three possibilities would exist. First, the bank could have a reserve deficiency precisely equal to $110,000. Under this possibility, full use would have been made of the carry-over from the previous period and the carry-forward to the next period would be zero.

Second, the bank could realize a reserve deficiency of less than $110,000 or even have excess reserves. In this event, the bank would not have fully utilized its carry-over allowance. If the bank had a reserve deficiency of less than $110,000, no carry-over would be allowed to the following week since reserves cannot be carried forward more than 1 week. If the bank had excess reserves, the carry-over would be limited to the size of the excess, provided it did not exceed the 2 per cent maximum allowable carry-over.

Third, if the bank experienced a reserve deficiency in excess of $110,000, the bank could, within the 2 per cent limit, establish a deficit carry-over to the next period. Full use would have been made of the $110,000 carry-over excess and the bank should offset the additional deficiency in the following week. Thus, a bank entering a settlement week with an excess carry-over would obtain full use of all reserves by establishing a deficit carry-forward to the following week.

reservable liabilities outstanding 2 weeks earlier, minus vault cash held 2 weeks earlier, and minus (plus) the allowable carry-over excess (deficiency) from the previous week. On Federal Reserve forms used in the Tenth District this concept is called *Cumulative Reserve Balances to be Maintained with Federal Reserve.*

TIMETABLE FOR RESERVE MANAGEMENT

Nearly 5 weeks may elapse between the beginning of a reserve assessment period and the time the books are closed on a reserve maintenance week. In this section the timetable for computing and meeting reserve requirements is reviewed chronologically.

Week I

For reserve purposes, the accounting week begins each Thursday and ends the following Wednesday. In reporting liabilities subject to reserve requirements to the Federal Reserve, banks use the closing figures for the day. On any day that a bank is not open for business, the closing balances for the previous business day are reported. Banks closed on Saturday and Sunday, for example, use Friday's closing figures for all 3 days. After the close of business on Wednesday, a bank could calculate its "total reserves required" for the settlement period beginning 1 week hence. However, the bank's required balance at the Federal Reserve cannot be determined until the next settlement week has ended and the carry-over allowance applicable to the third week is known.

Week II

At the end of the second week a bank able to track its reserve account precisely will know its carry-over allowance for the following settlement week. Projections of reserve balances, though, may be subject to error. While relatively few charges are made to a bank's reserve account without its prior knowledge, such entries do occassionally occur. The Treasury, for example, has at times drawn on tax and loan accounts before Reserve Banks have had an opportunity to notify member banks. To assist banks under these circumstances, the Federal Reserve provides all member banks with a daily statement showing reserve balances and any credits or debits to the reserve account. With this information a bank can follow and verify changes in its reserve balances.

Week III

The third week is the reserve maintenance or settlement week, the period for meeting the reserve requirements. On or before Monday of the third week, a bank will receive a statement from the Reserve Bank showing total cumulative reserves required for the current settlement week, the amount of reserves a bank would need to maintain at the Federal Reserve to have a zero carry-over to the following week. In addition, the maximum and minimum amounts of reserves that could be maintained at the Federal Reserve without exceeding the carry-over allowance to the following week are indicated. A sample of the statement used in the Tenth Federal Reserve District is shown in Table 2. With the figures for the carry-over from the second week now finalized, a bank can establish a definite target for reserves during the settlement period. The bank would have until the close of business on Wednesday to make any necessary adjustments in its reserve balance.[7]

---

[7] As in the case of computing reserve requirements, funds at the Federal Reserve count toward meeting reserve requirements only if they are on deposit at the close of business. On holidays and other nonbusiness days, the previous day's balance is repeated.

Table 2
Federal Reserve Bank of Kansas City
Advice of Reserves to be Carried
For Period Ending 04/20/77
(Amounts in Thousands)

AC75

Bank Number

Bank Name
City
State   Zip

Deposit Classification	Total Deposits For Period Ended 04/06/77	Percent Applied	Cumulative Reserves Required
Net Demand Deposits			
First 14.0 Million	14,000	7.00	980
Next 56.0 Million	20,000	9.50	1,900
Savings Deposits	15,000	3.00	450
Other Time Deposits			
30 to 179 Day Maturity			
First 35 Million	30,000	3.00	900
180 Days & Less than 4 Years Maturity	10,000	2.50	† 300
4 Years & Over Maturity	9,000	1.00	* 270
Total Cumulative Reserves Required			4,800
Less: Vault Cash for Period Ended 04/06/77		1,800	
Plus: Deficient Carryover From Previous Period		50	
Cumulative Reserve Balances to be Maintained with Federal Reserve			3,050

	Minimum	Midpoint	Maximum
Range of Cumulative Reserves to be Maintained to Realize Full Advantage of Carryover Provision	3,050	3,098	3,146
Daily Averages	436	443	449

†Reserves on maturities of 180 days to 4 years have been increased to bring reserves on total savings and time deposits to a minimum of 3 percent.

*Reserves on maturities of 4 years and over have been increased to bring reserves on total savings and time deposits to a minimum of 3 percent.

Weeks IV and V

On the Friday following the conclusion of the reserve maintenance week, the Federal Reserve sends each member bank a report on its reserve position during the maintenance period. This report lists the actual reserves maintained for the settlement week, indicates whether the bank had a reserve excess or deficiency, and states the allowable carry-over to the next reserve period.[8] If the bank had a carry-over deficiency, the form notes that the records is preliminary. A final record of the bank's reserve position would then be furnished at the completion of the following settlement period when the Federal Reserve could determine the portion of the carry-forward deficiency subsequently offset. If the carry-over were not wholly offset in the fourth week or if the amount of the deficiency in the third week exceeded the carry-forward allowance, the final report would also show the penalty on the deficiency and its disposition.[9] Examples of the preliminary and final reports used in the Tenth District are shown and described in the Appendix.

ESTABLISHING A TARGET RANGE FOR RESERVES

The "Advice of Reserves to be Carried" form indicates a target range for a bank's reserve balances at the Federal Reserve. The range is derived so as to

[8] In computing the reserves maintained during a settlement week, allowance must also be made for "as of" adjustments. These adjustments are a means of correcting for errors which may have occurred on a bank's daily reserve statement. For example, if a bank requested a wire transfer and the Federal Reserve debited the account of the wrong bank, both banks would receive modifications to their reserve accounts, effective "as of" the date of the transfer. Similarly, if the Federal Reserve were unable to complete a wire transfer on the day requested, the banks involved might each receive an "as of" correction. "As of" adjustments occur relatively infrequently, particularly in the case of smaller banks, but they must be taken into consideration when they do develop.

[9] The Federal Reserve Bank of Kansas City has established a set of guidelines to assist administrative officers in assessing or waiving penalties on reserve deficiencies. Present guidelines permit the granting of waivers in several situations.

1) A penalty may be waived if the amount is small. No specific limit has been established on the number of times a bank may have small penalties waived, but a waiver will not ordinarily be granted to banks with regular deficiencies.

2) A waiver may be granted if a bank has a net deficiency in its reserve account up to 5 per cent of total required reserves. This particular category is designed for banks with large deficiencies, but may be utilized by an individual bank only once every 2 years.

3) If a bank is leaving the Federal Reserve System, waivers may be granted during the final 2 weeks.

4) If a bank is placed in receivership or is in the process of being absorbed by another bank, waivers may be granted during this period.

5) If a bank is newly organized, switches from nonmember to member status, or merges with another bank, it is required to hold only a portion of normal reserve requirements during the next 2 years. Any penalties that would normally result from such reserve shortfalls are routinely waived.

Waivers granted under these five categories are semi-automatic and require no action on the part of the member bank. A final category has been established under which waivers could be granted if the penalty is attributable to errors. For example, a bank may be counting on a transfer of funds to its reserve account, but if the transfer is not made in time to be credited to reserves that day, a deficiency could arise. Such special waivers are considered only at the request of member banks.

It is important to recognize that these guidelines could be modified at any time and that the granting of any waiver is not totally automatic. All waivers are subject to the discretion of an administrative officer. Moreover, banks which regularly have reserve deficiencies could be subjected to Reserve Bank scrutiny or even legal action.

Finally, if penalties for deficiencies are assessed, the actual debit to a reserve account is made on the last business day of the month and includes the total of penalty charges for each settlement period ending during the month.

EXAMPLE

The "Advice of Reserves to be Carried" in Table 2 shows the calculations necessary to compute "total cumulative reserves required." The table begins with the cumulative totals of deposits held by the bank each day during the reserve assessment week. All dollar amounts are listed in thousands. It then shows that the bank has a reserve requirement of $4,800, that it maintained vault cash during the reserve assessment week of $1,800, and that it had a reserve deficiency in the previous settlement week of $50. Therefore, the reserve balance the bank should maintain on deposit at the Federal Reserve to meet current requirements and to offset the deficiency is $3,050 (=$4,800 − $1,800 + $50). However, if the bank held additional reserves it could establish a carry-over excess to the following week. The maximum allowable carry-over would be 2 per cent of total reserves required, or $96 (=2% of $4,800). Thus, the maximum reserves the bank should consider maintaining on deposit at the Federal Reserve would be $3,146 (=$3,050 + $96). Similarly, the minimum would be $3,050.

make full allowance for any reserve carry-over from the previous period while limiting deviations to the amount eligible for carry-over to the following period. Although the Federal Reserve provides this information to a bank, it arrives relatively late in the settlement week. To avoid major last minute adjustments, therefore, many banks estimate their target ranges relatively early in the settlement week by using the daily statement pro-

EXAMPLE

Suppose a bank's total reserves required for the current period are $5,000,000, that its vault cash 2 weeks earlier was $500,000, and that it has a reserve carry-over deficiency from the previous week of $60,000. The minimum amount of reserves the bank could carry at the Federal Reserve without incurring a reserve deficiency would be $4,560,000 (=$5,000,000 − $500,000 + $60,000). A reserve balance of this amount would meet the requirement for the current period and would make up the deficiency of the previous week.

The bank would have a maximum carry-forward allowance to the next period of 2 per cent of $5,000,000 or $100,000. The upper limit to the target range, therefore, would be $4,660,000 (=$4,560,000 + $100,000). Any larger amount would mean that the bank had held more in excess reserves than could be carried forward to the next period.

vided by the Federal Reserve. The methods for determining the target range differ slightly, depending on whether the bank is currently operating with an excess or a deficit carry-over.

Carry-Over Deficiency: If a bank is presently operating with a carry-over deficiency from the previous week, the *minimum* quantity of reserves the bank should seek to maintain at the Federal Reserve is equal to the sum of the amount required for the current period plus the amount necessary to offset the reserve deficiency. Any smaller amount of reserves would mean that the bank had not offset its carry-over deficiency with an equal amount of excess reserves and would, therefore, subject the bank to a penalty. The *maximum* reserve balances the bank should consider holding would exceed the minimum by 2 per cent of total reserves required in the current week. Maintenance of reserves in excess of this amount, while permissible, would involve an opportunity cost since these "surplus" reserves earn no interest and would not be allowable as a carry-forward to the next reserve period.

Carry-Over Excess: If a bank is presently operating with an excess carry-over allowance from the previous week, the *maximum* amount of reserves the bank should seek to maintain with the Federal Reserve is equal to the amount that would allow full utilization of the carry-over excess. Any additional balances would mean that the bank was not fully utilizing its excess reserve carry-over from the previous period. The *minimum* quantity of reserves the bank should maintain at a Reserve Bank would be less than the maximum level by 2 per cent of total reserves required. Any lesser amount of reserves would mean that the bank had a deficiency in excess of the carry-over allowance.

In developing the target range, one boundary will always be the balance a bank would need to maintain to offset any carry-over excess or deficiency from the previous period. On the "Advice of Reserves to be Carried" form shown in Table 2, this amount is labeled "Cumulative Reserve Balances to be

---

EXAMPLE

Instead of a deficiency, assume the bank in the previous example has an excess carry-over of $60,000. All other figures remain the same. In that event, the upper limit to the target range would be $4,440,000 (=$5,000,000 − $500,000 − $60,000). The lower limit to the range would be $4,340,000 (=$4,440,000 − $100,000).

Maintained with the Federal Reserve." It is equal to total reserves required, less vault cash from the reserve assessment period, plus (minus) the carry-over allowance for a reserve deficiency (excess) from the previous week. The other boundary will differ from this amount by 2 per cent of total reserves required, the maximum carry-forward allowance. Banks operating with an excess carry-over should aim to establish a carry-over deficiency, while those with a carry-over deficiency should seek a carry-over excess. This procedure requires that banks alternate weeks of carry-forward excesses and deficiencies. If a bank keeps its actual reserves within the target range, the bank will be able to count all its reserves toward meeting its requirements. In such cases, the bank is said to be operating with a "zero net reserve position." Those with a "non-zero net reserve position," in contrast, have not made full use of reserves. Banks in this situation, for example, may have had an excess or deficit carry-over in two consecutive weeks or may not have fully utilized an excess carry-over from a previous period.[10]

As a practical matter, a bank should probably aim at the midpoint of its target range since minor deviations in either direction would affect only the actual carry-over to the following week and would entail no costs. This target, however, must be examined with a view to the management philosophy of each bank. Some banks may view reserve deficiencies as being a much more serious problem than reserve excesses and would, accordingly, shade their target toward the upper end of the range. Alternatively, when money market rates are substantially above the penalty rate on deficiencies, some may reduce their target toward the lower boundary of the acceptable range, thus increasing the risk of a reserve deficiency.

ADHERING TO A TARGET RANGE

At any time numerous factors interact to cause increases or decreases in a bank's reserve balance at the Federal Reserve. Balances would tend to decline if the dollar amount of cash letters received from the Federal Reserve exceeded the credit becoming available on cash letters sent to the Federal Reserve, if payment from a bank's reserve account were made for purchases of securities, if Federal funds were sold, if currency or coin were shipped from a Reserve Bank, if drafts drawn on a reserve account were presented for collection, or if a Treasury tax and loan account were called. Similarly, balances would rise if securities held in safekeeping at Reserve Banks mature, if currency or coin is deposited, if Federal funds are borrowed or returned,

---

[10] The accounting department at each office of the Federal Reserve Bank of Kansas City has developed a computer report which summarizes the reserve behavior of individual banks for each week during a 9-month period. Examination of the "net position" column of this report indicates the frequency with which a bank operates with a zero net reserve position. Copies of this report are most helpful in pinpointing banks which may require special assistance in managing reserves. The report, which is available to banks upon request, can also be of use in measuring the success of reserve management programs.

or if the Federal Reserve credits banks with the interest received for securities held in safekeeping. Other factors could be cited, but these include some of the more significant ones causing reserve fluctuations. In reserve management, banks are shooting at a moving target.

Although maximum efficiency in reserve management requires that banks keep actual reserves within a target range, there are no inflexible guidelines that can be offered regarding the timing or method of making reserve adjustments to achieve this goal. If a sizable divergence from the target range develops at the beginning of a reserve period, a strong case could be made for taking corrective action promptly. The sale or purchase of securities at this time would reduce the likelihood of having to make a very large, but temporary, adjustment near the end of the period. Moreover, fully corrective action later could be impossible. Banks, for example, are not permitted to overdraw their reserve accounts to eliminate an excess and in some states the amount of Federal funds which can be sold to individual purchasers is subject to lending limit restrictions. Similarly, many correspondents restrict the amount of Federal funds sold to respondents to a specified fraction of the respondent's capital accounts. Early action, though, may not eliminate the need for further adjustment in reserve balances later in the period.

If a bank expects its actual reserves to diverge from the target range by a relatively small amount, any adjustment should probably be postponed until the reserve period is drawing to a close. Unforeseen credits or debits to a reserve account could always develop. Also, as the size of a comparatively small excess or deficiency grows, so does the maneuverability of the bank. Many midwestern and Rocky Mountain correspondents, for example, will buy Federal funds in multiples of $25,000, but stipulate a minimum purchase of $50,000. A bank with daily average excess reserves of $40,000 would have difficulty finding a purchaser for that amount, but would normally have no problems disposing of $300,000 for 1 day, $150,000 for 2 days, or even $100,000 for 3 days.

The frequency and size of changes in a bank's reserve account will also influence the optimal timing of adjustments. Many smaller banks maintain semi-dormant accounts at the Reserve Bank. These banks generally send outgoing cash letters to correspondents and have the reserve account of a correspondent debited for incoming cash letters. Cash letter activity, therefore, does not affect their reserve balances. The major factors causing reserve balance changes are such transactions as currency and coin ordered or deposited, calls on Treasury tax and loan accounts, payments for savings bonds sold or redeemed, and Federal funds sold or returned. In many instances the magnitude and timing of these transactions will be known several days in advance and could be manipulated within limits to influence a reserve balance. For banks with relatively inactive reserve accounts, it is generally recommended that an analysis of the week's reserve position be prepared on Monday. At that time, firm figures for 4 days will be available. Controllable transactions affecting the bank's reserve position will largely be known, making an estimate of the closing reserve balance on Monday, Tuesday, and Wednesday relatively precise. If the projected reserves do not fall within the previously established target range, the bank would then have 3 days to make any adjustment.[11]

Banks with greater activity in their reserve accounts have a more formidable task in projecting balances. These banks generally are the ones which send cash letters to the Federal Reserve for collection. In addition to the factors already listed, they would have to make allowance in reserve projections for the net effect of any wire transfers, charges for incoming cash letters, for deferred availability of credit on cash letters deposited, and for numerous miscellaneous transactions. As early as Friday, banks in such situations should begin to examine their reserve position and perhaps initiate corrective action. The analysis should then be reviewed frequently, with adjusting action being taken daily throughout the remainder of the settlement week.

The types of adjustments banks should consider in bringing their reserve balances within the target range would depend mainly on the magnitude of the deviation, its likely duration, the relative yields available on alternative types of investments, and on the cost of different sources of funds. As before, no firm guidelines can be offered. Banks anticipating a prolonged buildup of excess reserves may wish to acquire longer term investments, but if short-term interest rates are unusually high, sales of Federal funds could prove more profitable. Large banks have many alternatives, but smaller banks projecting a temporary excess or deficiency should consider such possibilities as the purchase or sale of Federal funds, transfers to or from correspondent accounts, the purchase or sale of securities either outright or under repurchase agreements, and the initiation or repaying of borrowing at the discount window.

The willingness and ability of banks to make reserve adjustments to achieve their target range is also likely to vary. If the transaction costs of making an adjustment are large compared to the interest that could be earned on surplus balances or to the size of a penalty on a deficiency, the incentive to make the adjustment will be less. Banks are likely to correct large deviations from the target, but might consider small divergences unimportant. The desire to alter reserves could be higher if a divergence is viewed as permanent rather than temporary or self-reversing. The ability of a bank to alter its reserve position is also an important consideration. Banks which do not have ready access to the Federal funds market, which have a relatively illiquid portfolio, which are reluctant to reduce correspondent balances, or which are unwilling to borrow at the discount window are less likely to be concerned about maximum reserve utilization. On the other hand, the possibility of Reserve Bank surveillance can be a powerful stimulus in preventing reserve deficiencies. Reserve managers should always consider all

---

[11] If a bank has its own reserve account debited for incoming cash letters, one weekly adjustment may not be adequate to ensure that a bank operates with a zero net reserve position. Since the dollar amount of incoming cash letters is highly variable and is largely unpredictable, unanticipated changes in reserve balances can often be substantial. Banks in this situation must be prepared to take further correcting action later in the settlement week, or alternatively should make arrangements to have the reserve account of a correspondent charged for incoming cash letters.

possibilities. Nevertheless, those banks which rarely operate with a zero net reserve position or which experience occasional large deviations from the target range could probably improve reserve management techniques and increase profits.

CONCLUDING REMARKS

Efficient reserve management involves obtaining full utilization of all reserves. The procedures outlined in this article should be effective and quick for most smaller banks. Larger banks will need to devote additional time and attention to reserve management. Obtaining effective use of all reserves, however, is but one aspect of the broader issue of optimum cash management. Optimum cash management involves holding the minimum in nonearning assets, given the liquidity and reserve needs of a bank in an uncertain world. A bank interested in maximizing profits must examine all operating and portfolio procedures. Effective reserve management is but a beginning.

APPENDIX

INTERPRETING THE REPORTS ON A BANK'S RESERVE POSITION

At the conclusion of a reserve week, the Federal Reserve sends each member bank a report on the reserves actually maintained during the settlement week. If the bank's reserves were deficient, the form notes that the record is preliminary. A final summation of the bank's position would then be furnished at the completion of the following settlement period when the Federal Reserve can determine the portion of any carryforward deficiency subsequently offset. The format of these reports varies among Federal Reserve districts, and the samples provided in this appendix are for the Tenth Federal Reserve District.

The example in this appendix corresponds to the bank portrayed in Table 2 and assumes the bank has two consecutive weeks of reserve deficiencies. This bank, it will be recalled, had total reserves required of $4,800, held vault cash during the reserve assessment week of $1,800, and had a carry-over deficiency of $50, making for a minimum required reserve balance at the Federal Reserve of $3,050 in order to offset the carryover reserve deficiency.

The "Preliminary Record" in Table 3 indicates that the bank actually held balances of $2,900 at the Federal Reserve during the settlement week. After allowance for the $50 reserve deficiency of the previous week, therefore, the reserves available to meet the current week's requirement of $4,800 were

Table 3
Federal Reserve Bank of Kansas City
Preliminary Record of Reserve Position
For Period Ending 04/20/77
(Amounts in Thousands)

AC66 Rev 1/77

Bank Number

Bank Name
City
State   Zip

Cumulative Reserves Required			4,800
Cumulative Reserves Maintained			
Vault Cash		1,800	
Reserve Balances		2,900	
Net "As Of" Adjustments		0	
	Subtotal		4,700
Minus: Deficient Carryover from Previous Period			50
	Total		4,650
Preliminary Reserve Position Deficiency			150
Allowable Deficiency Carryover to Next Period			96
Deficient Reserves Not Allowable for Carryover			4

$4,650 (=$2,900 + $1,800–$50). Thus the bank also experienced a reserve deficiency in the second week, with the amount of the shortfall being equal to $150 (=$4,800 − $4,650). If the bank had carried $150 more in reserve balances, the requirement for the current week would have been met and the carry-over from the previous week offset.

Of the $150 deficiency, $50 is attributable to the carry-over from the previous week. Since reserve excesses or deficiencies can be carried forward only one week, this amount is not eligible to be carried forward for another week. In computing the bank's "final" reserve position for the previous week, a penalty would be assessed for the $50 deficiency which was not offset. Given that the interest penalty will be charged, the bank's net reserve deficiency in the current week in effect becomes $100. However, with total reserves required of $4,800, the bank is eligible only to carry over a deficit of $96, leaving $4 of the reserve deficit which cannot be carried forward. Regardless of the excess reserves carried in the next period, this $4 shortfall will also be subject to a penalty. The final line of Table 3, therefore, is based on the assumption that the $96 carry-over deficiency will be fully offset in the following week and does not include the previous week's shortfall in reserves.

Table 4
Federal Reserve Bank of Kansas City
Final Record of Reserve Position
For Period Ending 04/20/77
(Amounts in Thousands Except Penalty Amounts)

Bank Number

Bank Name
City
State   Zip

Cumulative Reserves Required				4,800
Cumulative Reserves Maintained				
Vault Cash		1,800		
Reserve Balances		2,900		
Net "As Of" Adjustments		0		
	Subtotal		4,700	
Plus: Excess Carryover From Previous Period			0	
	Total			4,700
Preliminary Reserve Position	Deficiency			100
Allowable Carryover 96 Offset by Excess Reserves				96
Final Reserve Position	Deficiency			4
Penalty on Net Deficiency				$0.79

Disposition of Penalty

	Waived	$0.79

AC76 Rev 1/77

The final report which is provided 1 week later is shown in Table 4 and relates to the computation of any penalty on a reserve deficiency. Many of the figures are the same as in Table 3. Since the charge for the $50 deficiency would have already been established, the table indicates a zero carry-over from the earlier week. In addition, the table shows that the bank completely offset its $96 carry-over reserve deficiency with holdings of excess reserves. Therefore, the bank would be subject to an interest penalty only on the $4 deficiency which was ineligible for carry-over. The interest penalty is computed on this shortfall.

Part I
ASSET MANAGEMENT

B. COMMERCIAL LENDING

In the commercial lending section of Part I, the first of two articles by Randall C. Merris provides an overview of business-related lending policies and practices of commercial banks. The dramatic changes that have occurred in recent years also are highlighted. In his second article, Merris focuses on fee-based loan commitments. This topic is of increasing importance to bankers, borrowers, and regulators. The importance of loan commitments stems from the potentially excessive loan demand that could result from tight credit conditions.

In the next article, Gary R. Severson analyzes the loan pricing process. Such factors as the base interest rate, reserve requirements, compensating balances, and loan commitment fees are incorporated into the analysis. The ability to develop alternative pricing proposals plays a key role in the lending process. In his award-winning article, Hugh M. Durden examines legal and ethical issues facing the lending officer on a day-to-day basis. The use of insider information, conflicts of interest, disclosure of financial information, tie-ins, and gratuities are among the issues discussed. The last article in this section is by Stuart A. Schweitzer and provides a clear explanation of a complex topic, the loan loss reserve. The management implications of this reserve are examined with respect to income taxes, earnings, and financial solvency.

BUSINESS LOANS AT LARGE COMMERCIAL BANKS: POLICIES AND PRACTICES*

Randall C. Merris

3

Commercial bank lending was once a fairly simple business. Business loans were nearly all short term and carried fixed interest rates. Any other details, except possibly collateral requirements, were left to informal agreements between a bank and its customers.

Business lending began getting more complex in the 1930s as many banks started making term loans—loans with maturities of more than a year. Relations between banks and business borrowers have been growing more complex—and more formal—ever since, the formality of term loans now being applied to many short-term loans as well.

Part of the push for more complicated loan arrangements—and, therefore, a greater variety in the kinds of agreements—has been the need for banks and borrowers to protect themselves from movements in interest rates over the credit cycle. Increases in market rates boost bank costs of funding outstanding loans. They also increase the opportunities for more lucrative new credits elsewhere. Reductions in market rates lower the interest costs of other debt financing available to bank loan customers.

Floating rates have probably been the most important innovation in bank lending since the advent of the term loan. Provisions for adjusting loan rates periodically give banks and borrowers some protection against market rate fluctuations. By combining some of the advantages of term and short-term

*Reprinted from *Economic Perspectives*, November/December 1979, pp. 15-23, with permission from the Federal Reserve Bank of Chicago and the author.

loans, floating rates have allowed banks to compete effectively for their share of the business credit market—even in the face of increased competition from the commercial paper market and other nonbank credit suppliers. At the same time, use of floating rates has encouraged changes in the other terms and conditions of business lending.

This article examines business lending practices at large banks, especially toward commercial and industrial loans. These loans to businesses other than financial institutions most clearly reflect the recent directions in bank lending policy. Pricing, maturities, and other lending terms depend on the particular bank and borrower negotiating the credit, as well as the use of the loan proceeds—such as, to provide working capital or finance expenditures on plant and equipment.

TERM LOANS

Term loans range in maturity from just over a year to more than ten years. Banks once held loans with maximum maturities of five to seven years. For

---

Fall of the Real Bills Doctrine . . .

Though term loans were sometimes made for special purposes, most banks offered only short-term credit until well into this century. This was because bank policies were based on the commercial loan theory of credit, an American adaptation of the Real Bills Doctrine in England.

According to this doctrine, the only appropriate bank loans were short-term, self-liquidating notes. By self-liquidating, bankers meant loans that led to enough increase in sales and near-term profits to cover repayment. Loans for plant and equipment did not usually qualify, the reasoning being that several years might be needed before returns on fixed capital were enough to retire the debt.

Some business loans were renewed routinely, even as early as the 1830s, with the result that nominally short-term credit arrangements were actually long term. Not until the 1920s, however, was the commercial loan theory seriously challenged. The idea that loans needed to be self-liquidating began losing credibility for several reasons:

- The realization that the commercial loan theory did not provide the monetary policy advantages its proponents claimed.
- The practice of financing long-term projects by borrowing from one bank to pay off another—sequential bank financing.
- The emergence of the view that banks could gain liquidity better from their non-loan assets and their liabilities.

Proponents of the Real Bills Doctrine had long argued that the requirement that bank loans be self-liquidating made the money supply expand

customers that needed longer terms, banks participated with other lenders. A bank might, for example, take the first five years of credit, with an insurance company taking the rest to maturity, often under different terms and conditions. Banks are more inclined now to take all the term credits themselves or to participate with other banks, each taking part of the loan for the whole maturity.

With the future always uncertain, lengthening the maturity structure of bank loan portfolios might seem to mean banks were taking more risks. But at least half the term lending at large banks calls for periodic adjustment of loan rates.

Costs are nearly always higher for initiating term loans than short-term loans. Considerable negotiation is required, usually at top levels of management and often with legal staffs representing the bank and the borrower. And voluminous documentation is needed to cover both the terms and conditions of the loan. Administrative costs are also high, especially in the frequent situations where the bank and borrower need to keep in touch throughout the life of the loan.

Agreement has to be reached not only on the amount of the loan and its price but also any number of other points:

and contract with the needs of business. However, bankers became increasingly aware, especially in looking back on the Panic of 1907, that the policy did not prevent severe contractions, bank deposit runs, or bank failures.

Many banks, meanwhile, had imposed the rule that customers had to have all their loans at the bank paid up sometime during the year. This clean-up rule, meant to strengthen the commercial loan theory, actually had the opposite effect. Annual clean-ups tended to encourage short-term borrowing first at one bank, then another, and then back at the first bank—all to extend effective credit periods for fixed-capital purposes.

Renewals, sequential financing across banks, and the clean-up rule together debased the short-term loan doctrine. It took a new theory of bank management, however, to utterly discredit the commercial loan theory.

The new theory took the view that as most business loans were not actually liquid, they did not serve as a funding cushion against unexpected deposit withdrawals. In place of short-term loans, the theory turned for liquidity to other assets—such as government and corporate securities, bankers' acceptances, and commercial paper—that could be sold with little loss of their capital value. A forerunner to modern liability management, the new theory also noted that banks could acquire liquidity through Federal Reserve borrowings and interbank sale of bonds under repurchase agreements.

Together, these changes both in attitude and in the structure of banks' short-term investment portfolios helped foster some growth of term lending in the 1920s.

. . . and rise of term lending

Although Real Bills persisted into the 1930s, events gave impetus to term lending.

• The slack demand for short-term loans during the Depression—even at a prime rate of 1½ percent from 1933 on—gave banks incentives and opportunities to shift into some higher yielding term loans.

• The Banking Acts of 1933 and 1935 limited bank activities in corporate security markets, leading banks to substitute term lending.

• The establishment of deposit insurance in 1933 reduced the likelihood of financial panics and deposit runs, encouraging some lengthening of the maturity of bank loan portfolios.

• A change in Federal Reserve rules in 1933 allowing loans of all maturities to be used as assets for discounts and advances at Federal Reserve banks increased the liquidity of term loans.

Loan commitment—an arrangement for the borrower to draw down loans and sometimes even a schedule for disbursing the funds. As the funds are made available to the borrower whether he uses them or not, a fee is sometimes charged on the amount of the commitment not used.

Installment schedule—a timetable for paying down the principal and interest. Payments are most often due monthly, quarterly, or semiannually.

Supporting balance requirement—the borrower's obligation to maintain demand deposits that help offset the cost of funding the loan. A bank may require that even a loan commitment be backed by demand deposits.

Collateral—property put up against a loan. Banker and borrower must agree on the physical nature of the collateral, its value, and the care to be taken in its handling and protection.

Protective covenants—a requirement that the borrower do certain things, as for example, keep working capital above some minimum level during the credit term or furnish the bank periodic financial reports. Covenants can also require that the borrower not do certain things without the bank's approval— for example, expand its fixed assets, undertake further external financing, enter a merger, or acquire an affiliate.

Some of the costs of initiating and administering term loans are charged directly to borrowers as fees. But there is, of course, an interest rate at which banks are willing to absorb the remaining costs of term lending.

REVOLVING CREDITS

Revolving credits were once treated as short-term loans, which followed the banking convention that all loans had to be paid up sometime during the

• Under the revision of bank examination standards in 1934, term loans were no longer routinely classified as "slow."

• With modern amortization gaining general acceptance, term loans, which had usually called for payment of principal and interest at maturity, were made payable in annual, semiannual, quarterly, or monthly install-ments. Installment payments smoothed the flow of interest and principal back to the bank and, by demonstrating a borrower's ability to repay, helped banks monitor term loans and identify problem credits.

• Banks were encouraged to help finance the recovery, and followed the examples set by the Federal Reserve and Reconstruction Finance Corpor-ation in making direct term loans to business.

The change was marked. A Federal Reserve survey in 1939 showed term loans accounted for a fourth of the dollar volume of business loans at the banks sampled—39 percent at the banks sampled in New York. More than a third of the banks, however, showed no more than five term loans on their books. A 1946 survey of member banks showed term lending ac-counting for more than a third of the dollar volume of business loans.

year—the annual cleanup rule. They now fall somewhere between term loans and short-term loans. Customers with revolving credits can borrow and repay repeatedly over the life of the agreement (usually two or three years) as long as the debt outstanding does not exceed the amount originally agreed on.

As many banks have relaxed the clean-up rule, however, allowing contin-uous indebtedness, revolving credits often qualify now as an intermediate form of term lending. Some contracts, in fact, include conversion clauses that allow credits to continue as term loans when the revolving credit agree-ment expires. Under such contracts, the period of revolving credit is often viewed as the first years of a term loan.

SHORT-TERM AND TERM LOANS AS SUBSTITUTES

Distinctions between term and short-term loans have sometimes been misleading. The most detailed survey of continuous indebtedness through renewal of short-term loans was conducted nearly 25 years ago in the Cleve-land Federal Reserve District. The survey showed that half of the dollar holdings of short-term business loans outstanding at member banks in the district were obligations of borrowers continuously in debt to the same bank for at least two years. A fourth of the short-term credit was owed by busi-nesses in debt to the same bank continuously for at least five years. Only 8 percent of this credit was to customers in debt to the same bank no longer than three months.

As long as loans are renewable, some borrowers with long-term financing needs might actually prefer short-term loans. Initiation costs are lower. And as the contracts are less detailed, they are less likely to put operating con-straints on the borrower.

Continuous indebtedness of this kind may not be to the bank's advantage, however, especially if it has to renew credit to prevent a loan default or bolster future demand for loans or other bank services. The prospects of renewal requests increase uncertainties for the bank. A borrower may feel that the loan can be renewed. But the bank cannot be sure renewal will be requested. Even if a bank has done very well in predicting renewal requests and sorting out the loans it feels obligated to renew, this ability is a poor second for certain knowledge of the length of indebtedness agreed on when the credit was first made.

Short-term loan renewals can, of course, be appropriate at times, as for example, when the need for longer-term credit was not anticipated. But the flexibility of term loans nowadays reduces the need for renewals. The term loan itself can be written to capture one of the main advantages of short-term loan renewal—periodic adjustment in the interest rate. Floating rates substitute directly for the privilege of banks to change the interest rate when a short-term loan is renegotiated at maturity.

Both bank and borrower find advantages in negotiating the *effective* maturity at the outset instead of a *nominal* maturity that can be renewed. Sure of the maturity of a loan, a bank can absorb some of the other risks elsewhere in a loan agreement or lower the average loan rate. Assured of credit for the full term, a borrower is spared the real (albeit sometimes small) risk that a renewal request might be denied.

LOAN COMMITMENTS

Loan commitments, once informal credit lines available to customers that kept adequate balances at a bank, are now more apt to be firm agreements laying out a bank's obligation to provide credit in the future (including the amount of the credit and the rate to be charged) and often the customer's obligation to pay fees on the credit availability. The change has come with the growth of both term loans and revolving credits and the greater use made of formal commitments for short-term lending.

The Federal Reserve Survey of Loan Commitments at Selected Large Banks for April 1979 showed $68 billion outstanding in unused formal agreements. Of these unused formal commitments, 16 percent was for term loans, 71 percent was for revolving credits, and the remaining 13 percent was mostly for short-term credits. Loans that had been made under formal commitments totaled $76 billion.

Despite the trend toward formalization of loan commitments, informal but confirmed lines of credit still accounted for much of the unused commitments. A total of $95 billion in unused credit was available to business borrowers under informal but confirmed lines, compared with the $68 billion in formal commitments. Use of informal lines was much less, however. Loans outstanding under confirmed lines amounted to $29 billion, compared with the $76 billion in loans that had been made under formal commitments.

COMPENSATING BALANCES

Although many banks still require compensating (or supporting) balances, with the trend toward explicit pricing of bank services, less emphasis is put on these balances than in the past. As a result, required balances are being replaced in many cases by explicit fees and increases in lending rates.

Where demand deposit balances are still used, the requirement is usually stated as an average deposit balance equal to a percentage of the loan or commitment. A typical requirement is an average balance of 15 percent of the loan. Another is 10 percent of the loan plus 10 percent of the total commitment.

Negotiations sometimes result in higher requirements on the loan commitments than on the loans themselves. In other cases, balance requirements are set higher on loans than on commitments.

Pressure from a credit customer to shift the balance requirement may give the bank some indication of how the commitment is to be used. If the borrower wants the balance required on the commitment reduced enough to have the loan requirement raised an equal amount, he clearly expects to make little use of the loan commitment—less than half of it on the average.

Floating loan rates. . .

Banks have been devising alternatives to fixed-rate pricing of business loans for decades. Graduated rates on some term loans appeared in the late 1930s. This scheme, applying progressively higher rates to later years of maturity, did not provide floating rates, of course. Term premiums to be added to the loan rate for later years were set when the loan was originated. The loan rate did not move with market rates, and the bank had no influence on it over the life of the loan.

Floating rates came into use in the late 1940s, with the introduction of formulas involving the addition of a quarter of a percentage point or more to the Federal Reserve discount rate. Floating rates were not widely used, however, as long as the discount rate and other rates remained fairly stable.

When the discount rate began changing more often in the early 1950s— and lagging hikes in the prime rate—banks switched the floating-rate base to the prime, a rate more closely reflecting market forces. Floating rate provisions, limited almost entirely to term loans, were not nearly as common as today.

The big change came in the mid-1960s, with the advent of modern bank liability management, growth of money-market funds, and more changes in short-term rates. Floating rates gave banks a way of making sure returns on outstanding loans—both long and short-term—moved with the costs of funds.

. . . and the formulas for computing them

Essentially two types of prime-based formulas are used in calculating floating rates:

• Prime-plus. The more conventional of the two, this method calls for an add-on factor to adjust for default risk and provide a term premium for long-term credit. An example is the prime rate plus 2 percentage points— "prime *plus* 2."

• Times-prime. Becoming more common, this method calls for multiplication of the prime by a factor to adjust for credit risk and a term premium. An example is the prime multiplied by 1.2—"1.2 *times* prime."

With either example, a prime rate set initially at 10 percent results in a floating loan rate of 12 percent.

Differences follow, however, if the prime rate is any rate other than 10 percent. With reductions in the prime rate, floating rates based on times-prime pricing decline faster than plus-prime rates. And increments in the prime result in faster increases in times-prime rates than in plus-prime rates.

Suppose, for instance, that an initial 10 percent prime is hiked to 12 percent. The prime-plus-2 loan rate moves from 12 percent to 14. The 1.2-times-prime rate moves from 12 percent to 14.4. If the prime is lowered from 10 percent to 8, the plus-prime rate falls from 12 percent to 10, but the times-prime rate drops to 9.6 percent.

Banks sometimes combine the two methods. An example is 1.09 times the *sum* of prime plus 1 percentage point—a floating rate equal to 1.09 *times* the prime plus 1.09 percentage points. Again, if the prime rate is set initially at 10 percent, the combination method leads to about the same floating rate as the basic methods—for example, 1.09 times 10 per-

---

LOAN PREPAYMENTS

Prepayment provisions in loan contracts spell out the penalty costs (premiums) charged for paying a loan before it matures. Until the 1960s, banks usually did not charge premiums when loans were paid off (or paid down) before maturity, provided the funds came from operating earnings or other internal sources. Although substantial premiums were often imposed on prepayments, financed from other borrowing, especially from other banks, many banks in the 1950s actually encouraged prepayments from a firm's retained earnings.

Banks today often impose substantial penalties on the prepayment of fixed-rate loans, the intentions being to hold borrowers to the full terms of their contracts in return for the banks' having to risk a rise in interest rates.

cent plus 1.09 percentage points, or roughly 12 percent. Effects for the combination method at any other prime, however, are the same as times-prime pricing, given the same multiplicative factors in the formulas.

As times-prime rates vary more than plus-prime rates over the interest-rate cycle, they have greater implications for changing bank loan revenue and, therefore, total profits.

One of the main reasons for times-prime pricing is that when the prime rate is raised, bank costs of funding outstanding loans in interest-sensitive markets may go up faster than the prime. The greater-than-proportional increase in the loan rate from times-prime pricing helps compensate banks for lagged upward responses of the prime rate.

The drift away from compensating balances also helps explain the growing use of times-prime pricing. The trend toward higher loan rates and lower required demand-deposit balances has, in fact, been a major factor in the use of more complicated floating-rate formulas.

The idea is to raise the loan rate enough to offset the loss of loanable funds when compensating balance requirements are eased. But the cost to a bank of foregoing these balances varies over interest-rate and credit cycles. When credit demand rises and banks scramble for ever more costly money-market funds, earlier reductions in compensating balances become increasingly costly. If rates are adjusted by the times-prime formula, explicit reimbursement to the bank increases as the prime rate rises. That is, an escalating rate premium replaces the supporting deposit balances.

Against these advantages of floating rates must be set the main disadvantage—the greater variation in loan revenue over the credit cycle. The disadvantage of floating rates becomes most apparent when market rates are falling. If formula loan rates are geared to fall as fast as money market rates, or even faster, bank profit margins on outstanding loans can be squeezed. Banks can immunize part of their business-loan portfolios from movements in money-market rates and the prime by continuing to make fixed-rate loans to customers interested primarily in loan-rate certainty.

If term borrowers could prepay their loans at will, with no direct or implied costs, they would in effect control maturities. As banks could not be sure of the repayment dates, prime-setting decisions would have to be based on probable prepayments, with banks undoubtedly charging more to compensate for the uncertainty.

Prepayment of floating-rate loans is seldom a problem. Borrowers have little incentive to prepay loans when the rates move with the costs of credit generally. Even if other interest rates fall a little faster than the floating rate, or rise a little slower, the substantial costs of originating other credit are apt to lock a customer into the existing loan.

Whether the rates are fixed or floating, then, most term loans run to maturity. And as a result, outstanding term loans are essentially immune to changes in the prime rate.

There are limits, of course, to the changes that can be made in prime rates.

Profile of commercial and industrial loans

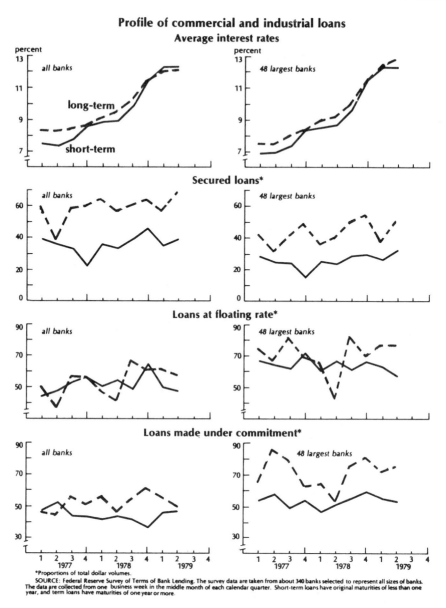

Average interest rates

percent   percent

Secured loans*

Loans at floating rate*

Loans made under commitment*

*Proportions of total dollar volumes.
SOURCE: Federal Reserve Survey of Terms of Bank Lending. The survey data are taken from about 340 banks selected to represent all sizes of banks. The data are collected from one business week in the middle month of each calendar quarter. Short-term loans have original maturities of less than one year, and term loans have maturities of one year or more.

If floating rates went up too much or did not respond to drastic reductions in market rates, borrowers would stand the prepayment penalties and term loans outstanding would fall.

SECURED LOANS

Although large corporations with top credit ratings routinely receive unsecured bank loans, many business borrowers have to post collateral. The amount of collateral and the type depend on the customer's credit rating, the size and maturity of the loan, and the purpose of the credit. Because of risk factors involved in some types of term credit, term loans are more apt to be secured than are short-term loans.

The most recent trend in secured bank lending is the kind of asset-based lending long handled by commercial finance companies. Large banks and their holding companies have become active in this specialized form of secured lending by acquiring existing finance companies, establishing new commercial-finance affiliates, and restructuring their own lending policies for closer management and monitoring of the collateral behind secured loans. The inroads large banks have made into asset-based lending represent a competitive response—especially to attract small business borrowers—and awareness of the need for adequate collateralization as an adjunct to the risk-bearing business of modern bank lending.

RECENT PRICING TACTICS

When loan demand eases and money-market rates fall, large money-center banks come under pressure to lower their prime-rate quotations in an effort to attract more new business loan customers. This was the situation in 1976 and 1977. Because of floating-rate provisions in outstanding business loans, however, reductions in the prime rate aimed at bolstering new loans call for forfeitures of revenue on floating-rate loans already on the books. Bank concern over loss of this revenue can slow the lowering of the prime.

When two large banks in a money center have significantly different proportions of their loan portfolios in floating-rate loans—especially if the loans are priced by different formulas (see box)—the one with the larger proportion may well be at a disadvantage in lowering its prime. These interbank differences in floating-rate loans help to explain split-rate primes—different prime rates at various money-center banks.

Large banks have tried several loan pricing policies aimed at bolstering loan demand and at the same time protecting profit margins on outstanding loans. One policy, dating from the 1950s, specifies ranges in which floating rates can be revised, as for example, an initial loan rate of 6 percent with the rate floating from 4 percent to 8 percent.

Some banks redesigned the cap-rate feature a few years ago by offering floating rates that would not average more than an agreed-on rate over the life of the loan. Because these cap rates combined the borrowing advantages of both fixed rates and floating rates, they gained some customer acceptance in 1971 and 1972.

When open-market rates rose, in 1973 and 1974, however, pushing up funding costs, profit margins on outstanding cap-rate loans dwindled. The upper limit on average interest costs became a ceiling that made further rate increases impossible. Banks have paid less attention to this type loan since. They have also shown few inclinations to adopt minimum-rate features that would limit the decline in loan rates when the prime was lowered.

Another technique for bolstering loan demand while protecting bank loan income has been floating rates tied to base rates other than the prime. This pricing feature is often tailored to the needs (and competitive environment) of large multinational corporations with access to credit markets abroad.

One of the rates that moves somewhat independently of the regular prime rate quotations governing other floating rates is the London Interbank Offering Rate (LIBOR); a short-term European money-market rate. Although this is the most common formula rate for these loans, such U.S. money-market rates as the commercial paper rate and secondary certificate of deposit rate are also used. In some cases, large banks have revised their overseas lending policies to provide credit in the European market at rates tied either to their U.S. prime rate or to LIBOR, depending on the expected changes in the prime-LIBOR rate spread.

Business lending strategies refined at large banks during a time of rising interest rates will be tested when demand for loans eases and interest rates fall. As pressures build for banks to lower their prime rates from the above-15 percent levels of recent months, a large part of their current loan portfolios will still be on the books.

Banks have been preparing for an eventual downturn by diversifying their business loans, interspersing fixed-rate loans with loans written to various formula rates based on prime and other rates. Their success in pursuing this diversification strategy will be reflected in how well their prime rates follow declines in market rates.

Since revisions in prime rates usually lag behind changes in market rates, the tendency is for the spread to widen when rates fall rapidly. If, after adjustment for the lag, the prime rate still responds sluggishly to easing market conditions, banks may have to rethink some of their explicit pricing methods for business lending.

LOAN COMMITMENTS AND FACILITY FEES*

Randall C. Merris

4

Commercial banks in recent years have begun to reevaluate their policies toward loan commitments—agreements in which banks obligate themselves to lend, upon customer demand, up to specified dollar limits over predetermined future time periods. These reappraisals have been prompted in part by concern on the part of both bankers and the monetary authorities over the high activation rates and large dollar volumes of loans extended under outstanding commitments during periods of tight credit.

The most recent such episode was in 1974 when tight money-market conditions and strong loan demand led major banks to boost the prime rate—the interest rate charged on business loans to banks' most creditworthy customers—to an unprecedented 12 percent. The monetary authorities' concern was that loan commitments made during earlier periods, when banks had easy access to funds, would require large-scale bank lending in 1974, hampering Federal Reserve efforts to restrict the growth of bank credit. Bank regulators were concerned that the high costs attached to honoring these commitments could threaten profitability and capital positions of some commercial banks.

Although bank loan commitments are not new financial instruments, these agreements have grown dramatically in dollar magnitudes and have assumed an increasingly critical position in bank management since World

*Reprinted from *Economic Perspectives*, March/April 1978, pp. 14-21, with permission from the Federal Reserve Bank of Chicago and the author.

War II. Of special importance has been the growth of fee-based commitments—contracts for which customers pay explicit bank charges called commitment facility fees (or simply facility or commitment fees). These fee-based commitments differ from credit lines, which are the traditional and still prevalent type of bank loan commitment. In place of explicit fees, credit line agreements typically require the customer to maintain compensating balances—minimum average checking account balances.

Growth of fee-based commitments has been spurred by a number of major banking developments since the early 1960s. A primary factor has been the increased reliance of commercial banks on open-market sources of funds to meet loan demands arising from commitments. The greater variability in the costs of these managed liabilities, compared with the relatively stable cost of traditional deposit sources of funds, has introduced additional uncertainties into bank management of loan commitments. At the same time fluctuations in interest rates applied to loans under commitments (i.e., takedowns) have been considerably greater in the post-1965 period. Increased variability of both bank costs and revenues has prompted many banks to analyze in detail the profitability of individual customer accounts and to make greater use of explicit pricing of loan commitments and other bank services.

For a long time loan commitments of commercial banks were viewed as a rather minor service performed as an adjunct to the actual loan contract. Nearly all loan commitments were in the form of credit lines related in a rather mechanical way to the volume of business loans. Largely as a consequence of the greater turbulence of financial markets in recent years, however, loan commitments have gained recognition as a distinct and separable service of commercial banks. This new view of commitments focuses on the financial advantages accruing to a business firm from assurance of future credit availability, a service that commands a price even if the commitment remains unused.

In general terms, loan commitments are viewed as insurance policies for which firms should be willing to pay a "premium"—either in the form of a facility fee or through compensating balances. Banks maintain some, but not complete, control over policyholder claims by reserving the right to vary interest rates applied on commitment takedowns in most of these contracts. It is extremely unlikely, in normal times, that all holders will decide to draw down their commitments simultaneously. As a result, banks are able to pool risks and forecast loan usage for commitments in much the same way that insurance companies use contingency tables to estimate claims.

Unlike claims under most forms of insurance, however, takedowns under loan commitments are not independent events ruled by accident or nature. Because takedowns occur at the discretion of business firms which are affected by tight credit conditions at about the same time, the possibility exists that a large proportion of commitment holders will turn to their banks for funds simultaneously. During periods of especially tight credit, such as in 1969 and 1974, takedowns were increased sharply enough by a sufficiently large number of commitment holders to engender concern.

COMMITMENT FEATURES

Loan commitment is a term loosely applied to a variety of agreements varying from informal understandings to legally binding contracts between commercial banks and their customers. A loan commitment may be negotiated between the parties and tailored to specific operating policies of the bank and particular credit needs of the customer. All major banks and many smaller ones have detailed operating policies regarding commitments. Any one bank frequently uses several standard types of commitments and further customizes these agreements to individual customers.

Even commercial banks are not always in agreement as to what constitutes a loan commitment. Some banks consider all or nearly all short-term business loans to arise from commitments, even if the bank has had no contact with the loan customer prior to the loan application. At the other extreme are banks that view themselves as making no commitments whatever. Fortunately, most banks' commitment policies are better defined and managed than either of these extreme views might suggest. Nevertheless, differences in terminology regarding commitments persist.

Loan commitments typically include four major elements—disclosure of the commitment to the customer, the dollar limit on loans under the agreement, interest rates on takedowns, and the time period during which the agreement is effective. While some banks have adopted internal guidelines for use in screening customer loan requests, these guidelines typically are not considered loan commitments unless they have been communicated to customers. Thus, terms such as "disclosed credit lines" or "confirmed lines" often are used to distinguish commitments from internal guidelines. Although all credit commitments involve disclosure to the customer, either orally or in writing, their treatment of the other major elements varies widely. Confirmed credit lines include lending limits but do not detail other terms and conditions of usage. Credit lines sometimes are open indefinitely or until further notice from the bank, but most often are on an annually renewable basis.

On the other hand, formal loan commitments, sometimes called "firm" commitments, include all four major elements of commitment agreements. Not only dollar loan limits, but also lending rates and the period for which the agreement is in force, are stated in writing. The lending rate is usually specified to bear a fixed relationship to the prime rate. The period during which formal commitments are in force is normally one to three years, depending on the purpose of the borrowing. There is usually a clause requiring a bank to show cause for not honoring a formal commitment, and proviso clauses stipulating that the customer must maintain minimum adequate working capital, limiting the customer's reliance on nonbank external financing, or imposing other controls on the firm's operations sometimes detail the conditions under which the bank may be released from its obligation to lend.

Two of the most important types of formal commitments are revolving credits and term loan commitments. A revolving credit entitles the customer to take down and repay loans repeatedly during the time the agreement is in effect, so long as the total loans outstanding at any time do not exceed the dollar limits of the commitment. Banks may require that a revolving credit be repaid in full for some part of each year. Term loan commitments are for bank loans having original maturities exceeding one year. Some commitments apply directly to term loans, whereas other commitments begin as revolving credits and allow conversion to term lending during the life or upon expiration of the revolving credit agreement. Revolving credits and term loan commitments are two principal types of commitments on which banks often charge explicit fees.

Another major category of formal commitments is the standby commitment, which is used to back an issuance of commercial paper—promissory notes issued by large corporations and used as a close substitute for bank loans. Although collateral is not required on commercial paper, investors typically require some assurance that issuers will be able to repay or refinance the debt upon maturity. Under standby commitments banks promise to provide refinancing through bank loans when the commercial paper matures. Corporations sometimes find bank refinancing less expensive than commercial paper, and take down large amounts of standby commitments. At other times, when commercial paper is relatively less expensive, standby commitments remain unused and serve only as credit assurance. In many instances a large corporation will have loan commitments outstanding from dozens of banks to cover its commercial paper. The fees charged for these commitments are referred to as standby fees.

Credit lines traditionally have been a major component of "customer relationships" —longstanding cooperative arrangements by which a bank provides total packages of bank services to business customers. Standing ready to provide loans, especially in times of tight credit, is vital to maintaining the loyalty of the customer and the long-run profitability of his account to the bank.

Advance commitment of funds also may serve as an important part of the loan approval mechanism used in major banks. So long as total loans to a given borrower remain within the dollar limits of the commitment, preapproved lending reduces administrative costs for a bank loan department by eliminating the need to review and approve each loan separately.

Knowing both the overall dollar volume of commitments and the totals for separate commitment categories, senior bank management is better able to forecast loan demand. However, knowledge of the usage rates of various types of commitments is also necessary.

USAGE RATES

Usage rates (i.e., the percentages of commitments taken down at any given time) vary significantly among credit lines, revolving credits, term loan commitments, and other types of commitments. Usage rates tend to be highest for formalized agreements, especially for fee-based commitments. Thus, term loan commitments and revolving credits have higher usage rates on average than confirmed credit lines.

Usage rates also display more cyclical variability for some categories of commitments than for others. Credit lines and revolving credits are designed to meet both foreseen and unforeseen short-term borrowing needs and so have more cyclical and seasonal usage than term loan commitments.

Nonbank financial institutions, especially finance companies, are major users of commitments, either directly or as backing for commercial paper, and are often treated as a separate commitment category. These commitments are most similar in form and usage to the revolving credits issued to commercial and industrial borrowers.

Banks also issue construction-loan and mortgage-loan commitments for loans secured by real estate, collectively called real estate commitments. Ultimate usage rates are near 100 percent for real estate commitments. A construction commitment is tied directly and formally to a specific construction project and includes a date for total takedown or a timetable for periodic takedowns increasing to 100 percent usage during the construction period. Similarly, a mortgage commitment is tied to a particular commercial or residential property as of a closing date. Real estate commitments are a totally separate entity and normally are not discussed along with "regular" commitments because the bank's uncertainty about usage rates, which is substantial for credit lines, revolving credits, and term commitments, is not as important for real estate commitments.

LENDING UNDER COMMITMENTS

Estimates from the latest available Federal Reserve survey of bank lending, covering loans contracted in the first full week of November 1977, indicate that slightly over 40 percent of the dollar amounts of short-term business loans (i.e., loans with maturities less than one year) and over 48 percent of long-term business loans were contracted through commitments. In general, the largest banks originate a larger proportion of their business lending through commitments than smaller banks. For example, 54 percent of the dollar volume of short-term business loans of the 48 largest banks in the November 1977 survey were made under commitments, compared to 33 percent of the same category of lending by other banks. Over 62 percent of the long-term business lending by the 48 largest banks was under commitments, compared to about 32 percent for other banks.

Generally, large loans are more likely to originate from commitments than are smaller loans. In the November 1977 survey, for example, only 19 percent of the dollar amount of short-term business loans in the $1-99 thousand size category arose from commitments, compared with 50 percent of short-term lending in the $100 thousand and over size category. Similarly, about 37 percent of the dollar amount of long-term loans in the $1-99 thousand category were made under commitments, compared to over 53 percent for the loans of $100 thousand and over. The prevalence of commitments for large loans is explained in part by the lead time for advance planning afforded by a loan commitment, which is especially critical when the loan represents a sizable portion of the bank's total lending and is to be outstanding for a long time.

PRICING COMMITMENTS

Facility fees, like interest rates, are quoted as annual percentages rates and are paid either in full when the commitment begins or at regular intervals during the life of the contract. Some banks use a base fee to which are added, depending on the customer, supplementary facility fees or compensating balance requirements related to the dollar amounts of the commitments or the takedowns.

During the 1950s and most of the 1960s, the basic facility fee was ¼ percent per annum on the unused dollar amount of the commitment but at times was increased by some banks to ½ percent on the unused amount.

The major purpose of the facility fee on commitments is to pay for the credit assurance services provided by the bank. Like prices of other goods and services, facility fees serve as an economic rationing device. They can be varied by the bank as a means of controlling the dollar volume of loan commitments. Increases in facility fees, other factors unchanged, will result in a reduction in dollar amounts of commitments demanded by new and existing customers.

Commercial banks change their basic facility fees very infrequently. One reason for "stickiness" of these fees is that banks have other methods available for influencing the volume of commitments. Commercial banks can change the availability of the funds borrowed under commitments by altering compensating balance requirements when applicable or can vary other elements of the commitment agreement. Interest and noninterest terms on the loans assured by the agreements also can be modified in lieu of changing the facility fee. For example, a business firm previously qualifying for loans at the prime rate might terminate the agreement or carry a smaller commitment when faced with a higher loan rate—say, prime plus one percent.

Inflexibility of facility fees also results from the manner in which fee charges influence loan demand, especially when the fee is applied to unused portions of commitments. The effects on loan demand are illustrated best by looking at changes in facility fees during two recent episodes of tight credit and strong loan demand.

• In the spring of 1969 several large New York City banks raised their facility fees from ¼ percent to ½ percent per annum on unused portions of new commitments and renewals of existing ones.

• In the fall of 1974 several major money-center banks imposed a ¼ percent fee on total dollar amounts of new and renewed commitments in addition to the ½ percent fee already levied against unused segments of their commitments.

Levying facility fees against the unused portions of commitments has significantly different implications for loan demand than placing fees on total commitments. The fee increase in 1969 was aimed at reducing the amount of outstanding commitments and thereby stemming the growth of business lending. However, increasing the fee only against unused commitments provided an offsetting incentive to commitment holders to *increase* the usage of the commitments that remained in force.

Given the size of the commitment, an increase in the fee on the unused portion amounts to a decrease in the effective loan rate on takedowns. Consider a commitment carrying a ¼ percent fee on the unused portion in early 1969 and obligating the bank to lend at the 7½ percent prime rate quoted from mid-March to early June 1969. The effective, or marginal, interest rate on loans under this commitment is 7¼ percent rather than 7½ percent because of the ¼ percent facility fee on unused commitment amounts. The borrower pays only 7¼ percent more by taking down the commitment since the ¼ percent fee is "saved" on each dollar of commitments used.

Now suppose that after the facility fee increase in 1969 from ¼ percent to ½ percent, the commitment holder chose to renew his commitment. With the prime rate still at 7½ percent, the new effective rate on takedowns would be 7 percent—the 7½ percent prime minus the ½ percent fee on unused commitment amounts. Thus, an increase in the commitment fee would result in a reduction in the effective cost of takedowns and probably would have the undesired effect of encouraging greater usage of commitments during a tight money situation.

It is noteworthy that the prime rate was increased in June 1969 from 7½ percent to 8½ percent—the largest single movement in the prime in modern history. This prime rate increase occurred soon after the ¼ percentage point increase in facility fees on unused commitments by some major banks. Some part of this hike in the prime rate may be explained by the need to adjust the loan rate to the new facility fee schedules.

Indirect evidence that banks learned a lesson in facility fee policy from the 1969 episode is provided by the experience of 1974. Banks that increased fees in 1974 avoided simultaneously decreasing effective loan rates on takedowns. Since the additional ¼ percent fee (or more in some cases) was placed on the total amount of new and renewed commitments, the commitment holder could not reduce the fee charge by simply taking down the commitment. From the banks' viewpoint the additional fee on total commitments had the advantage of reducing the dollar volume of commitments without stimulating an offsetting increase in takedowns.

Even when applied to total commitments, higher fees tend to increase observed usage rates because these agreements become a higher-cost financial resource. This is because the higher commitment fees lead holders to economize on the volume of unused commitments, resulting in higher observed usage rates.

REGULATION

It has been suggested on occasion that bank loan commitments should be subject to public regulation, either by placing reserve requirements on commitments or by limiting overall dollar volumes. Each of these alternatives, however, presents serious problems owing to the rather special nature of commitments—namely, that these contracts are contingent claims on the banking system. Because no transaction involving the actual transfer of funds is made until the commitment is taken down, commitments do not appear on bank balance sheets. Thus, regulation of commitments would not operate directly on an item appearing on the balance sheets of commercial banks.

If reserve requirements were placed on loan commitments, however, banks would need to alter accounts which do appear on their balance sheets—liquidating loans and investments or attracting additional deposits—in order to obtain funds to meet these requirements. By absorbing loanable funds, reserve requirements against loan commitments could prove a heavy burden on banks. The probable result would be that some banks would eliminate loan commitments (formal commitments at least) from the list of bank services provided. Many banks probably would impose additional compensating balance requirements, facility fees, and higher loan rates on commitment takedowns. In this way, the implied costs of reserve requirements against commitments would be shifted onto banks' credit customers.

The establishment of ceilings on dollar volumes of outstanding loan commitments would cause serious regulatory problems. Restrictions on loan commitments would have to be extended to entire business loan portfolios of commercial banks. Otherwise, banks simply could shift large volumes of lending from formal commitment status to lending without prior commitment or to agreements sufficiently informal as to avoid, at least technically, the official definition of a commitment. Unless all business lending and commitments were regulated in the same way, a reversal in the trend toward formal commitments would enable banks to circumvent quantitative controls on commitments.

If different quantitative restrictions (or reserve requirements) were imposed on different categories of business loans and loan commitments, the consequence would be bank credit allocation with its multitude of regulatory costs and inequities.

Despite the monetary authorities' occasional concern over the pro-cyclical effects of loan commitment usage, the need for regulatory control over loan commitments has not been clearly demonstrated. The fee revisions in 1969 and 1974 have shown that banks' control over outstanding formal commitments can be maintained during tight credit periods. Some firms holding bank credit lines in 1974 sought to convert them to fee-based commitments. While assuring customers that confirmed lines would be honored as readily as formal commitments, banks balked at converting these informal lines.

It should be remembered that commitment agreements expire and must be renegotiated. Even if many large, unused commitments accumulate during a period of slack loan demand, many of them expire as business credit demand recovers. After that occurs, and before credit pressures of the recovery have mounted, banks have several options. They can reduce the sizes of commitments, raise facility fees and compensating balance requirements, or alter other interest and noninterest terms on loans. Moreover, commitment holders have little incentive to accumulate commitments in anticipation of a credit crunch if the agreements are expected to expire before credit stringency appears.

Indeed, the otherwise minor difficulties that some banks encountered from loan pressures in 1974, as well as the resulting concern on the part of the monetary authorities, were exacerbated by efforts of public officials to hold bank lending rates—particularly the prime rate—below the level dictated by market forces. To the extent that banks yielded to pressures to restrain rate increases, they denied themselves the use of a major method for controlling commitment usage—raising the price of borrowings.

Though formal controls appear unwarranted, commitments nevertheless pose problems that merit the attention of bank management and supervisory authorities. Some banks still have fairly informal commitment policies and could benefit from specific guidelines and better internal data on loan commitments. Consideration should be given to uniform disclosure of dollar amounts of loan commitments, at least formal agreements, as addenda items on all bank balance sheets. Disclosure would enable investors to evaluate the impact of loan commitments on individual banks' risk positions, and also could contribute to more consistent and effective bank examination procedures.

DETERMINING PRICING ALTERNATIVES*

Gary R. Severson

5

The scenario is a familiar one to loan officers: After you've analyzed a prospective credit and proposed terms and pricing, the customer takes some exception to the price. Until recently, this reaction almost always centered on cost, but now it just as frequently reflects accounting, liquidity or cash flow considerations. Assuming that your original price fairly related return against risk, how do you determine pricing alternatives that assuage the customer's objections without compromising the yield on the credit? As an example, let us use a case where the proposed price for a line of credit is prime plus ½%. Additionally, you are charging a commitment fee of ½% on the unused portion and requiring that deposits equal 10% of the commitment plus 10% of the outstanding loan. The customer's reaction focuses on the deposit requirement, and he states that he can only maintain deposits up to the equivalent of 15% of the outstanding loan. He concedes that he could accept an increase in the nominal interest rate of up to an additional ¾% and asks that you propose some pricing alternatives for the line of credit that satisfy his constraints.

*Reprinted from the *Journal of Commercial Bank Lending*, November, 1974, pp. 2-8. Copyright 1974 by Robert Morris Associates. Reprinted with permission.

A METHOD OF YIELD CALCULATION

First, let us consider a method of yield calculation. Using the more common pricing elements of rate and deposits, yield can be derived initially as:

Formula 1:

$$Y = \frac{R \, (ALO)}{ALO - [(1 - RR) \, (FCD)]}$$

Where: Y   = yield
        R   = nominal interest rate
        ALO = average loan outstanding
        RR   = reserve requirement[1]
        FCD = free collected deposits provided by the borrower

In this formula, the numerator shows the gross revenue from a loan, and the denominator shows the bank's investment in that loan (average loan outstanding less those loanable funds provided by the customer). A simpler way of expressing these relationships for subsequent points in this discussion is to divide through the formula by the average loan outstanding leaving:

Formula 2:

$$Y = \frac{R}{1 - [(1 - RR) \, (FCD)]}$$

Where FCD is now redefined as free collected deposits as a percent of average loan outstanding.

Commitment fees contribute to the numerator in Formula 2 and can be defined in terms of their effective addition to the rate. In other words, we can translate a commitment fee into an equivalent interest rate and add it to our nominal interest rate. In the case of a fee charged on the unused portion of the commitment, that translation is shown as:

Formula 3:

$$EA = \frac{CF_u \, (1 - U)}{U}$$

Where: EA   = effective addition to nominal interest rate
        CF_u = commitment fee charged on unused portion of the commitment
        U   = utilization (ALO divided by commitment, and represented as a percent)

When a commitment fee is charged at the outset of a credit arrangement, irrespective of the anticipated utilization, the determination of the effective

---

[1] Our examples assume a reserve requirement of 18%.

addition is more difficult to represent precisely in a simple formula. However, from a sampling of our own commercial loan portfolio, the following heuristic was developed which provides reasonably well the equivalent increase in the nominal interest rate from a commitment fee collected on the front end:

Formula 4:

$$EA = \frac{CF_f\,(1.045)}{U}$$

Where: CF_f = commitment fee collected on the front end.

With the occurrence of either commitment fee in the pricing structure of a credit facility, the corresponding modification to our yield Formula 2 above is, therefore:

Formula 5:

$$Y = \frac{R + EA}{1 - [(1 - RR)\,(FCD)]}$$

THE DENOMINATOR AND FREE COLLECTED DEPOSITS

Brief attention should now be directed to the denominator, particularly the definition and determination of free collected deposits. This term refers to gross deposits provided by the borrower, less float and less that amount of collected deposits necessary to offset account activity charges. After applying the appropriate reserve requirement, the remainder is the deposit balance which directly contributes to the yield by reducing that portion of the loan that must be funded from other bank sources.

Free collected deposits are represented in Formulas 2 and 5 as a percent of the average loan outstanding. When deposits are required in a fixed amount, divide that amount by ALO to determine FCD:

Formula 6:

$$FCD = \frac{DR_f}{ALO}$$

Where: DR_f = fixed deposit requirement.

Formula 6 can also be used when, instead of a specific requirement, there is an expectation that deposits will average a particular amount.

When a deposit requirement is stated as a percent of commitment, express this relationship to average loan outstanding by dividing by utilization:

Formula 7:

$$FCD = \frac{DR_c}{U}$$

Where: DR_c = deposit requirement as a percent of commitment.

The resultant FCD from Formula 7 will vary, of course, dependent upon utilization. A deposit requirement already stated as a percent of outstanding, however, will maintain a constant relationship, represented simply as:

Formula 8:

$$FCD = DR_o$$

Where: DR_o = deposit requirement as a percent of outstanding.

As deposit requirements are frequently combined (most commonly a DR_c plus a DR_o, or the greater of a DR_c or a DR_o) it is necessary, of course, to make the appropriate additions or comparisons to reflect the overall FCD position.

CALCULATING THE YIELD

Based on the methodology discussed above, we can now return to our original example and calculate its yield, assuming prime to average 10 ½% during the period and utilization to average 60%. One must make estimates of rate and utilization to determine the yield in any variable rate line of credit. Rate projections are generally provided by the bank's Economics Department, and utilization estimates can be derived from the line's purpose, its past usage and the customer's own expectations. For the purpose of comparing alternative pricing structures, however, we can be assured reasonable validity if we use the same assumptions consistently. In our original pricing proposal, our givens and assumptions are then:

$$
\begin{aligned}
R &= 11\% = .11 \\
CF_u &= \tfrac{1}{2}\% = .005 \\
DR_c &= 10\% = .1 \\
DR_o &= 10\% = .1 \\
U &= 60\% = .6
\end{aligned}
$$

Formula 3 allows us to calculate the effective addition to our nominal interest rate from a commitment fee charged on the unused portion:

$$EA = \frac{.005\,(1 - .6)}{.6}$$
$$= .0033$$
$$= .33\%$$

Free collected deposits expected from the deposit requirement on the commitment, DR_c, is determined from Formulas 7 as:

$$FCD = \frac{.1}{.6}$$
$$= .167$$
$$= 16.7\%$$

Both deposit requirements must be separately satisfied, so the combined FCD is .267 (.167 as calculated above plus .1 (10%) from the deposit requirement on the outstanding).

We now have sufficient data to calculate the yield from Formula 5:

$$Y = \frac{.11 + .0033}{1 - [(1 - .18)(.267)]}$$

$$= \frac{.1133}{.781}$$

$$= .1451$$

$$= 14.51\%$$

With 14.51% as the yield from our original pricing proposal, it should be our objective to maintain this yield while considering our customer's objections. Concentrating first on his constraint that deposits cannot exceed 15% of outstanding, we can work "backward" through Formula 5 to determine the combination of rate and commitment fee necessary to maintain our yield:

$$.1451 = \frac{R + EA}{1 - [(1 - .18)(.15)]} \qquad R + EA = (.1451)(.877)$$
$$= .1273$$
$$= 12.73\%$$

Our original numerator was 11.33% so it now needs a 1.40% increase (.1273 − .1133) to offset the deposit constraint. If we take the .75% rate increase which the customer offered, we are still .65% short. One possible way of recouping this shortfall would be to charge a front end commitment fee of 3/8%.

$$\text{From Formula 4, } .0065 = \frac{CF_f(1.045)}{.6} \qquad CF_f = \frac{.0039}{1.045}$$
$$= .00373$$
$$= .373\%$$
$$\approx .375\% \text{ or } 3/8\%^2$$

The terms of our original proposal and our first alternative (I) are summarized in the following table:

	Original Proposal	Alternative I
R	11.0 %	11.75 %
Spread over Prime	.5 %	1.25 %
CF_u	.5 %	.5 %
CF_f	-	.375%
DR_c	10 %	-
DR_o	10 %	15 %
Y	14.51%	14.52 %

---

[2]The precision of the calculations is occasionally impractical to implement; in this example, rounding to the nearest 1/8% does not jeopardize the conclusions.

ADJUSTING THE YIELDS

We have thus far disregarded two additional pricing elements available to the loan officer: (1) the frequency of interest and fee collection and (2) the prerogative of charging interest and fees on a 360-day year basis. The above calculations both assume a quarterly collected yield on a 365-day year basis. Yields defined in this manner are more consistent with nominal costs of funds and provide a standard perspective for evaluating alternative pricing structures. We must, however, make the appropriate adjustment of yields that are collected or earned on different bases. For example, a yield collected on a monthly basis translates to a quarterly basis as follows:

Formula 9:

$$Y_q = 4 \left[\left(1 + \frac{Y_m}{12} \right)^3 - 1 \right]$$

Where:
Y_q = Yield, quarterly collected
Y_m = Yield, monthly collected

From: $\left(1 + \frac{Y_q}{4} \right)^4 = \left(1 + \frac{Y_m}{12} \right)^{12}$

which determines what quarterly collected yield compounded four times equals what monthly collected yield compounded twelve times or, in other words, which equates the effective annual yield of each.

Different collection frequencies can be similarly translated, but quarterly or monthly periods are the most common.

The adjustment for the 360-day year is made by simply multiplying the yield by the factor, $\frac{365}{360}$, or its decimal equivalent, 1.0139. It should be calculated before the collection frequency adjustment if both adjustments are required.

Considering these pricing elements, as well as those of rate, commitment fees and deposit requirements which we discussed earlier, the following table presents additional alternatives that would satisfy both the lender and the borrower in our original example:

	Alternatives					
	II	III	IV	V	VI	VII
R	11.75%	11.5 %	11.25%	11.25%	11.5 %	11.25%
Spread over Prime	1.25%	1.0 %	0.75%	0.75%	1.0 %	0.75%
CF_u	1.25%	0.5 %	1.5 %	-	0.75%	1.0 %
CF_f	0.25%	0.75%	-	1.0 %	0.5 %	0.5 %
DR_c	7.5 %	-	5 %	-	-	5 %
DR_o	-	10 %	5 %	10 %	12.5 %	5 %
360/365 day year	365	360	360	360	365	365
Collection frequency[3]	Q	Q	Q	M	M	M
Y_q	14.51%	14.51%	14.51%	14.51%	14.50%	14.51%

[3] Q = quarterly collection; M = monthly collection.

LEGAL RISKS IN COMMERCIAL LENDING†

Hugh M. Durden*

6

The legal and ethical dimensions of corporate responsibility for all U.S. businesses have been broadened considerably in the recent past. The banking industry is no exception, and bankers today must necessarily be more concerned than ever before with the public interpretation of their actions. Furthermore, weight of this increased responsibility, more often than not, rests squarely with the commercial lending officer because he personally confronts legal issues almost daily in the normal course of his relationship with customers.

Commercial lending officers as a group have traditionally had a deep appreciation for, and a commitment to, ethical conduct in their dealings with the public. This tradition was never more important than it is today. The fact remains, however, that the nature and the complexity of the legal issues in banking today have expanded beyond past precepts and require that the lending officer be constantly aware of current topics and decisions. For this reason, it is the purpose of this paper to outline the major legal issues in banking today, why they should concern the individual bank officer, and

†Reprinted from the *Journal of Commercial Bank Lending*, November 1973, pp. 11-18. Copyright 1973 by Robert Morris Associates. Reprinted with permission.

*The author is Executive Vice President, Wachovia Bank & Trust Company, N.A., Winston-Salem, North Carolina.

Mr. Durden's paper won second prize in the RMA National Paper Writing Competition, 1973. Mr. Durden's paper also earned first prize in the RMA Carolina-Virginias Chapter Annual Case Study and Special Subject Paper Writing Competition.

how his affairs should be conducted in order to prevent serious misunderstandings (or worse) between his bank, its customers, the public and various legal authorities.

Specifically, this paper will discuss the lending officer's responsibility in each of the following areas:

1. Securities Law, including:
   a. Insider information/conflicts of interest
   b. Disclosure of financial information
2. Tie-ins
3. Gratuities
4. Confidential information

SECURITIES LAW

Perhaps the most significant, and most complex, of these topics is the expansion of liability which is occurring in regard to Federal securities law. Since this represents the newest, and possibly the most all-encompassing, area of potential liability faced by many bankers, considerable attention will be devoted to this topic.

The legislative basis for the current expansion of liability in securities matters is not new, and is relatively straightforward in its language. There are essentially only two major references. The first is Section 16 of the Securities Exchange Act of 1934, which imposes strict requirements upon directors, officers and major stockholders in sales and/or purchases of equity securities of their respective corporation. Such insiders are accountable for any short-term (less than six months) equity transactions, and any profits derived therefrom are to be returned to the corporation. The second major point of reference is the SEC's Rule 10 b-5, which is also based upon powers derived from the 1934 Securities Exchange Act. This rule prohibits the action of any person who employs any artifice to deceive, makes false or misleading statements or engages in any practice which would operate deceitfully upon any other person in connection with the purchase or sale of a security. Although closely related, Section 16 deals primarily with inside information and conflicts of interest, while Rule 10 b-5 deals with disclosure of accurate information.

In general, then, Section 16 and Rule 10 b-5 are intended to protect the public investor from the unfair advantage that insiders might enjoy and from fraudulent and/or misleading influences upon the prices of listed securities. Both of these restrictions have for years been applied to brokers and dealers in securities as well as to insiders in the strictest sense—the officers, directors, and major stockholders of publicly traded companies. The interpretations of both rules have been steadily expanded and have been successfully applied to the role played by accountants, lawyers and underwriters in the sale and trading of securities. There is every indication, and in fact some concrete evidence, that commercial bankers will soon share in all forms of these liabilities. Recent trends in the case law for both areas are significant to lending officers.

Insider Information

In regard to insider information, probably the most well known case is the *SEC* vs. *Texas Gulf Sulphur Company*.[1] In this case, the firm legitimately concealed some important information concerning a mineral discovery in order to secure land options. However, during this period of withheld information some members of the firm's management made large purchases of the company's stock and then further complicated matters by issuing a misleading public statement concerning the discovery. Although this was a landmark case at the time (1964), today it seems apparent that this set of circumstances would be a misuse of insider knowledge as well as a violation in the release of false or misleading information. In another major case, Merrill Lynch was engaged in 1966 as an underwriter for an issue of Douglas Aircraft debentures.[2] In the course of the underwriting preparations, Merrill Lynch personnel became aware that financial information as yet unreleased would show earnings that were considerably lower than earlier published forecasts. This information was passed to selected brokers and in turn to certain institutional accounts who then sold Douglas stock. These accounts were reported to have avoided losses of about $4.5 million in the price decline which followed the release of the actual earnings. While not insiders in the strict traditional sense, the SEC charged that the underwriters were, in practice, insiders and that their subsequent actions were therefore illegal. Further, the investors favored with this inside knowledge were sued for fraud in their sales of Douglas stock to unsuspecting buyers. This case illustrated probably better than any other the extension of insider liability to what were heretofore independent groups.

The circumstances involved in these cases and others could be reproduced rather closely in the commercial banking field, and it appears to be only a matter of time until the regulatory authorities and the courts choose to extend legal liability to the commercial banker in analogous situations. In fact, a case filed in March 1973 by a large pension fund charges the Continental Illinois National Bank and Trust Company with a conflict of-interest arising from their insider position as both lender (through the commercial loan portfolio) and investor (through their trust department) in certain companies.[3] It is alleged that this conflict interfered with their fiduciary relationship in

---

[1] 401 F.2d 833 (2d CIR., 1968); Also companion case, 312F. Supp. 77 (S. D. N. Y., 1970). Wade M. Gallant, Jr., "Conflicts of Interest and the Commercial Banker," *The Journal of Commercial Bank Lending*, April, 1973, p. 15.

[2] SEC Act Release No. 8459, CCH Fed. Sec. L. Rep. 77, 629 (1968).

[3] "Continental Illinois Bank Sued Over Management of UAL Pension Fund," *Wall Street Journal*, March 29, 1973.

trust management and that pension funds assets suffered accordingly. The suit seeks $7 million as reimbursement for losses. In regard to the dollar value of such liability, one should not be misled by the statute's requirement for the return of profits gained through use of insider positions. In addition to that, a violator, either individual or corporate, might be sued for the losses of all other investors.

It seems rather clear that a strong possibility exists of lending officer involvement with insider information. The important definitions are those of "insider" and "conflict of interest." The exact legal form given these terms may vary from case to case. An insider is simple anyone who possesses or obtains "material inside information," which includes any information which might reasonably be expected to influence an investor in making his investment decision. The general theme of conflicts of interest is that they involve a conflict between self interest and a duty, loyalty or obligation to any other person, class or group. These definitions are rather open-ended, and that is typically how they are interpreted. A lending officer may easily become an insider; in fact, he may not be doing his job properly if he does not possess some form of "material inside information." His use of this information is thus the important determinant of potential legal liability. The general tenet for the banker then must be that his position, and the information obtained therefrom, cannot be used to advance the interest of himself or any other person or group. Such knowledge applied for gains in one's personal or family investments is obviously forbidden. Equally important is a prohibition against sharing such information with others, for example, his own bank's trust department.

Misrepresentations of a Customer's Financial Position

The second critical topic involving lending officers in securities litigation is that of misrepresentations of a customer's financial position. Rule 10 b-5 clearly prohibits misleading or erroneous information which might defraud or deceive an investor. Traditionally, bankers have had little or no involvement in this matter and disclosure was more or less left to a company and its accountants, and perhaps its legal counsel. The present view, however, is basically that anyone, to the extent that they affect the form or content of a company's financial condition, is to some degree responsible for the fair presentation of that condition to actual and/or potential investors. This responsibility is not likely to extend directly to a bank, but the bank could easily be involved if it "aided or abetted" the subsequent unlawful action of its customers.[4] This indirect responsibility carries, furthermore, the same liability as the offending business or person. "Window dressing" loans are the

---

[4] Martin Lipton, "Expanding Responsibilities of Commercial Banks and other Lenders Under Federal Securities Laws," *New York Law Journal*, July 10, 1972.

best example of a bank's ability to help a customer misrepresent his financial condition. It is fairly easy to see how such lending might be held as aiding and abetting a misrepresentation.

Unfortunately, other possible involvements in this matter are not as clear. A potentially much more important area revolves around the issues of distress loans and/or control positions by a bank. A lending officer might well know that a company's actual condition is worse than it may appear and that the company's future may in fact depend almost entirely upon the bank's continued credit. Taken one step further, the bank may feel that circumstances are such that it can and should call its loans. The current argument in such matters, as yet largely untested, is that the bank's responsibility now extends past the corporate body to the company's stockholders. This thesis could be based on either of two points: (1) the bank in fact controls the company; or (2) the bank knows more about the company than the stockholders and thus might have been assisting in misrepresenting the firm's condition. These issues were among several that were being contested in the *Stirling Homex* case.[5] In this case, the principal stockholders are suing their banks for alleged misrepresentations that had a material effect on the company's financial condition and claiming that the bank's actions were a direct cause of the firm's subsequent bankruptcy, all to the detriment of the stockholders' investment.

Other than the fairly straightforward area of window dressing loans, this subject of a bank's responsibility for its customers' financial condition and its fair disclosure is sufficiently complex to prevent the formulation of concrete rules for lending officers. There are, however, certain general principles that lending officers should be aware of in dealing with this matter. First, a lending officer should recognize his and his bank's potential liability in this matter—namely, that if he directly or indirectly aids or abets a misrepresentation to investors, legal liability for such action may ensue. Second, it may occasionally be appropriate to urge the company to disclose certain facts concerning its condition and relationship to the bank. Third, it may be wise to seek legal counsel in some matters, particularly when the rights of stockholders might be involved, such as in regard to distress loans and/or *de facto* control positions by the bank. The direct implication of present legal trends is that a banker can no longer take the position that he simply made the loan and left stockholder interests to be assumed by others. In fact, any time a bank's action, or lack of it, might have a serious and adverse effect upon a firm's investors, the bank must recognize its potential liability and condition its action accordingly.

TIE-INS

The rapid and continuing increase in bank diversification, particularly through bank holding companies, has raised an additional concern for many

---

[5] "Brothers Who Founded Stirling Homex Suing 2 Banks, Charge Fraud," *Wall Street Journal*, October 23, 1972.

banking officers. The prohibition against tie-ins and/or reciprocal dealings is now an important matter for many banks. This subject was addressed directly in the 1970 amendments to the 1956 Bank Holding Company Act. Section 106 of those amendments provides that a bank shall not extend credit or any service on the condition or requirement that the customer also obtain additional services from that bank or from any other subsidiary of the bank or its holding company. Traditional banking services such as maintaining deposits or a restriction of further debt are exempted from these prohibited tie-ins. The implications of this law, and the behavior it dictates for the lending officer, are fairly clear—thou shalt not employ any such methods that restrict a customer's right to free choice in selecting financial services. However, the problems created by the law are not quite that simple. Credit decisions are frequently very subjective matters, and the law does not curtail the exercise of individual judgment in such matters. The problem may arise when two customers are considered for a loan, both of whom appear to be equally qualified, and the loan is only granted to one of the two. If the decision is based upon one's subjective evaluation of a certain factor, for instance, the quality of management, and the customer receiving the loan has also had considerable involvement with one of the bank's subsidiaries, then the lending officer's decision must in fact have not been swayed by the existence of the other business. In this case, it may be well to have the subjective basis of your decision documented in one form or another.

The basic point is that tie-ins between a bank's traditional services and the use of other bank or subsidiary services are illegal *per se* and a lending officer would be well advised to avoid apparent as well as actual violations in this matter. This can be accomplished by logical, well-documented evaluations of each prospect on its own merits.

GRATUITIES

Most lending officers are familiar with the legal prohibitions against receiving gifts or other considerations because of a banking relationship or a transaction between the bank and a third party. It is possible that questions could arise in this regard where a bank officer receives a gift of nominal value from a personal friend or acquaintance who is also a borrowing customer of his bank. Such activity is not necessarily illegal. At the same time, since lending officers are frequently in the public view, it is advisable for the officer to avoid any apparent as well as actual compromises in this matter. A sound basis for one's behavior in this matter would be to refuse any gifts, entertainment or other consideration from a banking customer other than that of a nominal value that the officer could personally reciprocate if he so chose.

CONFIDENTIAL INFORMATION

Confidentiality of credit information is also a subject with which most lending officers are well aware. The Fair Credit Reporting Act of 1971 imposed certain restraints in this regard, but lending officers have by and large adapted well to this law and handle the applicable communications in a straightforward manner. However, indiscretions may still occur in such matters, either through carelessness or lack of awareness, and such slips can be harmful. A recent North Carolina case involves a businessman suing a bank and one of its officers for $10 million for allegedly severely damaging the plaintiff's reputation with "actual malice and in reckless, wanton and willful disregard of the plaintiff's rights."[6] The suit maintains that the bank officer replied to a third party's inquiry as to the status of a check issued by the plaintiff by stating that the customer was "kiting" checks and that the account was to be closed. In such a case, a bank may find itself required not only to prove that the customer was actually kiting checks in the strictest sense, but also to defend the bank officer's actions of so stating to a third party. It seems that it would have been more prudent to have held any necessary conversations of this nature only with the customer and to confine any third party remarks to documentary facts concerning the specific inquiry. The apparent lesson for lending officers is to limit strictly their disclosure to confidential information, especially of a derogatory nature, and to follow closely the letter and the spirit of the credit reporting legislation and the RMA Code of Ethics.

CONCLUSION

The unmistakable trend that one observes in any research into the current legal atmosphere of banking is one of increasing legal risk for bankers in general and lending officers in particular. Furthermore, these topics, securities law, tie-ins, etc., are not remote esoteric issues—they are matters which may easily impinge upon the normal, day-to-day activities of a commercial lending officer. The potential risks of litigation and/or prosecution in areas which were heretofore private matters between bankers and their customers simply cannot be ignored in the future. There are, however, certain basic principles that a bank and its officers can observe to minimize this risk. These include:

1. *Awareness.* The old advice of ignorance being no defense is still applicable. Bankers should make conscious efforts to stay aware of present devel-

---

[6] Various, *Winston-Salem Journal*, Winston-Salem, N. C., particularly October 25, 1972, and December 12, 1972.

opments in these fields. There are several excellent publications which can assist the lending officer in this need for up-to-date information.

2. *Securities law.* Conflicts of interest and insider information cannot be avoided in many instances. The lending officer's personal investments, his disclosure of information to others, and especially his communications with a trust department must be governed accordingly. In certain areas, the advice of legal counsel would be well worth seeking ("distress" loans, control positions and misleading company statements are good examples).

3. *Communication and documentation.* It is possible for a banker's honest, straightforward behavior to be misconstrued in certain cases. Having proof of one's good intentions and ethical behavior would then be helpful, to say the least.

4. *Code of ethics.* Many banks now have a formally adopted code of ethics covering many of the possible legal pitfalls for an officer and instructions as to how they should be avoided. Even if not written, some form of understanding and communication of ethical and legal standards should be shared within the organization.

Finally, it is logical to expect that banking will receive increased scrutiny in its customer relationships in the future. Also, it is perhaps unfortunate, but quite possible, that increasingly strict legal restrictions might be placed upon banking affairs. Long accustomed to dealing with economic and financial uncertainties, bankers must now adjust to these and other legal risks as they develop. In so doing, the bank's and the individual lending officer's best defenses are awareness, common sense and ethical conduct.

BANK LOAN LOSSES:
A FRESH PERSPECTIVE[†]

Stuart A. Schweitzer[*]

7

Nobody likes to be in default on a loan. Yet, even the best-intentioned borrowers are sometimes unable to pay their debts. And when they have difficulty paying their debts, their troubles fall right into the laps of their creditors. No wonder, then, that analysts of banks and the banking system pay particular attention to bank loan losses.

Loan loss rates at commercial banks have been on the rise for some time. And some bank experts say there's apt to be a record volume of loan defaults this year, as recession brings financial misfortune to many. That brings to the fore the issue of bank defenses against potential loan losses.

Analysts generally focus on a bank's "reserves for possible loan losses" as its principal defense against uncollectable loans. Yet, over the past five years banks haven't built up their loss reserves as rapidly as they have increased their vulnerability to loan losses. While this has distressed some observers, there is a line of reasoning which leads to the conclusion that there probably isn't that much real cause for concern. The logic goes something like this: Until recently, bank loan loss reserves have been unnecessarily large. In addition, most banks have substantial earnings streams and capital resources which can also be used to cover potential loan losses. Thus, according to this rea-

†Reprinted, with deletions, from the *Business Review*, September 1975, pp. 18-29, with permission from the Federal Reserve Bank of Philadelphia.

*Dr. Schweitzer, formerly a Senior Economist at the Federal Reserve Bank of Philadelphia, is now Assistant Economist at Morgan Guaranty Trust Company of New York. This article was prepared while the author was associated with the Bank.

soning, loan losses themselves pose much less of a threat to bank soundness than the danger of public overreaction to those losses.

SETTING AND SUBDIVIDING THE LOSS RESERVE

Most firms and individuals maintain reserves of some sort to assist them in managing their financial affairs. These reserves may be only a few dollars set aside in a cookie jar or millions of dollars invested in income-producing assets. But, in either case, they help tide the household or business over any financial rough spots that may occur. Since banks are forever advising the general public to "put something aside for a rainy day," it is only fitting that most banks do the same. Loss reserves are the device that most banks use to build protection against normal variation in loan losses. Banks usually plan to rely on their earnings and capital accounts to cover extraordinary loan losses.

A bank that adopts the "reserve method" for covering its loan losses makes an addition each year to its loan loss reserve.[1] The bank doesn't earmark particular assets as part of its loss reserve. Rather, the loss reserve becomes a claim upon the assets of the bank generally, as are the bank's liabilities and capital accounts. When a loan held by the bank proves uncollectable, the decline in the value of the bank's loan assets can be "charged off" against the loss reserve. That way, as long as losses don't exceed reserves, the bank's earnings do not have to absorb loan losses directly. Earnings are buffered from the potentially wide swings in loan losses from year to year. And the reserve helps to cushion the bank against insolvency as well.

Taxes and Accounting for the Loss Reserve. Besides offering smoother earnings and an insolvency cushion, the reserve method also offers banks smaller tax bills. A bank may take tax deductions for the funds it transfers to its loss reserves instead of for its actual loan losses. And the tax law's generous standard regarding the size of the loss reserve permits banks thereby to reduce their tax payments (Box 1).

The tax deduction gives banks the incentive to transfer the maximum amount allowed by law to their loan loss reserves, and most do just that. But they usually don't report all of those tax deductions as operating expenses in their published financial reports. Although it may seem unusual, it's quite legal for a bank to report larger expenses to the Government than to its shareholders. The tax authorities permit a bank to "pay" for a transfer to its loss

---

[1] Banks aren't required to use the reserve method for covering their loan losses. They are also permitted to be on the "direct charge-off method," whereby they use current earnings to meet loan losses as they occur.

BOX 1

THE TAX ADVANTAGES OF
BUILDING LOSS RESERVES

U. S. tax laws give recognition to the fact that a portion of the interest received by a bank eventually will be needed to cover its losses on uncollectable loans. Ever since 1921, banks have been permitted to deduct from taxable income a "reasonable" volume of transfers to a reserve for loan losses. Of course, since these tax deductions reduce a bank's taxes, it has always proven difficult for banks and the Government to agree as to what is reasonable. For a long while banks were permitted to build a reserve consistent with bank loss experiences during the 1930s. The last vestige of this was a U.S. Treasury ruling in 1965 permitting banks to maintain reserves in an amount up to 2.4 percent of their "eligible loans."* Tax reform has since sent this percentage lower.

The U.S. tax system is heading toward application of the principle that a bank should be able to shelter from income tax only those contributions to a loan loss reserve which are consistent with its recent loss experience. That principle is a part of the Tax Reform Act of 1969, but will not be fully effective until 1988. In the meantime, banks are permitted to shelter a reserve whose ratio to eligible loans is either based on the bank's loss experience or else is subject to a stipulated maximum.** The maximum ratio currently is 1.8 percent, but will drop down to 1.2 percent in 1976. It will drop further to 0.6 percent in 1982. Not until 1988 will banks be required to be on an "experience basis" for their loan loss reserves. Beginning in 1988, under current law, banks will be limited to a tax-free reserve no larger, as a fraction of their eligible loans, than the ratio of uncollected loans to eligible loans on an average basis over the prior six years.

Thus, under current law, the tax benefit to a bank from handling its loan losses via the reserve method will gradually decline. For a time, however, the size of the tax saving will continue to be substantial. The U.S. Treasury estimates that over one billion dollars of tax receipts will be lost to the Government in fiscal 1975 because of the generous allowance for loan loss reserves at banks and savings and loan associations combined. The tax loss is expected to remain close to that level in fiscal 1976. But it should decline after than, as the maximum ratio of the reserve to eligible loans drops to 1.2 percent on January 1, 1976. That reduction will have its impact in fiscal 1977.

---

*According to IRS rules, not all bank loans are eligible to serve as a basis for the reserve computation. The loans which are ineligible include Federal funds sold, loans backed by U.S. Government securities or bank deposit balances, and loans guaranteed by the U.S. Government.

**Regulations limit the size of the deduction for a transfer to the loss reserve during any single year to 0.6 percent of eligible loans.

reserve partly by provisions from operating expenses and partly by provisions from retained earnings. Either way, the bank's transfer to its loss reserve is tax-deductible. But the bank's operating earnings aren't reduced when retained earnings are used to build the reserve.

The Three Parts of the Loss Reserve.   In actual practice, most banks charge both retained earnings and operating expenses for transfers to their loss reserves. This leads to a loss reserve which has three components—a valuation reserve, a contingency reserve, and a deferred tax reserve. But the bank can't cover loan losses out of all of these components.

When a bank charges its operating expenses to provide for estimated loan losses, accountants record the result as an addition to the bank's *valuation reserve*. When a transfer is made from retained earnings to the bank's loss reserve, that's recorded as an addition to the bank's *contingency reserve*. When the bank cuts its tax bill by taking tax deductions for additions to its contingency reserve, its tax saving is recorded in the bank's *deferred tax reserve* (see Box 2 for a numerical example). In principle, this account is used only

---

BOX 2

THE THREE PARTS OF A LOSS RESERVE

All of the dollars in a bank's loan loss reserve are not created equally. Instead, each dollar comes from one of three sources—the bank's revenues, its retained earnings, or the taxes that it owes to the U.S. Government. An example will clarify just how this all happens. But first, it may be useful to know why things need be so complicated.

The answer is our tax laws. It's already been noted that banks are allowed to accumulate, free of corporate income taxes, more loan loss reserves than can be supported by loan loss experience. While banks are entirely willing to save on their taxes, they want to do so in a way which doesn't reduce the profits that they report to their shareholders. This requires some financial gymnastics, but it can be done. What it requires is that banks sort their loss reserves into three segments—the valuation, contingency, and deferred tax portions of the overall loss reserve.

An example will help clarify this. Consider the status of the mythical Small-Loss National Bank. Small-Loss National had revenues last year of $1000. Its operating expenses, before any provision for loan losses, were $700. Its loan portfolio equals $10,000, and its average annual loan-loss ratio equals 0.2 percent.

Small-Loss National has decided to "charge" its revenues with a $20 addition to its bad debt reserve ($20 equals 0.2 percent of $10,000). This $20 represents an addition to the bank's *valuation reserve*—it meets the test of being "charged" against revenue as a bank expense, and that's

for holding funds that will eventually be paid to the Government as taxes.

Of the three reserve components, accounting principles permit loan losses to be charged only against the valuation portion. While the contingency and deferred tax items are part of the bank's total loan loss reserve, they represent transfers made for Federal income tax purposes only. If a bank's loan losses should exhaust its valuation reserve, the bank's next resource would be its earnings rather than the other loss reserve elements.[2]

The 1969 Agreement on Valuation Reserves. The principle that the valuation reserve be the only reserve element available to cover a bank's loan losses is a long-standing accounting axiom. It became a banking rule, however, only after a 1969 agreement among the Securities and Exchange Commission, the Federal banking agencies, and the accounting profession. Under

[2] A bank could regain use of its contingency reserve by restoring that reserve to retained earnings and making a tax payment in the amount of the deferred tax reserve. But this would only be useful if the bank had exhausted both its valuation reserve and its earnings and was charging retained earnings to cover further loan losses.

what's required of funds added to the valuation reserve. The bank thus reports its net income before taxes as $280 ($1000 minus $700 minus $20).

This $280 figure is what Small-Loss National tells its shareholders and the public generally that it actually earned last year. In an effort to use legal means to reduce its tax liability, however, it tells Uncle Sam something else. Remember, the U.S. Government usually permits a bank to add more to its loss reserves—and therefore shelter more income from current taxation—than the bank may need to cover loan losses. Suppose that in Small-Loss National's case, the Government will permit it a $50 deduction for transfers to its loss reserve this year. Since it's only willing to take $20 for its loss reserve out of revenues, but it can shelter a total of $50 if it wants to, the bank looks elsewhere for the other $30.

Here's how the bank does it. Whereas shareholders were told that the bank actually earned $280, the Government hears a different story. Taxable income is reported to the Government as $250 ($280 less $30). That reduces Small-Loss National's tax obligation by $15 (assuming, for simplicity, that the bank's tax rate is 50 percent). This $15 tax saving is an addition to the *deferred tax* portion of the bank's loan reserve.

Now, only another $15 is needed to make the bank's total addition to its loss reserve equal to $50. That final $15 is the other half of the $30 the bank is looking for. It represents the shareholder's half of the difference between the bank's reported profit of $280 and its taxable profit of $250. This $15 would have gone into the bank's retained earnings if it hadn't been added to the loan loss reserve. It is assigned by accountants to the *contingency portion* of the loss reserve.

that agreement, the *entirety* of each bank's loan loss reserve as of January 1, 1969 became a valuation reserve. Additions to the valuation reserve had to be charged to the bank's income statement as expenses only beginning with 1969. And only since 1969 have the other elements of the valuation reserve been ineligible to cover loan losses.

Choosing the Size of the Valuation Reserve. The success of the reserve method as a device for handling loan losses depends on a bank's ability to anticipate its losses. Ideally, a bank should set aside funds which, over time, will just equal the loan amounts that end up being uncollectable. To do this, the bank must accurately assess the risk of loss on each loan it holds. This is quite simple for some kinds of loans—consumer loans, for example, generate highly predictable loss experiences. But some kinds of lending, often involving large loans to business, generate a more erratic flow of loan losses. It's quite difficult to compute a proper addition to the valuation reserve for such loans.

How large do a bank's valuation reserves need to be? Obviously, they need to be large enough to cover the normal losses which may be expected on the basis of actuarial principles. In addition, the valuation reserve might incude a cushion against unusual losses which may occur irregularly over time. But it would be impractical and unnecessary to make the valuation reserve large enough to cover all the bank's unusual losses. Current earnings and equity capital are always available to backstop the loss reserve. Translating these principles into action isn't simple, of course. And critics have been quite vocal in criticizing the quality of bank judgments about the size of their valuation reserves.

VALUATION RESERVES FAIL TO KEEP PACE

Current regulatory rules require each bank on the "reserve method" to make a minimum addition to its valuation reserve during each year, equal to its average rate of loan losses for the last five years, applied to its volume of loans outstanding on average during the current year.[3] This is only a minimum addition to the bank's loan loss reserve, however. Banks are instructed to reserve more than the minimum amounts if they anticipate loan charge-off rates significantly higher than their five-year average. That is where bank judgment comes into play. And critics quickly point out that bank judgment

---

[3] Regulations do permit banks to be only partially on the reserve method. That is, it would appear that banks can build a tax shelter from some of their income but still be on a direct charge-off basis for covering actual loan losses. Banks doing this will be considered *not* to be on the reserve method for the purposes of this article.

has produced declining loan loss coverage by valuation reserves over the past several years.

After 1969, when the agreement on expensing of the valuation reserve was reached, and through 1973, most banks provided only the minimum amounts required as an addition to their valuation reserves. In 1974, many banks altered this pattern and provided extra amounts above and beyond the minimum set by bank regulators. Evidence from quarterly earnings reports indicates many banks are continuing to provide extra amounts for loan losses in 1975. In fact, the formula for loan loss provisions seems to be playing a small part in bank's decisions about how much to provide for their loss reserves this year.

Between 1969 and 1974, while they were reliant on the formula, banks charged off nearly as much in uncollectable loans as they added to their valuation reserves. Hence, the valuation reserve as of year-end 1974 was only about 1 percent larger than it was at the start of 1969 (see Table). This relative constancy of bank valuation reserves contrasts sharply with the rapid growth of bank loans and loan losses. Bank loans have nearly doubled since the start of 1969 while the dollar volume of bank loan losses has risen nearly fourfold.

How could valuation reserves have fallen relatively so far behind? It's principally because banks' entire loan loss reserves were defined as valuation re-

**LOAN CHARGE-OFFS HAVE NEARLY OFFSET PROVISIONS
FOR THE LOSS RESERVE BY INSURED BANKS.
THUS, THE VALUATION RESERVE HASN'T RISEN
APPRECIABLY SINCE 1969**

(In Billions of Dollars)

Year	Valuation Reserves At Start of Year	Loan Charge-offs During Year	Provision for Loan Losses during Year	Valuation Reserves At Year-end
1969	$5.22	$ .49	$ .52	$5.25
1970	5.25	.98	.70	4.97
1971	4.97	1.09	.87	4.75
1972	4.75	.89	.97	4.84
1973	4.84	1.16	1.26	4.94
1974	4.94	1.95	2.29	5.28

TECHNICAL NOTE: The valuation reserve as of January 1, 1969 is the total loan loss reserves of all banks as of December 31, 1968. This is pursuant to the regulatory assignment of all loan loss reserves to the valuation reserve in 1969. Data on the valuation reserve as of successive year-end dates have not previously been published. These data have been computed for the purposes of this article as follows:

Year-end Valuation Reserve = Start-of-Year Valuation Reserve
+ Provision for Loan Losses during Year
− Loan Charge-offs during year

DATA SOURCE: All data from columns (2) and (3) and for the first entry in column (1) are from the FDIC.

serves when the accounting rules were changed in 1969. That change left the average bank with valuation reserves of nearly 2 percent of loans outstanding, which was enough to cover ten years of loan losses at the rate at which such losses occurred in the 1960s. Thus, even as loans and loan losses grew substantially after January 1969, few banks felt the need to charge their revenues with more than the minimum required amounts. The valuation reserve cushion that banks had when the '69 rules change was enacted left them comfortable with the small contributions made from '69 through '73.

It is notable that even during 1974, when many banks for the first time reserved more than the minimum amounts required under the '69 rules, the ratio of valuation reserves to loans continued to decline. And the ratio of these reserves to new loan charge-offs fell off even more. It is thus important to focus on the relative protection against loan losses afforded by valuation reserves and banks' other defenses, and to assess whether there's been a material weakening of banking soundness in this area.

LOSSES OUTPACE LOSS RESERVES: WHAT ARE THE IMPLICATIONS?

The failure of bank valuation reserves to keep pace with bank loans and loan losses since 1968 is indeed striking. But this development may say more about the meaningfulness of banks' prior earnings reports than it does about any changes in the industry's vulnerability. Bank valuation reserves smooth out a bank's earnings record and make that record more meaningful to investors in the face of irregular loan losses. But, as guarantors of bank solvency, they are quite limited. A bank's earnings and equity capital are more significant defenses against unusual loan losses.

Effect on Earnings. When a bank employs the reserve method, its earnings in any year are considerably insulated from its actual loan loss experience during that year. The bank's reported earnings in each year are reduced by that year's contributions out of revenues to its valuation reserve. As long as the bank follows the regulatory formula to compute its current minimum provision for loan losses—that is, if the bank bases its loan loss provision upon its latest five-year rate of charge-offs—a given year's loan loss will have an effect only 20 percent as large on the bank's earnings in that year.[4] Actual

---

[4] An example may help here. Suppose a bank has had loan charge-offs equal to 20¢ per $100 of loans during each of the past five years. Imagine that its current year charge-off rate was $1 per $100. Then its latest five-year average would equal

$$\frac{4 \times 0.20 + 1 \times 1.00}{5} = .36.$$

The bank would have to boost its valuation reserves this year by 36¢ for every $100 of loans outstanding. That's only 16¢ per $100 higher than last year's requirement of 20¢ per $100. And it's only 20 percent of the 80¢ per $100 runup in this year's loss ratio.

losses in a given year may be above or below the year's addition to the valuation reserve; if so, the valuation reserve will absorb the difference between the year's loss provision and the year's actual losses.[5] In this way, annual variations in a bank's loan loss experience which will end up offsetting one another within a five-year period have their biggest impact on the valuation reserve rather than on earnings.

The valuation reserve does more than just smooth out a bank's earnings record. The reserve also helps make that earnings record more meaningful as a statement of the bank's underlying profitability. That is, the buffering function of valuation reserves helps to prevent erroneous signals about bank profitability from being conveyed to the public because of a one-time change in the charge-off rate. But this only holds when banks adhere rigidly to the principle of the reserve method. Suppose a bank boosted its interest revenue by extending more risky loans. Since the loans are riskier than those the bank had been issuing, the fraction of those loans likely to prove uncollectable a year or two hence is higher than the bank has been charging off recently. If the bank takes proper account of this, it will provide extra amounts for its valuation reserve concurrent with its receipt of higher interest payments. That is, it will reduce its reported net income to reflect more meaningfully the profitability of its current operations.

Has this feature of the reserve method actually worked in the past few years? Apparently not. Until recently, banks have not felt compelled to build up their valuation reserves in order to handle their growing loan losses. The 1969 rule change left them with plenty of loan loss coverage. Now, to the extent that many banks have since used up the valuation reserve cushion that the rule change gave them, income statements will now begin to reflect relatively larger charges for the loan loss reserve than in the past. That is, banks' net operating earnings apparently have been somewhat overstated since 1969 because funds that might ordinarily have been "spent" to build loan loss reserves have not been expended.[6] Crude estimation suggests that during 1969-74, banks were spared enough loan loss expense to boost their net earnings after-tax by nearly 8 percent (Box 3). Now that valuation reserves seem no longer to be inflated, bank profits will not longer contain this bonus.

This may hold some implications for the success that banks will have in raising funds in both the debt and equity markets. While lenders and shareholders are, of course, concerned with bank soundness per se, they are also keenly interested in bank profitability. For one thing, sustained profitability is itself an indicator of bank soundness. For another, bank profits are a measure of the bank's ability to make additional interest or dividend payments. Thus, to the extent that banks lose the profits advantage they held in the years after 1969, they may also now lose some of their attractiveness to investors. Of course, investors may have previously recognized any overstate-

---

[5] Continuing with the above example, suppose the bank has $1000 in loans outstanding. Its charge-offs this year are 1 percent of $1000, or $10. Its contribution to the valuation reserve is 0.36 percent of $1000, or $3.60. Thus, the valuation reserve will decline this year by $6.40.

[6] Bank profits were overstated before 1969 as well. The focus here is on considerations following the 1969 rule change, however.

BOX 3

1969 RULING ON VALUATION RESERVES
BOOSTED BANK PROFITS

Computing the "right" volume of loan loss reserves for a bank to maintain is a very tricky procedure. But let's take an intellectual "giant step." Suppose that, for the banking system as a whole, valuation reserves ought to equal—as they did at year-end 1974—about 1 percent of loans outstanding. Many banking observers think a valuation reserve ratio of 1 percent is about right for the industry as a whole, so the assumption may be all right. We'll come back to this assumption shortly.

The valuation reserve ratio which the banking system held as of the start of 1969 was just under 2 percent. This high ratio was attained because banks were permitted to classify their entire loan loss reserve as a valuation reserve on January 1, 1969. This gave them $5.22 billion of valuation reserves as of that date.

Over the years since 1969, banks have added a net of only $.06 billion to their valuation reserves. That is, additions to bank valuation reserves have exceeded loan charge-offs against these reserves by only $.06 billion. This small addition to bank valuation reserves was concurrent, of course, with substantially increased loan and loan loss volumes. Banks got away with so small a net increase only because they had so much in valuation reserves to start with.

Now, back to that assumption. Imagine that banks had been assigned "the right" volume of valuation reserves back in 1969. Instead of $5.22 billion, they would have had only $2.65 (1 percent of $265 billion in loans) billion at that time. Then, banks would have had to work harder in order to reach the "correct" level of valuation reserves by year-end 1974. The banks would have had to charge their earnings—and reduce their profits by—a total of $2.57 billion more than they actually did over the 1969-74 period. This amounts to nearly 6 percent of bank operating earnings, pretax, and nearly 8 percent of bank net earnings, after-tax, during 1969-74. If valuation reserves are now at the "right" ratio to loans, then this profit bonus will no longer be available to banks.

ment of bank earnings and entered that into their analyses. If so, elimination of the artificial boost to profits from loss reserve provisions won't significantly affect bank fund-raising efforts.

Loss Reserves as Solvency Insurance.   While there is no substitute for loss reserves as an earnings stabilizer, earnings and equity capital are effective substitutes for loss reserves as solvency insurance. A bank with uncollectable loans runs the risk of insolvency. But if a bank should "run out of" valuation reserves in meeting a calamitous loan loss, its earnings and capital accounts could still absorb the loss.

A bank's net operating earnings would be its next line of defense should its valuation reserves be exhausted. And, for the banking system as a whole, there's a lot of room to cover loan losses out of earnings. Earnings, before tax, in 1974 were over four times as great as charge-offs. This meant that valuation reserves and earnings together were over 7.5 times as great as charge-offs. Furthermore, the banking system's equity capital represents an amount 30 times as great as 1974 charge-offs. An equity capital is what a bank turns to if its earnings are exhausted. While each of these multiples is substantially less than their values of a few years ago, it's difficult to argue that they aren't *now* high enough.

Thus, the combination of loan loss reserves, operating earnings, and equity capital appears sufficient to protect most banks from loan losses well above those they've been experiencing. Of course, those defenses may not be adequate to keep all banks afloat, should loan losses jump. But judgments about the adequacy of reserve provisions shouldn't rest solely on whether each individual bank is sound. A more important issue is whether the *banking system* as a *whole* is safe. If too many individual banks got into trouble from loan losses, that could endanger the entire system. But the dimensions of the capital, earnings, and loss reserve protection now existing render this most improbable.

Capital as the Ultimate Insurance against Loan Losses. It's good to know that the banking system is well buffered from loan losses. But it's troublesome to consider all of the attention that's been placed upon loss reserves by students of this issue. Loss reserves are one of the guarantors of bank solvency, but their role is small in comparison to that played by bank capital. The real issue surrounding the industry's ability to withstand higher loan losses is the same as that surrounding its ability to withstand higher losses in other areas—the adequacy of bank equity capital. True, there's lots of controversy over how much bank capital is needed. But that's where there ought to be controversy, for loss reserves are just a variation on the bank capital theme.

APPEARANCES ARE DECEIVING

As banks have expanded their roles as department stores of finance, their exposures to the risk of loan losses have also grown. With a severe recession on the books for 1975, the likelihood of particularly high loan losses at banks this year has raised questions about the ability of the industry to handle such losses.

While a recession needn't necessarily bring higher loan losses to commercial banks, the issue of adequate loan loss coverage is still meaningful at this juncture. Valuation reserves—the loan loss reserves out of which a bank normally "covers" loan losses—have grown very little over the past five or six years. Meanwhile, the volume of bank loans and loan losses has risen substantially. Thus, the degree of loan loss coverage which valuation reserves can provide has fallen substantially.

Banks are aware that they must have the resources to absorb loan losses internally. Otherwise, they realize, they can get into the same kind of financial hot water as their defaulting borrowers. Do banks need to cover more than three years' worth of losses with valuation reserves? That's how much coverage they had at year-end 1974, and it may be enough for all but a few institutions. Besides, loan loss reserves may not be the best measure of a bank's ability to remain solvent in the face of unusual losses. Loan loss reserves help stabilize a bank's earnings and are the bank's first line of defense when faced with loan losses. But the bank's earnings and equity capital are typically far more meaningful than loss reserves as resources in the battle against unforeseen loan losses. These resources must be available to cover a wider set of contingencies than just a bank's loan losses. But their sheer size relative to the historical experience which commercial banks have had with loan losses is reassuring indeed. Potential loan losses don't appear as overwhelming when viewed in the perspective as they would if loan loss reserves were a bank's principle defense.

ASSET MANAGEMENT

C. CONSUMER AND MORTGAGE LENDING

The lead article in this section is by Robert W. Johnson and focuses on the pricing policies related to bank credit cards. The results of his analysis show that dramatically different levels of profitability exist depending upon card user characteristics. Based on these user characteristics, alternative pricing and fee policies are proposed and examined. The next article by William C. Melton and Diane L. Heidt provides an excellent overview of the variable rate and rollover mortgage loans. The economic rationale, pricing, mechanics, and consumer safeguards related to these "floating" rate loans are among the topics discussed. In order to reduce the risk associated with volatile interest rates these instruments are becoming more widely used by banks and other depository-type institutions. In the following article, William C. Melton discusses another type of mortgage loan that is becoming more widely used. Al-though the graduated payment mortgage loan is a fixed-rate loan, the "tilted" payment stream makes housing more affordable, especially for the younger, first-time home-owners.

In addition to these new types of mortgage loans, the mortgage market itself has undergone significant change in recent years as discussed by Charles M. Sivesind. The ability of banks and other mortgage lenders to package and sell pools of mortgage loans to other investors in the form of pass-through securities enables mortgage money to be recycled within the institution's service area. Another mortgage-related security is the mortgage-backed bond which is issued primarily by savings and loan associations and mutual savings banks. Although banks may not issue mortgage-backed bonds, they usually act as a trustee on behalf of bond-holders.

PRICING OF BANK CARD SERVICES[†]

Robert W. Johnson[*]

8

This article examines whether the present pricing structure of bank cards is appropriate to the manner in which different classes of consumers use their cards. Finance rates paid by bank cardholders are related to the number of debits to their accounts (transaction services) and to their average daily balances (credit services). To explore which classes of consumers would benefit from legislation mandating a "free period" or prohibiting flat monthly or annual fees, levels of finance charges in relation to cardholders' age, education, and income are shown. Finally, various alternative pricing structures are briefly examined.

THE DATA BASE

During 1977, the Credit Research Center (CRC) at Purdue University, in cooperation with the Palo Alto Office of Management Analysis Center, Inc. (MAC) undertook a massive study of bank credit card operations in Califor-

†Reprinted by permission, *Journal of Retail Banking*, June 1979, pp. 16-22, © Consumer Bankers Association, 1725 K Street NW, Washington, D.C. 20006, and the author.

*Robert W. Johnson is Director, Credit Research Center, Krannert Graduate School of Management, Purdue University.

nia and Washington. MAC was retained by the Western Bank Card Association and the Bank of America to gather data under CRC's guidance, and CRC has had the responsibility for compiling and analyzing the data.

The basic data used here originated from a random sample of about 1,200 active bank card accounts drawn from ten California banks. Twelve-month histories were obtained showing daily transactions in each account. Statistical analyses of these account histories were prepared for CRC by Edward DeSpain, Sartain & DeSpain, Inc. CRC then arranged to have questionnaires sent to these cardholders. In each instance, the cooperating bank retained control over the names and addresses of the accounts involved, and neither CRC nor Edward DeSpain had any means of identifying the individuals whose accounts were included in the sample. The response rate to the questionnaire was remarkably good; over 50 percent. Analysis has not indicated a significant difference between respondents and nonrespondents. In summary, the data used in this paper are drawn from a representative sample of about 650 California back cardholders.

The accounts sampled were all active accounts, with at least one transaction during the 12-month period studied (Exhibit 1). Eighty percent of the accounts had some activity in each of the 12 months. Many of the accounts had a relatively low level of activity. Almost one-third of the accounts had an average of one debit or less per month, but 12 percnet had more than seven debits per month (Exhibit 2).

BENEFITS RECEIVED AND REVENUES PAID

Whether benefits received by consumers match the revenues they pay for bank card services is a matter of concern to consumers, banks, and legislators who attempt to limit the contractual arrangements between cardholders and their banks. Legislative concern is apparent in the rate ceilings established in many states and by the interest shown last year by some members of Congress who advocated a mandated "free period" on revolving credit in H.R. 8753.

To address these issues rationally a number of questions need to be answered. How do various groups of bank cardholders use their accounts? How does the usage rate compare with the rate of finance charges that they pay?

Exhibit 1. Number of Months Showing Activity			Exhibit 2. Debt Transactions Per Month		
Months of Activity	*N*	*Percent of Accounts*	*Number*	*N*	*Percent of Accounts*
1-4	22	3	1 or less	202	31
5-8	44	7	1.01-2	146	22
9-11	64	10	2.01-7	227	35
12	525	80	More than 7	80	12
	655	100		655	100

What changes in the pricing structure might be warranted by the manner in which consumers use their accounts? What types of consumers—especially what income groups—would be affected by a change in the pricing structure?

At the outset, it should be noted that the only revenues considered here are the finance charges paid by cardholders. Obviously, with their purchases these cardholders also generate merchant revenues, or merchant discounts, that are received by the merchant banks. These merchant discounts have not been considered here for several reasons. First, analysis for six-month periods from 1973 to 1975 showed that the incremental costs of handling the merchant accounts in California exceeded or about matched revenues in four of the six periods studied. Second, the cost analysis was made for a period prior to "duality," *i.e.,* the use of both MasterCard and Visa by the same bank. Reports suggest that merchant discounts have been significantly pared since 1975. Hence, at present it is unlikely that merchant revenues in the aggregate exceed the associated costs of handling the merchant accounts. Finally, it is not possible from the data to determine the merchant revenues generated by individual cardholders. The rate of merchant discount on individual debits is not recorded. Also, there is no way of knowing whether the debits to accounts were generated by charges at a merchant of the cardholders' bank or at some other bank's merchant. One would guess, for example, that upper-income consumers travel more widely and thus generate a higher proportion of interchange fees to merchant discounts than do lower-income consumers.

Transactions and Finance Rates Paid. Let us first consider whether the consumers who made frequent use of their accounts—and thereby benefited from that service—paid for the service (Exhibit 3). Compare the rate of charge paid over the 12-month period by the low users (one debit or less per month) with the rates paid by high users (over seven debits per month). Whereas 56 percent of the low users paid an annual rate exceeding 14 percent, 54 percent of the high users paid two percent or less.

It should be noted that this analysis excludes costs and relates only to the cardholder revenues (finance charges) received in return for the debit services provided cardholders. It may not be five times as costly for a bank to enter five debits in an account in a month than to enter only one debit per month.

Exhibit 3. Relationship of Account Use to Finance Rate Paid

Those whose average debits/ monthly were	Percentage paying APRs of			
	2% or less	*2-14%*	*Over 14%*	*Totals*
1 or less	28	16	56	100
1.01-2	25	26	49	100
2.01-7	36	28	36	100
Over 7	54	31	15	100
Totals	33	25	42	100

Source: Credit Research Center, California Bank Card Study

Exhibit 4. Relationship of Income and Frequency of Use of Account

Income ($)	N	Percent of Sample	Percentage having monthly debits of				
			1 or Less	1-2	2-7	Over 7	Totals
10,000 or less	66	10.5	48	20	27	5	100
10,001-15,000	102	16.1	30	32	32	5	100
15,001-20,000	107	16.9	38	19	34	8	100
20,001-25,000	114	18.0	27	28	36	9	100
25,001-30,000	96	15.2	34	10	38	18	100
30,001-40,000	82	13.0	21	27	42	10	100
Over $40,000	65	10.3	17	15	32	35	100
	632	100.0					

However, even if costs do not rise in direct proportion to the number of debits per month, it is apparent from Exhibit 3 that the more debit services consumers used, the *lower* the average rate they paid. The "high users" found their bank cards to be a convenient alternative to cash, but paid little or nothing to the banks for that service.

Who are the consumers receiving the highest levels of debit (transaction) services but paying relatively less than those making infrequent use of this service? As might be anticipated, they are upper-income consumers (Exhibit 4). Whereas only five percent of consumers with incomes under $15,000 had more than seven debits per month, 35 percent of those with incomes over $40,000 had this level of activity. Thus examination of Exhibit 4 shows that, in general, legislation mandating a "free period" or prohibiting a minimum monthly or annual fees on bank cards principally would benefit consumers with annual incomes of $25,000 and above; that is, consumers who actively use their accounts, but largely avoid paying for the service.

Average Balances and Rates Paid.   Another service provided by banks to their cardholders is credit. All of the active accounts studied had a positive average daily balance (ADB) over the 12-month period. At issue is whether the finance rates paid by the cardholders were related to their ADBs. About a fifth of California cardholders over the 12-month period carried ADBs of $80 or less, while another fifth had an ADB exceeding $500 (Exhibit 5). Five percent of the accounts had ADBs in excess of $1000.

Exhibit 5.
Average Daily Balance Per Account

Average daily balance ($)	N	Percentage of Accounts
80 or less	147	23
80.01-200	152	24
200.01-500	192	31
Over $500	141	22
	632	100

Exhibit 6.
Relationship of Account Balance to Finance Rate Paid

Those whose average balance/ monthly was	Percentage paying APRs of			
	2% or Less	2-14%	Over 14%	Totals
$80 or less	69	29	3	100
80.01-200	52	33	15	100
200.01-500	14	28	58	100
Over $500	1	7	92	100
Totals	33	25	42	100

Source: Credit Research Center, California Bank Card Study.

In contrast to the findings concerning the number of debits per month, it is apparent that consumers who carried large balances tended to pay for that service (Exhibit 6). In general, the higher the ADB, the more likely were cardholders to pay an APR exceeding 14 percent. Presumably, consumers carrying large ADBs were revolvers and paid a finance charge for that service.

One might expect that upper-income consumers would carry much larger ADBs than middle- or low-income consumers, but that is not the case (Exhibit 7). For example, 28 percent of those with incomes over $40,000 had ADBs over $500, but so did 27 percent of those with incomes from $15,000 to $20,000. Similarly, there seems to be little consistent relationship between income levels and ADBs in the range of $80 to $200.

Why should income levels and ADBs be largely unrelated? Other data from the study show that upper-income consumers carry more bank cards and travel and entertainment (T&E) cards than those having lower incomes. Thus, as shown in Exhibit 8, 22 percent of bank cardholders with incomes of $40,000 or more carried three or more cards. In contrast, only eight percent of consumers having incomes from $15,000 to $20,000 carried this many cards. Similarly, 57 percent of California bank cardholders having high incomes ($40,000 or more) used one or more T&E cards, in contrast to a corresponding figure of only 23 percent among consumers with incomes from $15,000 to $20,000. Thus, upper-income consumers spread their accounts among more credit grantors. While an annual fee is required to have a T&E

Exhibit 7. Relationship of Income and Average Daily Balance Owed

	Percentage having average balance of				
Income($)	*$80 or Less*	*80.01-200*	*200.01-500*	*Over 500*	*Totals*
10,000 or less	30	20	39	11	100
10,001-15,000	28	25	25	22	100
15,001-20,000	18	24	31	27	100
20,001-25,000	27	20	36	17	100
25,001-30,000	22	28	20	30	100
30,001-40,000	23	25	31	21	100
Over 40,000	12	26	22	28	100

Exhibit 8. Distribution of Bank Credit Card Accounts

Income ($)	*Percent of Sample*	*None[a]*	*One*	*Two*	*Three or more[b]*
No answer	4.2	•	32	68	•
10,000 or less	10.0	2	47	45	6
10,001-15,000	15.5	•	47	43	10
15,001-20,000	16.2	•	45	47	8
20,001-25,000	17.3	•	51	41	8
25,001-30,000	14.5	•	46	46	8
30,001-40,000	12.4	•	40	50	10
Over 40,000	9.8	•	23	55	22
All	100.0	•	43	47	10

Source: Credit Research Center, California Bank Card Study.

a. All respondents should have at least one bank credit card account since the sample was selected from active accounts.

b. Although it is possible to have more than two bank credit card accounts (two MasterCard accounts, for example, some respondents may also be reporting the number of cards owned.

card, consumers pay nothing extra to use additional bank cards. Indeed, it may make it easier for them to rotate multiple accounts and avoid paying finance charges. As a result, we can see from Exhibit 8 that 77 percent of high-income cardholders had two or more bank cards, whereas other data from the study show that only 15 percent of these same high-income consumers had two or more T&E cards. Consequently, the pricing structure of bank cards encourages multiple accounts, a costly process for banks taken in the aggregate, but not for the consumers holding multiple cards under current pricing structures.

Characteristics of Cardholders and Rates Paid. CRC's California Bank Card Study also developed data on the APRs paid by various types of consumers. These exhibits should be approached gingerly. First, different classes of consumers received different levels of transaction and credit services. Second, there is a considerable degree of correlation among age, education, and income. Ultimately, we want to combine these variables with data on transaction costs and credit costs to identify the types of consumers that are most profitable.

Subject to those caveats, we can observe that the older a consumer, the less likely is he or she to pay finance charges over 14 percent (Exhibit 9). Whereas just over half of cardholders under 30 paid what we might call a "full" finance charge, less than a third of those over 50 paid charges at this level.

As we might expect, the higher the level of education, the lower the APRs paid (Exhibit 10). Whereas 48 percent of cardholders with advanced degrees paid only a nominal finance rate, 53 percent of those with some high school or grade school education paid over 14 percent. These results are possibly associated with rate awareness, since other studies show that the level of education is strongly associated with rate awareness.

Finally, income levels are associated with APRs paid (Exhibit 11). The percentage of income groups paying a "full" rate declined from a high of 53 percent ($15,000 to $20,000) to a low of 36 percent (over $30,000).

Summary. Legislation that mandates free period or prohibits minimum monthly or annual fees is directed at preserving the status of consumers who are currently paying nominal (two percent or less) annual finance rates for

			Percentage paying APRs of			
Age	N	Percent of Sample	2% or less	2-14%	Over 14%	Totals
Under 30	91	13.9	19	29	52	100
30-39	181	27.6	27	25	48	100
40-49	156	23.8	32	22	46	100
50-64	178	27.1	41	27	32	100
65 and over	50	7.6	56	16	28	100
	656	100.0				

Exhibit 9. Relationship of Age to Finance Rate Paid

Exhibit 10. Relationship of Education to Rates of
Finance Charge Paid

| | Percentage Paying APRS of | | | |
| | 2% or | | Over | |
Education	Less	2-14%	14%	Totals
Some High or Less	27	20	53	100
High School	25	21	54	100
Some Coll.	28	29	43	100
Degree or				
Some Adv.	37	23	40	100
Adv. Degree	48	26	26	100
Totals	33	25	42	100

Exhibit 11. Relationship of Income to Rates of
Finance Charge Paid

| | Percentage Paying APRS of | | | |
| Income | 2% or | | Over | |
($000)	Less	2-14%	14%	Totals
10 or Less	32	21	47	100
10-15	29	29	42	100
15-20	27	20	53	100
20-25	31	26	43	100
25-30	32	27	41	100
Over 30	41	23	36	100
Totals	33	25	42	100

the use of the services provided by bank credit cards. The basic services provided have been classified here as transaction services (entering debits and credits, billing accounts, and so on) and credit services (providing the average daily balances used by consumers).

The data provided in this section identify clearly which consumers would benefit from legislation of this type; those who are over 50, with college or more advanced degrees, and with incomes over $25,000 or $30,000. It would benefit most particularly high-income consumers who use their accounts frequently by making numerous purchases during the course of a year. These affluent consumers evidently view the credit card as a convenient substitute for cash and largely avoid paying a finance charge for the services that they receive.

ALTERNATIVE RATE STRUCTURES

Several alternative rate structures have been proposed and, in some cases, have been put into effect. A number of savings and loan associations and credit unions have imposed a finance charge, perhaps one percent per month, that is assessed from date of purchase. The 12 percent yield provided by this billing method would reduce yields currently experienced by commercial banks, but not by as much as one might expect. It has been shown that under current billing procedures a sample of 17 California banks experienced gross yields ranging from 12.33 percent to 15.33 percent, rather far below the disclosed APR of 18 percent.[1] If a card issuer charging one percent per month from date of purchase also requires that cardholders maintain certain minimum deposits or share accounts, the effective yield may approach that currently realized by many commercial banks.

It is also worthwhile to observe that levying finance charges from date of purchase would be a stimulus to the development and use of debit cards. At the present time consumers can have the convenience of using credit cards at point-of-sale and gain in addition the use of credit for an average of about 25 or 30 days. If they pay their accounts in full each month, they obtain these services without paying the bank for providing them. The credit card is merely a very handy substitute for carrying cash. But, if finance charges are assessed from date of purchase on credit cards, debit cards may be preferred by consumers—most particularly those upper-income consumers who presently make extensive use of bank credit cards. Moreover, these are also the very consumers who are most likely to adopt electronic funds transfers. They belong to the group "that (1) generates a disproportionately large volume of checks and credit transactions; (2) has a high opportunity cost of time; (3) likes flexibility in managing its debts and cash flows; and (4) understands the use of credit and nonmoney payment mechanisms."[2]

An alternative approach would be to assess an annual fee.[3] Data from a representative California bank suggest that a minimum annual fee would have relatively little effect on revenues, if it is assumed that consumers' purchase and payment habits would remain unchanged.

Increase in gross finance charge
revenues from minimum annual fee of

$6— 6.1%
$10—10.9%

In contrast, a flat annual fee would add significantly to banks' revenues:

Increase in gross finance charge
revenues from flat annual fee of

$4— 7.7%
$6—15.4%
$10—25.7%
$15—38.6%

[1] Ray McAlister and Edward DeSpain, "Bank and Retail Credit Card Yields under Alternative Assessment Methods," Working Paper No. 21 (West Lafayette, Ind.: Credit Research Center, Purdue University, 1978), p. 19.

[2] William C. Dunkelberg and Robert W. Johnson, "EFTS and Consumer Credit," Working Paper No. 2 (Revised) (West Lafayette, Inc.: Credit Research Center, Purdue University, 1975). p. 60.

[3] There are two types of annual fees. A minimum annual fee would be charged unless interest income exceeded a certain amount. A flat annual fee is one that is charged regardless of the amount of interest income or card usage. (Editor's fn.)

In addition to increasing gross revenues, an annual fee would also have the effect of causing consumers to concentrate their credit use on a small number of bankcard accounts. The added fee income and whatever savings are realized from having a smaller number of large accounts might well enable banks to lower their finance charge from the current disclosed rate of 18 percent—a politically sensitive rate—to a lower level. In addition, the level of charges to various classes of customers might be related more closely to the transaction and credit services provided by banks.

While state and federal legislation obviously hinders innovative restructuring of the prices of bank card services, changes like those suggested above may well benefit both consumers and credit card issuers. The data from CRC's California Bank Card Study provide a basis for analysis of the impact of such changes. Since card-issuing banks have similar data in their own records, it is to be hoped that this analysis may stimulate further research and innovative pricing systems for bankcard services.

VARIABLE RATE MORTGAGES*

*William C. Melton and
Diane L. Heidt*

9

Recently, Federally chartered savings and loan associations were authorized to offer variable rate mortgages. Prior to that authorization, various forms of variable rate mortgage instruments were being offered in a number of states, and several states currently are considering introducing some form of them. This interest in variable rate mortgages is due to the difficulties which the standard fixed payment mortgage has created for many lenders in periods of volatile interest rates as well as the prospect that, as restrictions on deposit interest rates are relaxed, lenders' exposure to interest rate volatility is likely to increase.

As its name suggests, a variable rate mortgage (VRM) is a mortgage loan which provides for adjustment of its interest rate as market interest rates change. Often adjustments of VRM interest rates are linked to the movement of some reference market interest rate or index. As a result, the current interest rate on a VRM may differ from its origination rate, *i.e.,* the rate when the loan was made. This is the major difference between a VRM and the standard fixed payment mortgage (FPM), on which the interest rate and the monthly payment are constant throughout the term. Because VRM rates can increase over the term of the loan, VRM borrowers share with lenders the risk of rising interest rates.

*Reprinted from the *Quarterly Review*, Summer 1979, pp. 23-31, with permission from the Federal Reserve Bank of New York and the authors.

INTEREST RATE RISK

The major mortgage lenders obtain funds primarily from relatively short-term deposits. The FPM, which generally has a term of twenty-five to thirty years, has significant interest rate risk for them because the maturity imbalance between lenders' liabilities and their mortgage assets exposes them to the risk of short-term rates paid on deposits and borrowings rising above yields on outstanding mortgages.[1] In such a situation, the interest expense of lenders approaches their interest income, causing losses which, if great enough, could threaten their viability. As a result of the FPM's interest rate risk, lenders make mortgage credit available on less favorable terms than they otherwise would, and their large holdings of seasoned mortgages paying below-market interest rates have limited their ability to obtain funds by paying market rates on deposits.

During the 1950's and early 1960's, when the variability of interest rates was relatively mild and long-term rates consistently exceeded short-term rates, the maturity imbalance of the major mortgage lenders was of little importance. However, with the acceleration of inflation in the mid-1960's, the average level and variability of short-term interest rates rose much more than long-term rates. This increased the risk of borrowing short to lend long, and thrift institutions sought to reduce this risk by lengthening the maturities of their deposits. For example, in the period from 1969 to 1978, savings and loan associations (S&Ls) reduced the share of their total deposits accounted for by passbook accounts, which are effectively payable on demand, from 69 percent to 32 percent. Mutual savings banks reduced their passbook share from 99 percent to 51 percent. Nevertheless, the average maturity of thrift institutions' assets still far exceeds that of their liabilities.

The constant interest rate on an FPM protects borrowers from increases in mortgage interest costs.[2] Borrowers can also prepay their mortgages in advance of maturity, although penalties typically must be paid if the loan is repaid within three years of its origination, and there generally will be other, possibly substantial, costs involved in originating a new mortgage, such as fees for appraisal, title search, etc. Prepayment may be attractive to the borrower if the original loan can be replaced by a new loan bearing a significantly lower interest rate. These advantages for borrowers are mirrored by disadvantages for lenders, whose return on a mortgage may decline but will not increase.[3]

---

[1] Nondepository mortgage investors, such as life insurance companies and pension funds, typically have long-term liabilities, so that they are less exposed to interest rate risk through mortgage investments.

[2] Moreover, if the loan is assumable—*i.e.,* if it can be transferred from the original borrower to a buyer of the house without the terms of the loan being altered—then the borrower may realize a capital gain in the form of a higher price for his house if current rates rise above the original rate.

[3] However, the lender still has an opportunity for returns on a *portfolio* of mortgages to increase to some extent at times of rising interest rates, even if the rates on the individual FPMs which comprise the portfolio are constant. One reason is that, in a market with substantial housing turnover, many loans will be prepaid well before maturity, so that they can be replaced with loans bearing current yields. Also, as outstanding loans are amortized, new loans can be made at current yields.

The VRM changes the distribution of interest rate risk by allowing interest rates on outstanding loans to increase if current market rates rise. Should market rates decline, downward adjustment of VRM rates saves the borrower the transactions costs involved in prepayment of an FPM and refinancing. VRM contracts almost never provide for a minimum rate—which would be difficult to enforce when borrowers can prepay their loans without penalty.

VRM TERMS AND RATES

VRMs differ greatly in the extent to which they protect borrowers against increases in interest costs. For example, some VRMs provide a rate ceiling, while others do not. Obviously, the rate "cap" is advantageous to the borrower, since it places an upper bound on interest costs. However, it is important to realize that the major protection against interest rate increases may be current mortgage rates, not the rate cap. If lenders attempted to increase rates on outstanding VRMs above the current market rate, borrowers could prepay their VRMs and refinance the loans at current market rates. Thus, depending on the level of prepayment penalties and costs of originating a new mortgage, the current mortgage rate provides an effective ceiling on VRM rate increases. In practice, when lenders in California and other states have been allowed to raise VRM rates, many have not done so in cases where the new rate would have been higher than, or close to, the prevailing rate on new mortgages.

Like FPM rates, VRM origination rates are affected by expected future interest rates. However, the expected pattern of interest rates in the near future may cause origination rates on FPMs and VRMs to diverge. If rates are expected to rise, the VRM rate should be lower than the FPM rate. But, if interest rates are relatively high and expected to decline in the near future, a lender might well feel that, other things being equal, VRM rate reductions could be more costly to him than the possible prepayment of an FPM, especially if subject to prepayment penalties. In such a case, the lender would require a higher origination rate on a VRM than on an FPM.

Other features of VRM contracts which affect their origination rates are prepayment and assumability provisions. For reasons explained earlier, the absence of prepayment penalties significantly increases the borrower's ability to take advantage of rate declines and avoid rate increases. Similarly, assumability is valuable in that it may allow the borrower to sell a house more easily or to realize a capital gain if the loan rate is below current rates and is not subject to adjustment when the loan is assumed. Other things being equal, a mortgage loan which incorporates liberal prepayment and assumability provisions will carry a higher rate than one which does not.

In addition, VRM origination rates are affected by the index (if any) used for adjusting the rate and the magnitude and frequency or permissible adjustments. If the index does not reflect movements in current market rates—or if index changes may be incorporated into rate adjustments only infrequently—

Canadian Rollover Mortgages

Rollover mortgages (ROMs) incorporate interest rate adjustments by structuring the loan as a series of relatively short-term loans, each one of which carries a constant interest rate. At the end of the term of the preceding loan, a new loan is originated at the current interest rate.[1] Since amortization is scheduled over a long period of years, a borrower may "roll over" a series of successively smaller loans before the debt is paid off.

ROMs currently account for almost all Canadian single-family residential mortgages. Although they were first introduced in Canada in the 1930's, ROMs have been widely used only since the 1960's. ROMs exist both as conventional mortgage loans and as government-guaranteed loans authorized under the Canadian National Housing Act (NHA). Both types typically have five-year terms.[2] Amortization is scheduled over a twenty- to thirty-year period for conventional ROMs and twenty-five to forty years for NHA ROMs. At the end of the term, the loan is renewed at the current mortgage market rate.

The government first began to guarantee five-year ROMs in 1969 and last year allowed three-year ROMs to be included in the NHA program. The interest rate on a government-guaranteed ROM is usually lower than the rate on a conventional loan, and the amortization period is longer. Borrowers have the option to extend the maturity of NHA loans to a maximum of forty years to avoid higher monthly payments if the rate is increased when the loan is refinanced. Borrowers generally do not have this option with conventional ROMs.

During the first two years of the term, up to 10 percent of the principal balance of a NHA ROM may be prepaid with a three-month interest fee. Any amount may be prepaid after the two years with a fee equal to three months' interest. At the end of the term, the borrower may make a prepayment without incurring a fee simply by taking out a smaller loan. Prepayment penalties on conventional ROMs vary with the lender. Generally there is a charge of three months' interest for prepayment during the term, but any amount of the loan may be prepaid without penalty at the end of the term.

[1] Canadian law does not require the lender to guarantee to originate a new loan at the maturity of the preceding loan, but such commitments are the standard practice among mortgage lenders.

[2] ROMs with terms of from one to four years do exist but are less common.

VRMs may have little advantage to lenders over FPMs. If current mortgage rates decline to a level below the VRM rate, borrowers have an incentive to refinance their loans, just as if they had FPMs. Alternatively, VRM borrowers benefit if the loan carries a lower than market rate. Also, if restrictions on

VRM rate increases reduce the likelihood of borrowers being unable to meet their payments, VRM default risk will be little different from that on FPMs, and VRM origination rates will not have to incorporate a special risk premium.

Default risk may also be reduced if borrowers have the option of keeping their monthly payments constant by extending the maturities of their loans to offset VRM rate increases. However, if borrowers use the option, lenders may find that the reduction of VRM amortization payments largely offsets the favorable effect on their cash flow of increases in VRM rates. The small increase in cash flow would then do little to assist lenders to meet their rising cost of funds.[4]

VRM ACTIVITY IN THE UNITED STATES

In different forms variable rate lending has been for years a central feature of housing finance in many European countries.[5] In addition, rollover mortgages (ROMs) have been the major mortgage instrument in Canada since the 1960's (see box). In contrast, VRM activity in the United States is of more recent origin. Substantial numbers of VRMs have been made in a number of states in the last several years, and the recent authorization of VRMs for Federally chartered S&Ls should spur such activity further. To date, the bulk of VRM activity has been concentrated in California, and California's VRM regulations served as a model for the VRM regulations recently issued by the Federal Home Loan Bank Board (FHLBB).[6] As a result, there is a tendency in popular discussion to identify VRMs with the specific version employed in California. As the accompanying box on pages 114-117 makes clear, the California VRM regulations are different for S&Ls and commercial banks and also differ in important ways from the FHLBB's regulations. Currently the most common kind of VRM originated by state-chartered S&Ls in California must incorporate a 2½ percentage point cap on cumulative rate increases, and rate adjustments are indexed to the average cost of funds index for California S&Ls published by the San Francisco Federal Home Loan Bank. Rate increases are at the option of the lender, while rate decreases are mandatory.

In contrast to the widespread usage of VRMs in California, VRM activity elsewhere in the country has been uneven. While few states have legislation which specifically forbids VRMs, the law in most states is silent on the matter, and the uncertain legal authority in these states probably has discouraged their introduction. Also usury ceilings in many states preclude meaningful

[4]The seriousness of this possibility is illustrated by the response of California VRM borrowers to the August 1978 rate increase. About two thirds of the affected borrowers exercised their option to extend the maturities of their loans rather than allow their monthly payments to increase.

[5]For example, variable rate mortgages of various types are used extensively in the United Kingdom, France, and Germany. In addition, rollover mortgages are common in Switzerland and the Netherlands.

[6]Title 12, Code of Federal Regulations, Parts 545 and 555.

CALIFORNIA VARIABLE RATE MORTGAGES

VRM Regulations

Regulations governing California VRMs are the product of legislation and of regulation by the California Commissioner of Savings and Loan. In addition, Federally chartered savings and loan associations (S&Ls) in California are subject to the VRM regulations of the Federal Home Loan Bank Board.

Prior to November 23, 1970, VRM lending in California was unregulated. On that date, legislation became effective which allows lenders the option of increasing the VRM interest rate only if the index to which it is tied increases, but a decrease in the rate is mandatory if the index decreases. The index itself is not specified. Semiannual adjustments of VRM rates are provided, with a maximum adjustment of ¼ percentage point. Prepayment without penalty is permitted up to ninety days following notification of a rate increase. Also, the terms of the variable interest rate provision are required to be fully disclosed to the borrower before closing the loan and to be described in both the mortgage (or trust deed) and the note. The legislation was amended in 1976 to provide additional protection to borrowers by requiring a 2½ percentage point ceiling on the cumulative increase in the VRM interest rate. In addition, in the event of a rate increase, borrowers were given the option of extending the maturity of their loans to a maximum of forty years in order to keep monthly payments stable. In January 1978, lenders were also allowed to offer a VRM with rate adjustments every five years and a maximum rate increase of 2½ percentage points.[1] These regulations apply to all lenders in California.

In addition, California S&Ls are subject to the more restrictive regulations of the State Commissioner of Savings and Loan.[2] VRMs providing for semiannual interest rate adjustments must be indexed to the weighted average cost-of-funds index for all California S&Ls published by the Federal Home Loan Bank of San Francisco.[3] Effective June 23, 1979, VRMs

---

[1] To date this new variant does not seem to have attracted much attention.

[2] In practice, California commercial banks offering VRMs in most cases voluntarily adhere to the rulings and regulations of the Savings and Loan Commissioner.

[3] Between June 24, 1971 and January 1, 1976, S&Ls were required to use an index of the cost of funds of all S&Ls in the Eleventh Federal Home Loan Bank District, which includes Arizona, California, and Nevada.

The index now used with California VRMs is calculated by dividing California S&Ls' total annualized funds cost by their average total funds:

$$2 \times \frac{\begin{bmatrix} \text{total interest or dividends paid on:} \\ \text{savings capital, FHLB advances, debentures, and} \\ \text{other borrowings} \end{bmatrix}}{\begin{bmatrix} \text{averages of:} \\ \text{savings capital, advances, debentures, and other} \\ \text{borrowings outstanding} \end{bmatrix}}$$

The index is released semiannually, usually in February and August, for the six-month periods ended December 31 and June 30.

providing for interest rate adjustments every five years must be indexed to the average yield on accepted bids for commitments to sell conventional mortgages to the Federal Home Loan Mortgage Corporation. Also, the minimum rate increase which can be implemented is 1/10 percentage point, except that, for VRMs with semiannual rate adjustments, smaller increases may be implemented if the ¼ percentage point maximum prevented rates from being adjusted fully in the previous semiannual period. Index increases of less than 1/10 percentage point may be accumulated until they total at least 1/10 percentage point. Borrowers are also required to be notified at least thirty days in advance of any rate adjustments.

Effective January 1, 1979, the Federal Home Loan Bank Board (FHLBB) authorized VRM lending by Federally chartered S&Ls in areas where Federally chartered associations had faced a competitive disadvantage in the market. At the time, California was the only state which the FHLBB felt met this requirement. Most of the FHLBB's VRM regulations for Federally chartered S&Ls are essentially identical to those currently applicable to state-chartered S&Ls in California. However, Federally chartered S&Ls may make only annual rate adjustments no greater than ½ percentage point. Also, in the event of a rate decrease, Federal associations must decrease the maturity of the loan first—but not to less than the original maturity of the loan—and then adjust the monthly payments. Other FHLBB regulations are significantly more restrictive. Federally chartered S&Ls must offer fixed payment mortgages (FPMs) as well as VRMs and must provide detailed information to facilitate the borrower's intelligent choice between them. To force Federally chartered S&Ls to continue to offer FPMs on reasonable terms, VRM acquisitions are restricted to 50 percent of their total mortgage originations and purchases. Also, effective July 1, Federally chartered S&Ls must index their VRMs to the national cost-of-funds index published by the FHLBB.

Growth of VRMs

VRMs had a very slow start in California. In the mid-1960's, one state-chartered savings and loan association attempted to incorporate provisions for variable interest rates in its mortgage loan contracts, but strongly negative consumer response discouraged the effort. Two S&Ls tried to promote VRMs in 1970 but met with only modest success. In 1971 another S&L began offering VRMs more successfully. In 1975 VRM activity finally picked up, as a significant number of large lenders began to offer them. Currently there are about twenty-seven state-chartered S&Ls, two national banks, and two state-chartered banks offering VRMs in California. Federally chartered S&Ls are beginning to offer them as well.

From mid-1975 through 1977, the volume of VRMs increased rapidly, as large California VRM lenders had about 60 to 80 percent of their new loan originations in VRMs (chart). However, during 1978, as mortgage interest rates rose sharply, the VRM percentage declined to about 40 to 50 percent, and VRM growth has slowed. The reason apparently is that lenders are offering VRMs on less attractive terms relative to RPMs in anticipation

(Box continued)

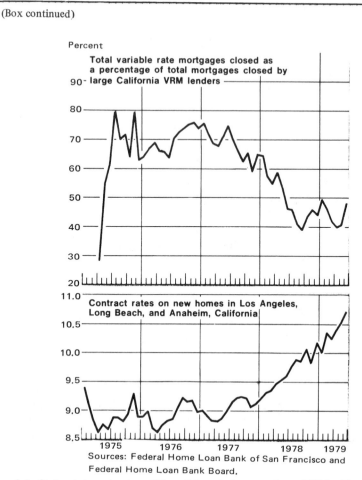

Percent

Total variable rate mortgages closed as a percentage of total mortgages closed by large California VRM lenders

Contract rates on new homes in Los Angeles, Long Beach, and Anaheim, California

1975   1976   1977   1978   1979

Sources: Federal Home Loan Bank of San Francisco and Federal Home Loan Bank Board.

of declining interest rates. Other things being equal, an FPM with prepayment penalties is more attractive to the lender in these circumstances since it locks in high interest rates.

After September 1978 the VRM percentage increased sharply, though it has resumed its decline since the beginning of this year. The resurgence was probably stimulated in part by the California Supreme Court's August 1978 decision in *Wellenkamp vs. Bank of America* that "due-on-sale"

VRM lending activity. Finally, until recently, Federally chartered S&Ls outside California were not authorized to offer VRMs.

Two states with considerable VRM activity are Ohio and Wisconsin. VRMs offered in Ohio are essentially similar to California VRMs, but the dominant form of VRM in Wisconsin differs from most others in that its rate is not tied to an index. Called the "escalator clause mortgage", it provides for a constant rate for three years, after which the rate may be adjusted once a year. The borrower is protected by restrictions on rate increases. The maximum initial rate increase is 1 percentage point, and a 0.5 percentage point maximum ap-

clauses in mortgage contracts cannot be exercised by lenders in order to increase interest rates on mortgages to current market levels.[4] The decision severely reduces lenders' ability to increase interest rates on FPMs in the active California housing market. Unless the law is changed or the Court reserves itself, VRMs should be even more attractive to California lenders in the future than they were in the past.

VRM Rate Changes

Interest rates on VRMs have decreased only once since 1970 but have increased several times. Following a rate decrease of 15 basis points in October 1972, the only S&L actively lending through VRMs implemented 25 basis point rate increases in April and October 1974 and in April 1975. The first rate increase implemented by a significant number of large lenders occurred following the August 1978 announcement that the cost-of-funds index increased in the first half of 1978 by 12.9 basis points. This increase in the cost of funds, plus earlier small accumulated increases, allowed about a 20 to 22 basis point rise in VRM rates, and twenty S&Ls out of twenty-one implemented it for most of their VRMs. There was very little consumer reaction to the increases. According to a survey conducted by the California Commissioner of Savings and Loan, only 4 percent of the borrowers who received notice that their rates were being raised wrote inquiries to lenders, and only 5 percent of the inquiries were complaints. A large majority of VRM borrowers—67 percent—decided to extend the maturity of their loans to avoid any increase in monthly payments. Most recently, the San Francisco FHLB announced in February of this year that, in the second half of 1978, the cost-of-funds index increased 30.1 basis points. This increase allowed lenders to raise their rates on most VRMs by the maximum increase of 25 basis points, with a further 5 basis point increase possible six months later.

[4] A due-on-sale clause is a device commonly used in real property security transactions to provide, at the lender's option, for acceleration of the maturity of the loan upon the sale of the real property security.

plies to successive increases. Borrowers are also protected to some extent by the option to prepay their loans without penalty within four months following a rate increase or anytime the rate is 2 percentage points or more above the original contract rate. For this kind of VRM, then, the current mortgage rate serves as an effective "index", since the virtual absence of prepayment penalties insures that lenders will not increase rates on outstanding VRMs above current mortgage rates.

Wisconsin lenders may offer a California-type VRM as well as the escalator clause mortgage. However, lenders strongly prefer the "escalator", and virtually all state-chartered S&Ls offer it, as do a number of Federally chartered S&Ls.[7] In contrast, activity in the California-type VRM is negligible. Though there were some complaints from borrowers who had their interest rates increased in 1974, following 1975 legislation governing the frequency and size of increases, rate adjustments seem generally to have been accepted by borrowers.

There has also been substantial VRM activity in several New England states, most notably Massachusetts.[8] VRMs in New England differ in a number of respects from those in California. Typically there is no cap on cumulative upward adjustments of VRM rates, and borrowers have either very limited options to extend maturities to offset rate increases or none at all. Indexes used also vary. In Maine and New Hampshire, VRM lenders generally have used as an index some measure of the cost of funds to lending institutions. In Massachusetts and Connecticut the norm is an index of current interest rates on new mortgages. Absence of a cap on rate increases and a maturity-extension option, together with indexation to mortgage rates, means that VRM borrowers in New England share more interest rate risk than their California counterparts. As a result, VRM lenders in New England must offer more attractive "discounts" off the FPM lending rate than do California VRM lenders. In New England the norm seems to be about a ½ percentage point reduction of the VRM rate relative to the FPM rate—considerably greater than the typical reductions of ¼ percentage point or less in California.

VRMs AS SHORT-TERM MORTGAGES

Borrowers seem to have responded to the substantial rate discounts offered in New England by favoring VRMs over FPMs when they expected to move, to sell their homes, and to prepay their mortgages in the near future. Although it is still too early to say so definitely, it appears that substantially lower initial rates on VRMs may lead to selection of borrowers preferring lower current interest rates in anticipation of prepaying their loans well before any substantial rate increases will have occurred. If this proves to be generally true, then VRMs, instead of functioning solely as a long-term variable-rate lending instrument, in effect would also be a device for making short-term mortgage loans. Indeed, at least one New England mortgage lender has specifically designed and marketed its VRM to appeal to "transient" homeowners who expect to move within a few years after originating their mortgages.

---

[7]There is some uncertainty as to whether an escalator clause mortgage complies with FHLBB regulations, which in general prohibit loans with an increasing sequence of monthly payments. Some Federally chartered S&Ls avoid the appearance of a conflict by extending the term of the mortgage to offset the effect of a rate increase on monthly payments. Others have interpreted the regulation as allowing them to increase monthly payments.

[8]A number of lenders in New England also offer ROMs similar to those used in Canada.

The major advantage to such a use of the VRM is that, under certain circumstances, it allows individuals who expect to be short-term borrowers to reduce their borrowing costs. In addition, borrowers avoid both the expense of writing a new loan upon maturity of a short-term loan and the risk that new finance might not be available then. Moreover, borrowers have flexibility in determining when to prepay or transfer their loans (if the loans are assumable). Thus, VRMs may provide a mechanism through which lenders, without attempting to screen short-term borrowers from long-term borrowers, may offer what are in effect short-term mortgage loans while retaining for borrowers many of the advantages of long-term financing.

CONSUMER PROTECTION

Consumer protection figures prominently in most discussions of VRMs. At the heart of the issue is disclosure of the terms of the mortgage contract. The FHLBB and a number of states have promulgated comprehensive regulations designed to insure that a borrower understands his potential mortgage costs with a VRM. By encouraging consumers to evaluate their borrowing options carefully and by insuring that lenders disclose to borrowers all information relevant for an intelligent choice between different mortgage instruments, these regulations facilitate the sound development of VRMs.

In addition to disclosure regulations, consumer protection measures have taken several other forms. For example, for many lenders the FPM is, for all practical purposes, the only mortgage design permitted. As a means for implementing consumer protection, such a draconian approach has obvious drawbacks.

Another approach to consumer protection is incorporated in the regulations issued by the FHLBB in December of last year, which required that any Federally chartered S&L offering VRMs also offer FPMs to prospective borrowers to assure them "the freedom to choose". While there are some mortgage lenders which lend only through VRMs, the great majority of VRM lenders also offer FPMs. There are two main reasons. First, since many individuals continue to prefer fixed monthly payments, it can still be profitable for lenders to offer FPMs. Second, for reasons developed more fully below, the VRM is likely to gain less acceptance in the secondary mortgage market than the FPM, so that lenders desiring to originate and sell mortgages have a strong incentive to offer FPMs. In light of these factors, the FHLBB's regulation will probably have little overall effect, though it may constrain some individual lenders.

Another, more important, way in which regulators and legislators occasionally have sought to protect the interest of borrowers is through placing restrictions on the form of the mortgage contract. For example, California VRMs have a 2½ percentage point cap on cumulative rate increases, and lenders must permit borrowers to extend the maturity of their loans (subject to certain limitations) to prevent rate increases from adding to their monthly payments. Since these features make VRMs more similar to FPMs and thus lessen their attractiveness to lenders, they contribute to limiting the rate discounts offered on California VRMs.

Also contributing to the smallness of the discounts is the linkage of most VRM rates to a statewide S&L cost-of-funds index. The California requirement resulted from a view that VRMs should enable lenders only to recoup variations in their average cost of funds and should not reflect movements in mortgage rates unrelated to movements in the cost of funds. While this view has an intuitive appeal as a means of insulating lenders' profits from fluctuations in the cost of funds, the insulation provided is only partial. In a period of rising interest rates, lenders' average returns on VRMs will rise about in tandem with their average funds costs, and their profit rates will be relatively stable. However, in a period of declining interest rates, yields on new mortgages will probably fall more than average funds costs, causing downward adjustments of VRM rates to lag behind the declining mortgage rates. Such a situation might lead to some consumer resentment until mortgage rates declined sufficiently to make it attractive for borrowers to prepay the VRMs and refinance them. As a result, returns on VRMs indexed to lenders' average cost of funds should rise roughly in tandem with average funds costs as rates rise, but probably will fall disproportionately as rates decline. This prospect clearly limits the magnitude of rate discounts which lenders can offer on VRMs.

Indexing VRM rates to funds costs also contributes to concerns that the progressive removal of deposit interest ceilings may raise funds costs and thus increase VRM rates, at least until the cap rates are encountered. The actual situation is more complex—and less threatening to borrowers—since they may prepay and refinance VRMs if their rates get out of line with market mortgage rates. No doubt some increases of mortgage rates will result from removal of deposit interest ceilings, but these will probably be substantially less than the increases in deposit interest rates.[9] The probable result, then, is that current mortgage rates will constrain increases in VRM rates resulting from indexing the rates to lenders' funds costs.

Since California VRMs are less attractive to lenders than those indexed to mortgage rates without rate caps and maturity extension options, it is not surprising that VRM rate discounts in California are relatively small. Ironically, though California VRMs do incorporate protections for consumers, they may also prevent individuals who expect to remain in their homes for relatively short periods of time from obtaining more favorable mortgage rates than long-term borrowers. In a housing market with turnover as high as that in California, the generally small rate discounts available to short-term borrowers may represent a considerable cost to consumers.

---

[9] Part of the reason is that as deposit interest ceilings are removed, lenders may initiate explicit charges for services heretofore provided free as a form of noninterest renumeration. In addition, many investors in the mortgage market—such as insurance companies and pension funds—are unaffected by deposit interest ceilings, and their demand for mortgages will dampen upward movements in mortgage rates relative to rates on alternative investments.

VRMs IN THE SECONDARY MORTGAGE MARKET

Because VRMs are a new mortgage instrument, sales of VRMs in the secondary mortgage market are a relatively new phenomenon. They are almost always arranged through negotiation between the originator and the investor—either directly or through a broker. However, in March 1978, the first public offering of VRM pass-through securities was made by the Home Savings and Loan Association of Los Angeles, the largest S&L in the country. The issue was well received by primarily institutional investors. A second issue in October met a somewhat poorer reception, and there have been no further public offerings of VRM pass-through securities since then. At this time, two main factors account for the relative unattractiveness of California VRMs in the secondary market. The California usury law limits the interest rate increases which out-of-state investors may expect.[10] Also, prevailing expectations of future declines in interest rates make fixed-rate investments more attractive to investors. Should rates decline significantly, public offerings of VRM pass-through securities could become attractive once again.

Nevertheless, a number of obstacles currently prevent VRMs from becoming a standard fixture of the secondary market. Since some states prohibit VRMs, lenders in such states may not buy them—either as whole loans or as participation certificates in pools of VRMs—for inclusion in their portfolios.[11] Moreover, even in states where VRMs are legal, Federally chartered S&Ls cannot purchase VRMs originated, for example, by California lenders with terms different from those authorized by the FHLBB. Also, Federal housing agencies such as the Federal National Mortgage Association and the Federal Home Loan Mortgage Corporation currently do not purchase VRMs.

The fundamental obstacle to purchases by the housing agencies as well as to trading VRMs in the secondary market is their lack of uniformity. Nonhomogeneous mortgage pass-through securities can be traded only after some detailed examination of the underlying mortgages. While newly issued Government National Mortgage Association pass-through securities bearing a given contract interest rate are uniform as to the contract rate and the original term, VRM pass-through securities, even if they have the same origination rate, may have different rate caps and different rate indexes. Moreover, although the indexes could be formally identical, different regional conditions affecting funds costs or current mortgage rates—especially state usury ceilings—might lead to variations in the pattern of implementation of VRM rate adjustments. Thus, with regional differences in deposit and mortgage markets, the origination rates as well as the course of rate adjustments will differ from one region to another. As a result, it will be difficult to trade VRM pass-

---

[10] Out-of-state lenders are subject to a 10 percent usury ceiling which does not apply to California S&Ls and commercial banks.

[11] However, since FHLBB regulations authorizing VRMs take precedence over such state laws, Federally chartered S&Ls in such states may offer VRMs.

through securities without some inspection of the underlying mortgages. This situation clearly favors determination of the terms of secondary market transactions in VRMs through negotiation between the buyer and seller, either directly or through a broker. Where the offering is large enough and the seller is sufficiently well-known to investors, it may be feasible to arrange a public offering. But, due to the lack of uniformity of VRMs, it will be difficult for securities dealers to "make markets" for them by posting the prices at which they stand ready to buy and sell.

To avoid such "fragmentation" of the secondary market for VRMs, a single, nationwide index has been suggested in place of the various local or regional indexes currently being used. The FHLBB lent support to this view in its recent regulations which required that all Federally chartered S&Ls offering VRMs after July 1 use the same nationwide cost-of-funds index. While widespread adoption of a uniform index clearly would reduce the variety of VRMs, several problems would remain. First, not all lenders would be attracted to the uniform index. For example, lenders in California might prefer to continue to index their VRMs to their average cost of funds. The California average cost of funds generally has tracked the national average very closely —the simple correlation coefficient between the two indexes is 0.99—but discrepancies have emerged, especially during periods of rising interest rates. Another reason why lenders might prefer to avoid using the nationwide index is that they might want to use VRMs to make short-term mortgage loans as described earlier, in which case they probably would want to index them to current mortgage rates. Moreover, even if all VRMs were tied to the nationwide index, local mortgage market conditions, including usury ceilings, would affect the ability of lenders to implement the VRM rate adjustments allowed by the national index. As a result, some heterogeneity would remain. Thus, use of a national index, though it will increase the uniformity of VRMs, does not appear likely to eliminate the fragmentation of the secondary market for VRMs.

OUTLOOK FOR VRMs

While it is difficult to predict the future growth and impact of VRMs, experience in California and elsewhere suggests that they should enjoy a ready market in states where they have not yet been introduced. In the near future VRMs are likely to spread more widely throughout the country. Effective July 1, the FHLBB authorized Federally chartered S&Ls in all states to offer VRMs and, as pressure grows to raise or eliminate deposit interest ceilings, interest in expanding lending through VRMs should increase. As more lenders are able to use VRMs to reduce the risk of lending long and borrowing short, VRMs should have a favorable impact on the supply of mortgage credit throughout the business cycle.

Experience to date illustrates the variety of feasible VRM designs, including nonindexed VRMs like the Canadian ROM and the "escalator clause" mortgage popular in Wisconsin, VRMs indexed to current mortgage rates as in New England, and VRMs indexed to a measure of lenders' funds costs as in California. Some of these VRMs provide borrowers considerable protection against future rate increases, though not so much as an FPM. But such protection is generally obtained only at the cost of higher origination rates, which may prevent short-term borrowers from reducing their borrowing costs with a VRM. Thus, in the future development of VRMs, the cost of imposing restrictions on the form of VRMs should be weighed carefully against the expected benefits.

GRADUATED PAYMENT MORTGAGES*

William C. Melton

10

In the space of a few years graduated payment mortgages have achieved fairly widespread acceptance. They presently are the most rapidly growing category of Federal Housing Administration (FHA)-insured mortgages, and legislation has recently been enacted which could expand their use still further. Moreover, the private sector has begun to offer a novel form of mortgage loan which allows the lender to receive a stream of constant payments while the borrower makes graduated payments.

The need to come to grips with the problems which high rates of inflation create for the standard fixed payment mortgage (FPM) has provided the impetus for two basic modifications of the FPM. Variable rate mortgages provide for interest rate adjustments to share the risk of interest rate changes between borrower and lender, but otherwise employ the same schedule of constant monthly payments of interest and principal as the FPM.[1] In contrast, the graduated payment mortgage (GPM) retains the constant interest rate of the FPM, but lowers the monthly payments in the early years of the loan and increases them according to a predetermined schedule.

This article would not have been possible without the assistance of Henry J. Cassidy, Chester C. Foster, Diane L. Heidt, and Warren Lasko, none of whom bear any responsibility for the views expressed herein.

*Reprinted from the *Quarterly Review*, Spring 1980, pp. 21-28, with permission from the Federal Reserve Bank of New York.

[1] See William C. Melton and Diane L. Heidt, "Variable Rate Mortgages", this *Review* (Summer 1979), pages 23-31.

FIXED PAYMENT MORTGAGES

The adoption of the fully amortizing, fixed rate, level-payment mortgage as the standard mortgage design owes a great deal to its ability to reduce mortgage defaults. Prior to the 1930s the fully amortizing loan contract—though apparently the most common form of mortgage loan—was nowhere nearly so prevalent as it is now.[2] Contracts often provided for no amortization or for only partial amortization of the principal amount prior to the maturity date. As a result, a "balloon" payment of principal often became due on maturity. Terms to maturity were frequently short, often only about five years. Common practice was for such loans to be renegotiated at maturity, with a new loan being made to refinance the part of the principal which the borrower did not pay down at that time.

This procedure entailed a number of risks, as became apparent during the depression of the 1930s. First, the short term to maturity, together with the balloon payment feature, meant that, if the borrower had not accumulated sufficient funds to repay the loan at maturity, he might be subject to foreclosure on his property unless he was able to negotiate a new loan for the unpaid balance of principal. Second, since a relatively small amount of amortization—or perhaps none at all—was required, the borrower's equity in the property did not necessarily increase significantly as time went by. As a result, in the event of a loss of income to the borrower or erosion of the value of the property, the temptation to default on the loan might be strong.

With the onset of the depression, loan defaults mushroomed, and many lenders were unable to roll over maturing loans, so that foreclosures surged to a massive rate. In response, the Congress took a variety of measures to reduce the short-term threat of foreclosures as well as to restructure the procedures of housing finance to avoid a recurrence.

Among these measures was Government mortgage insurance administered by the FHA. FHA insurance, begun in 1934, required that loans be long term and fully amortizing, with constant monthly payments. Similarly, Federally chartered savings and loan associations, first created in the 1930s, were limited almost exclusively to making mortgages with those characteristics, and many states passed legislation applying similar restrictions to mortgage lending institutions under their jurisdiction.[3] In addition, the Federal National Mortgage Association (FNMA), organized in 1938, restricted its secondary

---

[2] Almost all mortgages held by savings and loan associations during the 1920s and early 1930s were fully amortizing, but other lenders held primarily partially amortizing or nonamortizing mortgages. Available data indicate that a variety of short-term mortgages, partially amortizing or nonamortizing, constituted slightly more than half of all mortgages in lending institutions' portfolios before the depression. For more details, see Henry J. Cassidy, "The Changing Home Mortgage instrument in the United States", Federal Home Loan Bank Board *Journal* (December 1978), pages 11-17.

[3] With the exception of the recently authorized reverse annuity mortgages, Federally chartered savings and loan associations may make balloon residential mortgages with a maximum term of five years, but the value of the loan may not exceed 50 percent of the security (Federal Home Loan Bank Board, *Annotated Manual of Statutes and Regulations*, section 545.6-1). This regulation restricts balloon mortgages to the relatively few individuals capable of making a 50 percent downpayment on a home.

market mortgage purchases to Government-insured mortgages, thus giving still further impetus to the adoption of the FPM as the standard mortgage instrument.[4] As a result of these measures, by the early postwar period the FPM was by far the dominant residential mortgage loan contract.

The adoption of the FPM as the standard form of mortgage contract was successful in overcoming the major problems of the residential mortgage market which existed during the 1920s and the 1930s. Its weaknesses began to become apparent only during the 1960s and 1970s—a period of rapid inflation and historically high and variable interest rates.

One of the FPM's most severe problems is the burden it creates for young families acquiring a home for the first time. Such families require housing services to accommodate their growing households, yet their current income —which is of major importance for determining the monthly mortgage payments they can afford—is often substantially less than their expected future income. Unfortunately, the FPM, by keeping monthly payments constant, does not allow such families to tailor their payments to their expected income growth. This "life cycle" problem exists even in an environment of stable prices.

Inflation causes an additional problem by making the burden of real mortgage costs in the early years of the loan term even greater relative to borrowers' current income than it would have been with no inflation. As inflation comes to be expected, nominal interest rates adjust upward to compensate lenders, at least in part, for the loss of purchasing power expected to occur during the term of the loan. Thus, if the rate of interest on mortgages were 3 percent in an environment of stable prices, it might rise to about 11 percent if an 8 percent rate of inflation is expected over the term of the loan. If the term to maturity of an FPM is not altered, this increased nominal interest rate raises the monthly payment. However, if the expected rate of inflation actually turns out to be correct, the increased rate of interest is approximately offset by the progressive reduction in the purchasing power of the interest and principal payments, so that the real cost of the loan remains essentially unchanged at about 3 percent per annum.[5]

Though the real cost—*i.e.,* the value of the monthly payments adjusted for price changes—is almost unchanged, its distribution through the term of the loan changes dramatically. Since inflation erodes the value of the higher nominal payments only gradually, the real cost is significantly higher in the early years of the term and is lower during the later years. For example, an increase in the expected rate of inflation from zero to 8 percent, reflected in an increase in the mortgage interest rate from 3 percent to 11 percent, causes the real cost of the first year's monthly payments on a $60,000 mortgage with a thirty-year term to rise from $253 per month to about $550 (Chart 1). By the eleventh year of the term, the real cost of the 11 percent mortgage

---

[4] In February 1972, FNMA broadened its mortgage purchase program to include conventional mortgages as well.

[5] This statement abstracts from considerations such as the tax treatment of interest expense which would reduce the real cost of the 11 percent mortgage relative to that of the 3 percent mortgage.

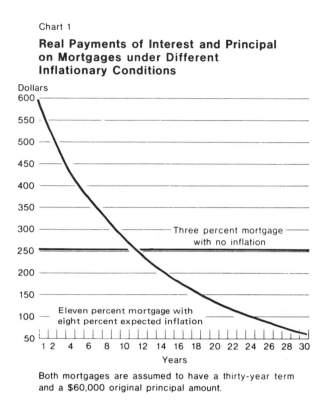

Chart 1

**Real Payments of Interest and Principal
on Mortgages under Different
Inflationary Conditions**

Both mortgages are assumed to have a thirty-year term
and a $60,000 original principal amount.

has declined almost to the real cost of the 3 percent mortgage; afterward it is less.

Most individuals are highly sensitive to the timing of real payments during the term of their mortgages, because they must make mortgage payments out of their current incomes and still have sufficient income remaining to meet other expenses. Hence the "front-end load" created by the concentration of the real payments in the early years can be a major burden. While the level of monthly payments can be reduced by decreasing the size of the loan (and increasing the down-payment), this alternative is generally impractical for young, first-time home buyers. In addition, the burden of other expenses relative to income is also likely to be substantial in the early years of home-ownership, when many younger persons are starting their families.

FHA-INSURED GRADUATED PAYMENT MORTGAGES

The development of GPMs was the outgrowth of the Experimental Finance Program of the United States Department of Housing and Urban Development (HUD), authorized by the Congress in 1974.[6] Section 245 of the National Housing Act as amended that year authorized HUD to initiate an experimental program to insure mortgages with "provisions of varying rates of amortization corresponding to anticipated variations in family income". The program was an effort to determine whether the problems of first-time home buyers could be alleviated within the framework of accepted mortgage lending practices. In 1977 the Housing and Community Development Act made the program permanent.

As their name suggests, FHA-insured GPMs have monthly payments which are low at first and rise gradually for a period of years before leveling off. Since they have a constant interest rate and a fixed term, the graduated payment feature means that the early monthly payments are insufficient to cover accrued interest. As the unpaid accrued interest is added to the principal balance of the loan, the outstanding loan principal increases; in other words, there is negative amortization in the early years of its term.

Like other FHA-insured loans, Section 245 GPMs are fully insured and intended to be made on an actuarially sound basis—*i.e.,* insurance premium payments are expected to be adequate to cover any losses. Originally, FHA-insured GPMs were subject to the same maximum loan-to-value ratio as FHA Section 203(b) FPMs and, since a GPM's principal increased in the early years, the minimum initial downpayment had to be greater than for an FPM. The Housing and Community Development Act of 1977 relaxed the requirement somewhat by allowing the principal amount of GPM loans to increase as high as 97 percent of the original estimated value.

Since the GPM program was new, HUD restricted it to five alternatives which differ according to the pattern of graduation of the initial payments. Three plans permit payments to increase at 2½, 5, and 7½ percent annually for five years, and two plans allow payments to increase at 2 and 3 percent annually for ten years. Monthly payments during each year are level; increases occur annually. After the final annual increase, the payments become constant for the remaining term of the loan. Payment schedules for an FPM and for Plan III and Plan V GPMs are illustrated in Chart 2. All the mortgages are assumed to have a thirty-year term and a $60,000 initial principal amount. The GPM payments are significantly less in the early years than those of the FPM. Indeed, during the first four years of the Plan III GPM, the total payments are $4,058 less than those for the FPM. Over the first six years of the Plan V GPM, total payments are $3,790 less than for the FPM. This early cost advantage is offset in two main respects. First, as noted earlier, the GPM plans require somewhat higher downpayments than the FPM. Second, when the GPM payments flatten out, they do so at a higher level than the FPM,

---

[6]The first kind of GPM authorized nationally was the "flexible payment mortgage" authorized by the Federal Home Loan Bank Board in February 1974. The idea behind it was to reduce the early monthly payments by omitting amortization in the early years of the term. However, since amortization constitutes only a small portion of the early payments for an FPM, the payment schedule for a flexible payment mortgage was not greatly different from that for an FPM, and the innovation never attracted much interest.

Chart 2

Monthly Payments of Interest and Principal for a Fixed Payment Mortgage and Two Graduated Payment Mortgages

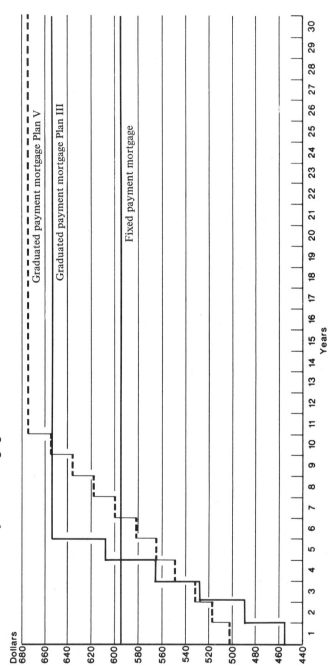

Dollars

Years

Graduated payment mortgage Plan V

Graduated payment mortgage Plan III

Fixed payment mortgage

A term of thirty-years and a contract rate of 11½ percent are assumed. Payments for mortgage insurance are not included.

owing to the negative amortization in the early years of term.[7] The result is that, while payments of interest and principal total $213,905 over the thirty-year term of the FPM, they are $14,155 (6.6 percent) more for the Plan III GPM and $17,217 (8.0 percent) more for the Plan V GPM.

The GPM program got off to a slow start. Regulations in some states against collecting compound interest on residential mortgage loans prevented many lenders from offering them. This problem was resolved by the Housing and Community Development Act of 1977, which exempted FHA-insured GPMs from such restrictions. Another problem which has yet to be resolved is that GPMs with negative amortization like those in the Section 245 program can increase the tax liability of taxpayers who calculate their income on an accrual basis—which includes most financial institutions. The reason is that, while the unpaid interest on such a GPM is added to the loan principal and not received by the lender in the year it was earned (accrued), it does increase the lender's tax liability for that year. Other things equal, this feature makes GPMs a less attractive investment than a standard FPM.

Expansion of the program was also slowed by the relative unattractiveness of the GPMs for the thrift institutions which originate most single-family mortgages. Since the low early payments of the FHA-insured GPMs initially produce less cash flow for lenders than do FPMs, they are not attractive to thrift institutions which rely largely on short-term sources of funds. The lack of enthusiasm on the part of thrift institutions, together with mortgage banks' traditional dominance of FHA originations, meant that mortgage banks accounted for almost all GPM originations. The statutory restriction of FHA single-family loans to $45,000—raised to $60,000 in 1977 and to $67,500 in 1979—also reduced the attractiveness of FHA financing in areas where housing prices are relatively high.

Since the GPM program was new, lenders also needed time to become familiar with the alternative designs, to make adjustments in their loan processing procedures, and then to market GPMs to potential borrowers. The result was that, out of a total of 321,118 FHA single-family mortgage insurance endorsements in 1977, only 331 were for GPMs. However, following the increase in the maximum FHA loan size, the Federal override of state laws barring collection of compound interest on residential mortgages, and the establishment of the Section 245 program on a permanent basis in late 1977, the situation changed dramatically. By December 1978, over 25 percent of total new single-family endorsements were GPMs. During 1979, about 27 percent of the total were GPMs.

The regional distribution of GPMs is highly uneven, with most activity taking place on the West Coast and in the southeastern part of the country. Indeed, by the end of 1979, California alone accounted for about a third of all GPMs in the country. This uneven pattern of introduction of GPMs is probably attributable to regional differences in the composition and strength of housing demand as well as state usury laws and other restrictions on the ability of lenders to offer them.

---

[7]There is a third small offset due to the insurance premium being larger for the increasing principal balance of the GPM than for the FPM.

Two provisions of the Housing and Community Development Amendments of 1979, signed into law on January 4, 1980, may expand the GPM program significantly. First, the maximum loan size for single-family mortgages insured by the FHA was increased from $60,000 to $67,500. Second, the GPM program was modified to increase the permissible GPM loan size when the initial home value is below or slightly above the maximum loan size. The new GPM authorized in Section 245(b)—the previous Section 245 is now renamed Section 245(a)—is similar to the earlier GPM and, for both programs, the loan balance at no time can exceed 97 percent of the value of the house. However, for the earlier program this was the initial appraised value; in the new Section 245(b) program the value of the home is assumed to increase over time, thus relaxing the 97 percent limitation. In projecting the future home value, HUD is authorized to employ a maximum 2½ percent annual rate of price appreciation—a rate well below that observed in recent years.

Depending on how the new program is implemented, the Section 245(b) GPMs may allow GPM borrowers to increase substantially their initial loan size and thus to reduce their downpayments.[8] The smaller downpayment would increase the attractiveness of GPMs for many people. However, the Congress placed a number of restrictions on the program. First, to concentrate the Section 245(b) program on first-time home buyers, applicants must not have owned a home in the preceding three years. Second, the number of mortgages insured in any fiscal year is limited to 10 percent of the aggregate initial principal amount of all one- to four-family mortgages insured under Section 245(b) during the preceding fiscal year or 50,000 mortgages, whichever is greater. Nevertheless, there appears to be ample scope for the new program to expand.

CONVENTIONAL GRADUATED PAYMENT MORTGAGES

The HUD program has given impetus to the development by the private sector of conventional—*i.e.,* nonFHA-insured—GPMs. First, the relatively low maximum FHA loan size, together with the rather demanding FHA construction standards and paperwork requirements, makes FHA loans of whatever form unattractive for many borrowers and lenders. Second, as noted earlier, the negative amortization in the early years of an FHA-insured GPM can create an increased tax liability and a cash flow pattern unattractive to many lenders. The former problem can be avoided through conventional financing. The latter problem has been alleviated through the development of a novel form of mortgage loan which allows the lender to receive a stream of constant monthly payments while the borrower makes graduated payments.

---

[8] As of this writing, HUD has not yet determined whether the new program would operate in the same Plans I-V as the Section 245(a) GPMs or whether new graduation periods and rates would be created.

WHO BORROWS THROUGH FHA-INSURED GRADUATED PAYMENT MORTGAGES?

Data collected in a special survey conducted by the United States Department of Housing and Urban Development indicate that the GPM (Section 245) borrower is on average 29-30 years old—one to two years younger than the average FPM (Section 203(b)) borrower. Most borrowers in both programs are married, but there is substantial singles participation as well. As one would expect, considering their lower average age, GPM borrowers generally have slightly fewer dependents than do FPM borrowers. A large majority—three qurters or more—of borrowers under both programs are first-time home buyers. However, GPM borrowers are somewhat more likely to own a home which is being sold to finance the purchase of a new home. The income of GPM borrowers is on the whole not very different from that of FPM borrowers—though in some individual markets GPM borrowers have markedly lower average incomes.

Though nationwide comparisons of FPM and GPM borrower characteristics are complicated by the fact that California has accounted for a disproportionate share of GPM volume, it appears that GPM borrowers buy significantly more expensive homes which they finance with larger mortgages. Because of the low early monthly payments of the GPM, this results in only a slightly greater burden of first-year housing expense relative to income for GPM borrowers, compared with FPM borrowers. GPM borrowers also put down significantly larger downpayments—in part because the most popular Plan III GPM requires a larger downpayment, but also because in many cases the maximum FHA loan size is a constraint. As a consequence, GPM borrowers generally have a lower loan-to-value ratio than FPM borrowers.

Average Characteristics of FPM and GPM Borrowers

Characteristic	FPM borrowers	GPM borrowers
Sales price	$36,130	$48,996
Mortgage amount	$34,427	$44,557
Total annual family income	$22,167	$22,128
Loan-to-value ratio	92.6%	89.8%
Total housing expense/ net effective income	30.9%	32.3%
Total fixed payments/ net effective income	51.7%	50.9%

Data are for loans on existing single-family structrues endorsed during the first quarter of 1979. Fixed payment mortgage loans (FPMs) are those endorsed under Section 203(b); graduated payment mortgage loans (GPMs) are those endorsed under Section 245.

Source: United States Department of Housing and Urban Development.

The loan is structured so that part of its proceeds is placed with the lending institution in a pledged savings account from which withdrawals are gradually made to supplement the borrower's early payments. The result is a loan with constant payments to the lender and graduated payments by the borrower. This means that the loan does not have the FHA-insured GPM's tax and cash flow disadvantages for lenders, who in addition acquire funds through the pledged account. Moreover, the pledged-account GPM circumvents many states' prohibitions against increasing monthly mortgage payments and the charging of interest on accrued interest—an important consideration, since the Housing and Community Development Act of 1977 overrode such state laws only for FHA-insured GPMs.

Finally, even though lenders typically pay only the passbook savings account interest rate on the pledged account, generally a tax saving will be realized which offsets or exceeds the loss of income created by borrowing funds at the mortgage rate and investing them at the passbook rate. The reason is that the borrower may deduct the withdrawals from the pledged account from his taxable income, since they are used to pay part of the mortgage interest. As a result, his deductible interest expense exceeds his actual out-of-pocket outlay for mortgage interest during the early years of the loan.

It is difficult to estimate the volume of originations of pledged-account GPMs. Since the loan is essentially an FPM from the standpoint of lenders, available data do not separate out the pledged-account GPMs from other mortgages. However, judging by the vigor with which they have been promoted, the volume of pledged-account GPMs may well be substantial.

GPMs IN THE SECONDARY MARKET

Additional impetus to GPM lending has been provided by the opening-up of the secondary mortgage market to FHA-insured GPMs. Initially, almost the only part of the secondary market in which FHA-insured GPMs were sold was the FNMA purchase program. Early in 1979, the Government National Mortgage Association (GNMA) expanded its pass-through certificate program to allow FHA-insured GPMs to be included in mortgage pools underlying the certificates.[9]

The GPM-GNMA certificates—familiarly referred to as "Jeeps"—provide an ownership interest in a pool containing mortgages with five-year graduation periods (Plans I-III). In practice, since the vast majority of GPM borrowers prefer Plan III, which has the steepest graduation schedule, the pools consist overwhelmingly of mortgages of this type. Because of the graduation feature, GPM-GNMAs have a slightly longer average maturity, or "duration", than do standard GNMAs. This is true both of the contracted term to matur-

---

[9]For a description of the GNMA certificate program, see Charles M. Sivesind, "Mortgage-Backed Securities: The Revolution in Real Estate Finance", this *Review* (Autumn 1979), pages 1-10.

ity and also of the average maturity calculated on the basis of prior experience with prepayments of FHA mortgages. As a result, the price of a GPM-GNMA security should be slightly more volatile than that of a standard GNMA security.

Yields of GNMA securities—including GPM-GNMAs—currently are quoted on the basis of a twelve-year prepayment assumption.[10] This is convenient for standard GNMA securities, since in most cases the yield distortions are not large. However, the assumption is less firmly grounded in the case of GPM-GNMAs, since there is no prior experience on which to base an evaluation of the accuracy of the approximation. On the one hand, if GPM borrowers are more likely to consider their homes as permanent investments and are less inclined to move than other borrowers, the GPM prepayment experience will be slower than prior FHA experience. On the other hand, if GPMs are especially attractive to upwardly mobile families inclined to move to a better house after a few years, then the GPM-GNMA prepayment rate could be faster than prior experience. In these circumstances, GNMA, for want of any better alternative, has applied the standard twelve-year prepayment assumption to yield calculations for GPM-GNMAs.

Trading in GPM-GNMAs has reflected the fact that the instrument is new, with few pools existing compared with standard GNMA securities. As a result of their less liquid market and their longer expected average term, GPM-GNMAs have traded at a discount of one to two points relative to level-payment GNMAs with the same coupon interest rate.

The number of GPM-GNMA pools has increased substantially—to 1,102 pools with an unpaid principal balance aggregating to $2.3 billion at the end of February 1980—and GNMA anticipates that the volume will expand in tandem with the growth of GPM originations. The liquidity of the market should improve in the future as the number of pools increases further.

Secondary market activity in pledged-account GPMs has been more modest. A number of sales of packages of GPMs carrying mortgage insurance provided by private mortgage insurance firms have occurred. Activity should be stimulated, however, when the Federal Home Loan Mortgage Corporation initiates its planned pilot purchase program.

EVALUATION OF GRADUATED PAYMENT MORTGAGES

As noted earlier, FHA-insured GPMs have expanded rapidly in the few years the program has existed. Though it is too early to make a definitive judgment, indications are that to some extent the expansion of Section 245 GPMs has been at the expense of Section 203(b) FPMs. If this pattern continues and also holds for conventionally financed GPMs, then the impact of continued growth of GPMs would not be primarily to expand the mortgage

---

[10] For a description of the calculation of yields on GNMA securities, see Sivesind, *loc. cit.*

market, though some increase would occur, but rather to allow borrowers to arrange their housing finance more conveniently than at present.

The major unanswered question concerning the growth and development of GPMs is not, however, a matter of relative rates of expansion; it is the implications of GPMs for loan defaults in the years ahead. As noted earlier, a key benefit obtained from adoption of the FPM as the standard mortgage design was to avoid any recurrence of the enormous volume of mortgage defaults which was precipitated by the depression of the 1930s. To the extent that the FPM is modified, defaults might once again become a source of concern.

In the past, the most important determinant of mortgage defaults has been the amount of equity which the borrower has in his house. Since equity is lowest in the early years of the mortgage term, the incentive to default—and its observed incidence—is greatest then. To the extent that a GPM with negative amortization—such as the FHA-insured GPM—increases the balance of the loan in the early years of the term, the owner's equity relative to the original purchase price declines. Other things equal, this should increase his incentive to default. This effect could be offset, however, if the rate of appreciation of the home's value exceeds the rate at which the loan balance increases. The requisite rate of increase in value depends on the level of the interest rate but is generally quite modest, on the order of 1 percent or so per year during the first five years of the thirty-year term of a Plan III GPM. The loan balance of pledged-account GPMs decreases continuously, but the larger initial loan size means that an additional default incentive is created, compared with both an FPM and an FHA-insured GPM. Both kinds of GPMs reduce the front-end load in the time pattern of the real payments on the mortgage, and this will probably reduce defaults in the early years, though they might be increased later on.

While the short period of time during which the FHA GPM program has been in operation precludes firm generalizations about default rates, there have been some indications that Section 245 GPMs have default rates which are either the same as, or lower than, Section 203(b) FPMs. However, more than ordinary caution is needed in interpreting this performance. First, downpayments on FHA-insured GPMs frequently have been greater than required under the program, and this should reduce defaults. The most likely reason for the larger downpayments is that the FHA's loan size limitation required buyers of more expensive homes to increase their downpayments to qualify for FHA insurance. In addition, since FHA-insured GPMs have a slower cash flow than FPMs of equal maturity and interest rate, persons financing through GPMs should expect to pay more points than with an FPM.[11] This also would tend to restrict the availability of GPM financing to borrowers capable of making larger downpayments. Finally, some GPM borrowers may have a

---

[11] A point is 1 percent of the principal value of a mortgage note. Since the maximum FHA mortgage rate is generally held well below market levels, points are charged to raise to market levels the yield on the funds actually advanced. While sellers are legally obligated to pay any points charged on an FHA mortgage, they generally attempt to shift this cost to the buyer by increasing the sale price and thus the downpayment required of the buyer.

preference for low monthly payments—to such an extent that they would be willing to reduce their liquid assets in order to lower the loan size and thus the monthly payments. This approach can make sense when the mortgage interest rate is substantially higher than the savings account interest rate, as has been the case during the FHA program's existence.

The absence of hard evidence concerning the default experience with FHA-insured GPMs raises the issue of precisely what an "actuarially sound" GPM is. The designers of the FHA program had in mind a mortgage contract in which the degree of graduation did not exceed the prospective rise in income of the borrower during the early years of the loan term. In fact, however, the available evidence suggests that income projections are not taken very seriously by GPM originators, with the result that Plan III—which has the steepest graduation rate—dominates all FHA's other GPM options. Now that the Congress has authorized the Section 245(b) GPM, in which an assumption is made concerning the future rate of price appreciation of the house, the evaluation of the soundness of GPMs has still less to do with actuarial methodology as usually understood. In the near future, continued inflation may ratify any such assumption and prevent the emergence of problems in the GPM program but, as inflation is brought under control, the validity of the assumption could be eroded. In such a case, as both inflation and mortgage interest rates declined, GPM borrowers—because of their larger loan sizes—would have an especially strong incentive to refinance their loans at lower interest rates. In addition, defaults and delinquencies might increase.

OUTLOOK FOR GRADUATED PAYMENT MORTGAGES

In the long run, the best way to deal with the front-end load induced in the real payments of an FPM is to reduce the rate of inflation. In the near-term, however, the GPM—whether FHA-insured or conventional—clearly has an important role to play in alleviating some of the problems created for many borrowers, especially young families, by exclusive reliance on the FPM as the standard mortgage design. GPMs will likely continue to expand at a brisk rate in the near future. Perhaps the principal obstacle to their doing so is the recent advent of single-family mortgages financed through issues of tax-exempt bonds. In areas where such programs have been actively employed, GPM activity has been very slight, for GPMs obviously are less attractive to house buyers than mortgages offered at below-market interest rates. Thus, the outlook for growth of GPMs will be influenced by the outcome of pending legislation to restrict issues of single-family mortgage revenue bonds.

In the longer term, even after inflation is brought under control, graduated payment mortgages are likely to remain an important innovation in the mortgage market, by virtue of providing greater flexibility in tailoring mortgage payments to anticipated income growth than does the fixed payment mortgage.

MORTGAGE-BACKED SECURITIES: THE REVOLUTION IN REAL ESTATE FINANCE *

Charles M. Sivesind

11

The rapid development of a variety of mortgage-backed securities has led to a radical transformation in real estate finance in recent years. By integrating the mortgage market into the traditional capital markets, these securities have broadened the financial base for home mortgages. During 1978, the $40 billion of mortgage-backed securities issued in this national market financed nearly one quarter of all home loan originations.

There are two major types of mortgage-backed securities: *bonds* with scheduled principal repayments that are secured by mortgage collateral and *pass-throughs* which provide ownership interest in the monthly payments from a pool of mortgages. Until recently, the market has been dominated by the bonds issued by the Federal National Mortgage Association (FNMA or "Fannie Mae") and the pass-through securities guaranteed by the Government National Mortgage Association (GNMA or "Ginnie Mae"), both backed by Government-insured mortgages. However, a variety of mortgage-backed securities are now financing conventional mortgage lending as well. Building on the success of pass-through securities issued by the Federal Home Loan

The author gratefully acknowledges the assistance of numerous market experts: Phil Cockerill, Arnold Diamond, Marcos Jones, Lee Kendall, Warren Lasko, Dan Laufenberg, Ken Rilander, Dave Seiders, Eric Sheetz, and Steve Shepherd.

*Reprinted from the *Quarterly Review*, Autumn 1979, pp. 1-10, with permission from the Federal Reserve Bank of New York.

Mortgage Corporation (FHLMC or "Freddie Mac"), pass-throughs backed by conventional loans are now being issued publicly by banks, savings and loan associations, and mortgage companies. Mortgage-related bonds are being used to finance mortgage loan portfolios of thrift institutions and various government-sponsored housing programs.

Mortgage-backed securities allow firms dealing in real estate finance either to specialize in originating and servicing mortgage loans (seller/servicing) or to focus on providing the long-term capital investment funds to finance lending activities (investment). Traditionally, commercial banks, savings and loan associations, and mutual savings banks performed both of these functions. Mortgage companies, on the other hand, mainly originated and serviced mortgage loans which they packaged for sale to such permanent investors as insurance companies and pension funds.

The widespread acceptance of mortgage-backed securities has encouraged a broad variety of institutional investors to invest in the mortgage market, once dominated by individuals and thrift institutions. This new market for mortgage-backed securities has reduced geographic and institutional barriers to mortgage lending by distant investors. By attracting a variety of new types of investors to the mortgage market and by integrating the mortgage market into the broader, more highly developed capital markets, mortgage-backed securities promise to stabilize the supply of funds to the housing sector of the economy—once an early casualty in any period of credit stringency.

THE CHANGING HOME MORTGAGE MARKET

The unique financing requirements brought about by widespread home-ownership have caused a continuing evolution in mortgage lending practices. But until recently the housing sector has been plagued by an insecure financial base. The real estate collapse of the 1930's led to a reorganization of mortgage lending practices, sparked by the creation of the mortgage guarantee program of the Federal Housing Administration (FHA) in 1934 and later by the Veterans Administration (VA) mortgage insurance program in 1944. The programs encouraged underwriting of mortgages with standardized terms, relatively low downpayments, and long maturities on properties meeting high-quality standards. Since low-risk FHA-VA loans could be sold to investors across the country, the programs facilitated the early development of an integrated, national mortgage market at little direct cost to the Government.

By encouraging the widespread adoption of the long-term, fully amortized, fixed-payment mortgage as the standard lending agreement, the FHA-VA programs also contributed to an increased role for institutional investors in home loans. The long-term nature of the contract lowered monthly payments, making homeownership affordable for a larger segment of the population, while monthly amortization of principal resulted in a gradual buildup of each homeowner's equity, reducing default risk. For investors, however, this type of contract presented several difficulties. The long maturity made evaluation of the future collateral value of the property particularly difficult, required the loans to be serviced over a long period, and emphasized the need for escrow of taxes and insurance. Liberal prepayment clauses, which were desired by borrowers to facilitate future real estate sales, created uncertainty of investment maturity. In addition, amortization resulted in relatively small but continuous principal repayments, complicating reinvestment options. These factors made mortgage investment attractive primarily to savings institutions and life insurance companies with larger portfolios than most individual investors.

The growth of institutional dominance in the mortgage market continued from the postwar housing boom into the mid-1960's. In 1946, households held over one quarter of the outstanding home mortgage debt (Chart 1). Commercial banks held about one fifth of the total, while thrift institutions and insurance companies held nearly half.

During the next twenty years, savings and loan associations provided most of the conventional financing in the rapidly growing sections of the country while households' relative mortgage holdings shrank. Over this period, strong housing demand made mortgage yields attractive relative to the returns available to institutional investors on many other long-term investments. Banks and thrift institutions, closely tied to their local markets, saw little need for FHA-VA insurance and tended to concentrate on conventional home loans. Life insurance companies, on the other hand, saw these Government-insured loans as a new type of high-yield, low-risk, long-term investment. Mainly to meet the needs of insurance companies for seller/servicing of FHA-VA loans in local communities, many mortgage companies were created during the postwar housing boom. These mortgage companies originated loans, nearly at cost, and sold them to final investors, continuing to earn servicing income over the life of the loan. Home mortgage investments of thrift institutions and insurance companies reached nearly three quarters of the outstanding total by the mid-1960's.

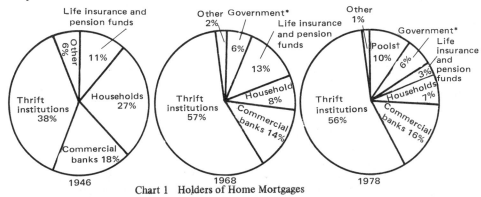

Chart 1   Holders of Home Mortgages

*Federal, state and local, including directly held mortgages and holdings of sponsored credit agencies.
†Pass-through securities backed by these pools are ultimately held by a variety of investor groups, including those listed here, but are carried on the books separately from direct mortgage holdings.
Source: Board of Governors of the Federal Reserve System, *Flow of Funds.*

The activities of mortgage companies began to change in the mid-1960's, when general increases in interest rates (in the face of FHA-VA ceilings which were held below market levels) encouraged life insurance companies to shift their lending focus away from one- to four-family houses toward multifamily dwellings and commercial buildings. Mortgage companies responded by becoming more active in multifamily and commercial lending, but they also were forced to seek new investors for home loans. At first the slack in the home loan market was taken up by the various Federally sponsored credit agencies (mainly FNMA) whose holdings of mortgages on one- to four-family dwellings increased from $2.5 billion in 1965 to $15.5 billion in 1970. Most of the loans sold to these agencies were originated and serviced by mortgage companies and consisted mainly of FHA-VA mortgages.

The search by mortgage companies for new investors took a new turn in the late 1960's with the creation of the first publicly traded pass-through securities backed by pools of mortgages. These new securities—mostly GNMA pass-throughs (see below)—in effect allowed mortgage companies to sell mortgages to investors who were located in other sections of the country and to institutions which had not invested in real estate loans in the past. By 1978, 15 percent of all newly originated home loans was placed in pass-through pools. These pools contained 10 percent of total home mortgage debt by the year-end. Meanwhile, as home mortgage rates declined relative to corporate bond yields, insurance companies and pension funds all but stopped buying home mortgages directly, although they continued to invest in pass-through securities and mortgage backed bonds.

THE INVENTION OF MORTGAGE-BACKED SECURITIES

The Government-related agencies—FNMA, GNMA, and FHLMC—may be credited with the development and widespread adoption of mortgage-backed securities as a means of financing home loans. Each agency fulfills a variety of roles, servicing one or more sectors of the mortgage market.[1] Some agencies subsidize certain types of housing. Some provide securities guarantees. Others purchase mortgages from originators and either package these loans into participation pools for resale to final investors or hold them in portfolio, financing the acquisitions by issuing notes and bonds. Some deal mainly in conventional loans, while others specialize in FHA-VA loans, which typically are made in connection with lower priced or older homes.

The FNMA was organized as a Government agency in 1938 to purchase

---

[1] The twelve Federal Home Loan Banks (FHLBs), while not usually treated as credit agencies, issue debt and lend the proceeds primarily to savings and loan associations on mortgage collateral. FHLB advances, which totaled $30 billion at the end of 1978, effectively increase the liquidity of mortgages held in savings and loan association portfolios but do not directly contribute to the marketability of mortgages.

Government-guaranteed mortgages. After its reorganization as a privately owned corporation in 1968, it began in 1971 to buy conventional mortgages. FNMA programs have been popular with mortgage bankers, who originate most of the loans it purchases, but it also buys from other approved FHA-VA lenders. In 1978, it purchased over $12 billion in mortgages, about half of which were conventional loans. At the end of 1978 it held mortgages with an unpaid principal balance of over $43 billion, one quarter of which were conventional loans. To finance its portfolio, FNMA issues short-term discount notes and intermediate-term debentures, effectively transforming mortgages into securities with a fixed maturity and a single principal repayment at the end.[2] Its short-term debt rose by $2.5 billion in 1978, and it issued debentures totaling $9.3 billion (Chart 2). FNMA purchases facilitate the separation of the seller/servicing and investment aspects of real estate finance, allowing local real estate markets to attract funds indirectly from distant geographic regions and from investors who do not wish to originate, service, or hold mortgage loans.

When FNMA was rechartered as a private corporation in 1968, programs requiring Government subsidies or other direct Federal support were assumed by GNMA, a newly organized Government corporation within the Department of Housing and Urban Development. There are now two major GNMA programs. One is the purchase of mortgages to support housing for low-income families for which private financing is not readily available. These special assistance programs provide mortgage funds at below market rates of

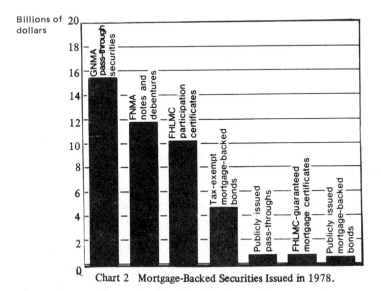

Chart 2   Mortgage-Backed Securities Issued in 1978.

[2] In the past, FNMA issued a few bonds explicitly collateralized by designated mortgages—the forerunner of mortgage-backed bonds now being used by savings and loan associations—but most of its debentures are not explicitly collateralized. All FNMA debt is treated as mortgage backed in this discussion. FNMA currently is considering the feasibility of marketing pass-through securities for conventional mortgages.

interest. In its "tandem plan" operations, GNMA issues commitments to purchase certain types of loans with interest rates below prevailing market levels and simultaneously sells these mortgages to FNMA or to private investors at prices resulting in market yields, absorbing as subsidy the difference between the prices paid and received.

The second major GNMA activity is its mortgage-backed securities program, which has revolutionized the secondary mortgage market. Under GNMA sponsorship beginning in 1970, the Government guarantees the timely payment of principal and interest on securities issued by private mortgage institutions and backed by pools of Government-insured or -guaranteed mortgages. These pass-through securities are designed to appeal to pension funds and other institutional investors not wishing to originate and service mortgage loans themselves. Pass-throughs are considered eligible real estate investments by most agencies that regulate commercial banks and thrift institutions, and for purposes of determining the tax status of thrift institutions. The securities provide a safe, easily marketable investment with an attractive long-term yield and a high cash flow each month resulting from interest and principal repayment.

GNMA pass-through securities provide for monthly installments of interest on the unpaid balance at the securities' stated certificate rate plus payment of scheduled principal amortization, whether or not collected by the servicer, together with any prepayment of other recoveries of principal. All mortgages placed in a pool must be issued at the same interest rate and cannot be more than one-year old. The GNMA certificate rate is 50 basis points below the contract rate of the underlying mortgages, 44 basis points going to the originator for servicing and 6 basis points to GNMA for providing its guarantee. Pass-throughs are issued in registered form with coupons. The issuer mails checks for interest and principal repayments to holders of record as of the end of each month to reach the recipient by the fifteenth.

Mortgage pools backing GNMA securities most frequently contain FHA-VA single-family mortgages, although pools may also be formed from other types of FHA-insured or VA- and Farmers Home Administration-guaranteed mortgages, subject to somewhat different terms than those described above. Single-family pools are formed in $1 million minimum amounts (pools for other mortgage types may be half that size), but many pools are substantially larger, containing $25 million or more in mortgages. Pass-through securities are issued in $25,000 minimum denominations with $5,000 increments, although in the national market a round-lot transaction is $1 million.

GNMA pass-through securities are issued by mortgage bankers (who account for three fourths of the annual total) as well as by thrift institutions and commercial banks that originate FHA-VA mortgages. Instead of selling the mortgages outright or financing them through deposits or other debt, the issuer forms a pool, sells pass-through securities, and continues to earn servicing income on the loans. Newly issued securities are marketed for immediate or forward delivery either directly by the issuer or, more typically, a securities dealer. There is a sizable annual volume of trading in seasoned issues, a direct result of the large volume of outstanding securities and their widespread distribution among all types of investors. In addition, there is an active futures market for the securities on the major commodities exchanges.

Until recently, GNMA pass-throughs have dominated the mortgage-backed securities market. There are over 800 active issuers of GNMA pass-throughs and over 33,000 pools. New issues in 1978 totaled $15 billion, financing over half of all new FHA-VA home loans and raising the outstanding unpaid principal balance of GNMA pass-throughs to $52 billion. In the first nine months of 1979, GNMA issues totaled over $16 billion.

FNMA and GNMA securities backed mainly by Government-guaranteed mortgages have dominated the mortgage-backed securities market during the past decade. Now, over 90 percent of all newly originated FHA-VA mortgages on single-family homes is placed in pass-throughs or sold to FNMA, but FHA-VA fixed-payment mortgages represent a declining fraction of total home loans. In May 1979, GNMA began to guarantee pass-through securities backed by graduated payment mortgages[3] insured by FHA, a potential fast-growth area for GNMA securities. However, the key to continued rapid growth of mortgage-backed securities lies in the conventional loan market and the housing bonds of state and local governments.

Mortgage-backed securities have been used only recently to finance conventional loans, which account for four-fifths of all home mortgages. The FHLMC, created by the Congress in 1970 and wholly owned by the Federal Home Loan Banks (FHLBs), has as its primary goal the development of a national secondary market in conventional mortgages. As a general rule, the FHLMC purchases conventional mortgage loans from savings and loan associations (four-fifths of its total purchases), mutual savings banks, commercial banks, and mortgage banks. At first the FHLMC purchased mainly participations and whole loans for its own portfolio, financing the acquisitions by borrowing from the Treasury and the FHLBs and by issuing its own mortgage-backed bonds. In 1974, however, the focus of its operations was shifted toward the sale of mortgage participation certificates (PCs) and guaranteed mortgage certificates (GMCs).

In many respects, PCs are similar to GNMA pass-through securities, although they are not backed by the full faith and credit of either the United States Government or the FHLBs. These certificates represent ownership interest in pools of conventional mortgages purchased by the FHLMC, which guarantees the monthly pass-through of interest, scheduled amortization of principal, and ultimate repayment of principal. Like GNMA pass-throughs, PCs are considered direct mortgage investments for most tax and regulatory purposes. PCs are marketed directly by the FHLMC and through a group of securities dealers who also maintain a secondary market in seasoned issues. The originator retains the obligation to service the loans for a fee of 3/8 percent and the spread between the price paid and received by the FHLMC, usually 30 to 50 basis points, provides a return to cover FHLMC insurance and administration costs.

---

[3] Graduated payment mortgages are a new and rapidly growing type of instrument having a lower monthly payment in the first few years than standard fixed-payment home loans.

PCs differ from GNMA pass-throughs in several respects because they are issued by the FHLMC rather than by individual mortgage lenders throughout the country. The mortgage pool underlying a typical PC comprises about 5,000 mortgage loans with a total value of about $100 million to $300 million. A given pool may contain mortgages issued at several rates, allowing PCs to contain loans issued in different sections of the country. Although the minimum PC denomination is $100,000, $5 million denominations are particularly popular since the unpaid principal balance will remain comfortably above the $1 million round-lot trading size for many years. In 1978, $5.6 billion in PCs was issued, bringing the outstanding unpaid balance to $10.2 billion at the year-end.

In 1974 the FHLMC created a new type of instrument, the GMC, to provide a mortgage investment instrument with much of the convenience of a bond. Like a GNMA pass-through, a GMC represents ownership interest in a pool of mortgages, but the interest on a GMC is paid semiannually and principal repayments are made annually, like some sinking fund bonds. The FHLMC guarantees timely payment on interest, full payment of principal, and promises to repurchase any principal that remains unretired after fifteen years. At irregular intervals, GMCs backed by mortgage pools totaling $200 million-$300 million are issued in minimum denominations of $100,000. In 1978 new issues totaled $700 million, bringing the outstanding unpaid balance to about $1.9 billion by the year-end.

NEW TYPES OF MORTGAGE-BACKED SECURITIES

The success of mortgage-backed securities guaranteed by the Federally related credit agencies has encouraged private mortgage originators to issue both mortgage-backed bonds and pass-through securities without Government involvement. Since 1975, thrift institutions have issued mortgage-backed bonds patterned after bonds issued by various Government-related credit agencies. The securities are similar in most respects to other corporate bonds. They are general obligations of the issuer with a stated maturity and fixed semi-annual interest payments. The bonds are collateralized by pools of mortgages, with a covenant obligating the issuer to maintain a stated level of collateral even when discounted to market value and adjusted for amortization and prepayments. Collateral maintenance levels are normally so high (usually 150 percent or more) that mortgage-backed bonds receive highest ratings.

Mortgage-backed bonds allow thrift institutions to borrow against their mortgage assets to obtain funds for new loans during periods of slow deposit growth, instead of borrowing from commercial banks or the FHLBs. These bonds are particularly attractive when the cost of alternative financing is above the bond rate, provided mortgage yields are higher than bond yields. Moreover, since the thrift institutions do not sell the mortgages outright, they may pledge old, relatively low-yielding loans as collateral without showing capital losses on their books. Most mortgage-backed bonds are issued with original maturities of five to ten years, roughly comparable to the expected average maturity of new mortgages. On the whole, these bonds allow thrift institutions to match more closely their asset and liability maturities and to broaden their funding base. Mortgage-backed bonds issued publicly in 1978 totaled $465 million, bringing the amount outstanding to $1.7 billion. In 1979, bonds totaling $1.0 billion were issued publicly in the first nine months.

Mortgage-related bonds have also become a prominent feature in the tax-exempt sector of the capital markets. State governments have supported single-family housing through general obligation bonds for a number of years (usually associated with veterans' benefit programs) and since 1970 through revenue bonds issued by housing finance agencies.[4] Housing-related revenue bonds were first issued by municipalities in 1978. These three types of bonds, designed to appeal to individuals and institutions who purchase other types of tax-exempt municipal securities, are used mainly to finance loans for low- and middle-income housing at below-market rates. New issues supporting single-family housing totaled $4.7 billion in 1978 and $6.5 billion in the first nine months of 1979.

The use of tax-exempt securities to finance mortgage lending has sparked considerable public debate. Proponents assert that the tax-exempt mortgage bond programs benefit the home buyer, the locality, and the housing industry by making homeownership affordable to more people. As a result, local neighborhoods are stabilized and, with demand pushing house prices higher, the tax base of the locality is enhanced. Critics charge that the use of tax-exempt bonds to finance housing increases borrowing costs to state and local governments for other purposes and reduces Treasury tax revenues and that mortgage funds generated in some programs are not channeled to those most in need of government subsidies. In response to these objections, Congressional legislation, H.R. 3712 and related bills, was introduced in April 1979 to restrict the use of tax-exempt revenue bonds to finance homeownership. The uncertainty about the outcome of this pending legislation has raised questions about the tax status of forthcoming issues.

In a promising application of mortgage-backed securities to the conventional loan market, banks, savings and loan associations, and subsidiaries of private mortgage insurance companies have placed a number of publicly issued pass-through securities (PIPs)[5] without any form of Government guarantee. PIPs provide a means for market pricing and public distribution of mortgage loans, substituting for private placement of whole loans and participations, or sale to a Government-related agency. The issuer forms a mortgage pool or trust, obtains private mortgage and hazard insurance and secures a rating, and sells the securities through an underwriting group—often to customers who regularly buy corporate bonds.

---

[4] Although six states formed housing finance agencies before 1970, only the New York housing finance agency issued bonds prior to that date. Such agencies are now found in forty states.

[5] A number of issuers have coined names for their securities—Connie Mac (Ticor), Pennie Mae (PMI), Maggie Mae (MGIC).

The first PIP was sold by Bank of America in September 1977, followed quickly by an offering of the First Federal Savings and Loan Association of Chicago in October. Securities totaling $728 million were sold in 1978 by four issuers and an additional $445 million was publicly placed in the first nine months of 1979. In a major extension of this market, "conduit" companies recently have begun to issue pass-through securities backed by conventional mortgages and serviced by thirty to forty lenders. This allows smaller originators access to the market, creating pools with broad geographic diversity.

PIPs offer several advantages over other loan sale alternatives. Public distribution provides a broader and deeper investment base than private placements, allowing large amounts of loans to be sold quickly at relatively attractive rates. In addition, details of the offering can be tailored to match the needs of the issuer rather than those of the Government-related credit agencies. For example, some agencies currently place limits on the maximum size of individual home loans that may be pooled as well as limit the amount of commitments accepted from any one seller. The agencies purchase loans in quantities determined by their own investment goals and require sellers to contract for delivery well in advance. Finally, many issuers feel they can provide insurance and administration at lower cost than the spread retained by the FHLMC when it issues PCs.

FORWARD COMMITMENTS

PCs and GNMA securities are sold mainly for forward delivery and settlement. These forward commitment procedures present a variety of new portfolio management options to investors more familiar with the immediate delivery conventions of the bond and equity markets. The necessity for a forward market arises from the special problems of originating home loans and packaging them for sale to final investors. Mortgage companies, thrift institutions, and other mortgage originators make commitments to lend funds in the future to builders and developers and to home buyers, although the borrowers are not obligated to take down the loans. Since home loans have long maturities and are often large relative to the borrowers' net worth, the time-consuming process of checking collateral and creditworthiness is particularly important.

It may take three to six months to accumulate a bundle of completed mortgage loans and process the necessary paperwork before selling the loans to a final investor. During this time, a mortgage originator bears the risk of capital loss if interest rates rise. For highly levered mortgage companies, even a small rate increase could be disastrous, making a purchase commitment from a future buyer desirable in many cases. "Firm" commitments require the loan seller to deliver mortgages at the commitment price; under a "standby" commitment, delivery is optional at the seller's discretion. Standby commitments are usually associated with more distant delivery horizons (often twelve months) and are accompanied by a nonrefundable fee of about 1 percent. To meet the demand for purchase commitments, particularly for twelve-month horizons or during tight money periods, standby commitments are often issued by banks and thrift institutions that may not desire delivery of the underlying mortgages but are willing to bear some price risk in return for the commitment fee. This can be done by fixing the strike price—the price at which delivery is made—at such a low level that the delivery option will not be exercised unless rates increase sharply.

In 1968 FNMA instituted a program for market determination of strike prices on its firm and standby forward commitments. FNMA now holds bi-weekly auctions in which lenders specify the rate at which they will offer various dollar amounts of mortgages. The volume of accepted offers is based on FNMA's cost of funds and the general tone of the mortgage market. Commitments are issued to successful bidders offering mortgages to FNMA at the highest yields (lowest strike prices). Since October 1971 four-month firm commitments have been auctioned biweekly, and since October 1972 twelve-month convertible standby commitments have been available as well. At the loan seller's option, these standby commitments may be converted to firm four-month commitments at the average price established in the most recent auction. These auction-market commitment procedures have not been imitated by other government or private loan purchasers, but an active over-the-counter forward market for pass-through securities serves much the same purpose.

This over-the-counter forward market—often called the "cash" market to differentiate it from the GNMA futures market on the commodities exchanges—is most active for GNMA securities, but similar procedures are followed in all pass-through markets. Dealers issue firm commitments to purchase or sell securities with stated certificate rates for delivery one to six months or more in the future.[6] The bid-asked spread is normally 1/8 percent for recently issued securities and somewhat higher for seasoned issues. Dealers may hedge their commitments with each other, with final investors, or in the futures market.

Some dealers also offer standby commitments that are essentially "put" options traded over the counter.[7] A potential seller of GNMA securities obtains a standby purchase commitment from the dealer for a negotiated fee, about 1 percent for the popular twelve-month contract. The strike price is

---

[6] These forward interest rates must be adjusted to get an unbiased estimate of future mortgage rates. As in any forward market for a durable commodity, forward prices tend to be lower than the cash prices expected to prevail on the delivery date when the cost of carry—anticipated capital gains plus any accrued interest less short-term interest rates and storage costs—is positive. With the usual upward-sloping yield curve and an unchanged interest rate forecast, forward commitment prices would normally be below prices quoted for immediate delivery.

[7] Although there is still some confusion on this point, the Commodity Futures Trading Commission is not expected to treat GNMA forwards as leverage instruments falling under its regulation. However, most regulations of financial institutions treat forward commitments as "puts" that may be questioned by examiners.

usually negotiated at a spread below the firm forward commitment price. The dealer may offset such a commitment by obtaining a standby commitment from a potential buyer, passing along most or all of the commitment fee.

Futures contracts—similar in many ways to firm GNMA forward commitments—may be arranged on the Chicago Board of Trade (CBT) and the Amex Commodities Exchange (ACE). At each exchange, contracts are available for delivery at three-month intervals going forward about two and one-half years. Delivery is guaranteed by the exchange, reducing the risk of delivery failures, and investors are required to post margin in the form of cash, securities, or a letter of credit. Contracts are evaluated at current market prices—marked to market—each day, and a maintenance margin is required to cover accumulated losses.

The contracts are issued in terms of a standard 8 percent GNMA certificate rate, but pass-throughs bearing other rates are deliverable according to an established price adjustment schedule. Because this schedule does not preserve equality of true yield to maturity for securities with different certificate rates, market participants generally find it advantageous to deliver a security with the highest allowable certificate rate. Under the new CBT contract and the ACE contract, only securities selling at or below par are deliverable, so that the "8 percent future", in fact, trades as if it were a contract for a GNMA issued at the current certificate rate.[8]

Because GNMA securities are Government backed, the forward market is exempt from most SEC (Securities and Exchange Commission) regulations. Unfortunately, it also has been associated with several well-publicized financial failures, leading to moves toward a restructuring of market practices.[9] Some dealers now request initial margin and mark outstanding contracts to market, requiring maintenance margins to cover accumulated losses.[10] Dealers also attempt to monitor the credit risk of customers, but a dealer generally has no means to determine a customer's total market exposure on a timely basis.

The risks inherent in issuing forward commitments for the purchase of pass-through securities (or taking the long side of a forward or futures contract) have caused regulators to question whether such activities are consistent with the fiduciary responsibilities of banks and thrift institutions. Firms

---

[8] Under the original CBT contract there was no "par cap", so that market participants tended to deliver securities with the highest available certificate rates.

[9] The three most widely publicized problems in GNMA trading have centered on forward commitment speculation resulting in delivery failures: The Winters Government Securities case involved questionable sales practices by a dealer. The University of Houston case resulted from overzealous investment plans of an investment officer. Most recently, the Reliance case involved massive failures by a mortgage banker to meet purchase commitments.

[10] The Justice Department has said that mandatory margin requirements proposed by the Mortgage-Backed Securities Dealers Association could constitute restraint of trade. Various forms of Government- and self-regulation are pending. These issues are discussed at length in *Analysis and Report on Alternative Approaches to Regulating the Trading of GNMA Securities* (November 7, 1978), prepared for GNMA by R. Shriver Associates.

may issue firm commitments with the hope of selling them prior to delivery at a speculative profit and may issue standby contracts for the fee income. Since delayed delivery contracts are an integral part of mortgage lending, the goal of regulation is to prevent abuses, while allowing financial intermediaries to perform this necessary role. To prevent portfolio managers from accumulating larger losses than can be accommodated at the time of settlement, most regulators and market participants support rules requiring all over-the-counter forward contracts to be marked to market and obligating buyers and sellers to post maintenance margins in the form of cash, securities, or letters of credit to cover any accumulated losses.[11] This would reduce the potential for the failure of one firm to create a chain reaction in the market but does little to insure that forward positions taken by individual investors are authorized by top management and are appropriate to the investment goals of the firm. Most market participants agree that, since little cash changes hands immediately, relative to the price exposure that is assumed in entering into a forward contract, operations of financial firms in either the forward or futures markets should be supervised at the highest management level.

OUTLOOK

The mortgage-backed securities market is coming of age. Up to this point, the market has been dominated by bonds issued by FNMA and by GNMA pass-through securities—both backed by FHA-VA loans. However, the relative importance of most types of Government-insured mortgages in the housing market is declining. Future growth of the pass-through market depends on the popularity of pass-through securities sold by the FHLMC and publicly issued by banks, savings and loan associations, and mortgage companies that are financing conventional mortgage loans. A second type of instrument, the mortgage-backed bond, is being used by thrift institutions to gain access to the capital markets, and tax-exempt bonds are being sold by state and local governments to support housing.

Mortgage-backed securities have important implications for economic efficiency and policy. By reducing geographic and institutional barriers to the movement of funds, the market facilitates a more efficient distribution of available financing to areas where housing demand is strongest. By allowing home buyers to compete for funds on favorable terms with corporate and governmental borrowers, the market contributes to general economic efficiency. Both of these effects increase the ability of the capital markets to generate mortgage funds by reducing the dependence of housing finance on interest-sensitive deposit flows. Thus, mortgage-backed securities help moderate the traditional "boom and bust" cycles in the housing sector by spreading the burden of high interest rates more evenly across all sectors of the economy.

[11] There is some feeling that contracts made by an approved mortgage issuer to sell any loans generated within the normal "production cycle" could be exempt from mark-to-market rules without undue risk of speculative abuse.

APPENDIX: ESTIMATING PASS-THROUGH YIELDS AND MATURITIES

The likelihood that many mortgages placed in a pass-through pool will be prepaid sometime before maturity creates uncertainty about the yield and average maturity of such an investment. Yields commonly quoted for pass-through securities are computed assuming there will be no prepayments until the twelfth year, at which time the entire remaining principal balance will be paid off. Monthly payments are assumed to be reinvested at the average yield, compounded monthly, until the end of the twelve-year horizon. This yield calculation probably does not give the best estimate of the rate of return, and a security's average maturity may differ significantly from twelve years.

To obtain a better estimate of the true yield of a pass-through security, a more realistic prepayment assumption must be employed. But, since pass-through securities are a relatively recent innovation, there is little direct prepayment evidence available. One strategy is to use the prepayment history of Federal Housing Administration (FHA) loans as a bench mark against which other mortgage pools may be measured.

Although few pools are likely to pay down precisely at the historical FHA rate, one plausible assumption is that the pattern of prepayments will be the same but will come in proportionately faster or slower. A "100 percent FHA" pool pays down at the historical FHA rate; a "200 percent FHA" pool pays down twice as fast (percentage of remaining balance that is prepaid each month, not dollar amount); a "0 percent FHA" pool has no prepayments (Chart 3).

Existing GNMA pools show a wide variation in prepayment experience. For example, 8 percent GNMA pass-throughs issued on December 1, 1970 had unpaid principal balances after eight and one-half years ranging from 70 to 29 percent of the original investment, corresponding to FHA pay-down rates ranging from 50 to 200 percent. As the various types of pass-through securities have time to establish prepayment track records, it should be possible to determine more precisely which geographic, demographic, and financial factors affect the prepayment profile. Until such fac-

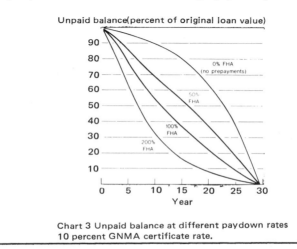

Chart 3 Unpaid balance at different paydown rates
10 percent GNMA certificate rate.

tors are analyzed more fully, buyers of newly issued pass-throughs will be unable to compute expected yields and average maturities with much precision. Similarly, the prepayment rate over the early years of the life of a pool need not give a good estimate of the subsequent prepayment rate.

Some prepayment assumption must be employed to produce a yield estimate well suited for comparison with returns on other types of instruments. If pass-through yields are to be compared with bonds, an adjustment must also be made for semiannual compounding. For example, a 9½ percent GNMA security priced at 96 has a quoted yield of 10.04 percent with the twelve-year paydown calculation. On a "true yield" basis, this security would yield 10.08 percent with a 100 percent FHA paydown or 10.21 percent with a 200 percent paydown. For securities such as this one, selling at prices close to par because they have certificate rates close to current market yields, the assumed prepayment rate does not have a large effect on yield. For securities selling at a deep discount (or premium), however, the prepayment assumption is a critical determinant of yield because the cash flow is assumed to be reinvested at the average yield rather than the certificate rate. As a result, an investor buying a deep discount GNMA pass-through would be willing to pay a premium price for a security backed by a "fast pay" pool expected to prepay at, say, a 400 percent FHA rate.

Because the cash flow from a pass-through security is concentrated in the early years, comparing pass-through yields with returns available in the bond market is not a straightforward exercise. The average maturity of a pass-through security—the proportion of the loan repaid each month times the number of months since the loan was originated—is sensitive to the prepayment assumption. A 9½ percent GNMA pool with no prepayments has an average life of 21.6 years. The average life under a standard twelve-year prepayment assumption is about 11.2 years, two years shorter than the 13.1-year average with a 100 percent FHA paydown. For a 200 percent FHA paydown, the average life drops to 8.9 years. These calculations suggest that most pass-through yields are roughly comparable to returns available on intermediate-term bonds.*

However, since pass-throughs return both principal and interest throughout their lives, reinvestment options must be considered carefully in light of interest rate expectations. When short-term interest rates are higher than the certificate rates on pass-throughs, fast pay pools appear attractive but, if short-term rates are expected to fall, investors would value such pools less highly. Rather than comparing pass-through yields with returns on bonds of similar average maturity, analysts can provide more useful information for investment decisions by comparing pass-through yields with returns on strips of bonds of various maturities weighted to produce a similar expected cash flow. This information may then be combined with estimates of possible reinvestment options, to decide whether the cash flow and yield characteristics of a particular pass-through are superior to the alternative presented by a given bond or combination of bonds.

---

*The calculation of average maturity and yield was recently discussed by Dexter Senft in "The 'True Yield' of a Pass-Through Security", *The Mortgage Banker* (September 1979).

Part I
ASSET MANAGEMENT

D. INVESTMENTS

The articles by Jimmie R. Monhollon and Jane F. Nelson describe the investment characteristics of Treasury bills and securities issued by agencies of the Federal government. Because of their high quality and liquidity, Treasury bills represent one of the main components of a bank's investment portfolio. Like Treasury bills, agency securities are exceptionally high in quality and, in the case of most short-term issues, are highly marketable and liquid. Also, like bills, most agency securities may be used to collateralize certain types of deposits and satisfy reserve requirements of some states.

One of the most crucial aspects of managing the investment account is the maturity policy. Ronald D. Watson addresses this issue by fo-

cusing on the liquidity and profit tradeoffs of various maturity strategies. Important operating constraints are imposed on the investment portfolio of most banks through so-called pledging requirements. The nature of these constraints and their impact on bank asset composition and liquidity is examined in Ronald A. Ratti's article. The significance of the bank investment account is underscored by the fact that regulatory agencies strongly advocate that each bank develop a written investment policy statement to guide day-to-day operations. In the article by David L. Hoffland, a model investment policy statement is presented. The detailed model may be readily adapted to meet the needs of individual banks.

TREASURY BILLS*

Jimmie R. Monhollon

12

For many years Treasury bills have been the single most important money market instrument. Before World War II the amount of these bills outstanding rarely exceeded $2.5 billion. By 1945 the total had risen to over $17 billion, and by June 1976 the outstanding volume was $161.2 billion. Treasury bills, which are the most widely held liquid investment, are an important tool in debt management and in the execution of monetary policy.

WHAT IS A TREASURY BILL?

A Treasury bill is an obligation of the United States Government to pay the bearer a fixed sum after a specified number of days from the date of issue. These debt instruments are sold by the Treasury at a discount through competitive bidding, and the return to the investor is the difference between the purchase price and the face or par value. The rate of return on a Treasury bill of a given maturity is calculated by dividing the discount by par and ex-

*Reprinted from *Instruments of the Money Market*, 4th edition, edited by Timothy Q. Cook, 1977, pp. 13-20, with permission from the Federal Reserve Bank of Richmond.

pressing this percentage as an annual rate, using a 360-day year. For example, a price of $97.45 per $100 of face amount for a 91-day bill would produce an annual rate of return equal to

$$\frac{100-97.45}{100} \times \frac{360}{91} = 10.088 \text{ per cent.}$$

Such a rate of return cannot be compared directly with the yield to maturity of a coupon-bearing issue having 91 days to maturity, since yields to maturity on coupon issues are calculated by using the purchase price instead of par as the divisor and by using a 365- instead of a 360-day year.

Treasury bills are issued in a variety of maturities and denomination tailored to meet the needs of a diverse group of investors seeking both liquidity and income in a single investment. Bills are currently offered on a regular schedule with maturities of 91 days, 182 days, and 52 weeks. The Treasury has also made occasional offerings of tax anticipation bills with maturities that have ranged up to nine months. In addition, the Treasury has at times "reopened" or sold additional amounts of outstanding maturities of bills. Reopenings are almost always for maturities that fall after one of the five major tax payment dates and, like tax anticipation bills, are designed to help finance the Treasury's requirements until tax payments are received. For this reason reopenings are generally referred to as "cash management" bills. Reopenings have been for bills with maturity dates as far away as 139 days. Usually, however, they are for bills maturing within a month, sometimes as soon as nine days; in such cases, they are often called "short-dated" bills. When the Treasury reopens a series of maturities at one time, as it has done occasionally, the bills sold are called a "strip" of bills. Treasury bills are currently issued in five denominations ranging from $10,000 to $1,000,000, although at times they have been issued in smaller denominations. All may be exchanged at maturity for new issues or redeemed for cash.

HISTORY

In their modern form, U.S. Treasury bills were first offered in 1929. The first issue, for $100 million, was sold in December 1929 and had a maturity of 90 days. From then until 1934, 30-, 60-, and 90-day maturities were offered. Between February 1934 and October 1937 the Treasury experimented with maturities of 182 days to 273 days in order to reduce the frequency with which they had to be rolled over. In 1937, largely at the insistence of commercial banks, the Treasury reverted to exclusive issue of 91-day bills. Then in December 1958 these were supplemented with six-month bills in the regular weekly auctions.

In 1959 the Treasury undertook to establish a pattern of one-year maturities coming due on a quarterly basis. The initial offering was for $2.0 billion, and subsequent offerings ranged from $1.5 billion to $2.5 billion. Replacement of the quarterly auction with a monthly auction of $1.0 billion of one-year bills began in August 1963. In September 1966 the Treasury added a nine-month maturity to the monthly auction of one-year bills. By offering $500 million of nine-month bills, and $900 million of one-year bills instead of the usual $1.0 billion, the Treasury raised $400 million of new money each month. The nine-month cycle was discontinued in late 1972, however, and since then the only regular bill cycles have been for maturities of 91 days, 6 months, and a year. As new money is needed, depending on the size of Federal borrowing requirements, the Treasury has added to the monthly and weekly bill auctions. In the first half of 1976, monthly sales of 52-week bills averaged $3.0 billion. During the same period, the weekly auctions of 13- and 26-week bills ranged from $5 to $7 billion, with about 40 to 45 per cent of that representing 13-week bills.

AUCTIONING NEW BILLS

New offerings of three- and six-month bills are made each week by the Treasury. Ordinarily, subscriptions, or bids, are invited on Thursdays, and the amounts of the offerings are set at that time. The auction is usually conducted on the following Monday, with delivery and payment on the following Thursday.

Bids, or tenders, in the weekly auctions must be presented at Federal Reserve Banks or their branches, which act as agents for the Treasury, by 1:30 p.m., New York time, on the day of the auction. Bids may be on a competitive or a noncompetitive basis. Competitive bids are usually made by large investors who are in close contact with the market. These bids comprise the largest portion of subscriptions on a dollar basis. In this type of tender the investor states the quantity of bills desired and the price he is willing to pay. A subscriber may enter more than one bid indicating the various quantities he is willing to take at different prices. Individuals and other small investors usually enter noncompetitive bids, which are awarded in full up to $500,000 on both the 91-day and the 182-day bills. Noncompetitive awards are sold at the average price of accepted competitive bids.

Subscription books at the various Federal Reserve Banks and branches close promptly at 1:30 p.m., and the bids are then opened, tabulated, and submitted to the Treasury for allocation. The Treasury first makes all noncompetitive awards. The remainder is then allocated to those competitive bidders submitting the highest offers, ranging downward from the highest bid until the amount offered is allocated. The "stop-out price" is the lowest price, or highest yield, at which bills are awarded. Usually only a portion of the total bids made at this price is accepted. The average issuing price, which is usually closer to the lowest accepted price than to the highest, is then computed on the basis of the competitive bids accepted. In the weekly auction of June 10, 1976, for example, bids for the three-month bills ranged from a high of $98.624 per $100 of face amount (equivalent to an annual rate of 5.444 per cent) to a stop-out price of $98.618 (5.467 per cent). A total of $2,309 million of bids were accepted, $445 million of which were noncompetitive tenders accepted at the average issuing price of $98.620 (5.460 per cent).

By bidding noncompetitively, small investors avoid several risks inherent in competitive bidding. In the first place, they do not risk losing their chance to buy through bidding too low. Nor do they run the risk of bidding too high and paying a price near the top. The dollar amount of noncompetitive awards as a per cent of total awards is generally quite small, usually less than 10 per cent. When market interest rates rise relative to the rates paid at deposit institutions, however, some small investors shift funds out of these institutions into alternative financial assets, such as Treasury bills. This phenomenon, known as "disintermediation," occurred in the late 1960's as market interest rates rose well above those permitted by Regulation Q on time deposits at commercial banks and thrift institutions. As a result, by January 1970 the ratio of noncompetitive to total awards had risen to 32 per cent. In reaction to this development, the Treasury raised the minimum bill award from $1,000 to $10,000. This change was designed to discourage noncompetitive bids by small investors in order to retain the Treasury bill as an instrument for attracting large quantities of funds primarily from institutional investors, to reduce the costs of processing many small subscriptions yielding only a small volume of funds, and to discourage the exodus of funds from financial intermediaries and the mortgage market.

The increase in the minimum bill award to $10,000 has not been entirely successful in deterring disintermediation. The ratio of noncompetitive to total awards continues to respond to interest rate movements, especially when rates rise well above Regulation Q ceilings. In September 1974, for example, when the three-month Treasury bill rate averaged 8 per cent, the share of noncompetitive awards in the 13- and 26-week auctions averaged 20 per cent.

In addition to the weekly auctions, monthly auctions are held for the 52-week bills and special auctions are held for short-dated bills, for other reopenings of outstanding maturities, and for tax anticipation bills. The auction procedure for these bills is similar to the regular weekly auctions of 91- and 182-day bills except that banks are sometimes permitted to make payment for tax bills by crediting their Treasury Tax and Loan Accounts.

ADVANTAGES OF AUCTIONS

Treasury bills are marketed by the Treasury solely through the auction technique. Treasury notes and bonds, however, are sold either using the auction technique or through subscriptions. Under the latter method the Treasury sets a price on the new issue and then receives subscriptions which are allotted completely and/or in part. Prior to sales of certificates, notes, and bonds, the Treasury discusses market conditions with representatives of the Federal Reserve System, Government securities dealers, and investor groups in order to assess the existing demand. An attempt is made to approximate how much the market can absorb in various maturity areas without disrupting price and yield relationships in the market as a whole. Only after such study does the Treasury decide what maturities and how much of each it will offer and what interest rates it will set. Decisions on interest rates are usually delayed until just before the financing is announced in order to appraise the mood of the market more exactly. Otherwise, interest rates might be selected which would either prove unattractive to investors or, conversely, provide them a windfall gain at the Treasury's expense. Under the auction method the Treasury takes the same care to assess market conditions. After doing so, however, it sets a coupon rate on the note or bond and sells the planned amount at the price range necessary to induce investors to purchase the desired amount. Consequently, the actual yield will be greater or less than the coupon rate depending on whether the security is sold at a price below or above the par value.

In general, the auction method is simpler and less time-consuming than the more involved subscription method. In auctions the market establishes a price, making it unnecessary for the Treasury to second-guess market conditions. Also, auctions eliminate the problems associated with oversubscriptions or undersubscriptions. The Treasury merely sets the amount of the offering and the market does the rest. For these reasons the Treasury in recent years has used the auction method not only for bills but also for most new longer-term issues, although it has continued to use periodically the subscription method when it needs to raise large amounts of new money.

Successful use of the auction technique presupposes a market of great depth and breadth. In periods of general market weakness, the market for long-term securities may be so thin that an offer of several hundred million dollars of new securities can not be absorbed without serious price reductions, i.e., yield increases. By contrast, the bill market is enormous and can absorb billions of dollars of new bills with only minimal impact on yields. The great popularity of the Treasury bill as a short-term liquid investment among banks, other financial institutions, nonfinancial corporations, state and local governments, and other investors underlies this characteristic of the bill market. It is largely because of this characteristic that the auction technique is especially suited to Treasury bills.

From the Treasury's standpoint, bill auctions provide an eminently convenient means of raising new cash. As noted above, the Treasury can raise large amounts of new money without upsetting the market and with a minimum of administrative cost. Also, the auctions provide the debt managers with a very flexible tool. When, for example, the Treasury needs new money and the total marketable public debt is close to the statutory limit, it can enter the market quickly and raise small amounts by adding to the supply of bills in the weekly auction. Conversely, it can squeeze under the debt ceiling by allowing bills to run off, that is, by failing to replace the full amount coming due.

Advantages also accrue to investors. Bill auctions are now part of the regular routine of the money market and as such have a minimum impact on investment values. They provide short-term investors with a predictable supply of highly liquid assets in a wide range of maturities.

RELATION TO MONETARY POLICY

Treasury bills perform an important role in the implementation of monetary policy since the Federal Reserve System influences the reserve positions of commercial banks primarily through the purchase and sale of bills. The Federal Reserve's purchases supply reserves to the banking system, and their sales have an opposite effect. While the Federal Reserve can and does operate outside the bill area, as a practical matter most of its purchases and sales must be concentrated in short maturities, principally Treasury bills. In an absolute sense, Federal Reserve transactions are very large and such operations in the relatively thin long-term market would result in wide swings in prices and yields.

INVESTMENT CHARACTERISTICS

Apart from their significance in the implementation of policy, Treasury bills comprise an important element in the general public's assets structure. The private sector's great demand for these bills is attributable chiefly to their high degree of liquidity or "nearness to money." Financial and nonfinancial institutions often find themselves with idle cash balances which may have been built up for payment of taxes or other outstanding debts, or as reserves against any of numerous contingencies. Often it is expedient to put such balances into short-term investments which can earn interest and which can be readily converted to cash with little risk of loss.

Treasury bills neatly fill these requirements. The highly organized market for bills insures their easy convertibility into cash and decreases the risk of loss should the investor need cash before the maturity of the bills. Their short maturities minimize the risk from price fluctuations associated with changing market conditions. Available in the market are dates and, like tax bills which range in maturity from a week or less to one year, and which are therefore appropriate to a variety of short-term investment needs. Moreover, yields on bills are generally competitive with other short-term investments.

Since Treasury bills meet so fully the requirements of a short-term investment, they constitute an important part of commercial banks' "secondary reserves." Through purchase of bills, banks can quickly convert excess reserves into earning assets with little loss of liquidity. Through sales, they can promptly acquire additional funds for lending or for meeting legal reserve requirements.

While selling Treasury bills is a highly convenient way for banks to raise cash, "turnaround" costs may make such sales a relatively unattractive way to cover very short-term reserve needs. Turnaround costs are the costs involved in selling bills one day and buying the same amount of bills back at a later date. In addition to incidental transaction costs such as phone calls and paper work, there are costs which arise because market dealers buy bills at a price slightly lower than the price at which they sell, the spread between the two prices representing their gross profit. Thus, if interest rates do not change, a bank seeking to raise funds for only one day would sell bills at a given price and buy them back the following day at a slightly higher price, simply because of the spread between bid and asked quotations. The typical dealer spread on actively traded Treasury bills, such as the current three- and six-month bills, is 2 to 4 basis points. Four basis points is equivalent to about $0.01 on each $100 par value of three-month bills. Thus a bank would have to pay one cent per $100 more than it received to sell bills one day and buy them back the next. Under such circumstances, the turnaround cost would be one cent per $100, or 3.65 per cent per year, and this cost would be in addition to the loss of interest on the bills. An alternative means of covering the one-day reserve need, say through borrowing Federal funds, would probably prove less costly. In terms of per cent per annum, turnaround costs of bill trading decline sharply the greater the time span between sale and repurchase, since the given cost of one cent per $100 is spread over more days. At the rates used in this example, a one-week turnaround would involve a cost of 0.52 per cent per annum. Thus, the attractiveness of bill sales as a means of raising funds varies with the time over which the funds are needed.

Bank holdings of Treasury bills typically vary seasonally and cyclically. When business is slack and loan demand is shrinking, banks generally turn to Treasury bills as a temporary investment outlet. Conversely, when business is expanding and loan demand is increasing, banks generally liquidate bills in order to expand loans.

Treasury bills are also important to corporations as a temporary investment and a potential source of ready cash. Rising interest rates in the postwar period have induced corporate treasurers to economize cash balances and to seek liquidity, where possible, in income-earning assets. In managing their cash positions, many corporate treasurers have become increasingly sophisticated in projecting future cash flows. Frequently they time the maturities of their short-term investments to coincide with future cash needs. On occasion, however, unforeseen cash needs arise and it becomes necessary to raise money in a hurry. For these purposes, Treasury bills are ideally suited. Bills are an equally advantageous investment for state and local governments in the management of their general funds and retirement funds.

According to the June 1976 Treasury Survey of Ownership, United States Government investment accounts together with the Federal Reserve Banks constituted the largest holder of bills. Other large holders are commercial banks, nonfinancial corporations, state and local governments (general funds), and foreigners.

FEDERAL AGENCY SECURITIES*

Jane F. Nelson

13

In the last decade the importance of the Federal and Federally-sponsored credit agencies in the nation's money and capital markets has grown dramatically. The outstanding debt of these agencies increased from $15.0 billion at the end of 1965 to $117.9 billion in mid-1976. Behind this rapid growth are a number of innovations in Federal budgetary and agency financing practices that have added new dimensions to both primary and secondary markets for agency securities. This article examines briefly the chief characteristics of agency securities, the markets for these securities, and recent developments affecting the relative importance of these markets.

THE ISSUING AGENCIES

Government-sponsored Agencies. Federal Government corporations and agencies, established by law to implement the Federal Government's various lending programs, issue securities to finance their activities. Five privately-owned, Government-sponsored corporations are responsible for most of the

*Reprinted from *Instruments of the Money Market*, 4th edition, edited by Timothy Q. Cook, 1977, pp. 85-93, with permission from the Federal Reserve Bank of Richmond.

growth in the agency market. They are the Federal National Mortgage Association (FNMA), Federal Land Banks, Federal Intermediate Credit Banks, Banks for Cooperatives, and Federal Home Loan Banks (FHLB). Included with the last agency is the Federal Home Loan Mortgage Corporation (FHLMC), all of whose capital stock is owned by the Federal Home Loan Banks. The primary function of the FHLB, the FHLMC, and FNMA is to provide funds to the mortgage and home-building markets. The other three corporations are part of the Farm Credit System, which provides credit primarily to farmers.

Most of the capital stock of the "big five" agencies was originally owned by the Treasury. In all cases, however, the Treasury's holdings have been redeemed and ownership has passed to member organizations and the general public. While the capital stock of the Federal Home Loan Banks has been owned entirely by member savings and loan associations since 1951, the other four agencies only completed the transition to private ownership following the passage of enabling legislation in the fall of 1968.

Federally Operated Agencies. Federally operated agencies include, among others, the Export-Import Bank, the Federal Housing Administration (FHA), Farmers Home Administration, Government National Mortgage Association (GNMA), the Tennessee Valley Authority (TVA), and the U.S. Postal Service. GNMA was established in 1968 to assume special assistance, management, and liquidating functions previously conducted by FNMA. The Export-Import Bank supports U.S. exports through loan guarantees and insurance. The FHA provides a system of mutual mortgage insurance for builders, buyers, and mortgage-lending institutions. As a part of the Department of Agriculture, the Farmers Home Administration extends loans in rural areas for farms, homes, and community facilities. The TVA was established by an Act of Congress to assist the development of the Tennessee River and the surrounding area. The Postal Service has the authority to issue debt obligations as needed to carry out its responsibility of operating the postal system. In contrast to other agencies, the Postal Service obligations are not necessarily guaranteed by the U.S., but may be at the discretion of the U.S. Treasury Department.

The Federal Financing Bank. A development that has had a major impact on the borrowing patterns of virtually all the Federally operated agencies was the establishment of the Federal Financing Bank in 1973. Prior to that time, each of the agencies raised its own funds in the financial markets through the sale of its own individual securities. As a consequence, the financial markets were faced with a growing number and variety of agency debt issues, which had various terms and guarantees. The Federal Financing Bank was established to consolidate the borrowing activity of these agencies. It was believed that it would lower the cost of raising agency funds because of the greater efficiency of the resulting fund-raising operation and the greater marketability of the regular Treasury debt issues sold instead.

The Federal Financing Bank can raise funds by borrowing from the Treasury or by selling its debt directly in the financial markets. The obligations acquired with these funds fall into three categories: debt obligations of on-budget and off-budget Federal agencies; assets sold by Federal agencies to the Federal Financing Bank; and Government-guaranteed borrowing by non-Federal borrowers. In practice, the agencies qualified to raise funds through the Federal Financing Bank include virtually all of the Federally operated credit agencies and one Federally-sponsored agency, the Student Loan Marketing Association.

As of June 1976 the Federal Financing Bank held $22.4 billion of Federal and Federally-sponsored agency obligations. It was originally widely expected that the Federal Financing Bank would raise a significant amount of its funds directly in the financial markets. With the exception of one issue of $1.5 billion of eight-month notes sold in July 1974, however, it has acquired all of its financing directly from the Treasury.

Since the establishment of the Federal Financing Bank, the eligible agencies, whose outstanding securities are described in the remainder of the section, have used it heavily or exclusively as a source of new funds. As of June 1976, seventeen agencies had acquired funds from the Federal Financing Bank. However, four of these agencies—the Farmers Home Administration, the Export-Import Bank, the Postal Service, and the Tennessee Valley Authority—accounted for 83 percent of the total funds supplied by the Federal Financing Bank.

INVESTMENT CHARACTERISTICS

Securities of Government-sponsored and Federally operated agencies consist of short-term notes, debentures, and participation certificates. Neither principal nor interest on most Government-sponsored agency issues is guaranteed by the Federal Government, although both are fully guaranteed by the issuing agencies. In contrast, the issues of Federally operated agencies are fully guaranteed by the Government.

There are three ways in which a new issue may be placed on the market. First, a Fiscal Agent, or middleman, may handle the security and organize his own selling group for distribution. Second, the agency may bypass the Fiscal Agent and place the issue directly with one or more syndicates. Third, the agency may sell the issue directly to the public. In each of these three cases the rate may be fixed, auctioned, or negotiated.

The eligibility of agency issues as investments of regulated financial institutions and as collateral for public deposits depends, to some extent, on the guaranteed or non-guaranteed status of the agency, and the maturity and marketability of the individual issue. Most agency issues are eligible as collateral for Treasury Tax and Loan Accounts and other public deposits. A few are acceptable collateral for all types of accounts which require a specific pledge of Treasury securities. Some, but not all, are eligible as collateral for Federal Reserve advances, and there are some which qualify as legal reserves of savings and loan associations.

Most agency securities bear a fixed rate of interest which, with the exception of the securities of the Farmers Home Administration, is paid semi-annually. Short-term discount notes, which pay interest equal to the difference between the discount price and the par value, were being offered by three agencies in 1976. Two of these, the FHLB and FNMA, have been selling these notes for many years. They were joined in January 1975 by the Farm Credit System, which began selling Consolidated Systemwide Discount Notes. As of June 1976 outstanding discount notes of these agencies totalled almost $3 billion.

The average maturity of Government-sponsored and Federal agency debt has lengthened considerably since 1969, as shown in the chart. In 1969 and 1970, agency financing was heavily concentrated in short-term issues to avoid being locked into long-term debt at the relatively high interest rates then prevailing. In 1971 and 1972 the agencies, primarily FNMA and the Federal Home Loan Banks, took advantage of lower interest rates to float longer-term issues and thus extend the average maturity of their outstanding issues. At the end of 1973 the proportion of agency debt maturing in less than a year was 30 percent. Since then this proportion has changed little; as of June 1976, it was 31.9 percent. Although the proportion of agency issues competing directly in the money market has declined, the volume of agency debt maturing in less than one year, which was $29.9 billion in June 1976, has continued to rise. The growth in overall agency debt plus the need to maintain a balanced debt structure should insure a key role for agency issues in the money market.

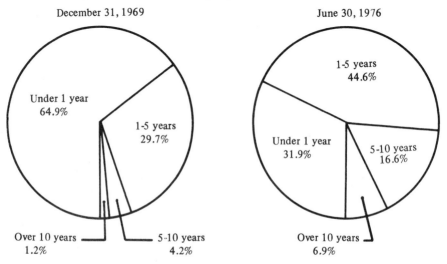

Maturity Distribution of Federal Agency Securities. Source: Treasury Bulletin

December 31, 1969

June 30, 1976

Under 1 year 64.9%

1-5 years 29.7%

Over 10 years 1.2%

5-10 years 4.2%

1-5 years 44.6%

Under 1 year 31.9%

5-10 years 16.6%

Over 10 years 6.9%

Interest income and principal on most agency issues are subject to all Federal taxes. Some agency issues are exempt from state and local taxes except inheritance and gift taxes. Others, however, are not exempt from any taxes. This is true of obligations of the Farmers Home Administration and securities issued directly or indirectly by FNMA and GNMA.

Call features also vary. Some agency issues are noncallable while others are callable by the issuing agency after a specified period of time. Export-Import Bank notes offer the investor the option of reselling the notes to the agency under certain conditions. Holders of Farmers Home Administration notes may extend the maturity of the notes or redeem them after a specified initial period.

CERTIFICATES OF PARTICIPATION

A certificate of participation (PC) represents a beneficial interest in a pool of agency loans or mortgages. It is a formal credit instrument carrying a contractual interest obligation on a specified principal. In contrast to an outright sale of assets in which the title to the asset actually is transferred to the investor, the investor does not acquire title to any of the pooled assets at any time. Rather, the issuing agency continues to hold the pooled loans and to receive interest and principal payments on them. These payments, in turn, are used to service the certificates. The Commodity Credit Corporation initiated sales of certificates of participation in a pool of crop loans in 1953, and the Export-Import Bank began selling participations in its loan portfolio in 1962. But the first sale of certificates of participation by FNMA in November 1964 market their beginning as a significant new instrument of agency financing.

With the passage of the Sales Participation Act of 1966, this method of financing was broadened significantly to include the pooling of assets of at least ten Governmental departments and agencies. The eligible loans include credit extended to farmers, small businesses, veterans, colleges, and numerous types of building projects. Under the terms of the Sales Participation Act of 1966, certificates of participation are, in effect, guaranteed. The law authorizes the selling agency to make "indefinite and unlimited" drawings on the Treasury, if indeed, to service the certificates. Because of this provision, the Attorney General of the United States has designated all participation certificates as direct obligations of the United States. By the end of 1966, about $39 billion of loans were eligible for pooling.

Prior to the implementation of the unified budget in fiscal 1969, certificate sales were not designated as debt in Governmental bookkeeping procedures. Proceeds from these sales were returned to the Treasury to be credited proportionately to the lending authorizations of the agencies represented in the pool. For budgetary purposes proceeds from the sales were counted as negative expenditures, and the budget was reduced correspondingly.

Under the old budgetary system, PC sales expanded rapidly and the volume outstanding reached a peak of $11.2 billion in August 1968. This was greater than the volume of securities outstanding for any single agency. Under the unified budget, however, PC's are considered an integral part of direct Federal debt, and their use has declined sharply. As of mid-1976, only $4.7 billion of PC's were outstanding.

PRIMARY MARKET

To facilitate primary market sales, most agencies have under contract a Fiscal Agent in New York City. One or more agencies may use the same Agent. When an offering is to be made, the Fiscal Agency assembles his selling group of securities dealers, brokerage houses, and dealer banks. Unlike syndicates formed for the sale of a specific stock or bond issue, members of the Agent's selling group do not bid against each other. Rather, each agency offering is made through only one selling group. To establish the price or price range of the new issues, the Fiscal Agent consults with the members of the selling group, the Treasury, the Trading Desk of the Federal Reserve Bank of New York, and the issuing agency regarding maturity, amount, coupon, and price. When the sale date arrives, the price is telegraphed by the Agent to the members of the group who then communicate subscriptions to the Agent. The Agent determines the allotments, which are usually a fraction of investor subscriptions.

This method of sale is used primarily by the five large Federally-sponsored agencies that account for the bulk of agency financing. Other agencies, almost all of which now are acquiring their funds from the Federal Financing Bank, often used other methods. For example, the Farmers Home Administration sold notes, representing long-term insured loans to farmers, directly to investors, primarily commercial banks. The Farmers Home Administration acts as a middleman between farmers and investors, servicing the loan and collecting interest and principal payments, which are forwarded to the owner of the note. The Export-Import Bank sold participations in its loan pool directly to commercial banks on an allotment basis, but in February 1967 it marketed a large issue through a syndicate for the first time. The Tennessee Valley Authority employed the auction method for selling its short-term paper. Certificates of participation were generally sold through syndicates headed by large brokerage houses and dealer banks.

SECONDARY MARKET

Some agency issues have an active secondary market while others do not. Obligations of the Federal Land Banks, the Federal Intermediate Credit Banks, the Banks of Cooperatives, the Federal Home Loan Banks, and the

Federal National Mortgage Association have well-established secondary markets. Dealers' inventories usually include large amounts of these securities. The spread between the bid and offered prices is narrow on short-term issues of these agencies, and trades of $1.0 to $5.0 million can generally be made without upsetting the market.

The secondary market for issues due in five or more years is a different story. Long-term maturities are usually available in comparatively small amounts, and the spread between bid and offered price is often as large as one dollar per hundred of face amount. Consequently, when new issues have been placed with investors, the secondary market has been able to give only a rough indication of the issues' current value. Actual trades, particularly of large amounts, are often negotiated on an individual basis.

In December 1966 the Federal Open Market Committee, pursuant to an Act of Congress, authorized the use of repurchase agreements involving agency obligations in its open market operations. These agreements are similar to those involving direct obligations of the United States insofar as terms and conditions are concerned. In August 1971 the Committee voted to conduct outright transactions in Federal agency securities. These developments not only increased the means available to the System for supplying and absorbing reserves but also tended to strengthen and broaden the secondary market for agencies.

Secondary sales of securities of smaller agencies are arranged in various ways. In the case of Farmers Home Administration notes, at least one dealer has made a special effort to provide a secondary market by "packaging" notes of smaller denominations into larger units for large investors.

Secondary market activity in agency issues has kept pace with the growth in the outstanding supply of agency debt. Daily average gross dealer transactions in agency securities grew steadily over the last decade from $140 million in 1965 to $1,043 million in 1975. About 37 percent of the 1975 dealer transactions were accounted for by issues maturing within one year. Daily average dealer positions in agency securities rose over the same period, although more erratically, from $337 million in 1965 to $939 million in 1975. Reflecting the relatively greater growth of longer-term agency issues, the percentage of dealer positions represented by issues maturing in less than a year declined from 69 percent in 1965 to 47 percent in 1975.

DEMAND

Agency issues have many desirable features; in particular, they have a very low degree of default risk and in many cases have well-developed secondary markets. It is not surprising, therefore, that the demand for them is broadly based. In fact, they are close substitutes for U.S. Government securities and, like U.S. securities, are held by virtually all sectors of the economy. A precise breakdown of relative shares is difficult, since in the Treasury's Survey of Ownership over half of the total outstanding are included in the residual "all other" category, which includes individuals, commercial bank trust departments, and all other institutions not covered by the Survey. Undoubtedly individuals hold a significant share. Among the reporting categories, the largest holder of agency issues throughout the history of the Survey has been commercial banks, which held 20.0 percent of the total as of June 1976. Next in line at that time were U.S. Government accounts and Federal Reserve Banks with 8.9 percent and state and local governments (including general and pension funds) with 7.0 percent.

The spectacular growth in Federal agency financing over the past decade emerges as the salient factor in the agency market. The growth of the Farm Credit System, FNMA, and the FHLB has been particularly rapid. The outstanding debt of the Farm Credit System rose $23.9 billion from 1965 to mid-1976. Over the same period the outstanding debt of FNMA and the FHLB rose $43.7 billion. The growth in the debt of these two agencies reflected their attempt to cushion the impact of rising interest rates on the residential mortgage market. In 1969, 1973, and 1974, three years in which the mortgage market was adversely affected by rising interest rates, these two agencies together raised $8.0 billion, $12.9 billion, and $12.2 billion of new funds.

The boom in agency financing has undoubtedly contributed to a broader and more active secondary market, thereby increasing the marketability of many agency issues. The average differentials between agency and U.S. Government short-term yields were 15 to 30 basis points in 1975 and 1976, lower than in most previous years. These relatively low differentials could reflect the enhanced marketability of agency issues, although it is difficult to say for sure since the relative yields on agencies and U.S. Governments also may be affected by other factors such as relative supplies. An unusually large supply of new U.S. Government debt was sold in 1975 and 1976 while the supply of new agency debt was quite moderate.

BANK BOND MANAGEMENT: THE MATURITY DILEMMA*

Ronald D. Watson

14

Had Gilbert and Sullivan been as familiar with managing bank investments as they were with policemen and pirates, they might well have intoned "a banker's [policeman's] lot is not a happy one."[1] The meter of this change of phrasing might have caused them some problems, but those difficulties pale when compared to the headaches of managing millions of dollars of government securities investments in today's financial markets. Recently bank investment officers have become aware that this complex job requires more than simply understanding the financial markets in which they ply their trade. They must also discern how their superiors will measure the success of their bond management performance. Recent developments in banking research suggest that the bond management script may need to be rewritten before future performances. At a minimum there are ways to make the leading role—that of the bond account manager—easier to play.

*Reprinted from the *Business Review*, March 1972, pp. 23-29, with permission from the Federal Reserve Bank of Philadelphia and the author.

[1] William S. Gilbert and Arthur Sullivan, *The Pirates of Penzance; or the Slave of Duty*, Act II.

SETTING THE STAGE:
BANK LIQUIDITY MANAGEMENT

Banks, just like any other business, come upon times when they could use more hard cash. When a bank wants money, say to meet a cash outflow, it has many sources to tap. Cash balances not currently held to meet reserve requirements might be reduced, additional deposits solicited, loan outflows curtailed, temporary borrowings made from the Federal Reserve Bank, or portions of the bond portfolio sold. As this incomplete list of possibilities indicates, management can convert earning assets into cash or acquire new liabilities to meet cash demands. The choice depends on the relative cost of the alternatives. This process is called *liquidity management*.

Before the mid-1960s, techniques for managing bank liquidity focused on *selling* assets, such as bonds, to generate additional cash. However, considerable attention has been devoted recently to solving these liquidity problems exclusively by *buying short-term liabilities* in the money markets as funds are needed. This strategy is known as *liability management*. Awareness and use of this option has added a new dimension to managing a bank's liquidity. Bankers now have more flexibility in meeting unexpected cash demands because this borrowing power enables them to avoid selling bonds or other assets when they find that prices are unfavorable.

However, the simple fact that these money markets are now well-developed sources of financing doesn't make them the most economical method for alleviating every financial pinch. The credit crunches of '66 and '70 showed the folly of presuming that money markets can accommodate all the banking community's liquidity demands at the borrowing rates it is willing to pay. Thus, bank assets, particularly government securities, and the men who control them continue to play key roles in bank liquidity management.

The Role of Government Bonds. Cash, U.S. Treasury securities (bills, notes, and bonds), government agency bonds, municipal bonds, and loans all have some value for meeting liquidity needs. Just as a playbill lists actors in order of appearance, the balance sheet ranking above suggests the probable order in which assets would be converted to cash and applied to satisfying a liquidity problem.

Cash is the most readily usable liquid asset, but much of a bank's cash is likely to be tied up meeting legal reserve requirements. Justifying an increase in the cash account beyond minimums required for reserves and daily business is difficult because the bank receives no income from this asset. At the other extreme, loans are a costly source of liquidity. There is no formal market in which to dispose of these obligations cheaply and easily. Hence, using loans to meet a liquidity pinch is impractical except as a last resort.

The assets which remain—the bank's portfolios of government securities—are a more practical source of liquidity. These bonds are formal obligations of borrowers who are financially sound, which can be traded in relatively well-organized markets. Some are more marketable than others, of course, but all can be converted into cash with little difficulty. The Treasury security, because of its ready marketability, has become the most common source of asset liquidity used by the men who manage bond portfolios at commercial banks.

The Role of the Bond Portfolio Manager. The man running the bond portfolio show has to be a first-rate director. His job is balancing the bank's liquidity requirements against bank earnings. An important part of this balancing act involves shaping the *maturity distribution of bonds*—the balance of short-, intermediate-, and long-term issues—in the securities portfolio.

There are no easy rules that will allow a banker to set a maturity distribution which enables him to meet cash outflows at a minimum cost. Sometimes short-term borrowings will be the cheapest and easiest source of funds. At other times the banker may be unable to use that market at all. Irregularities in the securities markets may make it advisable to raise cash by selling long-term rather than short-term bonds. A desire to take capital gains or capital losses for tax purposes may affect the selection of maturities to sell. Further, the choice of bonds to sell might depend on what the banker wants to leave in his securities portfolio for future liquidity protection. Despite the diverse circumstances, a bond portfolio manager's job in shaping the maturity distribution of the portfolio ultimately comes down to matching returns against risks.

ACT ONE: THE UNCERTAIN WORLD OF THE ACCOUNT MANAGER

The curtain rises with the bond manager at his desk scratching his head over the bewildering choice of bond maturities before him. In choosing which assets to hold and how long to hold them, he is out to achieve the highest possible returns for the bank without exposing it to unwanted risks. But this task is easier said than done. It is a simple fact of life that a portfolio which offers the expectation of above-average returns—either in the form of interest or capital gains—normally brings higher risks. The uncertainty of future interest rates lies behind much of this problem of balancing risks and returns.

A Problem with Interest Rates. Changes in interest rates cause changes in bank earnings and in the value of the portfolio. Thus, the vagaries of interest rates involve the portfolio of the manager in two kinds of troublesome risks: 1) the variations occurring in the interest income earned on bond investments, and 2) the capital losses resulting from an upward shift in market interest rates.[2] Managing these risks can be particularly difficult because reducing the portfolio's exposure to one often increases exposure to the other.

For example, suppose an account manager seeks to reduce exposure to the first risk, fluctuating interest income. He may be able to do this by putting more of his portfolio in longer-term maturities. Long-term bonds offer a steady flow of coupon or interest income as long as they are held. And since their rates tend to fluctuate less than short-term rates, reinvestment income is also more stable.

But what happens if interest rates in the market shift upward after this move to long-term bonds is made? Our manager has that unsettling experience of seeing his portfolio drop in value. This change in interest rates results in a loss because more interest income could now be earned with the same investment in a newly issued bond. Hence, no one would pay the old price for the bond, and its market price would be bid down until its effective yield matched the current market rate. Whether or not the account manager has to record or "realize" this capital loss would depend on whether he has to sell any long-term bonds to cover cash drains on the bank. If he does have to sell, say, a 15-year bond yielding 5 percent in a market where the current yield has risen to 6 percent, he will have to swallow a capital loss of nearly 10 percent.

Thus, by attempting to avoid the first risk of interest income fluctuation, our account manager falls victim to the second risk, capital loss, all because of the fickle nature of interest rates. Consequently, a portfolio manager's outlook for interest rates must necessarily shape his selections for the government bond account. Honing the accuracy of his interest rate predictions allows him to reduce capital losses or increase capital gains while still meeting the bank's liquidity demand. Moreover, top management could help by making its interest rate expectations clear. Senior management can hardly set the level of future interest rates by decree. However, interest rate forecasts have a strong impact on the maturity distribution appropriate for the portfolio. It only makes sense to insure that top management's expectations are considered in formulating portfolio policies so that these policies are consistent with those followed in other areas of the bank's operations.

To the extent that the portfolio manager is uncertain about future interest rates, he's likely to "hedge" his bets when balancing risks against returns by planning for a variety of contingencies.[3] The manager hedges by putting

---

[2] Falling interest rates create capital gains. However, this form of income instability is not viewed as a "problem" by portfolio managers.

[3] An important element of the portfolio maturity decision is the structure that is assumed for future interest rate movements. Until recently it had been common to presume that bond yields would generally rise as the maturity of the bond increased. Such an assumption implies that there will be a long-term improvement in a portfolio's income (after capital gains and losses) if maturities can be lengthened. In the last few years, short-term yields have exceeded long-term rates so frequently, that some bond managers are beginning to doubt the wisdom of trying to extend the portfolio's average maturity. The longer-term bonds still seem to offer an opportunity for more stable income flows, but their net return may not be higher. To the extent that one believes that interest rate movements will more closely mirror the recent past than the overall experience since 1951, the following discussion will have to be modified. Funds normally invested in long-term bonds, because their yield was expected to be high, might be shifted into shorter maturity issues.

some of his assets in long-term bonds while keeping others in short-term bonds. This provides some income stability plus a ready supply of emergency liquidity free of capital loss risk. In short, the hedging manager won't lose big, but he won't win big either.

Uncertainty for Top Management. Not only does an account manager run into uncertainty from interest rates but also from top management. Portfolio managers may be unsure as to how their bosses weigh the risks of unstable portfolio income as opposed to capital losses. That is, how much management is willing to forego in potential earnings to avoid or reduce exposure to each type of risk.

Quite likely those evaluating a bond manager's performance will be less than elated by significant capital losses, and some will be even more unhappy if the capital losses have to be "realized." These bankers usually try to keep realized losses at a minimum, because such losses stand out in the income statement. Thus, reporting them creates unfavorable publicity and embarrassment. This forces the portfolio manager to hold enough short-term securities (for instance, Treasury bills which are virtually free of capital loss risk) to cover any cash outflow likely to come down the pike.

Other portfolio managers may have to please bosses (or possibly stockholders) who are more concerned with the steadiness of the bank's overall income than with capital losses. This will encourage the portfolio manager to select more long-term bonds for the account. However, as income stability improves, the risk of capital losses climbs. Therefore, he will lengthen his maturities only as long as the combined effects create a more stable net income.

But often an account manager is uncertain as to the weight management attaches to these alternative forms of risk. As in the case of uncertainty about future interest rates, the manager is likely to shape the maturity distribution of the portfolio to hedge his bets. He will hold a supply of short-term securities sufficient to cover most cash drains without severe capital losses. He will also keep some longer maturities to steady the portfolio's interest earnings. Thus uncertainty about management's views on risk poses a difficult problem for the account manager in terms of balancing risks against returns.

ACT TWO: MANAGEMENT TECHNIQUES

Surrounded by the uncertainty of which risks his bosses most want to reduce along with a great deal of uncertainty about what the future holds for interest rates, the account manager seeks some method to guide him in plying his trade. The technique often chosen for selecting the bond portfolio is the "liquidity reserve classification system" (see Box.)

THE LIQUIDITY RESERVE SYSTEM FOR PORTFOLIO MANAGEMENT

The most common scheme for managing the bond portfolio's distribution is the reserve system. It is characterized by the wide variety of bond maturities included in the portfolio. According to this method of portfolio management, both the kinds of liquid assets available for bank investment and the sources of instability in the bank's cash flows are grouped into several categories. Assets needed for maintaining the bank's liquidity can be safely allocated to cash, short-term government securities, other short-term securities that are also highly liquid, and long-term government bonds. Paralleling this asset structure, sources of cash flow uncertainty are divided into daily, weekly, seasonal, and cyclical cash flows. Net cash inflows represent a liquidity problem for the bank only in an opportunity-cost sense, but net outflows are presumed to have specific causes and are met from specific sources of reserve funds.

The *primary reserve* is the part of a bank's cash account that exceeds its legally required reserves: ready money for meeting net outflows that occur in the normal course of the bank's daily activities. This reserve must be large enough to allow the bank to meet its current obligations without encountering embarrassing cash shortages. Yet primary reserves must be kept at a working minimum because they earn no interest.

The *secondary reserve* is composed of short-term, highly marketable government securities. Paramount is the requirement that these assets be readily convertible into cash at little or no risk of capital loss. Generally,

Liquidity Reserve Approach. Under the most common form of this system, each kind of investment is categorized (primary, secondary, tertiary, and investment) according to how liquid it is. Cash, of course, is the most obvious source of liquidity, but most of it is needed to meet the bank's reserve responsibilities. The short-term Treasury bill becomes part of the bank's secondary reserves which are held as the next line of defense against outflows. Long-term bonds are an investment reserve to be sold or "cashed in" when the bank is under the pressure of extended funds outflows.

Under this layered system of reserves the greatest concentration of invested funds occurs in the short-maturity Treasury bills and notes. However, some reserve funds are spread over a wide range of maturities to increase the average return on the portfolio and to stabilize the flow of interest income. By advocating an extension of a portion of the portfolio's investment funds into intermediate- and long-term securities, this management approach assumes that, on the average, short-term yields will be lower than long-term ones. Moreover, it implicitly assumes that stabilizing interest income is desirable as long as capital losses are under control. Avoidance of losses is the key to this philosophy as evidenced by a heavy concentration in short-term securi-

the most suitable security for this purpose is the Treasury bill. However, Treasury notes of less than two years to maturity or even government bonds which mature in the near future satisfy these requirements. This reserve provides a useful source of liquidity for seasonal cash outflows such as crop cycles, holiday periods, and tax deadlines.

A *tertiary reserve* might be held by the bank for protection against major cyclical outflows associated with either loss of deposits or with the heightening of loan demand, both phenomena occurring over a long period of time. The reserve for this kind of outflow need not be as liquid as the primary or secondary reserves, so it is generally composed of securities of somewhat longer maturities and higher yields. Government securities with maturities of two to five years could normally qualify for this reserve designation.

To the extent that bonds of still longer maturities have a reserve function, they are said to be part of the *investment reserve*. Securities of this type can be held to provide an additional cushion in case of severe financial stress. Combining assets held for each of these reserve purposes produces a spaced maturity portfolio.

Seldom is this one-to-one correspondence of reserve to function followed very rigorously in the banking community. Any sensible banker needing to convert a portion of his reserves to cash would analyze his portfolio to determine the most advantageous sale. However, the liquidity reserve system provides a banker with a rough tool for measuring his reserve needs for cash outflows and for protecting himself from serious losses in bond account dealings.

ties. Attaining a "reasonable" level of income without incurring high capital loss risks, rather than seeking high income, is the name of the game.

The problem with the liquidity reserve approach is that it is not designed to find a bank's *best* bond maturity distribution. It serves only to suggest one that will *suffice*. Therefore, the portfolio manager may be missing chances for higher returns that would not increase the bank's risks. Another difficulty encountered in following the liquidity reserve system is deciding which intermediate and long maturities to include in the portfolio. Specialists in the field sharply differ in their willingness to include maturities of more than five years because of the heavy capital losses that can occur in ten- and fifteen-year bonds. If long-term government bonds are held only as a backstop against catastrophic outflows, the longest maturities are suitable. "Forced sales" and hence realized capital losses will rarely occur. However, if these bonds are to be used frequently in absorbing cyclical liquidity demands, the chances of realizing capital losses are higher, and some authorities are reluctant to suggest commitments longer than five to seven years. In either case, the liquidity reserve approach yields a portfolio that is hedged with intermediate maturities.

Split Maturity Strategy. Some recent research may result in an eventual rewriting of the script for portfolio managers. It has uncovered a *split maturity strategy* as an alternative to the *liquidity reserve approach* to bond management. This recent addition to the banker's repertoire was uncovered by computer analysis, using techniques from operations research.[4] The preliminary results merit careful analysis for they contradict the liquidity reserve system under certain assumptions.

This research discloses that the bond maturity distributions which produce the most attractive combinations of risks and returns are structures comprised of either all short-term bonds, all long-term bonds, or combinations of the two (split maturity structures).[5] These maturity distributions contain no bonds maturing between five and fifteen years. This result depends heavily on the presumption that there is a yield advantage to investing in long-term bonds.

Split maturity strategies contradict the basic approach of the liquidity reserve system. Rather than trying to produce a "sufficient" return without heavy capital loss risks, the split maturity structures result from attempts to earn the highest return possible while controlling *probable* losses. These results suggest that it may be more efficient for a manager to control capital loss risks by investing only in the shortest maturities available and to seek income by investing in the maturity offering the highest expected yield rather than spreading investments over many maturities. The manager would then be investing in a portfolio of "balanced risks and returns" rather than one that is hedged with intermediate maturities.

A further point highlighted by this split portfolio research is the importance of the account manager's measure of risk. When the risk measure used in the analysis was "capital gains and losses," the entire short-term portion of the portfolio was invested in the shortest available maturity. However, altering the concept of risk to include both capital value changes and income instability made it more efficient to spread the short-term investments over a range of short maturities (up to four or five years to maturity). Extension of some short-term investments over several years increases the portfolio's capital loss risks, but it more than compensates by reducing interest income uncertainties. But even with this concept of risk, there remains a gap between the short and long maturities in the portfolio.

The split maturity strategy may help the portfolio manager improve his

---

[4] A detailed description of this research can be found in Charles R. Wolf, "A Model for Selecting Commercial Bank Government Security Portfolios," *Review of Economics and Statistics*, 5 (1969): 40-52 (a nonlinear mathematical programming model); Dwight B. Crane, "A Stochastic Programming Model for Commercial Bank Bond Portfolio Management," *Journal of Financial and Quantitative Analysis*, 6 (1971): 955-976 (a probabilistic linear programming model); Ronald D. Watson, "Tests of Maturity Structures for Commercial Bank Securities Portfolios—A Simulation Approach" (unpublished D.B.A. dissertation, Indiana University, Bloomington, Indiana, 1971) (a simulation model).

[5] For purposes of this discussion short-term bonds are defined as those being less than five years to maturity, intermediate from five to ten, and long-term from ten to fifteen years. In addition, this result is predicated on: 1) the bank's management being averse to taking risks, 2) the unequal trade-off of capital losses and increasing bond maturities, 3) the assumption that long-term interest rates normally exceed short-term rates.

performance in the face of changing interest rates, but it isn't a cure-all. He must still weigh the risks of capital losses versus income stability in allocating his investable funds. He must also make the decision of how risky he wishes his portfolio to be (relative to the bank's liquidity requirement). Finally, he must incorporate expectations of future interest rates into the managing of the bond account's maturity distribution. These decisions can be simplified when top management makes the ground rules clear, but it's still a delicate balancing act.

FINALE

Again, to paraphrase slightly Messrs. Gilbert and Sullivan, the portfolio manager's lot is certainly not a happy one. The performance of his bond portfolio is subject to forces beyond his control—the bank's liquidity requirement and the vagaries of interest rates. Estimating both of these is a tricky business. He may also face the dilemma of having his performance rated by a criterion that is unknown to him.

A bank's top management has a responsibility to reduce the difficulty of this job by helping the portfolio manager cope with this uncertainty. It should first decide how his performance will be evaluated (with a full understanding of the implication of each criterion) and make him aware of the decision. Then it should work out with the portfolio manager a set of interest rate projections to be used in managing the bond account. These two acts will enable the bond account manager to devise a strategy that is consistent with the objectives and expectations of the bank as a whole. When the plot has unfolded, the strategy could well be a split maturity structure. However, the important point is that the bond account manager should understand the constraints under which he must make his decision. If this can be done, the portfolio manager's lot will be a much more happy one.

PLEDGING REQUIREMENTS AND BANK ASSET PORTFOLIOS[†]

Ronald A. Ratti [*]

15

Under state and Federal law, commercial banks are required to hold government securities as a reserve against government deposits. While these pledging requirements are potentially important links between the asset and liability sides of a bank's portfolio, they have largely been ignored in the professional literature. This omission cannot be justified even if pledging requirements have no effect on bank demand for Government securities, because locking up Government securities as a pledge against public deposits forecloses their use as a source of bank liquidity and reduces flexibility in the management of bank assets. Moreover, if pledging requirements do have an impact on bank holdings of Government securities, fluctuations in the growth of government deposits will have important implications on the ability of banks to meet credit demands and on bank profitability.[1]

[†]Reprinted, with deletions, from the *Economic Review*, September/October 1979, pp. 13-23, with permission from the Federal Reserve Bank of Kansas City and the author.

[*]Ronald A. Ratti, associate professor of economics at the University of Missouri-Columbia, was formerly a visiting scholar at the Federal Reserve Bank of Kansas City.

[1] As of November 2, 1978, Treasury tax and loan account depositories may administer their accounts under either a note option or a remittance option. Both options require the pledge of acceptable collateral. The Treasury projects that there will be an average of around $8 to $8.5 billion in TT&L balances at depositories, compared with average balances of about $1.5 billion in recent years. This anticipated sharp upward swing in government funds at depositories can be expected to have an impact on bank asset portfolios.

The purpose of this article is to examine the role of pledging requirements and to determine their impact on the asset portfolio of banks and on bank profitability. The first section of the article reviews the pledging requirements on both Federal and state and local government deposits, with particular emphasis on the requirements of the seven states in the Tenth District. In the second section, the arguments—both favorable and critical—concerning the role of pledging requirements are presented, and possible alternative procedures are discussed. The third section summarizes the empirical evidence on the effectiveness and likely consequences of pledging with regard to bank profitability and asset composition.

STATUTORY PLEDGING REQUIREMENTS

Federal Government Deposits

Under Federal law, Federal Government deposits in excess of those insured by the Federal Deposit Insurance Corporation (FDIC) must be backed by eligible collateral at least equal to this amount.[2] Eligible collateral consists of obligations issued or insured by the U.S. Government or agencies at face value, obligations of the states at 90 per cent of face value, and obligations of other political subdivisions that are not in default at 80 per cent of face value.[3] All assets accepted as satisfactory collateral for Federal Government deposits are required to be physically located with a Federal Reserve Bank or its branches or with a custodian prescribed by the Federal Reserve.

State and Local Government Deposits

Thirty-eight states have similar pledging requirements for the deposits of state and local governments.[4] These laws and regulations differ widely regard-

[2]The provisions are included in the National Bank Act of 1919, the Second Liberty Bank Act of 1917, and U.S. Treasury Circulars Nos. 92, 176, and 848.

[3]Other eligible collateral, as set out in Treasury Circular No. 92, would be 1) the obligations issued or guaranteed by the International Bank for Reconstruction and Development, the Interamerican Development Bank, or the Asian Development Bank at face value; 2) loans to students which are insured by Federal insurance, a state agency, or nonprofit institutions or organizations, at face value; 3) obligations of domestic corporations, at 80 per cent of face value; or 4) commercial and agricultural paper and bankers' acceptances having a maturity of less than one year, at 90 per cent of face value. As of October 16, 1978, the acceptable maturity on this last category has been extended to two years. However, the items have also been restricted to obligations of domestic corporations. In the future, the obligations of individuals and partnerships and of foreign borrowers will not be acceptable.

[4]The states without laws requiring the pledging of assets for government deposits or where pledging is not practiced are Arkansas, Connecticut, Delaware, Indiana, Iowa, Maine, Massachusetts, New Hampshire, Rhode Island, Utah, Vermont, and Wisconsin.

ing the proportion of government deposits that must be covered by eligible collateral, what constitutes eligible collateral, how that collateral is valued, and its appropriate physical condition. For example, about half of these states have a uniform pledging requirement for state and local deposits that ranges from 5 per cent in South Dakota and New Jersey to 110 per cent in California, Minnesota, Mississippi, and Oklahoma.[5] Five states have no pledging requirements on county or municipal deposits but require a pledge against state deposits;[6] two states have no requirements on municipal deposits but do have them on state and county deposits;[7] and one state, North Dakota, has no pledging requirements on state deposits but does have them on county and municipal deposits. The remaining states that allow pledging have differential nonzero requirements on state, county, and municipal deposits. In these states the maximum pledging requirement is 120 per cent on state deposits and 110 per cent on county and municipal deposits.[8]

As to eligible collateral, direct obligations of the U.S. Government satisfy pledging requirements in all states. Obligations guaranteed by the United States and those of U.S. Government agencies are accepted by most states. Also widely accepted are state bonds, notes and certificates of indebtedness, county and municipal securities, and revenue bonds. It is very common, though, for states to restrict eligibility to obligations issued within their own jurisdiction. The method of valuation of eligible collateral for pledging purposes is either at par or at market value (usually not to exceed par value). In some jurisdictions it is at par value for some eligible items and market value for other eligible items. The market value criteria tend to be the most frequently applied.

Most state statutes require the physical transfer of pledged assets to a custodian. The designated custodian is usually either a Federal Reserve Bank or branch or a large correspondent bank. For member banks of the Federal Reserve System the custodian is the relevant regional Federal Reserve Bank or branch. Typically, prior approval of the custodian is required before additions or subtractions may be made in the pledged collateral.

Requirements in Tenth District States

The great variation in pledging requirements among states is illustrated by the requirements of states in the Tenth District, as summarized in Table 1. Six of the states have a uniform pledging ratio for various categories of local

---

[5] The other states with a uniform pledge for state and local deposits are Arizona, Colorado, Kansas, Louisiana, New Mexico, North Carolina, Ohio, Oklahoma, Oregon, Pennsylvania, Virginia, and Wyoming.

[6] These are Georgia, Michigan, South Carolina, Vermont, and West Virginia.

[7] Hawaii and West Virginia.

[8] The above summary on state pledging ratios was drawn from Appendix C, "Pledging Assets for Public Deposits," American Bankers Association, Washington, D.C. (1976).

government deposits, varying from 50 per cent in New Mexico, through 70 per cent in Kansas and 100 per cent in Colorado, Missouri, and Wyoming, to 110 per cent in Oklahoma. In Kansas, however, if a bank is successful in obtaining government funds and its bid is in excess of the rate on 3-month U.S. Treasury bills, the requirement becomes 100 per cent. Also, a resource pooling option is available to banks in Colorado that would lower their ratio to 50 per cent. In Nebraska, the ratio is 110 per cent on state funds and 100 per cent on county and municipal funds. All these pledging ratio requirements refer to government funds in excess of those insured by the FDIC.

Each of the Tenth District states accepts as eligible collateral the obligations issued or guaranteed by the United States or its agencies, their own state bonds, and their own state subdivision obligations. Missouri and Nebraska are the only states that find the bonds of other states acceptable, and Colorado and Kansas allow first mortgages as eligible collateral. Eligible collateral is valued on the basis of market value in Colorado and Wyoming, and face value in Kansas and Oklahoma. In New Mexico, the obligations of the state and its subdivisions are valued at face value, and other acceptable obligations are valued at market value. In Missouri and Nebraska, the statutes are silent regarding the method of valuing securities, and market value criteria have

Table 1
PLEDGING REGULATIONS OF TENTH DISTRICT STATES

| | Pledging Ratios on Deposits | | | Eligible Collateral | Valuation |
	State	County	Municipal	Includes*	Method
	(In per cent)				
Colorado	100[†]	100[†]	100[†]	First Mortgages	Market
Kansas	70[‡]	70[‡]	70[‡]	First Mortgages	Par
Missouri	100[§]	100	100	Other State Bonds	Market[#]
Nebraska	110	100	100	Other State Bonds [‖]	Market[**]
New Mexico	50	50	50		Mixed[††]
Oklahoma	110	110	110		Par
Wyoming	100	100	100		Market

*A blank indicates eligible security in that state is limited to obligations issued or guaranteed by the United States or its agencies, its own state bonds, and its own state subdivision obligations. An entry indicates the acceptability of the entry in addition to the preceding.

[†] A resource pooling option is available to the banks in Colorado that would lower the ratio to 50 per cent. To date it has not been utilized.

[‡] If the bank obtaining public funds placed a bid in excess of the current 3-month U.S. Treasury bill rate, the ratio rises to 100 per cent.

[§] The ratio on state funds in Missouri had been 110 per cent until 1975.

[‖] Restricted to those states whose bonds are purchased by the Board of Education Lands and Funds. This means virtually all states.

[#] Statutes silent. Market valuation method widely used.

[**] The statutes on state and county funds are silent regarding the valuation method, and market value criteria have come to be used. The statute regarding municipal deposits explicitly states face value to be the appropriate valuation method, but apparently market value is used.

[††] Par value for obligations of state of New Mexico and its subdivisions, market value for other obligations.

been adopted. Acceptable custodians for pledged securities are the Federal Reserve Bank of Kansas City, its branches, or a large correspondent bank. Also, subject to the approval of the state banking commissioner, banks in Nebraska, New Mexico, Oklahoma, and Wyoming that are not members of the Federal Reserve System may retain on their own premises the securities pledged against state and local government deposits.

THE ROLE OF PLEDGING REQUIREMENTS

The basic reason for the imposition of pledging requirements is to ensure the safety of government deposits in banks.[9] That is, a political entity whose deposits are backed entirely by securities is guaranteed no loss if the bank holding its deposits should fail. Pledging requirements thus serve to ensure that the political community with funds deposited in a failed bank will not endure any particular financial hardship. However, some observers have argued that the banking system is now much more regulated and stable than it was during the time pledging requirements were introduced, so that the argument concerning the safety of government deposits is not as valid. Moreover, some believe that the safety of these deposits can be guaranteed by alternative means within the existing regulatory framework.

A second argument used to support the use of pledging requirements is that they strengthen the market for Government securities. Most states rule ineligible for pledging purposes the obligations issued by other states or political subdivisions not in their jurisdiction. This has the effect of improving the market for their own debt and for that of their political subdivisions. If the argument concerning the strengthening of the market for Government securities is valid, however, the demand on the part of banks for other asset items, primarily loans, is reduced. This implies that bank credit becomes available on less favorable terms following imposition of the requirements. Thus, funding of government projects at lower costs has to be weighed against the increased cost of obtaining credit for private borrowers at commercial banks.

A third argument suggested in favor of pledging requirements is that they cause banks to hold more Government securities than would otherwise be the case, thereby making bank portfolios safer. However, if the existence of pledging requirements causes a bank to hold a larger quantity of Government securities, it is by no means obvious that the bank has a less risky portfolio

---

[9]The National Bank Act of 1864 contained a provision requiring that U.S. deposits in national banks be secured by a pledge of U.S. bonds or other securities. Prior to this act, Congress had required (since 1779) that the United States be first satisfied in the event of the insolvency of a debtor, including banks. In 1930, pledging by national banks was authorized for state and local government deposits, and shortly thereafter most states passed laws allowing state banks to pledge assets not only against state and local government deposits but also against deposits of the United States. Before this time, government deposits were secured by alternative means such as surety bonds.

than before.[10] Indeed, to the extent that holdings of nonpledged short-term securities are reduced, bank liquidity may be reduced as a result of the requirement.[11]

Another potential problem with pledging requirements is that they may lead to suboptimal portfolio behavior. That is, if the management of government deposits is subject to more restrictions than that of nongovernment deposits, the former can be expected to be less profitable. Hence, banks may not hold a portfolio of assets that would maximize either long-run profits or the well-being of their shareholders. This potential problem is complicated by an additional factor: since state laws on pledging differ widely regarding the fraction of government deposits that needs to be secured, there is a differential incidence of pledging requirements between states and differential regulatory burdens on banks in different states.

Possible Alternatives

Alternative proposals are usually designed to meet some of the problems referred to above. To be considered practical, however, the proposals must also ensure the security of government funds. One proposal that meets this requirement to some extent would grant preferred but unsecured status to government deposits.[12] The experience of the FDIC suggests that government funds would invariably be recoverable under this option, although only after a delay. A second proposal that would not involve such delays would be a state government insurance system.[13] Under this proposal, the insurance rates paid by commercial banks could be determined by the level of government funds on deposit and the characteristics of the depository institution. Insurance coverage up to some specified limit could be provided

[10] This argument is similar to one concerning reserve requirements and bank solvency. In this connection it is widely recognized that if the existence of the reserve requirement results in a level of excess reserves smaller than what the level of reserves would be in the absence of the requirement, bank liquidity has been reduced.

[11] In Appendix A of "The Pledging of Bank Assets: A Study of the Problem of Security for Public Deposits" (Chicago: Association of Reserve City Bankers, 1967), Charles F. Haywood reports the results of a survey of pledged assets at insured commercial banks in mid-1966. The survey revealed substantial immobilization of the security portfolio. It was found that 50 per cent of direct U.S. Government and almost 40 per cent of state and local governments were set aside.

[12] Adopted in Mississippi in addition to pledging requirements.

[13] State insurance schemes for government monies are run by the Public Deposit Protection Commission in Connecticut, by the State Treasurer's Sinking Fund in Iowa, the State Deposit Guarantee Fund in Wisconsin, and the Insurance Fund for Public Deposits in Indiana. An alternative to state insurance would be a private scheme involving the use of surety bonds. Its major drawback, however, is that it involves indirect pledging—i.e., acceptable collateral has to be pledged with the private company supplying the insurance. Since the use of surety bonds in lieu of pledging is allowable in most states, and banks typically do not elect this option, it cannot be considered a viable option.

on government deposits, with the balance secured by a pledge of government securities with the FDIC.

A final category of proposals involves standardizing pledging requirements by extending the role of the FDIC. These proposals vary from advocating 100 per cent FDIC insurance for all government funds to advocating the present insurance coverage plus the pledge of acceptable collateral equal to 100 per cent of the uninsured balances secured with the FDIC.

THE IMPACT OF PLEDGING REQUIREMENTS

Effect on Security Holdings

Changes in deposits of any type will normally cause banks to alter their Government security holdings. However, to the extent that pledging requirements influence security holdings, the impact of changes in government deposits will differ quantitatively from the impact of changes in private deposits.[14] The material below presents results of an empirical investigation into the effects of pledging requirements on holdings of Government securities by banks. In particular, the investigation focuses on the extent that pledging requirements cause banks to alter their holdings of Government securities in response to changes in the funds that governments deposit with them.

The impact of changes in government deposits was examined by applying regression analysis to data on member banks in the Tenth Federal Reserve District reported on call reports for 1977. The regression analysis was used to measure the impact on holdings of Government securities of various factors—such as changes in government deposits and changes in other deposits at banks.[15] From the analysis, estimates were derived of the extent that holdings of Government securities change due to changes in particular types of deposits.

---

[14] It should be borne in mind that other factors, such as different rates of turnover or interest rate payments between government and nongovernment deposits, could also cause a difference in impact.

[15] In order to obtain a single call report number for assets and liabilities for 1977, a weight of one-eighth was given to the December 1976 call, weights of one-quarter each to the March, June, and September 1977 calls, and a weight of one-eighth to the December 1977 call. It should be emphasized that the empirical results are based on data drawn from member banks of the Tenth Federal Reserve District. Although results for other banks during the same period are unlikely to be different, it is possible that results for other time periods may yield different conclusions. In particular, a major weakness of any cross section study is the absence of factors, such as interest rates, that change over time. A more elaborate study combining time and cross section data would allow an evaluation of these qualifications.

Table 2
REGRESSION RESULTS: IMPACT ON HOLDINGS OF GOVERNMENT
SECURITIES OF A $1 INCREASE IN DEPOSITS

Deposits	U.S. Government Securities	State and Local Securities	Loans	Cash
Total Demand	.382	−.222	−.184*	.152
Total Time	.475	−.187		
Total Savings	.473	−.030*		
Government Demand	.051*	.462	−.410	−.151
Government Time and Savings	.034*	.003*		

*Statistically insignificant variables. All others are statistically significant at the .005 level of confidence.

The results of the regression analysis are presented in Table 2.[16] They show the impact on bank holdings of governments of a $1 increase in various types of deposits, under the assumption that all other deposits and total resources do not change. For example, a $1 increase in total deposits leads to an increase of $.382 in holdings of U.S. Government securities and a decline of $.222 in holdings of state and local securities. These results can be explained in terms of general liquidity considerations. As deposits increase relative to bank capital, the bank compensates on the asset side by moving into items that are readily marketable, such as U.S. Government securities, and out of items such as state and local securities.

The results of the regression analysis indicate that pledging requirements do affect bank holdings of state and local government securities. As shown

[16]The regression equations underlying the results in the table are:

$$\text{U.S. Sec./TA} = \underset{(-3.52)}{-.301} + \underset{(3.43)}{.382 D/TA} + \underset{(5.10)}{.475 T/TA} + \underset{(4.88)}{.473 S/TA} + \underset{(8.09)}{.369(1/TA)}$$
$$+ \underset{(.29)}{.051 GD/TA} + \underset{(.43)}{.034 GTS/TA} + \text{State Dummy Variables}$$
$$R^2 = .200, F = 15.12, N = 740;$$

$$\text{SPS Sec./TA} = \underset{(5.04)}{.276} - \underset{(-3.11)}{.222 D/TA} - \underset{(-3.13)}{.187 T/TA} - \underset{(-.48)}{.030 S/TA} - \underset{(-7.54)}{.220(1/TA)}$$
$$+ \underset{(4.12)}{.462 GD/TA} + \underset{(.06)}{.003 GTS/TA} + \text{State Dummy Variables}$$
$$R^2 = .168, F = 12.24, N = 740;$$

$$\text{Total Loans/TA} = \underset{(6.88)}{.663} - \underset{(-1.47)}{.184 D/TA} - \underset{(-.67)}{.071 T/TA} - \underset{(-.93)}{.102 S/TA} - \underset{(-2.58)}{.132(1/TA)}$$
$$- \underset{(-2.08)}{.410 GD/TA} - \underset{(-.61)}{.055 GTS/TA} + \text{State Dummy Variables}$$
$$R^2 = .179, F = 13.21, N = 740;$$

$$\text{Cash Due/TA} = \underset{(4.90)}{.132} + \underset{(4.32)}{.152 D/TA} - \underset{(-.420)}{.123 T/TA} - \underset{(-2.57)}{.079 S/TA} - \underset{(-2.77)}{.040(1/TA)}$$
$$- \underset{(-2.73)}{.151 GD/TA} + \underset{(2.17)}{.055 GTS/TA} + \text{State Dummy Variables}$$
$$R^2 = .377, F = 36.61, N = 740;$$

where U.S. Sec. = U.S. Government securities, SPS Sec. = state and political subdivision securities, TA = total assets, D = total demand deposits, T = total time deposits, S = total savings deposits, GD = government demand deposits, GTS = government time and savings deposits.

in Table 2, banks increase their holdings of state and local government securities by $.462 in response to a $1 increase in government demand deposits. This is the net effect of the pledging requirement, since if government demand deposits increase by $1 and total demand deposits remain fixed, nongovernment demand deposits decline by $1. In the absence of pledging requirements, the effect of this change in the private-government composition of deposits would be zero. Table 2 also shows that changes in government time and savings deposits have no impact on holdings of state and local securities. The regression analysis indicates that the impact of a $1 change in the private-government composition of time and savings deposits leads to an increase in holdings of state and local securities of only $.003, an amount that is too small to be statistically significant.[17]

The analysis also indicates that pledging requirements do not affect holdings of U.S. Government securities by banks. The estimated changes in holdings of U.S. Government securities resulting from a $1 change in the ownership of both demand deposits and time and savings deposits are too small to be statistically significant. However, changes in total deposits do result in changes in holdings of U.S. Government securities. For example, an increase of $1 in demand, time, and savings deposits results in increases in U.S. security holdings of $.382, $.475, and $.473, respectively. Thus, the results suggest that banks use as a pledge against government deposits the U.S. Government securities they would have held anyway in the absence of pledging requirements.

Effect on Other Assets

The above results indicate that because of pledging requirements, the security portfolio of banks is $.462 larger for every dollar of government demand deposits than it would be with no pledging requirements. For a given level of total bank resources, this means that holdings of other assets—such as cash and loans—are lower. Regression analysis, similar to the above, was conduc ted to examine the impact on cash and total loans. As shown in Table 2, pledging requirements meant a reduction of $.410 in loans and $.151 in cash for each dollar in government demand deposits. That is, if total demand deposits remain fixed, and a change in the ownership of demand deposits occurs so that government deposits increase by $1 and nongovernment demand deposits fall by $1, loans would fall $.410 and bank cash would fall $.151.

Effect on Liquidity

Pledging requirements also may have an effect on bank liquidity. The extent of the effect, though, depends upon the definition of liquidity and the

---

[17]However, if the security portfolio is broken down by remaining maturity classes, the existence of the pledge on government time and savings deposits will cause banks to hold a significant, but small, extra amount of short-term state and local securities. These results are not reported here.

effectiveness of pledging requirements. The broadest definition of liquidity, which is employed here, is the sum of cash plus the security portfolio in excess of required reserves and pledged securities. The effect of the pledging requirement is assumed to be the differential impact on assets of a change in government deposits compared to a change in nongovernment deposits.

As summarized in Table 2, a shift in the ownership of $1 of demand deposits from the private to the government sector results in an increase in state and local securities of $.462 and a reduction in cash of $.151. That is, the sum of cash and the security portfolio rises by $.311 ($.462 minus $.151) as a result of the shift. However, the effect on liquidity is not simply $.311 — it will be $.311 minus any change in required reserves and pledged securities. Since government and nongovernment deposits are subject to the same reserve requirements, there is no effect on required reserves resulting from a change in the ownership of deposits. The situation is obviously different, however, for the amount of securities that must be pledged. For states in the Tenth District, as shown in Table 1, the smallest pledging ratio on state and local deposits is 50 per cent, and for five of the states at least 100 per cent. This observation, coupled with the 100 per cent pledging ratio on Federal Government deposits, implies that an increase in government demand deposits of $1 and a reduction in nongovernment demand deposits of $1 results in an increase in the amount of securities that needs to be pledged of at least $.50. These results imply that bank liquidity is reduced as a result of pledging.[18]

Effect on Profitability of Government Deposits

The existence of pledging requirements also may be expected to reduce profits because they are a restriction on the operating activities of banks. To examine this issue, an empirical investigation was made of the relative profitability of government and nongovernment deposits. Three alternative measures of net income were employed—net operating income (that is, net income before taxes, securities gains or losses, and loan loss provision), income before taxes, and net income after taxes.[19] These income measures were regressed

[18] If the definition of liquidity is restricted to cash due plus securities with a maturity of less than five years less required reserves and pledged securities, the negative effect on liquidity of the pledging requirement is even larger. According to results not reported in the text, a shift of $1 in the ownership of demand deposits from the private to the government sector results in an increase of about $.20 in cash due and securities with a maturity of less than five years. This value is far below the increase in the value of the securities that needs to be pledged.

[19] Net income before taxes, securities gains or losses, and loan loss provision is essentially the value of services sold, minus operating costs exclusive of loan loss provision. From the Consolidated Report of Income form for 1977 it would be given by "income before taxes and securities gains or losses" plus "provision for possible loan losses." Net income before taxes is calculated from the 1977 Consolidated Rport of Income by adding "securities gains (losses), gross" to "income before taxes and securities gains or losses."

in turn on asset and liability items drawn from consolidated reports of condition for member banks of the Tenth Federal Reserve District for 1977.[20]

The results indicate that pledging requirements raise the cost of government time and savings deposits by $.012 in terms of net operating income, $.030 in terms of net income before taxes, and $.020 in terms of net income after taxes. The effect of pledging on the cost of each dollar of government demand deposits is $.013, $.107, and $.015 in terms of net operating income, net income before taxes, and net income after taxes, respectively. These results are consistent with the view that government deposits are less profitable than private deposits.[21]

CONCLUSION

A major conclusion of this study is that demand by banks for state and local securities is greater as a result of the presence of pledging requirements. However, this strengthening in the demand side for state and local securities necessarily implies a weakening in banks' demand for other asset items. The item bearing the principal burden of this displacement was found to be private loans. Therefore, any argument advocating the use of pledging requirements on the grounds that they make government borrowing easier has to be tempered with the realization that they also make borrowing by the private sector more difficult.

Another conclusion is that pledging requirements tend to reduce the liquidity of banks below levels that would exist in their absence. Although the demand for government securities was increased as a result of pledging requirements, the increase was found to be less than the value of securities that needed to be pledged. This result, together with the finding concerning the displacement of cash, means that pledging requirements reduce bank liquidity, when the latter is defined as cash plus securities held in excess of pledging requirements. Therefore, the adverse effect of pledging requirements on bank liquidity should be carefully considered by those advocating the pledging of eligible collateral as a means of securing government funds.

---

[20] The asset items were taken to be gross loans, U.S. securities (sum of U.S. Treasury, U.S. agency and corporations' securities), the securities of state and political subdivisions, demand deposits at U.S. banks, and other noncash assets (a residual item amounting to total assets less loans, all government securities, and cash due from banks). The liability items were taken to be total demand deposits, total time deposits, total savings deposits, other liabilities (total liabilities minus deposits), government demand deposits, and government time and savings deposits. A scale variable (the inverse of total assets) and state dummy variables were also included.

[21] Strictly speaking, this conclusion only follows with any degree of confidence with regard to time and savings deposits. The effect of the pledging requirement on the cost of government demand deposits is not statistically significant.

A MODEL BANK INVESTMENT POLICY[†]

David L. Hoffland [*]

16

◄Every one of the nation's 14,600 banks should have a written investment policy. A written investment policy integrates the bank's investment activity with its other activities. Significant changes in cash position, borrowed funds, the quality and maturity of loans, the nature and stability of deposits, capital position or dividend payout will often require corresponding changes in investment strategy.

If too vague or general, a policy will not serve the purposes of bank managements, boards of directors and regulatory authorities, who prefer specific statements they hope will preclude unpleasant surprises. Bank investment officers, on the other hand, usually advocate general guidelines that permit wide latitude in carrying out their duties. The author presents a model investment policy that can be adapted to the specific needs of individual banks. It fixes responsibility for managing the investment portfolio and the broad limits of its composition, lists acceptable securities and specifies their approximate quality, and suggests how the portfolio should evolve in successive phases of the interest rate cycle.►

Written investment policies have become a lively topic now that the Comptroller of the Currency has joined the Federal Reserve Banks, the Federal

†Reprinted from the *Financial Analysts Journal*, May/June 1978, pp. 64-67, with permission from the publisher and the author.

*David Hoffland is a Vice President of Fifth Third Bank in Cincinnati and manager of its investment portfolio.

Deposit Insurance Corporation and the American Bankers Association in advocating that banks establish one. At present, however, only a small minority of the nation's banks—perhaps as few as 10 per cent—have such a written policy.

Of the banks in the U.S., 14,300 have less than $300 million in deposits, hence are unlikely to have a full-time, experienced investment officer. Investment activity in these banks is a secondary responsibility of the president, cashier or other officer, and often receives inadequate attention. If they exist, their written investment policies typically consist of two or three pages of general goals and objectives, outlining few restrictions if any, and perhaps a statement of strategy to be followed during the current year. In many of these banks investment policy is strongly influenced by visiting investment bankers. It is safe to say that written investment policies play an unimportant role in such banks.

There are, however, good reasons for having a written investment policy. It fixes responsibility and delegates authority for making investments. It states bank objectives and provides guidelines for carrying them out (including, sometimes, specification of acceptable securities and maturities). It integrates the bank's investment activity with its lending and other policies. Investing *is* complementary to other bank activity and, since consideration of total activity should properly precede development of an investment policy, the establishment of a written investment policy should promote management development of a comprehensive asset and liability policy.

There could be few objections to having a written investment policy other than the fact that one might be unnecessary. When investment policy is made at the top, and represents a key ingredient in total asset and liability planning, a written policy may be irrelevant. On the other hand, if investments are a stepchild operation, separated from the main body of bank planning, writing down a policy will not cure the problem. Problems most often occur where an investment officer (investment department) goes his (its) own way, oblivious to the rest of the bank.

Writing an investment policy is not easy. On one hand, a policy that is too vague and general will serve no purpose. On the other, a policy that is too specific and restrictive may have a negative effect on bank earnings. Bank investment officers usually prefer general guidelines that given them wide latitude in carrying out their duties. Bank managements and boards of directors, however, prefer specific statements, which they hope will preclude unpleasant surprises. Securities dealers, municipalities, bank managements, boards of directors and shareholders all have, along with the regulatory authorities, particular interests in bank investment policies.

In all banks, the investment policy-making process should be nearly the same. The policies that result, however, should not be the same. Each should be tailored to the individual bank's requirements, expertise and opportunities. The following policy was prepared to be used as a model by banks in writing their own investment policies. It provides a relatively conservative approach to investing without imposing boundaries of a specific nature. Banks under $300 million in deposits might use the model policy as written. Larger banks might use the basic elements, but will probably want to disperse investment responsibility among officers or departments.

A MODEL INVESTMENT POLICY

1. Basic Policy Objectives

The bank's investment portfolio represents a substantial share of its assets. It is expected to make a strong and stable contribution to bank earnings, but earnings are not its primary objective. The primary objective of the investment portfolio is to provide the liquidity necessary to meet day to day, cyclical and long-term changes in the mix of bank assets and liabilities. A second objective is to provide a suitable balance of quality and diversification to bank assets. A third objective is to provide a stable flow of dependable earnings. A fourth objective is to provide a countercyclical balance to earnings, by absorbing funds when loan demand is slack and by providing loanable funds when loan demand is strong.

It is the intention of the bank that day-to-day investment strategy be complementary to and interactive with certain key aspects of the bank's other activities. Cash position, borrowed funds, the quality, maturity, stability and earnings of loans, loan charge-off experience, the nature and stability of deposits, capital position, and dividend payout—consideration of all these areas is prerequisite to determination of investment strategy. Significant changes in any one of them may require changes in investment strategy.

While this investment policy sets some maximums, minimums and averages to be used as guidelines, it is intended to be a flexible tool of management and should be interpreted as such. It will be reviewed at least annually, or whenever changed conditions warrant a review.

We recognize that bank investments must be made over the course of a business cycle, often at inopportune times, and we adopt that (usually) three to five-year cycle as the proper time frame for establishing investment policy as well as measuring results. Although the investment policy may sometimes result in reduced portfolio earnings in the short run, it should significantly increase earnings in the longer run.

2. Responsibility

_____, _____, has the responsibility for
           name   title
managing our investment portfolio, and he will report to the board of directors monthly. His report will include comments on the condition of the bank, on national and local conditions, on the condition of the investment portfolio and on the type of investment strategy dictated by the foregoing in light of this policy statement.

3. Composition of Investments

The bank's investment portfolio consists of three sections:

1. Federal Funds Position. Normally we will sell approximately $_____ daily. We may purchase this amount for up to one month if necessary. Sales may be made only to the following banks, who must buy from us as principals, not as agents:

name	name

name	name

2. Liquidity Portfolio. We will maintain approximately $_____ (equal to at least 10 per cent of deposits) in U.S. Treasury and federal agency obligations, used interchangeably and consisting of not less than 10 items nor more than 20. At times this portfolio may be more than twice the minimum.

3. Income Portfolio. The remainder of available funds will be invested primarily in tax-exempt state and municipal obligations, and in some cases quality corporate bonds. The bank's level of taxable earnings may be an important criterion in determining the amount of tax-exempt investment. The bank's policy is not to minimize income taxes paid, but to maximize net income. Tax exempt investments will be used only to the degree that they contribute to this objective.

4. Acceptable Securities

Securities acceptable for the Liquidity Portfolio are:

1. U. S. Treasury obligations
2. U.S. federal agencies

    a. Federal National Mortgage Association
    b. Federal Home Loan Bank
    c. Federal Land Bank
    d. Banks for Cooperatives
    e. Federal Intermediate Credit Bank
    f. Export Import Bank (U.S. guaranteed)
    g. Farmers Home Administration (U.S. guaranteed)

3. Commercial paper of prime rated corporations that have at least $250 million in equity capital
4. Bankers acceptances of major, quality banks

5. Negotiable certificates of deposit of major, quality banks
6. Repurchase agreements utilizing U.S. Treasury or federal agency obligations with short maturities
7. Tax-exempt, federally guaranteed, project notes

Securities acceptable for the Income Portfolio are:

1. State and municipal tax-exempt bonds
2. Quality, highly marketable corporate bonds listed on the New York Bond Exchange

5. Maturities

For the Liquidity Portfolio:

an average maturity of approximately _____ years, a maximum maturity of _____ years for any item.

For the Income Portfolio:

an average maturity of approximately _____ years, a maximum maturity of _____ years for any item.

We expect to have some bonds coming due in nearly every year, but we will not follow a rigid ladder approach. We expect the average maturity in each portfolio to shorten or lengthen depending upon the phase of the interest rate cycle. When purchasing securities we will be guided, in part, by our perception of that cycle.

6. Quality and Diversification

We expect that the quality and diversification of our municipals will be, approximately (plus or minus five per cent):

Aaa _____%	General Oblig'tns	_____%	
Aa _____%	Revenue	_____%	
A _____%	Other	_____%	
Baa _____%	In-State	_____%	
N/R _____%	Out-of-State	_____%	

We expect that the quality of corporate bonds in the Income Portfolio will be Aa or Aaa listed bonds.

As a matter of policy we will purchase the unrated bonds of local municipalities in support of our service area, provided, of course, they appear to be reasonable credit risks. When not buying local area bonds we will attempt

to gain a broad diversification of marketable names, with approximately
_____% of the bonds being out of state. Except when buying local
area bonds, $25,000 will be a minimum purchase, and we normally will buy
in $_____ amounts.

We will purchase industrial development revenue bonds only when they
are in our service area or are obligations of a valued commercial customer,
except for a limited amount of pollution control bonds issued by the largest
corporations having Aaa and Aa ratings. We will purchase municipal revenue
bonds where financial information is readily available and where we believe
the enterprises to be sound and well established, with a strong pattern of
earnings and debt service coverage. All our securities will be marketable and
of investment grade whether or not they carry a rating. All credit judgments
will be our own, although we may use as supplementary evidence credit advice and information supplied by investment dealers, correspondent banks
and the rating services.

7. Making Portfolio Adjustments

Changes in the maturity structure of the Liquidity Portfolio and the Income Portfolio will be made in accordance with our perception of the interest rate cycle.* We recognize that the concept of any orderly cycle is a sim-
plification, that precise determination of each phase is difficult and that each
business cycle is unique. Nevertheless, keying maturity structure to the interest rate cycle is a useful guide to action and a constructive disciplinary force.

Phase I Conditions—maximum cyclical ease. This is the trough of the cycle. Economic activity is at a low ebb, having declined from a more prosper-
ous period. Demands for bank credit are weak and loan repayments probably

Phases of The Interest Rate Cycle

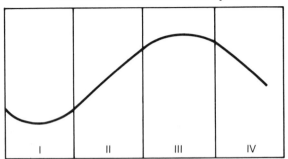

*This description of the interest rate cycle is similar but not identical, to that which appears in the
American Bankers Association publication, *Study Five: Adapting The Portfolio to Changing Conditions*,
pages 12-14. Study Five is a part of the series, *The Role of Investments in Bank Asset Management*,
published by the ABA in 1974.

exceed new extensions. Federal Reserve policy is aggressively easy, rates are relatively low and bond prices are high. Business is described as "poor." During this phase maturities should be shortened, profits taken on taxable bonds and new investments kept short. The Liquidity Portfolio will be relatively large.

Phase II Conditions—transition to tightness. Signs of business recovery are clear and activity is expanding, with an attendant increase in loan demand. Federal Reserve policy has moved away from aggressive ease, interest rates are rising from their previous lows and bond prices are retreating from recent highs. Leading indicators are expanding. Funds may be transferred from the Liquidity Portfolio to the Income Portfolio, and maturities extended.

Phase III Conditions—maximum cyclical tightness. This is the peak of the cycle. Most economic indicators are setting new highs. Credit demands are strong and lenders are forced to be selective in their loans because money is tight. Federal Reserve policy has shifted to restraint and bank reserves are under pressure. Interest rates are high and bond prices have fallen to new lows. Business appears to be booming. Maturities should be extended and tax loss programs executed in both portfolios. The Liquidity Portfolio may reach its minimum size. Add to the Income Portfolio if at all possible.

Phase IV Conditions—transition to ease. Business activity is retreating on a broad front and demand for credit has weakened. The Federal Reserve has shifted to a less restrictive policy. Leading indicators are falling. Interest rates have eased from their recent highs. Bond prices are showing a persistent rise. Maturities should be shortened somewhat and the Liquidity Portfolio will begin to grow.

8. Pledging

When pledging securities to secure public deposits, we will attempt first to pledge eligible municipal securities from the Income Portfolio. We will attempt to maintain free from pledge as many as possible of the securities in the Liquidity Portfolio.

9. Safekeeping

If a member of the Federal Reserve system, we will hold our securities in safekeeping at the Federal Reserve Bank (which is a free service) unless our major correspondent provides superior or specialized services at a small cost.

If a nonmember, we will concentrate our securities in safekeeping at one major correspondent. While safekeeping charges may be made by account analysis, we will investigate the charges used in such analysis and attempt to avoid unnecessary safekeeping expenses. We will not keep securities in our own vault except for short maturity local municipal notes or corporate bonds registered in the name of the bank.

10. Deliveries

Both when buying and selling securities, we will insist that deliveries be made against payment, either through our major correspondent or through the Federal Reserve system. We will not accept due bills under any circumstances and we will not pay for securities before delivery.

11. Computer Program

As long as our securities portfolio consists of 80 or more items we will maintain our portfolio on a computer program provided by a major correspondent. The benefits of accounting, record keeping, pricing and analysis make such a program relatively cheap.

12. Gains and Losses on Securities Sales

We recognize the benefits of taking tax losses on the sale of securities, both taxable and tax exempt, as being at least equal to the earnings on the amount of money not paid in taxes. We will attempt to execute tax loss programs during Phase III of the interest rate cycle. During Phase I of the cycle, we may execute sales of taxable securities to realize gains. Ordinarily, taking gains implies that maturities should be shortened, while taking losses implies that maturities should be lengthened.

13. Swapping of Securities

The idea that a security can be sold and a very similar one bought, with a net benefit to the bank, is based upon a concept that securities markets are imperfect. Detailed knowledge of markets and prices is necessary for success. We recognize the value of such security transactions and approve of a limited number of them, so long as the "swap" meets the following conditions:

(a) The yield differential gained is *more* than normally exists.

(b) The transactions conform to all other investment policies and objectives.

(c) Quality, maturity or yield is not unduly sacrificed.

(d) The transactions are reported independently of other investment activity and each swap is reported in detail.

(e) The transactions accumulate benefits, and such benefits are measured and reported no less than quarterly to the board of directors.

14. Trading Activity

Buying and selling securities in a brief period for profit is speculative. Nevertheless, there may be occasions when buying new issues of Treasuries or federal agencies for profits seems warranted. We will approve of such trading activity, one transaction at a time, in a maximum amount of $_____.

15. Credit Files

We will maintain a credit file on every municipal and corporate security in our Income Portfolio. Minimum contents will include a circular or official statement issued at the time of the bond sale. If the bond was purchased in the secondary market, a financial statement of the issuer and/or some type of analysis will be included. This credit information should cover population, gross and net bonded debt, assessed and full market values of taxable property, per capita or per customer debt, relative debt burden, relative tax burden, debt to net plant and debt service coverage.

16. Exceptions to This Policy

Before taking action that deviates *significantly* from this policy, approval will be secured from the Board of Directors. Minor exceptions are expected to occur frequently. The spirit of this policy is not to prevent exceptions, but to promote planning for investments and to integrate investment strategy with other bank activity.

Part II
LIABILITY AND
CAPITAL MANAGEMENT

A. DEPOSITS

The funds used by banks to maintain reserves and to acquire loans, investments, and fixed assets are obtained primarily from deposits, borrowed funds, and capital. In Part II, various aspects of these primary sources of funds are examined. The lead section deals with deposit-related issues. In the first article, Dwight B. Crane and Michael J. Riley focus on NOW account pricing strategies. In the mid-1970s, these interest-bearing transaction accounts were authorized for use by depository-type institutions in several New England states. However, beginning in 1981, these accounts may be offered nationwide by banks, S&Ls and mutual savings banks. Thus, the competitive strategies discussed in this article are

of interest to all bankers. The article by John R. Brick demonstrates several methods of calculating the yields on six-month money market certificates. Since the yield calculations on MMCs are unlike those of other savings deposits or financial assets, there is often considerable confusion on the part of bankers and the public as to the meaning of the figures advertised by issuers.

The next article by William C. Melton provides a comprehensive overview of the negotiable CD market. Closely related to domestic CDs are the Euro-dollar CDs. These dollar-denominated foreign deposits are playing an increasingly important role in the liability management of larger banks and the money market in general, as explained in Aubrey N. Snellings' article.

STRATEGIES FOR A NOW-ACCOUNT ENVIRONMENT[†]

Dwight B. Crane and Michael J. Riley[*]

17

The payment of interest on checking-type accounts has spread rapidly since the Consumer Savings Bank in Worcester, Massachusetts first introduced negotiable order of withdrawal (NOW) accounts in 1972. The concept spread quickly to savings banks in Massachusetts and New Hampshire, then to all institutions in these two states and to institutions in all six New England states as authority was granted. The federal government has now *extended* this authority to New York. With the advent of automatic transfers from savings to zero- or low-balance checking accounts, the payment of interest on transaction accounts has been allowed to spread nationwide, at least to commercial and savings banks. Other institutions are also moving in this direction, though, as thrift institutions in several states are allowed to offer non-interest-bearing checking accounts and many credit unions may offer share draft accounts.

The prospect of NOW accounts or their equivalents posed a number of questions for New England institutions, questions that are now being faced elsewhere. Will consumers want NOW accounts? Will they treat them like

†Reprinted by permission from the *Bankers Magazine*, Jan.-Feb. 1979, pp. 35-41. Copyright © 1979, Warren, Gorham & Lamont, Inc., 210 South Street, Boston, Massachusetts. All rights reserved.

*Dwight B. Crane is Professor of Business Administration at the Graduate School of Business Administration, Harvard University. Michael J. Riley is Executive Assistant to the President, Northeast Utilities. Drs. Crane and Riley have written *NOW Accounts*, recently published by Lexington Books, D.C. Heath & Company.

checking accounts that pay interest or like savings accounts with easy with-drawal privileges? What kind of pricing strategy will help the institution gain the most from these new accounts while minimizing any adverse impact on profitability?

To help answer these questions, we have studied the New England experience, including the pricing strategies adopted by a variety of institutions. One outcome of this study is a strategic framework that can be used both to help understand the evolution of pricing strategies that occurred in these states and to assist institutions in other states in developing their own strategy for interest-bearing transaction accounts.

CONSUMER ACCEPTANCE

The evidence from New England shows that customers have enthusiastically embraced NOW accounts. In doing so, they have changed their pattern of normal banking relationships. In June 1972, the demand deposits of individuals in Massachusetts were estimated to be approximately $1.5 billion;[1] by December 1977, NOW-account balances exceeded $1.9 billion. Since only individuals and nonprofit institutions may have NOW accounts, it is significant that NOW balances exceed the earlier checking account balances. The New Hampshire story is even more impressive: 1972 demand deposits were $181 million; by the end of 1977, NOW-account balances were approximately $275 million—50 percent more than checking account balances in only five years. Clearly, customers have accepted NOW accounts to such an extent that current balances exceed this earlier measure of their potential.

Perhaps even more interesting is the number of customers acquiring NOW

TABLE 1

CONSUMER ACCEPTANCE OF NOW ACCOUNTS
(December 1977)

	Dollar Balances in Thousands*	Number of Accounts in Thousands[1]	Number of Households in State (1975)**
Connecticut	$ 363	$ 137	$1,023
Maine	177	57	345
Massachusetts	1,928	1,386	1,936
New Hampshire	275	180	266
Rhode Island	157	N/A	307
Vermont	51	N/A	152
Total New England	$2,951	$1,810	$4,029

 * SOURCE: Statistical Section, Research Department, Federal Reserve Bank of Boston.
** SOURCE: Bureau of Census, Statistical Abstract of the United States.

[1]Longbrake & Cohen, "The NOW-Account Experiment," *Journal of Bank Research*, 77 (Summer 1974).

TABLE 2

**ACCEPTANCE OF NOW ACCOUNTS
BY FINANCIAL INSTITUTIONS**
(December 1977)

	Number of Institutions Offering NOW Accounts	*Number of Institutions*	*Percent Offering NOW Accounts*
Connecticut	117	172	68%
Maine	68	97	70%
Massachusetts	405	480	84%
New Hampshire	93	121	77%
Rhode Island	16	N/A	N/A
Vermont	22	N/A	N/A
	721	943	76%

accounts. Massachusetts had about 1.4 million NOW accounts at the end of 1977, compared to a total population of approximately 1.9 million households. This means that roughly three out of every four households in Massachusetts have active NOW accounts. The data for December 1977 (Table 1) show a remarkable story of customer acceptance.

Banks and thrifts responded rapidly to consumer interest in NOW accounts. Within two years of their introduction in June 1972, over three-quarters of Massachusetts savings banks were offering NOW accounts. Commercial banks didn't get this authority until January 1974, but within two years over 70 percent were offering NOW accounts. Similar trends occurred in the other New England States. Most of the financial institutions in New England have accepted NOW accounts, and their numbers continue to grow (Table 2). If other areas of the country follow similar trends, financial institutions will have little time to consider strategic alternatives after receiving NOW-account or equivalent authority.

WHAT ARE NOW ACCOUNTS—CHECKING OR SAVINGS?

Legally, NOW accounts are savings accounts, yet many bankers think of them simply as checking accounts that pay interest. Perhaps the most obvious and least understood lesson of the New England experience is that NOW accounts can be treated by consumers as either checking accounts or savings accounts, depending upon pricing. This distinction is important to a banker. Obviously, there is little benefit in trying to attract checking account balances from thrift institutions. With appropriate pricing, though, commercial banks may be able to attract savings account balances to their interest-bearing transaction accounts. The potential here is far greater since, nationwide, the majority of household funds are in savings accounts, not checking accounts.

In the first months after savings banks obtained NOW-account authority, they operated without competition from banks and other thrifts. This period

from June 1972 to December 1973 provides an interesting experiment, because Massachusetts savings banks followed distinctly different pricing strategies from New Hampshire savings banks. The Massachusetts savings banks
set interest rates at the savings rate level of 5¼ percent and charged 15 cents
for each draft processed. New Hampshire savings banks paid low interest
rates of 2 to 4 percent and required no service charges. As a result, Massachusetts savings banks attracted NOW accounts that looked much like savings accounts, while New Hampshire NOW accounts acted like checking accounts:

NOW-ACCOUNT CHARACTERISTICS
(January 1974)

	Massachusetts Savings Banks	New Hampshire Savings Banks
Average balance	$1,409	$585
Average number of drafts per month	5.2	10.8
Percentage of accounts with zero drafts	25%	15%

New Hampshire savings banks "learned their lesson." They began to increase the interest rate paid to the savings rate level, and significantly increased their average balances. Massachusetts savings banks also changed their
pricing strategy to be more attractive, generally dropping their service charges
per draft. The perhaps predictable result occurred: Account activity increased,
and average balances fell. It seems reasonable to conclude that a savings deposit interest rate will help attract large-balance accounts, while service charges
can significantly influence account activity.

STRATEGIC RESPONSES TO NOW ACCOUNTS

Institutions varied greatly in their response to the NOW-account environment in Massachusetts and New Hampshire. The typical thrift institution was
naturally more enthusiastic than its commercial bank counterpart. However,
there were also wide differences in strategy, even within the thrift group and
the commercial bank group:

☐ Commercial Bank Strategies   ☐ Thrift Institution Strategies

    • Bank resisters   • Concerned thrifts
    • Bank acceptors   • Aggressive thrifts
    • Bank enthusiasts   • Ambitious thrifts

Commercial Bank Responses

Most commercial banks initially opposed the introduction of NOW accounts, but when account erosion and other competitive pressures developed,

they accepted the idea and moved to offer terms attractive to customers, and yet with a minimum impact on profitability. These "acceptors" seemed willing to reevaluate and adjust strategy as trends developed, and as they assessed the operating results of strategies chosen. As a group, initially they tended to require 10 or 15 cents per draft service charges, then to go through an intermediate period with a trend toward "free" accounts, and finally to settle on terms that required significant minimum balances to avoid service charges.

The commercial bank "resisters" originally opposed and continue to strongly oppose the NOW-account concept. They typically see NOW accounts as substitutes for checking accounts; they often either refuse to offer NOW accounts, or they reluctantly provide the accounts with severe restrictions and heavy service charges. These banks seem much less willing to adjust pricing to competitive pressure and operating results, perhaps because a number of their managers believe that NOW accounts are unnatural and will, in time, be eliminated by legislation or by institutions themselves due to the additional cost.

A few commercial bankers welcomed NOW accounts as a new weapon to use in their aggressive pursuit of growth. These "enthusiasts" tended to quickly adopt NOW accounts, to offer the most attractive terms, and to advertise heavily. Despite their growth orientation, a few enthusiasts targeted their accounts toward customers with the most profitable business and through this and other means claimed to achieve both growth and favorable operating results, at least initially. However, less than 10 percent of the commercial banks in Massachusetts and New Hampshire still offer free NOW accounts.

Thrift Responses

Thrift institutions, in general, welcomed NOW accounts as a new source of funds in a period of disintermediation. The majority of accounts were opened by new customers bringing new money at a time of periodic deposit outflows. Most of the savings banks that initially offered NOW accounts in 1973 fell in the "aggressive" category. They were anxious to acquire new powers to counter a loss in savings deposit market share to commercial banks. These institutions were profit-oriented as were the commercial bank acceptors. Yet, unlike their commercial bank counterparts, they saw the introduction of NOW accounts as more of an opportunity and were willing to price more aggressively.

The "concerned thrifts" had strong reservations about their ability to handle the administrative burden and loss exposure of NOW accounts. The concept was novel and many managers felt unprepared to risk an undertaking outside their normal of business. The thrifts in this group that offered NOW accounts often did so as a result of customer requests and followed strategies to minimize their exposure. Often the thrift would refrain from advertising or limit advertising to signs and brochures within the branches. Terms tended to be less favorable, and in several cases NOW accounts were permitted only to existing customers.

"Ambitious thrifts" tended to seek market share aggressively. Several saw their traditional depositor base declining in number and used NOW accounts to try to build a new younger depositor base. These institutions were relatively indifferent to profitability in the short run as long as NOW accounts proved an aid to other strategic goals.

A STRATEGIC FRAMEWORK

As banks begin to pay interest on NOW or other transaction accounts, they will find it important to think carefully about their pricing strategy, paying particular attention to the desirability and profitability of different types of accounts. Which account types are profitable? Which accounts should the bank try to attract to the new service from the competition? Are there ways of making initially unprofitable accounts become profitable NOW accounts?

To answer such questions, we have developed a simple strategic framework that helps identify the implications of different pricing structures. In particular, it can help a bank think through the types of accounts that will be profitable or unprofitable under a proposed pricing structure, while at the same time identifying the kinds of accounts that will be attracted to the bank or discouraged, relative to competitive terms being offered. To illustrate the strategic framework, we can use it to help analyze the evolution of pricing strategies in the New England states.

The first step is to identify some sample accounts that could be transferred to NOW or similar accounts. Our list will be kept short to simplify the illustration, but a bank using this framework could choose as many account types as it desired.

SAMPLE TYPES OF NOW ACCOUNTS

☐ Checking-Type Accounts

- Special—small average balance, low to moderate activity
- Regular—average account size, moderate to high activity
- Large—high average balance, moderate to high activity

☐ Savings-Type Accounts

- Small—low average balance, very low activity
- Average—average size, very low activity
- Large—large accounts, very low activity

For a particular pricing scheme, a bank can assess the profitability of each of these account types, and it can assess whether customers would find the price structure attractive relative to their other alternatives. With this information, the accounts can be categorized into one of four groups as shown in the pricing table below:

PRICING IMPLICATIONS

	Attract Consumers	Discourage Consumers
Profitable Accounts	Block 1	Block 4
Unprofitable Accounts	Block 2	Block 3

For example, we could identify a pricing scheme that would be attractive to large checking accounts and still have these accounts be profitable to the bank. This would put large checking accounts into Block 1 of the table. Further analysis with this set of prices could be used to place the other account types in one of the four blocks, providing a profile of the profitability and consumer attractiveness of this pricing policy.

To see how the table might be used, consider the move to free NOW accounts that "aggressive" and "ambitious" Massachusetts savings banks made beginning in late 1973. This move would put all of our six accounts in the "attract" column, but probably only the large checking, average, and large savings accounts would be in the profitable row.

FREE 5% NOW ACCOUNTS

	Attract	Discourage
Profitable	Large checking Average savings Large savings	—
Unprofitable	Special checking Regular checking Small savings	—

All sizes of checking accounts would be attracted to a free 5 percent[2] NOW account because of the ability to receive 5 percent interest without incurring any service cost or meeting a minimum balance requirement. Savings accounts would also be attracted because customers could receive a commercial bank savings interest rate, while gaining the ability to write free drafts or checks. (Note that customers at savings banks and S&Ls have an incentive to keep some of their funds in savings accounts rather than NOW accounts because of the extra ¼ percent in the 5¼ percent savings rate allowed at thrift institutions. This rate differential contributes to the smaller average NOW-account balance at thrifts.)

---

[2] In 1973, Massachusetts savings banks paid 5¼ percent interest, the maximum permitted. The maximum NOW-account rate was lowered to 5 percent effective January 1, 1974.

To determine which of the individual account types are profitable under this or another pricing scheme requires some analysis and judgment on the part of bank management. For the purpose of our illustration, though, it is reasonable to assume that only three of the accounts are profitable with free NOW accounts paying 5 percent, as shown in the table.

Was the savings bank move to free 5 percent NOW accounts profitable? We don't know, but it might have been more profitable than commercial bankers are willing to admit, at least in the short run. The total profitability of the strategy depends on the relative amounts of profitable and unprofitable accounts that are attracted. Since holders of large accounts are more likely to be financially sophisticated than those of smaller accounts, the inflow of profitable accounts may have more than offset any losses on smaller accounts. There were other factors that also may have encouraged savings banks to price aggressively: a desire to quickly establish market share for strategic reasons, and the fact that, unlike commercial banks, they faced no cost increase from the switch over of non-interest-bearing checking accounts to NOW accounts.

Even if the total profitability of a free 5 percent NOW account is positive, the pricing table makes clear that some unprofitable accounts are attracted. Also, total profitability could be improved, at least in the longer run, by discouraging unprofitable accounts and/or by making them profitable through service charges.

A concern about profitability led many commercial banks and "concerned" thrift institutions in 1974 and 1975 to impose service charges of 10 to 15 cents per draft on NOW accounts. The implications of this strategy have mixed benefits as shown in the pricing table: The benefits are that unprofit-

10-15¢ PER DRAFT SERVICE CHARGE

	Attract	Discourage
Profitable	Average Savings Large Savings	Regular Checking Large Checking
Unprofitable	Small Savings	Special Checking

able checking-type accounts are shifted to the "discourage" column because more attractive terms are available in the marketplace. Free NOW accounts were available at some thrift institutions, an obviously attractive alternative, but special and regular checking account customers would also find attractive the free checking terms available at many commercial banks. From the customer's viewpoint, the 5 percent NOW-account interest on special and regular balances would be too small to justify paying the service charges.

Note that the special checking accounts are moved by this pricing policy from Block 2 to Block 3. These customers are discouraged, but if they open a NOW account, they are still unprofitable. In contrast, regular checking accounts move up to the profitable row (Block 4) because the draft charge combined with earnings from the larger average balance makes them profitable to the institution, a desirable feature of pricing structures.

Shifting special and regular checking accounts is a beneficial feature of this pricing policy. But the cost is that the profitable large checking accounts would also be discouraged, relative to free NOW accounts available in the marketplace. A solution to this difficulty is to set prices conditional on minimum or average balances maintained in the account. Several institutions, including commercial bank "acceptors," have adopted this strategy, which moves the large checking accounts that meet the conditions back to the "attract" column.

FREE NOW, CONDITIONAL ON MINIMUM BALANCE

	Attract	Discourage
Profitable	Large Checking Average Savings Large Savings	Regular Checking
Unprofitable	Small Savings	Special Checking

"Conditional pricing" in some form seems to have good long-run characteristics. It maximizes the number of account types that are both profitable and attracted to the institution (Block 1). Accounts in Block 2, unprofitable-attract, are minimized by prices that discourage accounts. In some cases, these prices are high enough to make selected "discouraged" accounts profitable if they open a NOW account at the bank, a desirable trait. Thus, good pricing strategies tend to have most accounts in the profitable row and very few in the unprofitable row. Ideally, it would be nice to make regular checking and other accounts as profitable as NOW accounts without discouraging them, but in competitive markets with free NOW accounts or even free checking available to consumers, this is impossible. Some difficult choices have to be made about the type of customer to attract and the pricing structure on NOW and automatic transfer accounts.

DYNAMICS OF STRATEGIES IN MASSACHUSETTS

The evolution of pricing strategies of Massachusetts institutions is both interesting and instructive, as illustrated in Table 3. Savings banks moved quickly and aggressively to market NOW accounts when they received authority. Although they initially imposed service charges, they paid a savings account interest rate and attracted high average-balance accounts. Beginning in Autumn 1973, the "aggressive" and "ambitious" thrifts began to drop service charges. In January 1974, 72 percent of the savings banks still had a charge for each draft, but a year later this dropped to 17 percent while the number offering free accounts rose to 71 percent. For a variety of reasons, these institutions sought to establish market position by offering attractive terms.

In January 1974, the pricing strategy of commercial banks offering NOW accounts was similar to savings banks, with 25 percent offering free accounts

TABLE 3

SERVICE CHARGE TRENDS

	Commercial Banks			Savings Banks		
	% Free	% 10¢-15¢	% Other*	% Free	% 10¢-15¢	% Other*
Massachusetts						
January 1974	25	58	17	27	72	1
July 1974	15	74	11	34	62	4
January 1975	21	44	35	71	17	12
July 1975	33	18	49	76	14	10
January 1976	31	16	53	75	7	18
July 1976	22	16	62	73	9	18
December 1976	20	11	69	71	10	19
June 1977	17	11	72	60	10	30
December 1977	16	10	74	60	10	30
June 1978	12	10	78	51	10	39
New Hampshire						
January 1974	0	67	33	75	19	6
July 1974	20	60	20	68	16	16
January 1975	50	17	33	67	5	29
July 1975	42	3	55	73	0	27
January 1976	35	2	63	74	0	26
July 1976	18	4	78	68	0	32
December 1976	16	4	80	68	0	32
June 1977	14	4	82	64	0	36
December 1977	13	4	84	62	0	38
June 1978	11	7	82	62	0	38

* "Other" includes minimum balance and other conditional pricing schemes.

(the enthusiasts) and the others imposing per item or other charges (the acceptors). The "resisters" were still waiting in the wings at this point. As savings banks shifted to free NOW accounts, commercial banks also moved, but in a different direction. They shifted to minimum balance or other conditional pricing schemes to be more selective in the types of accounts attracted and retained. In effect, they moved to encourage profitable NOW accounts, discourage unprofitable accounts, and make profitable the less desirable accounts that weren't sufficiently discouraged. More than one major bank went even further to use NOW accounts as a way of repricing all checking-type accounts to reposition themselves in the marketplace and improve profitability. By late 1976, almost 70 percent of the Massachusetts commercial banks had adopted conditional pricing policies of some sort.

By 1977, the trend to free NOW accounts reversed itself as some of the enthusiastic bankers and aggressive thrift institutions began to adopt conditional pricing. Part of the impetus for this reversal were lower earnings rates on assets and rising operating costs. However, the fact that less profitable and unprofitable accounts were being encouraged to find their way to the "free" institutions was probably also a factor. It is likely that more and more institutions will require their smaller accounts to pay service charges.

CONCLUSIONS

NOW accounts or their equivalent are coming, but we can learn some prepatory lessons from the New England experience.

- NOW accounts or their equivalent are likely to be more popular than you think (if you are not close to the New England experience).

Some private consumer surveys in states without NOW accounts suggest less than enthusiastic consumer acceptance of interest-bearing transaction accounts. But interest on checking accounts has lots of appeal when explained and marketed.

- Don't assume that a strategy for NOW accounts or automatic transfer accounts is not needed.

Bankers who adopt a casual wait-and-see attitude may be the ones hurt most. After all, the accounts most likely to move to a NOW-type account are the large-balance high-profit accounts. We are not suggesting that banks rush into a new product, but a prepared strategy or plan of action is important.

- High interest rates are needed to attract large average balances.

The contrast between the New Hampshire and Massachusetts experiences strongly suggests that higher rates will attract larger average balances and that competitive pressures will push the rate up to a savings account level. The larger average balances come partly from savings-type accounts, suggesting that the "integrity" or separateness of the savings account is not as solid as some believe. One Massachusetts commercial bank advertised that individuals should have two accounts, one for savings and one for checking. Savings banks countered with advertisements suggesting that two accounts were a good idea, but they could both be NOW accounts.

- NOW accounts provide an opportunity, as well as higher costs.

There is no question but that commercial bankers' lives are complicated by the advent of NOW accounts and by automatic transfers from savings to checkings. But there is also an opportunity to be creative, to reposition the institution in the marketplace. The opportunities will differ. For some, it will provide a means of attracting savings balances from other institutions; for others, an opportunity to shift or expand their customer base. The key to achieving the opportunity is to be ready with an understanding of the institution's cost structure, a knowledge of its present and potential customer base, and a pricing strategy that will help the bank achieve its objectives.

CALCULATING YIELDS ON MONEY MARKET CERTIFICATES[†]

John R. Brick [*]

18

In mid-1978, increasing interest rates raised the specter of disintermediation as savers began to bypass banks and thrift institutions in order to obtain market yields in excess of those allowed on savings accounts. Historically, this process caused cash flow problems for financial institutions and resulted in serious disruptions in the financial markets. Particularly adverse effects were felt in the mortgage market.

To overcome this problem, regulatory agencies allowed banks and thrifts to offer the so-called money market certificate, or MMC. This new instrument had a maturity of six months (or 182 days to be exact), with an offering yield tied to the weekly auction rate on six-month Treasury bills. Initially, institutions could increase the saver's return by compounding interest monthly, daily, or continuously. Furthermore, S&Ls and mutual savings banks could offer MMCs at a yield that was 25 basis points higher than the corresponding rate offered by banks. Since the yields on MMCs were then competitive with market rates, the threat of disintermediation and the resulting cash flow problems in thrift institutions subsided.

Although the MMC innovation was successful in preventing disintermediation, another problem was left in its wake. The operating costs of mortgage-

†Reprinted with permission from *The Examiner*, Summer 1979, pp. 13-15. *The Examiner* is a quarterly publication of the Society of Financial Examiners, 1406 Third National Building, Dayton, Ohio, 45402, (513) 223-0419.

*Associate Professor of Finance, Michigan State University.

oriented institutions increased rapidly as short-term rates increased and many savers shifted from low-yielding deposits to the higher yielding MMCs. In an effort to reduce the cost pressures facing S&Ls and mutual savings banks, regulators in March, 1979 prohibited the compounding of interest on MMCs. Also, when the bill rate was more than 9 percent, payment of the 25-basis point premium also was prohibited. (Subsequent regulations further limited the conditions under which thrift institutions may pay the 25-basis point premium. The conditions depend on the level of interest rates and may be changed in order to achieve regulatory objectives. Ed. note.)

Although these changes reduced the cost pressures facing thrift institutions and diminished the rampant demand for MMCs by savers, MMCs have become established as a permanent and important component of the savings program offered by banks and thrift institutions.

Since the interest rate on MMCs is tied to the rate on a money market instrument, the calculation of the effective yield involves several steps. This stems from the fact that the pricing of discount-type money market instruments is not directly compatible with the manner in which the yields on savings accounts are quoted. Furthermore, the pricing procedure involves several different interest rates that are not strictly comparable. As a result, the pricing procedure and yield relationships underlying MMCs are not widely understood. Such an understanding is important from the standpoint of managers of depository institutions in order to inform the public and avoid deceptive advertising practices. From an examiner's standpoint, an understanding of MMC calculations is essential in order to ensure compliance with regulations. The purpose of this paper is to clarify the pricing process related to MMCs. An alternative procedure is examined as is the relationship between the pricing of MMCs and other investments.

PRICING PROCEDURE

In order to demonstrate the presently used pricing procedure, an example is provided. On May 21, 1979, the six-month Treasury bill auction yield was 9.602 percent. During the following week many S&Ls, banks, and mutual savings banks were advertising the following figures for MMCs:

9.602%   Annual Rate

9.974%   Effective Yield

$485.43   Earned on $10,000 in 6 mo.

The interest earned and the effective yield are derived from the "annual rate" of 9.602 percent. In order to convert this rate to a 365-day "effective yield," the assumption is made that when the initial investment matures in 182 days, the principal and interest will be reinvested at the same "annual rate" for another 182-day period. Then, the entire principal and interest will be reinvested again at the same rate for one day bringing the total investment period to 365 days. Thus, on an original investment of $10,000 the interest earned during each period is as follows:

PERIOD 1:

$10,000.00 × .09602 × (182/360) = $485.43

PERIOD 2:

$10,485.43 × .09602 × (182/360) = $509.00

PERIOD 3:

$10,994.43 × .09602 × (1/360)   = $ 2.93

Total Interest   = $997.36

It is important to note that the "annual rate" used to calculate the dollar amount of interest is the Treasury bill discount rate which is based on an interest accrual period of 360 days. The term 182/360 represents the term of the investment relative to the interest accrual period. In this example, the total interest earned over a 365-day period would be $997.36. Since the original investment is $10,000, the "effective yield" is $997.36/10,000 = 9.974 percent.

The question may be raised—is it appropriate to assume the reinvestment of principal and interest at the same rate in future periods? Although it is unlikely that the future reinvestment rates will be the same for the entire year, the assumption complies with standard financial practice. For example, if a 5-year bond is bought to yield 9 percent to maturity, the assumption is made that the interest income will be reinvested at the same yield-to-maturity. Also, the assumption is necessary in order to calculate the "effective yield" which is usually the focus of promotional efforts for savings accounts.

The procedure used to find the effective rate is unlike that found in textbooks dealing with financial mathematics. Thus, another question arises— is this procedure consistent with the principles underlying financial mathematics? To address this question we will examine an alternative procedure.

AN ALTERNATIVE APPROACH

Another approach that may be used to calculate the effective yield is based on present value concepts. The basic financial model is:

$$FV_{mn} = PV\left(1 + \frac{r}{m}\right)^{mn}$$

where

FV_{mn} = future value of the investment at the end of m × n periods

PV = present value of the investment

r = nominal or quoted rate of interest

m = number of times per year that interest is compounded

n = term of investment in years.

From the preceding example we know that the future value of the MMC after initial investment is $10,485.43. Since the MMC is a six-month investment, the principal and interest may be reinvested semiannually so m = 2. The value of n is 182/365 = .49863 so mn = .99726. Substituting these values into the basic model we have

$$\$10,485.43 = \$10,000 \left(1 + \frac{r}{2}\right)^{.99726}$$

The nominal yield r that satisfies this relationship is 9.736% which is about 24 basis points lower than the advertised effective yield of 9.974 percent.[1] However, the two yields are not directly comparable in this form.

The discrepancy between the effective yield 9.974 percent and the nominal yield of 9.736 percent is a source of confusion. The reason is that savings accounts are quoted in terms of an effective yield and other financial assets are quoted in terms of their nominal yield. Letting i represent the effective interest rate and r represent the nominal interest rate, the relationship between the two rates is given by the model:

$$1 + i = \left(1 + \frac{r}{m}\right)^m \quad \text{or} \quad i = \left(1 + \frac{r}{m}\right)^m - 1.$$

Substituting the values of r and m into this equation, the effective rate is:

$$i = 1 + \left(\frac{.09736}{2}\right)^2 - 1$$

$$i = 9.973\%$$

which is virtually the same as that obtained from the presently used method. (The slight difference is due to rounding).

To sharpen the distinction between the *nominal* yield and the *effective* yield, consider the pricing of bonds and other types of saving accounts. If a one-year, 9 percent bond that pays interest semiannually is bought at par, the yield is obviously 9 percent. However, this is the nominal yield. The effective yield may be calculated using the present MMC averaging procedure or present value concepts. Using the averaging procedure we have:

PERIOD 1:

$10,000.00 × .09 × (1/2) = $450.00

PERIOD 2:

$10,450.00 × .09 × (1/2) = $470.25

Total Interest = $920.25.

---

[1] The value of r may be obtained directly on many modern calculators or by algebraically rearranging the basic model to get

$$r = [(FV_{mn}/PV)^{1/mn} - 1].$$

Using the values from our example,

$$r = [(\$10485.43/10,000)^{1/.99726} - 1] \text{ or } 9.736\%. \text{ (Ed. fn.)}$$

Thus the effective yield is $920.25/10,000=9.2025 percent. Alternatively, the effective yield may be derived from the nominal rate of 9 percent:

$$i = \left(1 + \frac{.09}{2}\right)^2 - 1$$
$$i = 9.2025\%.$$

Similarly, if a regular savings account pays a nominal rate of say 7 percent and compounds interest daily, the effective yield is:

$$i = \left(1 + \frac{.07}{365}\right)^{365} - 1$$
$$i = 7.25\%.$$

Another way of looking at the problem is to express the dollar amount of interest as a percent of the original investment and then adjust this rate for the number of investment periods in one year. In the MMC example above, the interest earned for 182 days is $485.43, or 4.8543 percent of the original $10,000 investment. In one year there are 365/182 = 2.00549 investment periods. Thus, the nominal interest rate is 2.00549 × 4.8543% = 9.735%. The effective rate would be calculated as shown above.

It is clear from the calculations shown here that the six-month money market certificate is priced in a manner unlike that of other savings accounts or financial assets. As a result, there has been considerable confusion surrounding the derivation and meaning of the figures advertised by issuers of MMCs. An understanding of the procedures is important from management's standpoint in that care must be exercised when promoting MMCs. Similarly, employees of issuing institutions should be able to explain the nature and meaning of the various figures to savers.

THE MARKET FOR LARGE NEGOTIABLE CDs*

William C. Melton

19

During the last fifteen years "liability management" has become accepted by large banks as a principal strategy for adjusting their lending capabilities. In tapping the domestic pool of short-term investable funds for the purposes of liability management, large negotiable certificates of deposit (CDs) are even more important to banks than trading in Federal funds or engaging in repurchase agreements (RPs) for Treasury bills. Because of the heavy bank reliance on the CD market, the monetary authorities have on numerous occasions used a wide variety of policy measures to influence bank use of CDs. In fact, since its introduction in 1961 no other vehicle for liability management has been subject to as many changes in regulations.

THE MECHANICS OF CDs

As its name suggests, a certificate of deposit is simply a receipt certifying that a certain amount of money has been deposited at the bank issuing the certificate. The certificate also specifies the rate of interest to be paid and the date on which the principal and interest may be withdrawn (the maturity

*Reprinted from the *Quarterly Review*, Winter 1977-78, pp. 22-34, with permission from the Federal Reserve Bank of New York and the author.

date). Large-denomination CDs, those in amounts of at least $100,000, are the ones used in liability management. They are generally negotiable, *i.e.,* the owner may sell title to the deposit to another investor prior to the maturity date.

Because CDs are time deposits, they are subject to Federal Reserve Regulation D, which requires time deposits to have a minimum maturity of thirty days. Time deposits are covered by deposit insurance up to the first $100,000 (formerly $40,000) of principal, and this is usually only a small fraction of the face value of large-denomination certificates. Therefore, investors must evaluate the likelihood of default by the issuing bank when considering purchase of a CD.

Since the computation of reserve requirements for deposits issued on a discount basis is cumbersome, CDs are almost always issued at par and traded on an interest-bearing basis. (Most other money market instruments, such as bankers' acceptances, commercial paper, and Treasury bills, are traded on a discount basis.) Should a CD be sold prior to maturity, the seller receives payment from the buyer for the principal—adjusted to current market value— and for all interest accrued from the original issue date to the date of the sale. If the buyer holds the CD to maturity, he of course receives both the principal and the full amount of interest indicated on the certificate.

Interest on CDs is computed on the basis of a 360-day year instead of the 365-day year used for bond yields. Issuing banks post rates for CDs of various maturities—30 days, 60 days, 90 days, etc.—but the actual rate is often negotiated between the issuer and the buyer (*i.e.,* the depositor) and is affected by the reputation of the issuing bank, the amount of funds it needs, the size of the CD, as well as its term to maturity. The new-issue market is called the primary CD market, and interest rates paid on newly issued CDs are primary rates. Transactions involving outstanding CDs take place in the secondary (dealer) market at what are termed secondary rates.

CDs are normally paid for in immediately available funds on the day of purchase, and they are redeemed in immediately available funds on the day they mature.[1] To facilitate settlement, CDs of many non-New York banks are often issued and redeemed through the issuer's correspondent bank in New York.

CDs are an attractive short-term, liquid investment for individuals, business firms, municipalities, and other organizations with large amounts of temporarily investable cash balances. Since CDs—unlike Treasury bills—are subject to at least some risk of default, they typically yield more than do bills of the same maturity. Thus, they are a tempting alternative for an investor willing to accept slightly more risk in return for a higher yield. Another advantage of CDs is that they may be issued for any desired maturity (of at least thirty days), whereas a Treasury bill maturing on a specific day, *e.g.,* a tax-payment day, may be difficult if not impossible to locate. Also, legal restrictions on the investment powers of state and local governments force

---

[1] See "Federal Funds and Repurchase Agreements", this *Review* (Summer 1977), pages 33-48, for a description of immediately available funds.

many to hold their temporarily investable funds in either government obligations or deposits in local commercial banks. Thus, these restrictions often make CDs the only instrument on which municipalities can obtain returns on short-term investments that are greater than those available on Treasury bills or other time deposits.

The present distribution of CDs among different types of investors is known only in broad outline. Some detailed information is available from surveys conducted in the early 1960's when there was only about $10 billion of large CDs outstanding, compared with about $70 billion at present. The results of those surveys, summarized in the table, showed that, as one would expect, business corporations were by far the largest original purchasers of CDs, while the remainder was bought, in about equal amounts by state and local governments, foreigners, and "others". The surveys also showed that smaller banks tended to sell relatively more of their negotiable CDs to individuals and to state and local governments and that these CDs were smaller on average than those issued to other types of investors.

The only recent source of information on the distribution of CD holdings is the breakdown of weekly reporting banks' outstanding CDs into those issued to individuals, partnerships, and corporations (PC) and those issued to all others. In most recent years, the share of CDs issued to IPC holders has been about two thirds. This suggests that the proportion of CDs originally purchased by businesses and individuals has not changed much from that shown in the table.

In liability management, banks actively seek more flexibility in expanding their lending capability in line with their profitable lending opportunities instead of adjusting their lending to deposits received more or less passively. Banks can do this by increasing their CDs when loan demand is strong and by allowing them to run off when loan demand turns sluggish. Only money-center and large regional banks have the ability to market their CDs effectively. The one hundred largest commercial banks with deposits in excess of $1 billion account for about 90 percent of all large-denomination CDs issued.

Orignal Purchasers of Large Negotiable CDs

In percentage of total Type of purchaser	December 5, 1962	June 30, 1964
Business	69	67
State and local governments. . . .	16	11
Foreign official institutions	6 }	12
All other foreign	1 }	
Individuals.	3	2
Others	6	9
Total	100	100

Numbers may not add to toals because of rounding.
Sources: 1962: Board of Governors of the Federal Reserve System; 1964: American Bankers Association.

On occasion, even a large bank may not issue all of its CDs directly to investors. For example, when a bank's liability management strategy requires it to market a large amount of CDs quickly, it may attempt to issue the CDs to dealers who are willing to purchase them for later sale or who are able to reach a broad array of potential investors quickly. When banks issue CDs into the secondary market in this way, the distinction between the primary (new-issue) and secondary (dealer) market becomes rather blurred.

CDs resemble other short-term money market instruments such as Treasury bills and bankers' acceptances in that they may be traded in a secondary market. The existence of such a market enhances their liquidity and makes them attractive relative to both non-negotiable instruments and negotiable instruments having poorly developed secondary markets. However, the secondary market rate generally exceeds the interest rate at which CDs are originally issued. The reason is that the CDs available in the secondary market may not match the maturities or be issued by the banks desired by investors, and investors have the option of buying CDs of any desired maturity of at least 30 days from preferred issuing banks. As a result, yields in the secondary market must often be increased relative to primary yields to induce investors to purchase them.

Generally, the spread between rates bid and asked in the secondary market averages about 10 basis points for maturities in the three- to six-month range and is somewhat greater for shorter maturities. These spreads, however, are representative only for CDs of the top twelve to fifteen banks whose certificates are traded regularly by the handful of dealers who maintain markets in CDs; bid-asked spreads for CDs issued by banks whose CDs are less frequently traded are naturally somewhat wider.

Moreover, there is generally a tiering (differentiation) of market rates according to market perception of the strength of the issuing bank and of the liquidity of its CDs. Less favored banks must pay somewhat higher rates on their CDs than the most favored money market banks.

In addition to issuing CDs in the domestic market, United States banks with foreign branches have the ability to secure time deposits from holders of offshore dollar balances—Eurodollars. Funds deposited in branches can then be re-lent by them to their United States head offices or lent abroad. Like the CD market, the Eurodollar market is a wholesale market in which the average denomination of deposits is quite large. A further similarity between the Eurodollar and CD markets is that some London branches of United States banks issue London dollar CDs (*i.e.,* dollar-denominated CDs redeemable only at the London branch of the issuing bank), which trade in a secondary market much as domestic CDs do. Since large banks have the option of selling CDs or similar liabilities in either the United States domestic money market or in the Eurodollar market, they change their relative reliance on the two markets according to where effective costs are lowest.[2]

---

[2]Two important differences between Eurodollars and CDs are: (1) Eurodollar deposits have no minimum term to maturity, while CDs have a minimum of 30 days, and (2) net Eurodollar borrowings of head offices of United States banks from their forign branches currently are subject to a 4 percent reserve requirement, while CDs are subject to reserve requirements of 1 to 6 percent, depending on their original term to maturity.

BEGINNINGS OF THE CD MARKET

The negotiable CD came into prominence only seventeen years ago. The conditions that fostered a large market for CDs were the gradual rising trend of interest rates during the 1950's and 1960's as well as the related development of sophisticated money management techniques by corporate treasurers. Since banks were prohibited from paying interest on demand deposits and since most were unwilling to pay interest on corporate time deposits, corporate treasurers actively began to use their temporarily investable balances to purchase short-term money market instruments. This investment strategy inhibited the growth of corporate deposits at large money market banks. In addition, the unavailability to banks of a flexible instrument with which to augment their conventional deposit sources meant that, in period of monetary restraint, the share of bank credit in total credit flows to nonfinancial sectors (business, state and local governments, housing, and consumers) declined.

Responding to this state of affairs, the First National City Bank of New York (now Citibank) began to offer CDs to domestic business corporations, public bodies, and foreign investors in February 1961. The primary objectives were to increase corporate deposits and to allow banks greater discretion over their sources of funds, so that in a period of rising loan demand and increasing interest rates they could accommodate increases in short-term credit demands by expanding their CDs. Otherwise, they would have to turn down profitable loan applications or sell some of their investments, possibly at a substantial loss. The ability of banks to "buy" funds by paying market rates of interest added greatly to their flexibility and was the key element in their ability to shift to liability management.

CDs had existed in negotiable form for years prior to 1961, but they could not become an important source of funds for banks until they could compete with other short-term money market instruments. To do so, they had to be readily marketable and to pay a market rate of return. The crucial innovation in February 1961 was the secondary market for large negotiable CDs (provided initially by the Discount Corporation of New York, a dealer in United States Government securities). The secondary market made CDs a truly liquid money market instrument by establishing a means through which an investor could sell his holdings quickly and at low cost prior to maturity. Other large banks promptly began to issue CDs, and other dealers soon entered the secondary CD market.

The expansion of CDs in the early 1960's was rapid and steady (Chart 1). The smooth and impressive growth of outstandings from February 1961 through the middle of 1966 reflected increasing acceptance of this new money market instrument. However, the CD rates which member banks—virtually the only banks issuing CDs—could pay were subject to the interest ceilings of the Federal Reserve's Regulation Q. The 1 percent ceiling rate on time deposits of less than three months' maturity prevented CDs in this range from being issued. Moreover, the market for longer term CDs was affected in late 1961, when three-month Treasury bill rates edged upward and exceeded

Billion of dollars

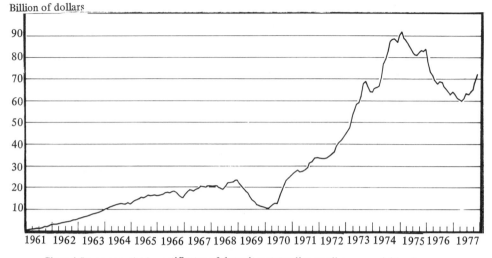

Chart 1 Large negotiable certificates of deposit outstanding at all commercial banks.
(Not seasonally adjusted)
Source: Board of Governors of the Federal Reserve System.

the 2½ percent ceiling rate in effect for three- to six-month CDs. At that point, only CDs of six-month or longer maturities on which the ceiling rate was 3 percent could be sold by banks, and these also became difficult to sell as the six-month Treasury bill rate approached 3 percent.

At the beginning of 1962, the Federal Reserve raised the ceiling rate for CDs of six- to twelve-month maturity to 3½ percent and that for CDs of twelve-month or greater maturity to 4 percent.[3] As a result of this change, banks were able once more to market CDs in the longer maturity range but were effectively prevented from issuing shorter maturities. A year and a half later, in July 1963, ceiling rates for CD maturities of three months and longer were fixed at 4 percent.

Meanwhile, the ceiling on one- to three-month CDs was deliberately held at an uncompetitive 1 percent level. This stimulated the growth of the secondary market which was then still in its infancy. The large spread between ceiling rates on long- and short-term CDs allowed dealers and corporations to buy long-term CDs, to hold them until only a short term to maturity remained, and then to sell them in the secondary market without fear of being undercut by banks offering competitive rates on newly issued short-term CDs. In addition, since long-term CD rates generally exceeded short-term CD rates, while both remained relatively stable, dealers profited during the first half of the 1960's by buying long-term CDs, holding them in inventory, and then selling them as short-term CDs. As long as rates were stable, this investment strategy—called "riding the yield curve"—increased their total interest return by an amount depending on the spread of the long-term CD rate over the short-term CD rate.

---

[3] In addition, time deposits of foreign official institutions were made exempt from Regulation Q interest rate ceilings in October 1962.

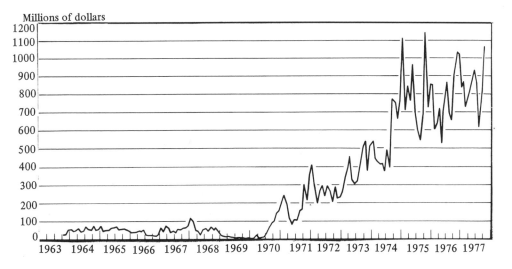

Chart 2 Dealer transactions in large negotiable certificates of deposit. (Monthly averages of daily figures not seasonally adjusted.) Source: Federal Reserve Bank of New York.

The artifically low Regulation Q ceiling on short-term CDs remained in effect until November 1964, when the maximum rate on CDs of 30- to 89-day maturities was raised to 4 percent, and the rate on longer term CDs was raised to 4½ percent. This change allowed banks to make competitive rate offers on CDs in the 30- to 89-day range for the first time. It thus put an end to the artificial stimulus to the growth of the secondary market. From the end of 1963 to the middle of 1966, the value of CDs outstanding nearly doubled, reaching $17.8 billion, while the daily average of gross dealer transactions changed little and remained at a modest level (Chart 2).

FIRST CRISIS: 1966

In response to rising interest rates, the existing Regulation Q ceiling rates were raised to a uniform 5½ percent for all CD maturities in December 1965 (Chart 3) in order to prevent banks from encountering difficulty when renewing (rolling over) their existing CDs. However, other market rates soon exceeded the new ceiling, and the CD market reacted immediately. Issuance of CDs began to slow, and outstandings started to fall.

Rates on CDs with longer maturities ran up against the ceiling in about the middle of 1966. Consequently, new issues of such maturities were greatly reduced, and the average maturity of outstanding CDs began a sharp decline (Chart 4). Shortly afterward rates on short-term CDs ran up against the ceiling, and new issues of short-term CDs also started to decline. The runoff of CDs from August to December 1966 reached a sizable $2.9 billion (Chart 1),

Chart 3
Interest Rates on Large Negotiable Certificates of Deposit

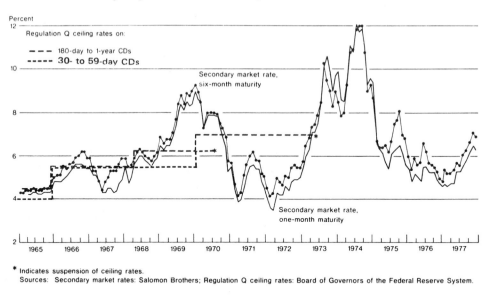

* Indicates suspension of ceiling rates.
   Sources: Secondary market rates: Salomon Brothers; Regulation Q ceiling rates: Board of Governors of the Federal Reserve System.

Chart 4
Average Maturity of Outstanding Large Negotiable Certificates of Deposit
Weekly reporting banks; not seasonally adjusted

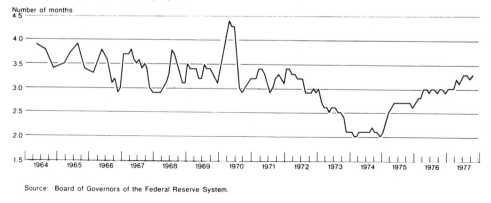

   Source: Board of Governors of the Federal Reserve System.

a decrease of about 16 percent from the August level. In the five years since
the introduction of negotiable CDs, banks had never undergone a comparable experience.

   The effects were also significant in the secondary market, where a rapid
rise in rates—to which Regulation Q, of course, did not apply—resulted in

considerable book losses for holders of outstanding CDs. Investors reacted by cutting back purchases of new CDs and holding to maturity the CDs already in their portfolios; thus market transactions as well as dealer positions were greatly reduced. Gross transactions in the secondary market declined to a level even lower than that observed in 1963, when data first began to be collected.

The pressures in the CD market caused by Regulation Q ceilings abated in December 1966, when interest rates started to decline rapidly. Pressures resumed in 1967 as rates on longer maturities again rose to the ceiling rate and made the average maturity of outstandings contract sharply. Early in 1968, when other market rates declined and the Regulation Q ceiling for longer term CDs was raided to 6¼ percent, pressures on the CD market were relieved once more.

During the 1966 "credit crunch", banks found that CDs were a potentially unreliable source of funds. In reaction, some large banks began to develop alternative sources of funds, particularly Eurodollars, on which rates were not subject to regulation. A few United States banks had used Eurodollars prior to 1966, but in that year gross borrowings from foreign branches rose to about $2 billion for the first time. It was also in the same year that the London dollar CD was introduced by the London branch of Citibank. The establishment of facilities for tapping the Eurodollar market during the 1966 credit cruch proved to be important during the 1969-70 crunch, when banks faced an even greater runoff of CDs.

In much of the postwar period, Regulation Q interest rate ceilings for member banks were set below the rates that thrift institutions specializing in housing finance were paying. In this way, *cross-intermediation,—i.e.,* the shift of deposits from thrift institutions to commercial banks—was prevented. It was widely thought that preventing such a shift would encourage home building.

The increase in time deposit rates paid by commercial banks after the December 1965 adjustment of Regulation Q ceiling rates appeared to observers to have contributed to outflows of deposits from thrift institutions in 1966. Accordingly, the monetary authorities were in part blamed for the difficulties of the housing market in that year. In response, the authorities requested, and the Congress promptly passed, legislation permitting different ceiling rates for time and savings deposits according to their size and, for the first time, also extending ceilings to rates paid on time and savings deposits by thrift institutions. In September 1966, the ceiling rate on commercial bank time deposits smaller than $100,000 was reduced to 5 percent while the ceiling rates for savings deposits and large negotiable CDs were left unchanged at 4 percent and 5½ percent, respectively. Although these actions may have reduced the threat of cross-intermediation, later events showed that rigid reliance on interest rate ceilings made both commercial banks and thrift institutions more susceptible to serious *disintermediation—i.e.,* the withdrawal of time and savings deposits to purchase higher yielding money market instruments.

SECOND CRISIS: 1969-70

Early in 1968, in response to rising market interest rates, Regulation Q ceiling rates were set at 5½ to 6¼ percent, according to maturity. However, despite the change in the ceilings, rates on new issues of CDs with shorter maturities were uncompetitive throughout most of 1968, and toward the end of that year the same happened to longer term CDs. In 1969, as monetary policy attempted to dampen inflationary pressures, market rates rose rapidly to the vicinity of 8 percent, which far exceeded Regulation Q rates. The ceilings were left unchanged, for the monetary authorities hoped that restriction of bank access to the CD market would both reduce the overall expansion of credit and cause banks to reduce the rate of their expansion of credit to business and thereby to lessen the financial squeeze on other sectors, such as housing and state and local governments. Consequently, between December 1968 and December 1969, banks were buffeted by the largest involuntary runoff of CDs ever, as investors sought more attractive returns available on other money market instruments. Outstandings declined by $12.6 billion, a loss of more than 50 percent from December 1968. Thereafter, outstandings stabilized at a depressed level during the first half of 1970.

The CD runoff during 1969-70 would have been even larger had not banks begun to take advantage of the exemption of deposits of foreign official institutions from Regulation Q ceilings. During the second half of 1969 and the first quarter of 1970, banks were able to increase CDs issued to foreign official institutions by about $2 billion, which offset some of the decline by CDs held by other investors.

The composition as well as the level of CDs was affected by the runoff. With the severe fall in new issues of CDs, the average maturity of outstandings actually rose sharply in the first half of 1970 (Chart 4) as large amounts of short-term CDs matured without being rolled over. (Because of the large proportion of short-term CDs, a runoff increases the average maturity of outstandings.)

While banks faced an unprecedented drop in outstanding CDs, the secondary market virtually dried up. Average daily gross dealer transactions dropped to the lowest levels since the inception of the market and were practically zero during the second half of 1969 and the first part of 1970. At the same time, dealer positions were almost completely eliminated. Hence, any potential investors in CDs were doubly deterred; the interest rates on alternative money market instruments substantially exceeded rates permitted on primary CDs, and the liquidity that had contributed to the earlier attractiveness of CDs no longer existed.

To compensate for the heavy loss of CDs, banks sold government securities, restricted lending to business, and sharply cut back purchases of municipal obligations (large banks were actually net sellers of municipals during the second half of 1969). Although the rate of expansion of bank lending to business was substantially reduced, business spending was not commensurately curtailed because many large firms were able to obtain funds by selling liquid assets and by utilizing sources of nonbank funds, *e.g.*, by selling commercial paper.

EURODOLLARS—A SUBSTITUTE FOR CDs

In addition to restraining lending and liquidating investments, banks also greatly increased their reliance on borrowings from their foreign branches. In fact, large New York banks, which had the best developed access to the Eurodollar market, were able to replace their CD losses almost dollar for dollar with such borrowings. As a result, Eurodollar borrowings from foreign branches soared in late 1968 and 1969; they reached an all-time high of $15 billion in October 1969.

Eurodollar borrowings were a highly attractive source of funds just then. In contrast to CDs, which were subject to Regulation Q ceilings, Eurodollar rates were unregulated. United States banks could therefore secure funds to offset their CD losses if they were willing to pay high interest rates, and their access to funds was potentially more reliable for the same reason. In addition —and again in contrast to CDs—the cost of Eurodollar borrowings was reduced somewhat because they were not subject to reserve requirements.

In October 1969, a 10 percent reserve requirement was imposed on net borrowings of United States banks from their foreign branches that were above a reserve-free base, defined in a rather complicated way. In essence, the base was equal to at least 3 percent of a bank's total deposits less its deposits due to foreign banks in any current four-week period. For banks that had average Eurodollar borrowings in excess of the 3 percent formula in the four-week period ended May 16, 1969, the base was raised to the May average. However, the base was automatically reduced if average borrowings fell below the May average in any subsequent four-week period. But in no case could the base be lower than that given by the 3 percent formula. The 3 percent formula was intended to avoid discriminating against banks which had been slow to enter the Eurodollar market and consequently did not have large levels of borrowings. The reserve-free base was adopted in order to motivate banks to refrain from reducing Eurodollar borrowings abruptly. Some banks were thus undoubtedly induced to maintain their borrowings for longer than they would have otherwise, and the net liability of United States banks to their foreign branches remained flat in the latter part of 1969 and declined only gradually in early 1970.

Because reserve requirements now applied to borrowings from foreign branches, banks turned to other sources of funds. The most important of these was outright sales of loans to bank affiliates, which in turn generally sold commercial paper to pay for the loans. Loan sales to affiliates at large weekly reporting banks increased from about $2.1 billion in May 1969 to

$3.0 billion by the year-end. In the first six months of 1970, loan sales doubled, and they reached an all-time high level of $8.1 billion at the end of July.

Meanwhile, in January 1970, the Board of Governors of the Federal Reserve System raised Regulation Q ceilings somewhat. The action was designed to limit outflows of CDs and other time deposits from commercial banks, but its impact was very modest. Even though market rates declined slightly around that time, they were still well above the new ceilings.

EFFECTS OF THE PENN CENTRAL CRISIS

On Friday, June 19, 1970, efforts to induce the United States Government to grant emergency credits to the Penn Central Transportation Company collapsed. Two days later, on Sunday, June 21, Penn Central filed its bankruptcy petition. The railroad then had in excess of $80 million of commercial paper outstanding, and the prospect of imminent default on this paper generated fears of a general liquidity crisis. For this reason, on Tuesday, June 23, the Federal Reserve took a variety of supportive actions, among which was suspension of the Regulation Q ceiling rate on CDs maturing in 30 to 89 days. The effect was to allow banks to reenter the short-term CD market, which they did with great alacrity. The massive acquisition of funds through new issues of CDs was crucial to banks' efforts to meet the financial needs of business. Many firms were unable to issue commercial paper during the weeks immediately after the Penn Central bankruptcy petition, and total commercial paper outstanding promptly contracted by about $3 billion.

Restoration of banks' access to the CD market also reduced their need to sell loans to affiliates and to raise funds indirectly through commercial paper. Accordingly, loan sales declined slightly in August, and they began to fall sharply after September, when reserve requirements were placed on bank-related commercial paper used to fund bank lending. By the end of 1970, outstandings of loans sold amounted to only $2.7 billion, well below the peak of $8.1 billion.

As banks resumed issuing CDs, the average maturity of outstandings declined rapidly from the all-time high of more than four months in early 1970 to a more normal range of about three months. In addition, the secondary market recovered almost immediately, and daily average transactions and dealer positions soon attained levels far exceeding all previous ones. A significant longer term effect was that participants in the financial markets assumed that the suspension of Regulation Q ceilings on the shortest maturities meant that the Federal Reserve would no longer employ rigid ceilings on CD rates as a tool of quantitative credit control.

After the Regulation Q ceiling on short-term CDs was suspended, deposits at foreign branches were 2 to 3 percentage points more expensive than domestic CDs. Thus, it was no longer attractive to maintain existing levels of

Eurodollar borrowings, and banks began to pay them down rapidly. The Federal Reserve Board raised the reserve requirement applying to net borrowings from foreign branches to 20 percent in January 1971. In addition, it announced that, if a bank defining its reserve-free base of Eurodollar borrowings as 3 percent of deposits reduced its borrowings below the reserve-free level, its base would be reduced accordingly. The intention was that the threat of higher reserve requirements on future borrowings would stimulate banks to maintain their current borrowings, thus counteracting the abrupt turnaround in international capital flows resulting from the reduction of borrowings from foreign branches. However, the inducement offered was evidently inadequate, since banks continued to repay them.

THE BOOM OF 1973-74

Credit demand began to revive in 1972, particularly demand for bank loans. Business loans increased rapidly during late 1972 and early 1973, in part because the prime rate was being held to a relatively low level under the influence of the Committee on Interest and Dividends in line with the price and wage control apparatus then in force. In May 1973, as interest rates on CDs with maturities of 90 days and more approached Regulation Q ceilings, these ceilings were suspended, an act that terminated Regulation Q ceilings on *all* large negotiable CDs. Thus the market's earlier assumption that, after the 1969-70 credit crunch, ceilings on CDs were no longer to be used as instruments of monetary policy turned out to be right. Had the ceiling on longer term CDs not been removed, the average maturity of CDs would have declined —an outcome that the authorities wished to avoid. As a result of their continued access to the CD market in 1973-74, banks were able—for the first time in the postwar period—to maintain their share in total credit flows to nonfinancial sectors during a period of monetary restraint.

In June 1973, the Federal Reserve attempted to slow the rapid rate of expansion of bank credit by introducing a marginal reserve requirement on CDs similar to the one applied earlier to Eurodollar borrowings. The existing 5 percent reserve requirement on a bank's base of CDs (defined as the amount of CDs outstanding on May 16, 1973) was continued. For CDs in excess of this base amount, the marginal reserve requirement was increased to 8 percent by addition of a supplementary reserve requirement of 3 percent.[4] At the same time, the authorities reduced the reserve requirement on Eurodollar borrowings by head offices of United States banks to 8 percent and announced a gradual elimination of the reserve-free base. This put reserve requirements for CDs and Eurodollars on a roughly equal basis. In September 1973 the Federal Reserve attempted to counteract expectations of an imminent easing

---

[4] This supplementary reserve requirement did not apply to banks with less than $10 million of CDs outstanding.

of monetary policy by announcing an increase in the marginal reserve requirement on CDs to 11 percent beginning October 4. The new reserve requirement, whatever its effect on market expectations, had little obvious effect on banks' utilization of CDs, for the volume of outstandings continued to increase. When strains on the credit markets temporarily eased in December 1973, the marginal reserve requirement was reduced to 8 percent again.

In September 1974, shortly after money market rates began to decline from their record highs, the authorities restructured CD reserve requirements by removing the 3 percent supplementary reserve requirement for CDs with an original maturity of four months or more. Thus, CDs in excess of the base amount that had an original maturity of less than four months continued to be subject to an 8 percent reserve requirement, while longer term CDs became subject to a reserve requirement of only 5 percent. This was the first time reserve requirements had been related to the maturity of CDs. The Federal Reserve wanted to induce banks to lengthen the average maturity of their CDs—by now reduced to an all-time low of slightly more than two months—by lowering somewhat the effective cost to banks of longer term CDs.

Other modifications to the reserve requirements came in December 1974. The marginal reserve requirement for CDs was eliminated, and reserve requirements were set at 6 percent for CDs with an original maturity of less than six months and at 3 percent for those with an original maturity of six months (180 days) or more. One problem with such a structure of reserve requirements is that banks may find themselves able to reduce their required reserves with adjustments of their CD maturities that leave the average maturity of CDs essentially unchanged. For example, issues of six-month CDs—which have a low reserve requirement—might be increased while issues of five-month CDs are reduced. This sort of change will reduce required reserves but will increase maturity only very slightly.

It is difficult to assess with precision the effect of these new reserve requirements on the maturity structure of CDs. However, the timing of changes in the average maturity of CDs sheds some light on the question. The average maturity of CDs actually declined slightly following the September revision and increased rapidly beginning in early 1975. Since the December revision in fact weakened the incentive banks had to lengthen CD maturities, the abrupt increase in the average maturity in early 1975 seems primarily attributable to the sharp runoff of CDs which began at that time.

Moreover, the actual changes in the spread of the six-month CD rate over the one-month rate were far greater than could have been produced by the modifications to reserve requirements. Simple calculations show that, all other things being equal, the change should have been an increase of 25-30 basis points in the spread of the six-month rate over the one-month rate. However, the spread increased by about 125 basis points from late 1974 to the end of 1975 and then was in large part reversed by the end of 1976 (Chart 3). This roughly followed the pattern of changes in the structure of interest rates in other markets. The actual behavior of the spreads thus suggests that market forces have a determining influence on the structure of interest rates in the CD market, while the influence of the differential reserve requirements is difficult to isolate.

A MULTITIER MARKET EMERGES

Though the CD market underwent a variety of shocks during the 1973-74 boom, it performed quite well. Unlike earlier booms, when Regulation Q ceilings precipitated a runoff of CDs and a severe thinning of the secondary market, in 1973-74 banks were generally able to market their CDs successfully—though they had to pay quite costly interest rates—and no discernible transactions decline occurred in the secondary market. The principal change was the advent of a "multitier" market, in which the rates paid by banks on CDs were tailored according to investors' perception of the riskiness of the issuing banks.

The collapse of the United States National Bank of San Diego in October 1973, followed by Herstatt in Germany and the Franklin National Bank in New York in 1974, had significant ramifications. For the first time since the 1930's, the specter of possible failure of even major financial institutions arose, making investors more sensitive to relative risk in evaluating CDs issued by different banks. Accordingly, investors did demand noticeably higher rates on the CDs of banks viewed as less stable. Since the early years of the CD market, distinctions had typically existed between rates paid by banks then classified as prime and nonprime, but the multitier market introduced a rather more refined differentiation. For the most part, in the new tier structure, the larger banks pay lower rates.

Bank size affected rates paid on CDs in two ways. Liquidity considerations favored the CDs of the large money market banks, since the secondary market for them is the most developed. And banks that attempted to place issues of their CDs beyond the circle of regular customers who knew them well had to pay a premium. For both reasons, regional banks trying to tap new sources of funds with their CDs in 1974 generally had to pay higher rates than did large money market banks. In 1975, when public attention began to focus on the financial crisis in New York City, even some large New York City banks found their CDs being less favorably received by investors than before. That change in the structure of CD rate tiers has since moderated significantly.

The development of a tiered market in CDs may betoken the maturation of the CD as a money market instrument. The earlier, relatively crude differentiation between prime and nonprime CDs was a rather peculiar feature of the CD market. A refined structure of tiered borrowing rates has, for example, long been a standard feature of the bond and commercial paper markets. In response to the development of tiering in the CD market, some banks may very well have changed their approach to lending or investing funds obtained through CDs, thus giving more emphasis to asset management relative to liability management. It is probably safe to conclude that banks are now far more conscious of the impact of their incremental CD exposure on their total cost of purchased funds than they were prior to 1974.

Another indication of the maturation of the CD market is that, as banks on the whole faced sluggish loan demand from the beginning of 1975 until relatively recently, they allowed their CDs to run down. At the same time, they restructured their balance sheets by expanding their investment portfolios considerably. This is the first time since 1961 that banks in the aggregate voluntarily reduced their CDs to any significant extent; earlier contractions had occurred when market rates exceeded Regulation Q ceilings. At other times CDs were always growing, even when loan demand was sluggish. This altered behavior may mean that the rapid growth stage of CDs has ended. From now on CDs will probably expand and contract in step with the movements of loan demand.

Developments in borrowings of United States banks from their foreign branches were less dramatic during 1973-74 than in 1969. Such borrowings were subject to reserve requirements during 1973-74 and, since Eurodollar rates typically exceeded CD rates, Eurodollars were generally a more expensive source of funds for United States banks than were CDs. Equally important, since the last remaining Regulation Q ceiling on CD rates was suspended in May 1973, CDs remained available—though they were extremely expensive—even during the tightest money market conditions in 1973-74.

Under these circumstances, banks relied very little on Eurodollars for domestic lending. In 1973, net borrowings from foreign branches remained in the neighborhood of $1.5 billion-$2 billion, far below the peak of over $15 billion in 1969. An unexpected tightening of the money market in early 1974 led to a rapid increase to about $3 billion, a level maintained through the summer. But a general weakening of demand for credit then became apparent, and starting in October net Eurodollar borrowings were rapidly repaid. Since February 1975, United States banks on balance have been net lenders to their foreign branches.

LESSONS OF THE PAST AND NEW DEVELOPMENTS

The lessons of the seventeen-year history of CDs primarily concern experience with the two means employed by the monetary authorities to influence the CD market: Regulation Q interest rate ceilings and reserve requirements.

While Regulation Q interest rate ceilings did restrict bank lending to business somewhat during the 1969-70 period, overall credit extended to business was affected much less. The rigidly maintained CD rate ceilings succeeded in preventing deposits from flowing from thrift institutions to commercial banks, but as a result both suffered severe deposit losses which greatly increased uncertainty in domestic financial markets. The further evolution of the financial system since that time and the increased ability of borrowers to secure funds from outside the banking system make it even more doubtful that Regulation Q can be used constructively as a means of monetary control in the future.

As to the various forms of reserve requirements applied to CDs, there is little evidence that they have had any appreciable effect on the market. This holds true for the marginal reserve requirements as well as for the current reserve requirements that are differentiated according to original maturity.

Further alterations of reserve requirements do not appear to be a promising means of increasing the average maturity of CDs. The demand for long-term CDs is mainly affected by three factors: the short period of time for which many investors have funds available, the thinness of the secondary market for long-term CDs, and the spread of the long-term CD rate over the short-term CD rate. Current reserve requirements influence the latter factor by penalizing short-term CDs. Given the tendency of the other factors to favor the purchase of short-term CDs, it seems likely that reserve requirements would have to incorporate a considerably greater differential to stimulate the issuance of long-term CDs. The legal limit on the range of reserve requirements that may be applied to time deposits, 3-10 percent, does not appear to allow much scope for creating such a differential.[5]

Of course, given the increased use of term loans in bank lending to business, there is a presumption that banks should lengthen the maturities of their deposits so as to maintain something of a balance between the maturities of their assets and their liabilities. In fact, the average maturity of CDs has recently tended to vary directly with the cyclical increase in the proportion of term loans in the portfolios of large banks. But, judging by the timing of maturity changes, very little of this variation appears to be attributable to the lowering of reserve requirements for long-term CDs in September and December 1974. The balancing of asset and liability maturities thus appears to take place over the business cycle independently of changes in reserve requirements.

The most interesting developments in the CD market in the last few years have been the innovations introduced by banks to extend the maturities of CDs. During the early 1975 the variable-rate CD was introduced. It has a minimum maturity of 360 days, and its interest rate, pegged at a specified spread over the issuing bank's current rate on 90-day CDs, is adjusted every 90 days. With such an instrument an investor can increase his total interest return over that obtainable by successively renewing short-term CDs without being committed to a fixed rate. The attraction to the issuing banks is that, on average, the total interest paid on a variable-rate CD will be less than that on a conventional (fixed-rate) CD of the same maturity. The reason is that the investor and the bank in effect split the risk premium included in the spread of the long-term conventional CD rate over the short-term CD rate. It is impossible to determine how many variable-rate CDs have been sold. The amount cannot be very large, since demand for long-term CDs is restricted by the scarcity of long-term investable funds and the relative illiquidity of long-term CDs.

Another recent innovation has the potential of altering somewhat the character of the market as well as lengthening maturities. It is the rollover CD introduced by Morgan Guaranty Trust in late 1976. The rollover CD was designed to overcome the limitation on a bank's ability to issue long-term CDs, due to six months being about the maximum maturity traded regularly

---

[5] Reserve requirements for specific kinds of time deposits have recently been set below 3 percent, but a bank's reserve requirement for all of its time deposits must nevertheless be at least 3 percent.

in the secondary market. Investors are naturally reluctant to purchase long-term CDs if they in large part lack the liquidity provided for short-term CDs by the secondary market. The rollover CD attempts to deal with the problem by packaging a series of six-month CDs into a commitment to roll them over for a longer period of time, *e.g.,* three years. Any one of the six-month CDs may be sold in the secondary market if the investor needs liquidity but, if he does so, he is nevertheless committed to roll over the CD by redepositing equivalent funds at each maturity date.

The rollover CD allows long-term CDs to be structured so as to be able to take advantage of the existing secondary market. Still, it is not so liquid as a conventional six-month CD, since the investor cannot at present sell his rollover commitment in the secondary market and since the rate of interest is fixed for the entire term of the commitment. Even so, the innovation could enhance considerably the liquidity of long-term CDs. A disadvantage to the issuing bank of the rollover CD, compared with a conventional long-term, single-maturity CD, is that the bank takes the risk, however small, that an investor may default on his future commitment to roll over the six-month CD. The additional risk may well limit the attractiveness of rollover CDs to banks until experience indicates that the risk is negligible or that it can be reduced to reasonable levels through careful management. The future of the rollover CD is still uncertain, and only a moderate amount has been sold by Morgan Guaranty.

The Federal Reserve has continued to encourage banks to lengthen the average maturity of their CDs by lowering reserve requirements for time deposits (including CDs) with long original terms to maturity. For example, in October 1975 the reserve requirement applying to CDs with original terms to maturity of four years or longer was reduced to 1 percent from 3 percent.[6] Since only a minute fraction of CDs outstanding at present have this long an original maturity, the effect of the change on the average maturity of CDs was probably nil. In January 1976 the reserve requirement applying to time deposits with an original maturity of at least 180 days up to four years was lowered to 2.5 percent from 3 percent. It seems unlikely that this small change had any appreciable effect on the average maturity of CDs.

It appears that the structure of reserve requirements on time deposits could well be simplified by eliminating different requirements for different maturities. As noted, it seems unlikely that these reserve requirements have had any significant effect on the average maturity of CDs, and they complicate considerably the calculation of banks' required reserves. There is also reason to question whether influencing the maturity structure of CDs is a desirable policy objective. If it is, consideration should be given to ways to encourage innovations such as the rollover CD; liquidity is likely to be more important to potential investors than the small extra return that might be created by low reserve requirements on long-term CDs.

---

[6] Morgan Guaranty initially hoped that rollover CDs of four years and longer maturity would be subject to the 1 percent reserve requirement applying to conventional CDs of such a maturity. But a recent Federal Reserve ruling held that, for calculation of required reserves, a rollover CD is equivalent to a six-month CD and thus is subject to a higher reserve requirement.

Another possible policy initiative would be to eliminate the 30-day minimum maturity of CDs. It is difficult to point to any important purpose served by this requirement, and its removal would probably contribute modestly to the smooth functioning of the market. Although removal would require a change in the legislation governing time deposits, such action is not inconceivable in light of recent trends toward payment of interest on demand deposits (NOW accounts, telephone transfers, etc.).

The availability of very short-term CDs would make CDs more attractive in investors' portfolios relative to finance company commercial paper, which often has only a few days' maturity. Most investors would probably find very short-term CDs attractive at only a modest spread over the RP rate. Very short-term CDs would also give banks a somewhat more flexible instrument for short-term adjustment of reserve positions than RPs, which must be backed by Treasury securities if they are to be exempt from demand deposit reserve requirements. Elimination of the 30-day minimum maturity would thus remove the artificial stimulus to secondary market trading in CDs of less than 30 days remaining maturity, much as was done for 30- to 89- day maturities by the November 1964 increase in the applicable Regulation Q ceiling from its earlier uncompetitive level. Finally, the availability of very short-term CDs would considerably simplify the cash management policies of municipalities, whose legal investment alternatives tend to be few.

PROSPECTS FOR CDs

An assessment of prospects must recognize that the CD market probably has reached maturity. Rates have become tiered to reflect investor perception of the relative riskiness of issuing banks—a standard feature of other financial markets. Perhaps more revealing of market maturity is the banks' voluntary reduction of outstanding CDs beginning in 1975, the first sustained voluntary retrenchment ever. There is thus little likelihood that bank reliance on CDs will increase at anything like the steady rate observed during much of the 1960's, when Regulation Q ceilings were not binding. The outlook, rather, is for CDs to behave much as they did in 1973-76; in that period, issues expanded in line with increased loan demand and contracted as loan demand declined.

Without a return to Regulation Q ceilings on CD rates or some other quantitative constraint on banks' liability management, United States banks' reliance on borrowings from their foreign branches as a source of funds will probably reflect primarily the relative cost of funds in the CD market and the Eurodollar market. Unless Eurodollar rates should at times get to be abnormally low relative to United States CD rates, such borrowings from now on should chiefly provide a source of funds with maturities of less than 30 days. Substitution between domestic CDs and Eurodollar time deposits at foreign branches will most likely be of appreciably smaller importance than it was in the past. For this reason, borrowings from foreign branches will probably grow much less than CDs whenever banks seek to expand their discretionary liabilities in response to growing loan demand.

THE EURO-DOLLAR MARKET*

Aubrey N. Snellings

20

The last two decades have witnessed the growth and development of an international money market which effectively links together national money markets in the world's major countries. This market is often referred to as the "Euro-currency" market, but this term is imprecise because non-European countries, notably Canada, Japan, and the Caribean countries, are quite important in the market. This brief article is concerned primarily with the foreign market in United States dollars, i.e., Euro-dollars, which make up about 75 to 80 percent of the broader market in foreign currencies.

WHAT ARE EURO-DOLLARS?

In the simplest terms, Euro-dollars are deposits, denominated in U.S. dollars, placed with banks outside the United States, including deposits at foreign branches of U.S. banks. Euro-dollar deposits arise when the owner of a demand deposit at a U.S. bank transfers ownership of that deposit to a foreign bank in exchange for a dollar-denominated deposit claim against the for-

*Reprinted from *Instruments of the Money Market*, 4th edition, edited by Timothy Q. Cook, 1977, pp. 94-101, with permisssion from the Federal Reserve Bank of Richmond.

eign bank. Euro-dollar deposits may be made by individuals, corporations, or other nonbanking institutions who may be depositing dollars acquired through a current or capital transaction already denominated in dollars or through purchase of dollars in the foreign exchange market. Other commercial banks may deposit funds obtained in the foreign exchange market or from the central bank, or they may redeposit funds obtained from other participants in the Euro-dollar market. Some deposits of central bank funds are made directly by the central bank, others indirectly through the Bank for International Settlements. Euro-dollar deposits usually take the form of a time deposit, but overnight and call deposits are also made. The foreign bank receiving the deposit may lend the dollars to another foreign bank, to a bank in the United States, to a nonbank abroad such as an importer, or to a U.S. company.

Trading in the Euro-dollar market may involve substantial pyramiding of Euro-dollar deposits. For example, a European bank holding a deposit in a U.S. bank may make a Euro-dollar deposit with another European bank, which in turn may deposit the proceeds with another bank, and so on. Each redeposit transfers ownership of the original deposit at the United States bank, and the transfer process could, of course, shift the deposit to another United States bank. Each such redeposit creates new Euro-dollar deposit liabilities on the books of the foreign bank involved, and the total Euro-dollars thus created may be several times the amount of the original claim on the United States bank. Of course, if these additional liabilities created simply represent a succession of interbank deposits, they do not expand the supply of credit to the nonbank public.

ORIGINS OF THE MARKET

The acceptance of deposits denominated in foreign currencies is a practice of long standing, but the Euro-dollar market as presently constituted goes back no earlier than the late 1950's. Some writers trace its beginnings to the early 1950's, when banks in Eastern Europe held dollar deposits with banks in Western Europe in preference to deposits in U.S. banks. The functioning of the market on its present scale, however, requires the free flow of short-term funds from country to country. This requirement became possible for the first time in 1958, when the major European countries, who had by then accumulated substantial reserves arising from U.S. balance of payments deficits, made their currencies freely convertible into the dollar. A second important development, which occurred a few months prior to the restoration of currency convertibility, was the imposition of restrictions by the British Government on the use of sterling to finance trade between nonresidents. These restrictions helped to stimulate use of dollar loans to foreigners by the British banking industry.

GROWTH OF THE MARKET

Precise data on the growth and size of the Euro-dollar market are not available. In recent years, however, the Bank for International Settlements has estimated the dimensions of the Euro-dollar and Euro-currency markets on the basis of reported foreign currency positions of banks located in eight European countries, Japan, and Canada.

The chart below is based on Bank for International Settlement data. In some respects, these data overstate the size of the Euro-dollar market.

Dollar Position of Commercial Banks in Selected Countries, vis-a-vis Nonresidents

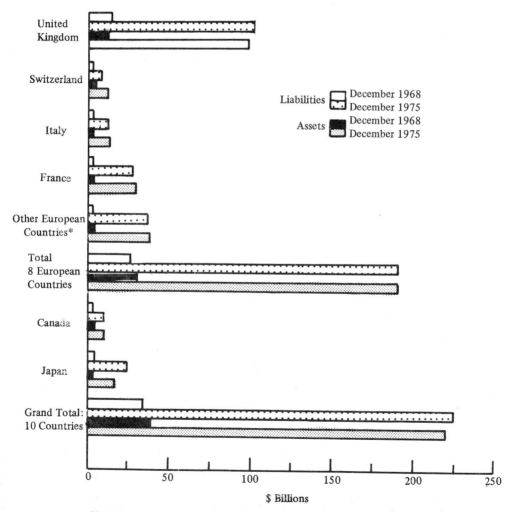

*Belgium, Germany, Netherlands, and Sweden.
Source: Bank for International Settlements, 39th and 46th Annual Reports.

Some of the assets and liabilities shown arose out of the pyramiding of deposits described above and thus overstate the amount of dollars available to nonbank borrowers. Some liabilities arose out of the use of credit lines with United States banks, while some assets represent normal working balances in United States banks that are not available for trading in the Euro-dollar market. On the other hand, the data do not reflect the dollar positions of these banks toward residents of their own countries and thus omit a substantial amount of dollars that are available to the market.

On the basis of such data, it is possible to estimate the approximate size of the Euro-dollar market. The growth of the market has been spectacular. According to the Bank for International Settlements estimates, dollar liabilities of commercial banks in the eight reporting European countries to non-residents grew from $26.9 billion at the end of 1968 to $151.7 billion in mid-1974. By then, however, certain developments had created an atmosphere of apprehension in the Euro-dollar market. The quadrupling of oil prices in late 1973 resulted in large balance of payments deficits for some countries that were borrowers in the Euro-dollar market, causing some doubt as to the quality of loans made to these countries. Also a few banks in the Euro-dollar market experienced large losses related to foreign exchange transactions. When foreign exchange losses led to the closing of a relatively small German bank, confidence in the Euro-dollar market was weakened, resulting in a highly unusual contraction in interbank deposits and gross Euro-dollar liabilities.

The events of 1974 led to widespread speculation about the future health of the Euro-dollar market. By early 1975, however, confidence in the Euro-dollar market had improved markedly, in part because of assurances in late 1974 from the Group of Ten central-bank Governors confirming their willingness to provide liquidity if needed for international banking and foreign currency operations of their respective countries. In any case, rapid growth in the Euro-dollar market resumed, and by the end of 1975 the dollar liabilities of commercial banks in the eight European countries to non-residents had risen to $189.5 billion.

London is the heart of the Euro-dollar market. In December 1975, banks in the United Kingdom (including branches there of non-UK-owned banks) accounted for 55.0 percent of the dollar liabilities reported by banks in the eight reporting European countries and about 46.2 percent of the total of the ten reporting countries. The fastest growing center of Euro-dollar activity in the recent past has been the Caribbean area, which now represents the largest Euro-dollar center after London.

CONTRIBUTING FACTORS

Confidence in the United States dollar is essential to the existence of the Euro-dollar market, but other factors have contributed importantly to its growth. Among the most important are interest rate differentials between the United States and foreign markets and legal and institutional restrictions on the movement and use of funds.

Euro-dollar deposits are for the most part interest-bearing time deposits of relatively short maturity, although maturities may be extended to five years, and interest is also paid on call money. Banks seeking to raise funds in this market must pay rates on deposits that are competitive with those on instruments of comparable quality, liquidity, and maturity in United States money markets. Loan rates, on the other hand, must be competitive with rates charged on local currency loans and in United States financial markets. This results in narrower margins between Euro-dollar borrowing and lending rates than generally exist between dollar borrowing and lending rates at U.S. commercial banks.

The Euro-dollar market makes possible the avoidance of numerous restrictions on the uses of funds or on rates that may be charged. Banks in the United States, for example, are prohibited from paying interest on demand deposits, and the rates they can pay on some classes of time deposits are limited by Regulation Q. No such restrictions apply to Euro-dollar deposit rates, so it is advantageous to many holders of dollars to deposit them in banks outside the United States. Likewise, United States banks may solicit funds in the Euro-dollar market at rates not subject to ceiling restrictions. Thus, in periods of high interest rates in the United States, when Regulation Q interest rate ceilings caused larger runoffs of certificates of deposits, U. S. banks could replace the lost funds by borrowing heavily from their foreign branches.

Another set of restrictions that influenced the growth of the Euro-dollar market consisted of controls on capital outflows initiated by the U.S. Government in an attempt to repress its chronic balance of payments deficits. These programs, started in the mid-1960's, included the interest Equalization Tax, which lowered the effective yield to U. S. investors on foreign securities; the Voluntary Foreign Credit Restraint Program, which set "guidelines" on foreign short-term bank loans; and the Foreign Direct Investment Program, which placed controls on new capital investments abroad by U. S. corporations financed with foreign earnings or dollars acquired in the United States. These programs diminished the ability of foreign subsidiaries of U. S. corporations and other borrowers to obtain funds in the United States, thereby stimulating demand for Euro-dollar loans and spurring growth of the market. All of these programs were terminated in January 1974.

IMPLICATIONS OF THE MARKET

The Euro-currency market is in a continuing state of evolution. Since the mid-1950's it has grown from a quite limited market in United States dollars into a worldwide market involving transactions in a number of major currencies. This evoluation toward a truly international money market has important implications for national monetary conditions, balance of payments positions, and the management of the money position of large commercial banks.

One result has been the development of an international interest rate structure independent of the rate structure within any individual country. This has tended to reduce interest rate differentials between national money markets and to limit to some extent the ability of monetary policymakers to influence the level of rates within particular countries. The impact of Euro-dollar rates on the rate structure of a particular country, however, depends on the size of Euro-dollar flows relative to total financial flows and upon the effort made to insulate domestic credit markets from the effects of Euro-dollar operations. But if a central bank attempts to hold interest rates in a particular country above those in money markets in other major countries, or if commerical banks try to maintain artificially high rates through cartel arrangements, a sharp influx of Euro-currency funds into that country is likely to put downward pressures on domestic rates. Conversely, countries attempting to hold rates below those prevailing in the Euro-dollar market have experienced outflows of funds which put pressure on their international reserves.

In recent years, commercial banks have made increased use of the Euro-dollar market to adjust their liquidity positions, and central banks have used it to supplement monetary policy operations in domestic money markets. During the decade of the 1960's, U. S. commercial banks placed increasing emphasis on the management of their liquidity positions from the liability rather than from the asset side. To some extent their increasing reliance on the Euro-dollar market was a part of this general change in policy. But in times of monetary stringency, Regulation Q ceilings sometimes prevented banks from having recourse to U. S. money markets through CD's. At such times they offset the loss of money market funds by borrowing heavily in the Euro-dollar market. In 1966, for example, liabilities of U. S. banks to their foreign branches rose from $1.7 billion in January to $4.0 billion in December, and in 1969, when interest rates rose sharply, these liabilities increased $7.0 billion. This particular stimulus to Euro-dollar borrowing was eliminated when interest rate ceilings on large CD's were suspended in June 1970 for deposits with maturities of less than 90 days and in May 1973 when rate ceilings were suspended for CD's with longer maturities.

The individual bank may increase its legal reserves by borrowing in the Euro-dollar market because this draws reserves from other banks. Such borrowings, however, do not increase the reserves of the banking system as a whole. Until October 1969 banks were not required to hold legal reserves against liabilities to foreign branches. Thus, until that time the substitution of a liability to a foreign branch for a domestic deposit liability could be used to reduce the required reserves of the banking system and increase the loanable funds of the system. The attractiveness of Euro-dollar funds was sharply reduced in 1969, however, when the Federal Reserve imposed a 10 percent reserve requirement on liabilities to foreign branches in excess of a reserve-free base level and against borrowings from nonaffiliated foreign

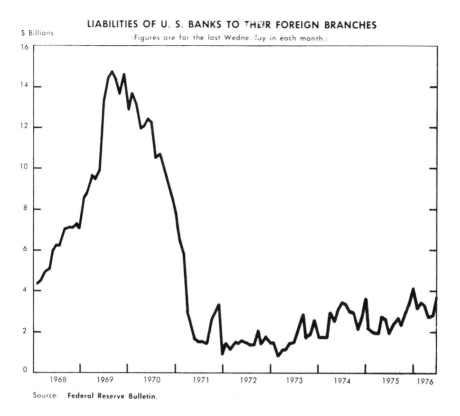

LIABILITIES OF U. S. BANKS TO THEIR FOREIGN BRANCHES
(Figures are for the last Wednesday in each month.)

$ Billions

Source: **Federal Reserve Bulletin.**

banks. This reserve requirement was raised to 20 percent in January 1971 and subsequently lowered to 8 percent in June 1973 and 4 percent in May 1975. The reserve-free base was eliminated in early 1974.

Periods of intense demand pressures in the Euro-dollar market have created special problems for central banks. To cite just one example, in 1966 heavy borrowings combined with year-end window dressing operations of European commercial banks put strong upward pressure on interest rates in the Euro-dollar market. Among other unfavorable results, these pressures threatened to pull funds out of sterling and to subject the spot sterling rate to intense pressure. To meet this situation, several European central banks, the Federal Reserve System, and the BIS took concerted action to relieve pressures in the Euro-dollar market. The Swiss National Bank, for example, bought spot dollars from commercial banks and sold them forward over the year-end. The dollars thus acquired were immediately channeled back into the Euro-dollar market. The BIS drew upon a $200 million swap line with the Federal Reserve and placed the dollars in the Euro-dollar market. The Netherlands Bank rechanneled funds into the market, while the German Federal Bank and the Bank of Italy took action to reduce the pullback of Euro-dollar placements by their banks.

Concerted action of this type by major central banks points up the growing recognition of the Euro-dollar market as an international money market.

In addition, central banks have for some years used operations in the market to influence domestic monetary conditions. The German Federal Bank, for example, has at times offered dollar swap facilities to commercial banks on favorable terms to encourage the banks to place funds abroad and thus reduce domestic liquidity. The Bank of Italy has provided similar swap facilities to Italian banks. On the other hand, a central bank may add to domestic liquidity by encouraging commercial banks to draw funds from the Euro-dollar market and convert them into the local currency. These operations in the Euro-dollar market, therefore, are quite similar in effect to central bank open market operations.

Part II
LIABILITY AND
CAPITAL MANAGEMENT

B. BORROWED FUNDS AND CAPITAL

In addition to deposits, several classes of debt-type instruments may be used by commercial banks to obtain funds. One of these sources of funds is the Federal Reserve's discount window. As explained by James Parthemos, the discount window is used primarily to meet short-term cash or reserve needs. However, since the Federal Reserve is the banking system's "lender of last resort," other forms of borrowing are available under certain conditions. Another source of funds used by larger banks is the banker's acceptance. The article by Jack L. Hervey explains how acceptances are created and used by commercial banks. If a time draft is "accepted" by a bank and sold in the money market, the bank in effect borrows the funds necessary to finance a specific transaction. The result is a money market instrument of exceptionally high quality.

In the first of his two articles on bank capital, Ronald D. Watson examines a hotly debated topic—the role of debt in the capital structure of banks. Such factors as the role of capital, regulatory concerns, leverage, and holding company effects are discussed. In his second article, Watson focuses on a perennial question—Is there a shortage of bank capital? This issue is important because bank expansion must be accompanied by a commensurate growth in capital. Watson argues that there is no shortage of capital but rather an unwillingness or inability to pay the high market rates for capital that have prevailed in recent years. Dividend policy, dilution, capital standards, and the cost of capital are among the issues analyzed by Watson.

THE DISCOUNT WINDOW*

James Parthemos

21

For bankers, the money market is important primarily as a focal center through which adjustments in their reserve positions are worked out. Member banks can make the same adjustments by borrowing at the discount window of their Federal Reserve Bank. Thus, a bank suffering an unexpected reserve loss can bring its reserve position back to the desired level by arranging a discount or advance at the Federal Reserve. Similarly, a bank experiencing a temporary buildup of reserves beyond desired levels may, before placing any funds in the money market, pay off any borrowings it may owe at the Federal Reserve. In any event, the Federal Reserve discount window affords to member banks an additional recourse in working out reserve adjustments and, from the standpoint of these banks, may be properly viewed as an operational part of the money market.

Reserve adjustments via the discount window differ in one important respect from adjustments effected in the money market proper. Trading in such instruments as Treasury bills, bankers' acceptances, and Federal funds among commercial banks or between commercial banks and their customers involves no net creation of new bank reserves. Rather, existing reserves are simply shifted about within the banking system. On the other hand, when borrowings or repayments at the discount window result in a net change in Federal Reserve credit outstanding, the volume of bank reserves is affected. Thus,

*Reprinted from *Instruments of the Money Market*, 4th edition, edited by Timothy Q. Cook, 1977, pp. 28-37, with permission from the Federal Reserve Bank of Richmond.

the choice by individual banks between the discount window and alternative means of reserve adjustment may influence the availability of credit and money in the economy at large.

Bankers' decisions to use the discount window or other segments of the money market for making reserve adjustments depend on the level of the Federal Reserve's discount rate relative to yields on money market investments, on institutional peculiarities in the several parts of the money market, and on legal and administrative arrangements regarding use of the discount window.

EARLY DISCOUNTING PRINCIPLES

Originally, the most important single function of the Federal Reserve System was to provide a pool of funds which could be drawn on by banks experiencing reserve difficulties. The ability of banks to draw on this pool, however, was not envisaged as an absolute right. Rather, it was linked to a widely held theory of commercial banking which is known to monetary students as the commercial loan or "real bills" principle. According to this doctrine, commercial banks should be allowed to borrow only against short-term, "self-liquidating" paper arising from the normal conduct of legitimate business. To ensure adherence to this principle, member banks were initially permitted to borrow only by rediscounting customer loans which met certain closely specified conditions based on the commercial loan theory. Promissory notes and other credit instruments meeting these specifications were defined as "eligible paper," that is, paper eligible for rediscount at the Federal Reserve.

By and large, the commercial loan principle dominated member bank use of the discount window until the banking crisis of 1933. During the 1920's trading in such money market instruments as short-term Government debt and Federal funds was not nearly so well developed as at present. While banks made extensive use of bankers' acceptances, commercial paper, and call loans against stock exchange collateral for reserve adjustment purposes, they also relied heavily on the discount window. Many bankers made it a regular practice to hold a supply of eligible paper which would be readily available for reserve adjustment through the discount window. Throughout the 1920's, average daily borrowings at the discount window usually exceeded $500 million and at times amounted to more than twice that figure.

FROM THE 1930'S TO THE ACCORD

The banking reforms of the 1930's incorporated features designed to encourage use of the discount window by banks. In some measure, these features were related to a growing conviction that the commercial loan principle and the eligibility requirements unduly restricted banks in their efforts to secure central bank assistance in times of stress. The effect of the reforms was to sweep away the real bills basis for discounting, although the concept of eligible paper was retained in the language of discount regulations.

At an early stage in Federal Reserve history, member banks were allowed to borrow on their own notes, secured by eligible paper or Government securities, instead of by rediscounting customer paper. Since 1933 direct advances against Government securities have accounted for most Federal Reserve lending. In addition, banking legislation of the 1930's incorporated a new section, 10(b), into the provisions of the Federal Reserve Act, authorizing Federal Reserve loans to member banks against any collateral satisfactory to the lending Reserve Bank.

Despite the encouragement of these changes and of low discount rates, banks used the discount window sparingly between 1933 and 1951. From 1935 to 1940 daily borrowings generally averaged below $10 million. For the most part, banks held large excess reserves and were under little pressure to borrow. Even after the business recovery of the early 1940's, borrowing remained at low levels. By that time, banks held large quantities of Government securities and the Federal Reserve's practice of pegging the market for these securities, instituted in 1942, eliminated the market risk of adjusting reserve positions through sales of Governments. The Treasury-Federal Reserve Accord in the spring of 1951, however, ended the pegged market for Government securities and began a new chapter in the history of the discount window.

DISCOUNTING SINCE THE ACCORD

Prices of Government securities fluctuated over a broader range after the Accord, and it became riskier for banks to rely on these securities as a source of reserves when adjustments were necessary. Consequently, banks began to reassess the relative attractiveness of the discount window. Partly for this reason, borrowings jumped sharply, reaching the $1.0 billion level in mid-1952 for the first time in more than 20 years. For most of the 1950's borrowings were at levels comparable in absolute (though not in relative) terms with those of the 1920's.

The renewed importance of the discount window, coming in an overall economic and credit environment quite different from that prevailing in the 1920's, suggested the need for a general review of the principles on which the discount privilege was based. In 1955, after an extended inquiry, the Board of Governors promulgated a major revision in its Regulation A, which sets forth the ground rules under which member banks use the discount window today. As embodied in Regulation A, administrative restrictions on use of the discount window relate to the broader aspects of the Federal Reserve's operations rather than to any particular banking theory. For example, Regulation A recognizes that borrowing by member banks creates new reserves and, unless subject to some restraint, could conflict with broader programs to achieve such national goals as economic and price stability. It also recognizes the necessity for ensuring that the public resources administered by the Federal Reserve are used not to support questionable banking practices but rather ensure continuity of effective banking services to the public.

Generally, Regulation A envisages use of the discount window as a temporary expedient open to member banks facing reserve adjustments necessitated by the workings of a dynamic economy. Thus, reserve needs occasioned by extraordinary seasonal swings in credit demand or in deposits may give rise to "appropriate" borrowing. Similarly, reserve problems associated with emergency situations affecting a community or a region, or with local or regional secular change, provide appropriate reasons for borrowing.

Continuous borrowing at the discount window is considered "inappropriate," whatever its purpose. Continuous discounting by an individual bank suggests use of central bank funds as a supplement to the borrowing bank's capital resources. It also implies that the borrowing bank has permanent reserve difficulties that should be corrected through basic portfolio adjustments. Regulation A enumerates other specific purposes for which use of the discount window is inappropriate. These include borrowing to obtain tax advantages, to profit from interest rate differentials, and to finance speculation in securities, real estate, or commodities.

Within the constraints embodied in Regulation A, the discount window is open to member banks in a variety of situations that may be considered more or less normal to commercial bank operations. For example, resort to the discount window for temporary aid in working out portfolio adjustments to meet especially meritorious local credit demands is also viewed as appropriate. More generally, as long as a bank demonstrates in its overall performance its intention to operate within the limits of its own resources, it can usually arrange temporary accommodation to cover a variety of problems.

In the fall of 1966, the provisions of Regulation A were supplemented for a brief time with special provisions designed to encourage banks to alter their lending and investing policies. This use of the discount window as a means of selective control was an attempt to cope with an unusual situation. Interest rates were rising rapidly, participants in the markets for fixed income obligations talked of the possibility of disorderly conditions, financial intermediaries were losing funds, and the flow of mortgage money had virtually stopped. At the same time, banks were expanding their loans, particularly business loans, at an unusually rapid pace, contributing to inflationary pressures. On September 1, 1966, the Presidents of the Federal Reserve Banks dispatched a letter to all member banks stating that banks that would respond to the pressures of tight monetary policy by adjusting their reserve positions through reduction of loan growth instead of through liquidation of securities in already jittery markets could qualify for longer-than-usual accommodation at the discount window. By December the unusual circumstances which prompted the September 1 letter had passed, and on December 27 the provisions of that letter were formally rescinded.

In April 1973 Regulation A was revised to permit less restricted use of the discount window for seasonal borrowing. Short-term access to the discount window had, of course, been available to member banks experiencing unusually strong seasonal reserve needs. In many instances, however, prolonged seasonal swings made it difficult for member banks, particularly smaller banks with limited access to national markets, to meet the need for funds through reasonable use of their own resources. The revision in Regulation A was designed specifically to assist those member banks that lacked reasonable access to national money markets in meeting seasonal needs arising out of expected patterns in deposits and loans.

Under the 1973 revision in Regulation A, a member bank could obtain Federal Reserve credit to assist it in meeting seasonal needs exceeding 5 per cent of its average annual deposits. In order to qualify for the seasonal borrowing privilege, the bank had to provide the Federal Reserve with sufficient advance evidence to indicate that the seasonal need would persist for at least eight consecutive weeks. The seasonal borrowing program initiated in 1973 was available only to banks with deposits of less than $250 million. Furthermore, member banks were not permitted to use the seasonal borrowing privilege and at the same time have net sales of Federal funds.

In August 1976 new revisions were made to Regulation A to liberalize the seasonal borrowing privilege. Under the revised regulations member banks can use the seasonal borrowing privilege to meet that part of their seasonal need for funds exceeding 4 per cent of their first $100 million of deposits the previous year; 7 per cent of their second $100 million; and 10 per cent of any deposits over $200 million. The period over which the seasonal need must persist was lowered from eight to four weeks and banks with deposits as great as $500 million, rather than $250 million, were made eligible for the seasonal borrowing privilege. In addition, the regulation was revised to allow net sales of Federal funds while banks are engaged in seasonal borrowing from the Federal Reserve; banks cannot, however, use the seasonal borrowing privilege to expand their net sales of Federal funds. The 1976 revision was made in recognition of the growing number of small banks that use the Federal funds market as a permanent source of liquidity.

Since the initiation of the seasonal borrowing program in 1973, seasonal borrowing has in each year been heaviest in the period from July through October. The magnitude of seasonal borrowing has also moved with the overall state of credit demand in the economy. In 1973 and 1974, when there was aggressive competition for bank loans, seasonal borrowing averaged $88.6 million and $84.8 million, respectively. In 1975 and 1976, however, when loan demand in general plummeted, average seasonal borrowing fell sharply to $23.3 million and $18.3 million, respectively.

ADMINISTRATION OF THE WINDOW

Currently, most Federal Reserve loans to member banks are made under the provisions of Section 13 of the Federal Reserve Act and are in the form of direct advances secured by Government obligations. Advances under Section 13 can also be made against eligible paper, which includes a variety of commercial, agricultural, and industrial paper, bankers' acceptances and other bills of exchange, construction loans, and factors' paper. The use of eligible paper as collateral was negligible in most of the postwar period, but there was a revival of interest in its use beginning in 1966 due to the diminished availability of Government securities collateral at banks.

Loans under Section 10(b), which may be secured by any collateral satisfactory to the lending Reserve Bank, are relatively unimportant in current discount activity. In part, this is because the rate charged on 10(b) loans is ½ percentage point higher than on Section 13 loans. Moreover, depending on the collateral offered, 10(b) loans may involve some delay. Banks borrowing under this Section usually have done so as a last resort and have offered chiefly municipal securities as collateral.

Maturities of up to 90 days are authorized on Section 13 loans, while the statutory limit on 10(b) maturities is four months. In practice, however, borrowings under either section are almost always for a maximum of 15 days. Notes may, of course, be paid in part or in full before maturity, in which case unearned discount is rebated. Unless the Federal Reserve is notified to the contrary, the amount due on the note is automatically charged against the borrowing bank's reserve account on the maturity date.

MECHANICS OF BORROWING

In order to borrow, a member bank must furnish the Federal Reserve Bank a certified copy of a resolution adopted by its Board of Directors specifying which of its officers are authorized to borrow on its behalf. Signatures on all notes submitted by a borrowing bank are checked against the bank's resolution and against the signature list held by the Bank Accounts Department of the Reserve Bank.

The type of borrowing most convenient for both the member bank and the Reserve Bank is the direct advance on a promissory note secured by direct obligations of the U. S. Government and by certain fully guaranteed Federal agency issues. To borrow on Government obligations, the member bank must execute an application and note, both of which must be received by a Federal Reserve Bank on or before the day of the borrowing. Any bank which wishes to do so may leave with the Reserve Bank a supply of signed notes with the dates and amounts left blank, to be filled in upon telephone requests of authorized officers of the member bank, followed by written confirmation. Loans on Government obligations are made for the face amount of the collateral. The collateral must be held by the Federal Reserve Bank unless prior arrangements have been made permitting another member bank to hold the securities under a custody receipt arrangement. Under such an arrangement the securities may be held by a member bank which in the usual course of business performs correspondent bank services, including the holding in custody of Government securities, for the borrowing bank.

While member banks may also rediscount eligible paper or borrow on their promissory note secured by eligible paper, this procedure is more time-consuming since the Reserve Bank must verify the eligibility of the collateral, then analyze and value it. Member banks, therefore, often submit eligible paper collateral in advance of the date of the borrowing. In 10(b) applications processing is prompt when municipal securities are offered as collateral, but delays may result when customer notes are offered.

BORROWING LEVELS

The volume of borrowings at the discount window fluctuates over a wide range, as shown in the chart. Both small and large banks use the discount window, but in most recent years large (Reserve City) banks have accounted for the greater dollar volume of borrowings. Borrowings generally increase in periods of rising interest rates and decline in periods of falling interest rates.

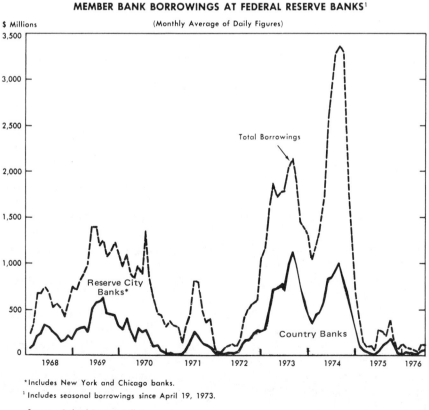

MEMBER BANK BORROWINGS AT FEDERAL RESERVE BANKS[1]

(Monthly Average of Daily Figures)

*Includes New York and Chicago banks.

[1] Includes seasonal borrowings since April 19, 1973.

Source: **Federal Reserve Bulletin.**

To a large extent this is because, in recent years especially, changes in the discount rate have lagged behind movements in money market rates. Consequently, in periods of rising rates, the cost of borrowing at the discount window becomes relatively more attractive compared to the cost of raising funds in other sectors of the money market.

Borrowings spurted sharply in the periods of credit tightness in 1969, 1973, and 1974. Considering the low level of the discount rate relative to the cost of alternative sources of reserve adjustment funds in those periods, however, the volume of borrowings would undoubtedly have been much greater without the use of discount administration as a rationing device.

LENDER OF LAST RESORT

A large part of the sharp rise in borrowing from the Federal Reserve in 1974 was by one bank, Franklin National Bank. Early in 1974 Franklin National reported poor operating earnings and substantial losses in foreign exchange operations. Its holding company announced on May 10, 1974 that it planned to suspend the regular dividend payment on both common and preferred stock. Massive withdrawals of deposits followed and on May 12 the Federal Reserve announced that, in its role of "lender of last resort," it would advance funds to Franklin National as needed. Subsequently, loans by the Fed to Franklin National reached as high as $1.75 billion in October 1975. In that month a merger was arranged with another bank, European-American, and an arrangement was worked out with the FDIC whereby it assumed the Federal Reserve loan and agreed to repay it over the next three years as collateral supplied by Franklin was liquidated.

In its role as "lender of last resort" the Federal Reserve has a responsibility to provide funds to banks when the consequences of failure to do so would aggravate or lead to a financial crisis. It was this role that the Chairman of the Federal Reserve Board, Arthur Burns, was taking when he announced that "The Federal Reserve, as lender of last resort, provided emergency assistance to Franklin beginning last May. By doing so, we kept Franklin's banking services available, prevented serious adverse consequences in financial markets both here and abroad, and provided the time necessary for the Comptroller of the Currency, the Federal Deposit Insurance Corporation, and the Federal Reserve to work out a satisfactory permanent solution."

The loan to Franklin was made at the discount rate of 8 per cent, which was at the time well below money market rates. As a reaction to this development, the Federal Reserve in September 1974 established a new category of discount borrowing under which a special discount rate could be applied to member banks requiring exceptionally large assistance over a prolonged period of time. That special discount rate, established under Section 10(b) of the Federal Reserve Act, has typically been set at one to two percentage points above the Section 13 rate.

DISCOUNTING VS. BUYING FEDERAL FUNDS

Banks that manage their reserve positions closely usually meet short-run reserve deficiencies either by borrowing from the Federal Reserve or by buying Federal funds. Large banks tend to incur reserve deficiencies more frequently than small banks and tend to rely more heavily on borrowed funds. The tendency to use both sources of funds increases rapidly with bank size. Most large banks borrow from both sources, but smaller banks tend to use one source or the other, but not both.

BANKERS' ACCEPTANCES*

Jack L. Hervey

22

Perhaps no other financial instrument—apart from money itself—has been as important to the development of international commerce as the bill of exchange and its more refined form, the banker's acceptance. By providing an efficient means of facilitating the shipment of goods through the extension of trade credit, these instruments have made it possible for two traders virtually unknown to each other and located in different parts of the world to enter into commercial transactions.

Economic historians trace the origin of early forms of these instruments to the twelfth century and attribute to their development the onset of the "commercial revolution." Over time, other instruments and means of settling international transactions were developed by banks, and consequently, bankers' acceptances have lost the unique place in international trade and finance they once enjoyed. Nevertheless, they continue to play in important role as modern financial instruments.

WHAT IS A BANKER'S ACCEPTANCE?

A banker's acceptance is a time draft, essentially an "order to pay" a specified sum of money at a specified date, drawn on and "accepted" by a bank.

*Reprinted from *Business Conditions*, May 1976, pp. 3-11, with permission from the Federal Reserve Bank of Chicago and the author.

By accepting the draft, a bank assumes the responsibility to make payment at maturity of the draft. Acceptance of a time draft by a bank serves to make the draft, already a negotiable instrument, more readily salable (marketable) because by its acceptance the bank lends its integrity and credit rating to the instrument. The drawing of the draft is frequently preauthorized by a "letter of credit" issued by either the bank on which the order is drawn or by that bank's correspondent bank in the country of the buyer. However, the major dollar volume of acceptances created takes the form of "outright" acceptances—that is, the instrument arises out of a contractual arrangement less formal than a letter of credit and is later supported by the appropriate documentation.

Bankers' acceptances possess several attributes that make them desirable financial instruments from the point of view of traders (exporters and importers), bankers, and investors. To the seller of goods the major advantage

---

The Life of an Acceptance

To illustrate the process by which an acceptance may be created, consider an example where a firm in Brussels contracts for the purchase of office equipment from a firm in Rockford, Illinois. (See flow chart for the sequence of events described below.) Following inquiries and an exchange of correspondence between the two firms, it is agreed that the Brussels firm will arrange for the issuance of a letter of credit in facvor of the Rockford supplier. The Brussels firm sends a "purchase order" to the Rockford firm (1), and also makes application to its local bank for a letter of credit (2), under a line of credit extended by the bank to the firm. The Brussels firm foresees a need for financing the office equipment for a period of 90 days from the time of shipment. Therefore, it stipulates in the letter of credit application that the draft is to be drawn at 90 days sight and further that it agrees to bear the charges for discounting of the draft in the United States by the Rockford firm. (The burden of who bears the cost of the discount varies with the relative bargaining power of the exporting and importing firms and may, as a result, rest with the exporter.) The Brussels bank issues a letter of credit available by draft at 90 days sight on its Chicago correspondent and mails it to the correspondent for delivery to the Rockford firm (3). Upon receipt of the letter of credit the Chicago bank verifies the authenticity of the signatures on the credit and mails it to the Rockford firm (4). The Rockford firm inspects the terms of the letter of credit and being satisfied with them, makes the shipment. It then collects the bill of lading and other documents called for under the letter of credit, draws a draft at 90 days sight on the Chicago bank and presents them to the bank along with the letter of credit (5). The Chicago bank satisfies itself that the documents are in compliance with the terms of the credit. It then accepts the 90 days draft, thereby creating a banker's acceptance (9), discounts it—charging discount and other charges to the account

in extending credit to the buyer through an acceptance lies in the fact that the instrument provides him with a bank's assurance of repayment. This feature has been particularly important in international trade, where the parties to the transaction may not be well known to each other or where the seller cannot readily ascertain the credit rating of the buyer. By using acceptance credit, the seller of goods in effect shifts the burden of guaranteeing the integrity of credit to the accepting bank.

The acceptance form of financing may be used to cover the shipment stage, which may amount to a substantial period—for example, an ocean shipment. The finance period may, however, extend into the period prior to shipment by the seller as well as into the marketing stage after receipt of the shipment by the buyer. To the trading party bearing the cost of the credit, bankers' acceptances also offer certain advantages over other forms of credit. A banker's acceptance usually compares favorably in cost with a conven-

---

of the Brussels bank—and pays the face amount of the draft to the Rockford firm (6). The shipping documents, the advice of debit covering the acceptance fee and other charges, and notification of the due date of the acceptance are mailed to the Brussels bank (7), which makes appropriate entries on its books. The documents are then forwarded to the Brussels firm, which will use them to clear the merchandise when it arrives (8).

The Chicago bank subsequently finds that it needs funds for its banking business. It sells the acceptance to an acceptance dealer (9) and receives the face amount of the acceptance less discount at the going bankers' acceptance rate for the number of days remaining to maturity (10). The Chicago bank has thus been able to replenish its reserves, earn some income arising from the difference in the rates at which it discounted the draft and sold it to the dealer, and earn interest for the period during which it held the draft. The dealer in turn sells the acceptance to an investor (11) and receives the net proceeds (12), after deduction of a discount, which should be slightly less than what he charged to the bank.

At maturity of the acceptance the investor presents it for payment to the Chicago bank (13) and receives the face amount of the draft in payment (14). The Chicago bank in the meantime will have received payment from the Brussels bank (15), which in turn has received payment from the Brussels firm (16).

Bankers' acceptances arise out of the financing of a U.S. import in a similar manner. The major difference is that if the foreign exporter submits the draft for acceptance, it does so to a U.S. bank that is a correspondent to its home bank. The reason the acceptance is not created by its home bank is that the U.S. acceptance market is the only one of consequence among the various national financial markets.

The procedure for a third-country acceptance may follow a similar procedure with the major difference being that the trading participants are outside the United States.

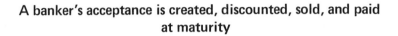

A banker's acceptance is created, discounted, sold, and paid at maturity

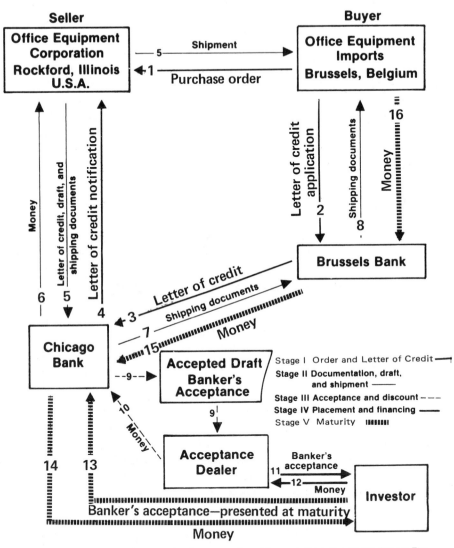

Note: This section was developed with the cooperation of Naran J. Patel, Operations Offizer, The Northern Trust Company, Chicago, Illinois.

tional bank loan despite the fact that the rate of interest charged (technically a discount on the face value of the acceptance) on credit extended through bankers' acceptances is often higher than the "prime rate" charged on conventional loans. In part this is because banks usually require conventional borrowers to maintain "compensating balances"—that is, the lending bank requires that a portion of the loan proceeds be maintained as a noninterest-bearing deposit. Because of this requirement, the effective cost of conventional credit is typically higher than the nominal quoted rate. Also, acceptance credit is typically more attractive for firms that are less than "prime" borrowers.

The attractiveness of an acceptance, as far as a bank is concerned, is that a bank earns a fee (usually 1½ percent per annum of the amount of the acceptance) for merely lending its name and credit rating by accepting a draft, without tying up any of its funds. The actual credit extension is, under these circumstances, undertaken by the seller of the goods. Only when the acceptance-creating bank purchases (discounts) the acceptance, from the seller of goods, for its own account does the bank tie up funds, earning not only the acceptance fee but also the discount charge on the acceptance credit. Even when the acceptance-creating bank purchases the acceptance (and thus, in effect extends the credit), the acceptance form of credit offers the bank certain advantages over a conventional loan. Unlike a conventional loan an acceptance is marketable and may be sold to an acceptance dealer, who in turn sells it to an investor that becomes the party financing the original transaction. As such, the acceptance when purchased by the bank serves as a form of secondary liquidity reserve. Finally, in the case of certain types of domestic shipment or storage drafts, acceptances are secured by title to the goods or a warehouse receipt (at the time the acceptance is created) and offer the accepting bank the advantage of good collateral. (See table for an outline of the applicable conditions.)

From the viewpoint of the investor bankers' acceptances hold two primary advantages. First, an acceptance is a relatively secure investment. By definition, an accepting bank assumes the primary obligation for payment of the face value of the acceptance at maturity. An acceptance is based on specific goods in transit or storage and, as noted above, in the case of domestic acceptances is in some cases secured by title or warehouse receipt. Further, an obligation for payment also rests with the drawer of the acceptance who assumes a liability contingent to that of the primary liability of the accepting bank (such an acceptance is sometimes referred to as "two-name paper"). While it is conceivable that these "lines of security" could break down, an acceptance is viewed by many as one of the safest forms of short-term investment. Second, acceptances are a relatively liquid investment. While the acceptance market is "thin" in comparison with the government securities market and concentrated with the relatively few New York acceptance dealers, quality acceptances are nevertheless readily marketable instruments.[1]

---

[1] The quality of an acceptance depends largely upon the familiarity of the accepting bank in the acceptance market, the financial soundness of the accepting bank, and the "eligibility" category of the acceptance itself. This is discussed in detail later.

Bankers' Acceptances–Conditions and Characteristics Governing
Eligibility, Reserve Requirements, and Acceptance Limits

Bankers' acceptance categories	Federal Reserve System treatment			
	Eligible for discount[1]	Eligible for purchase[2]	Reserve require-ments[3]	Aggregate acceptance limits[4]
1. To cover specific international transactions				
a. U.S. exports or imports.				
Maturity-6 months or less	yes[5]	yes	no	yes
6 months to 9 months.	no	yes	yes	no
more than 9 months.	no	no	yes	no
b. Shipment of goods *between* foreign countries.				
Maturity-6 months or less	yes[5]	yes	no	yes
6 months to 9 months.	no	yes	yes	no
more than 9 months.	no	no	yes	no
c. Shipment of goods *within* a foreign country.				
Maturity-any term	no	no	yes	no
d. Storage of goods within a foreign country (readily marketable staples secured by warehouse receipt).				
Maturity-6 months or less	yes[5]	no	no	yes
6 months to 9 months.	no	no	yes	no
more than 9 months.	no	no	yes	no
e. Dollar exchange–required by usages of trade in approved countries only.				
Maturity-3 months or less	yes	no	no	yes
more than 3 months.	no	no	yes	no
2. To cover specific domestic transactions (i.e., within the U.S.)				
a. Domestic shipment of goods–*with* documents conveying title attached at time of acceptance.				
Maturity-6 months or less	yes[5]	yes	no	yes
6 months to 9 months.	no	yes	yes	no
more than 9 months.	no	no	yes	no
b. Domestic shipment of goods–*without* documents conveying title.				
Maturity-6 months or less	no	yes	yes	no
6 months to 9 months.	no	yes	yes	no
more than 9 months.	no	no	yes	no

ACCEPTANCES BY TYPE OF TRANSACTION

Traditionally, the most typical use of bankers' acceptances has been in financing imports and exports. The rapid expansion in the volume of acceptances in this category during the past decade (1966-75) by and large paralleled

**Bankers' Acceptances—Conditions and Characteristics Governing
Eligibility, Reserve Requirements, and Acceptance Limits**

Bankers' acceptance categories	Federal Reserve System treatment			
	Eligible for discount[1]	Eligible for purchase[2]	Reserve require- ments[3]	Aggregate acceptance limits[4]
c. Domestic sotrage—*readily marketable staples* secured by warehouse receipt.				
Maturity-6 months or less	yes[5]	yes	no	yes
6 months to 9 months.	no	yes	yes	no
more than 9 months.	no	no	yes	no
d. Domestic storage—*any goods* in the U.S. under contract of sale or going into channels of trade and secured through- out their life by warehouse receipts.				
Maturity-6 months or less	no	yes	yes	no
6 months to 9 months.	no	yes	yes	no
more than 9 months.	no	no	yes	no
3. Marketable time deposits (finance bills or working capital acceptances) not related to any specific transaction.				
Maturity-any term	no	no	yes	no

NOTE: This table is based, in part, on an unpublished paper from the 7th Annual CIB Conference at New Orleans, October 13, 1975, by A. Bardenhagen, Vice President, Irving Trust Company, New York.

[1] In accordance with Regulation A of the Board of Governors as provided by the Federal Reserve Act.

[2] Authorizations for the purchase of acceptances as announced by the Federal Open Market Committee on April 1, 1974.*

[3] In accordance with Regulation D of the Board of Governors as provided by the Federal Reserve Act.

[4] Member banks may accept bills in an amount not exceeding at any time 50 percent (or 100 percent if approved by the Board of Governors of the Federal Reserve System) of unimpaired capital stock and surplus (as defined in FRB, Chicago Circular No. 2156 of April 2, 1971). Acceptances growing out of domestic transactions are not to exceed 50 percent of the unimpaired capital stock and surplus. The aggregate limit for a bank accepting dollar exchange bills is 50 percent of unimpaired capital stock and surplus over and above the aforementioned 100 percent limitation. (Section 13(7) and (12) of the Federal Reserve Act.)

[5] The maturity of nonagricultural bills may not exceed 90 days at the time of discount.

*On March 15, 1977, following the original publication of this article, the Federal Open Market Committee issued a directive indicating "... that the system should permit its existing holdings of bankers' acceptances to mature and that it should no longer purchase these instruments outright under ordinary circumstances." (Editor's footnote.)

the boom in U.S. and world trade. The value of U.S. exports and imports expanded by 3.7 times, while acceptances financing that trade increased 4.2 times. However, during the last five years the rate of expansion in trade substantially outstripped the growth in acceptances. While both exports and imports increased about 2.5 times, acceptances financing export and import trade were up 1.9 times. This recent lag in growth in acceptance financing of

U.S. trade is attributable to a relatively slower growth in acceptances financing imports, which were up only 1.4 times from December 1970 to December 1975. Over the same period export acceptances increased 2.6 times. By the end of 1975 there were $4 billion of export acceptances and $3.7 billion of import acceptances outstanding.

The most dramatic increase in acceptance financing in recent years took place in bills created to finance trade between foreign countries and goods stored abroad—the so-called "third-country" bills. At the end of 1975 over $10.3 billion, or 55 percent, of all bankers' acceptances outstanding were third-country bills. This amount was 3.9 times larger than at the end of 1970. The surge in third-country bills has been primarily due to increased utilization of the U.S. acceptance market by the Japanese. A large proportion of Japan's foreign trade—even with non-U.S. trade—has been denominated and settled in U.S. dollars, thus leading Japanese traders to utilize the U.S. acceptance market rather intensively.[2]

Domestic shipment and storage acceptances have accounted for a minor portion of total acceptances outstanding during most of the post-World War II period. At the end of 1975 just over 3 percent of outstanding acceptances were domestic—about $600 million. The lack of popularity for the domestic acceptance derives in part, from the requirement that to be *eligible for discount* by the Federal Reserve, the instrument must be secured by attached documents conveying title at the time of acceptance, or a warehouse receipt or other documents securing title to readily marketable staples (see table).

Another category of acceptances is the "dollar exchange" bill. The nominal purpose of "dollar exchange" acceptances is the short-term creation of dollar exchange for a foreign country. They may be utilized to alleviate temporary or seasonal shortages of dollar exchange, "as required by usages of trade." As such, dollar exchange acceptances are unique, among bankers' acceptances, in that they are not based on specific merchandise trade or storage transactions.

The creation of dollar-exchange acceptances has been restricted by the Federal Reserve Act. Member banks may accept dollar exchange bills only from certain countries that are eligible for this form of credit. Further, since April 1974 such acceptances cannot be purchased by the Federal Reserve (see table covering eligibility conditions). These restrictions—plus the availability of alternative, more flexible sources of credit—have made these acceptances rather unpopular. At the end of 1975 they accounted for less than 1 percent of total U.S. acceptances outstanding.

ACCEPTANCES AND THE FEDERAL RESERVE

The Federal Reserve Act of 1913, Sections 13 and 14, broadly outlined the authority of the Federal Reserve System with respect to regulation of

---

[2] It has been estimated that less than 15 percent of Japan's exports and 3 percent of its imports are settled in the Japanese yen.

the purchase and sale of bankers' acceptances. This authority, along with that contained in Sections 9 and 19 of the Act, was used to promulgate the detailed Regulations A, D, and H of the Board of Governors of the Federal Reserve System and the regulations relating to open market operations of the Federal Reserve System. The following highlights the nature of these regulations.

The Federal Reserve may "acquire" acceptances under three sets of conditions. First, it may initiate purchases (and sales) of bankers' acceptances in open market operations. Second, a bank that is a member of the Federal Reserve System may submit acceptances to its district Federal Reserve Bank for discount (technically rediscount) at the "discount window"; if the Fed discounts the acceptance, the proceeds are credited to the member bank's reserve account. Third, a member bank may pledge acceptances as security against an advance or loan requested from the Federal Reserve.

Ongoing involvement of the Federal Reserve in the acceptance market has been largely confined to open market dealings. Buying and selling activity in the open market is carried out for two primary reasons. First, as a part of the System's implementation of monetary policy, it may acquire acceptances from dealers to hold for its own account (outright purchases). Alternatively, the Fed may enter into repurchase agreements with acceptance dealers whereby the Fed acquires acceptances for a short period of time—typically a week or less. These purchases, or repurchase agreements, allow the Fed to temporarily increase the amount of reserves in the banking system in the same way as if it were to purchase, sell, or enter into repurchase agreements covering U.S. Treasury securities.

The second reason for which the Fed periodically enters the acceptance market is to function as an "agent" for foreign customers, primarily foreign central banks, who wish to acquire the instruments for investment purposes. Until recently, the Federal Reserve added its own endorsement (i.e., "guarantee" of payment), thus enhancing the security of the investment. This practice was discontinued in November 1974.

Acceptances that are purchased by the Federal Reserve, used as collateral against a loan to a member bank by the Federal Reserve, or discounted at the Federal Reserve must meet certain requirements (see table). In creating acceptances banks try to adhere to these requirements, even though they may have no intention of selling or discounting them with the Fed. This is for two major reasons. First, acceptances meeting the conditions for *eligibility for discount* or *eligibility for purchase* are more readily salable in the market than are acceptances that do not meet these conditions—*ineligible* acceptances. As such, they provide a greater degree of liquidity for the accepting bank. Second, as will be explained later, acceptances that are *eligible for discount* are not subject to reserve requirements.

The distinction between *eligible for discount* and *eligible for purchase* by the Federal Reserve is important for two reasons: one reason derives from certain restrictions imposed by the Federal Reserve Act.[3] Section 13(7) and

---

[3] The market's reaction to the technical distinction between acceptances *eligible for discount*, acceptances *eligible for purchase*, and *ineligible* acceptances does not appear to follow this clear differ-

(12) of the Act limits the amount of acceptances that a bank can create for any individual, and have eligible for discount by the Federal Reserve, to 10 percent of that bank's paidup and unimpaired capital and surplus (unless the acceptance is "adequately secured"). Further, the Act limits the aggregate amount of acceptances, *eligible for discount* with the Federal Reserve, created by a bank to 50 percent (100 percent with approval of the Board of Governors of the Federal Reserve System) of that bank's capital and surplus. Acceptances that are *eligible for purchase* or are *ineligible* for either discount or purchase by the Federal Reserve *are not* subject to Section 13 quantity limitations.

Second, as noted above, the applicability of reserve requirements to acceptances outstanding varies according to the "eligibility" category of the acceptance. According to Regulation D, Section 204.1 (f) 5, of the Federal Reserve Board a banker's acceptance that meets the conditions that make it *eligible for discount* may be sold by the creating and discounting bank without subjecting the proceeds of the sale to reserve requirements. Thus, a member bank that sells an acceptance that meets such eligibility requirements is free from the obligation to set aside a certain portion of its funds in non-interest-bearing balances with the Federal Reserve. Conversely, a member bank must maintain reserves against the proceeds of the sale of acceptances "undertaken . . . as a means to obtaining funds to be used in the banking business . . ." that do not meet the *eligibility for discount* conditions of Section 13 of the Federal Reserve Act.

Purchase of acceptances by the Federal Reserve is governed not only by the *eligibility* requirements, but also by the underlying "quality" of the instrument. The Federal Reserve purchases only "prime" acceptances. A prime classification is based upon a number of factors including the marketability of the instrument (which is importantly dependent upon the view held by the acceptance dealers), the financial condition of the banks accepting the paper, the volume of transactions in the acceptance market carried out by the accepting bank (bank size itself is not a determining factor), and a set of physical standards and forms of documentation that are to be adhered to in the instrument itself. Even the designation of an acceptance as prime does not guarantee that at any given time an acceptance created by a particular bank will be purchased by the Federal Reserve because of restrictions on the proportions of acceptances from any one source that the Federal Reserve will acquire.

---

entiation. As reflected by the terminology of bankers involved with acceptances and as reflected by rates quoted by acceptance dealers, *eligible* acceptances are those technically *eligible for discount. Ineligible* acceptances include the rest: *eligible for purchase* and *ineligible.* The relative willingness of acceptance dealers to deal in acceptances *eligible for purchase* as compared with *ineligible* acceptances appears to be the major distinction between these categories—a nonprice differentiation.

REGIONAL DISTRIBUTION OF ACCEPTANCES

Historically, the majority of bankers' acceptances outstanding have been acceptances of banks located in New York and San Francisco. At the end of 1975 nearly 84 percent of acceptances outstanding were from banks located in these two Federal Reserve districts. This stems from East and West Coast banks having been traditionally more heavily involved in international transactions and in financing international trade than the inland banks. Moreover, New York has been the traditional financial center of the United States, hosting the most active domestic money market where acceptances can be readily traded. It is also the home base for the relatively few dealers that are active in the acceptance market.

Chicago ranks as a distant third in the value of acceptances outstanding from banks in that Federal Reserve District—about 4.5 percent of the national total at the end of 1975. During the post-World War II period Chicago's share of acceptances outstanding has ranged from about 2.5 percent at the end of 1950 to 6 percent at the end of 1971. Of course, as noted earlier, the volume of acceptances outstanding nationwide increased markedly over the postwar period—more than 47 times from 1950 through 1975. The volume of acceptances outstanding from Chicago district banks increased more than 80 times over the same period. It has been over the last five years, however, that the bulk of the dollar volume surge has occurred. Chicago district acceptances outstanding increased from $353 million at the end of 1970 to $837 million at the end of 1975. Over the same five-year period bankers' acceptances outstanding nationwide increased from $7.1 billion to $18.7 billion.

CONCLUSION

For many years bankers' acceptances have been an important element in the financing of international trade. Over time, improved lines of communication between parties involved in international transactions and the development of other financial instruments and modes of settlement of international transactions have reduced the overall importance of the acceptance. Only a relatively small portion of world trade is financed by means of bankers' acceptances. For example, estimates based on the average amount of export and import acceptances outstanding during 1975, assuming a 90-day maturity, suggest that only about 15 percent of U.S. merchandise trade was financed by acceptances. Nevertheless, acceptances continue to play an important role as a highly specialized financial instrument for facilitating international commerce, a role for which they are ideally suited.

BANKING ON DEBT
FOR CAPITAL NEEDS*

Ronald D. Watson

23

Ninth National Bank is under fire from the bank supervisors. Convinced that the bank is undercapitalized, the regulators are demanding an additional $1,000,000 of capital stock. However, the bank's management knows that with stock prices depressed there will be severe dilution of the current stockholders' earnings and ownership control if new stock is sold. Instead, it counters with an offer to add $1,000,000 of long-term debt to the bank's capital structure, arguing that the debt will protect the depositors just as much as a new stock issue.

This alternative puts the regulators in an uncomfortable spot. Long-term debt has *some* of the characteristics of equity capital, but it's an imperfect substitute. Should they compromise and take whatever depositor protection is offered by long-term debt or insist that new stock be sold? The choice isn't easy, and the precedents that bank supervisors are now setting will greatly influence the profitability and solvency of the banking industry in years ahead. Debt may be a useful source of funds to the banks and a reserve cushion for the Federal Deposit Insurance Corporation, but its value in protecting society from bank failures is very limited. Bank supervisors may someday regret it if they sacrifice equity capital standards in the mistaken belief that debt is just as good.

*Reprinted from the *Business Review*, December 1974, pp. 17-28, with permission from the Federal Reserve Bank of Philadelphia and the author.

IS DEBT CAPITAL?

Suppose a bank wants to use debt as a substitute for equity in raising new capital—why should society care? If debt has characteristics that make it similar to common stock in the way it protects depositors from the bank's losses, the regulators have little cause for objecting to its use. But, if debt is substantially less effective than stock in protecting both the individual bank and the banking system, there is good reason for bank supervisors to prevent banks from treating it like equity capital.

Common Stock as Bank Capital.   For the functions that capital must perform in a commercial bank—protecting depositors and allowing the bank to absorb losses without failing—common stock has long been regarded as the best form of capital. It has no maturity date, so the bank need never worry about paying it off. In addition, dividend payments are not a legal obligation, so failure to pay them will not bring the bank's operations to a halt. Finally, as long as the equity capital accounts exceed any losses suffered, the bank is considered solvent. This last point is of critical importance.

Capital must be available to absorb both operating losses—the result of current expenses exceeding current revenues—and capital losses on investments—whether they result from falling bond prices, loan defaults, broken leases, or anything else. As long as losses can be fully offset against capital invested by the bank's owners, the legal claims of depositors or other creditors are not compromised, and the bank can continue to function. Charging losses against the bank's equity capital accounts is a normal business practice. It's only when losses are so great that they wipe out these capital accounts and impair the bank's ability to pay its liabilities in full, that the institution will be forced to close.[1]

Mild losses on investments and temporary operating deficits are sufficiently common in banking that it is in the best interests of the depositors, investors, and the economy for banks to have a cushion of equity capital. With capital to absorb losses, most banks can operate without interrupting their operations, forcing the FDIC to cover their depositors' claims or disrupting the public's confidence in its banking institutions. The key question that regulators must confront is "can the amount of capital needed to protect depositors differ from the amount of equity needed to keep the bank going?"

Debt as Bank Capital.   Long-term debt has characteristics quite different from common stock, and these differences are important to deciding whether

---

[1] Whenever the losses charged against a bank's capital are sufficient to offset its entire reserves, retained earnings, and surplus accounts and would partially impair its common stock account, regulators step in to reorganize, merge, or close the bank. As a practical matter, a bank must have a significant equity cushion to function for an extended period of time. If any bank realizes losses that wipe out most of its equity cushion, it would be obliged to raise new capital very quickly if it intends to stay in business.

it is a good capital substitute (see Box 1). First, the maturity of debt is fixed. Any bank debt issue of seven or more years to maturity can be classified as a capital note and listed on the balance sheet as a capital account item. Many debt issues have much longer maturities, but 25 years is normally an upper limit. Maturities of that length certainly differentiate these bonds from ordinary deposits which may be withdrawn on very short notice. A long-term issue must eventually be repaid, but the banker knows exactly when that payment obligation must be met and can plan ahead. In all probability the debt issue will be refinanced by the sale of new debt rather than repaid from internally generated funds.

However, the fact that the bank must be able to refinance the bonds sometime near the maturity date creates a risk that equity capital will never pose. The chance that credit markets would refuse to provide a bank with the volume of new money that it needs to refinance outstanding debt is small, but the possibility still exists. Inability to roll this debt over could put the bank in default on the obligation and lead to a failure.

Another key difference between long-term debt and common stock is the bank's legal obligation to pay interest when it becomes due. Distributing a dividend to stockholders regularly and punctually is very important to a bank that wants its stock to perform well in the markets, but in an emergency, dividends can be omitted. Interest cannot.

Surprisingly, the *cash costs* of servicing debt capital that carries no sinking fund provision[2] are no greater than the costs of most common stock. Bank stocks normally pay dividends of 3 to 6 percent of their current selling price, while debt issues must carry interest payments in the 7 to 10 percent range. However, interest expenses are tax deductible to the bank, so the after-tax cost of long-term debt is reduced to the 3½ to 5 percent level—roughly the same as the cash flows for dividends on a common stock issue. This means that debt is no more difficult for a bank to service than common stock *under normal conditions*. The difference is in servicing the two forms of financing during an emergency when interest payments are obligatory and dividends are not.

It is also possible for a bank which issues large amounts of long-term debt when interest rates are high to be stuck with very expensive funds if rates subsequently drop. Banks operate with very thin spreads between the return on their assets and the cost of the money they borrow. If the interest income on their loans and investments falls more rapidly than the cost of their funds, profit margins can turn into loss margins. The use of a "call provision," through which the bank can redeem its debt at a penalty price, is one way to control this risk. However, exercising this call privilege may take time, and the bank must continue to pay both the high interest and the penalty before it can rid itself of these costly funds.

A third characteristic of long-term debt that is important to the analysis is its claim to payment *vis-à-vis* depositors. Like equity capital, virtually all

---

[2] Sinking funds are provisions found in bond contracts which require the bank to make periodic repayments to reduce the principal amount of the debt. Most bank debt being sold currently makes explicit provision for some repayment of principal prior to the issue's final maturity date.

BOX 1

WHY DEBT?

Aggressive bank management finds long-term debt a very *appealing* way to raise new money. It has characteristics which make it ideal for simultaneously supporting new growth of assets, raising the return on common stock, and preserving existing shareholders' control of the business. The key advantages offered by long-term debt are. . .

Relatively Low Cost. Interest payments on debt are classified as a tax-deductible expense for the bank. Therefore, if its marginal tax rate is 48 percent, each $1 of interest expense will cut the bank's tax bill by 48 cents (giving the debt an effective after-tax cost of only 52 cents per dollar spent). A dollar distributed as common stock or preferred stock dividends is not tax-deductible, and, therefore, has an after-tax cost of $1.

The tax-deductibility of interest charges would be irrelevant if bankers were forced to pay twice as much for new debt as they pay for new common stock. However, they don't pay twice as much. Debt is normally a much less expensive form of new funding for a bank than new equity. Common stock issues normally pay a current dividend yield of only 4 to 7 percent compared to the market interest yield on debt of 8 to 10 percent. Yet, few investors would be willing to buy the stock if increases in those dividends were not probable. The after-tax *cash costs* of new bond and common stock issues may be comparable in the first year or two, but dividend hikes on the common stock will soon make the long-run costs of equity capital far higher than those of debt.

Another factor affecting the cost of new capital is flotation costs. Debt has the upper hand here also. While there are exceptions to any rule, the cost of raising debt capital by selling capital notes or debentures is usually lower than the cost of a common stock issue of the same size. It may also be easier to privately place debt issues than new stock issues—especially when current stockholders have preemptive rights to acquire proportionate shares of any new stock created.

long-term debt is subordinated—it receives payment of principal and interest only after the claims of depositors have been discharged fully. Debt outranks common stock in claiming whatever funds are left after depositors have been paid, but both serve to protect the interests of the depositor. Subordinated debt should increase public confidence in the safety of an uninsured bank deposit. It is this feature of bank debt that proponents hold out as its primary benefit and the reason that regulators should allow freer use of debt as a capital substitute.

Long-term debt may be cheap for other reasons as well. As long as the debt is not classified as a deposit, the bank is under no obligation to hold reserves against those funds. In addition, while Federal Reserve member banks are required to invest a portion of their equity capital funds in Federal Reserve Bank stock, this requirement doesn't apply to debt capital. Nor do banks have to pay a deposit insurance fee on these funds.

Leverage. The fixed and relatively low cost of long-term debt makes it ideal for levering a bank's earnings. As long as the return earned on the funds raised through a new debt issue exceeds the cost of borrowing these funds, these "excess" revenues can be distributed among the stockholders —amplifying their return (see Appendix). However, each dollar of debt issued by the bank represents a claim to earnings and assets that takes precedence over that of the shareholders. Those obligations are also legally binding. If the bank should fail to meet an interest or principal repayment, those creditors can ask the regulatory authorities to close it down. The *risk* that leverage entails may make debt unattractive when its proportion becomes sufficiently high.

Control. A bank's present ownership may also be attracted to debt because it represents a new source of long-term funds which will *not* have a voice in the management of the institution. If new common stock were issued to augment the bank's capital, the new shareholders would have the right to vote for the board of directors. Bondholders have no such privilege. Therefore, if the current stockholders are willing to bear the risk of added debt, they can expand their bank without relinquishing any control of the organization.

Soothing the Regulators. Many banks having capital adequacy problems with the supervisory authorities have turned to long-term debt as a source of new capital. Debt might be sufficiently attractive to some banks that it would be raised as a source of new funds regardless of whether it could be used as capital. The fact that regulators have been willing to accept modest amounts of it as a substitute for equity capital makes it all the more appealing.

Bankers Opt for More Debt. Arguing that long maturities and subordination of debtholders' claims to those of depositors make long-term debt a good substitute for equity, bankers are now eagerly adopting it as the cheapest and easiest way to raise new capital. While some banks used debt prior to the Great Depression, most of the emergency Government financing of the industry that took place during the 1930s was in the form of debt capital. Following this period, banks tried to rid themselves of this debt as quickly as possible because it was commonly interpreted as a sign of weakness. In 1962 the Comptroller of the Currency reestablished debt as an acceptable form of financing for national banks, and its use has been expanding rapidly ever since.

Between 1963 and 1973 the total capital of insured commercial banks more than doubled,[3] but the debt portion of "long-term capital" expanded to more than 30 times its original size—from $130 million to over $4 billion. Long-term debt now constitutes nearly 8 percent of all bank capital.

BANK REGULATORS AREN'T CONVINCED

While bank regulators have sanctioned the use of some debt, they are apprehensive about both the degree to which it is a substitute for equity and the amount of debt a bank can safely carry. The proportion of equity capital to risky assets in banks has declined markedly in the last 15 years, and supervisors fear that this has increased the risk of bank failures. Substituting debt for equity just magnifies the potential risks because it increases a bank's legal payment obligations. In addition, the development of bank holding companies has heightened the uncertainty since their capital positions may be quite complex and even harder to evaluate than those of the affiliate banks (Box 2).

Limits to Debt Use.   As a result of these risks, regulators are quite reluctant to allow banks to acquire more than modest amounts of long-term debt. Regulatory agencies normally maintain a basic standard which limits long-term debt to a third of the bank's total capital funds. Banks which might have difficulty managing this much debt are often limited to less. This is not an inconsequential proportion, but some banks would try to raise more if there were no supervisory restraint.

In principle, the capital markets themselves should also limit a bank's use of debt in its capital structure. As the proportion of debt financing grows, the risk inherent in the financial leverage it produces also grows. (Leverage is the use of funding whose cost is fixed to try to increase the profits of the shareholders. See Appendix) While replacing costly common stock with less expensive debt funds may be profitable when leverage is moderate, increasing leverage risk will eventually prompt investors to demand a higher yield from both the debt and equity securities of the bank. Eventually the average costs of the bank's long-term funds will begin to rise, and the institution will be discouraged from any further attempt to substitute debt for equity. However, there is little evidence to date that investors find the level of bank debt

---

[3]However, during the same period, the total assets of commercial banks expanded even more rapidly (from $311 billion to $827 billion) so the relative capitalization (including both debt and equity) of the industry was shrinking.

BOX 2

HOLDING COMPANIES COMPOUND
THE DEBT PROBLEM

If defining debt limits for a commercial bank seems a tangled problem, assessing the impact of a leveraged holding company owning a leveraged bank creates a "Gordian knot" for the supervisor. The evolution of bank holding companies (BHCs) has raised some very important regulatory questions, but so far no supervisory "Alexander" has discovered the sword which will allow him to carve out a solution to this analytical nightmare. There are three elements which make this problem particularly sticky, both for the regulator and the capital market which provides this debt.

Joint Operating Risks. Little information exists to help analysts determine the extent to which BHCs are either more or less risky than their component parts. Part of the theory behind forming BHCs is the complementarity of the related financial activities. The entrepreneurs who form these financial conglomerates argue that each affiliate in the BHC could help to backstop the others since periods of tight credit or recession would impact differently on each. Accordingly, many BHCs have been capitalized at less than the sum of the capital required to operate each business separately and have relied more heavily on borrowed funds to finance their activities. Whether this practice will create inordinate risks is difficult for either the market or the regulators to determine.

Who Backs the Holding Companies' Debt? A second point of great confusion is the extent to which the BHC can rely on its banking affiliate to guarantee loans to the parent corporation. Regulators are doing everything in their power to insulate the bank from the holding company, because they do not want the bank's soundness sacrificed to the aims and needs of the BHC.

Supervisory authorities have set firm guidelines on the extent to which banks can be tapped for support of the parent organization but those limits are not presently clear to the investing public. Recently a financial problem experienced by the parent holding company of the Beverly Hills National Bank in California caused a "run" by depositors on the subsidiary bank which was, at the time, quite sound. This run created such severe liquidity problems for the bank that it eventually failed. Until the public and the investing community become fully aware of the limitations on bank support of a BHC, the market may be prone to underestimate the risk of BHCs. This is important to society because underassessment of risk will lead to artificially low capital costs and overextension by the BHCs.

Double Leverage. The term sounds sinister and appropriately so. Double leverage is the practice of using debt money raised by the BHC parent to make equity investments in subsidiaries. It is an especially

Box 2 (continued)

useful way to get around regulatory requirements concerning the capital adequacy of subsidiaries. If bank supervisors insist that the bank subsidiary increase its equity capital, the holding company parent may borrow money to make such an investment. On the surface the bank is now safer because it does have more equity capital. But the larger BHC organization isn't any more safe. It will need the affiliate bank's dividends to pay the debt service on these new borrowings.

As long as the bank is fully insulated from the BHC, financial risk is being transferred from the bank to the parent corporation. There is nothing inherently wrong with this if the market for BHC securities is sensitive to this risks, can evaluate them correctly, and charges the parent a risk premium which accounts for the actual risk of the organization. However, imperfections in this evaluation process may cause problems like the Beverly Hills National Bank failure and wind up imposing a heavy cost on society.

EXAMPLE

Suppose, for example, a bank and its BHC are capitalized in the following way:

BHC

Banks stock $ 10	$ 0 Debt
Other stock 10	20 BHC common stock

BANK SUBSIDIARY		COMBINED OTHER SUBSIDIARIES	

Assets $100	$90 Deposits
	  10 Common
	        stock
		Assets $50	$40 Liabilities
			  10 Common
			        stock

If the bank regulators were to request another $10 of bank equity capital because they felt the bank was too risky, they would be saying that society's best interests require that this system have additional capital . . . as follows:

disturbing enough to make them demand substantially higher yields to cover this risk.

However, bank leverage creates risks for society at large beyond those borne by investors. As is common for regulated industries, investors can't be counted on to discipline borrowing banks because those investors don't bear all of the costs of the institution becoming overextended. In the case of a bank that receives assistance from the regulators to stay in business, the bond and stockholders are given a partial reprieve and may not pay any "Social Darwinist" piper for the risks taken by the bank. This regulatory backstopping hardly discourages the substitution of debt for equity and may enable the investors to make a higher return from the added leverage.

BHC	
Banks stock $20	$ 0 Debt
Other stock 10	30 Common stock

BANK		COMBINED OTHER SUBSIDIARIES	
Assets $110	$90 Deposits 20 Common stock	Assets $50	$40 Liabilities 10 Common stock

If the BHC were to resort to double leverage to satisfy the capital request, it would raise the needed $10 from debt sources rather than new stock . . .

BHC	
Bank stock $ 20	$10 Debt
Other stock 10	20 Common stock

BANK		COMBINED OTHER SUBSIDIARIES	
Assets $110	$90 Deposits 20 Common stock	Assets $50	$40 Liabilities 10 Common stock

The bank would have additional equity capital but the holding company system would not. Presumably the capital market will discipline BHCs' use of double leverage, but any imperfections in its collective analysis or in depositors' ability to differentiate financial problems of holding companies from those of the banking subsidiaries may generate great social costs not borne entirely by the investing community.

In the event that a bank fails, the security holders may lose everything they've invested, but the public may also incur costs as a result of the failure. A bank closing may undermine confidence in other banks or the financial system as a whole, and it may deprive the local community of needed services and competition. These "external" costs of the failure make it inappropriate for bank supervisory authorities to let the banks (interacting with the capital markets) have a free hand in setting debt capital standards.

Real Protection? Differences of opinion on bank debt as capital, therefore, boil down to the function assigned to capital. If capital's sole task is thought to be the protection of bank depositors—the stance taken by many bankers—then debt is a proper form of capital. In the event of a failure, the bank's losses would be offset against debt capital as well as equity capital before the FDIC or the depositors were required to absorb any losses.

However, if the function of *preventing failures* by absorbing losses is also assigned to bank capital, debt is less useful. Losses cannot be charged against debt capital in an operating bank, so debt capital will not reduce the risk of failure. To the extent that long-term debt is *substituted* for equity capital, the risk of bank failures is heightened and the attendant costs to society also increased. Since it is the job of the supervisory authorities to worry about the social costs of bank failures, most regulators are far less enthusiastic than the rest of the banking community about the growth of debt capital.

DEFINING A THEORETICAL LIMIT

Any ideal solution to the problem of setting limits on bank debt capital must come to grips with the fundamental economic factors just developed. First, bankers find leverage profitable, but only because capital markets do not consider most banks overleveraged. In addition, the inflexibility of a bank's obligation to pay interest and repay principal makes debt a riskier form of financing than equity capital. Investors in bank securities understand and accept this risk, but they don't bear all of the costs associated with a bank failure. Finally, long-term subordinated debt may serve one of the regulator's goals—protecting depositors—but it is of no use in absorbing the losses that *cause* banks to fail. Accordingly, it is of little use to the regulator who expects capital to prevent failures.

Even in principle, setting debt capacity rules which accommodate these factors is a difficult task. While regulators find debt riskier than equity, the only defensible reason for bank supervisors limiting its use is to make society better off. If debt, in fact, magnifies the likelihood of bank failures—and their resultant social costs—limiting it is reasonable. However, if debt allows banks to achieve greater profitability or to provide services at a lower cost without seriously jeopardizing society's interests, there are costs to restricting its use.[4] Any regulatory restriction placed on bank capital is apt to make the bank less efficient in using money. The institution may be forced to use more long-term capital or less debt than investors feel it needs. The result may be higher prices for bank services or less expansion of banking activity than would otherwise be the case.

Ideally, society's interests would be served best by limiting debt to the level where the added social costs associated with preventing banks from se-

---

[4] Since the most important reason for a business to prefer debt to equity is the tax-deductibility of interest payments, it isn't at all clear that society as a whole reaps any benefits from the alleged efficiencies of debt "capital". However, reassessing the logic of our corporate tax structure is beyond the scope of this article.

lecting the exact amount and composition of their capital structure are just offset by the additional social benefits of a lower bank failure rate.[5] It makes sense to use regulatory power to promote social goals, but it makes no sense to create a set of debt prohibitions which cost society more in the long run than the benefits produced are worth. Unfortunately, implementing the theoretical solution is far more difficult than simply stating it. Defining the actual dollar values of the costs and benefits described above would be a formidable undertaking.

SOME PRACTICAL SOLUTIONS?

Regulatory agencies have a number of possible options available to them for "solving" this problem of bank debt use. The first is simply to *prohibit* its use. This approach would prevent any possibility of a bank substituting debt for equity capital when, in fact, it needs the equity. However, this alternative is hardly sensible. It in no way solves the problem of assuring capital adequacy, and it deprives banks whose capital is "adequate" of a very useful source of additional funding.

The other extreme in the spectrum of options is to adopt a *market rule* for limiting debt. This would be the easiest road for bank supervisors to follow in the short run, but the existence of social costs to bank failure that are not borne by the investors make this an imperfect approach. Relying on the capital markets to discipline banks' use of debt capital would probably lead to greater use of debt than would be ideal from society's standpoint. A long-run solution probably lies in a middle-of-the-road approach.

Change the Terms on the Debt. A third possibility might be to require that banks using long-term debt as a capital supplement *alter the form of the debt securities* to offer additional protection against failure. There are three properties of long-term debt securities that regulators find bothersome: (1) losses cannot be charged against debt capital without liquidating the bank; (2) interest must be paid whether the bank is profitable or not; and (3) the debt must eventually be repaid or refunded. Nothing can be done about the first problem, but the second and third could be mitigated by using different kinds of debt securities.

The risk of a fixed interest commitment might be overcome if banks were to issue debt on which interest was paid only if earned (these are called income bonds or revenue bonds). Normally securities such as these are issued

[5]The benefits of debt ceiling regulations could be defined as the total cost to society of bank failures if there are *no limits* on debt *minus* the cost of failures when debt ceiling regulations are in effect. The tighter the debt limit, the greater the benefits from reduced bank failure. However, each tightening of the debt ceiling may force banks further from the capital structure they would most like, thus making them less efficient from the point of view of the private economy.

by corporations only when they are in financial trouble, so bankers would strongly argue that investors would not accept the bonds and the banks should not be required to use this kind of security. True perhaps, but 15 years ago issuing long-term debt or preferred stock was also considered a sign of weakness for a bank. Investors might need time to become accustomed to the idea, but if the bank is sound the additional risk to the debtholder (and the resultant risk premium in the interest rate) should be modest.

Requirements that sinking funds be established by banks to guarantee periodic repayments of debt principal are another possibility, although these provisions are already a common feature of new issues. This would not prevent banks from refinancing rather than retiring their bonds, but it would reduce the likelihood that very large quantities of debt capital would have to be refinanced all at once.

Endless variations in the terms of debt issues are possible—witness the recent floating rate capital notes—but any alteration attempted must meet the IRS guidelines which distinguish bonds from preferred stock. Once the bond issue begins to look like a preferred stock, the interest expense loses its tax-deductible status and its effective cost to the bank doubles.[6]

Of greater importance, however, is the fact that the modifications which change the surface details of long-term debt instruments don't eliminate the basic characteristics that make it a risky substitute for equity capital. Some risks can be reduced—and these might justify requiring banks to issue only income bonds or to use sinking funds with their debt—but they are the lesser ones from the standpoint of society. The debt must still be repaid at some future date, and the bank must be able to absorb losses out of capital accounts other than its long-term debt.

Variable Rate Deposit Insurance. Proposals to alter the terms of bank debt are aimed at reducing the social costs of failure by making it less likely to occur. A somewhat different tack might be to shift some of the social costs of insuring society against more bank failures back to the banks and their shareholders. If the FDIC varied the cost of its deposit insurance according to the risk of each bank it insures, the effect would be to raise the implicit cost of funds for banks that adopted particularly risky asset or liability portfolios. If a bank wished to substitute debt capital for equity capital, it would be free to do so but would be obliged to pay for the added costs its action imposed on society. Estimating these costs and setting deposit insurance fees based on risk would be extremely difficult, but it should be possible to construct a rational rate schedule. Despite potential imprecision, confronting the problem would still be preferred to the current practice of making no explicit attempt to calculate either the costs or benefits of bank regulation. This proposal was recently offered in the context of setting over-

---

[6]On October 8, 1974 President Gerald R. Ford proposed allowing corporations to deduct the fixed dividend costs of preferred stock issues from taxable income. If this suggestion were enacted, preferred stock should become a very attractive alternative to long-term debt.

all capital adequacy standards, but it also covers the problem of selecting a proper debt/equity mix of capital.[7]

SHORT-TERM REGULATION

Controlling social costs through variable deposit insurance rates might be the simplest and most flexible solution to this controversy. However, it is not a widely accepted solution and implementing it would take time even if it were adopted. In the meantime regulators still seek guidelines for restricting debt capital use to a level close to the theoretical ideal.

Unfortunately, no magical thumbrule exists. Each bank is different, and debt capacities vary widely. The "ideal" limit to a bank's use of long-term debt as a capital supplement depends on the risk that debt creates. The ability to utilize debt successfully depends on the quality and maturity structure of the bank's assets, the composition of its liabilities, the skill of its management, the stability of its competitive environment, and its access to money markets, among other factors.

The regulators' only guideline is the basic requirement that equity be sufficient to allow a bank to charge any reasonably predictable losses against capital without jeopardizing its basic existence. Beyond that, any debt supplement to capital that isn't potentially destablizing because of excessive debt service requirements would be a plus, because it would provide additional protection for the claims of depositors in case of a general banking emergency.

What the industry needs is some objective quantitative analysis of the real risks of long-term debt and the real social costs of bank failures. In the meantime, assessing the proper mix of debt and equity capital must remain a subjective judgment—a decision based on the regulators' concern not only for protecting the economy from a financial panic but also for minimizing the costs to the financial community of operating with less debt capital than it can successfully manage.

---

[7]For a more complete discussion of this point, see Ronald D. Watson, "Insuring Some Progress in the Bank Capital Hassle," *Business Review* of the Federal Reserve Bank of Philadelphia, July-August 1974, pp. 3-18.

APPENDIX
THE PURPOSE OF LEVERAGE

The potential advantages of long-term debt capital in a bank's capital structure can best be seen from a numerical example. Suppose your bank starts with a capital structure of $500,000 composed simply of 10,000 shares of common stock issued and selling for $50 each. If the bank were to realize net operating revenues of $100,000 per year before taxes the shareholder's return could be computed as follows:

Net Revenue	$100,000
—Income Tax (50 percent)	50,000
Earnings After Taxes	50,000
÷ 10,000 shares	
Earnings per share	5.00
Return per share	$= \dfrac{5.00}{50.00} = 10$ percent

Now suppose that the bank could change its capital structure by replacing some of its equity with long-term debt. If the bank could sell $250,000 of debt at an interest cost of 10 percent and could use the proceeds of this sale to repurchase its own common stock in the market, it would shift from an all-equity capital structure to one that is half equity and half debt. Even though the cost of the debt is 10 percent—the same as the return earned for the common shareholders—the remaining stockholders would see their earnings rise.* The increase in profits for the stockholders occurs because the interests costs are treated as tax-deductible expenses.

Net Revenue	$100,000
— Interest	25,000
Earnings Before Taxes	75,000
— Taxes (50 percent)	37,500
Earnings After Taxes	37,500
÷ 5,000 shares	
Earnings per share	7.50
Return per share	$\dfrac{7.50}{50.00} = 15$ percent

The long-term debt will also lever earnings if the bank's net revenues can be increased without additional capital. Suppose operating earnings were to rise 10 percent.

Net Revenue	$110,000
— Interest	25,000
Earnings Before Taxes	25,000
— Taxes (50 percent)	42,500
Earnings After Taxes	42,500
÷ 5000 shares	
Earnings per share	8.50

$$\text{Return per share} \quad = \quad \frac{8.50}{50.00} = 17 \text{ percent}$$

Without the leverage provided by the fixed cost of long-term debt a 10-percent jump in earnings would result in only a 10-percent increase in earnings per share (to $8.25). However, with the debt capital, earnings per share advance by more than 10 percent when there was a 10-percent increase in operating income.

A caveat: The sword of leveraged earnings cuts two ways. Just as a 10-percent increase in operating earnings will cause earnings per share to jump more than 10 percent, a *drop* in corporate earnings of 10 percent will result in a disproportionate erosion of earnings per share. Leverage can be a highly risky practice—especially in large doses—since a substantial drop in earnings may make it impossible for a firm to meet its debt repayment obligations. This is normally grounds for starting bankruptcy proceedings.

---

*Some increase in the return per share would be necessary to compensate stockholders for the higher risk they now bear.

BANKING'S CAPITAL SHORTAGE: THE MALAISE AND THE MYTH*

Ronald D. Watson

24

Is it possible that bank capital—like oil—is a scarce resource whose supply is in danger of being exhausted? To read the financial industry's trade journals a person might conclude that capital is a rare substance whose supply can grow only at a strictly limited rate. However, the current presumption that banks can't raise the funds they want for strengthening their capital positions and expanding deposits needs a lot of rethinking. Banks must have capital to inspire public confidence and absorb losses.[1] If they can't get the capital required to support their operations, maybe banks aren't serving the economy as effectively as is generally assumed.

Clearly, the banking industry must raise additional capital if it is to grow. Growth without new capital is possible, but only if bank regulators are willing to allow risks to increase, and that isn't likely. The "shortage" is occurring because banks are expanding their assets more rapidly than reinvested profits can boost capital. The obvious supplement to retained earnings is new capital from public issues of long-term debt and equity securities. But bankers claim that declining stock prices and higher interest rates have made the cost of this new money (especially the equity) too high. The problem is

*Reprinted from *Business Review*, September 1975, pp. 3-13, with permission from the Federal Reserve Bank of Philadelphia and the author.

[1] Ronald D. Watson, "Insuring Some Progress in the Bank Capital Hassle," *Business Review* of the Federal Reserve Bank of Philadelphia, July-August 1974, pp. 3-18.

compounded by generally weak markets for bank securities, especially in the wake of several failures of large banks in 1974. Most banks resort to outside financing only when other sources of funds are no longer readily available.

Restricting the industry's growth to the rate at which it can generate capital internally has been suggested, but most banks are reluctant to accept a policy that might mean losing ground to other financial intermediaries or even slowing the whole economy's growth. Yet, further growth for banking appears to be stymied. Internal generation of new capital is too slow, outside capital seems too costly, and the regulators are closing off the alternative of expanding without additional capital.

This should not—and need not—be an impasse. If the problem looks insurmountable, it may be that we are zeroing in on the wrong target. The issue should not be one of "how to get capital for future expansion," but "are the profit opportunities of this expansion great enough to justify raising new capital at today's prices?" If the profits are there, banks can afford to pay the going rate for capital. If they aren't, then the capital should go to industries that have better opportunities to use it. Bank capital markets may be in poor shape, but that alone shouldn't change the way the decision to expand is made.

THE CAPITAL CHASM

The bank capital "shortage" has been brewing for several years, but recent projections of enormous capital shortfalls over the next decade have significantly pepped up discussions of the problem. There have been prophecies of a capital "gap" (differences between probable capital accumulations and capital demands of the industry) of $16.7 billion[2] by 1978 or $32.0 billion[3] by 1979. These projections have intensified the industry's awareness that the methods used for financing growth in the '60s may not be equal to the task in the '70s.

Bankers have normally considered it impractical to try to close this gap with outside sources of funds. Data on bank financing is very sketchy, but the industry has a long history of depending heavily on earnings retention for additional long-term funds (as have most corporations). Of the new securities issued by banks the bulk has been debt (subordinated notes and debentures) rather than common or preferred stock.[4] In general, internal funds are more appealing as a source of capital than external funds because their cost seems very low. Retained earnings almost always look cheaper than new

[2] *The Capital Adequacy Problem in Commercial Banks*, 1974-1978 (Princeton, N.J.: The Institute for Financial Education, 1974), p. 8.

[3] Warren R. Marcus, *The Challenge to Banking: Capital Formation in the Seventies* (New York: Salomon Brothers, 1974), p. 6.

[4] "Report of Securities Issued by Commercial Banks and Holding Companies," Report #67, Corporate Financial Counseling Department of Irving Trust Company, New York, February 28, 1975.

common stock. A new stock issue may dilute the earnings of current share-holders, but retaining earnings never will. Furthermore, there are substantial transaction costs associated with floating new debt or equity issues publicly. Retained earnings may also seem less costly than long-term debt which carries an explicit obligation to pay interest.

Raising money through new issues of common stock has become even more expensive in the last few years because bank stock prices have declined dramatically even though earnings have been growing. Bankers accustomed to seeing their shares sell for 15 to 20 times earnings in the early 1960s were dismayed to see those prices drift into the 10 to 15 times earnings range in the late 1960s and early 1970s and then plummet to the 5 to 10 times earnings range in 1974.[5] As stock prices decline, the number of shares that must be sold to raise a fixed amount of new capital increases. When this occurs, the current stockholder's control of the bank is diluted and his future dividends diminish relative to what he would have received if the stock had been sold at a higher price. And each jump in equity cost has strengthened management's resolve to avoid paying the cost of raising funds with new stock issues.

Even debt capital has become more expensive in the last few years. Not long ago sound banks were able to sell their long-term obligations at an interest rate of 5 to 6 percent. However, an upward drift in rates and recent concern about bank soundness have made the going rate 8½ to 10 percent these days.

CURRENT REMEDIES FOR SPANNING THE GAP: A WEAK BRIDGE

Even though there is no universally accepted response to this problem, there have been any number of suggestions. Some have been directed toward loosening the regulatory constraint on expansion while other plans have been designed to reduce the industry's cost of capital. All of these proposals have some merit, but none constitutes a lasting solution to the problem.

Lower Capital Standards. Some effort has gone into convincing the regulatory agencies that banks don't really need all the capital that supervisors currently consider prudent. If capital standards were lowered, still more expansion could take place. Bankers point to the willingness of investors in the capital markets (until very recently) to advance debt funds to banks at interest rates nearly on a par with other high-quality corporate borrowers. This is

---

[5] *Keefe Bank Stock Manual* (New York: Keefe, Bruyette, and Woods Inc., 1974). Inflation and riskier bank portfolios have been important reasons for the rising cost of new debt and equity capital. However, many bankers claim that public statements by regulators warning of capital inadequacy problems have increased the cost of funds even to very conservative banks by making investors wary of all bank securities—not just banks that had been aggressive in using leverage.

interpreted as evidence that investors (who are the first to lose their money if banks fail) have considered banks to be good risks. If regulatory standards on capital are too conservative, reducing them would alleviate the current bind on growth. Reducing capital requirements might also enable banks to maintain the lower standard through retention of earnings. However, such a hope might be overly optimistic. A key reason that banks haven't maintained capital at the current standard through internal generation of profits is that they have been willing to sacrifice profits to achieve asset growth. If the regulator's capital constraint is relaxed without a simultaneous reexamination of the importance of maintaining profitability, the problem will just reappear in a couple of years. Asset growth will again be halted by the capital adequacy barrier, but this time it will be at an even lower standard.

More Debt. The second type of suggestion for closing the capital gap consists of plans for lowering the price that banks must pay for their capital funds. The most common proposal is that banks use more long-term debt as a substitute for equity capital. As long as debt hasn't been overused, it has a cost below that of equity and appears to be the cheapest way to raise outside capital. Debt is a particularly attractive form of capital in that it is the one form of long-term funds whose cost is a tax-deductible expense.[6]

Yet, substituting long-term debt for new equity is also only a partial solution. Long-term debt is an inadequate substitute for equity because it has legal characteristics which are different from those of common stock. Its claim to interest is secondary to that of depositors, so it backstops their claims. But interest and principal must be repaid on time if the bank is to avoid default, and operating losses cannot be charged against debt "capital" (except in liquidation) as they can against equity capital.

Accordingly, if a bank's asset growth is financed with debt capital rather than equity, the chance of incurring a large loss that would wipe out the remaining cushion of equity capital grows. The greater the amount by which the growth of risky assets exceeds expansion of the equity cushion, the greater the risk of failure. Bondholders are also wary of this heightened risk of failure. As the investors' risks grow, the yield they demand on their investment also climbs. As a result, heavy use of "cheap" debt capital will eventually raise the cost of new equity and debt (both new and refinanced) by causing the market price of these securities to decline. This risk "spillover" reduces the cost advantage of new debt. It also hurts the financial position of the current shareholders whose investment has now dropped in value. If a bank's debt position becomes excessive by market standards, management will find that by cutting back on the use of debt the shareholders' risk will be reduced, the stock's price will tend to rise, and the overall cost of funds will be lower (even new equity issues become relatively less costly than additional debt).

---

[6]There have recently been legislative proposals that all dividend payments be treated as tax-deductible expenses in the same way that interest payments are now deductible. If this change in the tax codes were enacted, it would make stock a relatively more attractive way to finance corporations.

New Securities. One of the problems preventing banks from using more debt capital is the poor marketability of these securities. Major banks that have market recognition are able to sell large amounts of debt at relatively low interest rates. However, smaller banks that lack this reputation aren't so fortunate. The market for their securities is normally restricted to their operating region, and borrowing costs may be higher than those of a large bank of the same risk. To overcome this disadvantages some smaller banks have borrowed debt capital from their big-city correspondents.[7] There have also been suggestions that smaller institutions use investment trusts (like mutual funds) to pool their securities. This device is intended to simplify the investor's diversification problems while providing a wider market for the securities of these banks.

Weakness in the stock and bond markets has prompted some authors to suggest that banks turn to convertible bonds for new capital. These are securities that can be converted into common stock if stock prices rise. Convertible bonds usually have an interest rate below that of nonconvertible debt. What's more, the price at which holders are allowed to convert their bonds into common stock can be set above the current market price of the stock. This type of security is supposed to give the issuer a cheap source of debt which will eventually be turned into equity at a better price than new stock issued right now—in a sense, the best of both worlds for the bank.

Investment trusts and convertible debt securities might be useful to a bank, but they won't make the cost of new capital substantially lower. Such a trust may improve the overall marketability of a bank's securities, making it easier for the institution to tap new sources of capital. However, an investor should be able to diversify his or her investments without the trust and has little reason other than convenience to accept a significantly lower return on pooled securities than for the individual issues.

Convertible bonds (and convertible preferred stocks) are also useful, but again they don't solve the problem. On the surface they look like a very cheap way to raise money. But this is not the case. If a bank offers a convertible bond, it may sell the securities at a low interest rate and attractive conversion price. However, it has still sold a debt issue, and debt is riskier for the bank than new equity. Holders of these bonds will only convert them to stock if the price of the bank's stock rises to a level above its conversion price in the future. If a bank really wants debt capital now and equity capital sometime in the future, it might be better off to float a bond issue initially, and then refinance it with a common stock issue later at the stock's higher price. In principle, there's no reason to expect a bank to be able to raise capital substantially more cheaply in the long run with convertible securities than with ordinary debt and stock.

Cut Dividend Payout. The high cost of new external capital has also prompted the suggestion that banks boost earnings retention by gradually

---

[7]This may make the smaller bank's capital position look more sound, but it hardly enhances the stability of the banking system.

cutting the proportion of earnings paid out as dividends. Retained earnings are an appealing way to build equity capital because the process doesn't create new shares which dilute earnings. The internal funds also increase the likelihood that there will be higher earnings in subsequent years.

But the suggestion that higher earnings retention be used when equity capital costs are high skips over some basic economics. If the cost of new equity is prohibitive, the cost of retained earnings should be treated as only "a bit less" than prohibitive. The cost of retained earnings is closely linked to the cost of new equity in the long run. In a world without taxes these costs would be identical except for the cost of underwriting new stock issues. Taxes make retained earnings slightly cheaper because investors whose profits are retained for reinvestment by the bank will avoid income taxes—at least until the reinvested profits produce higher dividends or until stockholders realize a capital gain on their investment. Realizing a capital gain would reduce the effective tax rate on the profits from reinvestment.

The connection between the cost of retained earnings and that of new common stock becomes clearer if we think of retained earnings as bank profits that are being reinvested within the organization for the benefit of the shareholders rather than being paid out to them in the form of dividends. Those same investors who want a very high return for investing in a new stock issue aren't likely to be happy to have their profits reinvested for them at significantly lower expected returns. If investors currently expect 15 percent as a return for investing in a bank's stock, they must feel that 15 percent is a competitive return given the risks of bank investment and the alternative uses they have for their money. If the bank can't earn enough profit on these retained earnings to give the shareholders that 15 percent return, it would make the investors better off by giving them the money as a dividend to invest as they see fit. In the long run, reinvestment of retained earnings at substandard rates will lower the bank's overall rate of return, and investors will bid down the price of the bank's stock. Therefore, reinvesting retained earnings when profit prospects don't warrant doing so is no solution to the capital problem.

Boost Earnings. The final proposal for closing the capital gap is one of speeding internal equity creation by increasing earnings margins. Greater profits would allow earnings to grow faster, equity to expand faster, and asset growth to be less impeded by capital. The proposal that banks raise their profit margins is the soundest and the most important of this crop of "solutions." It comes the closest to confronting the fundamental reason that the industry finds itself "unable" to raise adequate capital. It is also the basic component of a real solution.

THE FUNDAMENTAL PROBLEM

The problem that banks face isn't a shortage of capital but an unwillingness or inability to pay the "going rate." There is no question that capital costs are high right now. By the historical standard of the last three decades, the only time they were higher was in the latter part of 1974 when long-term interest rates were above their present levels and stock prices were extremely depressed. Adjusting to these rising capital costs is difficult for all business-men—and the reaction is likely to be slow. Many bankers have delayed rais-ing capital hoping that a future drop in market rates will reduce these capital costs.

Beyond the argument that rates may soon drop, many bank managers are simply unwilling to tolerate the dilution of earnings per share that could ac-company a new stock issue (spreading the existing earnings pool over a larger number of shares). Retained earnings may have a high implicit cost, but it's a difficult cost to pinpoint. Diluted earnings, however, suggest that manage-ment may have made some errors somewhere along the line. That makes di-lution a difficult path to accept (see Box).

Bankers may also be unwilling to pay the high cost of new capital for the sound economic reason that they cannot reinvest it at a sufficiently high re-turn. They may know that they need greater earnings to justify raising addi-tional funds yet may be unable to increase their margins because competitive pressures are too strong. Any move to raise earnings will be hard to sustain if other financial institutions don't consider themselves to be under the same pressures. If only one bank in an area raises its loan rate, its competitors will have an advantage in selling their services. In all probability the first bank will lose some of its share of the market. It's only when all banks feel the pressure to build their capital (and no one has a clear cost advantage) that profit margins can be raised successfully. Even then, banks may lose some business to other nonbank financial organizations unless those firms are un-der equivalent pressure to boost earnings.[8]

In the long run, the banking industry can only pay a higher price for cap-ital if it can pass these costs along to customers in the form of higher effec-tive interest rates or higher fees for other services provided. The ability to pass costs along depends in greater part on whether the industry can preserve its cost advantage over (or, at least, parity with) competing suppliers of fi-nancial services. If bank loan prices can't be competitive, profit opportunities will shrink and maintaining the industry's recent growth rate will be impos-sible.

THE FUNDAMENTAL SOLUTION

The industry can pay the going rate for capital if it is careful to use sound methods in analyzing its cost of funds and return available on new invest-

[8]This should not be interpreted as an approval of collusion to raise prices. Even though the entire industry has profits that are insufficient to attract new capital, each bank must respond to the prob-lem individually. However, the more widespread the profits squeeze, the more likely that individual banks will follow a move to raise prices rather than try to increase their market share by maintaining current prices for loans and services. In the long run, competitive markets will generate equal prices from all suppliers, but at a level which covers the cost of all factors of production including equity capital.

WHEN WILL DILUTION OCCUR?

A common argument advanced against the sale of new stock is the concern that the stock's earnings per share (E.P.S.) will be diluted by an increase in the number of shares outstanding. This is true, and to the extent that a bank's ability to pay dividends is tied to its E.P.S., it is undesirable to dilute earnings. However, this isn't the whole story.

New equity capital does more than simply dilute the current earnings of the existing shares. The new money can be invested profitably and used as a base for expanding other liabilities. It also reduces the risk of the bank's capital structure. It is quite possible that shareholders of a bank that sells new common stock can experience a mild dilution of their earnings but be better off. They have a sounder investment because their risk is lower and the bank now has a better equity base on which to expand in the future. As a practical matter, new stock issues *almost require* dilution in the short run. Stock must be sold in large enough blocks that the flotation and underwriting cost aren't too large a proportion of the total funds raised. But the new equity will then be sufficient for further expansion of fixed-cost liabilities and the bank can releverage the earnings to their former level.

Stock Price Dip. It's almost an article of faith that new stock can't be issued after a fall in the bank's stock price without diluting earnings. Dilution may well occur, but it isn't a foregone conclusion.

Suppose the Ninth National Bank's Balance sheet is the following.

Cash	(0%)*	$ 100	Deposits	(6%)	$ 600
Bonds	(7%)	500	Borrowing	(7%)	500
Loans	(11%)	600	Capital	(20 shares	100
				@ $5 per)	
Total		$1200	Total		$1200

Assuming the bank's tax rate is 50 percent, its earnings per share would then be

revenues   — expenses = income — taxes = profit
$(0 + 35 + 66) - (36 + 35) =$ 30   —   15 $= 15/20 = \$.75$ E.P.S.

Assuming that the stock's market price is equal to its par value, this is a 15 percent return on the stockholders' investment.

Suppose this bank had some attractive investment and lending opportunities but needed additional money to expand its assets. A total of $200 could be invested as follows:

20% in bonds at 7% = .014
80% in loans at 11% = .088

.102 = 10.2% before-tax yield
5.1% after-tax yield

Suppose, also, that the bank would have to rely heavily on purchased funds and new stock to raise this money but could get it in the following way:

20% from new deposits
70% from borrowings
10% from new common stock (4 new shares).

The average cost of these marginal sources of funds (adjusted for the tax deductibility of interest) would be

Proportion		Tax-Adjusted Cost		
.2	X	$(.06 \times .5 = .03)$	=	.0060
.7	X	$(.07 \times .5 = .035)$	=	.0245
.1	X	$(.15)$	=	.0150

.0455 = 4.55% tax-adjusted cost of funds

As long as funds can be raised at 4.55 percent and invested at 5.1 percent, the bank should expand.** In fact, if the bank makes this expansion its new balance sheet would be

Cash	(0%)	$ 100	Deposits	(6%)	$ 640
Bonds	(7%)	540	Borrowings	(7%)	640
Loans	(11%)	760	Capital	(24 shares	120
				@ $5 par)	
Total		$1400	Total		$1400

and the E.P.S. of the bank's stock (including the new shares) would jump to

revenues — expenses = income — taxes = profit
$(0 + 37.80 + 83.60) - (38.40 + 44.80) = 38.20 - 19.10 = 19.10/24 =$
$.796 E.P.S.

---

*The numbers in parentheses denote the effective *yield* on assets or the net cost of funds raised. Economic theory suggests that a firm should utilize a source of funds until the marginal cost of the next dollar raised from that source is exactly equal to the marginal cost of a dollar from any alternative source. If the bank described above really found that its cost of obtaining new deposits was below the cost of new short-term borrowings, it should tap that source until the marginal cost of deposits rises to the level of the cost of new borrowings.

**Bankers continually confront choices between greater return with higher risk or lesser returns with lesser risks. This analysis assumes that the bank's overall risk has not been altered by the expansion. The proportion of risk assets is up, but so is the bank's capital position. Therefore, the return expected by investors will not change.

Now suppose that inflation picks up or investors become worried about the long-run profitability of banks. The price of Ninth National's stock might drop from $5 to $4 a share. That represents a significant increase in the cost of new equity capital to the bank (15 percent to 18¾ percent), and it will now take five new shares rather than four to raise the $20 of new equity. However, the fact that these costs have risen is not sufficient reason to abandon the expansion. If profits from the new investments are high enough to cover the jump in equity costs, the bank should go ahead with its plans. If overall profits are unchanged the new E.P.S. will be ...

$$\$19.10/25 \text{ shares} = \$ .764 \text{ E.P.S.}$$

This is far less attractive than the 79.6¢ E.P.S. that the bank's shareholders would have received had the stock price remained $5 a share. But both new and old shareholders are still better off with the expansion than they would have been without it (76.4¢ versus 75¢).

In summary, an expansion that earns enough to benefit the new shareholders will automatically make the old ones better off. It's only when the new capital investment isn't profitable by the market's current standard of returns that expansion shouldn't be undertaken. Dilution will occur *only* when the wrong financial decision has been made or when the bank has exceeded the bounds of prudent leverage and has to sell more equity to get back to a safe capital structure.

ments. In the long run, solid financial analysis will be more effective in loosening the industry's growth constraints than plans to make bank securities more marketable. Management will also find that its own long-run interests are served by making sound financial decisions. Asset growth may be one measure of accomplishment, but consistent profitability over the long haul makes a banker's position more secure.

The Cost of Funds.   One of the most basic problems that industry must confront is estimating the costs of its own sources of funds. Bank management must determine where new money is coming from, what its full cost is, and what effect decisions to change the bank's capital structure (and, thereby, its risk) will have on the cost of these funds. The cost of funds to a bank depends in part on the riskiness of its capital structure—the proportions in which it raises long-term versus short-term funds and debt capital versus equity. A bank may raise its next dollar of funds from any of several specific sources, but it must carefully maintain a balance of debt and equity as it grows over time. If this week's funds come from debt sources, they will soon have to be balanced with new equity. Since increasing risk makes it impractical to expand indefinitely using only short-term borrowings, bankers must include the cost of funds from all of the sources that will eventually be tapped when they estimate the real cost of additional funds.[9] To be profitable, any investment made by the bank should earn enough profit to pay for all the funds used to finance it.

Lending money at rates which cover only the cost of funds borrowed to make the loan will quickly lead to profit problems. The cost of the new equity that must be raised to keep risk exposure constant must also be covered in the rate charged on the loan. Otherwise, the cost of the bank's funds will rise even further. If the cost of new capital is increasing, the signal to management should be clear: either reduce the bank's overall risk or be prepared to earn a high enough return on assets to pay for this capital. Successful operation over a long period requires that investors be given an expected return on their funds that is as high as returns available from other comparable securities. The fact that markets for the capital of smaller banks are especially imperfect doesn't alter the fact that those banks must have equity to expand and must pay whatever the "going market rate" is for that equity.

A Minimum Return. Once a bank has estimated the price it must pay for new funds it has a benchmark for judging alternative investments. A bank should only invest in loans or securities (or combinations of them) whose expected return is above the cost of the new funds required to finance them. That seems obvious. But the decision must be made on the basis of the current cost of all funds that will be raised during the next planning period rather than just the cost of a block of short-term debt which might be raised next week. It should also consider the full effect that any change in the bank's asset or liability risks will have on the cost of any funds raised. Furthermore, if the bank expects to have more funds than it needs to meet loan demand and liquidity requirements for an extended period, simply investing them in the highest yielding asset available may not be the best strategy. The investment must still yield enough to pay the full cost of these funds, or they should be returned to those who have loaned to or invested in the bank. This might be done by not replacing maturing debt issues or by paying extra dividends. In the long run, capital markets should eventually force a bank in the direction of managing its funds efficiently. (Limitations on entry into banking and imperfections in the market for bank securities may make market discipline less effective than it is in unregulated industries.)

Shrink, If Necessary. If investment prospects don't justify raising new funds, the institution shouldn't try to expand. Doing so isn't in the best in-

[9]A common technique for estimating a corporation's cost of new funds is the weighted average method. A business evaluates the net cost of raising additional funds from debt and equity sources by estimating the cost of each source and weighting the cost according to the proportion that those funds will represent of any new money raised. If a bank expects to finance 80 percent of its growth with short-term debt costing 4 percent after taxes and the other 20 percent of the expansion with new stock costing 12 percent, its weighted average cost of funds is $.8 \times .04 + .2 \times .12 = .032 + .024 = .056$ (5.6 percent). See Box for a more thorough explanation of this process.

terests of either shareholders or management. When the cost of funds exceeds the returns available to a bank, capital markets are giving management a signal that alternative uses for its shareholders' fund are relatively attractive. If the bank can't earn a competitive return on its equity, its stockholders can use the money for other investments. A bank that reinvests shareholder earnings when its return isn't on a par with other securities of similar risk is preventing shareholders from making better use of their own money. Eventually, the shareholders will sense this and try to sell their stock. The falling stock price will put pressure on management to correct the problem or answer to the stockholders.

The market is also signaling the bank that consumers and borrowers aren't sufficiently interested in its banking services to pay the prices that make the bank able to give investors a competitive return. Either another financial organization can provide that service at a lower cost or tastes have changed and people don't really want the service at all. Banks that can't afford to pay the going rate for funds (because they can't pass their higher costs on to their customers) should not expect to get additional money.

The Regulatory Constraint.   If banks were unregulated and absolutely free to buy money and sell services in a competitive business environment, these market forces could resolve the "capital shortage" automatically. But the fact is, they're not free and, therefore, they do not work perfectly. The industry, in fact, is tightly regulated, and the regulations influence bank profits. Exclusive rights to issue demand deposits and limitations on entry into the industry are examples of implicit subsidies from Government to commercial banks. Conversely, capital adequacy constraints, reserve requirements, and portfolio limitations tend to lower bank profits. The point is not that these constraints are "wrong" or "unjust," but that they influence the profitability and competitiveness of banks vis-á-vis other financial service organizations.

Firms operating in an unregulated world have the right to raise their prices enough to compete for the higher cost equity funds—as long as their customers are willing to pay those higher prices. Banks are free to make some price adjustments, but they may not be able to pass on higher money costs as effectively as unregulated financial corporations. If banking agency regulations or state usury statutes inadvertently hold earnings below the level needed to raise new capital, the industry's growth would be unnecessarily curtailed.[10]

There is no way to know, right now, whether this will be an important problem or not. Bank regulators must be vigilant in assuring that only the constraints that are necessary to promoting the financial system's stability are enforced. This problem becomes especially important as regulators weigh the pros and cons of changes in capital requirements and of expanded powers for both banks and thrift institutions.

---

[10] It is also possible that their regulated environment gives banks an advantage as money costs rise. In that instance, regulations are giving banks an unearned competitive edge and allowing them to increase their market shares at the expense of nonbank businesses. This results in just as great a misallocation of society's resources as occurs when bank profits and growth are unnecessarily restricted.

CONCLUSION

Any projection of historical trends in bank growth, profits, and dividend payout practices suggests that the banking system's demand for external capital will expand rapidly in the years immediately ahead. Yet the capital "gap" will probably sow the seeds of its own resolution. If banks curtail their growth because of an inability to find profitable new investments (or to circumvent the regulator's capital constraints), the least attractive investments can gradually be culled from their portfolios. By concentrating available resources on the more profitable business that remains, banks will be taking steps to build capital internally. Better profits and stronger capital positions, will cut risks, and banks will then be more able to compete for new external capital. Competition from the nonbank financial sector will remain, but these organizations must also pay high prices for additional capital. The key, however, is astute use by banks of the money available to them and prudence in raising only those funds that can be reinvested profitably. As long as the profit opportunities exist, banks will have the opportunity and the justification for raising whatever funds they need. When expected profitability is insufficient, the desire to expand must be held in check.

Regulators also face a challenge in the years ahead. They must not only protect the public's interest in its financial system but also try to keep the game "fair." The regulatory agencies can alter the competitive viability of the industries they regulate. If these industries are to serve society and their shareholders efficiently, they must be free to respond to their changing economic environment. The desire to expand banking's capital base rapidly is one development which can only be accomplished successfully if regulation doesn't prevent the industry from competing for funds, investing rationally, and passing rising costs along to customers who are willing to bear them.

Part III
INTERNATIONAL BANKING

In Part III several aspects of international banking are examined. In the first article, Janice M. Westerfield identifies several risks associated with foreign loans and discusses methods that may be used to shift or minimize the risks. A brief numerical analysis of international diversification is also provided. In the second article, Warren E. Moskowitz argues that the increasing size, complexity, and risks of international banking operations require a re-examination of the traditional asset-liability decision-making process. The advantages and drawbacks of the alternative "global approach" are examined by Moskowitz. Not surprisingly, the dramatic increase in international banking activity in recent years has drawn the attention of regulatory agencies. This is reflected in the third international banking article which was written by Roger M. Kubarych. Like domestic loans, foreign loans are examined with respect to credit risk. However, foreign loans also possess "country risk." Thus, an important facet of the examination process is an evaluation of the bank's ability to monitor and control its foreign loan exposure.

A PRIMER ON THE RISKS OF INTERNATIONAL LENDING AND HOW TO EVALUATE THEM*

Janice M. Westerfield

25

Among recent changes on the U. S. banking scene, surely one of the most dramatic has been the surge in international lending. Loans to foreign governments, firms, and individuals have grown both in volume and in earnings, and some aggressive international bankers have found that their foreign earnings actually exceed their domestic ones.

The steep upward trend in international involvement, which is tied in with overall trade expansion and new opportunities for profit, has brought different kinds of risks as well as substantial returns. The lender who makes loans in foreign countries has all the risks that he would have at home. But, beyond these, he has to consider risks which derive from the unique political, social, and economic conditions of the country in which the loan is placed.

These risks obviously are important to bankers because banking is a profit-making industry and risk affects profit. Now that international lending has become such a high-volume business, the possibility that foreign loan losses might have an adverse impact on the American banking industry as a whole has become a matter of concern to government and to the public.

Even the most careful risk management won't obviate all the hazards of lending in foreign countries. But bankers are working hard to identify, evaluate, and reduce the risks that go with foreign lending. And those who succeed in reducing their risks, through geographical diversification of their loans, or by other means, stand a good chance of receiving returns that repay their efforts abroad.

*Reprinted from the *Business Review*, July/August 1978, pp. 19-29, with permission from the Federal Reserve Bank of Philadelphia.

U. S. BANKS GO INTERNATIONAL

Since the beginning of the decade, U.S. banks have moved decisively into international finance, increasing their foreign claims and their earnings from foreign assets.

Growth . . . The statistics tell most of the international lending story.

Foreign claims of banks in the U.S. have grown from about $21 billion in 1972 to over $92 billion in 1977—a compound annual growth rate of 30 percent. And foreign branches of U.S. banks now have about double that volume of claims on foreigners. Earnings of foreign assets also are up sharply, especially in relation to domestic earnings. A Salomon Brothers study of thirteen large bank holding companies found that, from 1970 to 1976, their foreign earnings rose by about $700 million while earnings at home grew by less than $40 million.[1] Thus 95 percent of the increase in their total earnings came from international operations. By 1976, foreign earnings accounted for more than half of total earnings for six of these bank holding companies. For the whole group, foreign earnings averaged 43 percent of total earnings.

. . . And Its Causes. The growth of international banking operations is related to a number of developments, especially the overall expansion of U.S. trade with other countries. Also important have been the spread of multinational corporations, the effect of government regulation on domestic profit opportunities, and the impetus for financing trade deficits that changes in petroleum prices have generated in some foreign countries.

U.S. trade has increased. American merchandise exports rose from $50 billion in 1972 to $115 billion in 1976, and imports showed similar growth. Much of this growth in dollar value—part of it real, part of it caused by inflation—was financed by U.S. banks, through letters of credit and banker's acceptances and through other instruments. To take a simple illustration: An exporter may ship goods in July and desire payment immediately, but the importer probably won't have the funds to pay until he receives the goods in October. Under circumstances such as these, both parties may agree to have a bank forward payment to the exporter and lend money to the importer through creation of a banker's acceptance during the time the goods are in transit. Once the importer receives and processes his shipment, he reimburses the bank for the amount of the acceptance (including applicable interest). *Trade financing* of this sort has become commonplace for U.S. banks.

Many firms that first incorporated in the United States now operate through subsidiaries in other countries and have a significant percentage of their assets and employment positioned abroad. As these firms have expanded into foreign countries, they have brought their bankers with them. In Europe

[1] Thomas Hanley, Salomon Brothers, 1976, *U. S. Multinational Banking: Current and Prospective Strategies.*

alone, for example, *U.S. multinationals*, with substantial financing by U.S. banks, have upped their direct foreign investment to over $56 billion.

This investment has paid off. Over the period 1966-75, sales by American affiliates in Europe rose by about 9 percent per year in real terms. And although reduced earnings prodded U.S. businesses to cut their foreign subsidiaries somewhat in 1976 and 1977, there remains a significant amount of multinational activity in Europe, and in other parts of the world, for U.S. banks to finance.

Interest in foreign banking operations probably has been encouraged by the regulatory environment at home. It's certain that *domestic banking regulations* helped to shape the responses of U.S. banks to changes in trading patterns. In the 1960s, the Federal government imposed controls on outflows of U.S. financial capital. These controls encouraged American corporations to finance their foreign investments with foreign funds. But in order to accommodate their corporate customers, U.S. banks set up foreign branches that tapped foreign capital sources. For this reason and others, branches of U.S. banks became more firmly established abroad. And this result was abetted by Regulation Q, which, by limiting the interest rates paid on domestic deposits, further induced U.S. banks to set up foreign branches to supplement their traditional sources of funds. The number of overseas branches increased from 180 in 1965 to 732 in 1975.

Thus regulation, along with the internationalization of U.S. corporate activities, helped spur the growth of overseas branches. And despite some regulatory changes, there remain considerable incentives for setting up overseas offices to service multinational corporate customers.

Finally, *balance-of-payments deficits* in other countries have played an important role in the growth of U.S. bank claims on foreigners. Especially since the quadrupling of oil prices in 1973, many third-world countries have been unable to generate enough export earnings to pay their oil import bills without outside help. Among these countries, the poorest have had little access to credit markets; but others have found help in the form of medium-term loans from U.S. commercial banks. Substantial credits have been extended directly to foreign governments or their dependencies rather than to businesses or individuals.

Thus American banks have been responsive to large-scale developments in world trade as well as to regulation at home and payments shortfalls in other countries. And they are striving to consolidate the gains they have made so far as well as to explore new foreign profit opportunities. But their foreign operations have brought new kinds of risks—risks which deserve close scrutiny.

IDENTIFYING FOREIGN LOAN RISKS

The primary principles for foreign lending are the same as for domestic— define and assess risk exposure and then reduce the risk that borrowers will default. But when a prudent banker makes a loan abroad, whether the borrower is an individual, a firm, or a government, he'll be thinking about not only these principles but also country risk.

Basic Risks.   The chances that a loan will be repaid in full are affected by many characteristics of the borrower. The less sound the borrower is financially, the greater the risk that part of the interest or principal of the loan will not be repaid. Thus an understanding of the financial condition of the borrower is important for domestic and foreign loans alike.

Besides the amount of repayment, the time of repayment also affects risk. Just as his domestic counterpart, the international lender must consider what he needs to preserve the overall liquidity of his portfolio. Liquidity—the ability to meet day-to-day obligations—may be impaired by having too much money tied up in long-term investments. Loans maturing in, say, five years cannot be used to pay liabilities due in six months. Thus the lender has to know not only how much of a return he can expect on his loan but also when he can expect to get it. And there are circumstances which could make a lender less confident of his expectations when he deals with foreign borrowers than when he deals with domestic ones.

Country Risk.   There are certain risks that can attach to a loan just because it is placed in a foreign country. One kind of country risk is *sovereign risk*, which derives from the unique mix of political, social, and economic institutions that characterizes a sovereign state. Another kind is *currency risk*— the risk that a loss will be caused by currency restrictions or trade barriers.

Default occurs whenever a borrower fails to repay either the principal or the interest on a loan. Sometimes a borrower may want to reschedule debt— to stretch out payments because they can't be met out of current resources. When a loan is rescheduled, the borrower usually must pay an interest penalty to compensate the lender for the higher risk of eventual loss. But the lender still may lose out on part of his return; and even if he doesn't, his liquidity may be reduced by having his money tied up longer than expected. A foreign government that can offer assurances against default and rescheduling of loans to private borrowers and autonomous government agencies will make such loans more attractive to international lenders.

Sovereign risk is closely tied to political developments, particularly the attitudes of the government authorities towards foreign loans or investments. Some countries attempt to smooth the way for foreign funds, whether those funds are flowing to public or private borrowers. But others make it very difficult to establish and maintain profitable lending operations. Minor obstacles can appear in the form of wage-price controls, profit controls, tax and legal restrictions, and so on. These forms of government interference generally raise the costs of doing business and sometimes reduce the chances that the lender will be fully reimbursed. Further, they may be signs that the borrower should face up to the possibility of nationalization of an investment, expropriation of assets, or prohibition of foreign loan repayment—any of which could change the risk picture.[2] Although the chance of expropriation may be small, the loss associated with it is so complete that it cannot be ignored. Sometimes partial compensation is offered, but even this may be delayed for long periods while host governments negotiate with foreign investors or lenders.

Currency risk, which can occur by itself or in combination with sovereign risk, has to do with currency value changes and exchange controls. Some loans are denominated in foreign currency rather than in dollars, and if the currency in which the loan is made loses value against the dollar during the course of the loan, the repayment will be worth fewer dollars when the loan comes due (though the asset loss may be offset by liabilities in the same currency). Because not all foreign currency markets are well developed, international loans sometimes cannot be hedged to reduce this kind of currency risk. Credits that are denominated in dollars, as most are, also may be subject to currency risk. Exchange controls, which are relatively common in developing countries, may limit the cross-border movement of funds or restrict a currency's convertibility into dollars for repayment. Or exchange rate changes may affect the borrower's capacity to generate sufficient earnings to pay off dollar loans.

All in all, the lender who wants the returns that go with foreign operations must be prepared to make an extra effort to identify his risks. But that's only the beginning. Once it's known what *can* happen, the lender has to evaluate the likelihood that it *will* happen. And that takes information.

RISK EVALUATION

Lenders have different ways to evaluate risk. In some cases they use in-depth studies of foreign countries. In others they use statistics that indicate a borrower's financial condition or checklists that pull together economic, social, and political data.

In-depth studies usually are based on both statistics and other information about a country's economic and financial management. Depending upon the extent of a bank's international operations, its evaluations may be quite comprehensive. Besides background information on basic economic trends in the foreign economy, these evaluations often contain careful analyses of inflation, fiscal policies, trade and capital flows, debt accumulation, political stability, and other variables.[3] Since some circumstances that affect country

---

[2]There are few recorded cases of large-scale nationalization by a foreign government. Chile and Cuba appear to be two examples.

[3]The way country risk is assessed will depend somewhat upon the purpose for which the assessment is to be used. Bankers are interested primarily in avoiding debt-servicing difficulties and in making profitable loans. International Institutions such as the International Monetary Fund want country studies as background information for annual consultations or for approving drawings from one of the Fund's facilities. The World Bank does its country evaluation studies for the purpose of deciding how much to loan and what kind of technical assistance to provide to its various members.

risk cannot be captured in statistics, it is inevitable that practical judgment and experience also come into play. And lenders who maintain branches or representative offices abroad may rely on their staffs not only to generate business but also to help them keep up with local developments that aren't reflected in a timely way by indicators and checklists. So the overall in-depth evaluation of a country is likely to come from many sources.

When bankers find it too costly or time consuming to get in-depth analyses, they may turn to on-site reports, checklists, and statistical indicators—separately or in combination—for assessing the debt-servicing capabilities of prospective borrowers. These aids may not be long on theory, but they do provide ways to get a grip on the information that a loan officer has to grapple with.

Some of the statistical indicators are designed to measure foreign exchange earnings entering a country against outgoing expenditures for debt servicing. The debt-service ratio was the first such indicator to be used extensively. This ratio states a country's interest and amortization payments as a percentage of its export earnings from goods and services. Other indicators, such as the current account deficit, net interest payments, and growth rate of real GNP, have been developed to supplement the debt-service ratio. And sometimes, because any of these individual indicators used alone may be misleading, several of them will be combined to construct composite indicators for more reliable identification of problem borrowers (see STATISTICAL INDICATORS).

Somewhat similar are the checklists of economic, social, and political variables that some bankers use along with their statistical indicators. These checklists are designed to yield supplementary information about a country's economic and financial management. The checklists are not standard from bank to bank, but they usually include variables about GNP, money supply growth, foreign trade, debt accumulation, and so on. The checklist items generally are not ratios, as the statistical indicators are, but they can be assigned numerical ratings and aggregated into a total score for each country.

Neither the checklist nor the statistical indicators are reliable predictors of debt-servicing difficulties. Often they signal false alarms. Most of the indicators and checklists describe conditions as they were a year or two ago. Even when current, they describe the situation only as it now is; they do not tell how the picture will change in the future. And predicting debt-servicing difficulties is essentially peeking into the future. Nevertheless, these indicators may serve as warning signals that a prospective foreign borrower ought to be examined more closely.

Thus the lender has to decide how much information he needs to negotiate a loan with a prospective borrower, and then he has to go out and get it. If the information simply is not available, or if it indicates too high a risk for the expected rate of return, the loan applicant may be turned down. But even if the decision is made to go ahead with the loan, the prudent banker will want to reduce the risk of loss.

STATISTICAL INDICATORS

Several indicators are used by international lenders to gauge country risk. These indicators, and the techniques of using them, do not have a high degree of reliability as predictors of deb-servicing difficulties. But they still may provide useful information to lenders.

The *debt-service ratio*, which probably is the most commonly used statistical indicator, measures foreign exchange earnings channeled into debt servicing against total exchange earnings from (current account) exports.

The ratio of the current account deficit to export earnings from goods and services—the *current deficit-export ratio*—measures temporary balance-of-payments difficulties and may fluctuate considerably from year to year. When combined with the *cumulative deficit-export ratio* over, say, a three-year period, the current deficit-export ratio can give a longer term picture of the amount and rate of growth of a country's debt burden.

The *interest-reserve ratio* measures net interest payments on external debt against international reserves in the most recent period. The interest payments reflect the debt interest burden for all debt accumulated. (Amortization data, which is not comprehensive in any case, is excluded.) This ratio measures the short-run ability of a country to meet its interest payments—out of international reserves, if necessary. The focus is on reserves as a last source of funds to service debt.

A variant of this ratio which also uses net interest payments is the *interest-export ratio*. This measures the debt interest burden against average annual export receipts and is a proxy for the debt-export ratio.

Indicators such as these focus on a country's ability to repay its external debt out of current account export earnings. But a reduction in these earnings needn't lead to debt-servicing difficulties or attempts to cut back imports, since grant aid, capital inflows, and international reserves may be used along with export earnings to service debt. Thus a country may have more flexibility than is suggested by external debt indicators.

Other indicators, which chart both internal and external economic conditions, are used for overall ranking purposes as well as for in-depth country studies. Some measures suggested by the literature include economic growth rates of gross domestic product and money supply as well as export earnings stability and level of economic development.

METHODS OF REDUCING RISK

Bankers have several ways to cut risk. They can seek third-party support in the form of loan guarantees or management assistance for borrowers; they can share risk exposure with several lenders; or, most important, they can diversify their loans among several borrowers or areas. And the regulatory authorities may be able to assist international lenders in holding down their country risk exposure.

Third-Party Help. One way for a banker to reduce the risk on a loan is to get a third party to agree to pay back both principal and interest if the borrower defaults. Foreign governments and central banks sometimes act in this capacity. But the guarantee is good only so long as the backer is solvent and adheres to the contract. And if the same government or central bank guarantees several loans, there's a chance that its ability to supply the required funds might be strained if more than one of these loans were to require funds at the same time.

An alternative to the foreign government guarantee is the external guarantee by a parent company or outside institution. The Overseas Private Investment Corporation, for example, offers programs to insure bank loans against the risks of war, expropriation, and inconvertibility, as well as to finance loans directly. Also, the U.S. Export-Import Bank (Eximbank) guarantees medium-term loans made by commercial banks against both political and credit risk. And the Foreign Credit Insurance Association, acting as agent for member insurance companies and the Eximbank, offers insurance against these risks.

Another form of third-party help that many bankers find reassuring is the presence of institutions such as the International Monetary Fund. The IMF does not assist the lender directly. It does not, for example, provide commercial bankers with its country reports. But it can put the lender's mind more at ease by fostering conditions in a borrower country that increase the likelihood of loan repayment.

In the course of determining whether a country that has balance-of-payments difficulties is eligible to draw from its funding facilities, for instance, the IMF examines the prospective borrower's current condition and economic policies. And it negotiates measures that the borrower must take to qualify for eligibility. A country's adherence to these measures, which the IMF monitors, can increase the probability that the borrower will be able to repay without difficulty. Thus the international banker benefits indirectly but importantly from having the IMF on site.

Risk Pooling. When third-party assistance isn't available, bankers still can cut the risk for any one institution by making a participation loan. Under this kind of arrangement, several banks combine their funds to reduce exposure directly for individual banks. This type of effort may include a sharing of expertise among the participants, but generally each bank wants and is expected to make its own assessment. Since participation loans sometimes are large and involve big-name banks, the country that gets them probably will feel that its access to credit markets will be served best by prompt repayment.

While third-party presence may reduce default risk and pooling may lessen the exposure of individual banks, there is another strategy that deserves consideration. Instead of focusing on each loan prospect in isolation as it comes along, the banker can examine each one for its effect on risk to the total loan portfolio.

Diversification. The portfolio approach to managing assets is important to bankers because they want to maintain a steady stream of returns over time. The typical lender does not want to put all his eggs in one basket, where they all can be broken simultaneously. And, in any case, he is prevented from doing so by legal restrictions. Instead, he diversifies the portfolio by investing in a variety of loans, so that, in case one borrower defaults, the earnings from other investments will minimize the effect of the loan loss on the bank's total earnings.

But whether diversification reduces risk for a given portfolio depends on how the returns on individual loans are correlated with one another—to what extent they are affected in similar ways by common conditions or events. Diversification will be a source of potential risk reduction if returns on individual loans are *not* perfectly correlated.[4] Thus of two loans with the same rate of return and riskiness, the one that is less perfectly correlated with the rest of the portfolio will be the more attractive; and it may even happen that a loan with a relatively low rate of return will be a useful addition to a portfolio because it's imperfectly correlated with the rest of the portfolio's contents (see Appendix).

Portfolio diversification can be pursued in several ways, of which geographical dispersion may be the most obvious. When loans to a foreign recipient are under consideration, it's usually the country-specific aspects of the loan that are first considered. That is, everything else being held constant—the maturity, loan guarantee, characteristics of the firm and industry, and so on —it's the sovereign state that makes the difference. This element in the choice among countries is what is identified most commonly as country risk.

But the choice among countries may ignore another source of country exposure, and that is loan concentration. A bank develops expertise in certain countries and cultivates sources yielding first-hand information, which is essential to sound decisionmaking. Furthermore, detailed knowledge of the borrower is required in order to form opinions about probabilities of repayment. The argument can be made that expertise built up in a country over a

---

[4] Citicorp states this point in its 1976 annual report (p. 25) as follows: "Overseas earnings, which contributed over 70 percent of the total earnings in 1976, are derived from doing business in more than 100 countries. Citicorp's worldwide policy of broad diversification of both assets and liabilities helps maintain earnings stability and reduces the risk of excessive concentration in any one particular country, currency, or industry."

long period is hard to beat. But if several loans have already been generated in, say, Country A, an additional loan in Country A may actually be more risky than a first loan in, say, Country B. Why? Because risks of excessive concentration may not be fully offset by first-hand information.

The risks of undue concentration stem from the possibility that a common factor may have an adverse effect on all the loans in a given country. This is because the economic and political management of a country influences all its economic units. If some adverse development should occur, many units within the country would be similarly affected. Take the case of a country that depends on two or three export products for its foreign exchange earnings. Although foreign exchange may also be obtained from other sources such as capital inflows or reserves, many countries derive foreign currency supplies primarily from export earnings. When the export market for a country's products deteriorates and foreign exchange earnings fall short, the government, its agencies, and many businesses all may have insufficient earnings to repay debts on schedule.[5]

Besides the effects of sovereignty and concentration on country exposure, interaction effects between foreign and domestic loans are important for diversification. Thus a bank's portfolio ought to be considered in its entirety and not analyzed in separate foreign and domestic sections. Risk to the overall portfolio probably can be reduced when some foreign loans are added to a predominantly domestic portfolio. The reason is that the business cycles of most other countries differ in timing and magnitude from those of the U.S., and so foreign borrowers and domestic borrowers are unlikely to suffer from overall economic declines at the same time. Thus diversification can be construed broadly over country, currency, industry, maturity, and so on.

Reducing portfolio risk for the same expected return (or else increasing the return for the same risk level) is the benefit the banker hopes to get through diversification. It follows that international lenders have a lot to gain by diversifying their loan portfolios. Spreading out their loans to achieve a relatively constant return is the best hedge against crippling loan losses. Even though there may be great advantages to specializing in one country and becoming thoroughly acquainted with conditions there, bankers ought to be willing to sacrifice some information advantage for the security of diversification.

How Regulators Can Help. The agencies that regulate American banking have watched international developments more and more closely as the volume of lending has grown. They recognize that geographical expansion has brought a new kind of risk, and they are interested in assuring the soundness of U.S. banking efforts abroad.

The regulator's position is a delicate one. Mere acceptance of international lending guidelines that banks set for themselves may not provide an effective

---

[5] A few countries rely mainly on earnings from just one export to repay their debts. A fall in the price of this export can produce debt-servicing difficulties and consequent debt rescheduling.

SUPERVISION AND COUNTRY RISK

The growth of U. S. bank claims on foreigners and the increase of other capital flows are major developments requiring assessment by the U. S. monetary authorities. Because information about happenings in the rest of the world often is incomplete, this task is a difficult one. The first step may be to gather information about the magnitude and geographical distribution of foreign exposure. The Federal Reserve, the Office of the Comptroller of the Currency, and the Federal Deposit Insurance Corporation are doing just that in a semiannual country exposure report of more than 400 banks, their overseas branches, and subsidiaries. The detailed information on borrowers and maturities is designed to assist these agencies in judging the risks that banks face in their international lending.

Several policy proposals are being discussed now, such as guidelines that would guard against excessive loan concentration in one country in relation to a bank's total capital. Others involve closer monitoring of bank internal procedures. Further, last January the Comptroller of the Currency issued a ruling on loan concentration designed to clarify the interpretation of banking law which limits national bank loans to individual borrowers to 10 percent of total bank capital. This ruling attempts to define the conditions under which governments, their instrumentalities, and their agencies can be considered separate borrowers.

level of monitoring. But imposition of uniform limits on the volume of a bank's foreign loans, for example, could operate to restrict foreign profit opportunities severely, with consequent harmful effects on the overall health of the American banking system (see SUPERVISION AND COUNTRY RISK).

The answer appears to lie in helping banks improve their information on foreign borrowers and avoid unusually large concentrations of credit in a single country. At present, the agencies with the heaviest involvement in international lending—the Federal Reserve System, the Comptroller of the Currency, and the Federal Deposit Insurance Corporation—are moving deliberately forward with such an approach. They are developing a data collection system that will help banks track their foreign exposure by recording the volume and maturity of loans in a given country, whether the loans have external guarantees, and whether they are denominated in local or nonlocal currency (usually dollars). This approach provides an analysis of loan concentration by country with respect to a bank's overall financial capital. With this information in front of them, bank managers and examiners are in a position to evaluate lending procedures and portfolio risk.[6]

---

[6] See "A New Supervisory Approach to Foreign Lending," *Quarterly Review*, Federal Reserve Bank of New York, Spring 1978, pp. 1-6.

SUMMING UP

Lending to foreigners involves country risk exposure and requires an assessment of risks of government policies and risks of currency or trade restrictions. Commercial bankers perceive that the profitability of their foreign operations and thus a substantial portion of their earnings vary directly with how well they evaluate foreign risks. Government authorities, as well, stress the importance of a careful analysis of country risk to ensure sound banking practices.

Because of the problems associated with incomplete information, bankers, regulators, and other concerned parties have developed a mix of qualitative and quantitative methods to evaluate risks associated with foreign claims. Yet, in the past, these measures have tended to focus on a single country and its political, economic, and social fabric. While these indicators are useful, they generally ignore how a single event might adversely affect a whole country. Nor do they recognize how countries depend on one another in the trading, financial, political, and other spheres.

Since these common relations are reflected in returns on loans, appreciable gains may be made from examining how an individual claim fits into the overall portfolio. Diversification of loans is essential if risk to the total portfolio is to be kept at an acceptable level. And imperfect correlation of returns is the key to successful diversification. As international operations continue to grow, bankers can be expected increasingly to explore the benefits that diversification could bring to the world of foreign lending.

APPENDIX

DIVERSIFICATION CAN REDUCE RISK

Suppose that a U.S. bank has decided to allocate $1 million of its funds to foreign loans in Country A or Country B. The bank feels it has developed some expertise in Country A, and it already has made several loans to public or private borrowers there. It has no loans outstanding in Country B. The maturities of the loans will be the same in whichever country they're placed.

The bank's international experts know the rate of return over the maturity of each loan and the probability of default. Using these basic data, they can calculate both the expected return and the variance of return. (Variance of return measures risk and is a function of the probability of obtaining a return that differs from the expected return.)

The loan to Country A would have a yield to maturity of 10 percent and a default risk of 2 percent. The calculation for the loan's expected return then is:

$$E(R_A) = 0.98(0.10) + 0.02(0) = 0.098.$$

The calculation for its variance is:

$$\text{var}(R_A) = 0.98[0.10 - E(R_A)]^2 + 0.02[0 - E(R_A)]^2 = 0.00033.$$

Note that a 2-percent default risk means that the bank has a 2-percent chance of receiving no payment on its loan and a 98-percent chance of receiving the full 10-percent yield.

The loan to Country B would have a yield to maturity of 10.2 percent and a default risk of 4 percent. Calculations will show that the loan to Country B would have the same expected return as Country A's—0.098— but a higher variance—0.00040. Thus the whole picture would be as follows:

	Yield to Maturity	Default Risk	Expected Return	Variance of Return
Country A	10.0%	2%	0.098	0.00033
Country B	10.2%	4%	0.098	0.00040

Assume, however, that the bank wants to diversify by splitting the $1 million 50-50 between the two countries instead of lending the full amount to the country with the lower variance—Country A. Further, assume that the returns on the loans to Country A and Country B move together somewhat and have a correlation coefficient c = 0.4. Finally, assume that the portfolio has an expected return that is equal to the expected return on the loan to Country A while the variance is less than it would be if the full amount were loaned to Country A:

$$\text{var}(R_P) = X_A^2 \, \text{var}(R_A) + X_B^2 \, \text{var}(R_B) + 2c \, AB^X A^X B^\sigma A^\sigma B$$

$$= 0.00026.$$

The loan to Country B has the same expected return as, and a higher variance than, the loan to Country A. But when Country B is added to the portfolio, the variance of the portfolio as a whole is less than the variance of either individual loan. Thus the variance of return on the individual loans has been offset by the less than perfect correlation among the returns. Diversification has reduced portfolio risk for the same expected return.

If the bank desires to find out what percentage allocation to Country A would *minimize* the variance of the portfolio return, this percentage (X_A^*) can be computed as well.[†] The minimum-variance portfolio turns out to have 58 percent loaned to Country A and 42 percent loaned to Country B. Again, diversification reduces portfolio risk for the same expected return, although the variance—$\text{var}(R_P^*) = 0.00025$—is only marginally less than that of the 50-50 portfolio.

[†] $X_A^* = [\text{var}(R_B) - c_{BA} \, \sigma_B \sigma_A]/\text{var}(R_A) + \text{var}(R_B) - 2c_{BA}\sigma_B\sigma_A$

$= 0.58.$

$X_B^* = 1 - X_A^* = 0.42.$

GLOBAL ASSET AND LIABILITY MANAGEMENT AT COMMERCIAL BANKS*

Warren E. Moskowitz

26

A dramatic expansion of international banking in recent years has led banks to reexamine the traditional decision-making process. Many banks had found that their international operations had grown in size and complexity, particularly regarding funding and lending. Additional effort was thus required to monitor and coordinate these activities, especially with domestic money management. Accordingly, some banks have adopted, or are presently considering, bankwide procedures for coordinating their asset and liability decisions. Other banks have continued to rely considerably on decision making by branches and functional units.

The variety of approaches currently used stems from differences in views about the best practical approach to funds management. There is no disagreement that conceptually the consolidated balance sheet and overall profit statement are key accounting elements for bank decisions. Nor are institutional constraints an impediment to global management. Until five years ago, United States capital controls had limited the movement of funds, between domestic and foreign offices of banks, making it less necessary to have an overall perspective. Today, however, dollar funds move freely among major capital markets and the movement of other currencies is relatively unconstrained, particularly in offshore markets. In principle, there is no barrier to linking the activities of separate banking units. Operationally, however, a global decision process may not be best for all banks. It requires that senior

*Reprinted from the *Quarterly Review*, Spring 1979, pp. 42-48, with permission from the Federal Reserve Bank of New York.

management assimilate bankwide information quickly, assess opportunities in world markets, and communicate decisions within the organization. To integrate these activities effectively may be costly. Moreover, coordinating decisions may conflict with other goals of bank management. The decision to adopt a global management approach depends upon the circumstances at an individual bank and the philosophy of its management. This article, based on discussions in New York and other major money market centers, reviews the pros and cons of alternative methods of asset and liability management.

BANK MANAGEMENT IN A NUTSHELL

At the heart of the bank management process are committees of high-ranking officers representing the major functions of the bank. For asset and liability management, for example, the most important areas represented are investment, money market, and lending activities, both domestic and foreign, supported by the economic analysis function. The fundamental long-run task of top management is to chart the probable course of the bank, allowing for adequate funding and capitalization to accommodate planned needs. Rarely, if ever, will events proceed exactly as planned. Lending opportunities may be greater or less than anticipated, money market conditions may tighten or ease, or currencies may come under upward or downward pressures. There-fore, management's objective is to position the bank so that it can adapt profitably to whatever conditions arise. One of the facts of life for manage-ment is that a modern international bank is dependent upon funds borrowed in the money market for a large portion of its liabilities. A bank is able to at-tract these funds at a favorable cost in part because of the perceived safety and liquidity of its liabilities. The guidelines set by management for sound operations are, therefore, critical for maintaining the attractiveness of the bank. A checklist of management concerns would include the following.

(1) Adequate capital. As the ratio of assets to capital increases, the risk to shareholders and uninsured depositors increases but, as the ratio declines, the rate of return on capital falls off. The happy medium is hard to find. When achieved, it is a blend of what competitors are doing, what supervisory authorities view as appropriate, and what the bank's own management thinks is prudent. However an acceptable ratio is determined, it will affect manage-ment decisions. In the planning process, the ratio signals the need to raise ad-ditional capital in order to meet planned growth. If the capital cannot be raised at an acceptable cost, the expansion of the bank's activities may be impeded, in the long run, by the need to stay within the range of prudent capital coverage.

(2) Liquidity. It is the nature of banking to make commitments to receive and to pay out funds. Some commitments may be fixed in advance. The

bank may be required to make payment to the holder of a certificate of deposit or a Eurodollar account, to receive payment on a maturing Treasury bill, or to hold funds in its reserve account with the Federal Reserve. In other cases, the timing and the amount of the flows are, within limits, at the discretion of the customer. He may choose to draw down a deposit or a line of credit, to roll over a loan, to make payments against an outstanding loan, or to put funds into a demand or time deposit account. The liquidity problem for the bank is always to be able to honor commitments to make payments at an acceptable cost and without reliance on the Federal Reserve discount window. To do this, banks chart foreseeable inflows and outflows of funds. They prepare for anticipated outflows by arranging to obtain funds at the time that the funds are needed. They also try to reduce the likelihood of unforeseen shortfalls by using stable sources of funds, such as customer deposits and funds with long maturities, in order to reduce the volatility of liabilities. As a cushion on the asset side, they hold liquid assets. However, banks also rely on their capacity to borrow in money markets as an important alternative to holding liquid assets. The markets in Federal funds, repurchase agreements, bankers' acceptances, certificates of deposit, Eurodollar deposits, and the commercial paper of the bank holding companies are sources from which banks plan to obtain funds as needed (Table 1).

(3) Market exposure. Because banks depend so heavily on the money markets for liquidity, it is important for them not to exhaust their capacity to borrow. They do this by remaining within what they feel is their share of

Table 1

Selected Assets and Liabilities of Large Commercial Banks*
In billions of dollars

Year-end	(1) Net Federal funds purchased†	(2) Certificates of deposit	(3) Other liabilities for borrowed funds‡	(4) Net liabilities to foreign branches§	(5) Total loans and investments	Ratio to (1) to (5) (percent)	Ratio to (2) to (5) (percent)
1966 . . .	‖	15.7	6.8	‖	189.4	‖	8.3
1969 . . .	9.5	10.9	2.8	12.6	239.8	4.0	4.5
1970 . . .	10.8	26.1	1.3	6.5	261.0	4.1	10.0
1972 . . .	20.0	44.9	1.9	1.1	325.4	6.1	13.8
1974 . . .	28.4	92.8	4.3	− 1.3	410.2	6.9	22.6
1976 . . .	51.3	65.9	4.2	−15.5	416.4	12.3	15.8
1978 . . .	61.4	100.0	16.9	−17.6	503.6	12.2	19.9

*Weekly reporting banks.
†Net of Federal funds sold to other commercial banks. Includes securities sold under agreements to repurchase.
‡Excludes borrowing from the Federal Reserve.
§A negative number indicates net funding of foreign branches.
‖Not available.
Source: Federal Reserve *Bulletin*.

each segment of the market. The demand for funds beyond the customary level is an ambiguous indicator of a bank's condition. The funds may be wanted because of profitable opportunities or, if the bank is having problems, to honor commitments. Whatever the actual situation, there is the danger that the financial markets will take the pessimistic view that the bank is experiencing internal problems. Banks are, therefore, reluctant to exceed their normal share of the market for fear of tarnishing the value of their name and thereby running the risk that all segments of the market would then be closed to them.

(4) Foreign currency positions. A bank's net position in a foreign currency exposes it to the risk of fluctuation in the value of that currency. The bank may gain, but it also risks a loss. To limit potential losses, a bank establishes rules concerning who will take such risks and to what extent. The general practice is to limit foreign exchange risk by hedging most foreign currency positions. However, foreign exchange traders may take positions within preset limits and subject to review at a higher level.

(5) Maturity mismatches. Raising funds at a maturity different from that at which the funds are lent gives rise to two concerns. One is the commitment to provide funds, that is, the liquidity problem discussed above. The other is the commitment to a particular interest rate. Unexpected changes in market interest rates may result in gains or losses in the bank's portfolio. Losses may result if the bank finances its loans with relatively short-term funds and market rates rise or if relatively long-term funds are used and lending rates fall. Correspondingly, profits can be earned if interest rates move in the other direction. In practice, much of this risk is mitigated by tying the lending rate to the cost of funds. However, banks can profit from the usual interest rate differential inherent in borrowing short and lending long and from correctly anticipating changes in interest rates. Hence, to an extent, they try to harmonize the maturity structure of the portfolio with likely interest rate developments. If rates are expected to fall, for example, fixed rate loans and short-term borrowings would be preferred. As with foreign exchange positions, top management must set limits on maturity mismatches and, especially, it must see that these limits are consistent with expected money market developments.

Having established general policy for the bank and having set limits on discretionary decisions that can be made at lower management levels, senior management leaves actual operations and market strategy to officers with functional or regional responsibilities. Adherence to the limits is frequently checked in the asset and liability management process, but within the limits managers are expected to maximize profits from their activities. Typically, the performance of a funding or a lending area is judged in relation to a standard measure of the cost of funds to the bank. The three-month London interbank offer rate or the three-month certificate of deposit rate (adjusted for reserve requirements and deposit insurance) are common choices, although particular activities may be matched against other rates. A money market function would try to raise funds at a lower cost, whereas a lending function would try to obtain a higher yield. The extent to which each succeeds determines that unit's profits.

GLOBAL MANAGEMENT

The global approach to asset and liability management shares all the features of traditional bank management just described. The concerns of management are the same. Operating responsibilities are still divided by function and by region among profit center managers, each with limits placed on his discretionary decisions. At the same time, advocates of global management recognize that in the 1970's the world economy has become more integrated and, in some ways, riskier. The geographic division of responsibilities is seen as an insufficient approach to both decision making and risk management in worldwide markets. A unified approach to funds management is thought to be a better way to interface with today's highly integrated markets. Consequently, emphasis is placed on bridging the gap between strategic planning and the bank's day-to-day currency and money market decisions. Efforts are made to know aggregate bank positions on a timely basis, to understand and to assess market conditions, and to coordinate market positions in a way consistent with an overall strategy.

THE CHANGING ENVIRONMENT

The increased use of global management techniques is a logical response to the changes that occurred in the world economy during the early 1970's. First, United States capital controls were removed, allowing free interactions between the domestic and international operations of banks. Second, the volume of international banking transactions, particularly through offshore offices, had grown into a major component of the total business of United States banks. Last, fluctuating exchange rates and wider variations in interest rates added to the risk of open currency and maturity positions.

The Removal of Capital Controls

In the 1960's, United States authorities initiated three programs that limited the ability of banks to move funds internationally. In 1965, in the hope of alleviating persistent balance-of-payments outflows, the United States extended the coverage of its interest equalization tax (IET)—a tax on foreign equity and debt issues purchased by United States residents—to include long-term bank loans to foreigners. At the same time, voluntary limits on bank lending abroad were adopted under the voluntary foreign credit restraint (VFCR) program. In 1969, under Regulation M, the Federal Reserve adopted measures to stem inflows of funds from foreign branches of United States banks during the period of tight monetary policy. As the result of these restrictions, the domestic activities of United States banks tended to be isolated from their international ones.

The IET and VFCR restrictions on banks were removed early in 1974, and the Regulation M reserve requirement was reduced in stages between 1973 and 1978. The end of capital controls removed the main institutional wedge that had segmented the dollar financial markets. Consequently, the degree of interdependence between domestic and foreign operations increased significantly. Domestic funds could, and did, support foreign business; equally, foreign funds could support domestic business. When capital controls limited bank options, there had been no great cost in compartmentalizing the bank decision process; but with the end of these controls the cost of, and return from, funds became the primary concern—the more so with the increasing volume of business.

The Growth of International Banking

International banking, by United States banks and banks of other countries, has grown very rapidly since the 1960's. Claims on foreigners of United States banks (including their foreign branches) have increased 30 percent per year since 1969 (the earliest year for which reliable foreign branch data are available), while liabilities to foreigners have grown 21 percent per year during the same period. By comparison, assets of domestic offices of large United States banks have grown much more slowly, 9 percent per year. Abroad, Bank for International Settlements statistics indicate an eightfold jump in Eurocurrency deposits of banks in eight reporting European countries (including branches of United States banks located there) since 1969 (Table 2). The boom of United States banking abroad has been very profitable for banks. In recent years some United States banks have derived 50 percent or more of their total profits from international activities, compared with more modest earnings a decade ago.

The major factor behind the impressive growth of international banking activities is the increasing interdependence of the world's economies: the growth of world trade, the global investment of multinational corporations, the rapid economic growth of some developing countries, and the imbalance in world payments, particularly since the 1973 OPEC oil price increase. It is natural that much of the increased payments flows associated with these events would occur through banks.

Table 2

Selected Measures of the Growth of International Banking

In billions of dollars

| Year-end | Claims on United States banks on foreigners | | | Liabilities of United States banks to foreigners | | | Assets of United States offices of | Gross Eurocurrency deposits in |
	Head office*	Foreign branch†	Adjusted total‡	Head office*	Foreign branch†	Adjusted total‡	large banks §	eight countries‖
1962 . . .	7.3	¶	¶	22.0	¶	¶	168.4	¶
1966 . . .	12.0	¶	¶	29.1	¶	¶	242.2	¶
1969 . . .	19.9	15.9	28.1	42.6	27.8	59.2	316.4	56.9
1970 . . .	13.9	28.6	41.8	43.5	35.7	71.9	337.1	75.3
1972 . . .	20.7	59.8	79.5	61.7	61.0	120.6	410.2	131.9
1974 . . .	46.2	111.2	151.6	96.1	106.0	197.6	529.5	220.8
1976 . . .	79.3	158.5	218.1	110.7	135.6	241.9	552.4	310.7
1978 . . .	125.2	207.4	302.7	166.3	168.9	323.0	689.9	447.9**

* The figures include head-office claims on, and liabilities to, their own foreign branches. Custody claims and liabilities are not separable from the bank's own claims and liabilities prior to 1978. In 1978, head-office claims and liabilities net of custody claims and liabilities items were $114.2 billion and $77.8 billion, respectively.

† Net of claims on, or liabilities to, sister branches.

‡ Net of head-office claims on, or liabilities to, its own foreign branches.

§ Weekly reporting banks.

‖ The data do not include bank positions *vis-a-vis* residents of the country in which the bank is located. The reporting banks are those located in Belgium-Luxembourg, France, Germany, Italy, the Netherlands, Sweden, Siwtzerland, and the United Kingdom.

¶ Not available.

** September 1978.
Sources: Federal Reserve B

** September 1978.
Sources: Federal Reserve *Bulletin*: Bank for International Settlements. *Annual Report* ("External Positions of Reporting European Banks in Dollars and Other Foreign Currencies").

Significantly, much of the growth of international banking has occurred through offshore banking centers. Claims of foreign branches of United States banks on foreigners have grown at an annual rate of 33 percent since 1969, while their liabilities to foreigners have increased at a 22 percent rate (Table 2). The use of offshore centers is related mainly to the lower cost of bank activities there. The restricted access to the United States capital markets during the period of controls, helped to promote the use of offshore facilities during that period. More important, though, has been freedom from other regulations, particularly reserve requirements, deposit insurance, and interest rate ceilings. Alternative tax structures abroad also offer some cost advantages to offshore banking. Moreover, offshore centers offer a choice of location to some depositors who are concerned that their accounts may be blocked or expropriated.

As international activities grew, the impetus for top level bank management to monitor the international function increased. The consequence of errors was no longer small. Moreover, in the mid-1970's the risk from international activities seemed less hypothetical than before. Questions were being raised about the soundness of bank loans to tanker companies and to developing countries, while the failure of a few prominent banks underlined the need for sound management. The environment was right for head offices to take a closer look at their global operations.

Increasing Risks in the Marketplace

In the 1970's exchange rates and interest rates have become more variable than they had been in the recent past. Central banks stopped pegging exchange rates in 1973, allowing them to float (although some countries, such as those in the European Community maintained currency arrangements that provided for a degree of cohesiveness among their exchange rates). Whipsawed by events—widespread inflation, an oil embargo and price increases, recession in industrial countries followed by an uneven recovery, and persistent trade imbalances among major countries—both exchange rates and interest rates have moved by wider amounts than in the past.

For banks, this movement has accentuated the risks of foreign currency exposure and maturity mismatches discussed above. Because potential gains and losses have increased, the interest of bank management in managing these positions closely has also increased. For the bank as a whole, risk stems from exposures that do not net out from the overall balance sheet. In this sense, the interest in global management is directly related to an interest in managing foreign currency and maturity exposures.

PROS AND CONS OF CENTRAL COORDINATION

The growth of international banking and the greater interdependence and riskiness of money markets and foreign exchange markets increased the incentive for some banks to use a global approach. Not all banks involved with international business have adopted global asset and liability management, however. Bank managements differ in the assessment of the relative merits of global management versus decentralized management. Some banks feel that central coordination enables them to manage better the flow of funds within the organization and to initiate profitable transactions that otherwise would not have been undertaken. Other banks feel that they are more effective if operated as individual profit centers with the looser coordination inherent in the traditional management review process. Particularly, they are concerned with the way in which central coordination shifts responsibilities to head office personnel, reducing motivation at lower levels and in foreign branches.

Much of the impetus for global management comes from the desire for a unified approach toward sources of, and uses for, funds in world markets, particularly world dollar markets. The primary goal is for the bank to be more effective in its use of the money markets. To the extent that it succeeds, the bank will be more profitable.

In practical terms, global management may help a bank fund itself at the lowest rate and lend at the highest. Since all banks compare rates in various markets when seeking or placing funds, the advantage of centralized information flow may be small under usual circumstances. However, where timing is crucial—as with an unexpected change in market conditions, for example— the difference between the two banking arrangements may be important. The authority to act, as well as the information per se, may be critical. The officer in charge of global mangement not only has flexibility in his choice of markets, but generally has wider limits on the positions he can take than his counterparts at individual profit centers. By contrast, the relative effectiveness of officers of branch profit centers would depend in part upon the ease with which they could obtain permission from the head office to exceed their limits in special situations.

Global management may also enhance a bank's ability to arbitrage favorable rate differentials. For example, six-month dollar funds may be available at 10.50 percent (adjusting for reserve requirements and deposit insurance) in the New York certificate of deposit market but may earn 10.75 percent in the London Eurodollar market. By placing $1 million in the London market financed from funds raised in New York, the bank would earn a profit of $1,250. In the process of bidding for funds in one market and offering them in the other market, the bank helps to narrow the arbitrage differentials between the rates in the two markets. In that way, the degree of integration between the two segments of the market is increased. In some banks organized as separate profit centers, the arbitrage function is handled by having funds managers deal at arm's length with their counterparts in other locations within the bank. Each manager could initiate an arbitrage transaction. At most banks, however, the decision to transact simultaneously in two markets requires agreement between the managers responsible for each market. Without central coordination, they would have to decide on a means of splitting the profits ($1,250 in the example) and each would have to determine that the transaction is in the interest of his profit center. Global management facilitates arbitrage transactions by establishing a clear management responsibility to exploit such profit opportunities in the interest of the bank as a whole. Moreover, the close contact that the parent bank keeps with the world market through its branches provides an important flow of information which helps spot arbitrage opportunities.

Another way in which global asset and liability management may be beneficial to banks is by increasing their ability to net out opposing transactions before they reach the market. Not uncommonly, a branch at one location may need funds at the same time that another branch wishes to supply funds. If they recognize their offsetting needs, they would transact with each other. Otherwise, the transactions would be made in the market, potentially at a cost to the bank of the spread between the bid and offer rates for funds. With global asset and liability management, the parent bank maintains close contact with each branch. These communications increase the chance that the offsetting transfers are handled internally, enabling the bank to avoid the potential market cost.

Many banks take positions and earn profits on expected fluctuations in market rates over time. Proponents of both the global and decentralized approaches each regard their form of management as being the better way of handling these positions. Advocates of decentralized management take the view that there is no monopoly on information in the market and that local managers are as likely to exercise good judgment as their counterparts in the head office. By managing individually part of the total bank portfolio, they help assure that the bank will respond, at least in part, to favorable market opportunities. It is hoped that such errors in judgment as occur will be more than offset in other profit centers and that large mistakes will be avoided. Thus, the decentralized approach is seen as the best way to maximize the bank's profits.

By contrast, the view of globally managed banks is that it is better to formulate a single bank strategy. Because contacts are maintained with personnel in local markets, it is felt that the head office is not at a disadvantage with regard to either information or ideas, compared with the decentralized approach. If more astute managers are at the head office, their judgment may be better than that of lower level officers. Most important, however, is the greater control of the total position inherent in global management. Because the response to market events is closely monitored by top management, some banks have been more willing to take market positions after adopting global management techniques than they had been previously.

A major class of concerns about global asset and liability management involves personnel management. At a basic level, resistance to change from existing managers often makes a shift to global management awkward. People who have held important decision-making functions at various profit-making units tend to resent new lines of authority, particularly if they have less authority under the new arrangement. Reluctance to alienate key staff people has sometimes been a barrier to adopting the global view.

Lack of personnel who are generally familiar with various bank functions has also acted as a barrier to global management. Knowledge of both the domestic and foreign sides of banking is a key ingredient to coordinating global activities. Banks thin in personnel with this experience have difficulty in shifting to global management. The long-run solution is to rotate people in various jobs so that they receive the proper training.

Beyond these initial barriers to change, though, there are deeper reasons for questioning the viability of global management. Coordination at the center is crucially dependent upon information on conditions in diverse market locations. It requires tacticians who continually probe the markets, executive trades, and report on events. The danger in central coordination is that it could unintentionally supplant thinking and decision making on the periphery. If that were to happen, global management would no longer get the information it needs to function effectively.

For this reason, some banks prefer decentralized organization. The challenge to earn profits, the freedom to manage a department or trading position without daily direction from superiors, and the feeling of being trusted with responsibility motivates people to be effective bankers. In this way, decentralized organization also helps train and select people for higher positions. In the view of those who favor this approach, it is the more effective way to run a bank.

INTERMEDIATE CASES

The polar cases of global management of assets and liabilities and decentralized decision making are not the only possibilities. Intermediate cases exist. One large bank, for example, has a policy of never interfering with the decisions of local managers. Nonetheless, these managers report daily to the head office, which can hedge market positions that, in the aggregate, appear to it to be unsound. In that event, the offsetting transactions would be done at the head office to maintain the spirit of local autonomy.

Centralized management need not be extended to all of a bank's operations. Eurodollar activity booked in Nassau or the Cayman Islands is usually the first international area to be coordinated with domestic money market trading. London, because of its importance, is often next, followed by other Euromarket centers. The movement to at least partial integration of management at some banks is an indication of the current strength of the shift to global management. One interesting case is a bank whose highest level officers strongly endorse the autonomy of local units. Nevertheless, lower level officers in the domestic and international areas at the head office and in London have recognized the advantages of close central coordination. Informally, a supervisory unit at the parent bank has become a vehicle for coordinating much of their activities.

Thus, while there are grounds for debating the merits for global management methods in their purest form, banks continue to experiment with alternative approaches. The reasons for doing so are clear. Banks are adapting to their larger presence in world markets, the tighter integration of domestic and foreign markets, and increased risks inherent in the economic environment.

A NEW SUPERVISORY APPROACH TO FOREIGN LENDING*

Roger M. Kubarych

27

International lending activities by United States commercial banks have increased greatly in size, complexity, and geographical scope during recent years. International credits now make up a significant portion of major bank loan portfolios and represent an important source of bank earnings. Foreign lending, of course, involves special kinds of risk that are not ordinarily found in domestic lending, although banks' loss experience from foreign loans has in fact been better than from domestic loans in recent years. Nevertheless, the rapid growth of international banking activities has created the need for improved techniques on the part of both banks and bank supervisors for defining, monitoring, and controlling those special risks.

The Federal Reserve System responded by reviewing existing bank examination procedures for foreign credits. It also made a survey in early 1977 of risk management practices by United States banks. Drawing on these reviews, a System Committee on Foreign Lending recommended changes in Federal Reserve procedures to strengthen supervision of international banking. The Federal Reserve Bank of New York has adopted these procedures on a trial basis in its current examinations of international loan portfolios. Systemwide implementation would follow final approval by the Board of Governors.

The other Federal bank supervisory agencies—the Office of the Comptroller

*Reprinted from the *Quarterly Review*, Spring 1978, pp. 1-6, with permission from the Federal Reserve Bank of New York.

of the Currency (OCC) and the Federal Deposit Insurance Corporation (FDIC)—were in the meantime studying their respective systems for supervising foreign lending. The three agencies joined together in an effort to develop principles for a common approach to international bank supervision. The aim is an effective supervisory system to ensure that foreign lending does not have adverse effects on the safety and soundness of the United States banking system.

A broad measure of agreement has now been reached on the essentials of a new Federal supervisory approach to foreign lending. An important element is the development of a common reporting form, which measures overall international exposure and its components for each bank. Most banks in this country with international operations have been asked to provide information on their foreign exposure twice a year. That information would enable bank supervisors to evaluate the exposure by country of individual banks and of the United States banking system as a whole.

A further element involves changes in procedures for examination on bank international loan portfolios. The emphasis would be on identifying concentrations of lending that seem large relative to bank capital and country conditions. In addition, examiners would pay particular attention to a bank's own procedures for monitoring and controlling its exposure in each country where it does business.

This article provides some of the details of how the new approach was developed and how it is expected to work.

DEFINING THE SPECIAL RISKS OF INTERNATIONAL LENDING

Much of the risk in foreign lending is no different from that in domestic lending. The present and future standing of individual borrowers must be appraised and monitored in light of changes in economic and financial conditions. Well-managed companies may be adversely affected by a general economic slowdown in a country or by problems in a particular industry. Poorly managed companies may have difficulties even in a strengthening economy. Banks and bank examiners have found it useful to analyze *credit risk* in loan portfolios in terms of traditional risk categories.[1] These same categories are applied to individual international credits as well as to domestic credits.

In addition, international lending involves *country risk*. It is a principal factor that differentiates international lending from domestic lending. Country risk can be and has been defined in various ways. But, broadly speaking, it encompasses the whole spectrum of risks that arise from the economic, so-

---

[1] Three classifications of loans with above-normal risk are used by examiners: substandard, doubtful, and loss. In addition, some loans which are superior to those in the substandard class are specially mentioned as warranting more than usual management attention.

cial, legal, and political conditions of a foreign country and that may have potential favorable or adverse consequences for loans to borrowers in that country. More concretely, country risk includes the risks of political or social upheaval, nationalization or expropriation, government repudiation of external debts, exchange controls, or foreign exchange shortfalls that might make it impossible for a country to meet external obligations on time. In some cases, payment of interest or principal on loans may be delayed or loan terms may have to be restructured. In rare cases, the result may be actual loan defaults.

Events such as these might materially affect the condition of the United States banks that make loans to a foreign country. Consequently, the potential risks must be carefully considered by banks and bank examiners. The examiners are responsible for alerting bank management to those risks that might be difficult for a bank to absorb and might therefore jeopardize the liquidity or soundness of the bank.

THE FEDERAL RESERVE'S REVIEW OF INTERNATIONAL LENDING

In view of the growth of international lending by United States banks and the enlarged role of commercial banks in financing international payments imbalances, the Federal Reserve undertook a comprehensive review of the System's supervisory approach in this area. An *ad hoc* Committee on Foreign Lending was appointed in late 1976 to study procedures and techniques used by member banks in making foreign loans and by Federal Reserve examiners in appraising state-chartered member bank foreign lending.

The committee initially conducted a survey of the existing foreign lending practices of member banks. The survey took the form of detailed discussions with senior bank officers by representatives of Federal Reserve Banks and the staff of the Board of Governors. In addition, an OCC examiner attended each meeting with a national bank. In all, discussions were held with forty-six banks across the country, including the twenty-five largest banks, to obtain a broad cross section by bank size and location.

The discussions were structured around questions concerning a bank's procedures for appraising, monitoring, and controlling foreign credit exposure. Each bank was asked how it defined country exposure, how it distinguished between different types and maturities of credits, and how it treated such factors as guarantees, collateral, and contingencies. The bank was asked whether limits on credits or commitments to a country were established and how they were reviewed as a country's economic and financial conditions changed. Questions were posed on how economic projections for a country were considered in individual lending decisions. Finally, each bank was asked about its policy toward diversification of country credits.

The survey revealed that all banks visited had in place internal systems for monitoring and controlling foreign lending, although practices varied considerably from bank to bank. The range of procedures largely reflected differences in bank size and organization as well as the kinds of international business conducted by individual banks. But they also reflected the relative inexperience of some banks in defining country risk and in measuring exposure to that risk. As a result, the detailed measurement of country exposure differed among banks, both in the types of credits considered subject to country risk and in the methods for consolidating the exposure to a country of different offices of a bank.

Although banks would naturally wish to emphasize particular aspects of their country exposure depending upon their business, the survey suggested that a greater uniformity in measuring exposure would be useful. It would allow bank supervisors to compare banks and let individual banks compare their foreign loan portfolios with averages for others. But, given the diversity of bank size and organization, it would not be desirable to impose a uniform set of procedures for all banks to use in evaluating, monitoring, and controlling foreign lending. Instead, the survey suggested aspects of an effective risk management system could be drawn from the experience at a wide range of banks.

WHAT A NEW SUPERVISORY
APPROACH SHOULD INCLUDE

From this review, it became clear that a restructured supervisory approach to appraising foreign lending should incorporate several features.

It should provide for uniform measurement of a bank's country exposure and a systematic basis for calling bank management's attention to any relatively large exposure which might be potentially troublesome. There is no precise way of measuring country risk, *per se*, or of assigning probabilities to potentially adverse developments in a country. However, a bank's country exposure, the sum of its credits and commitments to a country, can be quantified. A consistent measure of exposure would allow examiners to compare portfolio management among different banks and to formulate standards for appropriate diversification within portfolios.

It should ensure that banks themselves have adequate internal systems for appraising, monitoring, and controlling country exposure. A bank supervisor can assess a bank's country exposure only at periodic intervals. But a bank's exposure may change from day to day. An effective internal control system is essential for maintaining continuous management oversight of international lending.

It should keep the appraisal of country exposure separate from the traditional risk classification system used for evaluating individual credits.

It should be capable of uniform application throughout the System. In the past, individual examiners had differing approaches to appraising international loan portfolios, and their individual judgments could vary.

It should provide a mechanism by which Federal Reserve Bank examiners would draw upon the knowledge and expertise of specialists within the System about country conditions to help identify potentially adverse developments in a country.

It should not give credit ratings to countries. Nor should it establish a list of particularly risky countries to which banks would be told not to lend. Bank supervisors are concerned with the condition of individual institutions as the components of a sound banking system. Actions of bank supervisors are not intended to result in the channeling of credit flows toward or away from specific countries or to lead to large disruptions of credit flows. In any case, there is no reason to believe that assessments about countries by bank supervisors would always be better than those of commercial banks.

It should recognize the great uncertainties that exist in any assessment of country risk and should stress that banks are best protected against adverse developments through diversification within their foreign loan portfolios.

Based on those criteria, new examination procedures and techniques were developed that would assist examiners in making more professional evaluations of individual loans and country exposures. They were field tested at state-chartered member banks in the New York, Chicago, and San Francisco Districts in the course of regular examinations. In addition, examination concepts and proposed techniques were discussed with senior officers of several other member banks.

Concurrently, work was in progress by the OCC and the FDIC to review their respective examination procedures for international lending. Discussions among the Federal Reserve and these other agencies suggested that a new Federal supervisory approach would provide the most effective and most equitable basis for examining United States banks' foreign lending portfolios. A broad measure of consensus has been reached on the basic elements of that approach. These are outlined in the following section.

THE NEW SUPERVISORY APPROACH

Under the new supervisory approach to international lending, credit risk would continue to be appraised using standard examination procedures and techniques. Individual credits would be reviewed to determine the creditworthiness of the borrowers. Credits identified as having an above-normal credit risk element would be classified by the examiner using the traditional groupings of substandard, doubtful, and loss.

Where the new examination approach would differ from previous procedures is in the treatment of country risk. The new approach would consist of three parts:

(1) Measurement of exposure in each country where a bank has a business relationship. In turn, individual bank exposure would be consolidated to show the overall exposure of the United States banking system to each country abroad.

(2) Analysis of exposure levels and concentrations of exposure in relation to the bank's capital resources and the economic and financial conditions of each country in which the bank has outstanding credits.

(3) Evaluation of the risk management system used by the bank in relation to the size and nature of its foreign lending activities.

The end product would be an examination report that reviews internal management systems and identifies certain concentrations of credit within the foreign loan portfolio that warrant management attention.

MEASUREMENT OF EXPOSURE

The Federal Reserve survey of United States commercial banks' foreign lending practices showed that there was no standard or uniform banking industry approach to measuring country exposure and no single best method among those used by different banks. Similarly, the Federal supervisory authorities had been defining country exposure differently.

The Federal supervisory authorities have now agreed on a uniform method for measuring exposure. It is based on a common reporting system for international lending information. That system benefited from earlier exercises in collecting international lending data conducted by the major central banks under the auspices of the Bank for International Settlements (BIS). But it goes further by measuring international exposure on a consolidated bank basis. Thus, loans to each foreign country would be included whether made by a bank's head office or by a branch or affiliate abroad. Information about foreign claims is provided by each reporting bank in a semiannual country exposure report, beginning with data for end-December 1977.[2] The report breaks down the bank's claims for each country by type of borrower and by maturity. Loan commitments and other contingencies are also detailed. Activities of a bank's foreign offices with local residents in local currencies are shown separately.

One feature of the country exposure report takes account of an important distinction in international lending. The location of a borrower may not coincide with the location of the ultimate country exposure. If, for example, a United States bank has made a loan to a borrower in country X and the loan is guaranteed by another institution in country Y, then the ultimate country exposure is allocated to country Y.

---

[2] The country exposure report is filed by all United States banks and bank holding companies with international activity above a specified level. For a description of the report see the Box.

In its exposure report, a bank is asked to reallocate credits and commitments to the country where the ultimate risk appears to reside. The examiner would then be able to analyze the foreign loan portfolio by this more comprehensive treatment of country exposure, as well as by country of location of borrower. The reallocation of exposure takes into account external guarantees or realizable collateral outside the country of the borrower. In the case of claims on foreign branches of other banks, ultimate exposure is reallocated to the location of those banks' head offices.

By consolidating the data for all reporting banks, the supervisory authorities also get a clearer picture, by location of credit and by country of ultimate risk, of the United States banking system's exposure to each country abroad. These aggregates allow the authorities to compare one bank's foreign loan portfolio with those of other United States banks.

In the examination process, the examiner would use the information from the country exposure report in analyzing a bank's international exposure. In particular, the examiner would express the overall measure of exposure for each country where a bank has outstanding credits as a ratio of the bank's capital funds. These ratios would give a picture of the bank's concentrations of lending relative to its own ultimate resources to absorb risk. They would serve also as an indicator to the examiner of which parts of a bank's international portfolio deserve a deeper look.

In summary, the country exposure data would enable the examiner: (1) to evaluate the amounts, location, maturities, and types of claims a bank has abroad, (2) to evaluate the amounts of claims reallocated to country of ultimate risk, and (3) to compare the exposure levels with the bank's capital and to suggest areas for further analysis.

ANALYSIS OF EXPOSURE LEVELS AND CONCENTRATIONS

The second part of the new examination approach would involve analysis of country exposure levels and concentrations of exposure. The objective would be to identify high concentrations of exposure relative to the bank's capital funds and relative to the economic and financial conditions of borrowing countries.

The analysis of country exposure levels would involve three steps:

(1) An evaluation of country conditions by research economists and country specialists. These evaluations would be made available to bank examiners for use as background to their analyses of foreign loan portfolios.

(2) Disaggregation by the examiner of aggregate exposure by referring to a bank's internal records. Particular attention would be paid to the types of borrowers and the maturity distribution of the bank's foreign claims.

Country Exposure Report

A semiannual country exposure report (FR 2036, CC 7610-88, or FDIC 6502/03) is filed by all United States banks and bank holding companies with international activity above a specified level. The report consolidates exposure for all domestic and foreign offices of an institution. Aggregate data from the country exposure report will be made public. The initial report provides data for end-1977. Results of a preliminary survey for June 1977 were released in January 1978.

Country exposure includes both outstanding claims on foreign residents and contingencies. Foreign claims are defined under three categories. (1) *Cross-border claims* are those of bank offices located in one country on residents of other countries. A loan to a company in Britain by a New York bank's head office is a cross-border claim. (2) *Nonlocal currency claims* are those of a bank's foreign offices on local residents denominated in currencies other than the local currency. A loan in dollars to a company in Britain by a New York bank's London branch is a nonlocal currency claim. (3) *Local currency claims* are those of a bank's foreign offices on local residents denominated in the local currency. A loan in pounds sterling to a company in Britain by a New York bank's London branch is a local currency claim.

On the report, cross-border and nonlocal currency claims are combined and shown by country of residence of the borrower. The total for each country is broken down by type of borrower: banks, public borrowers, and all other borrowers. The totals are also broken down by estimated time remaining to maturity. Four maturity categories are used: one year and under, one to two years, two to five years, and over five years.

Contingencies are shown separately. They are contractual commit-

(3) Examiner comments on the results of the analysis.

Countries that warrant in-depth review would be identified through simple statistical screening techniques. The techniques would be used to pick out countries which have, in relation to other countries, large current account deficits or heavy external debt service or low international reserve positions relative to the size of their own economies and their external trade. The aim is to base a screening mechanism on objective criteria. But the statistical indicators themselves are not designed to be, nor would they be used as, predictors of potential debt repayment difficulties.

For this limited screening purpose, indicators have been computed from reported balance-of-payments statistics and other financial data. One is a measure of short-term current account imbalance, while another is an indicator of medium-term current account imbalance and the rate of external debt-accumulation. Other indicators measure countries' debt interest burden in terms of such factors as current receipts (exports of goods and services) and

ments to extend credit, such as letters of credit and undisbursed portions of loans that are not subject to further bank approval. Contingencies are broken down into two categories: (1) public borrowers and (2) banks and other nonpublic borrowers.

Total cross-border and foreign office nonlocal currency claims are adjusted for each country to take account of external guarantees, collateral, and interbank placements that shift the ultimate country risk to another country. The reporting bank makes a separate tally by reallocating the claims from the country of the borrower to that of the guarantor. A similar reallocation is made for contingencies. The adjusted data show exposure by country of ultimate risk.

Guarantees are narrowly defined to include only formal and legal obligations by residents of countries other than the borrowers'. Claims collateralized by tangible and liquid assets (*e.g.*, cash, certificates of deposit, gold, marketable securities) are reallocated to the country where the pledged assets are held or where their value can be fully realized. In the case of marketable securities, for instance, the exposure would usually be shifted to the country where the security was issued. Interbank claims on a branch abroad are shifted to the country in which the head office is located. Claims on subsidiary banks are adjusted to the country of the parent only if formally guaranteed or collateralized in that country.

Local currency claims of a foreign office, the third category of claims noted above, are treated as a country exposure only to the extent that they are not offset by local currency liabilities. To provide a broader picture, local currency assets and liabilities by country are shown separately.

As a final entry, each reporting institution shows for each country in which it has offices the net amount "due to" or "due from" those offices. This reflects the cross-border flows of funds within a banking organization.

---

international reserves. The indicators would be regularly computed for the major borrowing countries in which United States banks have exposure.

The screening mechanism is intended to be suggestive only and not exhaustive. But its obvious advantage is its objectivity and relative simplicity. System research economists, moreover, continue assessing available economic statistics which could improve the screening process.

Countries identified through the screening process would be thoroughly reviewed. Comprehensive studies would be prepared for the examiner's use in raising questions with the bank under examination and in appraising country risk in portfolio concentrations. On the economic side, the focus would be on a country's balance of payments and its international reserves, both current and prospective. The review would also include an analysis of the country's domestic economic situation and government policies, foreign exchange rate behavior, and structural trends in the economy. In addition, conditions affecting political and social stability would be noted, especially as they may have a bearing on the overall economic environment.

These reviews of country conditions would provide background for the examiner's analysis of exposure concentrations in a bank's international loan portfolio. All country concentrations which appeared high would be looked at in detail. A bank's outstanding credits in a country would be examined by type of business (loans, acceptances, investments, placements, etc.), by maturity (short term versus long term), and by class of borrower (government, nonbank private sector borrowers, and banks).

Drawing on this analysis of exposure levels and the assessment of country conditions, the examiner would comment on those country exposures which appeared high in relation to the bank's ability to absorb risk and to the country's condition. Certain norms would be established to guide examiners in making critical comments on high concentrations by country. These would not be hard and fast rules. But the approach would ensure a reasonable level of uniformity, while allowing the examiners to exercise judgment and discretion in framing their comments.

Examiner comments might include references to a country's status with the International Monetary Fund or adherence to conditions imposed by the IMF on credit drawings. Comments might also be made where a bank's outstanding loans to a country represent a disproportionate share of the total lending by United States banks to that country, or where information maintained by the bank on a country or group of countries is deemed inadequate.

The objective of any critical commentary would be to encourage appropriate diversification in a bank's international lending portfolio. Diversification remains a bank's best protection against risk in an uncertain world.

EVALUATION OF RISK MANAGEMENT SYSTEMS

The third part of the new examination approach would involve an evaluation of the risk management systems used by banks in appraising and controlling their foreign credit exposure. All banks engaging in international business should have the capability to analyze their customers and risks independently. No bank should lend to a particular borrower, for example, simply because other banks are extending credits to that borrower.

As the Federal Reserve survey of bank foreign lending practices confirmed, banks involved in international business have already set up internal systems for controlling foreign lending. There are notable differences in approach among banks, although these mostly reflect differences in the size and organizational structure of banks as well as the composition of their business.

Whatever the differences of detail, certain general characteristics should be found in all internal control systems. The examiner would need to be satisfied that a bank's risk management system is comprehensive and covers all aspects of the bank's international business. The examiner would evaluate the bank's internal system for measuring exposure to each country where the bank does business. The bank's methods for assessing country conditions would be evaluated to see whether risk assessments are based on reliable and up-to-date information, reviewed with reasonable frequency, and kept separate from marketing considerations. The bank's procedures for monitoring and controlling country exposure would be analyzed. The analysis would consider how the bank limits its lending to individual countries. It would also focus on how and at what stage country risk assessments are considered by bank officers in making lending decisions and in modifying country exposure limits. Any inadequacies found by the examiner in the bank's country risk management system would be brought to management's attention in the examination report.

CONCLUDING REMARKS

The new approach to appraising international lending outlined in this article has several advantages. It emphasizes diversification of risk in individual bank portfolios. By doing so, it avoids any implications of official credit ratings of foreign countries. It underlines the role of bank managements in seeking diversified portfolios and in maintaining adequate internal mechanisms for monitoring and controlling country exposure. Details of this supervisory approach are still being developed, and discussions among the Federal supervisory agencies are continuing. There is every reason to hope that before long the technical groundwork will be completed and a new approach fully implemented.

Part IV

ASSET-LIABILITY MANAGEMENT

The management of individual asset and liability components such as loans, investments, and deposits is conducted within a framework known as asset-liability management. As the term suggests, there is a joint relationship or linkage between the management of assets and liabilities. In his two-part series John T. Clifford provides an explanation of this joint relationship. His articles highlight the implications of the so-called "gap" which provides an indication of the sensitivity of a bank's earnings to changes in interest rates. Various asset-liability management strategies are examined under different economic and interest rate scenarios.

In the next article Marcelle Arak and Christopher J. McCurdy provide a comprehensive overview of the interest rate futures market. In a related article, Carl Schwesar, Joseph Cole, and Lou D'Antonio work through the mechanics of a variety of bank-related interest rate futures transactions. The significance of these two articles stems from the fact that a volatile interest rate environment makes the bank manager's task of controlling interest rate risk extremely difficult. However, as the articles point out, the futures market provides the managers of banks and other financial institutions with an effective means of hedging against the adverse effects of interest rate changes. Thus, proper use of the futures market for hedging purposes is an important asset-liability management strategy. Although bank participation in the futures market has been limited because of regulatory restrictions and a lack of understanding on the part of many bankers, it is likely that hedging will play an increasingly prominent role in the future asset-liability practices of commercial banks.

In the final article in this section, Alfred Broaddus provides a simplified explanation linear programming as it applies to the asset-liability management problem of commercial banks. Using graphs and nonmathematical terms, Broaddus effectively demonstrates the interaction among bank operating objectives, constraining influences, and alternative courses of action.

A PERSPECTIVE ON ASSET-LIABILITY MANAGEMENT: PART I*

John T. Clifford

28

Recent economic and money market conditions have given rise to a renewed interest in bank asset and liability management and a re-appraisal of some past practices. The traditional "asset-funds allocation" methods gave way to a concentration on sophisticated "asset management" and investment concepts during the early 1960s. By the end of the decade, emphasis had switched toward a freewheeling "liability management" philosophy which stressed broad money market dependence to supplement the customer deposit base. In the early 1970s it became fashionable to seek balance sheet and earnings growth through high leveraging and marginal interest differential business.

The events of the 1973-74 period have been sobering to the expansion and diversification-minded banking industry. Now, in the face of diminished public confidence, there emerges an overwhelming concern for capital adequacy, liquidity, control of credit expansion and a clear need for a profitable but more conservative and integrated approach to asset-liability management.

A MATTER OF FUNDAMENTALS

There is, perhaps, no better basis for deriving an asset-liability management strategy than a thorough understanding of the individual bank, its cus-

Reprinted from the *Magazine of Bank Administration*, March 1975, pp. 16-21, with permission from the publisher, the Bank Administration Institute.

tomer mix and its economic environment. While countless techniques have been developed to deal with this issue, they are of questionable usefulness if not applied and interpreted with a full understanding of the nature of the particular bank's assets and liabilities. There is no single perspective, theory or structure that can be universally applied successfully to all banks nor will any combination of such approaches eliminate the necessity for the exercise of good business judgment. The approach discussed in this article is merely another way of dealing with the issue within the context of an analytical framework, highlighting certain inherent relationships and identifying the major underlying factors which must be evaluated as a first step toward the development of an asset-liability management strategy.

RATE MIX CLASSIFICATIONS

Figure 1 represents the structure of a hypothetical bank with assets and liabilities classified according to the interest rate characteristics. "Matched"

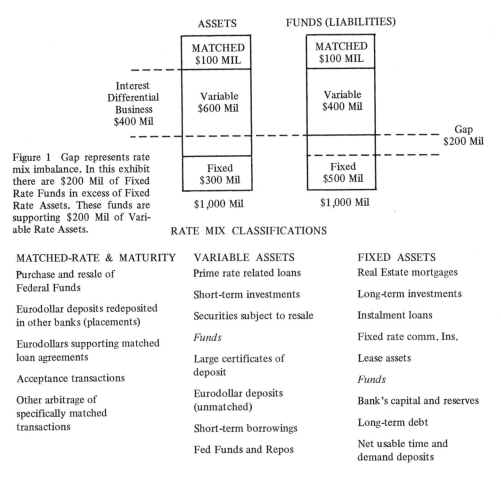

Figure 1 Gap represents rate mix imbalance. In this exhibit there are $200 Mil of Fixed Rate Funds in excess of Fixed Rate Assets. These funds are supporting $200 Mil of Variable Rate Assets.

RATE MIX CLASSIFICATIONS

MATCHED-RATE & MATURITY	VARIABLE ASSETS	FIXED ASSETS
Purchase and resale of Federal Funds	Prime rate related loans	Real Estate mortgages
	Short-term investments	Long-term investments
Eurodollar deposits redeposited in other banks (placements)	Securities subject to resale	Instalment loans
Eurodollars supporting matched loan agreements	*Funds*	Fixed rate comm. Ins.
Acceptance transactions	Large certificates of deposit	Lease assets
Other arbitrage of specifically matched transactions	Eurodollar deposits (unmatched)	*Funds*
		Bank's capital and reserves
	Short-term borrowings	Long-term debt
	Fed Funds and Repos	Net usable time and demand deposits

assets and liabilities represents specific sources and uses of funds in equal amounts which have identical predetermined maturities and a negotiated rate spread. "Variable" represents interest-bearing assets and liabilities where the rates fluctuate with general money market conditions. "Fixed" represents assets and liabilities that have a relatively fixed rate or supporting costs (demand deposits) over an extended period of time.

This form of rate-mix classification sets the stage for an evaluation of the potential profitability and liquidity impact during various phases of the economic cycle. This analytical structure, coupled with a full understanding of the cyclical interaction between rates and changes in balance sheet relationships, will provide some basic ingredients toward formulating an asset-liability strategy.

GAP ANALYSIS

The rate mix chart (Figure 1) demonstrates that our hypothetical bank has more fixed rate funds than fixed rate assets. These excess fixed rate funds (demand and savings deposits) support a portion of the bank's variable rate assets (commercial loans). This rate-mix imbalance is designated on the chart as a "GAP" equal to the amount by which fixed rate funds exceed fixed rate assets.

Changes in the size of the GAP at various money market rate levels can have a significant impact on earnings performance. A wide GAP during high rate phases of the cycle will produce strong earnings, but at low rate phases a wide gap will result in an earnings decline. This is because the rates on variable assets (commercial loans) will decline while the cost of supporting fixed rate funds remains the same. Using the asset-liability positions shown in Figure 1 and adding rates prevalent during mid-1974 (at the height of the cycle), the earnings impact can be observed in Figure. 2.

Figure 2 At High Rate Phase ($Mil) ASSETS	FUNDS		SPREAD	MARGIN	
Matched $100 Mil @ 13%	Matched $100 Mil @ 12%	=	1 %	$ 1.0	
Variable (Total $600) $400 @ 13%	Variable $400 @ 12%	=	1 %	4.0	
$200 @ 13%	$200 @ 6%	=	7 %	14.0	GAP
Fixed $300 @ 9%	Fixed (Total $500) $300 @ 6%	=	3 %	9.0	
Total: $1,000	$1,000		2.8%	$28.0	

Note that the GAP generated $14 million or 50% of the annualized margin during the high rate phase of the cycle. Let's assume that the rate cycle moves down to a lower level from the high of a 12% prime in mid-1974 to an 8% prime, and in process the following normal cyclical changes take place: 1) Disintermediation is partly reversed and fixed rate funds increase 5% ($25 million); and 2) the spread between variable rate assets and funds doubles to 2% (purchased funds vs. prime commercial loans). With the above assumptions, the margin analysis would appear as shown on Figure 3.

Despite the higher volume of lower cost fixed rate funds and the wider spread between variable rate assets and funds, there has been a decline in margin, at the low rate phase, of $4 million, down 13%. The GAP contribution has dropped more than $7 million, because no management action was taken to control the size of the GAP.

GAP MANAGEMENT

Any approach to asset-liability management requires that all balance sheet categories be integrated into a common strategy. This is particularly true in managing the GAP relationship, and certain principles flow directly from GAP analysis. Following are some of these principles:

■ Fixed rate funds must exceed the volume of fixed rate assets. If this does not occur, a portion of fixed rate assets would be supported by variable rate funds with attendant high risks in liquidity and profitability. At high rate phases of the cycle variable market sensitive funds are in short supply, and variable cost rates could cause narrow or negative spreads on previously existing fixed rate investments and loans.

■ The minimum GAP size is unique to each bank. The absolute minimum GAP size at the low rate phase of the cycle must be adequate to absorb the

Figure 3 At Low Rate Phase ($Mil)	ASSETS	FUNDS		SPREAD	MARGIN	
	Matched $100 Mil @ 9%	Matched $100 Mil @ 8%	=	1 %	$ 1.0	
	Variable (Total $600) $375 @ 9%	$375 @ 7%	=	2 %	7.5	
	$225 @ 9%	$225 @ 6%	=	3 %	6.8	GAP
	Fixed $300 @ 9%	Fixed (Total $525) $300 @ 6%	=	3 %	9.0	
	Total: $1,000	$1,000		2.4	$24.3	

effects of seasonal deposit fluctuations and potential disintermediation in a subsequent upward cyclical phase. The individual bank's deposit structure must be studied to determine the appropriate minimum GAP for adequate liquidity protection.

▪ GAP must be managed to expand and contract with rate cycle phases. The ideal GAP relationships to various pahses of the rate cycle are as follows:

Rising — Widening
Rates   GAP
High — Widest
Rates   GAP
Falling — Narrowing
Rates   GAP
Low — Narrowest
Rates   GAP

It is impossible to have the GAP at its "ideal" maximum position at all phases of the cycle. An excessively wide GAP at high rate phases may maximize earnings at that time, but if not narrowed while high rates are available on fixed rate assets, it will result in reduced earnings during a subsequent lower phase. The asset-liability strategy should be oriented toward optimizing gap relationships throughout a complete cycle and not maximizing at any one phase.

Management actions related to matched rate and maturity categories and those affecting variable rate categories will have absolutely no impact on the size of the GAP at any phase of the rate cycle. However, over expansion of matched or variable rate assets can restrict management actions related to the GAP because of excessive borrowing levels or leveraging beyond prudent capital adequacy limits.

The GAP size can only be controlled by changes in either fixed rate assets or fixed rate funds levels since, by definition, the GAP is the amount of difference between fixed rate assets and fixed rate funds. Management action relative to fixed rate funds (particularly deposits) is somewhat limited and subject to all the usual competitive pressures. There is no substitute for strong and consistent growth in retained earnings which builds the capital base for leveraging, provides fixed funds to directly support assets and establishes a favorable climate for attracting debt and equity funds from the capital markets with minimum cost and dilution.

The primary management control over the size of the GAP must come from the strategy and tactics employed in relation to fixed rate loans and investments. This strategy must encompass both additions to the fixed rate classifications of assets and the equally important reductions through preplanned maturity and sale. When adding to fixed rate portfolios at high rates, the maturity distribution must provide for bridging the future anticipated period of cyclical low rates to provide margin protection during that period. Likewise, the maturity distribution of existing securities and loans must be evaluated in preplanning the reduction of fixed rate assets through sale into a secondary market, if necessary, during low rate phases of the cycle. This widens the GAP for a subsequent upward cycle.

There are two very important tactical considerations in adding and disposing of fixed rate assets during the high and low rate phases. The first is to acquire the assets in resalable lots but not all at one time during the cyclical phase. Since no one has found a way to be sure that a rate cycle has either peaked or bottomed out, it is only prudent to space the acquisitions and sales over several months. This method is admittedly conservative, and in retrospect will appear not to have had the greatest profitability impact. However, one merely has to recall the experience of March 1974 when many banks acquired large volumes of investments when the cycle appeared to be turning downward only to experience a volatile reversal causing significant bond depreciation with little capacity remaining to take advantage of even higher yields available at the cyclical peak.

The second consideration also involves the unpredictability of the rate cycle and the need to pre-plan asset moves at predetermined market rate (price) levels. For example: As securities are acquired during high rate phases, there should be a specific identification of lower yielding securities which will be automatically sold during the declining or low rate phase of the cycle. This can either be a "delayed swap" transaction or simply a GAP or guideline control plan of action and applies equally in reverse to the preplanning of acquisitions prior to an ascending phase of the cycle. (See "threshold concept" below.)

Finally, management control strategy should avoid the interpretation of every minor rate fluctuation as a cycle and the attendant high risk "trading psychology" which is speculative rather than conservative in nature. Leave the trading functions outside the scope of asset-liability management strategy and provide, if necessary, a small, well controlled "sandbox" asset allocation where such instincts can be vented rather than jeopardizing the basic structure.

■ GAP management must be consistently applied to maintain stable earnings growth. GAP management should be one aspect of an integrated and conservative asset-liability strategy. It is designed to optimize earnings over a complete economic cycle without moving to an extreme position during any one phase and thereby risking vulnerability in a subsequent phase. Earnings volatility can be greatly reduced when margins are optimized over the life of a cycle resulting in increased investor confidence and enhancing the bank's ability to attract additional capital base for future growth.

■ There exists some longer range implications of GAP analysis on asset-liability strategy. The size of the GAP is determined by the level of fixed rate funds in excess of fixed rate assets. Management has direct control over the fixed rate assets, but much less control over the fixed rate funds position.

There are currently many uncertainties surrounding traditional savings and demand deposits. Reserve requirements on fixed rate deposits are subject to adjustment by regulatory authorities when implementing national economic or monetary policies. Currently the rate ceilings imposed by regulators cause disintermediation when market rates rise above those which banks are allowed to pay. There is increasing speculation as to when rate ceilings will be eliminated thereby converting previously fixed rate funds to variable rate status. Competitive pressures have brought about new innovations such as the NOW account which is offered by some thrift institutions and commercial banks. Tight cash management by large corporations and institutions has led to the "zero balance," "minimum balance" and "automatic investment" demand deposit accounts. These factors raise serious questions about the future reliability of such deposits and further indicate that a reappraisal of related asset strategy may be in order.

A significant decline in fixed rate deposits might result in a reverse GAP where variable rate funds were supporting fixed rate, long-term assets. This condition could lead to heavy GAP losses during high rate phases of the cycle rather than the favorable contributions enjoyed historically. Also, the vulnerability of the GAP from the deposit side should be hedged against on the asset side. The maturity distribution of fixed rate assets should be more closely matched to the availability of fixed rate funds. Long-term investments equal in volume to capital and long-term debt contain little maturity risk. Other fixed rate investments and loans, however, should be held to shorter maturity schedules more in keeping with the future uncertainty of low cost, fixed rate deposit availability.

A bank's asset-liability strategy must come to grips with a maturity policy on long-term investments—not only from the standpoint of rate-mix and GAP analysis, but also in consideration of market values. A review of historic yield trends on long-term bonds demonstrates that even if acquired at the peak of each cycle during the past 30 years, they were yielding below market within seven to ten years later. With continued high inflationary expectations and heavy capital demands, serious questions must be raised as to the maturity limits of bank investments and the banking purposes served by large, long-term bond portfolios.

FIXED RATE ASSETS THRESHOLD CONCEPT

Simply stated, the "threshold rate" is a rate established by management policy for each fixed rate asset category above which new assets may be acquired and below which lower yielding assets will be sold. It may be the existing average rate earned on the asset classification or a rate strategically determined by management as an appropriate decision threshold.

The objective of the threshold rate concept is to assure consideration of increasing average asset yields on each transaction of buying, selling, swapping, renewing, ect. In order for the concept to function, there must also be a maximum volume level established for each asset category the aggregate of which will represent the fixed rate asset guideline relative to the rate-mix GAP.

When applied to fixed rate loans, the policy must permit some replacement of maturing loans even at low rate phases of the cycle whenever continuity of market participation is necessary. Major emphasis on adding to fixed rate loan classifications should come during high rate periods when the yields are the most profitable and customer demand is strongest. This requires a disciplined management policy to avoid "loading up" during low rate periods. The fixed rate loans acquired during low rate phases should emphasize situations where other banking relationships are enhanced, and the form of the loan should be suitable for resale into an existing secondary market. The strategy should provide for operating well under the volume guideline during a low rate phase, so that heavier acquisitions can be made during the high rate phases without expanding overall asset levels beyond prudent capital and liquidity limits.

The threshold rate concept applied to investments should follow the same principles defined above for loans. Two additional "thresholds" could be integrated into an overall investment strategy. A "quality threshold" would represent the weighted average rating (i.e., Moody's Aa") that must be maintained on all commercial and municipal bond portfolios. The policy on quality would also include a minimum acceptable rating (i.e., "Baa") below which no security would be acquired. A "maturity threshold" policy would establish a range (i.e., 8-12 years) within which the weighted average maturity of the portfolio would be maintained. A high limit (i.e., 16 years) and a low limit (i.e., four years) could also be established for new security purchases to assure reasonable market protection from short-term volatility and long-term inflationary erosion.

The combination of three "thresholds" (rate, quality and maturity) plus the asset size guideline would represent the executive policy limits assigned to functional management within which they would be free to act.

SUMMARY

Asset-liability management involves much more than the establishment of a series of ratios to be applied to a balance sheet. It is a complex process that must encompass a thorough understanding of the particular bank's asset and liability mix, customer behavior and how these relate to the external economic and competitive pressures that the structure will encounter.

The strategy of asset-liability management, like the old adage, says "buy high and sell low," but the unanswerable question follows: "How do you know when it is high or low?" This question plagues any system and, for that matter, any lack of a system. Economic forecasting and the related timing of management actions are subject to wide margins of error. This, in itself, calls for a conservative approach rather than reaching for the elusive brass ring or being helplessly swept along by uncontrollable events. A conservative strategy will not maximize earnings in the short-term, but neither will it result in a pattern of margins that follows the erratic behavior of a short-term rate curve with potentially volatile swings.

The rate-mix approach presented above herein explores asset-liability management from one perspective and can contribute to a broader understanding of the subject when applied to a particular bank. The GAP and "threshold" concepts dealt primarily with the interrelationships of fixed rate assets and liabilities.

A PERSPECTIVE ON ASSET-LIABILITY MANAGEMENT: PART II *

John T. Clifford

29

The events of the 1973-74 period have been sobering to the expansion and diversification-minded banking industry. Now, in the face of diminished public confidence, there emerges an overwhelming concern for capital adequacy, liquidity, control of credit expansion and a clear need for a profitable but more conservative and well-integrated approach to asset-liability management.

Traditionally, banks concentrated on various allocation methods of matching specific funds sources with selected uses. Deposit funds were somewhat taken for granted as unique to the economic role of banking, and emphasis was directed more toward "asset management." Higher growth and profit objectives soon exceeded the ability of banks to develop increased deposit levels, and "liability management" came into vogue during the mid to late 1960s. The early 1970s found the industry embarking upon broad programs of diversification and expansion through holding companies with attendant high leveraging and the reliance upon money market funds to support marginal "interest differential business." By the mid '70s, however, a combination of official and public concern for capital adequacy and the extreme economic conditions prevailing throughout the work brought about a reappraisal of the strategies and structures employed in asset-liability management.

While countless techniques have been developed to assist management in this vital area, there is no substitute for a thorough understanding of the individual bank's customer behavior, economic and market environment, and

Reprinted from the *Magazine of Bank Administraion*, April 1975, pp. 32-36, with permission from the publisher, the Bank Administration Institute.

the functional relationships of its assets and liabilities. Part 1 of this series described an analytical approach involving the classification of assets and funds according to their interest rate characteristics (Figure 1, pg. 350).

The structure depicted in Figure 1 demonstrates the analytical relationships of assets and funds when classified according to rate behavior. *Matched Rate* represents specific sources and uses of funds in equal amounts which have identical predetermined maturities and a negotiated rate spread. Such transactions would include Eurodollar placements, federal funds purchased and resold, arbitrage agreements, special loan arrangements, etc. *Variable Rate* represents interest bearing assets and liabilities where rates fluctuate with general money market conditions. This classification would include prime rate related loans, short-term securities, securities subject to resale or repurchase agreements, large negotiable certificates of deposit, short-term borrowings, etc. *Fixed Rate* represents assets and liabilities that have relatively fixed rates (costs on demand deposits) over an extended period of time. Examples would include long-term investments, real estate mortgages, instalment loans, the bank's capital funds, long-term debt, net usable time and demand deposits, etc.

Each of the asset and funds rate-mix classifications will respond to various phases of the rate-economic cycle in a definable manner. A successful asset-liability management system must provide the means for controlling these responses in order to achieve profitability, liquidity and capital adequacy objectives. The rate-mix analytical approach enables management to simulate the interaction of rates and balances at various cyclical phases when applied to the structure of a particular bank. This requires a thorough knowledge of the individual bank's customer base and how it interacts with changes in the economic cycle. There are certain specific tendencies inherent in the rate-mix classifications, however, which can be evaluated generally to identify areas of high sensitivity in all banks.

Part 1 of this series concentrated on one of the more sensitive relationships highlighted through rate-mix analysis. This involved the degree to which fixed rate funds exceeded the level of fixed rate assets. This imbalance is designated on Figure 1 as the GAP. The excess fixed rate funds (i.e., capital and net usable savings and demand deposits) are employed to support an equal amount of variable rate assets (i.e., prime rate related commercial loans). The cost of funds in the GAP is relatively fixed throughout all phases of the economic cycle, while the income generated by the asset side will rise and fall with the level of money market rates. This creates a high level of earnings volatility, the intensity of which depends upon the size of the GAP and the actions of management to control its expansion and contraction during various phases of the rate cycle.

Since asset-liability management considerations of the GAP and the characteristics of fixed rate funds and assets were previously explored in Part 1, this article will concentrate on variable and matched rate classifications and a summary of rate cycle influences on asset-liability management strategy.

Variable rate assets and liabilities are also referred to as the "interest differential business" component of a bank's asset-liability structure. A portion of the variable rate assets (commercial loans) are supported by fixed rate funds (GAP relationship), but the remainder are supported by an equal amount of variable rate funds (purchased funds) as identified in Figure 1. Profitability of this interest differential business is determined by the ability of management to control the rate spread between purchased funds and commercial loans. There are highly competitive market pressures at work on both sides of the interest differential equation at all phases of the rate cycle. Despite the larger commitment of resources (assets and funds) to this category of business, the potential margin contribution may be substantially lower and less controllable than the margin attainable through GAP management. The enhancement of variable rate asset yields (commercial loans) contributes to higher margins on both the purely interest differential business and the GAP.

VARIABLE RATE ASSETS

Management control over the quality of credit and the industrial distribution of commercial loan customers has a heavy influence on the yields and overall profitability of commercial loans, but these subjects are outside the scope of this analysis. The cyclical expansion and contraction influences and the rate responsiveness of commercial loans are key elements to a bank's asset-liability management strategy. Both of these considerations are predetermined, to a large degree, at the time that the terms and conditions of credit lines are negotiated with the commercial customer. Unused credit lines are similar to an industrial firm's backlog of unfilled orders. Once they are activated, the profitability and expansion characteristics of credit lines flow directly into the bank's balance sheet and earnings statement—much the same as production costs and sales flow from the mix and prices pre-negotiated for factory orders. There is little that the average bank can do during high rate stress periods to improve its commercial loan yield, since the prime rate is established by the marketplace (with some government assistance) and the bank has firm commitments outstanding in the form of previously extended credit lines.

The potential expansion in the loan portfolio due to the credit line "backlog" should be controlled toward an asset size guideline that is within reasonable levels in relation to capital adequacy and borrowing or purchased funds capacity limits. This is obviously easier said than done, but failure to control the potential expansion of the loan portfolio can lead to serious adverse liquidity and profitability consequences. One of the first steps in a management control of this expansion is to thoroughly study the composition of its commercial loan customer mix and behavior in previous economic cycles. Any special industrial concentrations should be identified and studied to determine both seasonal behavior and how such industries react in relation to general economic cycles. Statistical techniques can assist greatly in evaluating potential expansion and contraction in commercial loan volume, but since no two cycles will be exactly the same there really is no substitute for exercising good management judgment based upon the environment of the individual bank. At a minimum, there should be a policy concerning the aggregate size of the credit lines outstanding with a defined approach to purging, extending, renewing and adding credit lines within the prescribed limits. The orientation of the management control strategy should be toward building and maintaining a core customer base while avoiding an imbalance of commitments to less predictable secondary relationships such as prestigious national accounts to be indirectly served through other primary banks.

The pricing formula for commercial loans is heavily influenced by competitive practices and credit judgment, but has an important relationship to both spread management and loan expansion. The overall effects of the competitive pricing structure can be influenced, in part, by management control over the mix of pricing formulas negotiated into credit lines. There is a double lag in commercial loan yields during an upward climb in interest rates. The cost of money market funds (CDs and borrowings) rises first, causing the beginnings of a rate squeeze. The margin impact and duration of this squeeze depends, in part, upon how quickly the prime rate moves up and how responsive the commercial loan rates are to a change in the prime. When there is a high percentage of commercial loans that are only periodically re-rated (i.e., 90 days), a second lag in rates occurs following a prime change which further intensifies the rate squeeze. On the downward side of the rate cycle, there is a favorable lag as money market cost rates tend to move down in advance of a drop in the prime rate which, in turn, is followed by lower loan rates. The favorable lag seldom makes up for the preceding unfavorable lag, since rate cycles usually move down more quickly than they go up and loan demand is diminishing on the downward side of the cycle. A loan pricing policy should incorporate features that would automatically increase loan rates with a change in the prime at least above a certain prime rate level. Large lines of credit could be priced for "normal" and "expansionary" levels of usage. The normal working capital portion of the line could be priced directly in relation to the prime while the expansionary portion could be priced as a fixed spread above the cost of incremental purchased funds. This was common banking practice applicable to credit line extensions (over lines) during the last two high rate cycles (1969-70 and 1973-74).

Other variable rate assets (primarily short-term investments) should be controlled through maturity guidelines relative to the source of supporting funds. The definition of one-year maturities as short-term seemed quite long during 1973 and 1974 whenever significant volumes were involved. Temporary investments should only be added with very short maturities (90-180 days) and limited to those situations where a low rate phase of the cycle is prolonged, and either customer accommodation deposits must be covered or where long-term funds are acquired to protect against an expected upturn in the rate cycle. The temporary investments should always be maintained at a shorter maturity than the underlying funds sources, otherwise there is a built-in rate and liquidity risk that would require a substantial spread to justify.

Short-term investments do not represent liquidity, they are merely a lower degree of illiquidity. It is the underlying longer-term funds that represent the availability of liquidity after the temporary investments have matured.

VARIABLE RATE LIABILITIES

Variable rate liabilities (purchased funds) such as negotiable certificates of deposit, federal funds purchased, commercial paper, domestic Eurodollars, etc. are priced according to general money market conditions, and little can be done to control the cost of acquiring new funds during an expansionary upward cycle. The requirement for such funds increases due to increased utilization of credit lines, and at certain rate levels disintermediation sets in resulting in more purchased funds acquisitions to replace the run-off in other time and demand deposit categories. Once the cycle has started, there is little that can be done to control the sequence of events. Virtually all asset-liability management actions must be pre-planned and, to some degree, activated in a phase of the cycle which precedes that phase requiring protection.

The rate squeeze prevalent in the upward phase of the cycle can be partly ameliorated by extending purchased funds maturities during the preceding low rate phase. This action will sacrifice some margin during the low rate period due to the higher rate premium paid for the longer fund maturities. Even during the declining phase of a rate cycle, it is prudent to begin to lengthen fund maturities to protect against a volatile reverse in the cycle such as occurred in March of 1974. Such extensions should be conservative in nature starting with small amounts and then larger amounts moving out in maturity gradually all through the declining phase. At the low level, most funds will have been extended and in a position to protect against the adverse effects of the next cyclical rise.

The objective in managing interest differential business is to maintain nearly constant spreads throughout all phases of the cycle. Any speculative moves anticipating precise cyclical turning points are at best a gamble and, even if successful, are apt to rebound adversely in a subsequent phase.

MATCHED ASSETS AND FUNDS

The profit characteristics of matched transactions are margin stability at all phases of the cycle since, by definition, the spreads are constant and the maturities are coterminous. There are, however, some important management considerations for matched asset-liability transactions:

Credit risk. The asset side of the transaction has the same credit risk as any other asset of similar quality.

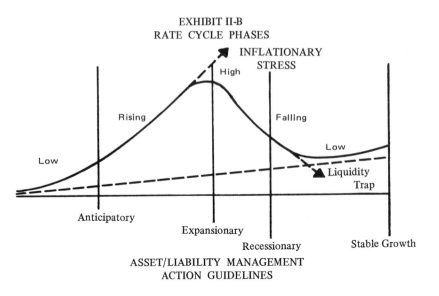

EXHIBIT II-B
RATE CYCLE PHASES

ASSET/LIABILITY MANAGEMENT
ACTION GUIDELINES

LOW RATE PHASE	HIGH RATE PHASE
Purge credit lines	Replenish credit lines
Lengthen funds maturities	Shorten funds maturities
Shorten invest. maturities	Lengthen invest. maturities
Raise long-term debt	Upgrade investment quality
Restrict fixed rate loans	Expand fixed rate loans
Update loan pricing policy	Plan investment sales
Sell investments	Acquire investments
Plan diversification	Execute diversification

TRANSITIONAL–RISING	TRANSITIONAL–FALLING
Gradually: (increasing emphasis on high side)	Gradually: (increasing emphasis on low side)
Shorten funds maturities	Lengthen funds maturities
Lengthen invest. maturities	Shorten invest. maturities
Expand fixed rate loans	Restrict fixed rate loans
Acquire investments	Sell investments
Execute acquisitions	Plan acquistions

GAP RELATIONSHIPS

Rising Rates	Widening Gap
High Rates	Widest Gap
Falling Rates	Narrowing Gap
Low Rates	Narrowest Gap

Adequacy of spread: Most matched transactions are competitive placements and spreads are narrow. Adequate spreads may not be available to compensate for credit risks and administrative costs unless other related business benefits accrue to the bank.

Relative value. The funds and assets employed in matched transactions consume a part of the bank's total capacity. There is a limit to the bank's ability to leverage on its capital base. Matched transactions with traditionally narrow spreads could become disproportionate in the asset-liability mix causing the bank to have an inflated size and a deflated R.O.A.

SUMMARY

There is no universally applicable asset-liability management system for all commercial banks. The cornerstone of a system for an individual bank is a thorough understanding of its customer base and market environment. An analysis and evaluation of the current asset-liability structure, including the perspective of rate-mix relationships, can serve as the basis for establishing a unique strategy for the particular bank. The objectives of asset-liability management must be realistic in relation to the existing capital base and the bank's access to funds sources of the type needed to reasonably assure liquidity and profitability. The dangers of operating at the outer edge of prudent leveraging do not assure maximum profitability and, on the contrary, can so reduce flexibility that highly profitable and sound asset-liability strategies cannot be exercised. The vision of management cannot be limited to the horizon of the current fiscal year or the short-term and often artificial growth comparisons with other members of the industry. Yesterday's heroes are still making headlines today but of a much different quality, and this will probably repeat itself again in the future. The economic cycle and its effects on asset-liability management must be accommodated, but not as a roulette wheel with win or lose riding on every turn. Risks are inherently a part of the banking business; but, as is true in any other industry, they should be proportionate to the opportunity and natural to the economic function that the bank is intended to fulfill.

The approach presented here is intended only as an analytical perspective leading toward the development of an asset-liability strategy that must, in turn, lead to the establishment of a structure that not only serves the needs of management, but also balances the legitimate interests of stockholders, customers and the public for whose benefit the bank was chartered.

INTEREST RATE FUTURES*

Marcelle Arak and Christofer J. McCurdy†

30

On a typical day in 1979, futures contracts representing about $7½ billion in three-month Treasury bills changed hands in the International Monetary Market (IMM) of the Chicago Mercantile Exchange in Chicago. This market and several other new markets for interest rate futures have very quickly become active trading arenas. For example, at the Chicago Board of Trade (CBT), futures contracts representing $820 million of long-term Treasury bonds were traded on a typical day; also, at the CBT, futures contracts representing $540 million of GNMAs (Government National Mortgage Association securities) changed hands on an average day.

Besides these three well-established interest rate futures contracts several new financial futures contracts have recently received the approval of the Commodity Futures Trading Commission (CFTC) and have begun trading. Futures contracts for intermediate-term Treasury notes commenced trading in the summer of 1979; in the fall, the Comex (Commodity Exchange, Inc.), which had traded many metals contracts, inaugurated a three-month bill futures contract, and the ACE (Amex Commodities Exchange, Inc., an affiliate of the American Stock Exchange) introduced a bond futures contract;

*Reprinted from the *Quarterly Review*, Winter 1979-80, pp. 33-46, with permission from the Federal Reserve Bank of New York.

†The authors wish to thank James Kurt Dew, Ronald Hobson, and Anthony Vignola for information and helpful comments. The foregoing do not necessarily agree with the views expressed herein, nor do they bear responsibility for any errors.

in addition, the New York Stock Exchange is intending to start a financial futures unit.

What accounts for the rapid growth of interest rate futures? Who are the most active participants in these markets? Some businesses such as financial institutions and securities dealers use it to hedge or manage interest rate risk. By and large, however, participants are involved for other reasons and help provide much of the markets' liquidity. A large portion of the activity in these markets is speculative—people and institutions betting on which way interest rates will move and how the interest rate in one month will move relative to another. Others are involved in these interest rate futures markets for tax reasons.

Both the enormous size of these futures markets and the nature of the participants are a matter of concern for the regulatory authorities. The Treasury and the Federal Reserve System have become aware of potential problems for the functioning of markets in Government securities; these problems include the possibility of corners or squeezes on certain Treasury issues and the disruption of orderly cash markets for Treasury securities. In addition, the regulatory authorities have become concerned that the substantial numbers of small investors participating in the markets may not be fully aware of the risks involved.

WHAT IS A FUTURES MARKET?

For as long as mankind has traded goods and services, people have made contracts which specify that commodities and money will change hands at some future date, at a price stated in the contract. Such contracts are called "forward" contracts. A forward contract tailored to one's needs offers obvious advantages—one can pick the exact date and the precise commodity desired. On the other hand, there are disadvantages. It may be difficult to locate a buyer or seller with exactly opposite needs. In addition, there is a risk that the other party to the transaction will default.

A *futures* contract is a standardized forward contract that is traded on an exchange. Usually the type and grade of commodity is specified as well as the date for delivery. Once a bargain is struck, the clearinghouse of the futures exchange itself becomes the opposite party to every transaction. Thus, it is the soundness of the exchange's clearinghouse rather than the credit-worthiness of the original buyer (or seller) that is of concern to the seller (or buyer) on the other side of the transaction. To ensure its viability, futures exchanges and their clearinghouses set up rules and regulations. These include the requirements that a clearing member firm and its customers put up "margin", that the contracts be marked-to-market daily, and that trading cease if daily price fluctuations move outside certain limits.

Among the oldest futures markets in the United States are those for wheat and corn which date back to the middle of the nineteenth century. Thereafter, futures markets for other farm products and raw materials gradually developed. One of the major purposes was to provide producers and processors with price insurance. Suppose a farmer expects to harvest wheat in July. Nobody knows with certainty what the price will be then; it depends upon the size of the harvest and conditions elsewhere in the world. However, by selling a futures contract for July wheat, the farmer can indirectly guarantee receiving a particular price. This is illustrated in Box 1.

Futures markets for commodities not only provide a forum for hedgers, but they also provide information. This information—about prices expected to prevail on future dates—is printed in the financial section of many daily newspapers. The farmer, for example, can use these futures prices to decide whether to plant corn or wheat. The food processor can gear up to can corn or beans depending upon the expected prices and the prospective consumer demand at those prices.

Interest rate futures are a relatively new development. In the fall of 1975, the CBT inaugurated a GNMA contract. Shortly thereafter, in early 1976, the IMM introduced a contract for ninety-day Treasury bills, and this was followed in 1977 by the CBT's Treasury bond futures contract. These three contracts—the CBT's original GNMA, the CBT's Treasury bond, and the IMM's three-month Treasury bill contract—have proved to be the most popular and heavily traded financial futures contracts. The amount of contracts outstanding, or open interest, in these markets has expanded significantly since their inception (Chart 1). Moreover, trading volume has also become quite large in relation to the underlying cash market securities. In 1979, daily average trading in the eight ninety-day Treasury bill contracts on the IMM was equivalent to about $7½ billion (at $1 million per contract), not much different from the daily volume of Treasury bills traded in the dealer market for United States Government securities.[1] Some interest rate futures contracts, however, have failed to attract much trading activity. For example, activity in the ninety-day commercial paper contract has remained quite light.[2]

HOW FINANCIAL FUTURES MARKETS OPERATE

The financial futures markets operate in the same manner as other futures markets. Their terms and methods are very different from those used in the money and bond markets. One of the most active financial futures markets

[1] The market is described in "The Dealer Market for United States Government Securities", Christopher McCurdy in this bank's *Quarterly Review* (Winter 1977-78), pages 35-47.

[2] One of the problems with this contract has been that commercial paper issuers have at times tended to sell paper with maturities much shorter than ninety days. Also, because the paper of a large number of companies is deliverable against the contract, this generates substantial uncertainty about which paper will be delivered. In addition, the original technical specifications of the contract engendered some confusion.

Box 1

Hedge in Wheat Futures

A farmer planning to harvest wheat in July sells a July wheat futures contract at $2.98 in March.

(1)	Suppose the price in July turns out to be......	$2.50	$3.00	$3.50
(2)	Gain or loss from offsetting futures contract [$2.98 − row (1)] ...	.48	−.02	−.52
(3)	Sales price of wheat in cash market [same as row (1)].......	2.50	3.00	3.50
(4)	Total earnings per bushel [row (2) + row (3)]......	2.98	2.98	2.98

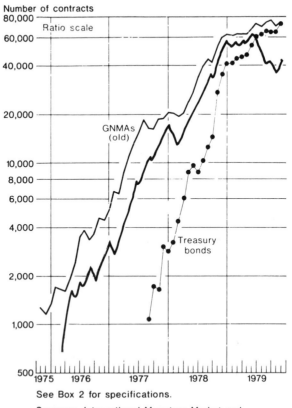

Number of contracts

See Box 2 for specifications.

Sources: International Monetary Market and Chicago Board of Trade.

is that for three-month Treasury bills at the IMM. Through this exchange, a customer could, for example, buy a contract to take delivery of (and pay for) $1 million of three-month Treasury bills on March 20, 1980. In all, there are eight contract delivery months on the IMM, extending at quarterly intervals for about two years into the future.

A customer places his order with a futures commission merchant—a firm registered with the CFTC and permitted to accept orders from the public—which sends the order to the trading floor of the exchange. There, a member of the exchange enters the trading pit and announces his intention to purchase the March 1980 contract. Another member who has an order to sell that contract shouts out his offer and, if the two can agree on a price, the trade is consummated. The trading in the pit is by *open outcry*, which is typical of futures exchanges and very unlike the over-the-telephone negotiations in the cash market for Treasury Securities.

The contract's price is quoted as the difference between 100 and the discount rate on the bill in question. Thus, a contract fixing a bill rate of 8.50 percent would be quoted at 91.50. This index preserves the normal futures market relationship in which the party obligated to take (make) delivery profits when the price rises (falls). The contract quote is not the price that would actually be paid for the bill at delivery. That price is computed by using the rate of discount in the standard bill price formula.

The clearinghouse interposes itself between the buyer and the seller, so that the buyer's contract is not with the seller but with the clearinghouse. (In the same fashion, the seller's contract is with the clearinghouse and not with the original buyer.)

A key ingredient in the financial viability of the clearinghouse is the margin that the clearing member firms must post on their contracts. For each outright purchase or sale of a three-month Treasury bill contract on the IMM, the firm must post margin of $1,200 per contract, which can be in the form of cash or bank letter of credit. The clearing member firm must, in turn, impose an initial margin of at least $1,500 on the customer. This may be posted in the form of cash, selected securities, or bank letters of credit. Futures firms can and often do require higher than the minimum margins of their customers. Margins formerly were more lenient, at one point down to $800 initial margin, but were raised following the greater volatility that emerged in the financial markets in the wake of the Federal Reserve System's policy actions in October 1979.

For as long as the position is outstanding, the contract will be *marked-to-market* by the clearinghouse at the end of each business day. For example a clearing member with a long position in the March contract would have its margin account credited with a profit if the price rises, or debited with a loss if it declines. The prices used in the calculations are the *final settlement prices*, which are determined by the exchange by examining the prices attached to the trades transacted at the end of trading each day.

Profits in the margin account may be withdrawn immediately. When losses occur and reduce the firm's margin below $1,200, the firm must pay the difference to the clearinghouse in cash before trading opens the next day. It is permissible for the value of a customer's margin account to fall below the initial $1,500 but, once the margin account falls below the $1,200 maintenance margin, the account must be replenished in full—brought back up to $1,500. Since the value of a 1 basis point change in the futures bill rate is $25 per contract, relatively small changes in interest rates can result in large changes in the value of a margin account.

The exchanges impose rules that prices may not change by more than a certain maximum amount from one day to the next. At the IMM, for example, no bill futures trades may be cleared if the price is more than 50 basis points above or below the final settlement price on the previous day although, if the *daily limit* restricts trading for a few days, then wider limits may be imposed on subsequent days. Margins are often temporarily increased during such periods.

When the customer wishes to get out of his contract before maturity, he must take an offsetting position. To cancel the contract he bought, he must sell another contract. His order is forwarded to the pit and a sales contract is executed, but not necessarily with the party who sold it to him in the first place. Once again, the clearinghouse interposes itself between the two parties and the latest sale will be offset against the original purchase. The customer's overall position will be canceled, and the funds in the margin account will be returned to him.

The lion's share of all contracts traded are terminated before maturity in this fashion. Only a very small percentage of contracts traded is delivered. In the case of Treasury bills, delivery takes place on the day after trading stops. The customer who has sold the contract (the short) delivers $1 million (par value) of Treasury bills that have ninety, ninety-one, or ninety-two days to maturity, and the customer who bought the contract (the long) pays for the bills with immediately available funds. The price paid for the bills is the settlement price on the last day of trading. (With the daily marking-to-market, almost all losses and gains have been realized before the final delivery takes place.)

Variations in procedures exist on different contracts and exchanges, but they generally adhere to the same principles: open outcry trading, interposition of the clearinghouse, posting of margin, and daily marking-to-market. Box 2 delineates the key specifications on financial futures contracts. Probably the most important difference among contracts is that some allow delivery of a variety of securities. The active Treasury bond contract, for example, permits delivery of bonds from a "market basket" of different bonds, all with maturity (or first call) beyond fifteen years. This has the effect of substantially increasing the deliverable supply of securities but generates some uncertainty among those taking delivery as to which bonds they might receive.

The formal organizational structure of futures trading stands in contrast to the informal nature of forward trading. Dealers in the market for United States Government securities often agree to transact trades that call for forward delivery of Treasury issues. These trades are negotiated in the same fashion as trades for immediate delivery. There is no standardized contract as in the futures market: the two parties must agree to the specific security involved, the exact delivery date, the size of trade, and the price. These terms are set according to the mutual convenience of the two parties. Often, there is no initial margin and no marking-to-market to account for gains and losses. Thus, each participant must size up the creditowrthiness of the other. Finally, these agreements, for the most part, are designed to result in delivery. (Some GNMA forward trades among a few firms can be offset through a clearinghouse arrangement.) If either side wishes to cancel the trade, it must go back to the other side and negotiate a termination.

PARTICIPANTS IN THE INTEREST RATE FUTURES MARKET

Many types of financial institutions participate in the markets for interest rate futures, but private individuals not acting in a business capacity account for the major part of interest rate futures positions in the three most active contracts (Chart 2).

According to a survey by the CFTC of positions outstanding on March 30, 1979, businesses other than the futures industry, commonly called "commercial traders", accounted for only about one quarter of open interest held in the most active contracts (ninety-day Treasury bills on the IMM, and Treasury bonds and the original GNMA contract on the CBT). In an earlier survey, such participants had held about three eighths of those contracts outstanding on November 30, 1977 (Table 1). The involvement of commercial traders is important because they are the only group that can use futures

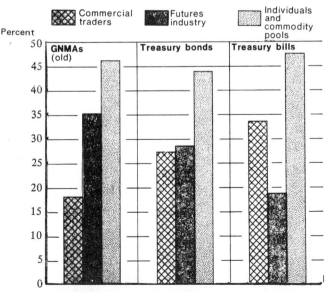

Chart 2 Furures Markets Participants, March 30, 1979. Source: Commodity Futures Trading Commission. Shares of open interest held by various groups.

Box 2

Futures Contracts on Treasury Securities (Currently Trading)

	Treasury bills				Intermediate-term Treasury coupon securities		Treasury bonds	
	ACE	*COMEX*	*IMM*	*IMM*	*CBT*	*IMM*	*ACE*	*CBT*
Deliverable items . . .	$1 million par value of Treasury bills with 90, 91, or 92 days to maturity	$1 million par value of Treasury bills with 90, 91, or 92 days to maturity	$1 million par value of Treasury bills with 90, 91, or 92 days to maturity	$250,000 par value of Treasury bills due in 52 weeks	$100,000 par value of Treasury notes and noncallable bonds with 4 to 6 years to maturity	$100,000 par value of Treasury notes maturing between 3½ years and 4½ years	$100,000 par value of Treasury bonds with at least 20 years to maturity	$100,000 par value of Treasury bonds with at least 15 years to first call or to maturity
Initial margin* (per contract)	$800	$800	$1,500	$600	$900	$500	$2,000	$2,000†
Maintenance margin* (per contract)	$600	$600	$1,200	$400	$600	$300	$1,500	$1,600†
Daily limits‡	50 basis points	60 basis points	50 basis points	50 basis points	1 point (32/32)	3/4 point (48/64)	1 point (32/32)§	2 points (64/32)
Delivery months (each year)	January, April, July, October	February, May, August, November	March, June, September, December	March, June, September, December	March, June, September, December	February, May, August, November	February, May, August, November	March, June, September, December
Total open interest (December 31, 1979)	106	913	36,495	435	715	265	207	90,676
Date trading began . .	June 26, 1979	October 2, 1979	January 6, 1979	September 11, 1978	June 25, 1979	July 10, 1979	November 14, 1979	August 22, 1977

Non-Treasury Securities Futures

| | Government National Mortgage Association (modified pass-through mortgage-backed certificates) | | | | Commercial paper | |
	CBT *(old)*	CBT *(new)*	ACE	COMEX	CTB *(30-day)*	CBT *(90-day)*
Deliverable items	Collateralized depository receipt covering $100,000 principal balance of GNMA certificates	$100,000 principal balance of GNMA certificates	$100,000 principal balance of GNMA certificates	$100,000 principal balance of GNMA certificates	$3 million face value of prime commercial paper rated A-1 by Standard & Poor's and P-1 by Moody's	$1 million face value of prime commercial paper rated A-1 by Standard & Poor's and P-1 by Moody's
Initial margin* (per contract)	$2,000	$2,000	$2,000	$1,500	$1,500	$1,500
Maintenance margin* (per contract)	$1,500	$1,500	$1,500	$1,125	$1,200	$1,200
Daily limits‡	1½ points (48/32)	1½ points (48/32)	3/4 point (24/32) §	1 point (64/64)	50/100 point	50/100 point
Delivery months (each year)	March, June, September, December	March, June, September, December	February, May, August, November	January, April July, October ‖	March, June, September, December	March, June, September, December
Total open interest (December 31 1979)	88,982	4,478	3,248	64	12	533
Date trading began	October 20, 1975	September 12, 1978	September 12, 1978	November 13, 1979	May 14, 1979	September 26, 1977

All specifications are as of year-end 1979.

*The speculative margin is shown where margins vary according to whether the contracts cover speculative, hedged, or spread positions.

†For all contracts but those which mature in current month. Then initial margin is increased to $2,500 and maintenance margin is raised to $2,000.

‡Exchanges frequently have rules allowing expansion of daily limits once they have been en effect for a few days (margins may change also).

§Limits in suspension as of the year-end.

‖Principal trading months; rules allow trading for current plus two succeeding months.

Table 1

Futures Markets Participants

November 30, 1977 and March 30, 1979
Average open interest; number of contracts

Type of participant	Government National Mortgage Association contract (old)				Treasury bond contract				Three-month Treasury bill contract			
	1977 amount	1977 as percentage of total	1979 amount	1979 as percentage of total	1977 amount	1977 as percentage of total	1979 amount	1979 as percentage of total	1977 amount	1977 as percentage of total	1979 amount	1979 as percentage of total
Commercial traders												
(total)	7,226	36.5	10,899	18.3	2,025	67.2	12,393	27.4	4,950	32.8	14,992	33.6
Securities dealers	3,395	17.1	4,270	7.2	1,534	50.9	8,226	18.2	2,758	18.3	5,596	12.5
Commercial banks	263	1.3	655	1.1	99	3.3	1,472	3.3	326	2.2	1,581	3.5
Savings and loan associations	494	2.5	2,500	4.2	—	—	394	0.9	56	0.4	136	0.3
Mortgage bankers	1,198	6.1	1,472	2.5	154	5.1	330	0.7	44	0.3	974	2.2
Other	1,875	9.5	2,003	3.4	238	7.9	1,971	4.4	1,767	11.7	6,706	15.0
Noncommercial traders (total)	12,588	63.5	48,705	81.7	989	32.8	32,826	72.6	10,154	67.2	29,661	66.4
Futures industry	7,353	37.1	21,113	35.4	477	15.8	12,924	28.6	2,765	18.3	8,434	18.9
Commodity pools	2,862	14.4	11,097	18.6	254	8.4	9,484	21.0	1,520	10.1	5,640	12.6
Individual traders	2,373	12.0	16,495	27.7	258	8.6	10,481	23.0	5,868	38.8	15,586	34.9
Total	19,814	100	59,604	100	3,014	100	45,219	100	15,104	100	44,654	100

Because of rounding, amounts and percentages may not add to totals.

Source: Commodity Futures Trading Commission Surveys. The 1977 survey covered all positions, but the 1979 survey excluded positions of fewer than five contracts.

contracts for hedging cash market positions to any meaningful extent. (See next section.)

Moreover, some of the businesses who participate in these futures markets are probably not trying to eliminate risk completely. Consider securities dealers, for example, who have been very active in interest rate futures markets—they held about 7 percent of total GNMA positions and about 18 percent of total bond positions in March 1979. Securities dealers are generally risk takers, trying to benefit from interest rate change, or arbitrageurs, trying to benefit from interest rate disparities, rather than hedgers. But, in meeting customers' needs and making a market in Government securities, they do make use of interest rate futures markets to manage their risk exposure.

Among other business participants, mortgage bankers and savings and loan associations combined held about 7 percent of total positions in GNMAs. Their participation in GNMAs is to be expected in view of their involvement in generating and investing in mortgages. A total of sixty-eight of these firms held positions on March 30, 1979, not much above the number reported in the earlier survey. Few commercial banks have been active in interest rate futures—twenty-four had open positions in bill futures, and fourteen in bond futures on March 30, 1979—accounting for a small fraction of total positions in these markets. Their relatively low level of participation may have reflected regulatory restrictions on their involvement in the futures market or some confusion about the regulators' policies.

Futures industry personnel and firms held a significant fraction of the open positions. This group includes many who are speculating on rate movements in general or on the spread relations between rates on successive contracts. Or they might be operating in both the cash and futures markets, arbitraging differences between the two markets.

Individuals and commodity pools—funds which purchase futures contracts—are very important participants in financial futures markets. They held almost half of the open positions in 1979, a substantial increase from their already significant participation in the earlier survey. Indeed, the 1979 share of total positions in financial contracts was certainly higher than that because positions of less than five contracts were not included in the second survey and individuals tend to hold the vast majority of such small positions.[3]

SERVICES PROVIDED BY INTEREST RATES FUTURES MARKETS

It is commonly believed that futures markets provide certain benefits—in the main, an inexpensive way to hedge risk and generate information on ex-

---

[3]Small positions in the bill futures contracts amounted to about 8,000 contracts at the end of March 1979 and thus would raise the combined share of individuals and commodity pools to a bit more than half of the bill futures market. Comparable calculations cannot be made for the CBT's bond and GMNA contracts because some small positions are posted on a net basis (*i.e.,* long positions are offset against short positions), compared with a gross basis as in the bill contracts.

pected prices. Interest rate futures markets also provide these benefits.

Several observers have noted that interest rate futures markets are not necessary to provide information on future interest rates or as a hedging mechanism. They point out that one can obtain information on future interest rates by comparing yields on outstanding securities which have different maturities. However, the interest rate futures markets do provide future interest rate information in a more convenient form.

It is also true that outstanding securities could be used to hedge market risk. Again, however, the futures market can provide a less cumbersome and expensive hedge. Suppose, for example, that a firm is planning to issue short-term securities three months in the future and is worried about the prospective short-term interest rate. The short sale of a Treasury bill with more than three months to maturity is one way to hedge the risk.[4] In the futures market, the interest rate risk on this prospective issue could be hedged by selling the Treasury bill contract for the month closest to the prospective issue date. If all short rates moved up, the hedger would make a gain on the futures market transaction which would offset the loss on the higher interest rate he would have to offer.

Banks, dealers, and other such financial institutions may find futures markets helpful in achieving a particular maturity structure for their portfolios while having adequate supplies of cash securities on hand. For example, a dealer may need to hold supplies of a six-month bill to be ready for customer orders. However, he may not want the risk exposure on this particular maturity because he thinks its rate is likely to rise. Or, a mortgage banker may wish to hedge the risk on rates between the time of the mortgage loan and the time of its sale as part of a large package of loans. By selling a GNMA futures contract while assembling the mortgage package, the banker can be insured against rate changes. If rates rise, the value of the mortgage portfolio will fall, but that will be offset by the profits on the short sale of the GNMA contract. If, on the other hand, rates fall, the gain on the mortgage portfolio is offset by the loss on the sale of GNMA futures. In this hedge, the banker foregoes the possibility of additional profit (or loss) and is content to profit from the origination and servicing fees associated with assembling the mortgages.

Not every financial transaction has an exact hedge in the futures market. When the cash asset is different from the security specified in the futures contract, the transaction is called a "cross hedge" and provides much less protection than an exact hedge. For example, a securities dealer might find it profitable to buy some certificates of deposit (CDs) and finance them for one month. To protect against a decline (increase) in the price (rates) of CDs over the interval, the dealer might sell Treasury bill futures contracts, assuming the movements in bill rates and CD rates will be similar over the interval.

---

[4]The prospective issuer could borrow a six-month Treasury bill and sell it immediately; three months hence he would buy a bill with the same maturity date to return. If interest rates for that future time interval rise, the security would be purchased more cheaply three months hence than is currently expected. The gain on this transaction would then offset the loss connected with issuing securities at the higher interest rate.

So long as the rates move in the same *direction* the dealer will be protected at least to some degree against adverse price movements. It is conceivable, however, that the rates could move in opposite directions. Thus, a cross hedge is really a speculation on the relationship between the particular cash market security held in position and the particular futures contract involved. In a cross hedge, the participants cannot deliver the cash security against the contract, so there is no threat of delivery that can be used to drive the prices on the two securities back into line as the expiration date approaches.

In contrast to financial businesses, nonfinancial businesses and private individuals are less likely to find a useful hedge in the interest rate futures market. Consider the typical nonfinancial business which is planning to issue securities to finance some capital purchase or inventory. If the rate of inflation accelerates, the firm will typically be able to sell its output at higher prices. Thus, its nominal profit and return from the investment will typically also rise.[5] This means that a rise in inflationary expectations, which is reflected in the nominal rate of interest, will tend to affect profits in the same direction as it does financing costs. Thus, to some extent, the firm is automatically hedged against inflation-induced changes in the interest rate.

A similar intrinsic hedge may be available to investors on any new funds they plan to invest. Presumably they want to be sure that their investment produces a certain real income or purchasing power in the future. If interest rates move down because anticipated inflation has fallen, then the return on any funds invested at the lower rate will be able to buy the same quantity of goods and services that they would have in the circumstances where inflation and interest rates were higher. (The real return on *past* savings, however will move in the opposite direction as inflation.)

Thus, to the extent that interest rate changes reflect revisions in inflationary expectations, many businesses and persons will not be in a very risky position with regard to saving or investment plans. If, as some contend, the variation in interest rates is largely connected with inflationary expectations, these groups would typically not obtain a very useful hedge in the interest rate futures market.

SPECULATION

While some participants use futures markets to hedge risk, others use them to speculate on price movements. Speculators like the high leverage obtainable and the low capital required for trades in futures markets relative to trades in cash markets. Speculation on interest rates could be accomplished in the cash markets but would typically involve greater costs than in futures

[5] The firm does not, however, tend to earn nominal profits in proportion to prices because the tax structure collects more in real terms during inflation. See M. Arak, "Can the Performance of the Stock Market Be Explained by Inflation Coupled with our Tax System?" (Federal Reserve Bank of New York Research Paper).

markets. For example, suppose one thinks that the three-month interest rate in the June-September period will be higher than the implicit forward rate for that time interval. The short sale of a September bill in March and its repurchase in June can produce a profit if those high rates materialize. The costs involved in these transactions include the dollar value of the bid-ask spread as well as the charges for borrowing a security. In addition, one must have sufficient capital to put up collateral equivalent in value to the securities borrowed or the credit standing to borrow the securities under a reverse repurchase agreement.

In futures markets, one does not pay for or receive money for the commodity in advance. The cost of trading in the futures market is the foregone interest on the margin deposit (if in the form of cash) plus the commission fees. Assuming a $70 commission, this would amount to about $125 on a three-month bill futures contract at current interest rates, if the contract were held for three months. A change in the discount rate on the futures contract of 5 basis points would therefore recompense the speculator for his costs (Table 2).

Besides speculating on the level of rates, some futures market participants may be speculating on the relationship among interest rates. Such speculation can take the form of a "spread" trade whereby the participant buys one contract and sells another, hoping that the rate on the contract bought will fall by more than (or rise by less than) the rate on the contract sold. Also, if participants believe that the slope of the yield curve will change in a predictable way when the level of the yield curve changes, a spread transaction (which involves a lower margin) can be a less expensive way to speculate on the level of rates.

Frequently, traders will take positions in futures contracts that are related to positions in cash market securities. A trader might think that the rate in the futures market is out of line with cash Treasury bills. If he feels the futures rate is low relative to the rates on outstanding bills, he might sell the

Table 2   **Change in Discount Rate on a Three-Month Treasury Bill Futures Contract Necessary to Cover Cost of a Futures Market Transaction**

In basis points

Holding period	Commission (in dollars)		
	$30	$50	$70
One month.	2.0	2.8	3.6
Three months	3.4	4.2	5.0
Six months.	5.7	6.5	7.3
Twelve months	10.2	11.0	11.8

$$\text{Basis point change} = \frac{C + \dfrac{h(.01i)m}{12}}{25}$$

where h is the number of months the contract is held, i is the rate of interest obtainable over the period h, m is the cash margin, and C is the commission on the futures trade. The numbers shown are based upon i = 15 percent and m = $1,500.

futures contract and buy the bills in the cash market. He could then carry the bill in position until the two rates move back to their more normal relationship. Then the bills would be sold and the short bill futures contract offset. These types of trades are often called "arbitrages" by participants in the cash market although they are not arbitrages in the strict sense in which a security is bought in one market and at the same time sold in another, thereby locking in an assured return. In fact, most arbitraging activity generally reflects speculation on the relationship between cash and futures rates.

USE OF FUTURES MARKETS TO
REDUCE TAX LIABILITY

Individuals and institutions have also used interest rate futures markets to reduce their taxes. One means was through spread transactions.

Until November 1978, spread transactions in the Treasury bill futures market were a popular means of postponing taxes. An individual would buy one contract and sell another, both for the next calendar year. For example, in 1976, the participant might have bought the March 1977 contract and sold the September 1977 contract. An important assumption was that interest rates on all contracts would tend to move together so that the net risk was relatively small. At some point before the end of 1976, whichever position had produced a loss would be closed out. (In the above example, the short position or the sale of the September 1977 contract was the item that showed a loss during the latter part of 1976.) That loss could then be deducted from other income for 1976, reducing the 1976 tax bill. The contract for March 1977, on which the gain had accrued, was not closed out until 1977 when it no longer affected the 1976 tax liability.[6]

What made Treasury bill futures particularly attractive for such spreads was the belief of many taxpayers that, just like actual Treasury bills, they were not capital assets. In contrast, it was clear that other types of futures contracts, not held exclusively for business purposes, were capital assets.[7] If Treasury bill futures were not capital assets, then losses on them could be fully subtracted from other ordinary income (providing that *net* ordinary income did not become negative). Capital losses, in contrast, could be subtracted from ordinary income to a very limited extent.[8]

This attraction of the Treasury bill futures market for tax postponement

[6] After the September 1977 contract was offset, another contract for 1977 would be sold to maintain a balanced position. In our example, the June 1977 contract would be sold to counterbalance the March 1977 contract that was still being held. Then sometime in early 1977, these two contracts would be closed out.

[7] *E.g.,* Faroll v. Jarecki, 231 F.2d 281 (7th Cir. 1956).

[8] Capital losses can be offset against capital gains with no limitation, but the excess of loss over gains that may be deducted from ordinary income in a single year is currently limited to $3,000.

[9] Rev. Rul. 78-414, 1978-2 C.B. 213.

[10] Rev. Rul. 77-185, 1977-1 C.B. 48.

was eliminated in November 1978 when the IRS declared that a futures contract for Treasury bills is a capital asset if neither held primarily for sale to customers in the ordinary course of business nor purchased as a hedge.[9] Further, the IRS, amplifying on an earlier ruling,[10] stated that the maintenance of a "spread" position, in transactions involving futures contracts for Treasury bills, may not result in allowance of deductions where no real economic loss is incurred.

A way that individuals can reduce taxes through the futures market is by indirectly converting part of the interest income on Treasury bills into long-term capital gains. Suppose that the discount rate on a bill is expected to fall as it matures. Since the market usually regards longer dated bills as less liquid (or as having more interest rate risk), an investor would typically expect that a bill maturing in, say, March 1981 would offer a higher annual discount rate in June 1980 than it would in February 1981. Similarly, the interest rate on futures contracts would tend to fall as they approach expiration (their price would rise). Pursuant to the November 1978 IRS ruling, the price increase in a Treasury bill futures contract should, in nonbusiness circumstances, be treated as a capital gain for an investor. In contrast, since a Treasury bill itself is not a capital asset, all the price appreciation on it—from date of purchase to date of sale—would be treated as ordinary income for tax purposes.

An investor would clearly prefer to have the price appreciation treated as a long-term gain rather than as ordinary income, since the long-term capital gains tax rate is only 40 percent of that for ordinary income. If a long position in a bill futures contract were held for more than six months, the profit would be a long-term capital gain. (Gains and losses on short positions in futures are always treated as short-term regardless of the holding period.) Consequently, some investors who might normally purchase 52-week bills would have an incentive to purchase distant futures contracts and, as those contracts matured, sell them off to take their capital gains. They could then invest their funds in three-month bills. These activities would tend to raise the discount rate on the 52-week bill. It would also tend to reduce the required discount rate on distant futures contracts. Thus, the discount rates on futures contracts would be pushed below the implicit forward discount rate on cash bills.

There are, of course, limits on the size of the wedge that can be driven between the forward rate on cash securities and the rate on futures contracts. Financial businesses cannot treat profits in bill futures as capital gains. For them, the futures contract has no tax advantage over a cash bill. When the wedge produced by investors exceeds the cost of arbitrage, these financial businesses will buy long-term bills and sell futures contracts to profit from disparities in rates.

RELATIONSHIP BETWEEN THE CASH AND FUTURES MARKETS

For many commodities, the spot price and the futures price are very closely related. Part of the explanation is that, if a commodity is storable, it can be bought today, stored, and sold at a future date. If the futures price were to exceed the spot price by more than the costs involved, arbitrageurs would buy the commodity in the spot market—raising the spot price—and would sell it in the futures market, lowering the futures price. These activities would reduce the disparity between the future price and the current price.

The relationship between cash and futures markets for bills is somewhat different from that for other commodities. A three-month Treasury bill cannot be stored for more than three months; it matures. However, a longer term bill could be "stored" until it has three months left to run. It is the cash market for that *longer term bill* which bears a relationship to the futures market that is typical of agricultural and industrial commodities. In the case of note and bond contracts, the deliverable item exists throughout the life of the contract.

For example, consider what cash market securities correspond to the IMM's June 1980 three-month Treasury bill contract. This contract calls for delivery of bills which have ninety-one days to run on June 19, 1980. Treasury bills having this maturity date will be sold by the Treasury in two auctions—as six-month bills on March 17, 1980 and as three-month bills on June 16, 1980. During the first three months of its life, the six-month bill issued on March 20, 1980 is the commodity that could be "stored" for delivery on the futures contract.

The funds used to purchase the six-month bill when it is initially issued could have been invested in three-month bills which mature on the contract expiration date. One measure of the interest cost involved in storage is therefore the foregone interest on the shorter bill—this is the "opportunity cost" of the decision to invest in the longer bill which is deliverable on the futures contract. It is common to subtract that opportunity cost from the bill price to get the "forward" price and the corresponding "forward" rate; this rate can then be compared with the discount rate on the futures contract.

Because in the past only three-month and six-month bills matured on Thursdays, only bills originally issued as three-month or six-month bills could be delivered on a ninety-day bill futures contract.[11] In fact, at any date, there was only one bill issue in existence that could be delivered on an IMM bill futures contract. That particular bill had between three and six months to maturity and could be delivered on the closest three-month bill futures contract. For longer bill futures contracts, there was usually no exact correspondence. There is no cash bill in existence today that could be delivered on the September 1980, December 1980, March 1981, and subsequent contracts traded on the IMM. However, there are bills which have a maturity date that may be quite close. For example, the 52-week bill maturing on September 16, 1980 will have eighty-nine days to run on June 19, 1980, while the June futures contract calls for bills which have ninety to ninety-two days to run on that date. By comparing the rate on this 52-week bill with the rate on the 52-week bill which matures twelve weeks earlier, a forward rate which covers

[11] Now that the Treasury has begun to issue 52-week bills maturing on Thursdays, there will be some occasions on which bills issued as 52-week bills will be deliverable against the three-month bill contracts.

an interval close to that of the futures contract bill can be calculated. Through this method, a rough forward rate in the period nine months prior to the contract's expiration can be obtained.

How does the rate on a three-month Treasury bill futures contract compare with the implicit forward rate in the cash market? The futures rate on the June 1979 contract and the "forward" rate on the corresponding cash bill (which matured September 21, 1979) moved very similarly in the last ninety-one days before the futures contract expired (Chart 3). Typically, the spread between the two rates was less than 25 basis points, with the forward rate somewhat higher than the futures rate. On most other futures contracts for three-month Treasury bills as well, the futures and forward rates were fairly close in the last ninety-one days or so before expiration.

When the contract's expiration date was far in the future, however, the link between its rate and the comparable forward rate was much weaker. In fact, spreads between forward and futures rates have at times been over 100 basis points in the three to nine months before the contract expired. Generally, in recent contracts, futures rates have been substantially below forward rates, and the spread between the two appears to have been wider than it was in earlier contracts.

Within three months of the expiration of the futures contract, futures and forward rates appear to be kept in reasonable alignment by investors and arbitrageurs. An investor, for example, can on the one hand hold a sixth-month bill, or, on the other hand, hold a three-month bill plus the futures contract

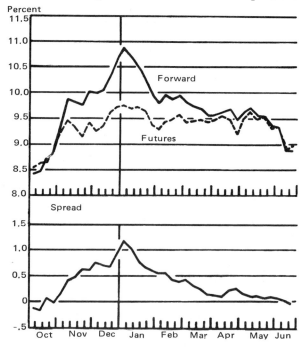

Chart 3 Discount rate on the June 1979 Treasury Bill futures contract (IMM) and the forward rate in the cash market. Spread equals forward rate minus futures rate.

for the month in which the three-month cash bill matures. If the six-month bill is yielding more than the other combination, investors will tend to prefer six-month bills. And their demand will tend to reduce its discount rate, bringing the forward rate down toward the futures rate. Similarly, if investors find the three-month cash bill plus the futures contract more profitable, their buying pressure on the futures contract will tend to reduce its discount rate, bringing it down closer to the forward rate.

Another group of market participants who help keep rates in line are arbitrageurs. If they observe that the six-month bill provides a forward rate which is high relative to the futures rate, they could buy six-month bills and sell them under a repurchase agreement for three months,[12] at the same time, they would sell a futures contract. They would then have no net investment position: the bill returned to them in three months corresponds to the commitment to sell in the futures market. But they would earn a profit equal to the futures price minus the six-month bill price, the transaction cost, and the financing cost. As arbitrageurs conduct these activities, they put upward pressure on the six-month bill's price by buying it and put downward pressure on the futures price by selling the futures contract. These activities of the arbitrageur usually tend to keep the forward and futures rates within certain bounds.

On contracts other than the nearest, however, there is no deliverable bill as yet outstanding—that is, no security exists that can be purchased, stored, and delivered against the contract. Consequently, arbitrageurs cannot lock in a profit by taking exactly offsetting positions in the two markets. If there is an order flow in the futures market that is persistent, sizable, and at variance with the prevailing view in the cash market, it is possible for speculators to drive a wedge between the rates on futures contracts and the implicit forward rates in the cash market.

One notable example occurred in the spring of 1979. Apparently, many small speculators purchased bill futures contracts due in mid-1980, in the belief that short-term interest rates had reached a cyclical peak and would begin to fall sometime within a year or so. From the end of April to the end of June, their holdings rose from about 25 percent to 35 percent of the total open interest and their net long positions expanded sharply. As a result of this buying pressure and purchases by those trying to get out of large short positions, rates dropped sharply, with the March 1980 and Jund 1980 contract rates falling by nearly 1¾ percentage points from mid-May to the end of June. Rates also fell on contracts with shorter maturities—those due in the latter half of 1979.

Many other participants were net short, and some of these were firms that felt they were arbitraging between the cash and futures market, holding in this case long positions in the cash bill market against short positions in futures contracts. One of the several cash futures operations they engaged in was a long position in bills in the six-month area (*i.e.*, due in November for the most part) versus a short in the September contract (calling for delivery

[12] A repurchase agreement specifies that the seller will rebuy at a prespecified date and price.

of the bill to mature on December 20 which had not been auctioned yet). As the rates on futures contracts fell, those with short positions faced sizable margin calls. To the extent that they then bought futures contracts to offset their short positions and also sold their cash bills, they greatly enlarged the wedge that was being driven between the rates in these two markets in late May and early June (Chart 4).

The widening wedge between the forward and futures rates made arbitrage involving futures contract sales even more profitable. But, after the shock of seeing large losses mount on short positions and show up in quarterly income statements, financial businesses were reluctant to expand their short positions. The futures and forward rates did not come back into alignment until late in the summer when interest rates started rising again.

PROS AND CONS OF INTEREST
RATE FUTURES MARKETS

Many observers of the new financial futures markets argue that these markets permit investors to obtain flexibility in ownership of securities at a very low cost. Someone who expects to have funds to invest in the period from

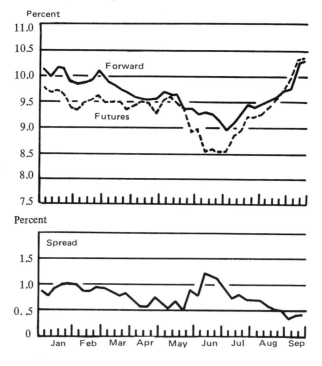

Chart 4 Discount rate on the September 1979 Treasury Bill futures contract (IMM) and the forward rate in the cash market. Soread equals forward rate minus futures rate.

mid-June to mid-September 1980, for example, can lock in an interest rate by purchasing a June Treasury bill futures contract. (For those who plan to purchase or issue other securities such as commercial paper or CDs, the links between the movements of rates in the bill futures market and the rates that obtain on these other instruments can be weak.)

By transferring the interest rate risk to those most willing to assume it, interest rate futures may increase the commitment of funds for some future time intervals. This could reduce the premium attached to funds committed for that future interval relative to funds committed for the nearer term. For example, the yield on 52-week and nine-month bills might fall. The resulting greater liquidity represents a gain to investors, while the lower interest rate on Government debt reduces the taxes necessary to service that debt.

While the provision of hedging facilities is a desirable aspect of interest rate futures markets, much of the activity appears to be speculative, and this has created some concern. One such concern is that speculation in the futures markets might push the prices of certain Treasury bills out of line with the prices of other securities. Because speculation is very inexpensive, entry into the futures market could be much more massive than entry into the cash market. Heavy demand in the futures market could be transmitted to the cash market by arbitrageurs. According to some analysts, the bill deliverable on the June 1979 contract was influenced by activities in the futures market. The June contract specified delivery on the Treasury bill due September 20 and only that bill. While the Treasury had sold $5.9 billion of bills with that maturity date, the Federal Reserve, foreign official accounts, and small investors held about one half. Thus, it appeared likely that the available trading supplies would amount to about $2 billion to $2½ billion.

However, open interest in the June 1979 contract stood at about 4,300 contracts, the equivalent of about $4.3 billion of bills at the end of May (Chart 5). This substantially exceeded the prospective trading supplies. During the spring, dealers reported that trading supplies in the September 20 bill were very thin and that it traded at a rate that was out of line with other bills. For example, it averaged about 4 basis points below the rate on the bill that was due a week earlier. Since investors usually require a higher rate when extending the maturity of their bill holdings, the 4 basis point difference provides a rough lower limit on the pressure that was exerted on the June contract and its spillover on the cash market.

Some observers argued that some investors were desirous of taking delivery because they thought there would be further declines in interest rates. Others pointed out that some people who had booked gains on long positions wanted to qualify for long-term capital gains. In any event, about a week before the contract expiration there was news of large increases in the money supply and industrial production which the market interpreted as indicating that a recession was not imminent and that interest rates would not fall immediately. This view probably contributed toward reducing pressure on the contract, and it was liquidated in an orderly fashion. Deliveries turned out to be a then record high of $706 million of bills due September 20, 1979, about a third of the available trading supplies of that bill. Deliveries on the Septem-

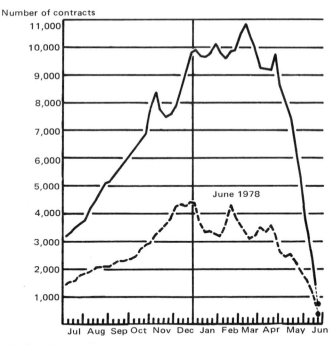

Chart 5 Open interest in Treasury bill futures contracts for June 1978 and June 1979.
Weekly averages, week ending each Wednesday. Total open interest as of last trading day is
indicated by dots. Source: International Monetary Market.

ber contract were somewhat lower, although still sizable (Chart 6), and deliveries on the December contract amounted to $1 billion.[13] Over the last month before delivery, the rate on the bill deliverable on the December contract averaged 8 basis points below the rate on the bill due one week earlier. As a result of these events, the question arises whether supplies of the deliverable bill are sufficient to prevent pricing dislocations.

In contrast to bill futures, other future contracts, notably in notes and bonds, have adopted a market basket approach to deliverable supplies. By allowing a variety of issues to be delivered, the contracts greatly reduce the possibility of a squeeze. If, for example, the September 13 bill had also been deliverable against the June contract, then traders would have had no incentive to deliver the September 20 bill at a rate that was below that on the September 13 bill. The mere availability of the other bill would therefore have provided a floor for the rate on the September 20 bill.

This analysis of bill futures has led some to suggest that, instead of a single deliverable issue, the deliverable security should be any one of a "basket" of Treasury bills with different maturity dates. However, others see disadvantages with the "basket" approach. In any event, the CFTC has authorized

[13] A part of the large amount of deliveries on the three 1979 contracts may reflect investor's preference for ordinary income losses instead of capital losses, a transformation that can be achieved by taking delivery on a contract on which one has booked a loss. See Arak, "Taxes, Treasury Bills, and Treasury Bill Futures".

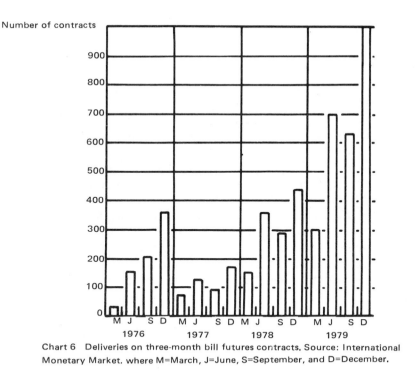

Number of contracts

Chart 6 Deliveries on three-month bill futures contracts. Source: International
Monetary Market. where M=March, J=June, S=September, and D=December.

the new exchanges such as the ACE and the Comex to trade futures which involve bills maturing in a different week of the quarter than the IMM bill contracts. If these markets grow and become more active, there should be less likelihood of pressure on the one particular March, June, September, or December bill whose futures contract is traded on the IMM.

Finally, to many of the regulators, the size of the required margin deposit is a key issue. Larger margins would help insure the exchanges against possible defaults as well as discourage excessive speculation with little capital. Moreover, they might make participants more aware of the possibilities of loss inherent in trading in interest rate futures. In early October 1979, the minimum initial margin on Treasury bill futures contracts at the IMM was only $800, and a 32 basis point move in the rate on one of those contracts could have wiped out the entire margin. Now that margin is $1,500, which gives better protection to the exchange and the contract.

CONCLUDING REMARKS

Interest rate futures markets have generated much new activity within a very short time; they have also generated some apprehension on the part of those concerned with orderly marketing and trading of the United States Government debt. Thus far, neither the extreme enthusiasm nor the worst worries appear to be justified.

Interest rate futures markets can provide inexpensive hedging facilities and flexibility in investment. But, to date, participation by financial institutions that might have such a need has not been large. Rather, it appears that participants have so far been primarily interested in either speculating on interest rates or reducing tax liabilities. These participants have been encouraged by fairly low margins. Until recently, the exchanges had shown a penchant for reducing these margins, but in October 1979 when interest rates fluctuated widely following the Federal Reserve System's adoption of new operating procedures, several exchanges raised margins substantially.

Most of the time, the financial futures markets have operated fairly smoothly. In general, there has been no greater volatility in the prices of bills which are deliverable on futures contracts than in the prices of other bills. And despite the huge run-up in open interest in some of the bill futures contracts, actual deliveries have not been large enough to disrupt the operation of the cash market. However, on several bill futures contracts, the price of the deliverable bill was pushed slightly out of line with prices on other issues with adjacent maturities. The CFTC, the Treasury, the Federal Reserve, and market participants themselves will have to continue to observe futures market activities to assure that significant problems are not building up.

Interest rate futures markets have already provided an arena for some institutions to manage interest rate risk. And, as these markets mature, their economic usefulness may come to be more widely appreciated.

HEDGING OPPORTUNITIES IN BANK RISK MANAGEMENT PROGRAMS †

Carl Schweser, Joseph Cole, and Lou D'Antonio *

31

Without effective asset and liability management, loan portfolios can't be effectively structured and funded. The following article shows how to reduce a bank's risk exposure through the use of hedging in the financial futures market. It includes one example in which the bank can help its borrower hedge the risk of adverse interest rate movement on a take-down under a line of credit. Such ideas should be of interest to the well-rounded banker/loan manager.

In recent years, the importance of bank risk management has been stressed as never before due to the increasing level of interest rate fluctuations. The perpetual tug of war between committing and obtaining funds has reached unbearable levels in these periods of rapidly changing interest rates. In the past, other segments of the economy faced exactly the same problems, and their experiments in coping with these problems eventually evolved into today's modern commodities markets. Despite the occasional bad press received by these financial markets, they provide our economy with a highly sophisticated risk management tool.

†Reprinted from the *Journal of Commercial Bank Lending*, January 1980, pp. 29-41. Copyright 1980 by Robert Morris Associates. Reprinted with permission.

The authors wish to thank Terrence Martell, Associate Professor of Finance at the University of Alabama, for his helpful comments. However, responsibility for any errors remains with the authors.

*The authors are on the faculty of the University of Iowa.

Country bankers have long aided agribusiness customers with hedging operations. But those same bankers have generally found such risk management techniques unnecessary for their own operations. Since 1965, however, price fluctuations in T-Bills, notes, bonds, and other credit instruments have increasingly exhibited a striking resemblance to the gyrations in farm commodity prices. Table 1 highlights the magnitude of the average weekly fluctuations in 13-week T-Bill yields. Individual swings in yields have been so extreme that in some cases they have exceeded 180 basis points in a single week.

In response to this clearly emerging risk source, the commodity exchanges have implemented several interest rate futures contracts. Successful and active contracts have evolved in T-Bills, T-Bonds, and GNMA mortgages. These contracts offer bankers the ability and flexibility to protect themselves against adverse price changes in the credit markets by adopting the same hedging techniques used by other major business segments in the economy.

The general level of acceptance of hedging in the interest rate futures market has not been widespread to date. Some bankers have taken a cautious wait-and-see- approach while others frankly don't understand the basics of hedging and the different hedging strategies that may be of use in the banking industry.

The purpose of this article is to present and analyze different types of banking transactions that present hedgeable risk exposure to the bank manager.[1] Examples will demonstrate that the use of hedging in the financial futures market can reduce a banker's risk exposure.[2] This presentation will show that the proper use of futures trading is truly a viable and vital risk management tool for the modern bank manager.

TYPES AND USES OF HEDGES

In concept, the theory of hedging is relatively simple while in practice it can appear to be complex and confusing. This confusion stems from the fact that many different banking situations can benefit from hedging, and each situation requires a different hedging approach. Whatever the situation and the hedging approach used, there are two basic types of hedges: the purchase of futures contracts and the sale of them.[3] When a hedger buys futures contracts, he is called a "long" hedger, and when he sells futures he is called a "short" hedger. Hedging can be used in both asset and liability management. Furthermore, it can be used to protect actual or anticipated commitments.

The best way to explain the use of hedging is to present several common

[1] U.S. Comptroller of the Currency Banking Circular No. 79, November 2, 1976, spells out the legal requirements national banks must meet to engage in futures trading.

[2] While hedging may be used to reduce risk, it is a practical impossibility for hedging to completely eliminate price risk. See page 3 of the Federal Reserve Bank of Dallas' *Review*, July 1977, for a further discussion of this topic.

[3] A futures contract is nothing more than an agreement to make or take delivery of a standardized amount of a commodity (in this case, securities) of a standardized quality during a specific future time period at a price determined at the time the agreement was made.

Table 1—Average Weekly Fluctuation in 13-Week T-Bill Auction Rates

Year	Basis Points	Year	Basis Points
1966	7.3	1972	12.7
1967	11.4	1973	22.4
1968	10.4	1974	33.4
1969	11.1	1975	17.0
1970	17.2	1976	8.9
1971	15.8	1977	6.4
		1978	14.8

Source for 1966 through 1976: *Opportunities in Interest Rates: Treasury Bill Futures*, November 1977, Chicago Mercantile Exchange.
Source for 1977 and 1978: *U.S. Financial Data*, Federal Reserve Bank of St. Louis.

banking situations that would benefit from hedging and show how hedging can be put into practice. We will take this approach, using actual market figures to add reality to the numbers and examples. Some specific comments concerning futures trading will be included in footnotes to increase your understanding of the market process.

Situation 1: Liability Management—Short Hedge

Through contacts with several of the bank's major customers, the bank anticipates the need for $10 million in additional funds in 30 days' time. To provide these funds, the bank decides to issue $10 million of 90-day CDs on October 5, 1978.

During the meeting authorizing the issue of CDs, one director expresses a fear that short-term rates will rise in the 30 days before the CDs are issued thus causing higher interest costs in servicing the CDs. It was decided that this risk should be hedged by selling 90-day T-Bill futures.[4] If rates increase before the issue date, the bank will have a gain from its futures position to offset the increased cost of issuing the CDs. Of course, if rates fall, there will be a loss in the futures position which will offset the reduced cost of issuing the CDs. Hedgers must remember the object of hedging is to reduce the risk of adverse price movements. However, once the hedge is placed, it also reduces the opportunity for windfall gains due to favorable price moves.

To get back to the hedged CD issue, the figures would have looked like those presented in Table 2 if a hedge was placed on September 5, 1978. The

---

[4]T-Bill futures were used for this CD hedge since there are no CD futures contracts and of the three active interest rate futures contracts, T-Bills, T-Bonds, and GNMAs, T-Bills yields most nearly parallel those of CDs. Hedging one commodity with a future in a second commodity is called cross hedging. Cross hedging only works if there is a high correlation between the price movements of both commodities. The Chicago Mercantile Exchange has done a correlation study between T-Bill futures and 13-week CDs and found them to be highly correlated (r = .854). (See page 18 of *Opportunities in Interest Rates: Treasury Bill Futures*, published by the Chicago Mercantile Exchange.) One should be cautioned, however, that this correlation does not hold for all periods as illustrated by the example in Table 3.

figures show that the CD rate did indeed go up, and the bank was forced to issue the CDs at 8.88% instead of the 8.25% prevailing in the market when the issue decision was made. This interest rate shift cost the bank $15,750 over the 90-day life of the CD issue. Fortunately, this risk was hedged, and the movement of the T-Bill futures paralleled the CD rate movement. December futures went from 7.66% to 8.34% giving the bank a profit of $17,000 before commission and approximately $16,400 after commission which more than offset the extra cost of issuing the CDs.

The fact that the CD yields and T-Bill futures yields didn't move exactly the same amount reflects basis risk, that is, the fact that the two yield series are not perfectly correlated. The basis is simply the difference in price (rate) between a current or anticipated asset or liability and a futures contract in a given month. The profit made on this trade (17,000 − 15,750 = 1,250) was caused by a narrowing of the spread between the CD market and the T-Bill market from 8.25% − 7.66% = .59% to 8.88% − 8.34% = .54%. This difference is the basis and is a key element in hedging.[5] Table 3 shows what happens if the basis widens while the hedge is in effect.

Situation 2: Asset Management—Short Hedge

In reviewing the bank's projected loan demand schedule, the loan committee has concluded that the bank will need to sell $1 million's worth of Treasury notes from its investment portfolio to meet this demand. If the committee's projections are correct, the funds will be needed at the end of January or about three months from now.

The notes selected for sale are 6¾% three-year Treasury notes that were purchased two years ago for $992,500 to yield 7.03%. The committee perceives the problems in this note sale as twofold. If the bank sells the bonds today, it will lose the income from the notes over the next three months. Furthermore, by selling the notes now, the bank will have to report a capital loss of $15,000 this year on the notes since they are currently selling at $977,500 to yield 8.67%. The alternative is to wait three months until the funds are needed to sell the notes. However, the committee fears interest rates will be even higher, and the capital loss will exceed what it currently is.

This situation is ideal for an asset management hedge, the mechanics of which are presented in Table 4. As the bank feared, the T-Note rate increased from 8.67% to 9.02% in the ensuing three months. The calculations in Table 4 show this increase would have cost the bank $3,250 in price depreciation. Since the decision was hedged, the bank gained $5,500 in the futures market which more than made up for the loss on the notes.

This hedge shows that the bank was able to keep the notes for three additional months thereby earning an additional $16,875 in interest income. At the same time, the risk of principal loss was lessened. If rates had turned around and started down after the hedge was placed, the futures transaction would have resulted in a loss. However, the loss would have been somewhat

---

[5] The total risk caused by price movements is reduced to the risk of basis movement for the hedger. The remaining risk is assumed by the speculator.

Table 2—Situation 1: Liability Management—Short Hedge
A Hedged Certificate of Deposit Issue

	CD Market Events		T-Bill Futures Market	
Sept. 5, 1978	Bank decides to issue $10 million in 90-day CD's on Oct. 5, 1978.		To hedge the risk of rising interest rates the bank sells 10^a contracts or $10 million of Dec. 78^b 90-day T-Bill	
	Current Sept. 5 CD Rate:	8.25%	futures^c at:	92.34 (7.66%)
Oct. 5, 1978	Bank issues the $10 million in 90-day CD's at the prevailing market rate:	8.88%	Bank closes out^d its hedge by buying 10 Dec. 78 T-Bill futures contracts at:	91.66 (8.34%)
	Yield loss due to rate increase in the CD market .63%		Yield gain on futures due to increase in T-Bill rate .68%	
	Dollar Cost of increase $\frac{90}{360} \times .0063 \times \$10,000,000 = \$15,750$		Dollar Gain from increase^e $\frac{90}{360} \times .0068 \times \$10,000,000 = \$17,000^f$	

^{a}A T-Bill futures contract calls for delivery of 90-day U.S. Treasury bills having a face value at maturity of $1,000,000.

^{b}T-Bill futures contracts are only sold for delivery in March, June, September and December. When a hedge is placed it is most effective when it is placed in the nearest contract month after the CD's will be issued.

^{c}T-Bill futures are quoted by subtracting the yield from 100%. This is done to put interest rate futures quotes on a similar basis as other commodities. Since, when interest rates rise, bond prices fall, you have an inverse relationship between prices and interest rate quotes. By stating the quote in its complementary form (one hundred minus the interest rate percentage), quotes and prices move in the same direction. The quote of 92.34 means an interest rate of 7.66%. It is also important to note that 92.34 is not the selling price for the 90 T-Bills. This price is determined by the following equation:

$\$1,000,000 - \frac{(\text{day to maturity} \times \text{T-bill yield} \times 1,000,000)}{360}$ = actual issue price

or in this example:

$\$1,000,000 - \frac{(90 \times .0766 \times 1,000,000)}{360}$ = \$980,850

^{d}In hedging you must remember that futures contracts are commitments to perform and not like options that will expire if left alone. Thus when you conclude the transaction in the CD market, you still have a commitment in the futures market. This commitment is easily offset (cancelled) by purchasing 10 Dec. T-Bill futures contracts.

^{e}A simpler way to calculate the gain or loss on a T-Bill futures contract is to know that one basis "point" (one-hundredth of a percent) equals exactly $25 in price movement per contract (68 points x $25 = $17,000).

^{f}This example does not consider commission costs on the 10 futures contracts. Commission costs are negotiable but could probably be estimated at $60 per contract. Commodity commissions cover both buying and selling (a round turn) the contract.

offset by the gain (smaller than expected loss) on the sale of the notes. In any case, the bank had protected itself from having to sell the notes sooner than desired and from further capital depreciation. Of additional concern to this example is the thin volume of trading in the one-year T-Bill futures mar-

Table 3—Liability Management—Short Hedge
A Hedged Certificate of Deposit Issue*

CD Market Events		T-Bill Futures Market	
Sept. 21, 1978	Bank decides to issue $10 million in 90-day CDs on Oct. 26, 1978 Current Sept. 21 CD rate:	8.65%	To hedge the risk of rising interest rates the bank sells 10 contracts of December 78 T-Bill futures at:	91.84
	Bank issues the $10 million in 90-day CDs at the prevailing market rate:	9.625%	Bank closes out its hedge by buying 10 December 78 futures at:	91.61
	Yield loss due to rate increase in the CD market	.975	Yield gain on futures due to increase in T-Bill rate	.23
	Dollar cost of increase $\frac{90}{360} \times .00975 \times \$10,000,000 = \$24,375$		Dollar gain from increase $\frac{90}{360} \times .0023 \times \$10,000,000 = \$5,750$	

* This example shows a short hedge that is not nearly as nice as the one in Table 2. The hedge is still valuable, but it can be seen that CD rates increased much faster than T-Bill rates. In this example, the basis (difference between the CD yield and the T-Bill yield) widened instead of narrowed as it did in Table 2. This basis variation is due mainly to the imperfect correlation between CD rates and T-Bill rates.

ket which may cause poor trade execution. However, as financial futures trading increases, this problem may be alleviated.

Two more examples of asset management hedges are presented on pages 398 and 399. Table 5 presents a long hedge which would have been used had the bank been faced with projected liquidity increases. In this case, the bank may want to preserve the prevailing high interest rate for those funds. Table 6 presents a T-Bond hedge which would be used if the securities to be sold were long-term instead of intermediate-term notes.

Situation 3: Lending Policy Management—Short Hedge

As financial futures acceptance increases, a bank should also be aware of possible customer uses. Consider the following example.

Your bank has extended a $5 million line of credit to one of its customers at a rate of prime plus 1%. The customer does not plan to use $1 million of the line of credit for about six months and is concerned that the prime rate may rise in the interim. To hedge such a risk, the customer, with the bank's assistance, could place and manage a short hedge in T-Bill futures. In that way, if interest rates rise, the customer's increased cost of borrowing should be offset to some extent by a profit from the short futures position. For example, the hedge could work as is shown in Table 7.

In this example, the prime rate increased 100 basis points before the $1 million of the credit line was borrowed. Table 7 shows that this increase would cost the borrower $10,000 over a one-year period. However, the hedge protected the borrower by reflecting this interest rate increase and giving the

Table 4—Situation 2: Asset Management—Short Hedge
A Hedged Treasury Note Sale

	Cash T-Note Market		T-Bill Futures Market	
Oct. 31, 1978	Bank decides to sell $1 million worth of T-notes (original price $992,500) in 3 months time. These notes have 15 months left to maturity and are currently priced to yield:	8.67%	To hedge the risk of rising interest rates the bank sells 4[a] March 79 contracts at:	91.55 (8.45)
Jan. 22, 1979	The bank sells $1 million worth of T-notes [b] at a price to yield: or $978,750	9.02%	The bank closes out its hedge by buying 4 March 79 1-year T-Bill futures at:	91.00 (9.00)
	Yield loss due to rate increase on the notes	.35%	Yield gain on futures due to increas in 1 year T-bill futures rate	.55%
	Dollar Cost of increase[c]	$3,250	Dollar Gain from increase[d] $\frac{360}{360}$ x .55% x 1,000,000 =	$5,500

[a]A 1 year T-Bill futures contract represents $250,000 at maturity.

[b]There are some additional risks in using the 1 year T-Bill market in that it is thinly traded. This lack of market activity may cause poorer trade executions and more price fluctuation than found in the other interest rate futures markets.

[c]When working with longer term bonds it must be remembered that even if interest rates remain constant the bond's price will vary over time. Discount bond prices will rise and premium bond prices will fall to par. Therefore, the $1,000,000 in notes discounted to $977,500 to yield 8.67% would have increased in value to $982,000 over the three month period if it still carried a 8.67% yield for a gain of $4,500 ($982,000-$977,500).

However, since the yield curve shifted upward, the bonds now offer a yield of 9.02 and are priced at $978,750. The loss on holding the notes then is the difference between what the price would have been, $982,000, and the actual price $978,750 which is $3,250.

The banks total capital loss on the notes is $13,750 which is the $992,500 purchase price minus the $978,750 selling price. This loss can be divided into two segments of $10,500 which is attributable to events that transpired before the decision to sell ($992,500-982,000) and $3,250 which is attributable to events which occurred after the sell decision ($982,000-978,750).

[d]The gain in futures, $5,500, exceeded the loss in the cash market, $3,250, because the basis between the cash T-note market and the T-Bill futures market (8.67-8.45=.22) narrowed over the three month period (9.02-9.00=.02). If the basis would have widened over this period the hedge would not have protected the full loss in the cash market.

borrower a $10,000 gain. It should again be pointed out that if interest rates fell, money would be lost in the futures, but this would be reflected in a lower cost of borrowing.

Table 5—Asset Management—Long Hedge
A Hedged T-Bill Purchase*

Your bank anticipates a reduction in business loan demand in about six months. As a result of the weak demand, the bank plans to invest $5 million in one-year T-Bills. To hedge against a potential decline in interest rates between now and six months from now when the bills are purchased, and hence a loss in interest earnings on the bills, the bank could buy one-year T-Bill futures. If rates do fall, the decline in earnings on the T-Bill investment would be offset by a gain on the futures transaction. For example, this hedge could work as follows:

	Cash T-Note Market		T-Bill Futures Market	
Oct. 1, 1978	Bank anticipates weak loan demand and hence a $5 million one-year investment. Current rate is:	8.20%	Bank buys $5 million of June 79 one-year T-Bill futures at 8.50%, or:	91.50
May 1, 1979	Bank invests $5 million in bills maturing 4/29/80 at:	7.85%	Bank sells $5 million of June 79 one-year T-Bill futures at:	91.85
	Yield loss due to rate increase:	.35%	Yield gain on futures due to rate increase:	.35%

Results of Hedge		Results of Hedge	
Invest $5 million in one-year (52 week) T-Bills at 8.20%; earnings are:	$414,555.56	Buy $5 million of one-year T-Bill futures at 91.50 (8.50%); value is:	$4,575,000.00
Invest $5 million in one-year (52 week) T-Bills at 7.85%; earnings are:	396,861.11	Sell $5 million of one-year T-Bill futures at 91.85 (8.15%); value is:	4,592,500.00
Interest opportunity loss:	$ 17,694.45	Profit:	$ 17,500.00

*The key to the effectiveness of the hedge is the stability of the relationship between cash market rates on one-year T-Bills and futures market rates on one-year T-Bills. A strong correlation between rate movements in the two markets provides the hedger with more certainty as to the outcome of the hedge transaction. In this example, we assumed that the rates in the two markets were perfectly correlated and that the 30 basis point spread remained constant. This resulted in a "perfect" hedge. (The hedger must realize, however, that hedges are rarely perfect.) If the spread had narrowed, the hedge would have been more effective, as the futures market gain would have offset more of the cash market loss. If the spread had widened, the opposite effect would result.

Table 6—Asset Management—Short Hedge
A Hedged Treasury Bonds Sale

	Cash T-Bond Market	T-Bond Futures Market
Oct. 17, 1978	Bank decides to sell $1 million worth of 8¼'s, 1990 May T-Bonds (originally pur-chased on 3/31/75 for $100.06[b] to yield 8.23%) in 3 months time. These bonds have 12½ years left to maturity and are currently priced at 97.22 to yield 8.53%	To hedge the risk of rising interest rates the bank sells 10[c] March 79 contracts of 15 year T-Bond futures at 93.07[d] yielding 8.74% 93.07
Jan. 19, 1978	The bank sells $1 million worth of T-Bonds at a price of 94.12 to yield 9.02%	The bank closes out its hedge by buying 10 March 79 15 year T-Bond futures at 90.15 yielding 9.039 90.15
	Yield loss due to rate increase .49%	Yield gain on futures due to increase in T-Bond futures rate. (9.039 - 8.74%) .299% Point gain[e] 88 points
	Dollar cost of increase $33,125	Dollar gain from increase[f] $27,500

[a]In this example the bank had purchased T-Bonds with long maturities. The hedging vehicle would need to be the T-Bond market instead of the T-Bill market since the higher the correlation between the cash market and the futures market the greater the reliability obtainable in the hedge.

[b]Bid prices are used in this example. 100.06 means 100 and 6/32nds of face value.

[c]A T-Bond futures contract represents an agreement to deliver a 15 year, 8% T-Bond worth $100,000 at maturity.

[d]T-Bond futures are quoted in 32nds. This quote is 93 and 7/32nds. Furthermore, it should be noted that T-Bond futures are actual prices and not the complement of the yield as is done in T-Bill futures.

[e]Calculated: 93 and 7/32nds - 90 and 15/32nds = 2 and 24/32nds or 88/32nds. Value points of 1/32nd in T-Bond futures represent a $31.25 gain or loss in the value of the contract.

[f]This gain can be calculated in two manners.
(1) Using the value point system:
   88 points at 31.25 each equals $2,750 per contract times 10 contracts equals $27,500.
(2) Calculating the T-Bond values:
   93.07 = 93,218.75 x 10 contracts = $932,187.50
   90.15 = 90,468.75 x 10 contracts = $904,687.50
                Subtracting $ 27,500.00

Table 7—Situation 3: Lending Policy—Short Hedge
Hedging Variable Loan Rate Exposure

Commercial Lending Market		T-Bill Futures Market	
Oct. 21, 1977	The bank's customer plans to use $1 million of its $5 million line of credit six months from now at prime + 1%. The borrowing rate is: 10.75%	The bank's customer sells $1 million of June 79 one-year T-Bill futures, to hedge an interest rate increase, at:	91.75 (8.25%)
Apr. 23, 1978	The bank's customer borrows $1 million against its line of credit. The prime rate is 10.75%, so the bank's customer borrows $1 million at: 11.75%	The bank's customer buys $1 million of June 79 one-year T-Bill futures to offset its short position at:	90.75 (9.25%)

Results of Hedge		Results of Hedge	
Borrow $1 million at annual rate of 11.75%; annual cost is:	$117,500	Sell $1 million of one-year T-Bill futures at 91.75 (8.75%); value is:	$912,500
Borrow $1 million at annual rate of 10.75%; annual cost is:	107,500	Buy $1 million of one-year T-Bill futures at 90.75 (9.75%); value is:	902,500
Interest Expense Increase:	$ 10,000	Profit (ignoring commissions):	$ 10,000

Situation 4: Asset Management—Hedged Yield Curve Ride

Bank portfolio managers have frequently been said to be riding the yield curve to higher profits. This statement means they purchase Treasury bills with maturities longer than their planned holding periods and consequently sell them before maturity when they need the funds. They do this to capitalize on the natural up trend in yields as time-to-maturity increases.

For example, a bank manager has a million dollars in excess funds. He knows these funds will be needed in 60 days' time. By looking over the T-Bill market, he sees he has two options. One, he can buy 60-day T-Bills paying a 7% discount for $988,333. Or two, he can buy 120-day T-Bills paying an 8% discount for $973,333 and then sell them at the end of 60 days. If he buys the 60-day T-Bills, he will earn $11,667 for an equivalent annual yield of 7.18%.[6] However, if he assumes the yield curve will not shift over the next

[6]To determine the T-Bills' actual issue price, use:

$$\$1,000,000 - \frac{(\text{days to maturity} \times \text{T-Bill yield} \times \$1,000,000)}{360}$$

Table 8—Situation 4: Asset Management
Hedging the Yield Curve Ride

100
Decision Date: July 21, 1978

Date Funds Needed:
September 21, 1978

Alternative 1: 7/21/78 Buy:	Standard T-Bill Purchase 9/21/78 T-Bill, hold till maturity Discount (61-day T-Bills) Purchase Price	6.70% $ 988,647	
9/21/78 Tender:	Terminal Value	$1,000,000	
	Gain	$ 11,353	
	Equivalent Yield	6.87%	
Alternative 2: 7/21/78 Buy:	Straight Yield Curve Ride 12/21/78 T-Bill, sell 9/21/78 Discount (152-day T-Bill) Purchase Price	7.26% $969,347	
9/21/78 Sell:	91-day Discount @ 9/21/78 Sale Price	8.13% $979,675	
	Gain	$ 10,328	
	Equivalent Yield	6.38%	
Alternative 3: 7/21/78 Buy:	Hedged Yield Curve Ride 12/21/78 T-Bill and hedge interest rate risk Discount (152-day T-Bill) Purchase Price	7.26% $969,347	
	Sell September T-Bill future		$92.61
9/21/78 Sell:	Discount (91-day T-Bill) Sale Price	8.13% $979,675	
	Buy September T-Bill future[a]		$91.87
	Gain on T-Bill Sale Gain on Futures (74 points @ $25)	$ 10,328	$1,850
	Total Gain	$ 12,178	
	Equivalent Yield over 60 days[b]	7.52%	

[a] It is possible to deliver the actual T-Bills owned to cancel the futures contract. Delivery can only be made if the T-Bills have a 90, 91, or 92-day life which will not fit all the general cases of yield curve rides. Furthermore, if the Banker can't plan on delivering against the futures contract, he would be better served by using the Dec. T-Bill contract month. This will eliminate the various difficulties encountered by holding an open contract in the delivery month.

[b] Hedged yield curve rides only work advantageously when the futures yield curve is upward sloping.

To determine the T-Bills' equivalent bond yield, use:

$$\frac{\text{(T-Bill face value}-\text{actual issue price)}}{\text{actual issue price}} \times \frac{365}{\text{days to maturity}}$$

six months (or interest rates won't rise), he will be able to buy the 120-day T-Bill for $973,330. He can hold the T-Bill for 60 days and then sell it for $988,333 to earn $15,000 for an equivalent annual yield of 9.38%.

This hypothetical example of riding the yield curve is very exciting except for one point: The yield curve can shift, and, if it's upward, it can make yield curve riding risky.

Riding the yield curve can be risky, but a hedged ride can reduce the risk considerably. The example shown in Table 8 portrays with actual data an unhedged yield curve ride that turned sour but would have been profitable had it been hedged.

Table 8 portrays a situation in which a banker has funds which can be invested for a 60-day period. The banker has three alternatives to follow in investing these funds. The first alternative is to buy a T-Bill with a 61-day maturity. This decision would have netted the banker a 6.87% equivalent bond yield over the 60-day period.

The second alternative available to the banker is to ride the yield curve by buying a 152-day T-Bill, holding it for 60 days, and then selling it. This procedure was shown in the previous discussion to be profitable if yields don't shift upward. In this example, yields did indeed shift upward causing actual T-Bill prices to fall below expectations. When the T-Bill was sold, the bank's equivalent bond yield calculates out to be 6.38%. This is considerably below what could have been obtained in Alternative 2.

The banker could have hedged the yield curve ride as is shown in Alternative 3. When the 152-day T-Bill is purchased, a September T-Bill futures contract is sold. At the end of 60 days, the T-Bill with 92 days of remaining life can be delivered against the open futures contract or, as in this example, sold in the open market. In this case, the equivalent bond yield for the 60-day holding period is 7.52% which is substantially above the resulting yields with the other two alternatives.

BIBLIOGRAPHY

1. *An Introduction to Interest Rate Futures Markets*, 1st Revised Edition. February 1978, The Chicago Board of Trade.
2. Duncan, Wallace H. "Treasury Bill Futures—Opportunities and Pitfalls." *Review*, Federal Reserve Bank of Dallas, July 1977, pp. 1-5.
3. *Hedging Interest Rate Risk*, 1st Revised Edition. September 1977, The Chicago Board of Trade.
4. *Opportunities in Interest Rates: Treasury Bill Futures*. November 1977, Chicago Mercantile Exchange.
5. Yardeni, Edward, "Hedged Rides in the T-Bill Futures Market." *Commodities*, August 1978, pp. 26-27.

LINEAR PROGRAMMING: A NEW APPROACH TO BANK PORTFOLIO MANAGEMENT*

Alfred Broaddus

32

Perhaps the most important and most difficult problem facing any commercial bank's senior management on a continuing basis is asset portfolio management. Portfolio decisions made at any given time directly affect a bank's current income and profits. Moreover, current decisions may significantly influence income and profit flows in future periods. What makes asset selection difficult is that alternative courses of action invariably present trade-offs between profits, liquidity, and risk. Evaluating and weighing these factors is an inherently complex task. The problem has been compounded during recent years by the pressure on commercial banks to maintain adequate profits in the face of increased competition for funds both from nonbank financial institutions and from various money market instruments.

As a result of this increased pressure, the commercial banking industry has begun to seek more sophisticated approaches to portfolio management. Management scientists are assisting the industry by devising improved decision techniques that can be understood and effectively employed by bankers.[1] One technique receiving considerable attention is linear programming. Linear programming is a basic analytical procedure, or "model," employed exten-

*Reprinted from the *Monthly Review*, November 1972, pp. 3-11, with permission from the Federal Reserve Bank of Richmond and the author.

[1] Two management scientists, Kalman J. Cohen and Frederick S. Hammer, have been instrumental in this effort. Their published work in this area, on which the present article draws extensively, is listed in the accompanying references.

sively in management science and operations research. Although the theory underlying the technique involved advanced mathematics, the model's structure is straightforward and can be understood by management personnel having only minimal training in mathematics. The purpose of this article is to describe the technique in a nonmathematical manner and to indicate how it can be used in the bank portfolio management process. Section I outlines two currently popular approaches to asset management and points out some of their principal deficiencies. Section II describes the linear programming model and uses a highly simplified numerical example to indicate the model's applicability to bank portfolio decisions. Section III discusses how banks might employ the model in practice and attempts to suggest the model's proper role in the overall portfolio decision process. Section IV summarizes the technique's advantages in banking applications and points out some of its limitations.

I. CURRENT APPROACHES

The typical bank's balance sheet lists a variety of assets and liabilities. Liabilities, such as demand and savings deposits, are sources of bank funds. Assets, such as business loans, consumer installment loans, and government securities, are uses of bank funds. The essence of the asset management problem is the need to achieve a proper balance between (1) income, (2) adequate liquidity to meet such contingencies as unanticipated loan demand and deposit withdrawals, and (3) the risk of default. The problem arises because assets carrying relatively high yields, such as consumer installment loans, are generally less liquid and riskier than assets having relatively low yields, such as short-term government securities.

The "Pooled-Funds" Approach. During the early postwar period, funds were generally available to banks in ample supply at low cost. Consequently, most banks followed what has been termed a "pooled-funds" approach in deciding how to allocate funds among competing assets. Under the pooled-funds concept, a bank begins its asset selection procedure by arbitrarily defining a fixed liquidity standard, usually some target ratio of reserves and secondary reserve assets to total deposits. Using this standard, the bank then allocates each dollar it attracts, from whatever source, in identical proportions among various categories of assets. A principal deficiency of this procedure is its failure to take into account variations in liquidity needs that arise from variations in the structure of liability and loan accounts.[2]

---

[2]The "structure" of an individual bank's liabilities refers to the proportionate allocation of total funds among various liability categories such as demand deposits, savings deposits, and certificates of deposit. Similarly, the structure of a bank's loan accounts refers to the allocation of total loans among various classes of loans.

The "Asset Allocation" Technique. The pooled-funds approach served most banks reasonably well during the late 1940's and early 1950's when funds were relatively plentiful and the majority of bank liabilities were non-interest-bearing demand deposits. Since that time, the financial environment in which banks operate has changed dramatically. Nonbank financial institutions, particularly savings and loan associations and mutual savings banks, began to compete vigorously with individual commercial banks for deposits during the 1950's. In addition, corporate treasurers, motivated by sharp increases in the yields of such money market instruments as Treasury bills and high-grade commercial paper, began to trim their working balances held in commercial bank demand deposits to bare minimums. The banking industry has responded to these deposit drains by developing new sources of funds, notably negotiable certificates of deposit, commercial paper issued through affiliates, and Eurodollar borrowings. While these innovations have permitted the banking industry to grow at an adequate rate, they have proved costly, resulting in increased pressure on bank profits. Therefore, a premium has been placed on efficient bank balance sheet management.

The management tool developed to meet the need for more sophisticated portfolio management was the so-called Asset Allocation technique.[3] The distinguishing feature of this procedure is that it takes explicit account of a bank's liability structure in guiding asset choice. More specifically, the Asset Allocation approach recognizes that the velocity of various types of liabilities differs systematically from one liability category to another.[4] The procedure specifies that funds obtained from liabilities with rapid turnover rates (such as demand deposits) should be invested relatively heavily in assets of short maturity, and, conversely, that funds obtained from low velocity liabilities (such as certificates of deposit) should be invested relatively heavily in long-term assets. In its most extreme form, the technique divides a bank into subsystems by liability classes: for example, a "demand deposit bank," a "time deposit bank," and a "Eurodollars bank." Funds flowing into each of these "banks," that is, funds obtained from each liability source, are then allocated proportionately among alternative assets using formulas that reflect liability velocities. For example, the demand deposit formula might specify relatively high proportions of short-term government securities and short-term business loans, while the time deposit formula might specify a relatively high proportion of mortgages.

Faced with an ever-widening range of diverse sources of funds, many bank portfolio managers have adopted the Asset Allocation approach because of its explicit attention to asset-liability linkages. But while the method represents an improvement over earlier procedures, it possesses several fundamen-

---

[3] The Asset Allocation or "conversion of funds" procedure was originally devised by Harold E. Zarker. See Harold E. Zarker, *Conversion of Commercial Bank Funds* (Cambridge, Massachusetts: Bankers Publishing Company, 1942).

[4] The velocity of a given liability account is the ratio of the dollar flow within that account during some specified time period to the average stock of dollars in the account during the same period. The reciprocal of velocity is then the length of time an average dollar remains in the account.

tal weaknesses.[5] First, velocity is a poor guide to the liquidity requirements imposed by a given class of liabilities. A far more relevant consideration is account stability, that is, the net daily variation of an account's total balance. It is widely recognized that no correlation necessarily exists between stability and velocity.[6] Second, the technique is arbitrary and inflexible. It is arbitrary because no clearly-defined bank goal (such as some form of constrained profit maximization) guides the determination of the various fund conversion formulas. It is inflexible because no systematic procedure is provided for altering the formulas in the face of changing external conditions, such as shifts in particular asset yields. Third, by compartmentalizing a bank into various subsystems, the method diverts attention from the overall goals of the bank's operations and fails to recognize important interactions between various bank activities. The linear programming approach described below avoids these difficulties.

II. THE LINEAR PROGRAMMING MODEL: AN EXAMPLE

Linear programming is a general mathematical procedure for maximizing target variables subject to constraints.[7] The linear programming model has been extensively applied in industrial production analysis, where the objective typically is to maximize profits by achieving the proper product mix within the constraints imposed by technical production procedures, resource availability, and resource costs. This section presents a simple numerical example designed to illustrate how the model can be used by bank portfolio managers. The example employs a set of graphs to assist readers unfamiliar with the model in grasping the essence of the technique's substantive content. While graphs are a useful explanatory device, their employment restricts the scope of the illustration. Consequently, the example is a necessarily artificial and unrealistic representation of the actual portfolio decision process. Nonetheless, the illustration conveys the flavor of the technique and demonstrates its applicability to bank balance sheet decisions.

Consider a hypothetical bank that holds two classes of liabilities, demand deposits (DD) and time deposits (TD), and that can choose between two classes of assets, loans (L) and securities (S). Hence, the bank's balance sheet takes the following form:

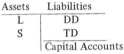

Assets	Liabilities
L	DD
S	TD
	Capital Accounts

[5] For a more extensive critique, see Kalman J. Cohen and Frederick S. Hammer, ed., *Analytical Methods in Banking* (Homewood, Illinois: Richard D. Irwin, Inc., 1966), pp. 45-53.

[6] See George R. Morrison and Richard T. Selden, *Time Deposit Growth and the Employment of Bank Funds* (Chicago: Association of Reserve City Bankers, 1965), p. 12.

[7] A comprehensive treatment of linear programming is contained in G. Hadley, *Linear Programming* (Reading, Massachusetts: Addison-Wesley Publishing Company, Inc., 1962).

Assume that the rate of return on loans is 10 percent during some relevant decision period, but that no loan matures and no loan can be sold during the period. Assume further that securities yield 5 percent during the period and can be liquidated at any time without the risk of capital loss. Total funds available to the bank are fixed at, say, $100 million, distributed as follows: $45 million in demand deposit accounts, $45 million in time deposit accounts, and $10 million in capital and surplus. Finally, assume for illustrative simplicity that the bank incurs no costs in attracting and maintaining deposits.

The bank would like to select an asset portfolio that maximizes its total return over the period. If this were all that were involved, the optimal asset selection decision would be obvious: channel all available funds into loans, the asset yielding the higher return. The bank recognizes, however, certain constraints upon its actions. In reality, the constraints are numerous. The present example will consider three.

Total Funds Constraint. As indicated above, the bank has $100 million to allocate between loans and securities. Consequently, the sum of its loan and securities balances cannot exceed $100 million. This constraint can be expressed mathematically as:

(1) $$L + S \leqslant 100 \text{ million}$$

where the symbol $\leqslant$ means "less than or equal to."[8] Chart 1 depicts this restriction graphically. Any point on the graph represents some combination

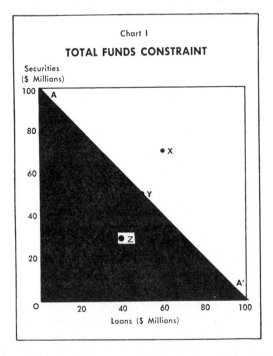

Chart I

TOTAL FUNDS CONSTRAINT

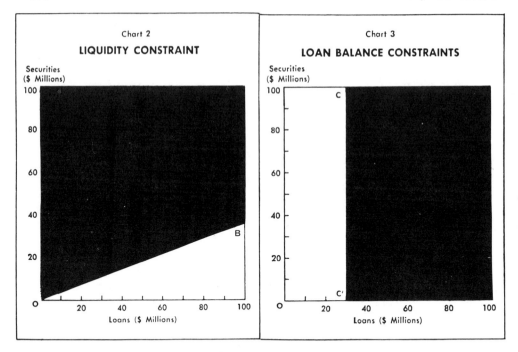

of loans and securities. For example, point X corresponds to a loan balance of $60 million and a securities balance of $70 million. The diagonal line AA' (the graphical representation of the equation L + S = 100 million) is the locus of points at which loans and securities total $100 million. At point Y, for example, the loan balance is $50 million, the securities balance is $50 million, and total assets are therefore $100 million. At any point above and to the right of line AA', such as X, total assets exceed $100 million. At any point below and to the left of AA', such as Z, total assets are less than $100 million. The total funds constraint requires that the point representing the bank's asset portfolio either fall on AA' or within the shaded region below and to the left of AA'.[9]

Liquidity Constraint. The bank recognizes that, because loans cannot be liquidated during the time period under consideration, some quantity of negotiable securities must be held to meet unanticipated deposit withdrawals. Therefore, the bank makes it a rule always to maintain some minimum ratio of securities to total assets. Assume that, with $45 million of demand deposits and $45 million of time deposits, the bank always maintains a securities balance equal to or greater than 25 percent of total assets. The mathematical expression for this constraint is:

[9] Strictly, with total funds equal to $100 million, the balance sheet identity requires that L + S equal exactly $100 million, that is, that the point representing the bank's asset portfolio fall *on* line AA'. For the purpose of illustrating the linear programming technique, it is helpful to treat the constraint as an inequality rather than an equality. This deviation will not affect the example's solution.

(2) $$S \geq .25 \, (L + S),$$

or equivalently and more conveniently, as:

(3) $$S \geq .33 \, (L).$$

Constraint (3) is depicted graphically by Chart 2. It requires that the bank's asset portfolio fall on line OB or at some point in the shaded region above the line.

On the presumption that time deposits are generally more stable than demand deposits, the bank's management varies its liquidity ratio inversely with shifts in the ratio of time to total deposits. Hence, an increase in the ratio would cause line OB to rotate downward, thereby enlarging the shaded area of acceptable portfolio. Conversely, a reduction in the ratio would rotate OB upward, diminishing the area of acceptable portfolios. The effects of such shifts will be considered below.

Loan Balance Constraint. Because the bank considers lending its most important activity, it imposes certain restrictions on its loan balance. Specifically, the bank attempts to satisfy all of the requests for loans submitted by its principal customers. Assume that the aggregate demand of these customers totals $30 million during the period. This constraint is depicted by Chart 3. The restriction requires the bank's portfolio to fall on or to the right of line CC'. The mathematical statement of the constraint is:

(4) $$L \geq 30 \text{ million.}$$

The Feasible Region. The three constraints just outlined are all relevant when the bank's management meets to allocate available funds between loans and securities. Chart 4 shows how the constraints taken as a group restrict the bank's range of choice. Any asset portfolio represented by a point outside the shaded region EFG violates one or more of the constraints. Conversely, any portfolio represented by a point within or on one of the boundaries of this region satisfies all of the constraints. Therefore, the portfolio selected must lie within the region or on one of its boundaries. For this reason, the area is called the "feasible region."

The Objective Function. The reader will recall the assumption that loans yield 10 percent and securities 5 percent during the relevant time period. Consequently, the bank's total income during the period equals 10 percent of its loan balance plus 5 percent of its securities balance.[10] Mathematically:

(5) $$\text{Income} = .10 \, (L) + .05 \, (S).$$

[10] For simplicity, the possibility of loan default is ignored.

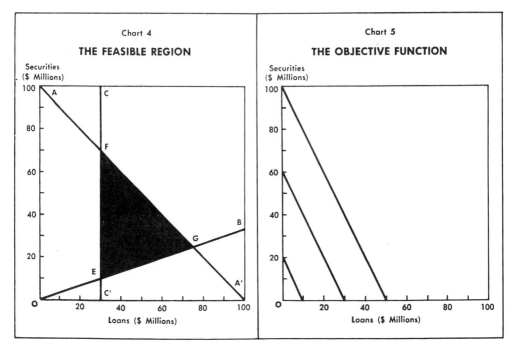

Chart 4

THE FEASIBLE REGION

Chart 5

THE OBJECTIVE FUNCTION

Expression 5 is called the objective function of the linear programming problem. Chart 5 depicts the "family" of objective functions represented by equation 5. Each member of the family, that is, each of the parallel lines on the graph, corresponds to some unique income level. On the graph, the line closest to point 0 corresponds to income of $1 million, the middle line to income of $3 million, and the outermost line to income of $5 million.[11] Hence, the bank's income increases as the objective function shifts upward and to the right.

The Optimal Asset Portfolio. All of the elements relevant to the bank's portfolio decision have now been developed. The linear programming problem is summarized by the following mathematical statement:

(6)   Maximize income = .10 (L) + .05 (S)

Subject to:

$$L + S \leq 100 \text{ million}$$
$$S \geq .33 (L)$$
$$L \geq 30 \text{ million.}$$

---

[11] The reader can easily confirm that *any* point on one of these lines represents a portfolio that yields the designated income.

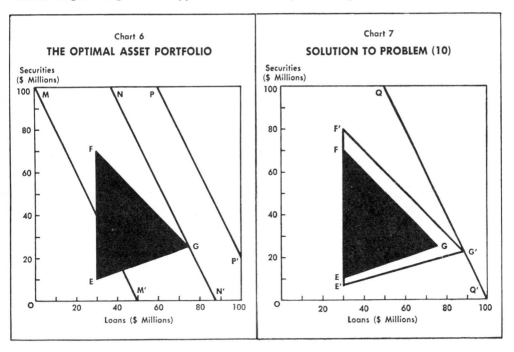

The solution to the problem is depicted graphically by Chart 6, which reproduces the feasible region of Chart 4 along with several members of equation 5's family of objective functions. From what has been said, it should be clear that the bank can find its income-maximizing portfolio by pushing the objective function outward as far as possible without going beyond the point where some part of the function lies within the feasible region. Clearly, the income-maximizing objective function in this case in line NN'. This line barely touches the feasible region at point G. Any line to the right of NN', such as PP', lies entirely outside the feasible region. Lines to the left of NN', such as MM', may contain points within the feasible region but correspond to income levels less than that represented by NN'. The solution to the problem is given by point G. The bank can maximize its income, while observing all constraints, by choosing the combination of loans and securities represented by point G: that is, by allocating \$75 million to loans and \$25 million fo securities.[12] This portfolio would yield \$8.75 million of income during the period. The linear programming model has provided the bank an objective procedure for determining its optimal portfolio. The model has taken explicit and simultaneous account of the various factors assumed relevant to the decision.

Analytical uses of the Model. The linear programming model can perform a number of useful analytical tasks for the bank in addition to suggesting reasonable approximations to income-maximizing portfolios. In particular, the

[12] For simplicity, the solution values are rounded to the nearest million.

model can specify how the bank's optimal portfolio changes when one of the constraints changes. Through analysis of this sort, the bank can determine the costs, in terms of foregone income, of the various constraints under which it operates. Knowledge of these costs, in turn, can assist the bank in such diverse tasks as deciding how much interest to pay depositors, determining the rate of return on capital, and deciding whether to borrow or lend in the Federal funds market. A simple extension of the above example will serve to illustrate.

It will be recalled that the bank's deposits total $90 million: $45 million of demand deposits and $45 million of time deposits. Imagine that the bank gains access to an additional $10 million of *time* deposits. These additional time deposits affect two of the constraints in problem (6). First, the total funds constraint is eased to:

(7) $L + S \leqslant 100$ million.

Second, it will be recalled that, by assumption, the bank's management varies the minimum ratio of securities to total assets inversely with the ratio of time to total deposits. Assume that, with $55 million of time deposits and $45 million of demand deposits, management considers a 20 percent liquidity ratio constraint adequate. Under these conditions, the restriction becomes:

(8) $S \geqslant .20 (L + S),$

or:

(9) $L \geqslant 30$ million.

With these modifications, the mathematical statement of the bank's problem is changed from (6) to:

(10)   Maximize income $= .10 (L) + .05 (S)$

                      Subject to:

$$L + S \leqslant 110 \text{ million}$$
$$S \geqslant .25 (L)$$
$$S \geqslant 30 \text{ million.}$$

Chart 7 depicts the altered situation graphically. EFG is the feasible region of the preceding problem. $E'F'G'$ is the extended feasible region of the new problem that results from the easing of the total funds and liquidity constraints attendant upon the $10 million increase in time deposits. Point G' represents the solution to the new problem, with the objective function in position QQ'. As indicated by G', the bank's new income-maximizing portfolio contains $88 million of loans and $22 million of securities. Since yields have not changed, the bank's income is now $9.9 million.

The solutions to problems (6) and (10) can assist the bank in determining how much to pay depositors for the $10 million increment of time deposits. Comparing incomes in the two cases, it is clear that the additional deposits produce $1.15 million of additional income ($9.9 million − $8.75 million), or $.115 per additional time deposit dollar. Consequently, the bank can afford to pay up to a rate of 11.5 percent for each additional time deposit dollar.[13] At first glance, management might consider it ridiculous to contemplate incurring additional deposit costs at a rate that exceeds the available return on either loans or securities. The reason it is profitable to do so is that the additional time deposits have both a direct and a secondary effect on the bank's income. The direct effect in this case is the additional income resulting from the investment of the extra funds. The secondary effect is the additional income generated by the reallocation of the bank's original $100 million of funds to a higher proportion of loans made possible by the eased liquidity constraint. The linear programming technique takes account of such secondary effects automatically. This illustration demonstrates the potential usefulness of the comprehensive decision framework that characterizes the model.[14]

III. APPLYING THE MODEL IN PRACTICE

The example presented in the preceding section has conveyed something of the flavor of the linear programming technique. This section builds on the example to describe more fully how the model might be applied to portfolio management in practice. The section concludes with a few remarkes regarding actual use of the technique at one large commercial bank.

Decision Variables and Constraints. The example developed above considered only two decision variables: that is, only two variables over which the bank had direct control. These were the bank's loan and securities balances. In reality, of course, bank balance sheets break assets down into far more detailed categories. (They also show a much wider variety of liabilities than the twofold deposit classification used in the example.) To exploit the model fully, a bank should define as many asset decision variables as there are assets of significantly different yield, liquidity, and risk in its portfolio. The model is capable of handling any number of decision variables. Problems containing more than two or three variables cannot be solved using graphs. Several standardized solution procedures (known as algorithms) exist, however, for solving large problems.[15]

---

[13] It should be emphasized that this conclusion applies only to *additional* time deposits, not to deposits already held. A bank could pay a higher rate for additional deposits by, for example, issuing a new certificate of deposit.

[14] In actual linear programming applications, questions of the sort just discussed are analyzed in a more sophisticated manner, using the so-called "dual" linear program. For an elementary treatment of duality in linear programming, see William J. Baumol, *Economic Theory and Operations Analysis*. 2nd ed. (Englewood Cliffs, New Jersey: Prentice-Hall, Inc., 1967), pp. 103-28.

[15] The most widely used algorithm is the so-called "simplex" method. See Baumol, *op. cit.*, pp. 82-97.

In addition to handling as many decision variables as necessary, the linear programming model can accommodate as many constraints as bank managers consider relevant to the portfolio decision process. Specifically, detailed and realistic sets of liquidity constraints can be built into the model reflecting liability and capital structures, cash flow patterns, seasonal fluctuations in loan demand, and miscellaneous restrictions imposed by management on the basis of experience.[16] A variety of other constraints are conceivable, taking account of such operating factors as legal reserve requirements, corresponding balances, and the use of certain assets as collateral to support government deposits.

Dynamic Considerations. The Section II illustration was static. That is, the bank's decision process was cast in terms of a single time period. Actual portfolio management is anything but static, and no rational portfolio manager can confine his attention myopically to the present. For example, current portfolios should provide adequate liquidity to accommodate anticipated future loan demand. As a second example, loan decisions in the current period may affect deposit levels in future periods. One of the distinct advantages of the linear programming framework is its capacity to treat such inter-temporal linkages explicitly. In portfolio decision applications, the model can be designed in such a way that it takes account of anticipated future conditions and generates optimal portfolios for several future periods as well as for the current period. The reader should not infer that management would, at some point, use the model to suggest desirable portfolios for, say, the next five quarters, and then slavishly follow the presciptions for each quarter as time passes. Obviously, the model should be updated and solved again as forecasts are superseded by knowledge of actual events. Rather, the value of explicit attention to the future lies in the resulting clarification of the factors relevant to current decisions.

Bank Goals. It was assumed in the illustration that the bank's objective was to maximize gross income during the single time period considered. Obviously, actual banks must define more refined objectives. First, deposit interest and other operating expenses have to be considered. In the terminology of the model, the variable maximized should be net income in some form. The model can easily meet this requirement by treating bank expenses as negative increments in the objective function. Second, if, as suggested earlier, a multiperiod time framework is employed, management must select a means of discounting future income to present value equivalents. A number of alternative procedures are available, any of which can be explicitly incorpor-

---

[16] In their pioneering application of the linear programming method to bank portfolio management, Chambers and Charnes developed a detailed system of capital adequacy-liquidity constraints using some of the bank examination criteria employed by the Federal Reserve System. See D. Chambers and A. Charnes, "Inter-Temporal Analysis and Optimization of Bank Portfolios," *Management Science, 7* (July 1961), 393-410.

ated in the model.[17] The model cannot itself select an objective; however, the model forces management to define some operating goal. Moreover, the model is structured in such a way that each specific portfolio decision has a definite quantitative effect on the goal variable and can be evaluated on this basis.

Use of the Model at Bankers Trust Company   During the 1960's, a group of management scientists developed a linear programming model at Bankers Trust Company in New York to assist that bank's management in reaching portfolio decisions.[18] The model is quite detailed. It employs a multiperiod decision framework, a large number of balance sheet categories as decision variables, and numerous constraints of the type described above.

Perhaps the most interesting aspect of the Bankers Trust experiment is the role played by the model in the overall decision process. The model has not served in any sense as a substitute for the judgment of management. Rather, its principal function has been to clarify the consequences of alternative decisions. An excellent example is provided by management's use of the model to analyze liquidity ratio constraints.

When the consulting team initially formulated the model, they included no constraint on the ratio of government securities to total assets. The bank's executive management was troubled by this omission. They feared possibly adverse consequences in the market for the bank's stock should the Bankers Trust balance sheet show a much lower ratio than the balance sheets of other large New York banks. Informed of this criticism, the consulting team reformulated the model to include a minimum ratio of 16 percent. Subsequently, the scientists used the model to specify the effects on profits of small reductions in the ratio. The model indicated that quite small reductions could increase profits significantly. Management was unaware of this sensitivity. On the basis of this information, a more flexible policy was adopted.

This experience demonstrates the kind of informative dialogue that can develop between a bank's executives and a team of management scientists using a relatively sophisticated linear programming model. It is precisely in such interchanges that the model's value to management lies.

IV. CONCLUSIONS

This article has described the linear programming technique and has indicated how it can be applied to bank balance sheet management decisions. A

---

[17]For a comparative discussion of these alternatives, see Kalman J. Cohen and Frederick S. Hammer, "Linear Programming and Optimal Bank Asset Management Decisions," *The Journal of Finance, 22* (May 1967), 159-62.

[18]Kalman J. Cohen served as a principal consultant in the Bankers Trust project. The following remarks summarize his description of the model and its application. See Cohen, "Dynamic Balance Sheet Management: A Management Science Approach," *Journal of Bank Research, 2* (Winter 1972), 11-18.

few cautionary remarks and a brief summing up are now in order.

Although the linear programming model is a powerful analytical tool, it is in no sense an automatic procedure for generating optimal portfolio decisions. The complex and continually changing conditions faced by banks cannot be fully specified by a set of equations. It is unlikely that any bank will ever know, precisely and definitively, its optimal portfolio at a point in time. At best, techniques such as linear programming can only suggest a range within which the "best" portfolio is likely to fall.

Nor is the model a substitute for the judgment of experienced portfolio managers. While it is unnecessary for executives to understand in detail the mathematical theory underlying the model or its computational procedures, management must be directly involved in the construction and application of any operational model. Specifically, management must define the objectives of the bank's operations so that the model can reflect these objectives. Further, management must specify the constraints it considers relevant to asset selection decisions in order that these constraints can be built into the model. Finally, management must determine the specific questions that the model is used to analyze. In short, the model does not reduce the need for managerial judgment. On the contrary, it challenges that judgment in a very comprehensive manner.

With due attention to the proper role of the model in the decision process, it seems clear that the linear programming approach has several distinct advantages over many alternative asset management tools, such as the Asset Allocation method described earlier. First, the structure of the model forces a bank's management to establish a definite operational objective and provides a convenient framework for considering factors relevant to portfolio choice. Second, the model simultaneously determines each element of a bank's optimal portfolio, given the particular goals and constraints specified by management. Because of its simultaneous approach, the model automatically takes account of trade-offs between decisions with respect to one element of the portfolio and decisions with respect to another element of the portfolio. Third, the model provides a convenient tool for evaluating (1) the comparative consequences of alternative decisions, (2) the effect of alternative constraints on bank profits, and (3) how portfolios should be adjusted when economic and financial conditions change.

The application of linear programming to asset management appears to be one of the more important recent developments in banking.[19] Small banks may find the costs of constructing and operating linear programming models prohibitive. If the technique becomes widespread among larger banks, however, small banks may find themselves exposed to the procedure through the portfolio management services provided by correspondents. Consequently, all bankers should be aware of the technique and its implications.

---

[19] In this regard, it should be pointed out that linear programming is only one, and by no means the most advanced, of the modern quantitative models currently being employed in private industry. It is quite possible that in the future one or several of the other techniques may prove more useful in banking applications than linear programming.

REFERENCES

I.   General Treatments of Linear Programming

Two excellent and relatively nontechnical introductions to linear programming are:

Baumol, William J. *Economic Theory and Operations Analysis.* 2nd ed. Englewood Cliffs, New Jersey: Prentice-Hall, Inc., 1965, pp. 70-128.

Dorfman, Robert, "Mathematical or 'Linear' Programming." *American Economic Review*, 43 (December 1953), 797-825.

Advanced treatments of the technique are:

Gass, Saul. *Linear Programming: Methods and Applications.* New York: McGraw-Hill Book Company, 1958.

Hadley, G. *Linear Programming.* Reading, Massachusetts: Addison-Wesley Publishing Company, Inc., 1962.

II. Applications of Linear Programming to Bank Portfolio Management

Chambers, D. and A. Charnes. "Inter-Temporal Analysis and Optimization of Bank Portfolios." *Management Science, 7* (July 1961), 393-410.

Cohen, Kalman J. "Dynamic Balance Sheet Management: A Management Science Approach." *Journal of Bank Research, 2* (Winter 1972), 9-19.

Cohen, Kalman J. and Frederick S. Hammer. "Linear Programming and Optimal Bank Asset Management Decisions." *The Journal of Finance, 22* (May 1967), 147-65.

Cohen, Kalman J., Frederick S. Hammer, and Howard M. Schneider. "Harnessing Computers for Bank Asset Management." *The Bankers Magazine*, 150 (Summer 1967), 72-80.

Part V
COST AND PROFITABILITY CONCEPTS

The articles in Part V focus on cost and profitability concepts. The first article in this section is by Ronald D. Watson and deals with estimating the cost of bank funds. Watson examines both the historical and marginal cost approaches as well as their financial implications. As he demonstrates, inaccurate estimates result in inappropriate lending or investment decisions with adverse effects on profitability and stockholder returns. One of the tools used as a benchmark for analyzing specific bank costs and profitability is the Functional Cost Analysis of the Federal Reserve Banks. As explained in Paul S. Anderson's article, the Functional Cost Analysis enables management to compare the profit performance of specific bank functions with those of comparable banks. This information has extremely important implications for pricing bank services and activities. In the next article, Robert E. Knight provides a detailed procedure for analyzing the profitability of individual corporate accounts. As Knight demonstrates, determining customer profitability requires a systematic analysis of all aspects of the bank's relationship with the customer.

As pointed out in an earlier article dealing with yield calculations on money market certificates, interest calculations often are a source of confusion for consumers and sometimes bankers. However, since various procedures may be used for both loans and deposits, the problem is not limited to money market certificates. Various interest calculating procedures are summarized in Anne Marie L. Gonczy's article.

The last article in this section is by William F. Ford and Dennis A. Olson. Analyzing Federal Deposit Insurance Corporation Data, the authors provide a financial and statistical profile of the so-called High-Performance Banks. Their purpose was to find the key financial characteristics that distinguish the best-performing banks from all other banks. Thus, the results presented in this article provide a basis for analyzing a bank's overall financial performance and placing it in perspective.

ESTIMATING THE COST OF YOUR BANK'S FUNDS[†]

Ronald D. Watson [*]

33

By the time Franklin National Bank finally succumbed in 1974, it had been assured an honored spot in modern banking theory as the textbook example of how *not* to run a bank. One of Franklin's weaknesses was the incorrect method its management used to estimate the cost of the bank's funds.[1] During a period of high interest rates, the bank consistently underestimated the cost of raising money. In fact, the cost of the money that Franklin borrowed to invest was higher than the return on the investments it was making.

Most bankers are far more sensitive to this problem than Franklin's management was, but being aware of how important it is to know the cost of money and being able to make an accurate estimate of that cost are two very different things. Making good cost estimates takes time and requires a thorough understanding of how investors make their decisions. Further, these estimates must reflect current conditions in the money markets instead of being based on costs in the past; and they must take account of the effect that the bank's choice of a capital structure may have on its cost of funds. Getting an accurate estimate of the cost of funds poses some tough computational problems, but there isn't any other way to find out what rate of return is required to make a profit.

[†]Reprinted from the *Business Review*, May/June 1978, pp. 3-11, with permission from the Federal Reserve Bank of Philadelphia and the author.

[*]Ronald D. Watson is Research Officer, Economist, and Assistant Secretary at the Philadelphia Fed, where he has served since 1971.

[1]Sanford Rose, "What Really Went Wrong at Franklin National," *Fortune* (October 1974), p. 118.

THE OLD WAY:
HISTORICAL AVERAGE COSTS

In the past, the most common method of estimating the cost of a bank's funds was to add together all the net expenses (interest, reserve requirements, and other expenses less service charge income) of borrowing current funds and divide the total by the amount being borrowed. This gave an historical estimate of the average return that had to be earned on assets acquired with these funds for the bank to break even in its investment activities. If the shareholders were to receive a return on the funds they supplied, a profit margin had to be added to this basic historical cost of funds estimate (see Appendix).

But historical costs can be extremely unreliable as a pricing guide if conditions are changing over time. When interest rates are rising, the average cost of funds already obtained will be below the cost of replacing those funds by new borrowing, and the bank may accept new investments it should reject. When rates are dropping, the historical cost of funds will be higher than replacement costs, and the bank may be led to set too high a standard for new investments, passing up opportunities to make profits. Historical estimates can be unreliable also when a bank's capital structure is changing. If a bank's debt is increasing faster than its equity, for example, it may come to be regarded as a riskier operation, and this perception of added risk may raise the cost of the bank's funds from all sources. It's because of drawbacks such as these that bankers have turned from historical cost estimates to some basic economic principles for generating cost estimates.

THE NEW WAY: A BIT OF THEORY

The theory behind this new cost estimating method starts from a reasonable premise—that bank managers should make investment decisions which make the bank more profitable. This theory rationalizes the rules of thumb that many bankers actually use when they look at profitability—rules such as adding in a desired long-term profit margin as they try to gauge the expected cost of funds over time.

Matching Added Costs With Added Revenues. To obtain the largest profit available, a bank should compare the expected return from an investment with the current cost of obtaining the money needed to finance that investment. If the return (in the long run) from a new loan or security doesn't exceed the probable cost of financing that asset while the bank owns it, the bank would do better not to acquire it.[2] The added amount that would be brought in by lending one more unit of money to a borrower is the *marginal revenue*. The added amount that would be paid out to procure one more unit of loanable funds is the *marginal cost*.

The use of current information in making the cost of funds estimates is extremely important. The cost of a bank's funds normally will change as market interest rates move. Some cost changes, as for CDs and Federal funds, will be highly visible, while others, as for demand deposits and savings accounts, will not be so obvious. The banker must keep abreast of both. As interest rates rise, a banker will find that other financial institutions will compete more vigorously for these funds, and the depositors themselves will make an effort to shift into the more lucrative investments. To attract and hold these monies a bank may have to step up its advertising, resort to premiums, and expand its menu of depositor services. The result will be a higher cost to the bank for funds from these sources.

Less obvious will be the rising cost of equity funds—the bank's common stock. The target rate that a bank's management sets for returns to shareholders should be adjusted to reflect any changes in yields on other long-term investments. Investors who have the alternative of investing in long-term bonds at 8 or 9 percent with little risk must expect to receive more than that from an investment in common stock, or they will stay with the safer security. When long-term interest rates rise 1 or 2 percentage points, the return to common shareholders must move by a similar amount. In a competitive money market, the bank's shareholders always will have investment options that offer the current market rates. Even though a bank may not be selling a brand new stock issue in this high-rate environment, it still must aim to earn the competitive rate for its current owners. If it doesn't, the owners would be better off to instruct management to pay the maximum dividend possible. The stockholders then could use the extra dividends to make investments elsewhere at the higher prevailing rates.

When New Costs Don't Match Old. The decision on a new investment should be made on the basis of the cost of new money. Even if a bank were lucky enough to obtain a large pool of funds at rates that are below current market levels, shareholders, who bear the risk of loss, should be the beneficiaries of this good fortune. If historical costs are used to set current loan rates, the benefits of having these relatively cheap funds will be transferred to the borrowers rather than being retained for the common stockholders. If circumstances were reversed, it's unlikely that borrowers would be willing to pay high interest rates on loans from a bank which has unusually *high* average costs. The fact that the bank had the misfortune of being stuck with

[2] Statement of the MC = MR principle is intentionally very general, so that complications such as tied-product returns and discounted future benefits can be accommodated within the definition.

large amounts of funds acquired when rates were very high wouldn't matter if cheaper sources were available elsewhere. Regardless of costs or the effect on profits available for stockholders, bankers can't charge borrowers a rate that is much higher than rates available elsewhere. So historical costs should not be considered in making today's investment decisions. Rather, the cost of an additional dollar of funds should be compared with the return that will be realized when that additional dollar is invested. So much for the theory.

But how should an estimate of the marginal cost of funds be made? Although averaging historical costs is relatively easy, figuring out the full cost of a new dollar of funds is another matter—especially if it's necessary to estimate the impact that using various sources of funds will have on the cost of other sources.

MARGINAL COST ESTIMATION METHODS

Two basic options are available to the banker who is trying to make a marginal cost estimate. One is to identify the source of funds that the bank currently is using to raise new money. Once this source is identified, an estimate might be made of the cost of raising another block of these funds. This estimate of the marginal cost of a single source will serve as the *hurdle rate*—the minimum required rate of return—for any new investment of average riskiness. The other strategy is to estimate the marginal cost of each of the sources being employed within the bank. By weighting the cost of new dollars drawn from each source by the amount to be raised from that source, bankers can construct a weighted average of marginal costs. The second method sounds more complex, but it has some advantages over the first that make it worth considering.

The Marginal Cost of a Single Source. The most straightforward approach is to determine which source of funds the bank wants to use, compute its marginal cost, and use that estimate as the hurdle rate. Presumably, the source selected will be the cheapest one available to the bank. For example, if CDs are the source a banker turns to, the cost of additional dollars borrowed in that market is the relevant marginal cost. The interest rate on CDs is easy enough to determine, but this rate is only part of the real marginal cost of these funds.

Suppose a bank—for example, the hypothetical Ninth National Bank—wants to borrow $1 million for expansion. If it turns to the CD market and pays 7 percent, that interest rate is the base for the bank's cost calculations. But the job of estimating the marginal cost of this source is just beginning. The bank will incur a small cost in acquiring and repaying this money, and that cost should be included in the estimate. Also, there will be a reserve requirement against this source of funds (currently 1 percent to 6 percent, depending on term to maturity),[3] any obligation to keep a portion of the borrowed money in the form of idle cash raises the effective cost of the funds. These adjustments to the basic interest cost are relatively easy to make.

A much more difficult adjustment to the cost is the one required to compensate suppliers of other sources of funds for the added risk created by this new borrowing. Ninth National's leverage—its ratio of debt to equity—will be increased by the addition of more CD funds. Since higher leverage produces more risk for the bank, other creditors and shareholders may not be as willing to continue supplying Ninth National with funds at the same interest rates as before. Depositors whose funds are covered by deposit insurance probably won't care. But the holders of big deposits and CDs might, because they are not fully insured, and their concern could cause them to shift their funds to another bank or demand a higher return from Ninth National. In either case, the bank's cost to attract and hold such deposits is likely to rise.

The same thing will occur with the capital note holders and the common stockholders. When they sense that risks are increasing, they'll seek a higher return on their investments. The ones that presently own these securities can't automatically start charging the bank a higher rate for funds that already have been committed, but investors will demand a higher return for any new invested funds. The bank will be obliged to increase its earnings and ultimately its dividends to stockholders in order to compensate them for their higher risk. If it doesn't, the interests of the current shareholders will be harmed. and that would be inconsistent with management's obligation to run the bank in a way which enhances the shareholders' wealth (see THE SIN—GLE MARGINAL SOURCE CALCULATION).

In any event, it should be clear that the impact which heavy use of one source of funding has on the cost of other sources should be included in any analysis of the cost of marginal funds. This risk spillover cost is very difficult to measure, but it must be included in the calculation. Accordingly, the cost of new CD money can be found only after considering the direct interest cost, any acquisition and servicing costs, reserve requirements, and risk spillover costs.[4]

The same principles apply to estimating the cost of demand and time deposits (handling, acquisition, reserve requirement, and deposit insurance costs are likely to be higher than for CDs) or capital notes (risk spillover may raise the cost of the bank's CDs and uninsured deposits as well as the cost of its common stock). Similarly, the nominal, before-tax cost of new common stock may overstate its real cost because it will have the effect of reducing overall risk and is likely to lower the net cost of other debt sources.

---

[3] See "Member Bank Reserve Requirements," Federal Reserve *Bulletin*, August 1977, A9.

[4] A more technical explanation of this calculation can be found in Ronald D. Watson, "The Marginal Cost of Funds Concept in Banking," Research Paper No. 19, Federal Reserve Bank of Philadelphia, January 1977; reprinted with revisions in the *Journal of Bank Research 8* (Autumn 1977), pp. 136-147.

THE SINGLE MARGINAL SOURCE CALCULATION

Suppose the management of Ninth National is looking for another $100 and wants to raise the money by issuing CDs. It will be obliged to pay the going market interest rate for funds (say, 7 percent). It must then add to this amount several surcharges which raise the effective rate. The cost of reserve requirements on the CD funds might, for example, be 3 percent (annualized), the cost to acquire such funds 0.5 percent (annualized), and the cost of servicing the funds 0.3 percent (annualized). Using the formula

$$\text{cost of funds} = \frac{(\text{interest rate} + \text{servicing costs} + \text{acquisition costs} + \text{insurance})}{(1 - \text{reserve requirement})}$$

the explicit cost of the CD funds is found to be 0.0804 or about 8 percent.

This is only part of the job. Since the bank now is being more heavily financed with short-term borrowed funds, the risk is greater. Both the other suppliers of borrowed funds and the shareholders may wish to raise the cost of future funds they provide for this bank. This additional indirect cost must be added to the explicit cost estimate. Suppose that raising $100 of new CD funds created $.20 in added costs for other sources of funds. The *real* marginal cost of the CD funds would be estimated as their explicit cost plus the risk spillover cost:

marginal cost = 8.04 percent + 0.2 percent = 8.24 percent.

Failure to include all of these costs other than interest in the estimate will lead to a hurdle rate for new investments that understates the real cost of new funds.

Averaging All Marginal Costs. The other approach to calculating a bank's marginal cost is to presume that the institution will be financed during the next few months in pretty much the same way as it's being financed now. Checking and savings accounts will open and close and the bank will experience deposits and withdrawals. But as long as advertising doesn't diminish and services don't deteriorate, total dollars from each retail source will change only gradually. The bank will wind up paying the going rate to hold funds from each of these sources. Similarly, market rates (plus associated costs) will be paid for any CDs sold even if they are simply replacements for maturing issues. Finally, the bank will have to pay competitive returns for capital if it expects to keep access to these sources of funds. In short, the mix of sources doesn't change, and the bank must pay current rates for each source used (see THE AVERAGE OF MARGINAL COSTS CALCULATION).

If Ninth National is trying to calculate the overall cost of this pool of funds, it will need an estimate of the marginal cost of each source employed. That estimate must include any explicit interest payments, acquisition and

THE AVERAGE OF MARGINAL COSTS CALCULATION

Since figuring out the risk spillover costs is very difficult, the banker might prefer to calculate his explicit marginal costs for each source of funds and average those estimates to find out what the entire pool of funds presently is costing. Suppose that the bank is structured as follows:

	Added Dollars	Explicit Cost*	
Demand deposits	$ 30	.05	$1.50
Time deposits	40	.07	2.80
CDs	10	.08	.80
Capital notes	10	.09	.90
Common stock	10	.22	2.20
	$100		$8.20

The Ninth National's estimate would be: marginal cost $= \dfrac{\$8.20}{\$100.00} = 0.082$ = 8.2 percent.

---

*With acquisition, servicing, and reserve costs included.

servicing costs, deposit insurance, and reserve requirements. Such a calculation will be straightforward for CDs and capital notes but very difficult for demand and time deposits (even if the bank has a reliable cost accounting system). Estimating the percentage of the advertising budget that goes to keeping demand deposit levels steady or the additional advertising that would be required to increase time and savings deposits by a few percent is a very uncertain undertaking. At best it will involve a substantial amount of informed judgment.

When management is satisfied with these marginal cost estimates, an overall average can be calculated by multiplying each estimate by the fraction of the bank's funds that will be raised from this source in the near future. The weighted average will indicate the cost to the bank of buying the funds that will be used for investments or loans made during that time and it will serve as a minimum target rate of return for a new investment of average risk.

For all its complexity, this estimate has an advantage over the single-source cost estimate. With the weighted average approach there is no need to try to calculate the impact that risk spillovers have on the cost of other sources. The present level of the bank's leverage risk already is reflected in the prices of its liabilities and equity securities. If the composition of the pool of funds doesn't change, the risks aren't going to change significantly. The risk spillover that each source of funds creates for the other sources is neutralized in this pooling process and need not be estimated separately. As a result, estimates of the current marginal cost of each source, averaged across all sources, will provide a correct estimate of the bank's pool of funds without further risk adjustments.

CHOOSE YOUR POISON

Both of the cost estimation methods just described have pitfalls. Calculating the marginal cost of a single source such as CDs looks easy. The interest rate is known and the reserve and handling costs are measurable. But estimating the size of the risk spillover adjustment that should be added to the other costs to get the real marginal cost is very difficult.

In addition, one of the basic principles of economic theory is that businesses should tap each source of funds until the cost of the next dollar raised from that source is the same as the cost of a dollar from each other available source. That's the way to maximize profit, since it keeps money costs as low as possible. If a bank concentrates its attention on the cost of just one source, it may lose sight of the availability of funds from other sources that are cheaper.

Computing a weighted average of marginal costs keeps a banker looking at all of his costs simultaneously. Estimating the marginal cost of the bank's demand and time deposits remains a sticky problem, but the uncertainties of calculating risk spillover adjustments are avoided. This method will not provide the manager with the information needed to balance the marginal cost of one source against the marginal cost of another. For that he needs a marginal cost estimate that includes the risk spillover adjustment for each type of funds used. But the banker doesn't have to worry about risk spillover adjustments when he uses this method. He may not be getting the cheapest mix of funds, especially if he has overlooked a relatively cheap source; but he will be getting an accurate estimate of the cost of the pool of funds he's using. In this he has an advantage over his counterpart who computes the marginal cost of a single source but then continues to raise funds from all of the available sources. If the real marginal costs of each source are not really equal, use of the single-source technique will produce a faulty estimate.

A Sensible Procedure.   Both processes produce the right answer when used correctly. And both are difficult to use correctly. The best approach is to remember that both methods *can* give the right answer. Calculate the bank's cost of funds both ways. Use a sharp pencil. Analyze the cost estimates employed. Think about the effect that leverage risk has on the cost of various sources of funds. Analyze what you're really paying for demand deposits.

If both methods can give a correct answer, the calculations you make should give the same *answer*. If they do, you have a cost of funds estimate. If they don't, you had better try to figure out why. Do you need better data about your costs? Is the bank being financed with too expensive a mix of sources? Are the institution's costs under both calculations higher than previously thought? Has the bank been adding new business at a loss rather than a profit?

The exercise may be frustrating. It may be disturbing. But a sharp banker has to go through it if he's to do a first-rate job of managing profits.

APPENDIX

AN EXAMPLE OF HISTORICAL AVERAGE COST CALCULATIONS

Consider the case of the hypothetical Ninth National Bank. This bank gets its funds from demand and time deposits, CDs, subordinated capital notes, and common stock (see BALANCE SHEET). The full cost of each source of funds (interest and servicing cost of all funds obtained from that source) is indicated in parentheses.

NINTH NATIONAL BANK BALANCE SHEET

Cash and due	$ 100	Demand deposits	(4%)	$ 300
Investments	300	Time deposits	(6%)	400
Loans	600	CDs	(6%)	100
		Capital notes	(8%)	100
		Common stock	(20%)	100
Total	$1000	Total		$1000

Since management wants to insure that the shareholders' funds earn a return of 20 percent (10 percent after taxes if the tax rate is 50 percent), it must include this profit objective in its average cost of funds estimate.

Demand deposits	.04 × $300 =	$12
Time deposits	.06 × 400 =	24
CDs	.06 × 100 =	6
Capital notes	.08 × 100 =	8
Common stock	.20 × 100 =	20 (before taxes)
	$1000	$70

$$\text{Cost of funds} = \frac{\$70}{\$1000} = 0.07 = 7.0 \text{ percent.}$$

Only if Ninth National is able to average a 7-percent return on all invested funds will it be able to pay shareholders that target 10-percent return (after taxes).

Most banks would have little trouble computing this breakeven return, and it would appear to solve the problem of estimating a cost of funds which could be used as a minimum required rate of return (hurdle rate) for new investment decisions. But, this will work only when interest rates are perfectly steady. Otherwise, using actual average costs to set the hurdle rate for new investments will give the wrong answer.

As an illustration, suppose that the inflation rate increases, and one consequence of this change is a jump in interest rates on most securities. For simplicity, let's say that all rates go up 1 percentage point. The cost of *replacing* all Ninth National's deposits, CDs, and capital funds might now be:

Demand deposits	5%
Time deposits	7%
CDs	7%
Capital notes	9%
Common stock	11% (after taxes).

The weighted average cost of a new pool of funds would be over 8 percent rather than the 7 percent that Ninth National has been paying for its funds. What happens if the bank continues to use that historical cost hurdle rate of 7 percent?

One thing that will happen is that Ninth National might be tempted to take on new loans and investments that yield only 7½%. If the bank invests in a $100 bond that yields 7½%, it will be earning $7.50 per year. But as long as the composition of the bank's sources of funds doesn't change, the cost of new funds acquired to make that investment is:

Demand deposits	.05 × $30 = $1.50
Time deposits	.07 × 40 = 2.80
CDs	.07 × 10 = .70
Capital notes	.09 × 10 = .90
Common stock	.22 × 10 = 2.20
	$100 $8.10.

Since shareholders are the last to be paid, this shortfall will come out of their part of the bank's income:

$7.50	income
−5.90	cost of debt sources
1.60	earnings before taxes
−.80	taxes
$ .80	earnings after taxes.

Return on new shareholder equity $= \dfrac{\$.80}{\$10.00} = 0.08 = 8$ percent.

This return is not high enough to pay shareholders the return of 11 percent (after taxes) that they expect from their investment in the bank's stock. The ones that are dissatisfied will want to sell their stock and its price will be forced downward. All of the shareholders will be worse off because of the incorrect investment decision.

COSTS AND PROFITABILITY OF BANK FUNCTIONS[†]

Paul S. Anderson[*]

34

As lenders to business, commercial banks have to be able to judge the operating efficiency of their borrowers in order to insure as far as possible the safety of their loans. Banks have acquired the reputation of being coldly efficient in making these judgments. In this article the tables are turned and the operating efficiency of banks is investigated, using the data compiled in the Functional Cost Analysis of the Federal Reserve Banks. According to this analysis, some banking functions are persistently much more profitable than others, while some actually entail losses year after year. These variations in profitability and their persistence seem to contradict the cold efficiency of banks. The relative costs and profitability of the various functions are relevant to public policy because many banking laws and regulations impinge on the operations of banks.

THE FUNCTIONAL COST ANALYSIS

About 20 years ago, the Federal Reserve Bank of Boston undertook an annual cost survey among its member banks of the costs of various bank functions. This survey was an outgrowth of less elaborate bank cost analyses which

[†]Reprinted from the *New England Economic Review*, March/April 1979, pp. 43-61, with permission from the Federal Reserve Bank of Boston.

[*]Assistant Vice President and Economist, Federal Reserve Bank of Boston. The opinions expressed are the author's and do not necessarily reflect the views of the Federal Reserve Bank or the Federal Reserve System.

were being made by the Federal Reserve Banks of Boston and New York. The functions which were first covered included demand and time deposits, capital funds, loans, securities, safe deposit boxes and trust administration. Since then, credit card, computer services to customers and the computer department functions have been added. Providing the data for this analysis requires quite a bit of bank time and effort but this was the only feasible way for smaller and medium-sized banks to obtain usable cost data. Later other Federal Reserve banks joined in the survey so that it is now nationwide.

The Functional Cost Analysis is an exceptionally useful management tool for participating banks. They can compare their costs for each function from year to year with averages of banks of similar size and deposit structure. Such comparisons with the actual operating results of like businesses are not available or even possible in most industries.

Each reporting bank presents, at the minimum, the total amount of direct labor costs per function. Because some employees work at several functions, banks carry out periodic time studies of such employees to establish a basis for allocating their wages. Tellers' wage costs for example, while largely assigned to demand deposits, also apply partly to savings deposits and various loan categories.

The difficulty in cost accounting is how to apportion the remaining costs among functions. Some of these other costs, supplies, for example, could be allocated directly if detailed records were kept of usage, but that is often not feasible particularly for smaller banks. Most other costs, like the president's salary, are true overhead costs and no direct method of allocation is possible. In the Functional Cost Analysis, all costs that are not allocated directly are distributed on the basis of a continuously analyzed relation of such costs to direct wage and salary costs per function.

While any method of allocation of indirect, overhead costs is a matter of judgment and thus could be challenged, there is a double check on accuracy in total functional costing. Since all overhead costs have to be assigned to some function, too much in one means that another has too little, so any misallocation shows up in at least two functions. Each year the methods of allocation are reviewed and revised if evidence warrants it.

Similar to the problem of distributing indirect or joint costs is that of evaluating the cost of interrelated functions. A clear example of interrelation is the close connection between business demand deposits and business loans. These two functions (as well as others) are treated as a package in dealings with business customers. It might contribute to overall bank profitability, for example, to provide more favorable lending terms in order to attract business deposits which are above average in profitability. Because of such interrelations, the cost results for each function must be viewed from an overall bank perspective.

The distribution of all costs provides a total cost for each function. This total is then divided by the size of each function to yield a percentage cost which is useful for comparative analysis. An an example, in 1977 the total cost of the demand deposit function of reporting banks averaged near 3.5 percent while that of time deposits was just over 6 percent.

For the demand deposit, time deposit and consumer instalment loan functions, the total costs are also divided among the activities or processes involved in each function. Demand deposits, for example, involve receiving deposits, processing incoming and outgoing checks (home debits and transit items), cashing checks and maintaining the account. The relative time spent on each of these activities is estimated from time studies so that each type of activity can be measured in terms of "weight units." The cost per weight unit is obtained by dividing the total cost of the demand deposit function by the total number of such weight units. This cost per unit times the number of units involved in a single processing operation gives its cost. The average cost of cashing a check in 1977, for example, averaged just over 20 cents at the largest reporting banks. Costs of specific processes in the time deposit function are obtained in a similar manner while in the consumer instalment loan function, costs are derived for making each loan and for collecting each payment.

Once all costs are distributed, the primary goal of the Functional Cost Analysis has been reached. But a further refinement is made, that of calculating the profitability of each function by cross-allocating costs and incomes. Those functions which are funds sources, like demand and time deposits, involve costs but practically no income. But the funds-using functions, investments and loans, are the opposite; they generate practically all the income but have relatively little direct costs. To impute income to the funds-providing functions like deposits, it is assumed that their investible funds (total funds minus cash and reserve requirements) are invested proportionately among all loans and investments and thus receive the overall average rate of return. The loan and investment functions are assumed to get their funds from the source functions at the overall average cost. Thus the cross-allocation of costs and incomes uses the pool-of-funds rule rather than a procedure of trying to match specific sources with specific uses, for example, savings deposits with real estate mortgage loans.

The functions which do not involve the funds of the banks, namely, safe deposit, trust and computer services, generate their own incomes. Their costs are allocated in the cost distribution and their profitability can be computed directly.

Shown in Table 1 is a brief overall summary view of the results provided by the Functional Cost Survey. Incomes and net earnings are presented for each function. The most notable result in the funds-providing section is the wide disparity in the net expenses among these functions. Net time deposit expenses were 6.17 percent in 1977 while net demand deposit expenses were less than half as much at 2.63 percent. This difference has persisted since 1966 so it is not a temporary and abnormal result. The cost of capital and borrowed funds combined is low but this is because no "profits cost" is imputed to capital funds.

In the funds-using, or earning assets, group gross yields vary considerably, ranging from 7¾ percent for securities (on a taxable equivalent basis) to almost 20 percent for credit cards. But associated investment expenses have a similar range so that net yields vary much less. Even so, the net earnings rate

TABLE 1
Summary of Functional Costs and Incomes, 1977
(Average of Small, Medium, and Large Reporting Banks)

Funds-Providing Functions	Total expenses	Less service charges, fees, etc.	Net expenses	Earnings on funds	Net earnings
	(Percent of funds provided)				
Demand deposits	3.52	.88	2.63	5.66	3.03
Time deposits	6.18	.01	6.17	7.07	.90
Capital and borrowed funds	4.07	.10	3.97	7.44	3.47

Funds-Using Functions	Gross yield	Expenses	Net yield	Cost of funds	Net earnings
	(Percent of funds used)				
Real estate mortgage loans	8.72	.92	7.80	4.84	2.96
Instalment loans (mainly consumer)	11.33	3.59	7.74	4.82	2.92
Credit card loans	19.81	13.49	6.33	4.79	1.54
Commercial and other loans	8.59	1.78	6.81	4.82	1.99
Securities (taxable basis)	7.77	.16	7.60	4.82	2.78

Nonfunds Departments	Income	Expenses	Net earnings
	(Average department)		
Safe deposit	$60,000	$103,000	−$43,000
Trust services	$561,000	$675,000	−$114,000
Computer services	$307,000	$366,000	−$59,000
Other (largely international)	$1,478,000	$1,326,000	$152,000

SOURCE: *Functional Cost Analysis* based on data furnished by 846 banks in 12 Federal Reserve Districts.

on credit cards is only a little over half that of most other earning assets.

The nonfunds groups such as safe deposits and trust services has the most surprising results. All operated at losses except the "other" category which is a miscellaneous collection of activities but is dominated by the international departments of the large banks. All these nonfund functions with losses in 1977 also have had losses in practically every year since this survey began so these 1977 results are not due to temporary aberrations in the data.

The cost and profit results for each of the functions are discussed in detail in subsequent sections. Then some of the broader implications of the survey are considered.

DEMAND DEPOSITS

The demand deposit function is by far the largest banking function as measured by the number of employees. But since the early 1960s, it has ranked second at most banks to time deposits in terms of either dollar volume of funds involved or total costs. But demand deposits still contribute most to overall bank profitability because they are the lowest cost source of funds.

Interest payments on demand deposits have been illegal since 1933, so the only cost of acquiring them has been the handling expenses. In the Functional Cost Analysis, these handling or processing activities have been divided into the following four major operations:

Home debits—processing checks drawn on account.
Deposits—handling currency and checks deposited in account.
Transit checks—handling and sending out for collection checks drawn on other banks which were received for deposit or for cashing.
Account maintenance—statement preparation and mailing.

The average costs of these operations, which are calculated by use of weight units as described earlier, are as follows for 1977:

Each home debit	10 cents
Each deposit	20 cents
Handling and sending out each transit check	5 cents
Account maintenance per month	$2.70

A simple measure of the costs of checking accounts is the total cost per check written. In 1977, expenses totaled around $7.00 per account per month while an average of 22 checks were written, yielding a total handling cost of just over 30 cents per check.

Over time, total handling costs per check are subject to the same two influences as the unit costs of other goods and services, namely, changes in wage rates and changes in productivity. Bank wages have been rising over the postwar period, like all other wages, and the rise has accelerated during the past ten years. Productivity rises in check handling have about offset the increase in wage rates since the late 1950s so that the total cost per check is now about where it was then, around 30 cents. But the productivity changes have been uneven, spurting in the early 1960s so that the total cost per check declined to 20 cents in 1966 but rising very little since then. The total handling cost per check is now back to just over 30 cents and is still rising.

The sharp decline in check processing costs in the early 1960s evidently reflected for the most part the widespread introduction of combination bookkeeping-adding machines called "tronics" which automated account bookkeeping substantially. Except for adding machines, these tronic machines were really the only clear advance in check processing technology since the beginning of banking. Until they were introduced, checks had been entered into accounts by hand just as Tiny Tim's father did in Scrooge's counting house.

The bookkeeping clerk simply inserted the account statement into the tronic machine and then entered the transaction amount. The machine would post the transaction and the new balance into the account. These tronic machines were essentially limited-program computers where the magnetic back of the statement sheet was the memory. They were much cheaper than regular computers, however, and evidently were much less error-prone than computers have proven to be up to now.

Tronic technology began to be replaced during the latter 1960s by computer processing of magnetically encoded checks which can be read by machine. The new technology has increased productivity only modestly, at least up to the present, as reflected in the comparative rises in wages and in processing costs. Wage levels in check processing rose about 92 percent at reporting banks over the past 11 years while total check processing costs per check written rose almost as much, about 85 percent.

The advent of computer processing has affected the costs of the four main demand deposit processing operations quite differently, as shown in the following table:

Table 2
Average Item Costs of Reporting Banks

	1966	1977	Percentage rise
	(cents)		%
Home debit	6.6	9.6	45
Deposit	9.2	19.7	114
Transit check	2.4	5.3	120
Account maintenance (per month)	145.0	268.0	85

Source: Same as Table 1.

Processing costs of deposits and transit checks actually increased more than wages while the cost of each home debit increased only half as much as wages. The explanation for most of the divergence in cost trends is the impact of magnetic ink encoding on various operations.

Banks have to encode the amount on every check which is received for deposit or for cashing. Encoding actually requires more handling than entering a deposit or check on a tronics machine. Thus computer processing provided very little saving of processing time in these two operations. The rise in item costs in excess of the wage rise probably was largely due to the allocation of the rather expensive computer cost. But in the case of home debits, over half on average are initially deposited or cashed at another bank which encodes them. Thus the home bank saves the encoding expense on those on-us checks which are transit items at another bank.

While computer processing did little to reduce costs initially, it does provide the capacity to process a large volume of transactions without having to increase the number of employees. It also makes available data which were previously not obtainable without great effort. For example, the computer performs "account analysis" for the determination of service charges.

INDIVIDUAL AND COMMERCIAL CHECKING ACCOUNTS

Demand deposits can be divided into two major categories, individual and all other, mainly commercial. These two categories differ substantially in average size, activity, costs and profitability, as seen in the following average 1977 figures for those Functional Cost reporting banks which provided separate data for the two groups.

Commercial accounts are typically a lot more active than personal accounts and their handling costs are two and a half times larger. But because their average balance is nearly ten times that of personal accounts, their expenses, on an annual basis, amount to only 1.7 percent of average balances as compared to 6.6 percent for personal accounts.

The investment earnings rate on balances is assumed to be the same for both accounts under the pool of investment funds concept used in the analysis. Income from service charges and fees adds significantly to the gross earnings of personal accounts but relatively little to the much larger commercial account. But because the expense ratio of the average personal account is so high, its net earnings are only ½ of 1 percent as compared to 4 percent for the average commercial account. Quite clearly the overall profitability of demand deposits arises from the commercial category while personal accounts do little more than break even. Most banks offer special checking accounts for individuals which have somewhat higher service charges (about $1.70 per month) than do regular personal accounts ($1.23 per month). But usually no minimum balance is required and these special checking accounts have average balances of just over $400. The additional service charges are not sufficient to offset the low investment income from the small average balance, so that these accounts were even less profitable on average in 1977 than regular personal accounts, losing about 30 cents per account per month while regular accounts made an average profit of 40 cents per month.

New England banks that offered NOW checking accounts which paid 5 cent interest had large balances in these accounts, averaging $2500. But this large average size was not sufficient to offset the 5 percent interest expense so that these accounts entailed an average monthly loss of about 5 cents. Furthermore, since most of these NOW accounts had formerly been profitable regular checking accounts due to their large size, the banks essentially also lost the 5 percent interest which they previously did not pay. This amounts to around $10 a month per account. In effect, a previous regular checking account averaging $2,500 which earned the bank about $10 a month was converted to a NOW account which lost 5 cents a month. With current levels of costs and earnings rates on loans and investments, a bank cannot

TABLE 3
Comparison of Individual and Commercial Demand Deposits, 1977
Functional Cost Reporting Banks

	Individual Demand Deposits	*Commercial Demand Deposits*
Average size	$ 921	$ 8,850
Checks written per month	15	43
Total cost per month	$ 5.05	$ 12.90
Gross investment earnings on account balances per month	4.24	40.91
Service charges and fees per month	1.23	2.03
Net earnings after costs per month	.42	30.04
Total cost per year, percent of average balance	6.6%	1.7%
Net earnings per year, percent of average balance	0.5%	4.1%

Source: Same as Table 1

both pay 5 percent and offer free checking on NOW accounts with average balances of less than about $3,000 and still make a profit.

SAVINGS AND TIME DEPOSITS

Handling expenses of savings and time deposits are low because these accounts have little activity, around three to five deposits and withdrawals per year. Consequently their expense ratios are also low, just over 1 percent for regular savings accounts, about ¼ of 1 percent for special notice time accounts and only 1/10 of 1 percent for time certificates of deposit. These expense percentages mainly reflect the average sizes and handling required of these three categories; savings account balances run just below $2,000 while special notice accounts and certificates of deposit are near $7,000. The certificate of deposit average is lower than might be expected because Functional Cost reporting banks include few of the billion dollar size banks, the bulk of whose certificates average well over $100,000 in size. The expense ratio of such giant accounts would be essentially zero, of course.

With those low expense expense ratios, the cost of savings and time deposits then depends primarily on the interest rate which is paid. These rates are limited by legal interest rate ceilings (so-called Regulation Q ceilings) on all but certificates of deposit of $100,000 or larger. Thus when earnings rates on assets are high, as in 1974, the profitability of these accounts is naturally higher than when earnings rates are lower, as in 1976 and 1977. In 1977, these accounts had average net earnings of just over 1 percent which made them more profitable than personal checking accounts but much less profitable than commercial checking accounts.

An interesting minor category in the time deposit department are the Christmas (and some other) club accounts. These are savings plans in which savers sign up to deposit a small amount regularly, typically $5 weekly. The deposits are withdrawable several weeks before Christmas (or some other date). Most banks pay interest on these accounts with a 4 percent rate being common. Usually the plan provides for no interest payment if the deposit is withdrawn before completion of the planned period. Some banks pay no interest at all and, as a result, the overall average interest cost for this category is just over 3 percent.

The weekly deposits make for quite a bit of handling. This, together with opening and closing expenses, brings the annual cost of servicing the account to over $7. Since the balance averages only about $110 over the year, servicing costs amount to over 6 percent of average outstanding balances. This is less than banks earn from these balances so these accounts are slightly unprofitable even before the interest cost is considered.

CAPITAL AND BORROWED FUNDS

Equity accounts provide about 8 percent of total funds at Functional Cost banks. In the cost calculations, their expenses are very small, less than 1 percent, because they exclude net income which is traditionally considered the cost of equity funds. The expenses assigned to equity are such minor items as handling expenses of dividend checks, unallocated directors' fees and outside examinations.

Various forms of borrowing account for only 2 percent of total funds at the smallest Functional Cost banks but over 10 percent at the largest. The large banks are usually net buyers (borrowers) of Federal funds, the chief source of borrowed funds, while the small banks are usually net sellers. Credit conditions were rather easy throughout 1977 and the average cost of borrowings was fairly low, around 6 percent, approximately the same as the total average cost, including handling expenses, of time and savings deposits.

CONSUMER LOANS

Like deposits, bank loans vary in their characteristics, differing substantially as to type of borrowers, average size, maturity, security, loss rate, and costs of making and servicing. At one extreme are loans to prime business borrowers who already have an approved line of credit that cost very little to make and service. They are also very large so their percentage cost is practically zero. At the other extreme, credit card loans to consumers involve quite a lot of processing and are very small, on average around $25 for each credit card sale, and their handling cost is around 12 percent.

The most detailed Functional Cost lending analysis has been made of consumer instalment loans. The average outstanding balance on these loans is near $2,000. Since at any given time an instalment loan held by a bank is one-half paid off, the average initial size of these loans is about $4,000, a rather large size reflecting the fact that the majority of these loans are made for the purchase of new automobiles. Also included in this category are relatively small amounts of mobile home loans and inventory, or "floor plan," loans to auto dealers, which are much larger, as well as home appliance and check credit loans which are on average much smaller.

The average cost of extending a consumer instalment loan is about $45. This is roughly equal to one average day's pay per bank employee (including officers), meaning that it takes one person-day in total to extend a consumer loan. This includes time spent in helping the applicant fill out an application, making the credit check, typing all the forms and finally extending the actual loan. Considering all the operations involved, banks are quite efficient in extending these loans. But Functional Cost banks now process about 10 percent fewer loans on average per worker than they did in 1966. By contrast, in the demand deposit function, they handle over 20 percent more check volume per worker than in 1966. One reason cited by bankers for this drop in instalment loans processed per worker is that regulations, especially those concerned with "truth in lending," have slowed down the processing of these loans.

The cost of collecting each payment is about $3, or $45 for the 15-month life of the average loan. This is equal to the costs of making the loan and thus seems quite high. By comparison, the cost of recording a deposit to a checking account was only about 20 cents, as noted earlier, so the $3.00 cost of collecting a payment seems excessive. The explanation is that all costs subsequent to the making of the loan are included in payment costs, whereas in costing checking accounts, the cost of maintaining the account is separated from the costs of handling checks written and deposits made. Since the cost of maintaining a checking account is approximately $2.70 per month, the payment collection cost of $3.00 monthly is reasonable.

Other costs involved in lending are losses and the cost of funds. Following are these costs for 1977, together with the gross income on consumer loans and the net earnings (in percent):

Income

Gross interest income	10.8
Other income (minimum fees, penalties, etc.)	0.5
Total income	11.3

Costs

Making loans	1.8
Collecting payments	1.4
Loan losses	0.4
Cost of funds	4.8

Total Costs 8.4

Net Earnings 2.9

Loan losses on consumer loans are relatively low, reflecting the fact that banks impose fairly high credit standards on borrowers. Loss rates on loans at consumer, or small, loan companies are roughly four times higher, which is a consequence of their lower standards. Small loan companies have to charge higher rates, of course, as a result.

CREDIT CARDS

Credit card loans are a recent innovation in banking. They were widely introduced during the 1960s and many thought they would result in a largely cashless society. But their impact has been much less than anticipated. Initially banks granted credit cards rather indiscriminately and many holders used them fraudulently by stealing cards or submitting fictitious names on applications or else simply neglected to pay amounts owed. As a result, losses were far above those experienced on other loan types. Even after losses were reduced by more prudent issuance, handling expenses were so large that most banks had operating losses. With the decline in the cost of funds from 1974 to 1977, more than half of the banks reporting on their credit card operations in the Functional Cost survey have finally been able to make profits on this function, although for all reporting banks combined the profit rate is significantly below the average for other loans.

Gross income earned on credit cards is high, near 20 percent. It is composed of two parts, merchant discount and interest earned on balances which are outstanding beyond the noninterest period, which usually extends for some 25 days after the first billing. Merchant discounts are the amounts banks charge retail stores for handling their credit card sales; these discounts average around 2.3 percent for reporting banks. Thus, on the average $25 credit card purchase, a bank pays about $24.40 to the retail store submitting the charges but bills the customer for the full $25, resulting in a gain of 60¢ per sales slip.

On average, about 40 days elapse from the time the bank pays the retail store until it begins charging interest to the customer. This free credit period is an outright loss to the bank because costs are accruing on the funds it has tied up in these free credit balances. If the customer does not pay the balance within the free credit period, the bank begins earning interest at a rate which is generally 18 percent on the first $500 and 12 percent on amounts above $500.

The smallest size group of Functional Cost reporting banks, those with deposits up to $50 million, had losses of 0.3 percent on their credit card operations in 1977. The two larger groups with $50-200 million and over $200 million in deposits, had net earnings of 1.6 and 3.0 percent respectively. A comparison of these differing profit experiences brings out the major factors affecting profitability.

The small banks were actually more efficient in operations than were the two larger size groups. On average, each small-bank employee in the credit card function processed about 650 sales slips per week as compared to 400 and 580, respectively, in the two larger size groups. Also, total expenses per employee were about $28,000 per year at the smallest banks and $31,000 and $33,000, respectively, at the larger banks. Thus, in the two areas over which banks had direct control, the smallest banks were above average in efficiency.

But in areas which were largely beyond the bank's control, the larger banks had more favorable experiences. The average size of their sales slips were some 50 percent larger, about $27 versus only $19 at the smallest banks. As a result, the smallest banks processed $630,000 worth of sales slips per year per employee, only a little more than the medium banks' $580,000, despite the fact that the smallest banks processed over 50 percent more sales slips per employee. The largest banks processed $730,000 per employee per year. This dollar volume generates the merchant discount income at the rate of about 2.3 percent.

In addition, around 38 percent of the sales charges at the larger banks remained unpaid after the free credit period and thus began earning interest, while only 33 percent of sales charges at the smallest banks lasted long enough to earn interest. Consequently, annual interest income per employee at the biggest banks was $42,000, at the medium-size banks $28,000, and at the smallest banks only $22,000.

Losses on credit card charges were about 1.3 percent in 1977, down substantially from earlier rates. But even the 1.3 level is still significantly higher than the loss rate on regular consumer instalment loans, real estate mortgage loans or business loans. (Fraud losses are not included in these bad debt losses because they are considered nonrecurring rather than ordinary operating expenses.)

MORTGAGE AND BUSINESS LOANS AND SECURITIES

Costs of making and collecting real estate and commercial (including agricultural) loans are substantially higher than those of consumer instalment loans. The annual operating costs of mortgage loans in 1977 were around $170 per loan outstanding while those of commercial loans were about $250, both well over double the $72 expense of handling consumer loans. But because mortgage and commercial loans are roughly ten times larger on average than consumer loans ($18,000-$22,000 versus $2,000), handling costs are lower, only 0.8 percent for real estate and 1.4 percent for commercial loans.

The costs of making a real estate mortgage loan amounts to around $500, far above the average $45 cost of making a consumer loan, but because mortgage loans have average lives of over five years, the annual cost is below $100. Receiving and processing applications and performing credit checks and property appraisals involve a lot more time for mortgage loans than for consumer instalment loans. This is particularly the case with commercial mortgage loans which are an appreciable share of the loans made by most commercial banks. Collection costs on real estate loans are probably somewhat higher than on consumer instalment loans because the bank usually also collects payments for real estate taxes and these must be transferred periodically to the local governmental unit.

Commercial and agricultural loans are quite a bit more varied than are real estate loans. Included are such types as conventional single-payment loans, accounts receivable loans, leased equipment loans and term loans with floating rates. Costs of making these loans likewise vary greatly. A single payment loan to a prime borrower with a line of credit involves very little cost, while a leased equipment loan would involve a lot of advance investigation and preparation and much subsequent supervision.

The average size of loan in the commercial, agricultural and other category is a relatively small $18,000. This is smaller than might be expected because business loans are usually thought to be quite large, certainly larger than home mortgage loans. Furthermore, the average Functional Cost reporting bank can make loans as large as $2 million, which is one-tenth of average capital accounts of $20 million. While these banks do make some maximum size loans, they make many more small loans to businesses which brings the average below that of real estate loans.

Loan losses have risen on both mortgage and commercial loans over the past ten years. In the mid-1960s, these losses were practically zero, and they are still less than 0.1 percent on real estate loans and around 0.4 percent on commercial loans. Unlike the largest banks in the country, most Functional Cost reporting banks had not financed real estate investment trusts to any extent, nor had they made many construction and development loans. These are the real estate loan types that in many cases have turned sour since 1973.

The costs of acquiring investments—including U.S. Government securities, tas-exempt securities, and Federal funds sold—are low, below 0.2 percent. Investments have been somewhat more profitable than loans on average over the past ten years, as market interest rates have risen faster than the cost of funds. Before the mid-1960s, investments had significantly lower net earnings than loans.

NONFUNDS DEPARTMENTS

As noted earlier, the distinguishing feature of the nonfunds department operations is that all except the foreign department had losses which have persisted since the beginning of Functional Cost analysis. While banks have raised their fees and charges over time for safe deposit boxes, trust functions, computer services and other miscellaneous activities, costs have kept pace so that losses continue. Why banks tolerate the protracted deficits in these operations will be discussed later, along with marketing and pricing operations concerning all bank functions.

The persistent losses of trust departments in the Functional Cost survey contrasts with profits often recorded in summaries of trust department operations compiled by several Federal Reserve banks at the request of the participating trust departments in their districts. The major reason for the different results is that the trust expenses reported in the special trust surveys generally include significantly less overhead costs than the Functional Cost analysis allocates to trust departments. The allocations of overhead expenses in the special surveys are made by the trust officers submitting the reports, usually without an outside check. Overhead allocation in the Functional Cost analysis is subject to check in that the respective amounts to the various functions and departments allow comparisons for reasonableness. This aspect is, of course, one of the chief strengths of the Functional Cost procedures.

POSSIBLE OPERATING ADJUSTMENTS IN THE FUTURE

Banking has the reputation of being a stable industry, doing business in traditional ways year in and year out. Bankers are reluctant to make changes, especially those that involve eliminating services to customers or raising charges sharply.

But developments might occur which would reduce bank profitability substantially and force banks to make offsetting operating adjustments. One possible development that would reduce profitability, but would actually be very desirable for other reasons, is a return to price stability which would almost certainly also lead to a reduction in interest rates to more normal levels.

A reduction in interest rates to levels prevailing in the early 1960s, for example, would cut the income of banks almost in half. Average yields on earning assets, net of lending expenses, were about 7.5 percent at Functional Cost banks in 1977, while from 1960 to 1965, average yields were only around 4 percent. Although interest costs of banks would also decline with a reduction in rates, these costs amount to only about half the interest income of banks. As a result, a given percentage point drop in both interest income and interest costs would reduce revenues twice as much as costs.

Another possible development which could cut bank profits by up to 50 percent is the removal of the prohibition of interest on all demand deposits. The legalization of NOW accounts (checkable savings accounts) in New England had already had an impact on bank earnings.[1]

The authorization of automatic transfers from savings to checking accounts throughout the Nation is also predicted to reduce earnings as individual demand deposits are pared down as a result. But these NOW accounts and automatic transfers apply only to individuals whose accounts make up only about a third of demand deposits. If interest payments on all demand deposits were allowed and competition led to average payments, net after service charges, of 3 to 4 percent, earnings of the typical Functional Cost bank would be reduced by nearly 50 percent.

What adjustments could banks make to offset a general fall in interest rates, or the payment of interest on demand deposits? One frequently mentioned in debates over bank costs is adjusting bank loan rates—raising them above current levels to cover interest on demand deposits or reducing them less than other interest rates if the general level of interest rates falls. But such interest rate adjustments are not really possible for banks because the general level of loan rates is set by demand and supply conditions in the market. Business loan rates tend to follow rates on commercial paper and negotiable certificates of deposit. Mortgage loan rates tend to follow bond rates and, in addition, are strongly influenced by thrift institutions. Consumer loan rates tend to remain quite stable and even though banks are the most important consumer lenders, they can hardly raise their rates above prevailing levels without losing market shares.

A second possible adjustment which, however, would not likely be successful either is to reduce interest rates on savings and time deposits. Banks would lose deposits to competing thrift institutions if they were to lower rates paid significantly. While a lowering of the rate ceilings under Regulation Q would accomplish the purpose of reducing bank costs, these ceilings have never been lowered, except for some minor adjustments, since they were imposed on commercial banks in 1935.

If banks are not able to offset reduced earnings by raising interest rates on earning assets or reducing interest costs on sources of funds, the only remaining avenues open are to reduce operating expenses or else to impose or raise charges for banking services provided. The opportunities for reducing operating expenses are probably fairly limited because banks presumably are already striving to hold them down. Expenses could be reduced by eliminating some functions entirely but this is hardly acceptable if banks wish to retain their image as full service institutions. One area in which banks have retrenched is in branching. Branching has been mainly aimed at attracting individual accounts, but, as noted earlier, these have declined in profitability over the past 15 years or so.

The focus of possible future operating adjustments will have to be on the pricing of services. These prices, or charges, would, of course, be related to

[1] See Ralph C. Kimball, "Impacts of NOW Accounts and Thrift Institution Competition on Selected Small Commercial Banks in Massachusetts and New Hampshire, 1974-75." *New England Economic Review*, January/February 1977, pp. 22-38.

the cost of the services. The following tabulation shows the average distribution of noninterest operating expenses of Functional Cost banks among the various functions.

TABLE 4
Distribution of
Noninterest Operating Expenses, 1977

Function	Percent of total non-interest expenses
Demand deposits	37
Time deposits	12
Instalment loans	15
Commercial loans	14
Real estate loans	6
Credit card loans	4
Securities	2
Trust department	6
Safe deposit boxes	1
All other (excluding international)	3
Total	100

Source: Same as Table 1.

Some of these functions are much more easily priced explicitly than others due to the inherent nature of the function or the competitive situation.

Demand Deposits

Because this function is by far the most costly and because its profitability level would change drastically if interest were paid or even if the level of earnings rates declined appreciably, charging for check handling would undoubtedly be the first area banks would explore in making adjustments to offset inadequate earnings. If interest were allowed, activity charges could subtracted from the interest credit so that those depositors with large balances would be earning net interest even with full charges for activity. As noted earlier, a full charge currently would be at least 30 cents per check, or the equivalent in separate charges per check, per deposit and for deposit maintenance. If full cost were charged for check handling, then banks could pay almost 4 percent currently on demand deposits. This rate seems low compared to the rate paid on time deposits but almost one-fourth of demand deposits goes into cash assets (vault cash, reserves and uncollected cash items) which do not earn a return. Furthermore, earnings on time deposits are below average, so earnings on demand deposits will have to do better.

The public relations problem in introducing full-cost service charges will be with the smaller, mainly personal, accounts which now either have no service charges or relatively low charges, such as 10 cents per check. Roughly half of all personal accounts are below $400. With an interest credit of, say, 4 percent and activity of 15 checks per month, a $400 account would entail net charges of over $3 per month. The account would have to average over $1,300 before the interest credit would offset a 30 cent per check service charge. This would be quite a drastic change from present arrangements. The first banks in a market area that introduced full-cost charges would likely lose a number of accounts. The dollar losses would probably be quite small, however, since the smallest accounts are most likely to be withdrawn. Some banks have already taken steps with regard to low-earning, small individual accounts. Several have raised service charges substantially while others have notified individuals with small balances that they should either raise their average balances or close out their accounts.

Proponents of "retail banking," which emphasizes maximum service to consumers as a method of holding and increasing deposits, consumer loans and, perhaps, some other services, would tend to oppose instituting charges that result in the loss of a significant number of personal deposits. While holding on to "loss" deposits might generate additional consumer loans or other business, the pertinent question is, what is the cost? For example, charging 10 cents per check might result in the retention of most small deposits that would be lost if 30 cents were charged. The 20 cents per check lost income amounts to $36 per average individual account per year. Assuming that one consumer loan arises from every two individual demand deposits (which is about the average ratio), this means that $72 of service charge income per year is foregone for each consumer loan gained. This is not profititable since the net earnings on consumer loans after the cost of money averages only about $50 per year. Other services individuals might use, such as credit cards or safe deposit boxes, are far less profitable than consumer loans so they would do even less in offsetting the cost of foregone charges for check handling. Thus, it is not profitable to try to attract and hold demand deposits by offering them at less than processing costs in order to gain other kinds of business.

Time Deposits

This area would not appear to offer much opportunity to reduce costs or impose service charges because rates paid are largely governed by competition and ceilings while handling costs are quite low. But, as in the demand deposit function, the overall time deposit figures conceal much diversity in profitability. Again, as in the case of demand deposits, this diversity in profitability arises from the size structure of savings deposits.

Half of the savings deposits of Functional Cost banks are less than $200 in size. The other half averages around $3,500. Handling expenses are around $20 per account which makes for a handling expense of around 15 percent annually for the below $200 accounts and about 0.5 percent for the top half of these deposits. These figures are based on the assumption that the activity levels of the small and large savings accounts are the same. The small accounts may well have more activity, that is, deposits and withdrawals, than the large accounts because many of them are used as convenience, transactions accounts. Thus the expense ratio of the smaller accounts could be higher than 15 percent.

These small savings accounts are clearly unprofitable, but what to do with them is a difficult question. A simple and direct approach is to place some lower limit on the size of savings accounts. This was actually proposed by a Detroit bank several years ago; it announced a minimum size of $50 on savings accounts, but the proposal aroused so much criticism that the bank abandoned it. Such a limitation appears to be a slap at the thrift ethic. But a Houston bank has installed a $100 minimum size.

Another approach is to impose service charges. To meet costs, these charges should be about $10 per year for account maintenance and, perhaps, $1 for each deposit or withdrawal which would also almost cover the costs of opening, closing and interest posting. With such charges, banks could give a 6 percent interest credit with the limitation, however, that any actual interest payment would not exceed the legal ceiling of 5 percent. For example, a $1,000 account with five deposits and five withdrawals per year would have charges of $20 ($10 for maintenance, $5 for deposits and $5 for withdrawals) against an interest credit of $60, for the net interest paid of $40. Accounts smaller than $333 would have net charges because the 6 percent interest credit would be less than the $20 in charges. The Houston bank noted above has imposed similar charges on savings account activity.

Such a charge plan for savings deposits would also be criticized just as the $50 minimum limit was. But criticism does not dispose of the basic problem which is that small savings deposits are loss operations. Should banks have to bear this loss? Also, the imposition of deposit and withdrawal charges will likely cause savers to change their use of this function. They would probably make fewer, but larger, deposits and fewer withdrawals. This could well result in larger savings balances and thereby encourage thrift. Also they might begin using checking accounts for their transactions needs which would both lower bank costs since it should reduce teller needs and eliminate frequent waiting in lines by depositors. Processing a check costs a bank about 10 cents while a withdrawal from a savings account costs about 80 cents.

Instalment Loans

Total costs of the instalment loan function are the second highest of all commercial bank functions exceeded only by the costs of handling demand deposits. Thus this function would appear to offer good possibilities for either reducing costs or imposing service charges in order to increase income. But consumer loans are quite profitable already and trying to extract more income from this function could result in a loss of business.

The profitability of consumer loans actually resembles that of savings deposits. Large loans are very profitable while small loans do not cover costs, due to the fixed costs of making loans and collecting payments. The average cost of making a consumer loan is around $45 while annual collection costs are about $36. Thus, just to cover these fixed costs and the 5 percent average cost of funds (in 1977), a one-year loan (at 11 percent of the outstanding balance) has to be about $2,500 while a two-year loan has to be almost $1,700. Smaller initial loans than these do not cover costs while large loans make a profit.

As with savings deposits, the way to insure that every consumer loan makes a profit is to impose separate charges for the costs of making the loan and collecting payments. As an offset, the interest rate could then be reduced to a level about 3 percentage points above the average cost of funds which currently would place it at 8 percent rather than the prevailing 11 percent.

Such a change would make large loans somewhat less expensive than the current procedure but would make small loans, like those used to finance appliance and furniture purchases, much more expensive. For example, a $1,000, one-year loan for the purchase of a bedroom suite would cost about $125 under the separate charge, 8 percent plan as compared to $60 under the current 11 percent rate. But a $5,000 auto loan for three years would cost only $720 with separate charges and 8 percent, while it costs almost $900 under the present 11 percent rate.

The relatively high cost of small loans under the separate charge plan should persuade borrowers of smaller amounts to shift to credit cards. For example, a $1,000, one-year loan would cost $125 under the separate charge, 8 percent plan but only $75 as a credit card purchase with the first month's credit free and 12 percent on the outstanding amount over $500 and 18 percent below. Such a loan would also be much more profitable to the bank than existing credit card charges which barely break even, as noted earlier, because they average only $25 per charge and often are repaid during the free interest period.

Credit Cards

Total expenses of this function are quite small so any feasible change in this function would not significantly affect overall costs or profits. Nevertheless, efforts should continue to make credit cards a contributor to profits rather than a drag. But increasing credit card income is not easy or simple as shown by the case of the large New York bank which imposed a 50 cents a month fee on each card but had to rescind it because it was ruled illegal under state law.

Among the remaining possibilities for increasing credit card income are: 1) increasing the discount charged merchants, 2) raising the interest rate, 3) eliminating the free interest period, 4) imposing a minimum size per charge, and 5) imposing a small service fee on each charge. None of these changes would be easy to initiate because some are restricted by law while all would involve public relations problems.

Obviously those that benefit from the credit card service should bear its operating cost. The problem is that both merchants and consumers benefit and there are difficulties in apportioning costs between them. The 2 to 3 percent typical discount charged merchants seems to be about as much as they feel they can afford. Most stores with small margins on their sales, like groceries, have decided they cannot afford to accept credit cards.

The remaining cost of credit cards, including a reasonable profit to banks, should logically be paid by the consumer, but state laws have raised such obstacles as mandatory free interest periods, interest rate ceilings and prohibition of card fees. Thus either these laws will have to be changed or banks will have to try to impose a fee on each sales slip processed. Conceivably this fee could be credited against any interest paid so those who allowed their charge to remain past the free interest period would pay no fee.

As it is, those consumers who repay their charges within the free interest period are really benefiting at the expense of all others. This free ride forces the two other charges, merchant discounts and interest on balances owed after the free interest period, to be higher than they would have to be if there were not this free ride. Those consumers that pay cash are also penalized. They pay the higher prices merchants must charge to cover the cost of credit card discounts even though they are not causing these extra costs.

To be fair to cash customers, merchants should give them a discount equivalent to the credit card discount charged by banks. Congress did consider requiring such a discount but it was not enacted. Currently merchants have the option of granting such a cash discount up to 5 percent if they wish without being liable for implicitly charging above ceiling rates to credit card customers who would be paying an extra 5 percent for using credit. A few merchants, including a large gasoline retailer, have granted discounts on cash purchases.

Business Loans

The expenses of the commercial, industrial and agricultural loan functions are quite high but this function is really a basic activity of commercial banks so sizable expenses would be expected. Business loans are negotiated on an individual basis and are part of the customer "package" which includes credit limits, interest rates, deposit balance requirements and activity charges and other services. As noted earler, the total business customer relationship is currently quite profitable.

But if interest were allowed on all demand deposits, changes would likely occur in the business customer package. Banks would undoubtedly have to offset interest payments with new or higher activity charges but with individual negotiation, no unmanageable difficulties should arise.

Real Estate Loans and Securities

Both these investment functions have fairly low expenses so not much leeway is available for reduction. On the income side, rates on both are largely set by the market so banks have little discretion in making adjustments to increase income.

Safe Deposit, Trust, and Computer Departments

Because these departments are generally already unprofitable, banks have the incentive to make adjustments to improve results even under current conditions when overall profits are generally satisfactory. But the required adjustments are especially difficult in the safe deposit and trust functions. Both of these functions are traditional bank services so they have to be available to support the image of a "full-service bank."

The losses of the safe deposit and trust departments might be rationalized on the basis that they mainly serve individuals with large demand deposit balances which are very profitable. But so far as the safe deposit department is concerned, many more boxes are available than customers with large balances. It is estimated that only about 5 percent of individual depositors have balances of $5,000 or more, but the number of boxes on average is equal to about 25 percent of total individual depositors. Thus more of the boxes in use must be rented to individuals with only average demand balances which are not very profitable as noted earlier.

About the only remedy banks have for the losses in the safe deposit function is to increase rental charges. But the required increases are quite modest —an additional 50 cents per box per month would bring the function above the break-even point at the average Functional Cost bank.

The trust department serves both businesses and individuals. For businesses it provides such functions as bond trustee, pension fund management, stock registration and stock transfer. Most trust customers, however, are individuals and some three-quarters of total trust income comes from them. But evidently the losses arise mainly from services to individuals also judging from the fact that the largest Functional Cost Banks, which have a larger proportion of their trust income from business services than do the smaller banks, have relatively smaller losses.

Trust services for individuals are extremely varied and include the administration of trust funds for such activities as placing flowers in cemeteries and maintaining parks. But the typical service is the administration of funds for educational and living expenses of beneficiaries. These trust services are expensive because they require much personal attention from trust officers. Banks have taken one important step to reduce trust expenses, that of combining small trust funds into one common trust fund. Other opportunities for reducing costs seem to be fairly limited so increasing trust fees is about the only effective action for eliminating the operating losses.

The computer customer service department is also a net loss function at most Functional Cost banks. The major services provided by the department are demand deposit and credit card accounting for other banks and payroll accounting for various types of commercial customers. Evidently the established pattern of charges for these services has been at too low a level for profitability because many offering banks have had excess computer capacity in the past and viewed any extra income from outside jobs as a way to help pay for the basic cost or rental of the computer equipment.

But over time the in-bank uses of its computers have generally increased leaving no excess capacity. To continue serving customers, new capacity for this purpose had to be acquired and charges had to be sufficient to cover full costs plus a reasonable profit. Many banks calculated that such a level of charges was significantly above the prevailing pattern and that it simply was not feasible to raise charges that much so they have announced they are going out of the business of providing computer services to customers.

Thus, as contrasted with the general lack of action on the loss problems in the safe deposit and trust departments, a number of banks have taken corrective steps with regard to computer services. But such corrective action was easier in the computer area because it was a new service as opposed to the other two which have been bank functions for literally centuries. Also, not many customers were involved in computer services and alternative nonbank suppliers of these services were available so that the possible loss of a significant number of customers to other banks was not much of a danger.

Functional Cost banks in New England made significant progress during 1977 with regard to losses in their Trust departments. On average they actually had slight profits in 1977 for the first item since the Functional Cost survey was instituted. But the average New England bank still had losses in the Safe Deposit function although only about half the average size of the losses nationwide. As noted earlier, New England banks have been less profitable than their counterparts in the Nation so they probably have been under somewhat more pressure to adjust fee schedules and reduce costs.

SUMMARY

The Functional Cost survey conducted by the Federal Reserve banks in cooperation with nearly a thousand member commercial banks is a valuable cost analysis which is unique in comprehensiveness and detail among business cost surveys. Its prime purpose is to provide participating banks with comparative cost data covering the standard banking functions. This information enables banks to identify those operating areas which appear to be below standard in efficiency so that improvements can be undertaken.

The broader interest in the survey arises from the insight it gives on banking operations. Overall, demand deposits are by far the cheapest, and therefore the most profitable, source of funds because they have no interest cost. But within the demand deposit category large commercial accounts are very profitable but individual accounts are barely above the break-even point. NOW accounts paying 5 percent interest are actually slightly unprofitable at most banks even though their average size is three times that of regular individual checking accounts.

Among earning assets, real estate and consumer instalment loans were the most profitable in 1977 while credit card loans were the least. While the rates charged on credit cards are high, typically 18 percent on the first $500 and 12 percent on amounts above, credit card processing costs are also high, reducing net yields. While the credit card function is a loss operation at some banks, its profitability has improved on average since it was introduced.

Commercial loans were somewhat below average in profitability in 1977 but that was largely due to the fact that market interest rates were at their lowest level in recent years. Yields on commercial loans fluctuate more than does the average cost of funds because the latter includes the cost of zero-interest demand deposits. When the general level of market rates is high, as in 1974, commercial loans are much more profitable than real estate or consumer loans whose average yields fluctuate less than the cost of funds.

A surprising result of the cost survey was that all three major service departments—safe deposit, trust and customer computer service—have been unprofitable over the entire period that these data have been compiled. Even though most banks are now aware of these losses, most have not succeeded in taking corrective steps. A number of banks have phased out customer computer services but such action is not possible in the safe deposit and trust functions. The latter two departments are standard, traditional and often legally contracted services of banks, as well as involving a heavy fixed investment, so they can hardly be discontinued. Improving their profitability will require substantial adjustments in fee schedules.

Among the interesting findings of the survey were the costs of various detailed activities. Following are examples of handling costs: a check drawn by a depositor, almost 10 cents; deposit to a checking account, 20 cents; a (transit) check drawn on another bank, 5 cents; withdrawal from a savings account, 80 cents; posting interest to a savings account, $1.55; making a consumer instalment loan, $45; collecting a payment on a consumer loan, $3.

Profits have been quite good overall during the postwar period so banks have not been under special pressure to increase operating margins. But some possible developments in the future could affect bank profits substantially. The two that loom as most important are allowing interest to be paid on demand deposits and a reduction in the general level of interest rates to more normal levels. Either of these developments could cut net operating income of the average bank by as much as one-half unless offsetting actions were taken.

To counter reductions in income, banks would probably not be successful in raising interest rates on their loans nor in reducing interest paid on time and savings deposits. Competition is quite active in both these areas and if banks move loan rates up or deposit rates down unilaterally, competitors such as thrift institutions, insurance, commercial and consumer loan companies would cut in on the banks' share of the savings and lending markets.

The remaining options for banks are to reduce noninterest operating expenses and to charge for services performed. They probably do not have much leeway for reducing expenses if they are to continue providing their standard services. Thus they will have to consider raising those charges which they have already installed and to impose charges on services which they now provide free. Among services for which charges could be imposed or raised are the following: checking activity, deposits and withdrawals from savings accounts, making consumer loans, collecting payments on consumer loans and posting credit card charges.

CUSTOMER PROFITABILITY ANALYSIS[†]

*Robert E. Knight**

35

In recent years banks have become increasingly aware of the need to measure the profitability of corporate customer relationships. Past emphasis on deposit size as a measure of rank has gradually given way to the realization that large banks are not necessarily the most profitable and that loans, not deposits, generate most bank earnings. At many larger banks, profitability analysis, essentially a sophisticated version of standard account analysis,[1] has been introduced to assist in measuring individual customer profitability. This article describes the objectives of profitability analysis, discusses some of the general principles involved in constructing an analysis, and considers the alternative types of profitability measures commonly utilized. A sample profitability analysis statement is presented to illustrate the interrelationships among variables.

*Reprinted from the *Monthly Review*, April 1975, pp. 11-20, with permission from the Federal Reserve Bank of Philadelphia.

†The author is President of the Alliance National Bank, Alliance, Nebraska.

[1] A detailed description of account analysis procedures used in correspondent banking can be found in the article, "Account Analysis." in the December 1971 issue of the *Monthly Review* of the Federal Reserve Bank of Kansas City. Since 1971, the Kansas City Reserve Bank has collected figures annually on the account analysis practices of major correspondents. The 1973 survey results were reported in "How Correspondents Analyze Accounts for Profitability," *Banking*, Journal of the American Bankers Association, Vol. 66, No. 10 (April 1974).

ACCOUNT ANALYSIS

The application of standard account analysis to both corporate and corres-pondent accounts became widespread in the mid-1960's when banks feared they might be caught in a profit squeeze. During that period the costs of pro-viding bank services escalated rapidly as inflation became more pronounced and as the variety of bank services increased greatly. Corporate treasurers, while asking for larger loans and for highly specialized services, were simul-taneously reducing noninterest bearing balances to invest the funds directly in the securities market. As interest rates rose, smaller banks began to sell large amounts of Federal funds, occasionally producing negative collected balances at correspondents. Meanwhile, bank liquidity was declining and lia-bility management techniques were not proving fully satisfactory in meeting the demands for loanable funds when Regulation Q interest rate ceilings were binding. Under these circumstances larger banks initially developed ac-count analysis techniques to ensure not only that adequate compensating balances would be maintained, but also that the needs of the most profitable customers could be given priority.

In performing a standard account analysis, a bank determines the revenue from a customer's account by multiplying the average collected balance, gen-erally adjusted for reserve requirements, by an earnings credit or allowance. The expenses of servicing the account are computed by multiplying the num-ber of times a given service is utilized by the cost (generally including an al-lowance for profit) of providing the service. A typical account analysis schedule is shown in Table 1.

While the account analysis represents an important step in determining the profitability of a customer relationship, it is not a measure of total profit-ability. For example, the analysis tends to focus on activity charges for which compensating balances are maintained—account maintenance, items depos-ited, ledger entries, wire transfers, etc.—but rarely makes allowance for other types of services such as loans, investment counseling, Federal funds transac-tions, trust services, or data processing. Its value, therefore, is primarily in analyzing the accounts of nonborrowers with heavy activity charges, such as respondent banks. For other customers, the omission of loan relationships has at times allowed the double or even triple use of compensating balances. Since cross-checking is frequently not automatic, a compensating balance required for a loan might at times be used to compensate for activity charges and also serve as a justification for a future call on credit.[2]

The primary objectives of account analysis are to measure the adequacy of

---

[2] Increasingly, banks have sought to correct the double use of balances by deducting both the com-pensating balance for a loan and required reserves from the collected balances shown in an account analysis. While this approach represents a step in the right direction, it does not allow for an analysis of the profitability of the loan. Possible tradeoffs between interest rates on loans and compensating balances are not shown. Moreover, the costs of making loans, variations in risk, necessary return on capital, etc., cannot readily be handled in this framework. By comparison, profitability analysis seeks to determine the total relative profitability of a customer relationship.

Table 1
FIRST NATIONAL BANK

Account Analysis for:
Month of:

EARNINGS ALLOWANCE

Average Ledger Balance		$_____
Less Average Uncollected Funds		$_____
Average Collected Balance		$_____
Less Legal Reserve of (17½%)		$_____
Average Balance Available for Investment		$_____
Earnings Allowance (%)		
INVESTMENT VALUE		$_____

EXPENSES

Account Maintenance	$2.00	$_____
Credits	7¢ each	$_____
Debits	7¢ each	$_____
Deposited Items		
Not Encoded	3¢ each	$_____
Encoded	2¢ each	$_____
Returned Items	25¢ each	$_____
Stop Payments	$2.00 each	$_____
Wire Transfers	$1.50 each	$_____
Coupon Envelopes		$_____
Currency Transactions		$_____
Coin Shipped		$_____
Account Reconciliation		$_____
Lockbox Services		$_____
Float Overdrafts		$_____
_____		$_____
_____		$_____
_____		$_____
TOTAL EXPENSES		$_____
NET PROFIT (OR LOSS)		$_____

compensating balances and to obtain an indication of the profits generated by an account relationship. The meaning of the profit figure obtained, however, is generally uncertain and can rarely be related directly to the profits of the bank. Since the price of a service often includes a markup, a high volume customer is likely to be more profitable than a low volume relationship, even though the computed profits are identical. Moreover, some banks build in an additional profit margin by granting an earnings allowance on investable funds below the actual earnings value of those funds or by making a deduction for reserves which exceeds actual requirements. In either case, the computed profits would tend to be understated. However, some bank services, such as consulting, credit checks on accounts receivable, loan participations, and security safekeeping, are often not included in the analysis, with the result that the estimated profits could be biased upward. For these reasons, many banks avoid a listing for profits at the bottom of an analysis statement, preferring instead to show net revenue as the amount available to compensate for other nonlisted services.

A SAMPLE PROFITABILITY STATEMENT

Profitability analysis seeks to overcome some of the shortcomings of regular account analysis by presenting considerably more detailed income statements for major customers. Multiple accounts for a single corporate relationship are consolidated, including those of subsidiaries and perhaps even major officers. Losses on one account, therefore, can be offset with profits on others. The earnings and expenses associated with loans and various fee services, such as the purchase and sale of securities, not typically considered in an account analysis are likely to be included in a profitability statement. Rather than emphasizing activity charges, however, profitability analysis focuses on the commercial lending function of banks and is of the greatest use in determining the profitability of net borrowers.

In the profitability analysis, the net amount of funds borrowed is computed and the estimated profit or loss from the income statement is generally assumed to raise or lower the return on funds loaned. Since estimated profitability tends to be strongly influenced by the terms on loans—compensating balances, interest rates, and associated fees—the analysis has often been proposed as a means of determining the loan terms necessary to meet a minimum profit goal for a bank. It can also be a helpful guide in allocating bank resources since the analysis tends to highlight the most profitable types of customers and loans. In some banks the analysis is also used to evaluate the performance of lending officers.

As might be expected for a relatively new technique, the methods of computing customer profitability vary significantly among banks. In part these variations arise from differences in management philosophy about the types of services deserving emphasis and the appropriate base to which profits should be related. Other factors include the amount of effort a bank may wish to devote to a partially nonautomated process, the degree of precision the bank expects from the figures, and differences in concepts, judgment, and sophistication in the measurement of certain variables. The more common methods of measuring profitability will be discussed in a forthcoming article, but one possible approach which demonstrates the general principles involved is shown in Table 2.

Sources and Uses of Funds

The first section of the profitability statement contains an analysis of the sources and uses of bank funds. Multiple loans to a customer are first consolidated to obtain average total loans outstanding (line 1).[3] As in the account

---

[3] In computing average loans and deposits, allowance must generally be made for the time period under consideration. For example, suppose a bank is conducting an annual profitability analysis on a customer relationship. During the year the customer borrowed $1 million for 9 months at an 8 per cent rate of interest. On an annual basis, this loan could be represented as $750,000 at 8 per cent or alternatively $1 million at 6 per cent. In most instances, the specific approach used would have no direct effect on the relative profitability ranking of individual customers but could affect comparisons of the computed profitability index with such external indicators as the prime loan rate. Consequently, the

Table 2
FIRST NATIONAL BANK
Customer Profitability Analysis

Account: XYZ Manufacturing

Affiliated Accounts:_____

_____

_____

Date: July 20, 1975

Period: 12/31 - 6/30

Type of Loan:_____

	CURRENT PERIOD	LAST 12 MONTHS
SOURCES AND USES OF FUNDS		
1. Average Loan Balance:	$_____	$_____
2. Average Collected Balance:	$_____	$_____
a. Investable Balance (17.5% reserve):	$_____	$_____
3. Average Time Balance:	$_____	$_____
a. Investable Balance (3% reserve):	$_____	$_____
4. Total Loanable Funds (2a + 3a):	$_____	$_____
5. Bank Funds Used by Customer (1 - 4):	$_____	$_____
a. Allocated Capital (8% of 1):	$_____	$_____
b. Funds Transferred from Pool (5 - 5a):	$_____	$_____
INCOME		
6. Gross Interest Income on Loans:	$_____	$_____
7. Earnings on Deposits (*xxx*% of 4):	$_____	$_____
8. Fees Paid:		
a: Service Charge Fees:	$_____	$_____
b: Loan Commitments:	$_____	$_____
c: Data Processing:	$_____	$_____
d: Total (8a + 8b + 8c):	$_____	$_____
9. Total Income (6 + 7 + 8):	$_____	$_____
EXPENSES		
10. Activity Costs from Account Analysis:	$_____	$_____
11. Interest Accrued on Time Deposits:	$_____	$_____
12. Charge for Bank Funds Used:		
a: Allocated Capital (20% of 5a):	$_____	$_____
b: Pool Funds (*xxx*% of 5b):	$_____	$_____
c: Total (12a + 12b):	$_____	$_____
13. Loan Handling Expenses:	$_____	$_____
14. Cost of Fee Services:	$_____	$_____
15. Data Processing:	$_____	$_____
16. Total Expenses (10 + 11 + 12 + 13 + 14 + 15):	$_____	$_____
NET INCOME		
17. Net Income Before Taxes (9 - 16):	$_____	$_____
PROFITABILITY MEASURES		
18. Allocated Capital Index (17 ÷ 5a):	_____%	_____%
19. Net Profits/Net Funds Used (17 ÷ 5):	_____%	_____%
20. Net Profits/Gross Amount Borrowed (17 ÷ 1):	_____%	_____%
21. Gross Profits/Net Funds Used [(17 + 12c)÷5] :	_____%	_____%

method of adjustment should be selected with a view to the ultimate objectives for which the profitability analysis is being conducted. Of course, if the analysis is being conducted on a more frequent basis (e.g., monthly or quarterly), adjustment of both the average balances and interest rates is likely to be necessary.

analysis, average investable or loanable funds provided to the bank by the customer (line 4) are obtained by deducting cash items in process of collection and an allowance for reserve requirements from gross ledger balances. Some banks also make deductions for the compensating balances required to cover the activity charges in the account analysis. Regardless, the deposit figure remaining after the various deductions have been subtracted is then netted against average loans outstanding to obtain the average net bank funds used by the customer (line 5). The customer, in other words, is assumed to borrow his own funds first.

For many banks the previous step completes the analysis of bank funds advanced to a customer. If the bank, however, wishes to relate the profit on the relationship to the return on bank capital, as is the case in the example, the net funds loaned to the customer must be subdivided into at least two categories. The first is the proportion of funds supplied from the bank's capital account. Allocated capital (line 5a) is frequently a flat percentage of gross loans. Some banks, though, assign capital in proportion to the estimated risk on loans, while others assume capital is also required to support the customer's deposits. Since profits will ultimately be related to the assigned capital, variations in its allocation can have a significant impact on the estimated profitability of a relationship. All other things being equal, a higher capital allocation tends to reduce the profit rate. In any event, if the return on capital is to be a measure of actual profitability, the capital assigned to a customer relationship should be selected in such a way that for the bank as a whole the total assigned capital is equal to the bank's actual capital.

The remaining category of bank funds supplied (line 5b) is a residual and represents funds obtained from sources other than the capital accounts. If the bank chooses to differentiate further among alternative sources of funds, such as purchased funds and deposit funds, this entry could be subdivided. The use of multiple pools of funds, however, is relatively uncommon.

Income

The second section of the profitability statement lists the major sources of income derived by the bank from the customer relationship. Most of the entries shown are self-explanatory. Gross interest income (line 6) includes the interest accruing on loans during the analysis period. Interest earnings on deposits (line 7) are imputed on the loanable funds supplied by the customer. This entry is required to give the customer income credit for compensating balances maintained. Service charges (line 8a) represent any fees paid to the bank to cover deposit activity costs or any charges associated with obtaining loans, such as points. Since these charges are most likely to arise when compensating balances are inadequate, provision must be made for their inclusion. Under the loan commitment entry (line 8b), a figure would be entered only if the customer had paid an outright fee for a commitment or a line of credit. If a compensating balance had been maintained instead, these funds would be reflected in the sources and uses section of the table and earnings accordingly imputed. In addition, net bank funds used by the customer would be reduced, resulting in a lower charge for bank funds loaned in the expense section of the analysis. If the analysis and the charges were internally consistent, either approach would have the same effect on estimated profits.

The inclusion of income from data processing services (line 8c) is somewhat controversial. Some banks feel income should be included only to the extent it is related to regular bank services or loans. Under this view, specialized services, such as EDP or trust departments, are treated independently of normal bank operations. These functions serve as separate profit centers but any income and expenses are not included in a profitability analysis related to loans. Others, however, feel that an accurate picture of the profitability of a customer relationship can be obtained only if all income and expenses from services are included. Banks in this latter groups often believe that customers are not likely to differentiate among different profit centers in considering the compensation for a bundle of bank services. On balance, neither approach is wholly satisfactory and practices vary among banks. Nevertheless, if a bank includes the funds received for a specialized service in the income portion of the profitability statement, the charge for providing that service should also be listed under expenses.

Expenses

The third major section of the profitability table derives the bank's total expenses associated with servicing the customer relationship. The first entry, charge for activity services (line 10), could be approached two ways. The bank in the example has implicitly opted to assign any profit from activity services to general profits associated with loans. Thus, it has based the entry on the actual costs of providing services, ideally making sure that the charge includes the expenses of all services provided for compensating balances. To the extent a customer maintains compensating balances based on the price of services rather than the cost, the earnings on the compensating balances would exceed the bank's cost of services. Other banks, however, often feel that it is inappropriate to allocate all profits to loans. According to these banks, the users of services requiring much labor and equipment should be expected to contribute to the profitability of those services. The charges for the activity services performed by the latter group of banks are usually based on the prices used in the account analysis. The price approach, moreover, allows banks to vary the profit margin on different services.

Either option could be justified. Banks relatively confident that they have developed accurate cost figures for all important services would perhaps find the cost approach superior since the total profits on the relationship are made more explicit. On the other hand, if a bank has not fully costed all services or if the accuracy of the cost figures is uncertain, the latter approach may be preferable. The use of prices would tend to build in a margin for services not included in the account analysis. In recognition of these difficulties, some banks compute profitability using both costs and prices. Regardless, either method is capable of suffering from the same types of biases previously discussed in conjuction with the account analysis.

In a similar vein, the charge for bank funds used (line 12) can be handled in a variety of ways. The example assumes the bank has established a specific pretax profit goal on capital. This target is simply built in as an expense. The target, however, must be realistic given projected interest rates and earnings. Alternatively, some banks do not establish a formal goal for return on capital. In these instances, the total of net bank funds supplied to the customer is usually assumed to come from the general fund pool. Under this approach, the computed profits are ultimately related to allocated capital, but the expected return on capital is not built in as an expense. Variations can also arise among banks in the interest charge for pool funds (line 12b). Some prefer to use an estimate of the bank's average cost of loanable funds, while others choose to use a measure of the cost of purchased funds.

The remaining items in the expense section are largely self-explanatory. Interest accrued on time deposits (line 11) includes interest earned by the customer on any time and savings deposits listed in the sources and uses section of the table. Many banks include time deposits in the profitability analysis only if they are noninterest earning or carry interest rates well below market levels. Large denomination CD's bearing competitive rates are often excluded from the analysis since these deposits are generally viewed as investments by corporate treasurers and are not likely to be bound to a bank by a customer relationship. Credit and loan handling expenses (line 13) are designed to cover the costs of making loans. Charges would be based on the operation and maintenance of the loan department, salaries of loan analysts, an allowance for bank overhead, and any outright expenses the bank has incurred in making the loan, such as legal fees. The entry for fee services (line 14) should make allowance for the cost of any services included in the income portion of the statement which have not been classified elsewhere under expenses. Possible examples might be charges for account reconciliation, lockboxes, payroll preparation, and night depository services. Finally, the inclusion of data processing expenses (line 15) is required, as discussed earlier, to ensure consistency in the treatment of income and expenses.

Net Income and Profitability

The last lines of the profitability statement are used to derive different indicators of the profitability of the customer relationship. Total profits or net income is shown in line 17. In line 18, the allocated capital index is computed by dividing profit by allocated capital. If greater than zero, this index indicates that the bank is actually realizing a higher profit rate on customer relationships than the goal previously established by the bank. A negative figure would suggest that profits were not sufficient to meet the target, while a zero figure would imply the goal had just been met.

The return on capital is by necessity an important criterion in judging the profitability of a customer relationship, but it is not the sole concern. For example, it provides no indication of the size of the relationship. The index could be high, but profits low. The amount of capital allocated to a relationship is also somewhat arbitrary, possibly leading to distortions in the index number. These types of considerations have caused many banks to compute more than one profitability ratio. One possibility is to determine profits as a percentage of net bank funds borrowed by the customer (line 19).

While the specific methods of computing customer profitability differ greatly among banks, the general objectives are often quite similar. Not only does the analysis provide a guide to whether a customer is adequately contributing to the profits of an institution, but it also formalizes the tradeoff between the terms on loans. For example, if the interest rate on a loan were to increase, income, net profits, and the profitability indexes would all rise accordingly. Similarly, if larger compensating balances were to be maintained, profitability would also rise as the imputed interest on deposits increased and as the charge for net bank funds borrowed declined. Some profitability statements even contain a series of entries at the conclusion of the analysis specifying what interest rates on loans would be necessary to meet bank profit objectives given differing compensating balance requirements. Regardless, the applicability of profitability analysis tends to be limited largely to customers who borrow. If the customer in the example were a nonborrower, the profitability indexes would be meaningless, although capital could perhaps be allocated on some basis other than gross loans.

Some caution must be exercised in analyzing the sample profitability statement. While the sample illustrates the general principles involved in computing customer profitability, the specific entries and the precise approach cannot be taken as representative of the analysis methods at all banks. There are wide differences among banks, not only in the approaches used to measure customer profitability, but also in the items included in the analysis. Many banks exclude some deposits or some loans in measuring the sources and uses of funds. The range of services for which income and expenses are listed can also vary greatly.

Differences in the structure of an analysis can have a significant impact on estimated profits. Most banks, for example, determine only the total of investable funds represented by deposits, implicitly allowing those balances to serve as compensation for either loans or activity services, but some also make an explicit deduction from collected funds for the compensating balances required for activity services. The effect of this latter approach is to increase net funds borrowed, thus lowering the estimated profitability of a given customer at those banks using a net funds borrowed ratio. Some banks allocate capital to borrowings while others assign an explicit expense charge for risk and loss.

Similarly, some banks charge customers the cost of money on the gross amount borrowed and give an interest credit on gross investable funds. By comparison, others charge only for net funds borrowed. For these two methods to yield identical results, the interest rates used for funds borrowed and supplied must be identical, yet such is not always the case. Some banks compute the profitability of loan and investment services separately to avoid having to allocate all profits to loans and some use slightly different formulas for calculating the profitability of different types of customers. Additional examples could be cited, but these demonstrate a few of the differences that exist among banks in the techniques of computing customer profitability.

INDEXES OF CUSTOMER PROFITABILITY

Just as a bank has numerous options in designing a profitability analysis, a wide variety of profitability measures could be computed. Nevertheless, at most banks, profitability is generally judged on the basis of a handful of standard indicators. These include the ratio of gross profits to net funds used, net profits to net funds used, net profits to gross amount borrowed, and net profits to allocated capital.[4] While only one of these commonly used indexes makes any explicit reference to bank capital, the alternative ratios can often be related in a fairly direct way to earnings on capital. As a result, the desired return on capital can set minimum acceptable values to the noncapital ratios.

Gross Profits/Net Funds Used

One of the profitability measures least likely to be subject to sizable distortion, and therefore one of the most credible, is the ratio of gross profits to net funds loaned. Gross profits are equal to total profits when the cost of money is not included in expenses. Under this approach, customers are assumed to borrow their own funds first and funds supplied by a customer are implicitly granted an earnings allowance equal to the average rate on the customer's loans. In mathematical terms the standard formula is:

$$\frac{\text{Gross Profits}}{\text{Net Funds Used}} = \frac{Y - E}{L - D}$$

where Y equals gross income derived from the customer relationship; E equals all costs of servicing the relationship other than the cost of funds; L equals average loans attributable to the relationship; and D equals average loanable or investable funds provided by the customer.[5]

The behavior of this ratio under varying circumstances can be readily seen. By eliminating the costs of funds from the analysis, a bank can avoid a situation in which the profitability index for customers with fixed rate loans and compensating balances varies inversely as money market interest rates rise

---

[4] A detailed discussion of alternative types of profitability measures is presented by Kenneth E. Reich and Dennis C. Neff in *Customer Profitability Analysis: A Tool for Improving Bank Profits*, a booklet published by the Bank Administration Institute and the Robert Morris Associates (1972).

[5] In terms of Table 2, this measure corresponds to line 21.

and fall. The index, though, would be sensitive to changes in loan terms. Since the interest paid on loans is reflected in Y and the compensating balances maintained are included in D, the index would rise if either of these variables increased. If net funds borrowed declines, the ratio—other things equal—will approach infinity. This tendency implies that large borrowers unable to keep sizable compensating balances may have a comparatively low profitability ratio and that smaller borrowers are likely to rank higher. If the customer is a net borrower, the value of the index can be compared directly to the bank's cost of funds or money market rates. As long as the ratio exceeds the bank's cost of funds, the relationship would be profitable. To ensure that a target return on capital is realized, however, the value of the index must exceed the bank's cost of funds by a sufficient margin.[6]

The gross profits/net funds used ratio has two important limitations. First, it is of little use in analyzing the profitability of a net depositor. Since the denominator would be negative, the ratio would imply that a bank was losing money on net depositors, which, of course, is incorrect. Second, the index makes no allowance for the size of the customer relationship. Among customers with identical rates of return on net funds used, those using relatively more funds are likely to be more important to the total profitability of the bank. While these qualifications are hardly unique to this particular measure, they do demonstrate the need for examining the figures underlying the computation of an index number before drawing any conclusions. Not only is the value of the index itself of importance, but also the relative weight or significance that should be attached to it.

Net Profits/Net Funds Used

Despite the relative ease in computing gross profits, most banks prefer to base an analysis of customer profitability on net profits. Net profits are gross profits minus an allowance for the cost of funds loaned.[7] The basic formula for this profitability index is:

$$\frac{\text{Net Profits}}{\text{Net Funds Used}} = \frac{Y\text{-}E\text{-}C}{L\text{-}D} = \frac{Y\text{-}E}{L\text{-}D} - \frac{C}{L\text{-}D}$$

where C equals the cost of net funds used. This profitability indicator differs from the gross profits/net funds used measure only in that the cost of funds (expressed as a percentage of net funds used) is subtracted from the gross profit yield. If the gross profit index, for example, were 10 per cent, and the cost of funds were 6 per cent, net profits/net funds used would be 4 per cent. Obviously, a positive ratio implies the relationship is profitable. A zero ratio

---

[6] An interesting analysis of the philosophy underlying the development and usage of the gross profits/net funds used indicator at the First National Bank of Boston is contained in a thesis by Peter W. Stanton, "A Management Information System for the Commercial Lending Function" (unpublished thesis, Stonier Graduate School of Banking, Rutgers University, 1974).

[7] In terms of Table 2, this measure corresponds to line 19.

would suggest a break-even situation, and a negative one, losses. As a result of the parallelism between these two profitability measures, both have the same limitations and behave in a generally similar fashion.

Net Profits/Gross Amount Borrowed

A slightly different measure of customer profitability is the ratio of net profits to gross amount borrowed. Since this approach combines methods previously discussed, little further explanation is necessary.[8] The basic formula is:

$$\frac{\text{Net Profits}}{\text{Gross Amount Borrowed}} = \frac{Y\text{-}E\text{-}C}{L}$$

This profitability index is applicable only to borrowers, but unlike the previous measures does not require the borrower to be a net user of funds. While comparisons between the index value and money market interest rates are not meaningful, the index varies directly with the average interest rate on loans. If the average loan rate rises 1 per cent, so would the profitability index. This measure, therefore, has the advantage of showing directly any change in loan interest rates necessary to meet minimum profit objectives. In general, a zero value for the ratio would imply a break-even situation. Banks utilizing this formula, though, generally seek a minimum return on gross loans of 1½ to 2½ per cent to realize a desired return on capital.

Net Profits/Allocated Capital

The final commonly used profitability measure is the ratio of net profits to allocated capital. Since the example at the beginning of this article used the capital allocation approach, little need be added about the general description of the method.[9] Mathematically, the formula is:

$$\frac{\text{Net Profits}}{\text{Allocated Capital}} = \frac{Y\text{-}E\text{-}C}{K}$$

where K represents capital allocated to a customer relationship. If capital is allocated to both earning assets and deposits, this index is perhaps the most versatile of those widely used. The profitability of all customers, whether or not they are borrowers, could be analyzed.[10]

---

[8] In terms of Table 2, this measure corresponds to line 20.

[9] In terms of Table 2, this measure corresponds to line 18.

[10] The pioneering work in the capital allocation method of measuring customer profitability was performed by Philadelphia National Bank. A detailed description of the analysis methods used at Philadelphia National is contained in a publication the bank has prepared entitled "Profitability Analysis of Commercial Customers."

Other Measures of Profitability

In addition to the four basic ratios, many banks have adopted additional indexes of customer profitability. These include such ratios as net or gross profits/total revenue, net profits/total expenses, total income/net funds borrowed, gross profits/total loans, actual income/target income, and total revenue/total expenses. Some banks simply compute net or gross profits but do not relate the figure to any specific indicator of the size of a customer relationship. Although each indicator has unique properties and should be selected to reflect management objectives, the choice of a particular indicator is not likely to be a crucial matter. Under normal circumstances, most indicators produce roughly the same ranking of customers.

CONCLUDING REMARK

In the future, bank profitability is likely to depend increasingly on the differential between loan rates and the cost of funds. Since profitability analysis tends to focus on this spread, it represents an important innovation for commercial banks. By combining numerous aspects of a customer relationship into a single analysis, it allows for a more accurate measure of customer profitability and overcomes some of the limitations of an account analysis. While the mathematics of customer profitability analysis are relatively simple, the emphasis on one or two index numbers tends to mask the numerous choices which must be made in constructing a profitability formula. On the first level, there is the question of what to include in a measure of a customer relationship, and on the secondary level, the issue of how to measure those items that are included. A balance between theoretical precision and practicality is always necessary. As a result, each portion of a profitability analysis has some controversial features.

ABCs OF FIGURING INTEREST*

Anne Marie L. Gonczy

36

Although Shakespeare cautioned "neither a borrower nor a lender be," using and providing credit has become a way of life for many individuals in today's economy. Examples of borrowing by individuals are numerous—home mortgages, car loans, credit cards, etc. While perhaps more commonly thought of as investing, many examples of lending by individuals can be identified. By opening a savings account, an individual makes a loan to the bank; by purchasing a Treasury bill, an individual makes a loan to the government.

As with goods and services that an individual might buy or sell, the use or extension of credit has a price attached to it, namely the interest paid or earned. And, just as consumers shop for the best price on a particular item of merchandise, so too should consumers "comparison shop" for credit—whether borrowing or lending.

But comparing prices for credit can, at times, be confusing. Although the price of credit is generally stated as a rate of interest, the amount of interest paid or earned depends on a number of other factors, including the method used to calculate interest.

To an extent, the Truth-in-Lending law passed in 1968 has eliminated some of the confusion concerning what it costs a consumer to borrow. Rules

*This is a revised edition of an earlier article originally published by the Federal Reserve Bank of Chicago in the September 1973 issue of *Business Conditions*. The original article and the revision were written by Anne Marie L. Gonczy. Reprinted with permission from the Federal Reserve Bank of Chicago. The article is presently a part of the Bank's *Readings in Economics and Finance*.

defining creditor responsibilities under Truth-in-Lending are covered in the Federal Reserve's Regulation Z. Most importantly, creditors are required to disclose both the Annual Percentage Rate (APR) and the total dollar Finance Charge to the borrowing consumer. Simply put, the APR is the relative cost of credit expressed in percentage terms on the basis of one year. Just as "unit pricing" gives the consumer a basis for comparing prices of different-sized packages of the same product, the APR enables the consumer to compare the prices of different loans regardless of the amount, maturity, or other terms.

Even with Truth-in-Lending, various interest calculation methods continue to be used. And no similar laws apply to help the consumer who is "lending" rather than borrowing. While Truth-in-Savings legislation, aimed at clarifying how much a consumer earns on savings accounts, has been introduced in Congress a number of times, it has not yet passed. Thus, confusion concerning the amount of interest paid or earned by a consumer persists. The confusion can be lessened, however, if the relationships between the different methods used to calculate interest are understood.

INTEREST CALCULATIONS

Interest represents the price borrowers pay to lenders for credit over specified periods of time. The amount of interest paid depends on a number of factors; the dollar amount lent or borrowed, the length of time involved in the transaction, the stated (or nominal) annual rate of interest, the repayment schedule, and the method used to calculate interest.

If, for example, an individual deposits $1,000 for one year in a bank paying 5 percent interest on savings, then at the end of the year the depositor may receive interest of $50, or he may receive some other amount, depending on the way interest is calculated. Alternatively, an individual who borrows $1,000 for one year at 5 percent and repays the loan in one payment at the end of a year may pay $50 in interest, or he may pay some other amount, again depending on the calculation method used.

SIMPLE INTEREST

The various methods used to calculate interest are basically variations of the simple interest calculation method.

The basic concept underlying simple interest is that interest is paid only on the original amount borrowed for the length of time the borrower has use of the credit. The amount borrowed is referred to as the principal. In the simple interest calculation, interest is computed only on that portion of the original principal still owed.

Example 1: Suppose $1,000 is borrowed at 5 percent and repaid in one payment at the end of one year. Using the simple interest calculation, the interest amount would be 5 percent of $1,000 for one year or $50 since the borrower had use of $1,000 for the entire year.

When more than one payment is made on a simple interest loan, the method of computing interest is referred to as "interest on the declining balance." Since the borrower only pays interest on that amount of original principal which has not yet been repaid, interest paid will be smaller the more frequent the payments. At the same time, of course, the amount of credit the borrower has at his disposal is also smaller.

Example 2: Using simple interest on the declining balance to compute interest charges, a 5 percent, $1,000 loan repaid in two payments—one at the end of the first half-year and another at the end of the second half-year—would accumulate total interest charges of $37.50. The first payment would be $500 plus $25 (5 percent of $1,000 for one-half year), or $525; the second payment would be $500 plus $12.50 (5 percent of $500 for one-half year), or $512.50. The total amount paid would be $525 plus $512.50, or $1,037.50. Interest equals the difference between the amount repaid and the amount borrowed, or $37.50. If four quarterly payments of $250 plus interest were made, the interest amount would be $31.25; if 12 monthly payments of $83.33 plus interest were made, the interest amount would be $27.08.

Example 3: When interest on the declining balance method is applied to a 5 percent, $1,000 loan that is to be repaid in two equal payments, payments of $518.83 would be made at the end of the first half-year and at the end of the second half-year. Interest due at the end of the first half-year remains $25; therefore, with the first payment the balance is reduced by $493.83 ($518.83 less $25), leaving the borrower $506.17 to use during the second half-year. The interest for the second half-year is 5 percent of $506.17 for one-half year, or $12.66. The final $518.83 payment, then, covers interest of $12.66 plus the outstanding balance of $506.17. Total interest paid is $25 plus $12.66, or $37.66, slightly more than in Example 2.

This equal payment variation is commonly used with mortgage payment schedules. Each payment over the duration of the loan is split into two parts. Part one is the interest due at the time the payment is made, and part two—the remainder—is applied to the balance or amount still owed. In addition to mortgage lenders, credit unions typically use the simple interest/declining balance calculation method for computing interest on loans. In recent years, a number of banks have also offered personal loans using this method.

OTHER CALCULATION METHODS

Add-on interest, bank discount, and compound interest calculation methods differ from the simple interest method as to when, how, and on what balance interest is paid. The "effective annual rate," or the Annual Percentage Rate (APR), for these methods is that annual rate of interest which when used in the simple interest rate formula equals the amount of interest payable in these other calculation methods. For the declining balance method, the effective annual rate of interest is the stated or nominal annual rate of interest. For the methods to be described below, the effective annual rate of interest differs from the nominal rate.

Add-on Interest. When the add-on interest method is used, interest is calculated on the full amount of the original principal. The interest amount is immediately added to the original principal, and payments are determined by dividing principal plus interest by the number of payments to be made. When only one payment is involved, this method produces the same effective interest rate as the simple interest method. When two or more payments are to be made, however, use of the add-on interest method results in an effective rate of interest that is greater than the nominal rate. True, the interest amount is calculated by applying the nominal rate to the total amount borrowed, but the borrower does not have use of the total amount for the entire time period if two or more payments are made.

Example 4: Consider, again, the two-payment loan in Example 3. Using the add-on interest method, interest of $50 (5 percent of $1,000 for one year) is added to the $1,000 borrowed, giving $1,050 to be repaid; half (or $525) at the end of the first half-year and the other half at the end of the second half-year.

Recall that in Example 3, where the declining balance method was used, an effective rate of 5 percent meant two equal payments of $518.83 were to be made. Now with the add-on interest method each payment is $525. The effective rate of this 5 percent add-on rate loan, then, is greater than 5 percent. In fact, the corresponding effective rate is 6.631 percent. This rate takes into account the fact that the borrower does not have use of $1,000 for the entire year, but rather use of $1,000 for the first half-year and use of about $500 for the second half-year.

To see that a one-year, two equal-payment, 5 percent add-on rate loan is equivalent to a one-year, two equal-payment, 6.631 percent declining balance loan, consider the following. When the first $525 payment is made, $33.15 in interest is due (6.631 percent of $1,000 for one-half year). Deducting the $33.15 from $525 leaves $491.85 to be applied to the outstanding balance of $1,000, leaving the borrower with $508.15 to use during the second half-year. The second $525 payment covers $16.85 in interest (6.631 percent of $508.15 for one-half year) and the $508.15 balance due.

In this particular example, using the add-on interest method means that no matter how many payments are to be made, the interest will always be $50. As the number of payments increases, the borrower has use of less and less credit over the year. For example, if four quarterly payments of $262.50 are made, the borrower has the use of $1,000 during the first quarter, around

Add-on interest: the more frequent the payments, the higher the effective rate

effective annual rate*
(percent)

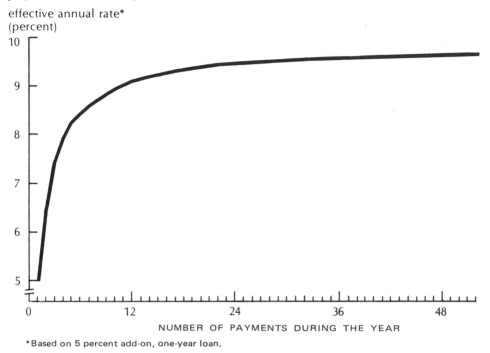

NUMBER OF PAYMENTS DURING THE YEAR

*Based on 5 percent add-on, one-year loan.

$750 during the second quarter, around $500 during the third quarter, and around $250 during the fourth and final quarter. Therefore, as the number of payments increases, the effective rate of interest also increases. For instance, in the current example, if four quarterly payments are made, the effective rate of interest would be 7.922 percent; if 12 monthly payments are made, the effective interest rates would be 9.105 percent. The add-on interest method is commonly used by finance companies and some banks in determining interest on consumer loans.

Bank Discount. When the bank discount rate calculation method is used, interest is calculated cn the amount to be paid back and the borrower receives the difference between the amount to be paid back and the interest amount. In Example 1, a 5 percent, $1,000 loan is to be paid back at the end of one year. Using the bank discount rate method, two approaches are possible.

Example 5: The first approach would be to deduct the interest amount of $50 from the $1,000, leaving the borrower with $950 to use over the year. At the end of the year, he pays $1,000. The interest amount of $50 is the same as in Example 1. The borrower in Example 1, however, had the use of $1,000 over the year. Thus, the effective rate of interest using the bank discount rate method is greater than that for the simple interest rate calculation. The effective rate of interest here would be 5.263 percent—i.e., $50 ÷ $950 —compared to 5 percent in Example 1.

Example 6: The second approach would be to determine the amount that would have to be paid back so that once the interest amount was deducted, the borrower would have the use of $1,000 over the year. This amount is $1,052.63, and this becomes the face value of the note on which interest is calculated. The interest amount (5 percent of $1,052.63 for one year) is $52.63, and this is deducted, leaving the borrower with $1,000 to use over the year. The effective rate of interest, again, is 5.263 percent. The bank discount method is commonly used with short-term business loans. Generally, there are no intermediate payments and the duration of the loan is one year or less.

Compound Interest. When the compound interest calculation is used, interest is calculated on the original principal plus all interest accrued to that point in time. Since interest is paid on interest as well as on the amount borrowed, the effective interest rate is greater than the nominal interest rate. The compound interest rate method is often used by banks and savings institutions in determining interest they pay on savings deposits "loaned" to the institutions by the depositors.

Example 7: Suppose $1,000 is deposited in a bank that pays a 5 percent nominal annual rate of interest, compounded semiannually (i.e., twice a year). At the end of the first half-year, $25 in interest (5 percent of $1,000 for one-half year) is payable. At the end of the year, the interest amount is calculated on the $1,000 plus the $25 in interest already paid, so that the second interest payment is $25.63 (5 percent of $1,025 for one-half year). The interest amount payable for the year, then, is $25 plus $25.63, or $50.63. The effective rate of interest is 5.063 percent, which is greater than the nominal 5 percent rate.

The more often interest is compounded within a particular time period, the greater will be the effective rate of interest. In a year, a 5 percent nominal annual rate of interest compounded four times (quarterly) results in an effective annual rate of 5.0945 percent; compounded 12 times (monthly), 5.1162 percent; and compounded 365 times (daily), 5.1267 percent. When the interval of time between compoundings approaches zero (even shorter than a second), then the method is known as continuous compounding. Five percent continuously compounded for one year will result in an effective annual rate of 5.1271 percent.

HOW LONG IS A YEAR?

In the above examples, a year is assumed to be 365 days long. Historically, in order to simplify interest calculations, financial institutions have often

Compound interest: over time, compounding increases the amount of interest paid

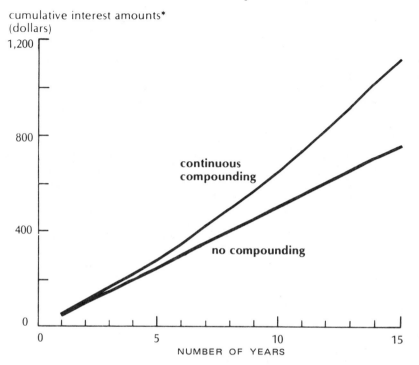

cumulative interest amounts*
(dollars)

*Amount paid on $1000 at 5 percent annual interest rate.

used twelve 30-day months, yielding a 360-day year. If a 360-day year is assumed in the calculation and the amount borrowed is actually used by the borrower for one full year (365 or 366 days), then interest is paid for an additional 5/360 or 6/360 of a "year." For any given nominal rate of interest, the effective rate of interest will be greater when a 360-day year is used in the interest rate calculation than when a 365-day year is used. This has come to be known as the 365-360 method.

Example 8: Suppose $1,000 is deposited in a bank paying a 5 percent nominal annual rate of interest, compounded daily. As pointed out earlier, the effective annual rate of interest for one year, based on a 365-day year, is 5.1267 percent. The interest payable on the 365th day would be $51.27. Daily compounding means that each day the daily rate of 0.0137 percent (5 percent divided by 365 days) was paid on the $1,000 deposit plus all interest payable up to that day. Now suppose a 360-day year is used in the calculation. The daily rate paid becomes 0.0139 percent (5 percent divided by 360 days) so that on the 365th day the interest amount payable would be $52. The effective annual rate of interest, based on a 360-day year would be 5.1997 percent.

Example 9: Suppose that a $1,000 note is discounted at 5 percent and payable in 365 days. This is the situation discussed in Example 5 where, based on a 365-day year, the effective rate of interest was 5.263 percent. If the bank discount rate calculation assumes a 360-day year, then the length of time is computed to be 365/360 or 1-1/72 years instead of one year, the interest deducted (the discount) equals $50.69 instead of $50, and the effective annual rate of interest is 5.34 percent.

WHEN REPAYMENT IS EARLY

In the above examples, it was assumed that periodic loan payments were always made exactly when due. Often, however, a loan may be completely repaid before it is due. When the declining balance method for calculating interest is used, the borrower is not penalized for prepayment since interest is paid only on the balance outstanding for the length of time that amount is owed. When the add-on interest calculation is used, however, prepayment implies that the lender obtains some interest which is unearned. The borrower then is actually paying an even higher effective rate since he does not use the funds for the length of time of the original loan contract.

Some loan contracts make provisions for an interest rebate if the loan is prepaid. One of the common methods used in determining the amount of the interest rebate is referred to as the "Rule of 78." Application of the Rule of 78 yields the percentage of the total interest amount that is to be returned to the borrower in the event of prepayment. The percentage figure is arrived at by dividing the sum of the integer numbers (digits) from one to the number of payments remaining by the sum of the digits from one to the total number of payments specified in the original loan contract. For example, if a five-month loan is paid off by the end of the second month (i.e., there are three payments remaining), the percentage of the interest that the lender would rebate is $(1+2+3) \div (1+2+3+4+5) = (6 \div 15)$, or 40 percent. The name derives from the fact that 78 is the sum of the digits from one to 12 and, therefore, is the denominator in calculating interest rebate percentages for all 12-period loans.

Application of the Rule of 78 results in the borrower paying somewhat more interest than he would have paid with a comparable declining balance loan. How much more depends on the effective rate of interest charged and the total number of payments specified in the original loan contract. The higher the effective rate of interest charged and the greater the specified total number of payments, the greater the amount of interest figured under the Rule of 78 exceeds that under the declining balance method. (See chart on page 477).

The difference between the Rule of 78 interest and the declining balance interest also varies depending upon when the prepayment occurs. This difference over the term of the loan tends to increase up to about the one-third point of the term and then decrease after this point. For example, with a 12-month term, the difference with prepayment occurring in the second month would be greater than the difference that would occur with prepayment in the first month; the third-month difference would be greater than the second-month difference; the fourth month (being the one-third point) would be greater than both the third-month difference and the fifth-month difference. After the fifth month, each succeeding month's difference would be less than the previous month's difference.

Example 10: Suppose that there are two $1,000 loans that are to be repaid over 12 months. Interest on the first loans is calculated using a 5 percent add-on method which results in equal payments of $87.50 due at the end of each month ($1,000 plus $50 interest divided by 12 months). The effective annual rate of interest for this loan is 9.105 percent. Any interest rebate due because of prepayment is to be determined by the Rule of 78.

Interest on the second loan is calculated using a declining balance method where the annual rate of interest is the effective annual rate of interest from the first loan, or 9.105 percent. Equal payments of $87.50 are also due at the end of each month for the second loan.

Suppose that repayment on both loans occurs after one-sixth of the term of the loan has passed, i.e., at the end of the second month, with the regular

Interest paid under the Rule of 78 is always more than under the declining balance—

but how much more depends on:

The term of the original loan contract

The effective annual rate of interest

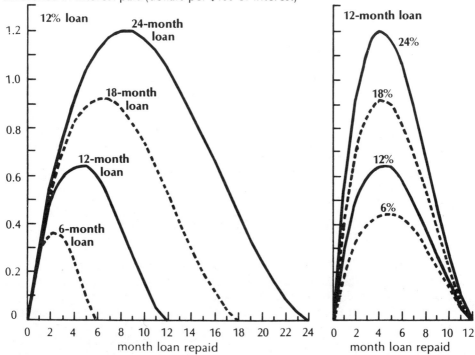

difference in interest paid (dollars per $100 of interest)

first month's payment being made for both loans. The interest paid on the first loan will be $14.74, while the interest paid on the second loan will be $14.57, a difference of 17 cents. If the prepayment occurs at the one-third point, i.e., at the end of the fourth month (regular payments having been made at the end of the first, second, and third months), interest of $26.92 is paid on the first loan and interest of $26.69 on the second loan, a difference of 23 cents. If the prepayment occurs later, say at the three-fourths point, i.e., at the end of the ninth month (regular payments having been made at the end of the first through eighth months), $46.16 in interest is paid on the first loan and $46.07 in interest paid on the second loan, a difference of but 9 cents.

BONUS INTEREST

Savings institutions are permitted to pay interest from the first calendar day of the month on deposits received by the tenth calendar day of the month, and also on deposits withdrawn during the last three business days of a month ending a regular quarterly or semiannual interest period. If a savings institution chooses to do this, then it is paying for the use of the depositor's money for some period of time during which the savings institution does not have the use of the money. The effective rate of interest is, therefore, greater than it would be otherwise.

Example 11: Suppose that on January 10, $1,000 is deposited in a bank paying 5 percent interest compounded daily based on a 365-day year and that funds deposited by the tenth of any month earn interest from the first of that month. On the following December 31, 355 days after the deposit is made, interest for 365 days is payable on the deposit, or $51.27. The bank, however, had the use of the funds for only 355 days. The effective rate of interest, or that rate which when compounded daily for 355 days would yield the interest amount $51.27, is 5.1408 percent.

Although savings institutions choosing to pay interest for these grace periods are prohibited from advertising an effective yield which takes this into account, depositors should be aware of the effect such practice has on the price paid for the use of their money.

CHARGES OTHER THAN INTEREST

In addition to the interest which must be paid, loan agreements often will include other provisions that must be satisfied. Two of these provisions are mortgage points and required (compensating) deposit balances.

Mortgage Points. Mortgage lenders will sometimes require the borrower to pay a charge in addition to the interest. This extra charge is calculated as a certain percentage of the mortgage amount and is referred to as mortgage points. For example, if 2 points are charged on a $50,000 mortgage, then 2 percent of $50,000, or $1,000, must be paid in addition to the stated interest. The borrower, therefore, is paying a higher price than if points were not charged—i.e., the effective rate of interest is increased. In order to determine what the effective rate of interest is when points are charged, it is necessary to deduct the dollar amount resulting from the point calculation from the mortgage amount and add it to the interest amount to be paid. The borrower is viewed as having the mortgage amount less the point charge amount rather than the entire mortgage amount.

Example 12: Suppose that 2 points are charged on a 25-year, $50,000 mortgage where the rate of interest (declining balance calculation) is 12 percent. The payments are to be $526.61 per month. Once the borrower pays the $1,000 point charge, he starts out with $49,000 to use. With payments of $526.61 a month over 25 years, the result of the 2 point charge is an effective rate of 12.29 percent.

The longer the time period of the mortgage, the lower will be the effective rate of interest when points are charged because the point charge is spread out over more payments. In the above example, if the mortgage had been for 30 years instead of 25 years, the effective rate of interest would have been 12.27 percent.

Required (Compensating) Deposit Balances. A bank may require that a borrower maintain a certain percentage of the loan amount on deposit as a condition for obtaining the loan. The borrower, then, does not have the use of the entire loan amount but rather the use of the loan amount less the amount that must be kept on deposit. The effective rate of interest is greater than it would be if no compensating deposit balance were required.

Example 13: Suppose that $1,000 is borrowed at 5 percent from a bank to be paid back at the end of one year. Suppose, further, that the lending bank requires that 10 percent of the loan amount be kept on deposit. The borrower, therefore, has the use of only $900 ($1,000 less 10 percent) on which he pays an interest amount of $50 (5 percent of $1,000 for one year). The effective rate of interest is therefore, 5.556 percent as opposed to 5 percent when no compensating balance is required.

SUMMARY

Although not an exhaustive list, the methods of calculating interest described here are some of the more common methods in use. They serve to indicate that the method of interest calculation can substantially affect the amount of interest paid, and that savers and borrowers should be aware not only of nominal interest rates but also of how nominal rates are used in calculating total interest charges.

HOW 1,000 HIGH-PERFORMANCE BANKS WEATHERED THE RECENT RECESSION[†]

William F. Ford and Dennis A. Olson[*]

37

The five years 1972-1976 saw several major stress indicators in the banking industry reach their postwar peaks.

For example, loan losses absorbed by banking increased four-fold during this period—from about $900 million (net of recoveries) in 1972 to $3.5 billion in 1976.

The cost of purchased funds also soared into the double-digit range, sharply reducing net interest spreads.

And the widely-publicized failures of a few large banks—including Franklin National of New York and U.S. National Bank of San Diego—led the media and the public to believe that the entire industry was on the brink of disaster.

But in spite of all these problems, the banking industry's net earnings actually increased every year, from $5.65 billion in 1972 to $7.85 billion in 1976. And our preliminary estimates for 1977 suggest that the banks collectively experienced earnings gains on the order of $500 million to $800 million last year.

Moreover, *our extensive studies of the FDIC's earnings data base shows*

---

†Reprinted with special permission from the April 1978 issue of *Banking*, Journal of the American Bankers Association. Copyright 1978 by the ABA.

*William A. Ford is President of the Federal Reserve Bank of Atlanta. Dennis Olson is Chief, Analysis Section, Federal Deposit Insurance Corporation. At the time this article was written, Dr. Ford was Senior Vice President of the Wells Fargo Bank and Mr. Olson was an Associate with Golembe Associates, Inc.

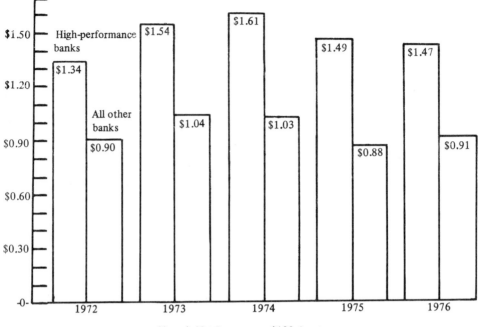

Chart 1 Net Income per $100 Assets.

that the 1,000 most profitable banks in our industry, on average, earned about 20% per year on their equity from 1972 through 1976, as noted in Chart 2. We call this elite subset of companies high-performance banks (HPBs) —roughly the top 7% of 14,000 banks. Their return on equity was 69% greater than the rest of the industry (20.8% vs. 12.3%).

HOW HPBs ARE ISOLATED

Before we go on to analyze how they did this, a few words about our HPB selection criteria may be in order.

To be included in our sample of 1,000 high-performance banks, two tests must be met: First, a bank must have a very high average rate of return for the last five years. Second, to ensure that performance has not fallen off, it must rank in at least the top 50% in profitability for 1976. The 1,000 banks with the highest five-year rates of return on equity that also met the second criterion were designated HPBs.

Our analysis has excluded a few hundred banks for which five years of operating history were not available. This exclusion of new banks from the analysis was intentional, because in the past we have found that new banks tend to have such unusual operating characteristics that comparisons against them are not too meaningful.

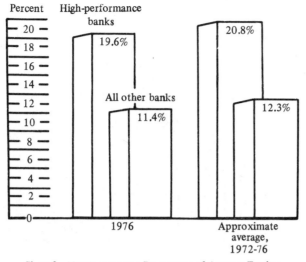

Chart 2   Net Income as a Percentage of Average Equity.

TABLE 1

Key Characteristics of High-Performance Banks

1.   **Maximization of revenues**

High loan income attained through appropriate pricing and avoidance of non-accruing loans, rather than relatively high volume

Maximization of income from tax-exempt securities

Maintenance of sufficient flexibility in asset structure to take advantage of changes in interest rates

2.   **Expense control**

Low investment in fixed assets, lower occupancy expense

Proper control of overhead and discretionary costs such as "other operating expense"

Minimization of loan losses through proper credit analysis

Control of personnel expense through efficient use of fewer employees, rather than through low salaries

3.   **Consistently good management**

Large comparative advantages in the management of smaller, controllable factors

Smaller comparative—but large absolute—advantages in management of larger, less controllable factors

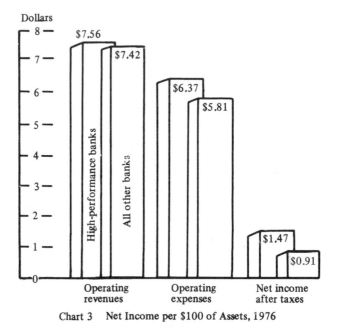

Chart 3   Net Income per $100 of Assets, 1976

ANALYSIS OF PERFORMANCE

With this new background, let's leave the historic data for now and concentrate on 1976, to see if we can figure out how this group of 1,000 banks so substantially outperformed the rest of the industry. Chart 3 presents the basic income equation for 1976.

The high-performance sample had a slightly higher yield on total assets. They generated $7.56 in operating revenues for every $100 of assets, compared with $7.42 for all other banks—a difference of 14¢, or about 2%.

But the high-performance banks had much lower expenses than other banks. In fact, they had total operating expenses of only $5.81 per $100 of assets, compared with $6.37 for the industry—a difference of 56¢, or 8.8%.

These two factors contributed to a substantial difference in net income after taxes. Whereas HPBs brought $1.47 per $100 of assets down to the bottom line, all other banks attained only 91¢. Thus the after-tax rate of return on assets was 56¢ higher than for all other banks, which means that HPBs were fully 61.5% above the industry average. The figures in Table 2 trace the year-by-year net income advantage of the HPBs over other banks, for the entire 5 year period, 1972-1976.

Now let's compare, for 1976 only, the asset-management strategies of HPBs vs. all other banks. As shown in Table 3, HPBs deploy their assets in a pattern distinctly different from that of other banks.

The key differences that we consider significant are the following:

First, HPBs as a group deployed less of their assets in taxable treasury securities (11.80% vs. 13.15%). Second, the same goes for other taxable government securities—mainly Fannie Maes and Ginnie Maes—where the investment in 1976 was 6.15% vs. 7.20% of assets.

TABLE 2

Revenue, Expenses, and Net Income per $100 of Assets, 1972-76

	1972	1973	1974	1975	1976
All other banks					
Revenues	$6.28	$6.76	$7.42	$7.28	$7.42
Expenses	5.14	5.39	6.04	6.20	6.37
NET INCOME	$0.90	$1.04	$1.03	$0.88	$0.91
HPBs					
Revenues	$6.41	$6.88	$7.53	$7.35	$7.56
Expenses	4.70	4.82	5.32	5.48	5.81
NET INCOME	$1.34	$1.54	$1.61	$1.49	$1.47
Difference					
Revenues	$0.13	$0.12	$0.11	$0.07	$0.14
Expenses	0.44	0.57	0.72	0.72	0.56
NET INCOME	$0.44	$0.50	$0.58	$0.61	$0.56

On the other hand, we find that HPBs deploy significantly more of their assets (15.50% vs. 11.60%) in tax-exempt securities. For the typical community bank with high pre-tax earnings, this strategy is appealing because it provides very attractive tax-equivalent yields compared with other assets. Or, stated in another way, a large tax-exempt-bond portfolio is used effectively to provide a tax shelter for high earnings from other sources.

Although it is not shown in the table, we should also note that the HPBs achieve higher yields on their large portfolio of tax-exempt bonds than do other banks. In 1976, HPBs had a tax-equivalent yield of 10.24% on these securities compared with 9.86% for other banks.

Third, with regard to the loan portfolio, the 1976 data confirmed our previous findings—namely, HPBs as a group are less "loaned up" than other banks. This finding is significant because it disproves the typical belief that high profits follow from a high loan volume.

With respect to pricing, we found, as in the past, that HPBs achieved higher yields on their smaller loan portfolios than the other banks. Specifically,

TABLE 3

Asset Composition, 1976

	Percentage of assets		
	HPBs	All other banks	Percentage difference
Cash and due	8.80%	9.40%	(6.4)%
Treasury securities	11.80%	13.15%	(10.3)%
Other govt. securities	6.15%	7.20%	(14.6)%
Tax-exempt securities	15.50%	11.60%	33.6 %
Loans, net	51.10%	51.50%	(0.8)%
Fixed assets	1.35%	1.80%	(25.0)%
Other assets	5.30%	5.35%	(0.9)%
	100.00%	100.00%	

in 1976 the HPBs earned 9.14% on their loans (including interest and fee income) against 8.96% for other banks. And this yield advantage of 18 basis points was achieved while maintaining better-than-average quality in the loan portfolio, as we shall see later.

The fourth asset-management key to high performance banking shown in Table 3 concerns fixed assets. Here, as in all previous years studied, we found the HPBs deploying significantly less of their funds in these non-earning assets—the negative difference being 1.35 vs. 1.80, or 25% less invested in fixed assets.

The difference in "cash and due" asset allocations shown in Table 3 are probably not significant because of differences in reserve requirements levied on HPBs vs. other banks. HPBs, by and large, are banks in the $10 million to $100 million size class. They tend therefore to benefit from the lower reserves required on small deposit bases.

Table 4 addresses the composition of the other side of the balance sheet— liabilities and capital.

Generally, the differences can be summed up very easily—there really aren't any big ones. In the past, we usually found that HPBs have had a higher proportion of demand deposits than other banks, and less time and savings. While this is still the case, the differences in 1976 werew minor. Similarly in the past we have found that HPBs generally had a lower relative amount of equity. This is now only marginally true. The question of capitalization is one we shall return to a bit later.

With regard to the interest cost on time-deposit funds, we found that in 1976 there was a difference of only 1¢ per $100 of deposits. The HPBs paid $5.67 per $100 for all types of time deposits, while other banks paid $5.66. In short, high-earning banks, as a group, did not make more money than other banks in 1976 by having significantly fewer time deposits, or by paying much less for them. In the same vein, in 1976 we found only a 1¢ difference in service-charge income per $100 of deposits between HPBs and other banks (90¢ per $100 for HPBs vs. 91¢ for other banks).

Now let's turn to the critically important subject of loan quality, which we alluded to earlier.

The basic message which Table 5 conveys could not be clearer: HPBs have much cleaner loan portfolios than other banks, and much better "loss coverage ratios." (The loss-coverage ratio is the multiple by which pre-tax net

TABLE 4

Composition of Liabilities and Capital, 1976

| | Percentage of total | | |
	HPBs	All other banks	Percentage difference
Demand deposits	32.95%	32.10%	2.6 %
Time & savings	57.25%	57.95%	(1.3)%
Total deposits	90.20%	90.05%	0.2 %
Other liabilities	1.90%	1.85%	2.7 %
Equity	7.90%	8.10%	(2.5)%

TABLE 5

Analysis of Loan Losses, 1976

	HPBs	All other banks	Percentage advantage
Provision for loan losses as percentage of average loans	0.38%	0.59%	35.6%
Net loan losses as percentage of average loans	0.28%	0.48%	41.7%
Recoveries as percentage of prior year's charge-offs	32.8%	30.1%	9.0%
Loan loss coverage ratio*	14.8×	5.7×	159.6%

*The loan loss coverage ratio is the multiple by which the sum of pre-tax net operating income plus the provision for loan losses exceeds net loan losses.

earnings, plus the provision made for loan losses, exceeds net loan losses.)

Starting at the top, in 1976 HPBs made a 35.6% smaller provision for losses than did other banks. They could do this because their net write-offs, as a percentage of loans, were 41.7% smaller than for other banks. The third row suggests the HPBs have not been underproviding for expected losses. And the bottom line shows that the loss-coverage ratios for HPBs are more than 2½ times as high.

To summarize our comments on loan portfolio management, 1976 experience confirms our previous findings:

HPBs deploy less of their assets in loans than do other banks. They stay less "loaned up."

They earn higher yields on their loans (20 basis points in 1976).

But they also take fewer losses and recover more of those losses.

Moreover, they cover the losses they do take with a much thicker protective layer of pre-tax income.

That, in turn, permits them to operate with slightly less capital than other banks—further enhancing their advantage over other banks in return on equity.

Now let's turn to our favorite aspect of HPB strategy: the all-important area of overhead expense controls. Table 6 shows what happened in 1976, as well as the previous 4 years.

First, let's review payroll costs (wages, salaries, and benefits). In 1976, as in previous years, HPBs managed to get by with much lower "people costs" per $100 of footings than other banks. The difference was 22¢ per $100 of assets ($1.52 for other banks vs. $1.30 for HPBs).

Note, too, that this people-cost-control advantage grew every year during the five years shown. We always are asked: How do they do it? Fewer people, or lower salaries? Table 7 provides an unambiguous answer: HPBs have fewer employees, but they pay them better.

TABLE 6

Selected Overhead Expenses per $100 of assets, 1972-76

	1972	1973	1974	1975	1976
Salaries, wages, and benefits					
All other banks	$1.43	$1.43	$1.48	$1.50	$1.52
HPBs	$1.34	1.28	1.29	1.30	1.30
HPBs' advantage	$ .09	$ .15	$ .10	$ .20	$ .22
Occupancy expense					
All other banks	$ .20	$ .19	$ .20	$ .23	$ .23
HPBs	.16	.14	.14	.15	.17
HPBs' advantage	$ .04	$ .05	$ .06	$ .08	$ .06
Other operating expense*					
All other banks	$ .96	$ .97	$1.05	$1.10	$1.11
HPBs	.87	.86	.91	.93	.95
HPBs' advantage	$ .09	$ .11	$ .14	$ .17	$ .16
Sum of three overhead expense items					
All other banks	$2.59	$2.59	$2.73	$2.83	$2.86
HPBs	2.37	2.28	2.34	2.38	2.42
HPBs' advantage	$ .22	$ .31	$ .39	$ .45	$ .44

*"Other operating expense" plus furniture and equipment.

TABLE 7

Employee Utilization Ratios, 1976

	HPBs	All other banks	Percentage advantage
Wages and benefits as a percentage of average assets	1.30%	1.52%	14.5%
Wages and benefits as a percentage of operating revenue	17.2%	20.5%	16.1%
Average wages and benefits per employee	$11,019	$10,843	(1.6)%
Average assets per employee	$887,783	$761,904	16.5%
Average loans per employee	$459,881	$390,151	17.9%
Net operating income per employee (pre-tax)	$14,333	$7,217	98.6%
Net income per employee	$12,039	$6,315	90.6%

HPB employees, in 1976, managed 16.5% more assets per person than employees of other banks; 17.9% more loans; and, most importantly, brought down to the bottom line 90.6% more net income per person.

Getting back to the other overhead items shown in Table 6, the HPBs again did a better job of controlling occupancy expenses in 1976 than did the other banks. As in the past, it's a big difference in a small but significant item.

The same goes for the long and costly list of "other operating expenses"— including the phone bills, light bills, postage, T&E expenses, etc.

And when it's all added up at the bottom of Table 6, we see that total overhead expenses were 15.4%, or 44¢ per $100 of assets, lower than other banks'. That 44¢ due to superior overhead control goes a long way toward explaining the 56¢ advantage for HPBs in net income per $100 of assets shown back in Chart 3.

ENVIRONMENTAL FACTORS

The next issue we shall look at is the question of whether there are certain factors that influence profitability but that are out of control of bank management. That is, were the larger profits of our high-performance banks caused by factors they could control, or were there some other reasons?

We tested several factors likely to be influential, using a statistical technique called regression analysis. Essentially all that technique does is tell us how closely one factor—say, for example, the growth rate of personal income in a given state—correlates with another factor, in this case the rate of return on capital for banks in that state. If the correlation is high and meets certain statistical standards, then we can often conclude that a causal relationship exists—that differences in the variable tested do in fact cause profits to be higher or lower.

We should note initially that some of the data we used in our testing procedure were not the best. Further, the data were based on statewide information, and states are not always very good proxies for relevant banking markets. Thus, the data deficiencies and mixed results indicate the findings should be considered suggestive, not definitive. Also, these tests were done using 1975 data and may be somewhat out of date. But in the past we have found these relationships don't change much over time.

A good economic climate is one factor which would be expected to influence banking rates of return favorably. We tested 1975's rate of return on bank capital against each state's rate of increase in total personal income both from 1974 to 1975 and for the longer-run, 1969-1975. Both showed a positive correlation with profitability, with the longer-run growth rate showing the better correlation. Although both were "statistically significant," they did not go very far in explaining differences in profitability.

Rather interestingly, the one factor we discovered which correlated most closely with banks' rate of return in a given state was agricultural loans as a percentage of assets—the higher the percentage of banks' agricultural lending in a state, the higher the average rate of return for banks in that state. In this instance, however, there is reason to believe the relationship is more coincidental than causal. That is, the incidence of greater agricultural lending did not of itself contribute to the higher rate of return; but rather, for the period tested, agriculture was enjoying unusually better economic conditions than business in general. Further, there is some evidence that states with relatively large proportions of agricultural activity have certain structural characteristics which correlate with above-average profitability for banks.

Thus, although banks in agricultural areas have had excellent profits the last couple of years, we would be hard pressed to conclude that it was due solely to the higher proportion of agricultural lending.

Several factors we examined appeared to depress bank profitability. The most important of these seems to be competition from thrift institutions— savings and loan associations and mutual savings banks. As the proportion of a state's deposit base controlled by thrift institution increases, the rate of return for banks decreases. There are other factors complicating the situation; for example, states with relatively large thrift industries have tended to have had slower economic growth in recent years. But the degree of correlation seems sufficiently high to conclude that *strong competition from thrifts does indeed reduce bank profitability*.

Two factors that are related to each other also appear to detract from bank profitability: (1) extensive branching activity, and (2) high proportions of fixed assets (land and buildings) to total assets.

In testing branching activity, we wanted a measure of the actual pervasiveness of branching rather than just the "unit" and "limited-statewide" branching classifications, which can be deceptive because of home-office protection clauses and related factors. A good proxy for the actual extent of branching seems to be the percentage of all offices in a state that are branch offices— the higher this percentage, the more liberal the branching laws are presumed to be. Using this measure, *as the number of branch offices relative to total offices increases, banking's rate of return decreases.*

Similarly, high fixed investments in land and buildings were correlated both with more extensive branching and lower rates of return.

Finally, several factors tested revealed inconclusive or unusual results.

For example, high loan-to-asset ratios and high ratios of demand deposits to total deposits—factors which some would expect to correlate with high profitability—did not. Those factors were actually correlated with lower profitability, especially the loan-to-asset ratio, but the correlations were not close.

We could not find any clear evidence that the level of interest rates—either rates paid on deposits or rates charged on loans—had any consistent relationship with profitability.

Also surprising was the fact that low populations per bank office—a factor often assumed to be a measure of overbanking—did not correlate with lower returns. but with slightly higher returns.

Overall, our tests of non-management factors were not very conclusive. *Although it appears that economic growth stimulates bank profitability and that extensive branching and strong competition from thrift institutions can depress profitability, the amount of variation that can be explained by these factors is not high.* This, coupled with the fact that rates of return for banks within the same state (and even with more localized markets) exhibit substantial differences, suggests that non-management factors influence only modestly banks' rate of return; most of the variation in profitability seems to be caused by factors which management should be able to control.

THE GROWTH ISSUE

The final question we address is that of growth. Did HPBs attain their high profits by sacrificing growth?

A quick look at Chart 4 shows that the answer to this question is a resounding no.

In each category shown—assets, loans, capital, and net income—the average annual growth rate from 1972 to 1976 is higher for HPBs than it is for all other banks. The lowest difference was with respect to deposit growth and the greatest difference was in equity growth.

(We did not analyze it in 1976, but in 1975 the largest difference was with respect to dividends—where the annual growth rate for HPBs was more than triple the industry average. We have no reason to suspect that this would not again be the greatest difference in 1976.)

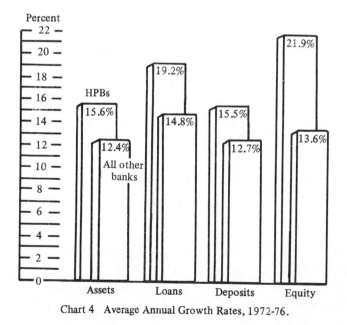

Chart 4 Average Annual Growth Rates, 1972-76.

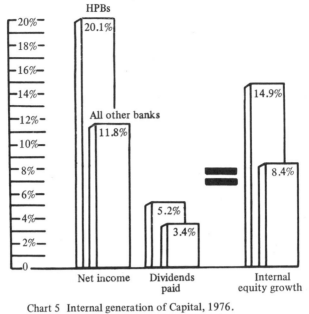

Chart 5 Internal generation of Capital, 1976.
Approximate percentages of average equity.

Actually, the question of growth should perhaps have been ignored because, almost by definition, HPBs will grow at an above-normal rate, at least in the 1972-76 type of environment. For most banks, the severest factor constraining growth is capital. If you don't have the capital to support growth, the regulators—if not normal businsss prudence—will insure that the growth doesn't occur. And the primary souce of capital is earnings retained from net income.

Chart 5 illustrates growth potential vividly. Net income and dividends are shown as a percentage of the existing equity base. Here, dividends paid are subtracted from net income to arrive at a fairly accurate estimate of retained earnings. The retained-earnings figure essentially represents the growth rate that can be supported from the internal generation of capital—that is, the maximum growth rate that could be attained without new capital issues or a decline in capital-to-asset ratios. Average retained earnings as a percentage of capital was 14.9% for HPBs and only 8.4% for all banks.

SUMMARY

In Table 1, we summarized what we believe are the key ingredients or characteristics of high-performance banks.

Maximization of revenues is one prime area. Partially, this comes from relatively higher loan income than the average for all other banks. The higher loan income appears to be derived not from high loan volume, but from appropriate pricing and margins. A secondary factor in the above-average loan yields, we suspect, comes not from higher rates charged but from the avoidance of non-accruing loans and the subsequent decrease in loan income.

Consistently, the maximization of income from tax-exempt securities has been a distinguishing characteristic of HPBs.

Finally, higher revenues seem to result from the maintenance of sufficient flexibility in the balance sheet to recognize and take advantage of changes in the level of interest rates.

Important as higher revenues are, proper expense control is a more distinguishing characteristic of high-performance banks. We believe this is simply because financial markets are becoming increasingly competitive; as that happens, there is less that management can do in terms of the revenue side.

In controlling expenses, there seem to be four key areas. The first is a minimization of investment in fixed assets to obtain below-average occupancy expense—in other words, marble palaces don't do much for the bottom line.

Proper control of overhead costs, as illustrated by lower "other operating expense," appears to be another key.

Reduced loan losses through effective credit analysis has recently received great attention, but our studies suggest that, even before loan losses presented such obvious problems, this was a key characteristic of HPBs.

Low personnel costs are another real key, and our data suggest that such savings come not from low salaries but from high productivity—greater output per employee.

The main key to becoming a high-performance bank lies in consistently good management. In virtually every one of the factors we reviewed, HPBs had some advantage. In the big ticket items, the percentage advantage was usually small, but the total contribution to higher earnings was significant. On the other hand, in the smaller items—such as loan losses and occupancy expense—the *absolute* contribution might not have been as great, but in *comparative* terms it was large.

These smaller items are the ones where management has the greatest discretion. And when these are properly attended to, the bigger items seems to come along too.

As we reviewed all of the various factors that distinguish HPBs, each could be classified into one of three functional areas: planning, organizing, and controlling. And those functions—at least according to our textbook—are the definition of management.

Part VI
REGULATORY ISSUES

One of the most emotionally charged issues in the regulation of banks and other depository-type institutions is "redlining." This term refers to the arbitrary denial of mortgage credit to creditworthy customers because of the geographical location of the property. In essence, it is discrimination and causes or contributes to urban blight. However, the underlying issues are not clearcut. For example, does the lack of mortgage loans in a specific area mean an institution is discriminating? Or does it mean that there is a lack of loan demand stemming from the area's undesirable social and living conditions? In an attempt to prevent redlining and "encourage" lenders to actively seek creditworthy borrowers, the Community Reinvestment Act was passed in 1977 and implemented in 1979. This Act and its implications are discussed in the article by Donald T. Savage. The provisions of the Community Reinvestment Act and other antidiscrimination laws pose a number of management problems. For example, an "affirmative marketing" program must be established. Furthermore, it is insufficient to simply avoid overt discrimination because under the so-called "effects test" seemingly neutral policies can be discriminatory. These and other legal issues are addressed in a comprehensive article by Warren L. Dennis, a civil rights attorney.

One of the key aspects of bank regulation is the financial examination process. Almost all banks are subjected to such an examination *by at least one of three federal agencies: the Federal Reserve Board, Office of the Comptroller of the Currency, or the Federal Deposit Insurance Corporation. Because these agencies carry out the task of evaluating the soundness of most of the nation's commercial banks, it is essential that a uniform rating system be used. For this purpose, the Uniform Interagency Bank Rating System was developed. This system, as explained in George R. Juncker's article, focuses on five critical aspects of a bank's operations and condition. Based on these and other factors, a composite judgmental rating is then made by the examiners.*

Most states have usury laws that are designed to limit the interest rates that may be charged on certain types of loans. Thus, during periods of high interest rates when such laws are binding, lenders either divert funds to investments with higher unregulated rates or they impose stringent non-price terms to ration their funds. As a result, serious market distortions arise as discussed in the article by Paul S. Anderson and James R. Ostas.[1] Other distortions arise when market interest rates exceed the Regulation Q ceilings on deposits of banks and thrift institutions. Seeking higher market yields, many savers bypass depository-type institutions and invest directly in money market instruments or indirectly via money market funds. The nature of these funds is examined in the article by Donald R. Fraser. Although the Regulation Q ceilings will be phased out in the 1980s, money market funds will continue to represent a significant competitive force.

---

[1] *Since this article was written, the Federal Government in 1980 passed a law overriding state usury laws on home mortgages. This preemption is permanent unless state legislatures reinstate their mortgage laws by 1983. Other consumer-related usury laws are unaffected by the Federal law.*

CRA AND COMMUNITY CREDIT NEEDS[†]

*Donald T. Savage**

38

Legislation, such as the Community Reinvestment Act (CRA), and regulatory actions in states, such as Massachusetts, have placed new emphasis on the responsibility of financial institutions to meet the credit needs of their communities. These new laws and regulations have been applauded by community antiredlining groups and attacked by many financial institutions as both unnecessary and as a move toward a credit allocation system. Regardless of how one feels, it seems that the "convenience and needs" analysis involved in regulatory decisions on bank charters, branches, mergers, and holding company formations and bank acquisitions is being modified to give greater weight to the community lending record of financial institutions.

STATE DEVELOPMENTS

A small, but increasing, number of states have adopted rules requiring financial institutions to make greater efforts to serve the credit needs of all segments of their community. Perhaps the most far-reaching of these state

---

†Reprinted by permission from the *Bankers Magazine*, Jan.-Feb. 1979, pp. 49-53. Copyright ® 1979, Warren, Gorham, & Lamont, Inc., 210 South Street, Boston, Massachusettes. All rights reserved.

*Donald T. Savage is an Economist in the Financial Structure Section, Division of Research and Statistics, Board of Governors of the Federal Reserve System.

regulations are in Massachusetts. Massachusetts' state-chartered institutions seeking approval to establish or relocate a branch, merge, or form or expand a holding company must file an affidavit attesting to their commitment to serving the credit needs of the community. Included in the affidavit are factors such as: willingness to provide loan application forms and accept applications for all types of loans at all offices; maintenance of a loan inquiry register, including telephone inquiries; local media advertising; communication of lending policies to real estate brokers; willingness to discuss lending policies with community groups; and, for mutual institutions, governing bodies that are representative of the community.

In addition to regulator-initiated actions, formal loan agreements have been formulated between community groups and financial institutions in New York and the District of Columbia. In several instances, community groups have intervened in the branch office approval process and have gained pledges of greater community lending as a condition for withdrawing their protest of the application.

FEDERAL LEGISLATION

New federal action in the area of stressing credit needs in the total analysis of convenience and needs is contained in Title VIII of the Housing and Community Redevelopment Act of 1977. Title VIII was introduced by Senator Proxmire and is generally known as the Community Reinvestment Act of 1977.

The CRA instructs the federal financial supervisory agencies—the Federal Reserve System, the Comptroller of the Currency, the Federal Deposit Insurance Corporation and the Federal Home Loan Bank Board—to encourage financial institutions to help meet the credit needs of their entire communities, including low- and moderate-income neighborhoods, consistent with the safe and sound operation of the institutions. Under regulations effective in November 1978, the agencies are required, in the course of regular bank examinations, to assess each institution's record of meeting community credit needs. This record is to be taken into account when evaluating applications for branches, mergers, bank holding company formations and acquisitions, and other changes in financial institution structure.

The federal agencies responsible for administering the law held public hearings in Spring 1978 in Washington, D.C. and six other cities. The hearings produced conflicting suggestions from consumer groups and financial institutions. Most consumer groups perceived the law as necessary to prevent redlining and to require institutions to reinvest deposits in home-mortgage, home-improvement, and small-business loans in older urban neighborhoods. Financial institution representatives, in general, argued that they were already meeting all reasonable credit needs, and that the law would require banks to make high-risk unsound loans and be a move toward credit allocation.

The Unmet Credit Needs Question

The basic premises behind the CRA seem to be that (1) there are many creditworthy people, especially in low- and moderate-income neighborhoods, who are unable to obtain credit from financial institutions; and (2) moreover, the financial regulatory agencies have not given sufficient attention, in assessing convenience and needs, to whether institutions were meeting the credit needs of their entire community. Numerous consumer group studies have concluded that there are unmet credit needs resulting from redlining, but methodological problems make it difficult to reach unambiguous conclusions on this issue.

The first analytical problem is the definition of "credit needs." Neither the CRA nor the regulatory agencies have attempted to define "credit needs." Indeed, credit needs may be undefinable. In a quantitative sense, credit needs are significantly different from credit demands, given that the former may be based on social objectives and the latter are based on willingness and ability to pay. In a market system, needs are important only as they create a basis for, and are reflected in, demands. A low-income neighborhood may have a need for housing rehabilitation credit, but most property owners may lack the income necessary to be considered demanders of credit. Thus, needs would remain even though demands were being met at the going market price of credit. Even the quantity demanded at a zero interest rate would not fill all credit needs, given that even interest-free loans have to be repaid. Credit needs for housing rehabilitation, for example, would be based on the total quantity of credit required to rehabilitate all homes in a specified neighborhood or banking market. With repayment ability limited, this standard would not be workable; the CRA recognized this limitation and requires only that institutions *"help meet* the credit needs . . ."" (emphasis added.) Meeting all credit needs is not feasible for a free enterprise banking system; only a government subsidized banking program could possibly meet all credit needs.

Are financial institutions meeting the credit demands of low- and moderate-income neighborhoods? While the banks argue that they are answering all reasonable demands for credit, allegations of unreasonable credit denials continue; most frequently these allegations are associated with charges of redlining on home mortgages and home-rehabilitation and improvement loans.

The Question of Redlining

The economic theory against redlining is presented persuasively by George Benston.[1] Basic microeconomic theory would not allow for the existence of

---

[1] Bentson, *The Anti-Redlining Rules: An Analysis of the Federal Home Loan Bank Board's Proposed Nondiscrimination Requirements* 2-7 (Law and Economics Center, University of Miami School of Law, 1978).

redlining. If there is a profitable lending opportunity and perfect flow of information, some institution should be willing to make the loan, regardless of the geographic location of the property used as collateral. Given the persistence and widespread nature of redlining charges, however, one wonders whether the market is working as efficiently as Benston suggests.

Perhaps there is a possible reconciliation of microtheory, the very limited empirical evidence, and the redlining allegations. Consider the following line of reasoning: First, rather than establishing a unique set of loan terms—interest rate, down payment and maturity—for each loan, lenders may establish one set of loan terms for a given type of loan, and then accept or deny individual applications for loans on those terms. The Benston findings in Rochester, New York would tend to support the one-set-of terms argument, because the terms on mortgage loans made in the central city were not significantly different, except for average maturity of loans, from terms on loans in the suburb used as a control area.

Second, lenders may either overestimate the risk of urban lending, or that risk may be significantly higher than the risk of suburban lending. While many bank representatives testifying at the CRA hearings indicated that lending in older neighborhoods was very risky, no one presented any evidence to support these assertions. Consumer groups, on the other hand, argued that careful appraisal and lending policies could produce urban loss rates equal to those of other areas. Systematic empirical evidence is needed to resolve this issue; studies of loan loss experience of institutions that do extensive lending in urban areas would contribute to resolution of this question.

Third, the costs associated with lending in older areas may be higher. General mortgage servicing costs are relatively fixed; on a small mortgage, such as would be associated with a lower-priced urban dwelling, the cost per dollar of mortgage debt would be higher than the comparable cost for a large mortgage on a suburban home. If, in addition, there are special costs associated with urban lending, such as the need for more detailed property appraisal, urban lending costs are increased relative to those of lending on standardized suburban tract homes.

A possible rationale for the existence of what seems to be redlining can be developed from the above points. Assume that risk and lending costs are higher in urban areas and that lenders make all loans at the market-determined equilibrium interest rate. Given that lenders will accept lowest-risk lowest-cost applications first, the proportion of accepted suburban applications will be higher than the proportion of accepted urban applications. At the market-clearing interest rate, the quantity of loans demanded in the urban area is greater than the quantity supplied, and there is an unmet credit demand. To eliminate the excess quantity demanded in the urban portion of the market, interest rates would have to be higher in that portion of the market than in the total market.

Why don't lenders charge different prices in the urban area than in the suburban portion of the market to account for any higher risks and lending costs? Or, why isn't there a unique interest rate for each loan to reflect the specific level of risks and costs associated with that loan? A number of reasons could be suggested, including the hypothesis that the setting of a unique interest rate for each loan would be more expensive than simply making all loans at one rate. In the present setting, it is likely that a dual pricing system for urban and suburban areas or individual loan pricing would encounter strong objections from urban consumer groups. In addition, in some states, usury ceilings might preclude establishing an urban lending rate at the market-clearing level.

How would the quantity of credit demanded by potential urban borrowers be reduced to the quantity institutions were willing to supply at the below-market-clearing interest rate? This could be accomplished by various pre-screening techniques such as discouraging formal applications, not operating branches in low-income areas, not accepting mortgage loan applications in those areas, charging high application fees, not advertising mortgage loan availability in the media in low-income areas, or any of the other practices alleged by antiredlining groups. The Benston *et al.* study does not really account for this type of demand reduction. Benston's groups contacted prospective sellers, rather than prospective buyers; the sellers could not be expected to have full information on the availability of mortgages to prospective buyers for their homes.

The above analysis, while consistent with theory, Benston's analysis, and antiredlining groups' charges, like most of the work in the area, has not been tested empirically. If, for whatever reason, there is some failure to lend in urban areas, what effect could one expect the CRA to have on this phenomenon?

HOW THE CRA CAN HELP

The major contribution of the CRA and similar state regulations may lie in the area of requiring institutions to be aware of, and consider plans for helping to meet, the credit needs of the entire community. Under the regulations, each institution's Board of Directors will approve a CRA statement outlining the institution's community or communities and the types of loans that the institution will be willing to provide within the community. Agency examiners will review these statements for reasonableness and to ascertain that low- and moderate-income neighborhoods have not been excluded.

The factors to be examined by the agencies in assessing the institution's record do not require any specific lending pattern or loan standards for types of loans, but rather examine the institution's stated lending policies and conformance to those policies. Does the institution do those things that would be expected of an institution dedicated to service to the entire community in which it operates?

Some of the questions to be considered by the examiners reflect the concern with service to the entire community. For example, does the institution attempt to assess community credit needs? Does it discourage formal loan applications? Is it willing to meet with interested community groups? Does it advertise its willingness to consider applications for various types of loans? Does it maintain offices throughout its community and provide credit services at all its offices? Does it participate in loans to, or purchase securities issued to finance community development projects?

From the consumer group point of view, the CRA statement provides an indication of what services the financial institution will make available in its community. The antiredlining groups can check the CRA statement and the bank's definition of its "community" and can register any opposition with both the institution and the appropriate regulatory agency. Members of the antiredlining groups can test whether or not the institution is living up to its CRA statements.

For the regulatory agencies, the CRA statement provides a measure against which the institution's performance can be examined over time; this information will be available when the agency is considering an application from the institution. Public comments on the CRA statement and/or the institution's performance also will be available for examiner review.

The CRA may also reduce one aspect of the total risk of lending in older urban neighborhoods. Assume that one institution is willing to lend on a given piece of property, but knows that no other instutution will be willing to supply financing when this property is resold in the future. This institution is accepting a higher degree of risk than would be required if it could assume that many lenders would be willing to lend to subsequent purchasers of the property. The institution, fearing the possible negative impact on its position of the actions of other institutions, may decide not to accept the risk. If the CRA has the effect of encouraging many institutions to lend in urban areas, the risk to any given institution may be reduced by the greater assurance of the availability of credit for future purchasers in that area.

What the CRA Will Not Do

The CRA is not a panacea for the ills of urban areas. The problems of the cities are much more far-reaching than merely a possible lack of credit. Credit alone will not improve the tax base, upgrade municipal services, attract new employment-creating investments, or reverse years of economic decline.

The CRA is not an income-redistribution measure. It does not require institutions to subsidize loans to low-income borrowers. While institutions may become more willing to lend to low- and moderate-income individuals, it is unlikely that the credit standards required to maintain the lender's safety and soundness will be relaxed. Thus, those without the income necessary to repay loans will not benefit directly by any change resulting from the CRA.

It also seems unlikely that the CRA will result in lower interest rates in urban areas. In fact, assuming that there is an unmet demand for loans in the urban portion of the market, the CRA could have the effect of increasing urban interest rates. If, in compliance with the CRA, the alleged demand reduction or prescreening devices are eliminated, separate urban and suburban loan rates, reflecting different costs and loss experiences would be a reasonable lender response. It would then be incumbent upon the lenders to justify this interest rate difference to protesting urban consumer groups by reference to its lending cost and loan loss data.

The impact of the CRA on the provision of convenient banking services in low- and moderate-income neighborhoods is questionable. On the one hand, the Act may encourage banks to establish branches in these areas; on the other hand, the law does not require banks to maintain unprofitable office locations. Naturally, the CRA does not change the branching prohibitions which may limit the ability of banks to provide convenient offices in those areas which could generate enough business for a profitable branch but not enough business to justify the establishment of a de novo bank.

CRA RISKS AND POTENTIAL

The risk mentioned most often in the testimony at the public hearings held by the agencies was that enforcement would become a form of credit allocation. Other witnesses, however, quoted Senator Proxmire to the effect that the measure was not an attempt to create an agency-managed credit allocation system. The regulatory agencies have not indicated any desire or tendency to use this law as a credit allocation device.

Possible loss of the benefits of institutional specialization is another risk presented by the CRA. The extent to which the regulations permit specialization by financial institutions is unclear. Although institutions would seem to be free to specialize, all institutions do have a continuing and affirmative obligation to help meet the credit needs of their entire community. A bank that made only yacht loans to people residing outside of its geographic community would probably be hard pressed to convince its regulator that it was meeting the credit needs of its entire community, including low- and moderate-income neighborhoods.

While not a panacea for the problems of urban areas and carrying some risks, the CRA does have some promise in the area of increasing the flow of funds to creditworthy low- and moderate-income borrowers. Even if it merely ensures that all potential borrowers are granted the opportunity to apply for credit and have their application appraised on its merits, the CRA will have contributed to the more equitable treatment of all customers of financial institutions.

HOW DO YOU KNOW YOU'RE NOT DISCRIMINATING?*

Warren L. Dennis

39

There is an ancient curse intoned against only the most formidable of enemies which states "May you live in a time of change." In recent times, this curse seems to have been invoked upon both lenders and the regulators of lenders for, during the past several years, the lending and credit industries have faced an assortment of new laws, regulations and judicial interpretations which appear to be placing ever narrower limitations on the lender's traditional freedom to exercise unfettered business judgment.

After the initial indignation fades, lenders have the serious responsibility of determining exactly what is expected of them and their employees. To do this, it is necessary to be familiar not only with the text of applicable laws and regulations, but also with the patterns of social and economic history which preceded the legal developments and with the reasoning behind them.

The laws and regulations which we will examine bracket a period of more than 110 years from enactment of the first to the effective date of the most recent.

They are: the Civil Rights Act of 1866; the Fair Housing Act of 1968; the 1974 amendment to the Fair Housing Act; the Federal Home Loan Bank Board's Fair Housing Regulations and opinions of Counsel; the Equal Credit Opportunity Act of 1974; the Home Mortgage Disclosure Act of 1975, Regulation C; the Equal Credit Opportunity Act of 1976; and Regulation B.

*Reprinted from the *Federal Home Loan Bank Board Journal*, May 1977, Vol. 10, No. 5, pp. 15-24.

These laws and the other civil rights statutes enacted on the Federal, State and local levels are unique in the history of legal systems. No society has made so thorough an attempt to eliminate legal distinctions based "on immutable characteristics of birth" as our own. While there may be disagreement upon the degrees of success which we can claim to have achieved in eliminating such distinctions, each of the laws and regulations cited above can be viewed as part of a progressive, ongoing effort to reverse whole sets of historical circumstances which heretofore had defined the ways in which we interacted.

GENERAL OBSERVATIONS

Here it may be useful to review a list of seven general observations about civil rights law enforcement which have particular application to our discussion. Such a review will help place in context our expectations about the scope and effect of recent legal developments.

1. We can probably never completely eliminate all personal prejudice or bias. It would be naive to assume that an act of Congress can effectively remove habits of intolerance which have grown up over many years. This is as unlikely as the possibility that laws against fraud and embezzlement can effectively eliminate greed. The laws are intended to prohibit discrimination in the course of commercial conduct and if individual animus and antagonism are diminished at the same time, this is a welcome dividend. Ultimately, however, after a period of resistance the intensity of personal bias will most likely decrease.

2. Each of the modern civil rights laws which affect lending practices has both a social and a business purpose. In enacting these laws, Congress has gone beyond making only social policy determinations. The legislators studied the business practices involved and made a considered judgment that these practices were unsound from an economic or business point of view.

For example, in the preamble to the first Equal Credit Opportunity Act (Section 502) Congress provided a statement of "Findings and Purpose" which reflected its judgment that discrimination on the basis of sex or marital status detracts from the soundness of loans and the strength of the financial system.

This observation is important because it demonstrates that Congress, far from being insensitive to the industry's legitimate concern with the preservation of sound underwriting practices, aggressively attempted to address this concern and assess the underlying validity of the practices being regulated.

3. The most effective method of achieving widespread compliance with the law is the institutionalization of its enforcement. When enforcement becomes routine, rather than remarkable, it signals an era of acceptance of new legal requirements.

Several years ago, in the public accommodations field (hotels, restaurants, places of entertainment), the Department of Justice was very active in conducting investigations and bringing lawsuits against the owners of public facilities who resisted integration.

Because of the routine and vigorous official response to violation, this type of overt discrimination was eliminated relatively quickly. In addition, widespread voluntary compliance was encouraged.

In the lending field, the incorporation of a comprehensive nondiscrimination review into the regularly scheduled examination contributes substantially to the institutionalization of civil rights enforcement and compliance. By making civil rights compliance a normal part of the examination process, compliance becomes a normal part of the business routine. This provides the lending industry with a sense of the priority which the regulatory agency attaches to this area of law and enhances the day-to-day familiarity of the lender with the provisions of the fair lending regulations. Significantly, it also provides a strong measure of accountability and complements a program of vigorous enforcement through litigation.

4. The ability of an investigation to uncover unlawful discrimination decreases in direct proportion to the effort to uncover it.

This probably occurs for two reasons: (1) The overt forms of discrimination are soon eliminated, and (2) in the face of strong enforcement efforts, subtle methods of discrimination become even more subtle. Ultimately, persons who challenge lenders' practices on the basis of discrimination will have to acquire a more sophisticated knowledge of the industry, and lenders or persons who defend lenders in connection with such challenges will have to acquire a more sophisticated understanding of civil rights law.

5. Increasingly, modern discriminatory lending practices are motivated not by traditional concepts of animus and invidious intent, but by perceived connections on the part of the lenders between some racial or gender-based factor and economic risk.

This lack of an invidious intention to discriminate, however, does not make a discriminatory practice any less unlawful or less vulnerable to challenge. But it is important to understand this source of motivation so that challenges to practices based upon it can successfully address the justification of the practice which the lender is likely to advance.

Many of the discriminatory practices we encounter are the "accidental by-product of a traditional way of thinking" and, although something "more than accident is necessary" to justify these practices, the traditions themselves are an important part of the analysis.

It is also important to keep in mind that, in most instances, the officers of lending institutions also are motivated by what they perceive to be their fiduciary responsibilities to depositors or shareholders and are not necessarily persons motivated by personal bias or invidious intent.

As a practical matter, incidentally, it does not enhance the credibility of persons who legitimately challenge discriminatory lending practices nor does it increase the likelihood of a succesful dialogue to misrepresent the motivations of representatives of the lending industry.

6. Many of the evils which the Government passes laws to correct were created or perpetuated by the action or inaction of the Government itself. For example, the housing policies of the Federal Government beginning in the early years of the New Deal frequently incorporated and built upon discriminatory practices developed in the private sector.

In introducing the Fair Housing Act, the then Senator Walter F. Mondale (D.-Minn.) referred to the "sordid story of which all Americans should be ashamed developed by this country in the immediate post World War II era, during which the FHA, the VA and other Federal agencies encouraged, assisted and made easy the flight of white people from the central cities of white America, leaving behind only the Negroes and others unable to take advantage of these liberalized extensions of credit, and credit guarantees."

Placed in this context, the efforts of the Government to correct discriminatory practices are all the more important.

7. No individual or agency has an exclusive patent on the correct interpretation of the civil rights laws or the application of these laws to lending patterns.

Courts frequently disagree on points of legal interpretation. Even the Supreme Court redefines its position as new cases with new facts come before it. There will be many issues under the ECOA, Fair Housing Act, and other laws upon which reasonable people will disagree. Even the four Federal financial regulatory agencies may not agree on certain issues.

Lenders, in evaluating their own practices, can derive the most security, after consultation with their counsel, by understanding the way the laws work and the reasons they were enacted and by developing a systematic procedure for analyzing their own practices in view of the legislative purposes of the law.

ANALYZING DISCRIMINATION

Over the years, a number of rules or guidelines to the interpretation of civil rights statutes have been evolved by the courts and regulatory agencies. It is not necessary for loan officers and others who work in the credit industry to have a law professor's understanding of these principles (and the inconsistencies which they frequently contain) and it probably isn't possible to neatly classify all of the many interpretations in the judicial and regulatory literature into simple rules of thumb.

We can, however, distill many of the generic rules and provide a set of categories or pigeonholes to serve as a useful guide in evaluating lending practices and determining if they are likely to be regarded as discriminatory.

An important point to be kept in mind in this undertaking is that the Equal Credit Opportunity Act, like the Fair Housing Act, is primarily a civil rights statute with broad remedial purposes. It is not only a consumer protection law, or a financial regulatory act. Accordingly, the courts are likely to interpret the ECOA more expansively than other parts of the Consumer Credit Protection Act, consistent with precedents established under other civil rights litigation.

We can suggest four general classifications of discriminatory conduct, each consisting of different tests and rules of construction and some having sub-classifications. They are:

1. Purposeful discrimination:
   a. Overt, or facial;
   b. Through use of pretext (pretextual).
2. Standards which are unduly subjective:
3. Present effects of prior practices:
   a. Failure to take adequate affirmative steps to correct prior discrimination;
   b. Freezing in/freezing out.
4. The effects test.

PURPOSEFUL DISCRIMINATION

A person engages in purposeful discrimination if his or her conduct is motivated by considerations which include or relate to one of the prohibited bases (race, color, sex, etc.) or if his or her conduct should reasonably have been anticipated to lead to discriminatory consequences.

To engage in purposeful discrimination, it is not, as we have already noted, necessary to have an evil motivation or an intent to deny to persons protected by the act a right granted by the act. The courts have held that "any course of conduct or way of doing business which actually or predictably results in different treatment of whites and blacks is a discriminatory pattern or practice, irrespective of motivation."

For instance, if a person's principal motivation is to make money, sell property or make loans, and not to deprive applicants of rights granted by law, but if that person tries to avoid dealing with members of a protected class because of fears about how other customers will react, a violation still can occur.

It is of little solace to the victim of discrimination that the perpetrator did it in good faith, and fear of adverse financial consequences is not a defense to purposeful discrimination.

Overt Purposeful Discrimination: Overt or "facial" discrimination occurs when, in some criteria or course of conduct, a prohibited basis is openly considered; i.e., it appears "on the face" of a standard or is an obvious element of a transaction.

Examples would include different treatment of similarly situated persons of different races; instructions to employees not to rent, sell or lend to black persons, or to do so only on special terms and conditions; failure to provide one group with the same preliminary information needed to process an application as is provided to others; or racial statements to a loan applicant or the use of racial codes for the purpose of segregating or rejecting applicants.

In the lending area, an overt form of discrimination might be evidenced by a policy, written or simply understood by employees, of not lending in an area because of racial integration which may be occurring there. Another example would be a rule of discounting a wife's income, or requiring a cosigner for a single woman. The fact that a policy of the kind described above is not written down does not make it less of an overtly discriminatory policy.

Overt discrimination is not limited to policy items and may occur if discriminatory acts are engaged in by the employees of an institution without a policy guideline. Disparate treatment is the touchstone.

Purposeful Discrimination Through Use of Pretext: This is characterized by the assertion of an ostensibly nondiscriminatory reason to justify discriminatory acts or practices. Typically, it involves an attempt to show reasons why a rejection was justified or that a rejection was in accordance with some legitimate, nondiscriminatory policy.

Examples would include a rule limiting occupancy in an apartment house near a military base to military personnel over the rank of major in circumstances where this predictably would exclude blacks and where there had been a history of purposeful discrimination by a landlord; use of fictitious or dummy contracts to avoid selling to minorities; referral of a black home-seeker to a black-managed real estate company by an officer of a white real estate company, because, as an officer, he does not "sell" homes; use of more stringent credit history evaluations for blacks than for whites; or the use of pregnancy-related characteristics as an excuse or pretext for treating women differently than men.

In the lending field, it might be construed as a pretext to rely on social considerations in underwriting properties whereas once racial factors were considered. The use of euphemisms or code words in property underwriting, such as "commercialism" or "traffic congestion," where these factors are used negatively in integrated, but not white, neighborhoods, might be regarded as a pretext for racial redlining.

Initiation of new underwriting rules soon after the enactment of fair lending laws may create an inference of discrimination through pretext. For instance, determining to count only the highest income when a couple applies for a loan and both husband and wife are working might be viewed as a pretext for continuing to discount a wife's income, if this practice had been engaged in prior to the change in law.

Initiating new questions such as "Do you expect any interruptions in income over the term of this loan?" or "What is your anticipated income over the term of this loan?" might be suspect—even if asked of both male and female applicants—if it had not been asked before the advent of the new law and if normal income verification procedures still were used and worked well.

In this case, an inference might be raised that questions were intended to learn about child-bearing plans, particularly if questions about child-bearing had been asked before the law was enacted. Obviously, a lender's practices before passage of the new law would be highly relevant to an inquiry of this kind.

Similar problems might be presented by new criteria which tighten up credit standards in direct response to new fair lending laws, the implication being that the creditor believes that the extension of credit to protected classes is "risky" and requires narrower credit standards in order to exclude greater numbers of these people.

The Prima Facie Case: The courts have recognized that "most persons will not admit publicly that they entertain any bias or prejudice . . ." and that discrimination is often accomplished through indirect means without any actual mention of race.

However, the law prohibits "sophisticated as well as simpleminded modes of discrimination," and to deal with this problem, the courts have applied the concept of the "prima facie" case to civil rights litigation.

This concept merely provides a set of rules for determining when the plaintiff or person complaining of discrimination has adduced enough facts to raise a legal inference of discrimination. The defendant then has an opportunity to show that the practice was not discriminatory. If nothing is done to refute the inference, or if the rebuttal evidence is insufficient, then the discrimination is considered proven and the plaintiff wins.

The rules for a prima facie case appear to be slightly different for cases alleging "purposeful discrimination" than for pure effects test cases, and it appears that plaintiffs may seek to prove their cases under either or both alternatives.

In the purposeful category, the rule which seems most applicable is that set down by the Supreme Court in an employment case called *McDonnell Douglas Corp. v. Green,* 411 U.S. 792 (1972). This rule has been applied to cases under the Fair Housing Act.

We can, then, assume that, even without direct evidence of overt discrimination, a complainant may make out a prima facie case by showing that he or she:

1. Is a member of a protected class;
2. Applied and was qualified for the credit (or housing or job) which was being offered;
3. Despite being qualified, was rejected;
4. After the rejection, learned and is able to show that others were able to obtain similar credit (or housing or jobs).

Once the complainant has shown these things, the burden shifts to the other side to show some legitimate, nondiscriminatory reason for the rejection.

In determining whether the reasons offered to show that the conduct was not a pretext for discrimination are or are not valid, the court may look to evidence such as the respondent's general policy and practice with respect to minorities, including statistical evidence or proof of disproportionate impact.

When alleged purposeful discrimination is being considered, proof of a statistically disproportionate impact, while not the sole touchstone, may provide "an important starting point" for a "sensitive inquiry" into such circumstantial and direct evidence of intent as may be available.

Other types of evidence which can be looked at include "the historical background of the decision in question" and "the specific sequence of events leading up to the challenged decision."

There are many additional rules of construction in this area. We should be familiar with some of the more important ones:

Partial Discrimination: Use of factors relating to race, sex or other prohibited bases in any aspect of a housing or credit decision is unlawful. Accordingly, use of such a factor "cannot be brushed aside because it was neither the sole reason for discrimination nor the total factor of discrimination." There is no room in the law for "partial discrimination."

Delegated Duty: The duty to comply with the Fair Housing Act cannot be delegated. Principals are liable for discrimination by their agents, both under the principle of *respondent superior* and because the duty to comply may not be delegated away.

Even a silent partner in an apartment project has been held liable in a discrimination case. Recently, the owner of a mortgage company was held jointly liable with his employee for compensatory damages of $5,000 because of discriminatory remarks and conduct by the employee. It was no defense that the employer had instructed employees not to discriminate.

Statistics: The probative value of statistical showings in cases of this kind should not be underestimated. It has been held that "in cases of racial discrimination, statistics often tell much and courts listen" and that ". . . nothing is as emphatic as zero."

Some courts have held that a statistical showing alone can create a prima facie case of discrimination. Moreover, when statistics do show a lack of loans in a certain neighborhood, it may not be a defense to claim "lack of demand" for the loans, for the statistics may not really indicate lack of interest so much as a sense of futility in applying for loans in this neighborhood.

Good Faith: Once a case of unlawful discrimination has been proved, injunctions are not issued grudgingly. Further, their scope is broad so as to ensure an end to the practice. The courts not only have the authority, but the duty to order affirmative relief which will correct the present effects of past discrimination. Neither good faith alone nor protestations of repentance and reform are sufficient to justify the withholding of equitable relief.

Even the voluntary adoption of a far-reaching affirmative action plan may not be sufficient defense if certain practices still result in discrimination. Further, lack of a discriminatory motive on the part of the lender will not prevent the award of compensatory damages to victims of discrimination.

The next two classifications of discriminatory conduct can be viewed as hybrids, conceptually somewhere between "purposeful discrimination" and the "effects test," depending upon the degree of discriminatory motivation involved. Accordingly, we should examine them separately.

STANDARDS WHICH ARE UNDULY SUBJECTIVE

Subjectivity and even instinct are frequently necessary and unavoidable elements of a credit underwriting or evaluation process. However, there is a principle set down in cases under the civil rights laws that "procedures for evaluating applicants should be as objective and uniform as possible . . . ." This is especially so where statistics indicate fewer rentals or loans to minorities.

For instance, rejection of an applicant because of "incompatibility" with other residents is too vague and too easily subject to discriminatory considerations.

In the employment area, it has been held that systems of evaluation which require a subjective opinion concerning the candidate's "adaptability," "bearing," "demeanor," "manner," "appearance," "maturity," "drive" and "social behavior" can be discriminatory.

In *Rowe v. General Motors*, 457 F. 2d 348, 558-559 (5th Cir. 1972), Title VII violations were found in circumstances where the person making a promotion decision was given no written instructions pertaining to the qualifications necessary for promotion and where the controlling standards were found to be "vague and subjective" and where there were "no safeguards in the procedure designed to avert discriminatory practices."

When these principles are applied to the credit area, it appears that violations might arguably be based merely upon the lack of objective, uniform, written criteria or upon the existence of vague criteria, together with a statistical showing of a low level of lending to minorities or to women.

For instance, use of general judgments as to "character" or "good pay" on the presumption that "I know a good loan when I see it," or the belief that "all houses in that area are poor collateral," without some objective economic measuring rods may be a dangerous course to pursue, particularly if there are several employees involved in granting loans.

It appears that some lenders may train employees by a somewhat mystical "laying on of hands" by which the knowledge of the senior is passed to the junior in an osmosis-like manner. Without guidelines that reduce to written form the standards which are to be used (allowing for needed flexibility, of course), it is difficult to see how a lender would be able to justify certain decisions in the face of a challenge on the basis of alleged discrimination. As held in *United States v. Youritan Construction Co.*, "Just as vague and undefined employment standards which result in whites, but not blacks, being hired are unlawfully discriminatory, so too are arbitrary and uncontrolled apartment rental procedures which produce otherwise unexplained racially discriminatory results." There is every reason to believe that the same rules of construction will apply under ECOA. (370 F. Supp. 643 (N.D. Calif. 1973) (conclusion of law No. 8 (aff'd. per curiam 509 F. 2d 623) 9th Cir. 1975.)

PRESENT EFFECTS OF PRIOR PRACTICES

Failure to Take Adequate Affirmative Steps: If any point has been emphasized throughout this presentation it is the impact of past history on present
practices.

In civil rights law, past practices have an important legal significance. We
have already pointed out that prior practices can have an important influence on how we interpret current procedures which are alleged to be pretexts
for discrimination. There are other implications of past practices of which
we should be aware.

First, discriminatory practices which were engaged in before a change in
the law *are presumed to continue* in the absence of a clear showing to the
contrary, and evidence of such past practices is admissible to shed light on
present circumstances.

Second, there is an obligation to take all reasonable and necessary steps
to correct the continuing, present effects of past practices.

The maintenance of an image in the public mind which is associated with
discriminatory practices, standing alone, can be evidence of discrimination,
and failure to take steps to correct this image can be actionable.

Also, the failure to affirmatively make employees aware of a change in
policy after a new law is enacted constitutes a discriminatory course of conduct, for the natural consequences are that discrimination will continue.

The legislative history of ECOA and of the 1974 sex amendment to the
Fair Housing Act reveals the presence of an industry-wide discrimination
with respect to women. Employees have been taught and have practiced discrimination under these old standards, and members of the public who
inquired about credit availability were frequently given information or discouraged from applying on the basis of these standards. One example is income discounting.

It can be argued that each creditor who, at one time, engaged in discriminatory practices has an obligation not just to comprehensively review present
procedures, but to take scrupulous care to make sure that all employees are
disabused of older notions which they may not yet have abandoned and to
ensure that they thoroughly understand new requirements.

With respect to problems of image, it can be argued that there is an obligation on the part of creditors to take affirmative steps to make known their
new policies in the market place, particularly among dealers, brokers, and
others who may have done business with the lender under older discriminatory policies.

Freezing In/Freezing Out: There is a principle in civil rights law which
prohibits the preservation of standards and criteria which, while neutral on
their face, perpetuate prior discriminatory practices whether the prior practices occurred before or after the new laws were passed and regardless of
motivation.

An example would be admission criteria for an organization which requires the applicant to obtain the recommendation of persons who are already members of the organization, the membership having grown under discriminatory conditions.

This is sometimes referred to as the "freezing out" of applicants because of the effect of past discriminatory practices on present operations and the "freezing in" of the effects of these previous discriminatory policies.

Another instance of the "freezing in" type of discrimination occurs when, for example, seniority promotion policies, which may be neutral on their face, have the effect of locking in minorities who, because of many years of a discriminatory employment policy, had been limited to less desirable positions in the company. Even when ended, the transfer and seniority provisions perpetuated the effects of prior discrimination.

A possible application of these principles in the credit area might include a policy of limiting extensions of credit to present savers or to prior loan customers or a policy of lending only in areas where loans are already outstanding.

Another possible application might be the limitation of extensions of credit to persons who already have a credit history. If previous discrimination has prevented a person from obtaining individual credit or from having his or her credit history reported in his or her own name, for example, a policy of tying new extensions of credit to a prior history would "freeze out" this person and "freeze in" the old patterns of discrimination.

Regulation B addresses this, in part, by requiring consideration of a person's contribution to a joint credit history.

THE EFFECTS TEST

Each of the tests which we have already discussed had one element in common. Under each, there had to be either a showing or a presumption of purposeful discrimination either overtly or through pretext somewhere in the scheme of proof or reasoning. Also, by exercising a reasonable degree of precaution and self-examination, a lender could most likely find and correct practices which fall into the categories already discussed.

Under a "pure effects test," however, we are examining practices which are not only neutral on their face, but which were adopted with no discriminatory motivation of any kind.

These are practices which a reasonable person could *not* necessarily predict would lead to discriminatory consequences, but which, upon a statistical showning, are proved to have a disproportionate impact on a protected class.

Accordingly, because it is more difficult to recognize such practices and because this leads to some uncertainty, there appears to be a good deal of uneasiness in the industry about the potential application of the effects test.

There also may be some feeling that, as a matter of principle, an organization should not be liable for the effects of practices which are not motivated by any unlawful purpose and which are difficult to diagnose.

Some have pointed to three recent Supreme Court decisions which, they claim, indicate that the Court is unhappy with the effects test, that the Court may be changing the concept of "necessity" under the test, and that the Court may be changing the standard for the statistical showing needed to prove a "discriminatory effect."

At the present time, however, the effects test is fully applicable to interpretations of the Fair Housing Act and the ECOA. We will see why after we first explore what the effects test is.

The effects test was first articulated in *Griggs v. Duke Power Co.* and later referred to in *Moody v. Albemarle Paper Co.* In *Griggs*, there had been a challenge to the use of a high school diploma requirement and an intelligence test for certain jobs which previously had been held only by whites. Although the Court noted the existence of prior discrimination by the company and discrimination by society in general, it found that there was no purposeful discrimination in the application of the diploma and test requirements. These were applied equally to blacks and whites.

The Court nevertheless invalidated these standards because they had a "discriminatory effect." The Court found that the broad remedial purpose of the Fair Employment law expressed a congressional intent to remove "artificial, arbitrary and unnecessary barriers" which present "built-in headwinds" for minority groups regardless of the motivation or purpose behind the standard.

In *Moody v. Albemarle*, the Court provided guidance as to the way that this effects test was to operate. In essence, the Court found that the purpose of the law was to eliminate practices which are not economically sound or necessary to the business and which make it harder for minorities to qualify.

We can express the effects in the following ways:

1. When it can be shown that a practice, even though neutral on its face and adopted without a discriminatory purpose, has a statistically disproportionate impact on a protected group (e.g., has a greater adverse impact on blacks than whites, women than men), a prima facie case of discrimination has been made out, and the burden shifts to the proponent of the practice to justify it.

2. To retain the practice, it must be shown that the practice serves a genuine business need. This includes proof that the practice has a demonstrable or manifest relationship to the business goal for which it was adopted and that the goal fulfills this "genuine business need."

3. If it is shown that the practice is a business necessity, as defined above, the challengers to the practice still can prevail if they can demonstrate the availability of other devices which serve the same legitimate business goals, but which have a less discriminatory impact.

CREDIT APPLICATIONS

The requirements for establishing a prima facie case in an effects test challenge suggest some potential applications in the credit field.

A credit scoring system, like an intelligence test or psychological test in the employment context, is a device which purports to predict performance. If, through the use of such a system, a greater proportion of blacks than whites or women than men is rejected, a prima facie case is made and the lender must show the validity of the criteria used in the credit scoring system.

Likewise a criterion such as prior homeownership or type of occupation (white collar, blue collar, etc.), if it correlates closely and adversely to the rejection rates for minorities or women, will require a showing not only of the "predictiveness" of the factor used, but also of the genuine business need to use that factor to the exclusion of others.

With respect to redlining issues, factors traditionally used in property underwriting include the age of property and neighborhood features such as conformity of improvements, or architectural considerations such as lot and building widths, or room count. If these ostensibly neutral factors operate, in effect, to limit the number of loans made in racially integrated areas, lenders may have the burden of demonstrating the necessity of relying on these factors.

Further, if a plaintiff makes a statistical showing of a very low rate of conventional lending in an area which is minority-occupied or integrated and a correspondingly high rate of conventional lending in other areas, the lender may then have the burden of coming forward and explaining why.

Likewise, if a lender, rather than underwriting each loan individually, excludes an entire geographic area from the areas eligible for conventional lending and, in so doing excludes areas of high minority concentration, the lender may then have to justify this practice.

Refusal to process FHA or VA loans solely because of administrative inconvenience or expense also might conceivably have a discriminatory effect, depending on the population statistics, the racial characteristics of the pool of persons eligible for such loans but ineligible for conventional financing, the general availability of such loans in the area, and the lender's other loans to minorities.

These challenges are not as draconian as they may at first appear. Underlying the analysis in each instance is the assumption that the lender will have an opportunity to demonstrate the validity of the criteria used.

It stands to reason, however, that, if the lender cannot demonstrate the validity, or has never undertaken a real examination of the validity of the criteria used, the criteria should probably *not* be used.

From a simple safety and soundness point of view, criteria and standards which do not bear a demonstrable relationship to creditworthiness or soundness probably should not be sustained.

To garner some idea of what is required to show "business necessity," consider the following quotation:

... a neutral policy, which is inherently discriminatory, may be valid if it has overriding business justification . . . . However, this doctrine of business necessity, which has arisen as an exception to the amenability of discriminatory practices, connotes an irrestible demand. The system in question must not only *foster* safety and efficiency, but must be *essential* to that goal. In other words, there must be no acceptable alternative that will accomplish that goal "equally well with a lesser differential racial impact."[1]

Business necessity requires more than a showing of inconvenience, annoyance, and expense.

DIAGNOSE YOUR INSTITUTION

To some extent the lending industry is being called on to examine its own foundations and its historically accepted premises. In the long run, this can only be a helpful and healthy exercise.

From our analysis of the way the fair lending laws are most likely to be applied in equal credit cases, several tools suggest themselves for self-diagnostic purposes. They are:

1. Statistics: (a) Where are loans being made? (b) To whom are loans being made? (c) What are the implications of home mortgage disclosure data? (d) What are the implications of racial notation data?

2. Prior practices: Review all old and new forms. Review older loan files and older training and policy memoranda.

3. Comparison of similarly situated persons: Look at loan files; interview employees with front line exposure; review all work sheets; interview unsuccessful applicants.

4. Policy: Review the articulated policy of the institution, both written and unwritten. Include policy and training manuals, staff meeting presentations, etc.

5. Image: Discover the image your institution has. What are the perceptions of the institution as held by dealers, brokers, public interest groups?

By gathering accurate information in each of these categories and seeing whether any practices fit into the "pigeonholes" we have discussed, a lender can be alerted to practices which may require change.

---

[1] *United States v. St. Louis-San Francisco Ry. Co.,* 464 F.2d 301 (8th Cir. 1972) (en banc), *cert. denied,* 409 U.S. 1116 (1973) and many cases there cited.

A NEW SUPERVISORY SYSTEM FOR RATING BANKS[*]

George R. Juncker

40

The commercial banking system which serves the United States is a very diverse one. Its nearly 14,500 banks range from single-office institutions, with less than $1 million in assets and serving a limited market area, to the international banking giants with hundreds of offices located in the world's financial centers and with assets which total many billions of dollars. Federal supervision of such a diverse banking system is necessarily a complex and demanding task for the three agencies that share responsibility for seeing that the banking system is safe and sound and serves the financial needs of the nation. While all three Federal agencies have approached the analysis of bank condition in a somewhat similar way, past differences in bank rating procedures and techniques used by the agencies had complicated the task of evaluating the condition of the banking system as a whole. In May, the Federal Reserve System, the Office of the Comptroller of the Currency, and the Federal Deposit Insurance Corporation (FDIC) announced adoption of a uniform system for rating the condition of the nation's commercial banks.

The new rating system gives senior officials at the supervisory agencies a capsule summary of the condition of individual banks as well as an indication of the health of groups of banks or the overall banking system. The ratings are intended as a tool to focus attention on real and potential problems and to permit the effective allocation of supervisory resources among the banks.

*Reprinted from the *Quarterly Review*, Summer 1978, pp. 47-50, with permission from the Federal Reserve Bank of New York.

Federal law gives primary supervisory responsibility for the nation's 4,700 national banks to the Office of the Comptroller of the Currency. The Federal Reserve System exercises direct supervisory authority over about 1,000 banks that are chartered by state banking authorities and that are members of the Federal Reserve System. The FDIC provides Federal supervision over more than 8,700 insured, state-chartered commercial banks that are not members of the Federal Reserve System. In addition, the Federal Reserve System is charged with primary responsibilities for supervising the more than 2,000 bank holding companies in the United States with one or more commercial bank subsidiaries.

The new Uniform Interagency Bank Rating System will help ensure consistency in the way the Federal bank supervisors view individual banks within the banking system. The new rating system has two main elements:

(1) An assessment by Federal bank examiners or analysts of five critical aspects of a bank's operations and condition. These are adequacy of the bank's capital, the quality of the bank's assets (primarily its loans and investments), the ability of the bank's management and administration, the quality of the bank's earnings, and the level of its liquidity.

(2) An overall judgment incorporating these basic factors and other factors considered significant by the examiners or analysts, expressed as a single composite rating of the bank's condition and soundness. Banks will be placed in one of five groups, ranging from banks that are sound in almost every respect to those with excessive weaknesses requiring urgent aid.

The new rating system builds upon the foundation of earlier systems used by the three agencies. These rating systems date back to at least as early as 1926 when the Federal Reserve Bank of New York used a simple system to categorize over 900 member banks then in the Second District.[1] Each of the three Federal banking supervisors adopted its own rating system in the mid-1930's after extensive interagency discussion. These systems tended to be very complex and attempted to combine subjective judgments and quantitative standards.[2] Probably because of their rigidity and complexity, coupled with improvements in the strength and stability of the nation's economy and banking system, these rating systems began to fall into disfavor in the 1940's as simplified approaches were sought. In 1952, the Federal Reserve System and the Office of the Comptroller of the Currency agreed on the basic structure of a rating system. That system, like the new uniform system, provided

---

[1] This rating system went by the name of MERIT. Based heavily upon management and asset quality in relation to capital, a rating of M was assigned for banks in good condition, E for satisfactory condition, R for fair, I for unsatisfactory, and T for serious.

[2] One system "scored" six characteristics—management, loans, securities, capital account, deposit growth, and earnings—and combined these numeric scores with a series of weighting factors. Judgmental inputs on factors not specifically measured were not permitted, making the resulting score difficult to interpret either as an absolute measure of condition or even in its relationship to other scores.

for separate ratings for capital adequacy, asset quality, and management and included an overall judgment of the bank's condition.[3]

The Federal Reserve's responsibility for supervising the activities of the nation's registered bank holding companies created particular interest in the design of an improved system for rating banks which could be used by all three Federal bank regulatory agencies. The new uniform system was designed, in large part, by a group headed by Eugene A. Thomas, vice president of the Federal Reserve Bank of San Francisco, working under the direction of the Federal Reserve Bank Presidents' Conference Committee on Regulations, Bank Supervision, and Legislation.

Under the new system, each performance characteristic and the composite is rated on a scale from one to five, which indicates the extent of the bank's strength or weakness. A rating of "1" indicates strength, "5" indicates a degree of weakness requiring urgent corrective actions. Thus, the strongest possible rating for a bank would be:

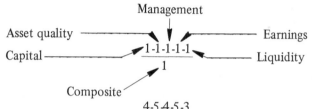

On the other hand, a rating of $\frac{4\text{-}5\text{-}4\text{-}5\text{-}3}{4}$ would indicate a bank with critical problems with asset quality and earnings and an overall condition that is less than satisfactory. Close supervisory attention and financial monitoring would be indicated by such a rating.

The examiner-analyst in using the new system evaluates each of the five elements of a bank's condition and the composite rating independently according to specifically defined standards. (See box for the definitions of each composite rating and the description of each performance zone as agreed upon by the three agencies.) While the five performance dimensions are somewhat interdependent, each is rated separately. Similarly, the composite is not determined by calculating an average of the separate components but rather is based on an independent judgment of the overall condition of the bank. Other factors, such as local economic conditions and prospects, trends in financial performance, and affiliation with a bank holding company, are evaluated by the examiner-analyst and incorporated into his overall assessment of the bank's condition.

Arriving at a six number representation of a bank's condition is an exercise which requires sound analytical judgment. It is admittedly an attempt to reduce to quantified terms a very complex judgmental evaluation process. A single ratio or group of ratios cannot fully or accurately describe all the un-

---

[3] The Federal Reserve and the Comptroller of the Currency have used what is essentially this rating system almost continuously since it was originally adopted. The specific definitions used in that system were included in former Governor Robert Holland's testimony before the Committee on Banking, Housing, and Urban Affairs, United States Senate (February 6, 1976).

I. Composite Rating

The five composite ratings are defined as follows:

Composite 1
Banks in this group are sound institutions in almost every respect; any critical findings are basically of a minor nature and can be handled in a routine manner. Such banks are resistant to external economic and financial disturbances and capable of withstanding the vagaries of the business cycle more ably than banks with lower composite ratings.

Composite 2
Banks in this group are also fundamentally sound institutions but may reflect modest weaknesses correctable in the normal course of business. Such banks are stable and also able to withstand business fluctuations well; however, areas of weakness could develop into conditions of greater concern. To the extent that the minor adjustments are handled in the normal course of business, the supervisory response is limited.

Composite 3
Banks in this group exhibit a combination of weaknesses ranging from moderately severe to unsatisfactory. Such banks are only nominally resistant to the onset of adverse business conditions and could easily deteriorate if concerted action is not effective in correcting the areas of weakness. Consequently, such banks are vulnerable and require more than normal supervision. Overall strength and financial capacity, however, are still such as to make failure only a remote possibility.

Composite 4
Banks in this group have an immoderate volume of asset weaknesses, or a combination of other conditions that are less than satisfactory. Unless prompt action is taken to correct these conditions, they could reasonably develop into a situation that could impair future viability. A potential for failure is present but is not pronounced. Banks in this category require close supervisory attention and monitoring of financial condition.

derlying factors that influence a bank's past, present, or future performance. Thus, consistency in the new system depends not, for example, on rigid definitions of what constitutes adequate earnings but rather on an appreciation by the examiner-analyst of the several roles earnings play in making a bank sound and the matching of the bank's particular and peculiar situation to the agreed-upon definitions.

Composite 5

This category is reserved for banks whose conditions are worse than those defined under Composite 4. The intensity and nature of weaknesses are such as to require urgent aid from the shareholders or other sources. Such banks require immediate corrective action and constant supervisory attention. The probability of failure is high for these banks.

II. Performance Evaluation

The five key performance dimensions—capital adequacy, asset quality, management-administration, earnings, and liquidity—are evaluated on a scale of one to five defined as follows:

Rating No. 1 indicates *strong* performance. It is the highest rating and is indicative of performance that is significantly higher than average.

Rating No. 2 reflects *satisfactory* performance. It reflects performance that is average or above; it includes performance that adequately provides for the safe and sound operation of the bank.

Rating No. 3 represents performance that is flawed to some degree; as such, is considered *fair*. It is neither satisfactory nor marginal but is characterized by performance of below-average quality.

Rating No. 4 represents *marginal* performance which is significantly below average; if left unchecked, such performance might evolve into weaknesses or conditions that could threaten the viability of the institution.

Rating No. 5 is considered *unsatisfactory*. It is the lowest rating and is indicative of performance that is critically deficient and in need of immediate remedial attention. Such performance by itself, or in combination with other weaknesses, could threaten the viability of the institution.

The first of the five performance dimensions—*capital adequacy*—gives recognition to the role that capital plays as the foundation supporting business risks within the bank. The greater the risks faced by a bank, the greater is its need for a strong capital base. In appraising these risks, the Federal supervisors review the risk "mix" of the asset portfolio as well as the skill with which management plans ahead and minimizes risks. The vitality of a bank's market area is also included in the analysis. The examiner-analyst also reviews the bank's capital-to-risk assets relationship, its trend, and a comparison of the bank's ratio with other banks of similar size and doing similar types of business.

An appraisal of the quality and collectibility of a bank's loans and investments has traditionally been one of the key parts of a Federal supervisory examination. The *asset quality* performance rating is largely based upon data on the overall quality of the assets held by the bank as developed during a supervisory examination. The new system, like earlier ones, relies heavily upon the classification of the bank's credits into loss, doubtful, and substandard categories according to the likelihood of the bank's actually absorbing a loss on a credit.[4] Loan and investment policies, the adequacy of valuation reserves, and management's demonstrated ability to collect problem credits would also be considered by the examiner-analyst in coming to a judgment regarding overall asset quality.

The third element in the rating evaluates the quality of a bank's corporate *management* including its board of directors. Management's technical competence, leadership, and administrative ability are evaluated along with the internal controls and operating procedures that have been installed. The bank's compliance with banking laws and regulations is another factor in the appraisal, as are the provisions for management succession. Judgments regarding management's willingness and ability to serve the legitimate banking needs of the community are also considered.

The strength of the bank's *earnings* is the fourth element in the performance rating. Here, a judgment is rendered on the adequacy of earnings to provide a sufficient return to the bank's stockholders, to generate sufficient cash flows for the normal needs of borrowers, and to provide for the future needs through the development of capital. The "quality" of earnings is also analyzed, with particular attention paid to the adequacy of the bank's additions to valuation reserves and to the tax effects on net income. Peer-group comparisons and trends in earnings provide additional quantitative evidence for the rating.

The *liquidity* rating is based upon the bank's ability to manage its assets and liabilities in such a way as to ensure that it can meet the demands of both depositors and borrowers without undue strain. Among the factors considered in evaluating liquidity are the availability of assets readily convertible into cash, the bank's formal and informal commitments for future lending or investment, the structure and volatility of deposits, the reliance on interest-sensitive funds including money market instruments and other sources of borrowing, and the ability to adjust rates on loans when rates on interest-sensitive sources of funds fluctuate. The examiner-analyst will review the frequency and level of borrowings and include judgments of the bank's ability to sustain any level of borrowings over the business cycle or to attract new sources of funds. These judgments also include analyses of the bank's present

---

[4] The usual rule of thumb used for interpreting these classifications is that all credits classified loss will indeed represent eventual losses, 50 percent of aggregate credits classified doubtful will be charged off, as well as 20 percent of substandard classifications. Of course, actual loss experiences vary from credit to credit and bank to bank depending upon a wide variety of circumstances.

and future access to traditional money market sources of funds and other domestic and foreign sources. The bank's average liquidity experience over a period of time, as well as its liquidity position on the examination date, would be considered. For Federal Reserve member banks, the use of the discount window is also reviewed to determine if borrowings are for other than seasonal or short-term adjustment purposes.

After analyzing the five key factors, the examiner-analyst arrives at a *composite rating* which summarizes the agency's overall view of the bank's condition and reflects the level of continuing supervisory attention which the bank's condition seems to warrant. A composite "1" rated bank would receive little supervisory attention between examinations, while a composite "5" bank would be subject to constant monitoring and a corrective action program developed by the bank's management and directors and accepted by its Federal supervisors.

The new rating system provides a uniform structure for use by the three Federal supervisory agencies in evaluating the condition of the nation's commercial banks. This uniformity of approach is expected to lead to more consistent and even-handed supervisory treatment. It should also enable more informed judgments regarding trends in the condition of the banking system as a whole.

PRIVATE CREDIT RATIONING[†]

Paul S. Anderson and James R. Ostas[*]

41

It is fall, 1974 in Boston. Savings banks have very little money to lend on home mortgages because depositors have been withdrawing substantial amounts from their savings to invest in securities paying much higher rates than banks pay on savings. What loanable funds a certain savings bank has can be:

(a) used to buy corporate bonds yielding almost 11 percent, and having no servicing expenses, or
(b) lent out at 9½ percent to a long-standing depositor on a mortgage loan which has servicing costs of just under ½ of 1 percent.

Question: Does the savings bank choose (a) or (b)? Most students of economics, as well as most of the public, would choose answer (a). But savings bankers, the people who count usually choose (b). Instead of lending funds to the highest bidders, savings bankers and other institutional lenders choose to charge less and then to distribute, or *ration*, their credit on some basis other than rate paid.

At the present time, funds for lending are plentiful and the question of credit rationing a remote one. However, periods of monetary restraint have been a recurring phenomenon in our economy, and problems of credit ra-

† Reprinted from the *New England Economic Review*, May/June 1977, pp. 24-37, with permission from the Federal Reserve Bank of Boston.

*Paul S. Anderson is an Assistant Vice President and Financial Economist at the Federal Reserve Bank of Boston and James R. Ostas is an Associate Professor of Economics at Bowling Green University.

tioning may return at some future time. The very concept of private credit rationing remains controversial, and its importance in implementing monetary policy is still questioned by many.[1] However, particularly during periods of credit restraint, the allocation of available funds among borrowers clearly is not based entirely upon the interest rate paid.

The impact of direct rationing of some prospective borrowers out of the market necessarily differs from the effect of an increase in interest rates. Specific attempts to measure these factors have been far less frequent than the development of theories to explain credit rationing, however. This article will be confined to a description of some of the lending practices related to credit rationing in the commercial, consumer, and mortgage loan fields.

I. THE RATIONING PHENOMENON

For most people, rationing refers to the procedure used primarily during wartime to allocate goods in short supply. Ration coupons that permitted the purchase of a set amount of the rationed item per time period were parceled out on a per capita basis. Economists call this nonprice rationing, as opposed to the common way of allocating goods by price rationing, which is charging a price that equalizes supply and demand. In price rationing, each dollar bill is, in effect, a ration coupon.

Rationing is defined in this article as the way goods or credit are allocated when their price is set at so low a level that more is demanded than is available. The rationing phenomenon has two aspects, the setting of a below-market or "too-low" price and the method of allocation at this price. Three combinations can be distinguished according to who sets the price and who determines the allocation scheme:

1. Price and rationing method both determined by government. This is the World War II type of rationing where the government controlled the price of goods in short supply and specified, by the use of ration coupons, how the short supply was to be distributed.
2. Price determined by government but rationing carried out by private sector. This type occurred at the time of the 1974 gasoline shortage. The government set the price at a level where more was demanded than was available. The short supply of gasoline was distributed privately, generally on the basis of first come, first served.
3. Both price and rationing determined in private sector. A striking example of this type of rationing occurred in the post World War II years after price controls were abolished in 1946. Auto manufacturers did

---

[1] For a review of the continuing debate in the literature about credit rationing, see Benjamin M. Friedman, "Credit Rationing: A Review," Board of Governors of the Federal Reserve System, *Staff Economic Studies*, 72, 1972, 27 pp. One of the more recent attempts to measure credit rationing used the Federal Reserve System's Quarterly Survey of Changes in Bank Lending Practices. See Duane G. Harris, "Credit Rationing at Commercial Banks: Some Empirical Evidence," *Journal of Money Credit and Banking*, Vol VI, No. 2 (May 1974), pp. 227-240.

not set prices at a level which would equalize demands with supplies, but at a lower level. More cars were demanded at these prices than were available and the automobile manufacturers permitted their dealers to distribute cars according to their best judgment.

All these examples were drawn from the markets for goods, but the rationing phenomenon also occurs in the credit markets. Most credit rationing falls into the second and third types. Examples of the first type, where the government sets both price and the rationing scheme, are rare in this country but have been common in some other countries, such as France.[2] The concept of rationing used here is the process by which lenders allocate their loanable funds when they do not (or cannot) charge a high enough interest rate to balance demands for loans with supplies of funds.

II. USURY LAWS

The most obvious example of "too low" interest rates occurs where usury laws set low ceilings on interest rates that can be charged on loans. Forty-eight states have usury laws which vary in coverage and the level of the ceiling, but most apply only to loans to individuals and noncorporate businesses.[3] Usually small consumer instalment loans are exempt from these general usury ceilings but are covered by special, higher ceilings. Loans to corporations most often are exempted entirely or covered by higher ceilings. As a result, usury ceilings primarily affect personal loans to consumers, mortgage loans to home buyers, and business loans to unincorporated firms.

The intent of usury laws is to protect "unsophisticated" borrowers against "exorbitant" interest rates. While such an intent can be applauded, usury laws really cannot do the job. The basic difficulty is that usury ceilings conflict with the law of supply and demand which sets prices in the market place. If the usury ceiling is below the market interest rate which lenders can get, lenders will tend not to lend to those borrowers, who are "protected" by the ceiling. For example, if conditions are such that the interest rate on mortgage loans should be 9 percent in order to balance demands for loans with supplies of funds but the ceiling on loans is 7½ percent (as it was in Vermont until April 1974), then more funds are demanded at 7½ percent than are available and credit rationing results. What funds banks do lend at the ceiling, they will lend to long-standing customers. Thus those borrowers that do benefit from usury ceilings generally would get favored treatment anyway because they are known to the lender or can provide good security.

---

[2] Donald R. Hodgman, "The French System of Monetary and Credit Controls" Banca Nazionale del Lavoro, *Quarterly Review*, No. 99 (December 1971), pp. 324-353; Donald R. Hodgman, "Credit Controls in Western Europe: An Evaluation Review," and Jacques H. David and Marcus H. Miller, "Discussion," in *Credit Allocation Techniques and Monetary Policy*, Federal Reserve Bank of Boston, Conference Series No. 11, September 1973, pp. 137-177.

[3] Norman W. Bowsher, "Usury Laws: Harmful When Effective," *Federal Reserve Bank of St. Louis Review*, Vol. 56, No. 8 (August 1974), pp. 16-23.

Available evidence suggests that in those states with usury ceilings below the market interest rate, thrift institutions increase their lending on out-of-state mortgages and other credit instruments.[4] As a result, funds lent on local conventional mortgages are reduced, as are new housing starts.[5] While FHA and VA mortgages are exempt from usury laws in several states, they do not serve to fill the "financing gap" that results from usury ceilings on conventional mortgages. FHA and VA mortgages involve a lot of "red tape." Their rates are set in Washington, and while the effective rate can be raised by discounting, many borrowers, and even lenders, object to this practice.

Of the 48 states with usury laws, a large number have raised the ceilings or relaxed the provisions of the law in the last ten years. They recognized that the net effect of usury ceilings substantially below market rates was on balance more injurious than helpful.

III. EVIDENCE OF PRIVATE CREDIT RATIONING ACTIVITY

It is obvious why interest rates on loans can become "too low" when usury ceilings are in force. But even where usury ceilings do not apply, loan rates are often "too low" during periods when funds are in short supply. At such times lenders do not raise rates to levels which would reduce demand to the volume of funds available, but hold rates at a lower level. At this lower level, the demand for funds exceeds the supply and lenders allocate or ration available funds to borrowers on some basis other than willingness to pay.

Borrowers become aware of the rationing phenomenon when they apply for loans. Normally lenders inquire about the applicant's credit rating and then state the terms of the loan. But when funds are in short supply, the lender will first determine whether the applicant is entitled to credit on the basis of his past relationship with the lender. If the applicant is not, he will probably be turned down with no discussion of what rates would be charged and whether the applicant would be willing to pay these rates.

Shown in the chart are comparisons of interest rates which indicate periods when rates charged for loans were lower than rates paid on comparable investments, which is a standard symptom that credit rationing is occurring. In the top panel are rates charged on conventional mortgage loans and the rate prevailing in the secondary or wholesale market for government-insured (FHA) mortgage loans. During periods when supplies of mortgage funds were

---

[4] Suzanne Cutler, "The Public Policy Objectives of the Regulation of Depository Institutions," in Leonard Lapidus et al., *Public Policy Toward Mutual Savings Banks in New York State: Proposals for Change*, Federal Reserve Bank of New York and New York State Banking Department, June 1974, p. 111.

[5] James R. Ostas, "Effects of Usury Ceilings in the Mortgage Market," *Journal of Finance*, Vol. XXXI (June, 1976), pp. 821-834; Arthur J. Rolnick, Stanley L. Graham, and David S. Dahl, "Minnesota's Usury Law: An Evaluation," *Ninth District Quarterly*, Federal Reserve Bank of Minneapolis, April 1975, pp. 16-25; Norman W. Bowsher, *op. cit.*, p. 19, and Robins, Philip K., "The Effects of State Usury Ceilings on Single Family Homebuilding," *Journal of Finance*, Vol. XXIX, (March 1974), pp. 227-235.

LOAN RATES, MARKET RATES AND INTEREST COSTS
(1965-1976)

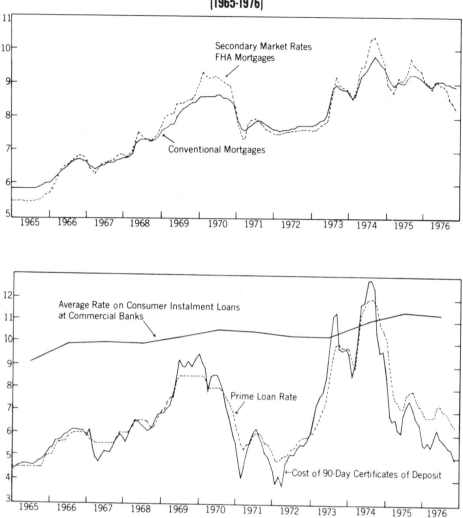

Note-The mortgage rate series are those compiled by the Department of Housing and Urban Development. The cost of 90 day CDs includes the cost of carrying reserves against these time deposits. The consumer loan rate is an estimate based on the Functional Cost survey of the Federal Reserve prior to 1971 and on a sample survey since then.

short, particularly in 1969-70 and 1974, rates in the secondary market rose 50 basis points or more above rates charged conventional borrowers. Not only does this indicate that rates charged for conventional mortgages were relatively low, but that lenders accepted these lower rates when they could have bought insured mortgage loans in the secondary market at a higher rate of return.

The lower panel in the chart compares the prime business loan rate with the cost of 90-day certificates of deposit (CDs) adjusted for reserve requirements. This adjusted CD rate is a measure of a bank's marginal cost of funds. Normally the prime loan rate approximates or slightly exceeds the CD cost, but in 1973 and again in 1974 the prime loan rate did not even keep up with the adjusted CD cost.[6] Again, banks were charging less for these loans than they were paying for their marginal source of funds.

Also shown in the lower panel are rates for consumer loans, which have been relatively stable. From a level of about 9 percent in 1963, rates on consumer loans by banks rose slowly to about 10½ percent in 1970-72 and then more rapidly to 11½ percent in 1974. Since the servicing expenses of these loans amount to around 3 percent per year, the net return on these loans did not cover the marginal cost of funds as represented by the CD rate. Obviously the rate on consumer loans was also below what might be expected during tight money periods.[7]

Why are lenders reluctant to charge what the market will bear? Several factors influence lenders to act circumspectly. They involve the image lenders want to gain and maintain before both governmental bodies and customers. Federal and state governments are quick to express concern if they believe that lenders are raising loan rates to unwarranted levels. In the past, some state governments have imposed restrictive usury ceilings, which can severely limit the operations of lenders.

Possible reactions of borrowers and the public generally also make lenders hesitant about raising loan rates rapidly. Maintaining good relationships with existing customers is important for long-run profit maximization. This is especially the case where the "products" are loans and deposits and one lender's products are practically identical to another's. Lending institutions strive to develop good relations with their customers and rapid and aggressive raising of loan rates can easily alienate them. Thus, lenders tend to delay raising loan rates until most comparable money market rates have risen and even then to raise their loan rates a little less than these other rates. In essence, lenders sacrifice short-run profits because they think that course is more profitable in the long run.

It should be noted that, as contrasted with credit rationing caused by low usury ceilings, voluntary credit rationing diminishes with the passage of time. Lenders do gradually raise their lending rates, and if tight conditions persist long enough, rates may eventually reach the "correct" level so rationing is

---

[6] A special factor serving to hold down the prime loan rate in 1973 and 1974 was the Federal Government's Committee on Interest and Dividends which monitored interest rate and dividend payment developments during this period.

[7] Construction lending provides an interesting contrast to the lending areas discussed in this article because it has little rationing—lenders generally charge the going market rate. The chief construction lenders are commercial banks, savings and loan associations, and real estate investment trusts. The characteristics of construction lending probably explain why credit is allocated on the basis of rate rather than being rationed when credit is tight. Construction lending is risky and the failure rate among builders and developers is much higher than the average among borrowers in general. The soundness of a loan depends on both the competence of the builder and the profitability of the completed project. Builders generally do not have substantial assets of their own, so they cannot provide much additional security. In addition, the construction industry is fairly small so little public attention is paid to its credit costs.

not needed. Also, as tight credit conditions become more common, as has happended since 1966, lenders adjust their interest rates more quickly. This can be seen in the chart; rates on all three types of loans shown were raised more quickly and to a greater extent in 1973-74 than in the two preceding restraint periods. Thus voluntary credit rationing is really a temporary phenomenon and may well become less important in the future as the country becomes more accustomed to large fluctuations in interest rates.

Mortgage Loans

The chief home mortgage lenders are thrift institutions—savings and loan associations and savings banks. These lenders present themselves as "people's institutions" and in the past Congress has granted them various types of favored treatment such as somewhat higher interest rate ceilings than commercial banks. Thrift institutions have also been successful in gaining a favorable and sympathetic attitude from the public. Residential mortgage borrowers have usually obtained more attractive terms than offered by other lenders. This favorable public attitude would be jeopardized if thrift institutions began raising mortgage rates as rapidly as competitive conditions allowed during periods of credit restraint.

Business Loans

Most business borrowers are much more interested in the availability of bank loans than in the current rate of interest. So long as they believe they are not paying more than other business borrowers in the same situation, they will accept higher rates, even though reluctantly. But elected officials express a great deal of concern about rapid rises in business loan rates. If Congress becomes sufficiently antagonistic to banks, it can pass penalizing legislation restricting bank operations and profits. Commercial banks have been quite successful in the postwar years in obtaining greater "tax equality," and they could jeopardize this trend by too aggressive rate-setting. A clear example of banks bowing to governmental pressure occurred in 1973 when the Government Committee on Interest and Dividends requested banks to raise the prime rate slowly and banks complied, even though they were under no legal requirement to do so.

Furthermore, banks do not have to raise the prime rate to the highest point possible in order to make good profits during a period of restraint. This is the case even though the cost of funds rises so rapidly during periods of restraint that for a time the *marginal* cost of funds borrowed by a bank exceeds the interest received from many, if not most, of its borrowers. However, the *average* cost of bank funds does not rise as quickly as do yields on earning assets because about one-third of bank funds on average are obtained from demand deposits which pay no interest. The net result is that although the costs of *additional* funds (those obtained through CDs, for example) rise above the yield on business loans, average costs of funds are low enough to provide a very profitable spread. Moreover, loan rates usually decline more slowly than CD rates when credit conditions ease. As the chart shows, a profitable spread opened up between the prime rate and the net cost of CDs in the easy credit periods of 1971-72 and 1975-76. Thus, when the credit cycle is viewed as a whole, bank profits suffer little, if at all, as a consequence of charging lower-than-market rates on business loans during a tight period.

Banks can also make up a part of the undercharges on business loans by other adjustments. The most common of these is to increase the compensating balances the borrower must hold. For example, if this balance is increased from 10 to 20 percent of the loan or the line of credit, the borrower really gets 10 percent less from his loan, yet his interest payment is the same as before, so his actual cost per $1 used is about 10 percent higher. Banks can also make up for "too-low" interest rates on business loans by adjusting commitment fees, fees for handling trust and pension accounts, and other charges. Still another adjustment is to add a premium to the prime rate, often done with new customers. Even though the new borrower may be as creditworthy as existing prime borrowers, the bank may charge him, say, prime plus 1 percent. This premium charge is continued until a regular customer relationship is established. Thus, for all these reasons the actual level of the prime rate on business loans may not accurately reflect the real cost of lending to any given borrower or its overall profitability to the bank.

These adjustments in the terms of the customer relationship are, at best, only a partial substitute for raising the business loan rate. Like the below-market level of the loan rate, they are symptoms of the fact that an imbalance, or disequilibrium, exists in the supply and demand for funds which requires rationing. If banks felt they could raise rates rapidly enough to balance supplies and demands, they would undoubtedly do so rather than adjusting these other lending terms because interest rate changes are much simpler than the other adjustments which usually involve individual negotiations with borrowers.

But it is not practical for banks (or other lenders) to change loan rates whenever market conditions change, even if they felt they could. Market interest rates, such as on Treasury bills or commercial paper, change continuously. Lenders prefer to delay changing their rates until they are fairly certain that the change will not have to be reversed soon.

Also, business demands for funds are so intense, or inelastic, at times that even fairly substantial rises in the lending rate do little to dampen these demands. For example, a lending officer of a large midwestern bank that was especially short of loanable funds stated that his bank raised the rate for some prime customers by three percentage points above the prevailing prime rate but that resulted in no withdrawals of loan requests.

In sum, there are frictions in rate setting on loans that make it practically impossible for lenders to allocate credit on the basis of rate alone. Thus, whenever credit conditions tighten rapidly, some rationing is inevitable.

Consumer Loans

Rates on consumer loans of banks are by far the most stable of the three types discussed in this article. The explanation involves the marketing strategies of banks adopted as a response to the history of consumer credit. In the 1920s, when consumer loans were first extended in any significant amount, they were considered risky and the rates charged were high. But these loans proved surprisingly sound in the depression of the 1930s. Their loss ratio was small; in fact, the percentage of failures among banks was much higher than the loss percentage on consumer loans. The relatively high interest yield combined with low losses made these loans very profitable during the 1930s, 1940s, and early 1950s when other yields were historically low.

Successful consumer lending requires sufficient volume so that processing costs per loan are moderate. At best, processing costs tend to run over 3 percent, and if not well controlled can easily rise to more than twice that level. But it is difficult to develop consumer loan business "off the street." It takes persistent advertising to gain recognition and habitual acceptance as a low-cost consumer lender with "low bank rates." Such advertising is aimed at influencing the habits of the borrowing public rather than convincing the public the institution merits special treatment.

This marketing effort is a long-term operation—it cannot be turned off when interest rates rise and then resumed with any success when rates decline. Because of this, banks believe it is good marketing policy to hold consumer loan rates as stable as possible during tight money in order to maintain the bank's reputation as a comparatively low cost lender. Thus banks are willing to charge less than is warranted during high rate periods in order to preserve their public acceptance and to profit by it when rates decline.

The other major consumer lenders, sales and consumer finance companies, dominated this market until commercial banks entered on a wide scale in the late 1930s. Since then, the finance companies have gradually lost market shares to commercial banks. Their cost of funds averages higher than that of banks and they typically charge higher rates—about 13 percent on new car loans, for example, as compared to about 11 percent by banks. But they cannot set their rates too far above bank rates or they will lose their market share even faster. Thus their rates tend to be determined by the level of bank rates. On small personal loans, which generally have the highest rates of the various types of consumer loans, usury ceilings often determine the level of interest rates.

IV. HOW LOANS ARE RATIONED

Rationing Mortgage Funds

During tight money periods, the inflow of funds to mortgage lenders declines substantially. Since lenders generally chose not to raise lending rates enough to reduce applications to the volume of available funds, they have a large gap between supplies of funds and demands for them. Their problem is how to parcel out the limited supply.

First, of course, lenders must honor prior loan commitments. Then their first general rationing action is to turn down all out-of-area applicants. According to all mortgage lenders who were interviewed, they want to satisfy borrowers in their main market area first. They also generally refuse all applications for credit for purchases of vacation homes. They believe primary home purchasers deserve priority.

Beyond these criteria, they rank borrowers by group. The following order is fairly typical of the priorities of thrift institutions:

1) Long-established depositors.
2) Buyers of houses on which lenders already have mortgages (refinancing loans).
3) Borrowers referred by brokers and builders who have a long-established association with lender.
4) Commercial mortgage borrowers.
5) Applicants "off the street" with no ties to lender.

Some institutions may tend to have somewhat different rankings and vary in their lending policies. Some lenders, attracted by the high rates paid, will rank large commercial mortgage borrowers second or third in their priority of applicants. Lenders who prize their broker and builder contacts might rank this group second.

Borrowers are further ranked by their relative safety. Those receive preference who can provide a high downpayment, 30 percent or even more, and can pay off the loan within 20 years. Not only do such terms make the loan less risky but they help the liquidity position of the lender by reducing the funds loaned out and increasing the rate of repayment.

A refinancing loan (giving a new loan on the same house on which the bank already held a mortgage) has been attractive in recent years because it allows the lender to obtain a higher rate of interest on what is essentially an old loan and on which the interest rate is usually lower than the prevailing rate. Such loans combined with a high downpayment are particularly attractive since the lender needs to advance less additional cash than for an original mortgage. Lenders will often grant a rate somewhat lower than the prevailing rate on such refinancing loans, in order to expedite the home sale and enable the lender to turn over the loan and get a higher rate than on the original mortgage.

A few mortgage lenders, however, may rely entirely on price to determine their lending policies. For example, one New England savings bank in a predominantly retirement and resort area, finding itself with a large inflow of savings during a period of general restraint, nevertheless charged all applicants a mortgage rate in line with corporate bond rates and higher than the prevailing mortgage rate charged by other thrift institutions. Similarly, a large commercial bank made a substantial short-term profit during a tight money period by lending for home mortgages at a high rate of interest and realizing a capital gain by selling the mortgage loans to a Federal agency at a lower rate of interest.

Normally, most new borrowers are referred by brokers and builders or come to the bank "off the street." Therefore when these two groups are rationed out, the lender has voluntarily cut out most of its new mortgage market. Unless disintermediation is severe, he will still be able to satisfy long-established depositors and the demand for refinancing loans, and occasionally, commercial mortgage borrowers as well. Of course, the lender is not strictly bound by any ranking and he will accommodate new applicants who seem to have an especially urgent need or who appear especially likely to become long-run customers.

Rationing Business Loans

Most business borrowers are long-time depositors of commercial banks, so a close relationship exists between the bank and the business borrower. These long-time depositors traditionally are entitled to a certain quota or line of credit and they generally are more interested in its availability than its cost during a period of restraint, because many profitable business opportunities are usually available at such times. The difficulty is that demands for business loans substantially exceed the volume of funds available then. In fact, a tight money period is generally characterized by rapid increases in business demands for funds which are not accommodated by monetary policy.

During such a period of credit restraint, the first priority of commercial banks is to grant all loan requests that fall within established credit lines. These are considered binding obligations by most banks whether or not a formal commitment fee has been paid. Beyond this, banks provide additional credit on a selective basis using such criteria as credit-worthiness, length or permanence of the customer relationship, profitability of the account over time in relation to bank services provided, proposed use of funds, including analysis of the feasibility of the project, degree of need, and availability of alternative sources of funds. Of course, banks run the risk of alienating customers by unfavorable loan decisions but they also know that applicants will have difficulty obtaining a loan at another bank as well.

Since in rationing business loans, banks first limit their lending to regular customers and to the accommodation of their usual needs, the new venture, the unusual or the risky project, the acquisition loan and the unexpectedly large demand for funds becomes casualties during a tight money period. Thus previous commitments tend to limit the supply of funds available for innovation and expansion. This must be counted an important cost of monetary restraint.

Shown in the accompanying table is a comparison of business lending practices of large commercial banks during easy and tight credit periods. While changes in the interest rate are the most common reaction to ease or tightness, many other reinforcing changes are made in loan terms and in

Changes in Bank Lending Practices at
Selected Large Commercial Banks
on Loans to Nonfinancial Businesses

	Easy credit period: three months to Feb. 1971		Tight credit period: three months to Aug. 1974	
	Firmer	Easier	Firmer	Easier
	(percentages of reporting banks)			
Loan terms:				
Interest rate	0	85	77	0
Compensating balances	2	25	68	0
Credit standards	5	5	60	0
Maturity of term loans	1	26	55	0
Value of applicant as depositor or source of other business	5	19	69	0
Intended use of loan	2	27	64	0

Source: Federal Reserve System Quarterly Survey of Bank Lending Practices.

lending attitudes. This listing of lending adjustments demonstrates that the bank-business borrower relationship includes many facets in addition to the rate charged. A small percentage of banks tightened various noninterest terms in early 1971 even though that was an easing period and no banks raised rates. Presumably this represents a completion of tightening actions these banks had begun during the preceding tight money period of 1969-70 and is further evidence that the loan rate itself does not fully reflect the costs of borrowing.

It is a common assumption that small business gets rationed out of the business loan market at such times. It is a fact that bank lending to large business generally does increase greatly as a proportion of total business lending during a tight money period. For example, between 1972 and 1974, the dollar amount of total new short-term business loans of $1 million and over nearly doubled, according to the Quarterly Survey of Interest Rates conducted by the Federal Reserve System, while the total of similar loans of under $1 million grew less than 10 percent.

However, the substantial increase in bank lending to large business during credit tightness probably reflects cyclically greater use of credit lines by large borrowers rather than changing credit standards. In most cases the bank is the small firm's only source of credit, and the small firm uses this source almost continuously. While large firms maintain compensating balances and lines of credit during times of ease, large firms also use stock issues, commercial paper, loans from insurance companies, and other sources to obtain their funds, and not just bank loans as in the case of small firms. When credit is restricted and other sources of funds such as commercial paper become too expensive or are unavailable, the large firm then relies more heavily on its bank lines of credit, and bank lending to large businesses increases.

Rationing Consumer Loans

The two main lenders of consumer credit, commercial banks and finance companies, are in somewhat different situations with regard to making consumer loans when money is tight. According to the bankers interviewed, the primary goal of most commercial banks is to provide the maximum amount of funds to their priority customers, businesses, and to limit other uses of funds including consumer lending as much as possible. But in trying to limit consumer lending, they must be careful not to tarnish their image as "the bank that likes to say yes." They raise credit standards, but this does not eliminate many applicants because banks typically get the better risks anyway. They discontinue advertising consumer lending, but this has little impact on their established clientele. Banks can do especially little about limiting credit card lending. Once cards have been issued and contracts made with stores to honor them, the volume of credit extended is essentially in the hands of the consumers. Thus, in the final analysis, commercial banks do little effective rationing of consumer credit.

Consumer lending is the priority operation of finance companies, both sales finance and consumer finance. They encounter a severe profits squeeze during a tight credit period because interest costs on their borrowerd funds, of which short-term bank loans and commercial paper are a large share, rise rapidly while their interest income rises little since consumer lending rates are so sluggish. Some finance companies also face a reduction in the availability of funds during such periods because banks that are short of loanable funds often single out finance company credit lines as the area to be cut back. In addition, commercial paper tends to become difficult to market unless the seller maintains an excellent credit standing.

Because of lowered profitability and the reduced availability of funds, finance companies ration credit mainly by raising credit standards. This is quite effective in limiting their lending because their applicants span a wide range of creditworthiness. The result is that the higher-risk, and usually lower-income, consumers get rationed out. Thus charging relatively low rates and rationing loans have the same impact as usury ceilings on consumer loans. Low-risk, high-income consumers pay relatively low rates for their loans, while higher-risk, low-income consumers have difficulty gaining access to conventional sources of credit.

Sales finance companies, which do most of their consumer lending indirectly by purchasing consumer loans from auto and appliance dealers, could conceivably reduce their lending by dropping some of these dealers during tight money periods. But if they were to do so, they would lose the business from those dealers permanently because the disappointed dealers would turn to another source of funds. Therefore, if a sales finance company intends to retain its share of the market during times when lending is profitable, it must do its best to serve its dealers when money is tight. Dealers must then, in turn, limit their credit sales to the better credit risks. Some finance companies did discontinue purchasing mobile home "paper" entirely during the 1973-

74 tight money period even though this meant that they would have difficulty reentering that market if they decided to do so in the future. Mobile home paper had become less profitable than other consumer lending lines and it also absorbed a larger amount of funds per loan.

Other consumer lenders have also had diverse experiences in recent years. Savings banks and savings and loan associations in some states have been empowered to make consumer loans, and some of them aggressively competed with the commercial banks for better-risk loans. But they have been thwarted by their funds shortages during the recent periods of credit restraint. As a result some of them had to stop practically all such lending, and this made it difficult for them to regain a share of the market when fund supplies became more plentiful after 1974. Credit unions, however, have had substantial inflows of funds even in the tight money periods, because they paid somewhat higher rates on their savings than other institutions and they usually had the advantage of convenience as well. As a result, they did not have to ration their loans and they increased their share of the market substantially so that they are now approaching commercial banks in the growth of consumer loans.

V. IMPACT ON LENDERS

Discussions of credit rationing usually focus on the impact on borrowers— who gets credit under rationing and who does not. Often overlooked is the impact on lenders. Since rationing entails a lower interest rate than could be charged, it results in at least a short-term loss to lenders.

The chief lenders to business, commercial banks, probably suffer least among lenders who ration credit. They can generally recoup any loss of income resulting from low rates by making adjustments in other facets of customer service. In any case, during periods of tight credit yields on commercial bank assets, which are almost entirely short-term, rise rapidly (even though less rapidly than they could), while their average costs rise more slowly because a good share of their funds comes from demand deposits on which no interest is paid. As a result, their earnings increase; from 1972 to 1974, for example, the net earnings spread (gross income minus total expenses) of commercial banks rose from 0.66 percent of total assets to 0.81 percent.

Among consumer lenders, sales and consumer finance companies tend to have reductions in net income during periods of credit rationing. For example, net income of these companies declined from a base of 100 in 1972 to 85 in 1973 and 89 in 1974, according to data compiled by the Citibank of New York, while net income of commercial banks rose from 100 in 1972 to 118 in 1973 and 127 in 1974. Rates on consumer loans rise very sluggishly at such times but interest costs of finance companies rise rapidly because they rely heavily on short-term debt, both commercial paper and bank loans, on which rates rise substantially. With respect to their consumer loans, commercial banks are in somewhat the same situation, but consumer loans are a relatively small portion of their assets, just over 10 percent, while these loans are well over 50 percent of the assets of most sales and consumer finance companies.

The chief mortgage lenders, thrift institutions, are affected most severely during tight money periods. Their earning assets are mostly long-term mortgages on which the returns do not rise, of course, when current market rates rise. Therefore they cannot afford to raise rates paid on savings (and are in fact prevented from doing so by Regulation Q requirements). At such times depositors tend to withdraw their funds to invest in higher-yielding assets such as U.S. Treasury bills and notes.

As a result of such savings withdrawals, thrift institutions have few funds to invest. They parcel or ration their funds primarily into mortgages at lower rates than it would be possible to obtain from other investments. This limits their earnings growth, but only slightly because the amount of funds involved is usually very small at such times.

Although savings banks do not sacrifice much income by charging below market rates for home mortgages when their funds are short, they do forego a substantial amount of extra income in years when funds are plentiful by not investing in the highest-yielding assets. For example, since 1967, home mortgage rates have usually been below corporate bond rates on a net yield basis after mortgage servicing expenses. These servicing expenses amount to around ½ of 1 percent, so corporate bonds are more profitable than mortgages if their market yields are within ½ of 1 percent of mortgage yields. Bond yields since late 1967 have usually been within that range of home mortgage yields and, in fact, exceeded mortgage yields in 1969, 1970, 1971, 1974, and 1975. Therefore, for maximum income, savings banks should have invested only in corporate bonds over this period or raised their mortgage lending rate to an equivalent net yield level. In some of these years, notably 1970 through 1972, savings banks had substantial amounts of deposit inflows to invest, so they sacrificed a good deal of income by placing the major part of their available funds into mortgages. This form of rationing is explained by the same factors that lay behind rationing of mortgage loans to customers —savings banks had to maintain their image as "people's institutions."

Another current influence which compounds the earnings problem of thrift institutions is the array of governmental restrictions and programs which are aimed at holding down mortgage rates. Usury ceilings, discussed earlier, are one example. Other rate-depressing actions include the activities of various government and government-sponsored agencies such as the Federal National Mortgage Association, the Government National Mortgage Association, and the Federal Home Loan Mortgage Corporation. These agencies obtain funds from the U.S. Treasury or by borrowing in the credit market and they then channel these funds into the single-family home mortgage market with the express purpose of holding down mortgage rates. This results, of course, in reduced earnings of thrift institutions and serves to weaken their financial positions, particularly in the case of federally chartered savings and loan institutions which do not have the power to invest in corporate bonds as well. While these government efforts to hold down mortgage rates are not directly connected with rationing, the same concept lies behind them, namely, that high mortgage rates should be opposed, whatever the general level or trend of interest rates. Such a public policy attitude must be altered if thrift institutions are to continue to be healthy and viable institutions.

Thrift institutions are, however, modifying their lending behavior as a result of these experiences. Savings banks, which are not restricted to mortgage lending to the same extent as savings and loan associations, have been investing about three-quarters of their net funds inflows since 1974 in bonds. Also, since 1973 both types of thrift institutions have raised their mortgage lending rates somewhat more rapidly when credit markets showed signs of tightening, as seen in the chart. Finally, many thrift institutions are actively selling off the mortgage loans they originate to the government-sponsored agencies. As thrifts do this, they will be forced to raise their rates to keep up with rates in this resale market to avoid a capital loss. As seen in the chart, rates in the secondary market fluctuate more widely than primary rates for conventional loans.

SUMMARY

Credit rationing occurs during tight money periods in mortgage, business, and consumer loan markets because lenders are reluctant to raise interest rates as rapidly as market conditions might indicate, and so must use nonprice criteria to distribute scarce funds. Credit rationing is a phenomenon understood by lenders and borrowers alike, despite the nontangible aspects of some of its operations. It may be characterized as one of the costs of contracyclical monetary policy, with the highest price paid by new and high-risk ventures. But credit rationing may also be described as a sound business practice, operating in the best long-run interest of lenders and borrowers who have long-standing relationships.

The most pronounced form of credit rationing now takes place in the home mortgage loan market, where supplies of funds decrease sharply during a period of restraint due to disintermediation at thrift institutions. Funds shortages are not nearly as acute in the business and consumer loan markets, so that rationing is not as severe.

Methods of rationing differ among lenders, but the general pattern at thrift institutions has been to grant first priority to long-established depositors. Since they account for only a small fraction of mortgage loan applicants, this shuts out most would-be borrowers. Second priority is usually given to refinancing loans, while third are applicants referred by realtors and builders with whom the lender has a long-standing relationship. The business loan market differs from the mortgage loan market, in that most large commercial banks in periods of restraint do have access to additional funds to try to satisfy increased demands for business loans. However, commercial banks do not raise rates on business loans enough to reduce demand to the level of available funds, and they also do some rationing.

Rates in the consumer loan market are the most sluggish of the three loan areas. Because demands for such loans generally do not rise much and because severe funds shortages do not occur, drastic rationing is not necessary despite the rate sluggishness. Whatever rationing is needed is achieved by raising credit standards.

Generally lenders are affected only slightly by credit rationing because tight money periods tend to be relatively brief. But in recent years mortgage lenders, and in particular thrift institutions, have been burdened by a rationing effect even when credit was relatively plentiful; home mortgage rates have been kept below competitive levels by a variety of governmental programs, yet thrift institutions are pressured into channeling the bulk of their funds into this market. This has had a long-run unfavorable impact in their earnings, and has weakened their financial position and ability to attract savings.

THE MONEY MARKET FUND AS A FINANCIAL INTERMEDIARY[†]

Donald R. Fraser[*]

42

Most of the flow of funds in the United States occurs through financial intermediaries—commercial banks, savings and loan associations, mutual savings banks, and other such institutions. For example, from 1970 through 1975 financial intermediaries provided about 90 percent of the more than $800 billion of private funds advanced in the credit markets of the nation.[1] This dominance of the flow of funds by financial intermediaries (the intermediation process) is no accident but rather reflects the important functions performed by financial intermediaries for both borrowers and lenders. Recently, there has appeared among the diverse group of financial intermediaries a new type of institution: the money market fund. While a number of articles have examined the money market fund from an investment perspective, there has been little discussion of how these funds mesh with the other institutions in the financial system.[2] It is the purpose of this article to put the money market fund within a financial intermediation context. It is first nec-

[†]Reprinted, with deletions, from *MSU Business Topics*, Spring 1977, No. 2, Vol. 25, pp. 5-11, by permission of the publisher, Division of Research, Graduate School of Business Administration, Michigan State University, and the author.

[*]Donald R. Fraser is a faculty member in finance at Texas A&M University.

[1]Board of Governors of the Federal Reserve System, *Flow of Funds Accounts*, 1946-1975 (Washintgon, D.C.: 1976), p. 9.

[2]For a discussion of the use of the money market funds as an investment vehicle, see Joseph E. Miles, "Money Market Funds Can Produce Income from Cash Reserves," *Pensions and Investments* 4 (19 July 1976): 21-22.

essary to discuss the nature of financial intermediaries and intermediation and then provide information on the nature of money market funds.

Financial intermediaries perform a number of services. These include providing a low risk outlet for the funds of individuals and businesses in the form of demand and time and savings deposits as well as in other financial instruments; assisting in fulfilling the credit or borrowing needs of the various sectors of the economy (consumer, business, and government); providing the mechanism for the payments and collections system of the United States; offering trust services; and providing a large variety of specific (miscellaneous) services necessary for the efficient operation of the business and financial system. More generally, however, financial intermediaries may be said to provide the following services which have (collectively) resulted in their dominance of the flow of funds process: denomination intermediation, default risk intermediation, and maturity intermediation. The first of these refers to the ability of the financial intermediary to reduce the problems associated with lenders who frequently desire small denomination securities and businesses that often prefer to issue securities in large denominations. This conflict is resolved by financial intermediaries who purchase a small number of large denomination securities and finance the purchase with the issue of a large number of small denomination securities. The commercial bank, for example, often makes large loans to major business firms while obtaining funds from small, individual savings and checking accounts. In essence, the financial intermediary pools the savings of a large number of individuals and provides funds to a much smaller group of borrowers.

The second vital function performed by financial intermediaries is default risk intermediation. Lenders frequently wish to purchase securities which have relatively little risk of loss. Conversely, many businesses and even government units are only able to sell securities which have substantial risk that the issuer will be unable to meet obligations to pay interest and principal in a timely fashion. Again there is a conflict between the preferences of lender and borrower. The financial intermediary reduces this conflict by purchasing the relatively high risk securities of businesses and governments and, in turn, issuing its own securities which have relatively low risk. This is possible for a number of reasons. Through diversification of the assets in its portfolio the financial intermediary may be able to reduce the risk of its portfolio below the risk level on any of its individual assets. In addition, the financial intermediary should be able to employ individuals with specialized skill in order to appraise more accurately the degree of risk involved in the purchase of any given security. It must be admitted, however, that there is some question as to the validity of this argument given the heavy losses suffered by commercial banks and other intermediaries in recent years. Government insurance has reduced the default risk on the securities of depository financial intermediaries (commercial banks, mutual savings banks, savings and loan associations, and credit unions).

Financial intermediaries also engage in the third function mentioned—maturity intermediation. Lenders often want to hold securities which have relatively short maturity and which therefore have relatively high liquidity.

However, borrowers—especially if they are applying the hedging principle of financial theory—wish to issue relatively longer term securities.[3] Financial intermediaries resolve these different maturity preferences by purchasing long-term securities and financing the purchase by issuing relatively short maturity securities. This is possible in the case of deposit institutions since the financial intermediary can expect that a substantial proportion of its deposit withdrawals will be offset by deposit inflow over any given period. However, the existence of maturity intermediation does mean that all financial intermediaries are necessarily illiquid and subject to problems when facing large demands for funds from depositors. The plight of the savings and loan industry in periods of high interest rates provides important evidence of this problem.

Financial intermediaries perform two other functions that are especially important. They may offer economies of scale in the lending and investing of funds, due to the specialized nature of the institution, such that savings may be made available to the ultimate investor at lower cost. Similarly, financial intermediaries may offer convenience to the investor in terms of physical location, record keeping, and the ability to shift from one investment to another quickly and with low transaction costs. The element of convenience may be especially important in the development of the money market fund.

MONEY MARKET FUNDS

Money market funds are investment trusts which exist for the purpose of holding money market instruments (Treasury bills, commercial paper, and other varieties of short-term, low credit risk financial instruments). These funds may be either closed end (a fixed number of shares) or open end (an unlimited number of shares), although most are open end.[4] If the investment trusts are closed end, then the number of shares which are outstanding is fixed. Shares of closed end funds may be traded on the open market at a price determined by supply and demand, although the underwriters of most closed end money market funds have agreed to purchase shares at net asset value. For the dominant type of fund—the open end money market fund—repurchase of the shares is done by the funds, again usually at net asset value. In this case, the price of the fund is set by the offer to buy or sell shares by

[3]The hedging principle suggests that the maturity of the sources of funds (such as borrowings) for an economic unit should be matched with the maturity of the investments or uses of funds of that economic unit. Hence, an economic unit with a large investment in fixed assets should have a large proportion of its funds from permanent sources such as long-term debt and equity. Conversely, an economic unit with highly seasonal investments in current assets should obtain most of its funds from temporary sources such as short-term borrowings.

[4]The closed end funds are referred to as unit investment trusts. A number of these were formed in 1974, apparently for the purpose of investing in certificates of deposit. At the time, it was possible for these unit trusts to provide FDIC insurance for their shareholders despite investing in CDs in denominations in excess of the FDIC insurance ceilings. This possibility was eliminated by the FDIC in late 1974.

the fund itself and not by supply and demand conditions in the market.[5] Money market funds also may be either load or no-load. Load funds are sold with a sales charge, while no-load funds are sold at net asset value with no sales charge. Most money market funds are no-load.

Money market funds, as their name implies, invest primarily in money market instruments. These include any financial instruments with the following characteristics: short term in maturity (generally less than one year), low credit or default risk, and a good secondary market. These characteristics create a financial instrument which is stable in price and carried limited risk to the holder. (They also, of course, create a financial instrument with a relatively low rate of return). Specifically, these financial instruments include Treasury bills, commercial paper, certificates of deposit issued by the major banks, bankers' acceptances, and others. Treasury bills are the short-term (one year or less) debt issues of the U.S. government; commercial paper refers to the short-term (270 days or less) debt instruments issued by large business firms, particularly the finance subsidiaries of manufacturing firms such as General Motors Acceptance Corporation; certificates of deposit represent the deposits at commercial banks of substantial amounts of funds (usually over $100,000) for a specified period of time (generally under one year); and bankers' acceptances are drafts drawn by a business firm on a commercial bank where the bank has accepted or guaranteed payment of the draft at maturity.[6]

The specific composition of money market instruments at individual funds, as well as the maturity of different instruments at these funds, varies widely. As of 31 December 1975, the two largest investments for all funds were in certificates of deposit (almost 60 percent of total money market fund assets) and U.S. government securities (almost 30 percent of total assets). However, the composition of the assets of individual funds and thus the risk to shareholders varies widely. There are funds which invest only in U.S. government securities. Other funds frequently concentrate their assets in certificates of deposit or CDs. Moreover, the composition of assets of individual funds shifts over time as the returns on some securities become more attractive relative to those on other securities and as fund managers change their expectations regarding the behavior of interest rates.

As of 31 December 1975, Capital Preservation Fund held 100 percent of its assets in the form of U.S. Treasury bills and notes. In contrast, Money Market Management, Inc., had 96 percent of its assets invested in bank certificates of deposits as of the same date, and J. B. Cabot Short-Term Fund had 80.3 percent of its assets in the form of bankers' acceptances. Many of these differences reflect judgments by management on the best portfolio strategy as of a particular time. However, a number of money market funds are restricted, through their prospectus, to investments in a selected group of money market instruments. For example, Fund for Government Investors is

---

[5]Given the nature of the assets held by money market funds it is unlikely that the market price established by supply and demand would vary widely from the net asset value.

[6]For additional information, see Federal Reserve Bank of Richmond, *Instruments of the Money Market* (Richmond: 1974), pp. 5-96.

restricted in its asset holdings to short-term securities issued by the U.S. government and its agencies.

Money market funds are a relatively new phenomenon in the investment community, dating back only to early 1974. They developed in response to two factors. First, interest rates on short-term financial instruments (money market instruments) reached unprecedented levels in 1974. The prime rate rose to 12 percent, the rate on three-month Treasury bills was almost 10 percent, and the yields available on commercial paper and certificates of deposit were well over 10 percent. Second, the returns available to the small investor (consumer or business person) at commercial banks or savings and loan associations were restrained to low levels by Regulation Q ceilings, which specify maximum rates payable on deposit accounts. Maximum rates on savings deposits were 5 percent for commercial banks and 5.25 percent for savings and loan associations. In a sense, the development of money market funds represents the attempt by market participants to avoid artificial restraints on investors which limit the efficiency of financial markets.

Money market fund managers quickly moved into this gap with the money market fund as an innovative financial intermediary. Shares in these funds were offered as being attractive not only to consumers, but also to business firms which were not large enough to manage effectively their own liquidity position and also to fiduciary institutions such as trust departments in relatively small banks. Growth of assets under management and expansion in the number of funds were explosive. From virtually nothing in 1973, total money market fund assets expanded to more than $2 billion by late 1974 and to an estimated $3.6 billion by the end of 1975. (Since this article was written, the assets of money market funds increased dramatically. By mid-1980, industry assets exceeded $80 billion. Ed. note.) Similarly, the number of money market funds grew from a handful in 1973 to more than 30 by late 1974 and to almost 40 by late 1975. Open market interest rates peaked in late 1974 and declined in the following months (except for the summer of 1975). As a result of the narrowing gap between open market rates and the rates payable by banks and savings and loan associations, the rate of growth of the assets of money market funds slowed throughout 1975 and 1976.

The reduction in open market rates in 1975 and 1976 produced speculation that the money market fund movement was a transitory phenomenon associated with periods of high interest rates and that its viability would be eroded with the return to "normal" interest rate levels. Moreover, it appears to be only a matter of time before commercial banks and other financial institutions are freed from the restraints of Regulation Q and allowed to offer a rate on savings and time accounts which is determined by the management of the institution and not by the regulatory authorities. Such a development would certainly have important implications for the money market fund. Undoubtedly, the enormous growth of these funds in 1974-1975 does reflect the existence of unusual rate relationships. However, if the money market fund is indeed an important financial innovation, its viability should not be destroyed by these developments, although the growth rate of the industry certainly would be affected. Indeed, completely apart from the flow of funds in periods of high interest rates, it may be argued that the money market fund represents a continuation of the post-World War II emphasis on developing more efficient devices for the use of cash resources.

The money market fund represents a financial innovation from a number of perspectives. Certainly, it offers maturity intermediation (since it provides instant liquidity to holders of shares but invests in a longer term portfolio of assets) and also risk intermediation (since it provides a diversified portfolio of securities managed by professionals in the field). However, the most important service perhaps relates to the function of denomination intermediation. Shareholders are able to acquire a part of a money market instrument with a small (usually $100 to $500) original investment. These instruments could not be acquired directly without having available a substantially larger amount of funds. For example. the minimum denomination of Treausry bills at original issue is $10,000. Similarly, while commercial paper and certificates of deposit may be purchased in a number of denominations, investments of less than $100,000 are difficult to execute at acceptable rate levels. Indeed, the normal round lot for certificates of deposit is $1 million, while commercial paper is usually available in denominations of $100,000, $250,000, $500,000, and $1 million (although the minimum round lot size usually available from a dealer is $250,000).

One important reason for the rapid growth of money market funds is that special services are offered. For example, a number of these funds have expedited redemption procedures. A shareholder usually may contact the fund by toll free telephone (or by letter) and have all or a portion of the value of his or her holdings wire transferred to his or her bank on the next business day. Moreover, many money market funds have check-writing redemption privileges. The fund maintains a program with a commercial bank, and the investor may write a check (for an amount above some minimum) against the assets in the fund. When the check is presented to the bank for payment through the normal clearing mechanism, the bank sells sufficient shares to provide funds to pay the check. One advantage of this procedure is that the holder of shares in the money market fund continues to receive interest until the check clears the bank. Hence, the shareholder can "play the float game." While perhaps of limited significance for small accounts, this service should be especially valuable for larger, business shareholders. In addition, many mutual fund management companies have established money market funds in order to offer a full range of investment vehicles to their customers. In a number of cases, the investor may shift from one fund to another (bond to stock to money market fund, for example) of the same management company at no charge. This offers substantial convenience to the customer.

CONCLUSIONS

Financial intermediaries and financial markets usually find methods to circumvent regulatory constraints which interfere with the flow of funds on the basis of risk/return considerations. The development of the money market fund provides an example. Limitations on rates available from depository financial intermediaries during the 1974 period of high interest rates produced a net advantage to investors who moved funds from deposit accounts to this new financial intermediary. Certainly, such movements will occur in future periods of high interest rates as long as ceilings prevail on the yields that depository financial institutions can offer their customers. However, these money market funds provide a number of important services and fulfill a variety of functions as financial intermediaries which are important even in periods of "normal" interest rate levels.